797,885 Books
are available to read at

www.ForgottenBooks.com

Forgotten Books' App
Available for mobile, tablet & eReader

ISBN 978-1-333-54029-6
PIBN 10517320

This book is a reproduction of an important historical work. Forgotten Books uses state-of-the-art technology to digitally reconstruct the work, preserving the original format whilst repairing imperfections present in the aged copy. In rare cases, an imperfection in the original, such as a blemish or missing page, may be replicated in our edition. We do, however, repair the vast majority of imperfections successfully; any imperfections that remain are intentionally left to preserve the state of such historical works.

Forgotten Books is a registered trademark of FB &c Ltd.
Copyright © 2015 FB &c Ltd.
FB &c Ltd, Dalton House, 60 Windsor Avenue, London, SW19 2RR.
Company number 08720141. Registered in England and Wales.

For support please visit www.forgottenbooks.com

1 MONTH OF FREE READING

at
www.ForgottenBooks.com

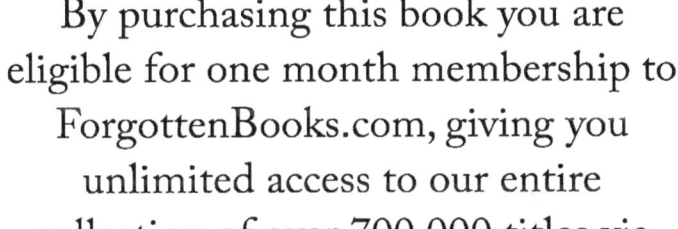

By purchasing this book you are eligible for one month membership to ForgottenBooks.com, giving you unlimited access to our entire collection of over 700,000 titles via our web site and mobile apps.

To claim your free month visit:
www.forgottenbooks.com/free517320

* Offer is valid for 45 days from date of purchase. Terms and conditions apply.

English
Français
Deutsche
Italiano
Español
Português

www.forgottenbooks.com

Mythology Photography **Fiction**
Fishing Christianity **Art** Cooking
Essays Buddhism Freemasonry
Medicine **Biology** Music **Ancient Egypt** Evolution Carpentry Physics
Dance Geology **Mathematics** Fitness
Shakespeare **Folklore** Yoga Marketing
Confidence Immortality Biographies
Poetry **Psychology** Witchcraft
Electronics Chemistry History **Law**
Accounting **Philosophy** Anthropology
Alchemy Drama Quantum Mechanics
Atheism Sexual Health **Ancient History**
Entrepreneurship Languages Sport
Paleontology Needlework Islam
Metaphysics Investment Archaeology
Parenting Statistics Criminology
Motivational

SAN FRANCISCO

A HISTORY
OF THE PACIFIC COAST
METROPOLIS

By JOHN P. YOUNG

VOLUME I

THE S. J. CLARKE PUBLISHING COMPANY
Chronicle Building, San Francisco
Pontiac Building, Chicago

SAN FRANCISCO

A HISTORY
OF THE PACIFIC COAST
METROPOLIS

By JOHN P. YOUNG

VOLUME I

THE S. J. CLARKE PUBLISHING COMPANY
CHRONICLE BUILDING, SAN FRANCISCO
PONTIAC BUILDING, CHICAGO

PREFACE

The reader who will take the trouble to peruse these pages will discover that the writer has dealt with events rather than with the men who brought them about or who figured in them. A variety of reasons prompted this course, but among them is not included lack of appreciation of the value of biography, nor of the interest which most people take in the doings of those who took part in acts worth recording, and of scenes meriting description. These can be more fittingly treated separately, and under circumstances which will permit their authors to preserve the sense of historical proportion, which suffers disturbance when the personal element forms too large a part of the narrative of a people's progress, thus subordinating the actions of the whole community, which after all that may be said on the subject, makes or mars its own fortunes and shapes its own destiny.

Although the period of active life of San Francisco has been a short one, as historical periods go, it has been crowded with incident. Enough of the latter could be found to present a vivid picture of the career of the metropolis of the Pacific coast, but in this work something more has been attempted than a mere recital of occurrences. It has been the purpose of the author to trace the causes of the growth of the City, and to describe the manifold activities of its citizens. In his effort to do so he has discovered an urgent necessity for condensation, and the elimination of a vast quantity of material at his command. Had he used a tithe of that placed at his disposal the history would have attained enormous proportions. This data, provided by accommodating and zealous friends, to whom I here wish to express my gratitude and obligations, is of a character which would permit of the writing of many monographs with an amplitude of detail which would perhaps make them more interesting to the special reader than these two volumes will be to the public generally.

If the general reader whose familiarity with particular phases of metropolitan life finds that their treatment has been inadequate, he is begged to recall that the activities of a great city are numerous, and that opinions respecting their importance are almost as varied as the number who give them consideration. He is reminded that the writer has sought to deal with a hundred subjects, half, or more, of which would lend themselves to amplification of the sort the minute reader exacts, but which in these volumes the exigencies of space have compelled the compression into a few pages, and sometimes into paragraphs. Episodes in the history of the City which other writers have ably dealt with at great length have necessarily been epitomized in order that a more comprehensive survey of the period in which they occurred might be taken, and because of the writer's belief that their details will grow less interesting as the years wear on until at last they become a mere speck in the historical perspective of San Francisco.

Perhaps that will be the fate of most of that which we now regard as important. In the multitude of happenings which the universal historian has to draw upon he finds comparatively few that he deems worth recording, and fewer still to which he devotes pages of description. Appalling calamities he passes over with a mere mention. Gibbon in his monumental history of Rome tells of the destruction of 250,000 lives in a great earthquake which nearly destroyed the city of Antioch in 551 A. D., and furnishes the reader no other information concerning it than is contained in his conjecture that "the domestic population of the city was swollen by the conflux of strangers to the festival of the Ascension," and he passes over the calamity which befell the Roman world in the second year of the reign of Valentinian with a mere reference to a tidal wave which drowned 50,000 people and to the disruption of a mountain; and his relation of the seismic disaster which overthrew the Colossus of Rhodes is confined to the recital of that fact coupled with a statement of the disposition made of the metal of the statue, which he appears to have introduced, more for the purpose of giving an idea of its size than to illustrate the misfortunes of the Rhodians.

The information, and the imagination necessary to present a graphic and more extended account were not lacking, but the historian was dealing with the events of centuries, and was compelled, while observing the limitations of space, to preserve the sense of proportion. To him tragedies and great calamities were as the ripples on the surface of a pond when a stone is thrown into its depths. When the transitory disturbance ceased the stone was forgotten. Whether consciously or unconsciously Gibbon recognized that it is the sum total of human happenings and experience which make history, and by a process of condensation which permitted him to momentarily turn the limelight of his genius on significant occurrences he succeeded in producing a picture from which a vivid impression is derived, although the canvas is crowded in places to the point of confusion.

On a lesser scale the annalist of a municipality seeks to accomplish the same result. He cannot succeed unless he pursues the same method. The description of a few events, no matter how important they may have seemed to those who participated in them, cannot truthfully portray the growth of a community. Their exceptional character stamps them as aberrations. It is only by the relation of the manner in which a people works out the problem of its everyday existence that a truthful idea of its status can be conveyed. Ebullitions on the surface show that there is heat under the caldron, but they do not tell the story of the causes that produced the heat.

The caldron has boiled fiercely at times in San Francisco and has brought a deal of scum to the top, but when skimmed off and thrown to the side, it is seen that the liquor beneath has been purified in the process. This story is an attempt to truthfully describe the boiling and the clarification. In doing so it has been found necessary to consider many activities and briefly review them, incidentally reciting the causes that have made their practice possible. In the following pages will be found not merely an enumeration and relation of events; they contain, it is hoped, sufficient information to enable the reader to form a judgment of the progress of the people of San Francisco both spiritually and materially.

There is something about the great industries of the State of California which have made the growth of the metropolis possible. The trade of the City and its commerce with foreign nations are treated. The development of the facilities of the great Bay of San Francisco is traced. The banking operations of the City at various periods, and its monetary troubles are noted. The labor troubles of the community, and its effort to promote manufacturing are dealt with. Its civic aspirations and accomplishments in the way of public improvements, receive attention, not in the spirit of the booster, but in a candid fashion which recognizes failures as well as successes. The shortcomings of the people in the administration of the affairs of the municipality, are described, and the blame for them placed where the author thinks it belongs. The recreations of the community: its sports and its amusements; its educational facilities; its libraries and its literature; its fraternal and social organizations; its celebrations; its journalism and periodical publications; its homes and its hotel and restaurant life; its art and its architecture; its churches and its charities are all included in the survey, and it is hoped that all these varied activities have been so correlated that the reader will find it possible to form a correct judgment of the present status of the metropolis and of the means by which it has been attained.

It has not been deemed necessary by the author to encumber his pages with the sources of his information. He freely confesses his obligations to writers who have dealt with the early periods, and disavows all claims to special research. For information concerning the events since 1877 he has depended on personal observation and information derived from so many sources that an attempt to make acknowledgment in detail would consume as much space as that required for their description. But he cannot refrain from renewing his expression of gratitude to those in authority, and in a position to know, for the trouble they have taken to provide him with the data upon which the story of the years after 1877 is largely based, and which he hopes has been told without other bias than that which conviction produces. JOHN P. YOUNG.

SAN FRANCISCO, October 1, 1912.

CONTENTS

CHAPTER I

THE SPANISH HUNT FOR A SHORT CUT TO THE INDIES

BALBOA SEES THE PACIFIC—THE SETTLEMENT OF PANAMA—SEEKING A SAFE HARBOR SPANISH TREASURE FLEETS—SIR FRANCIS DRAKE AND HIS PURSUITS—THE SEARCH FOR ANIAN—SETTLEMENT OF CALIFORNIA ORDERED—THE HARBOR OF MONTEREY—SPANISH NEGLIGENCE OF OPPORTUNITIES—A HUNT FOR ISLANDS OF GOLD—REVIVAL OF INTEREST IN THE SHORT CUT...................................... 3

CHAPTER II

SPAIN'S PURPOSE IN OCCUPYING CALIFORNIA

HALF WAY HOUSE FOR SHIPS IN THE PHILIPPINE TRADE—THE SANDWICH ISLANDS OVERLOOKED—RUSSIA COVETED CALIFORNIA—EFFECTS OF MISSIONARY ZEAL—THE BELIEF IN THE INSULARITY OF CALIFORNIA—INVESTIGATIONS OF FATHER KING—SPANISH PROJECTS SLUMBER—THE FRANCISCAN ORDER—EXPULSION OF JESUITS—FATHER JUNIPERO SERRA—SEARCHING FOR MONTEREY—PORTOLA'S DISAPPOINTMENT—DISCOVERY OF SAN FRANCISCO BAY............................ 9

CHAPTER III

THE ESTABLISHMENT OF THE MISSION OF ST. FRANCIS

SEARCH FOR THE BAY OF MONTEREY CONTINUED—LIEUTENANT DE AYALA ENTERS THE GOLDEN GATE—THE EXPEDITION TO SAN FRANCISCO BAY—SELECTION OF A SITE ON MISSION BAY—THE PRESIDIO ESTABLISHED—FATHER SERRA REACHES MISSION DOLORES—SPANISH DRY ROT COMMUNICATES ITSELF TO THE NEW COUNTRY—SPAIN'S TRADE WITH THE PHILIPPINES—THE MISSION INDIANS—THE LIFE AND LABORS OF PADRE SERRA.. 15

CONTENTS

CHAPTER IV

RESULT OF THE LABORS OF THE MISSIONARIES

DEATH OF PADRE SERRA AT MONTEREY—SPANIARDS POOR COLONISTS—MANAGEMENT OF THE MISSIONS—THE MISSION INDIANS—THE AIMS OF THE PADRES—CHARACTER OF CALIFORNIA INDIANS—INDIANS LOW IN THE HUMAN SCALE—WORKING ON UNPROMISING MATERIAL—INDIANS TAUGHT AGRICULTURE—PRACTICAL ENSLAVEMENT OF THE INDIAN—THE ABORIGINES MELT AWAY UNDER CIVILIZING INFLUENCES... 23

CHAPTER V

THE UNPRACTICAL CHARACTER OF THE MISSIONARIES

THEIR FAILURE TO INCOURAGE COMMUNICATION—THEY NEGLECT TRAVEL FACILITIES—PASTORAL PURSUITS IN CALIFORNIA—WRETCHED CONDITION OF SETTLERS—YANKEE TRADERS VISIT CALIFORNIA—LARGE NUMBERS OF HORSES AND HORNED STOCK RAISED PRODUCT OF THE MISSIONS IN 1839—OCCASIONAL INDIAN UPRISINGS—ARCHITECTURE OF THE MISSIONS—INDOLENCE OF SETTLERS—LIFE ON THE RANCHES—PASTORAL PURSUITS TEND TO INDOLENCE—AGRICULTURE NEGLECTED AND MANUFACTURING IGNORED—NO TRADE EXCEPTING WITH SMUGGLERS............... 29

CHAPTER VI

SPANISH DISCOURAGEMENT OF RELATIONS WITH OUTSIDERS

UNCOMMERCIAL METHODS OF SPAIN—THE PREDICTION OF A PADRE CONCERNING SAN FRANCISCO BAY—EARLY YANKEE AMBITIONS—SPANISH FEAR OF THE RUSSIANS—THE VISIT OF RAZENOFF AND HIS ADVICE TO THE CALIFORNIANS—NAVIGATION OF THE BAY DISCOURAGED BY GOVERNOR SOLA—EARLIEST TRAFFIC ON THE BAY OF SAN FRANCISCO—CAPTAIN MORRELL MAKES A SUGGESTION—UNCLE SAM SEEKS AN OUTLET—REPORT OF COLONEL BUTLER ON CALIFORNIA—MEXICO UNAPPRECIATIVE OF CALIFORNIA—ARGUELLO LAUDS POSSIBILITIES OF PROVINCE—THE EARLY IMMIGRANTS WELCOMED—SHIPS DROP INTO SAN FRANCISCO BAY—THE FOUNDATION OF YERBA BUENA.. 35

CHAPTER VII

FOUNDATION OF THE VILLAGE OF YERBA BUENA

YERBA BUENA IN 1839—THE FIRST HOUSE ERECTED IN YERBA BUENA—DEDICATION OF THE MISSION OF ST. FRANCIS—REZANOFF'S VISIT TO SAN FRANCISCO BAY IN 1806—THE RUSSIAN IS WELCOMED—A ROMANCE OF YERBA BUENA—REZANOFF SECURES SUPPLIES FOR THE ESTABLISHMENT OF THE RUSSIANS IN SITKA—DEATH OF REZANOFF IN SIBERIA—RUSSIAN METHODS IN CALIFORNIA—FEW BOOKS IN CALIFORNIA BEFORE ARRIVAL OF AMERICANS—DANCING FORBIDDEN BY THE PADRES—PATERNAL RULE ON THE RANCHES—THE INFLUENCE OF THE CHURCH...... 41

CONTENTS

CHAPTER VIII

LIFE OF NATIVE CALIFORNIANS ON THEIR RANCHES

HOSPITALITY OF THE NATIVE CALIFORNIANS—NATIVE CALIFORNIANS AND THEIR HORSES—THE FEASTING AND MERRYMAKING OF THE PEOPLE—DANCING AND MUSIC AT FIESTAS—LOVE OF FINERY—SOCIAL DISTINCTIONS—INDOLENCE A BESETTING SIN—AN EASILY CONTENTED PEOPLE—A GREAT LACK OF CREATURE COMFORTS—SOAP SPARINGLY USED—SIMPLE DIET OF THE NATIVE CALIFORNIAN—HE DID NOT EXERT HIMSELF TO PROVIDE FOR THE TABLE.................... 49

CHAPTER IX

LIFE IN CALIFORNIA BEFORE THE AMERICAN OCCUPATION

SOME SQUALID FEATURES—DRINKING AND GAMBLING—VICES ADOPTED BY NEW COMERS—THE CALIFORNIA BULL RING—EXTRAVAGANT HABITS EASILY ACQUIRED—TRADING INSTINCT NOT HIGHLY DEVELOPED—EXCESSIVE FEAR OF LUXURIOUS HABITS—THE TROUBLESOME RUSSIANS—CAUSES OF CALIFORNIAN BACKWARDNESS—YANKEE TRADERS ON THE COAST—SMUGGLING A FINE ART—CELEBRATIONS AT THE MISSION ST. FRANCIS—AN UNCONVENTIONAL PEOPLE—SEXUAL MORALITY............... 57

CHAPTER X

BEGINNING OF THE AMERICAN INVASION OF CALIFORNIA

THE FIRST SETTLERS OF SAN FRANCISCO—MEXICAN OPINION OF CALIFORNIA—AMERICAN CRITICISM OF SPANISH METHODS—RESTRICTIONS ON IMMIGRATION—FOREIGNERS WELCOMED BY CALIFORNIA WOMEN—THE FIRST AMERICAN INTRUDERS—RUMORED SEIZURE OF THE PORT OF SAN FRANCISCO—FRICTION WITH FOREIGNERS—INTRIGUING AMERICANS—TRADE WITH NEW MEXICO—ADVANCE GUARD OF THE AMERICAN INVASION—AGGRESSIVENESS OF AMERICAN IMMIGRANTS................... 65

CHAPTER XI

COVETOUS EYES CAST ON THE BAY OF SAN FRANCISCO

SEVERAL NATIONS ENVIOUS OF SPAIN—THE SPANISH FAILURE TO MAKE USE OF THE PORT OF SAN FRANCISCO—THE PADRES AND THE MILITARY—THE FATHERS OPPOSED TO REPUBLICAN GOVERNMENT—POLITICAL SQUABBLES IN CALIFORNIA—OFFICIAL LIFE UNDER SPANISH AND MEXICAN RULE—MEXICO UNCONCERNED ABOUT THE FATE OF CALIFORNIA—CONCILIATORY AMERICANS—FRENCH AND BRITISH INTRIGUES—STIMULATING DISLIKE OF AMERICANS—FREMONT APPEARS ON THE SCENE—THE "PATHFINDERS'" ACTIONS EXCITE SUSPICION................. 71

CONTENTS

CHAPTER XII

LABOR PROBLEM BEFORE AMERICAN OCCUPATION

CALIFORNIA AND THE SLAVEHOLDERS OF THE UNITED STATES—CHINESE LABOR SUGGESTED AS EARLY AS 1806—INDIANS AS SLAVES—THE INDIAN AN OBJECT OF DREAD—THE ATTEMPT TO ELEVATE THE INDIAN—ENSLAVEMENT OF INDIAN CHILDREN INDIANS CRUELLY TREATED—NO REWARDS FOR THE INDIAN LABORER—OPPOSITION TO INDIAN PUEBLOS—INDIAN PUEBLOS NOT A SUCCESS—RELIGIOUS TRAINING OF MISSION INDIANS—UNSATISFACTORY RESULTS............................. 77

CHAPTER XIII

THE SPANISH LAND GRANT SYSTEM IN CALIFORNIA

FIRST LAND GRANTS IN 1773—LIBERAL ALLOTMENTS DID NOT ATTRACT SETTLERS—LARGE RANCHES PRODUCTIVE OF INDOLENCE—THE NEGLECTED STOCK OF THE NATIVE CALIFORNIANS—PARALYZING EFFECTS OF THE BAD LAND LAWS—SUPPLIES RECEIVED FROM ALASKA—NO MANUFACTURING SKILL DEVELOPED—EARLY CONSERVATION SUGGESTIONS—LUMBER SCARCE—CALIFORNIANS NOT LOVERS OF THE SEA—MONTEREY OVERSHADOWS SAN FRANCISCO IN IMPORTANCE................. 83

CHAPTER XIV

EARLY TRADING TROUBLES OF THE CALIFORNIANS

SPANISH AND MEXICAN ATTEMPTS TO REPRESS TRADING—SMUGGLING POPULARLY APPROVED—THE FUR TRADE—SPAIN SURRENDERS NORTHWEST COAST—VISITS OF YANKEE SHIPS TO CALIFORNIA—THE FORT ROSS ESTABLISHMENT—AN AMICABLE ARRANGEMENT WITH THE RUSSIANS—SUTTER AND VALLEJO QUARREL—THE TRADE IN HIDES AND TALLOW—THE WHALERS AND THE WHALING INDUSTRY—HONOLULU A RIVAL OF SAN FRANCISCO—FIRST MERCANTILE ESTABLISHMENT IN YERBA BUENA—CONTINUED IMPORTANCE OF MONTEREY—SAN FRANCISCO'S FIRST PUBLIC IMPROVEMENT—SEVENTY YEARS OF INACTIVITY................................ 91

CHAPTER XV

THE EVE OF THE OCCUPATION BY AMERICANS

SPANISH FAILURE TO DISCOVER GOLD IN QUANTITY—A FEW OUNCES FOUND IN LOS ANGELES BEFORE THE SUTTER FORT DISCOVERY—HOPES OF THE AMERICAN SETTLERS—SOUTHERNERS HOODWINK THE NORTHERN PEOPLE—THE PLOTS OF THE SLAVEHOLDERS—JACKSON'S OFFER TO PURCHASE SAN FRANCISCO BAY—THE WAR WITH MEXICO—FREMONT'S EXPEDITION—FREMONT'S POLICY OF PROVOCATION—WASHINGTON AUTHORITIES MISLED—FREMONT AND IDE—THE BEAR FLAG EPISODE—WHAT MIGHT HAVE HAPPENED.. 99

CONTENTS

CHAPTER XVI

ACQUISITION OF CALIFORNIA BY THE UNITED STATES

THE CONQUEST OF CALIFORNIA—YERBA BUENA—EARLY INHABITANTS OF THE VILLAGE—ARRIVAL OF MORMONS—THE DONNER PARTY—YERBA BUENA GROWING—OCCUPATIONS OF THE FIRST SETTLERS—COMMERCE OF THE PORT IN 1847—TEMPTING THE WHALERS—TRADE WITH NEW MEXICO—THE MISSION DOLORES—MISSION ARCHITECTURE—YERBA BUENA CHANGED TO SAN FRANCISCO—FIRST REAL ESTATE TRANSACTIONS—THE ORIGINAL STREETS OF YERBA BUENA...................... 111

CHAPTER XVII

THE BAY OF SAN FRANCISCO AND ITS GREAT IMPORTANCE

SURROUNDED BY A WILDERNESS—THE "GOLDEN GATE" NAMED BY FREMONT—THE NAME "CALIFORNIA"—THE ENTRANCE TO THE HARBOR—THE SHORES OF THE BAY OF SAN FRANCISCO—A NATURAL BASIN FILLED IN BY THE PIONEERS—CONTOUR OF THE BAY NOT GREATLY CHANGED—FIRST STEAM VESSEL ON THE BAY—RUSSIANS IN ALASKA—ALASKA A SOURCE OF SUPPLIES—COMMERCE OF THE PORT IN 1848—HUNDREDS OF SHIPS IN THE HARBOR—THE DAWN OF COMMERCIAL GREATNESS. 121

CHAPTER XVIII

THE DISCOVERY OF GOLD AT SUTTER'S MILL IN 1848

EFFECTS OF THE DISCOVERY—THE CAREER OF SUTTER—A POORLY KEPT SECRET—BEGINNING OF THE RUSH TO CALIFORNIA—MILITARY GOVERNOR RICHARD B. MASON—PROPOSAL TO CONSERVE THE GOLD—MARSHALL'S LIFE THREATENED—SAN FRANCISCO BECOMES THE MINER'S MECCA—MINING AND TEMPERAMENT—EFFECTS OF THE GOLD LURE—THE GOLD HUNTERS—THE RUSH IN 1849—POPULATION IN 1849 IMMIGRANTS POURING INTO CALIFORNIA—UNSTABLE CHARACTER OF THE NEW POPULATION—DEPENDENCE ON MINING................................ 131

CHAPTER XIX

MANY VICISSITUDES EXPERIENCED BY THE PIONEERS

A FLIMSILY CONSTRUCTED CITY—SAN FRANCISCO IN 1848—THE BIG FIRES OF EARLY DAYS—LACK OF PRECAUTIONS AGAINST FIRE—FIVE CONFLAGRATIONS—METHODS OF CONSTRUCTION IMPROVING—FIRST STORE BUILDING IN SAN FRANCISCO—GOOD ARCHITECTS—EXPENSIVE BUILDING MATERIALS AND HIGH COST OF LABOR—MISSION STYLE NOT FAVORED BY THE PIONEERS—JERRY BUILDING—NUMEROUS BRICK STRUCTURES—APPEARANCE OF THE CITY IN 1854—EARLY LAND GRABBING—LAYING UP TROUBLE FOR THE FUTURE.. 139

CONTENTS

CHAPTER XX

LAND TITLES AND TROUBLES OF PIONEER DAYS

BIG DEMAND FOR TOWN LOTS—WATER FRONT LOTS EAGERLY BOUGHT—ATTEMPT TO VALIDATE FRAUDULENT LAND GRANTS—COLTON GRANTS DECLARED FRAUDULENT—TROUBLESOME SQUATTERS—FEDERAL DETERMINATION OF TITLES—CONFUSION CONCERNING PUEBLOS—AMERICAN ALCALDES IMITATE THEIR PREDECESSORS—OFFICIALS CONNIVE WITH SPECULATORS—THE SQUATTERS' ARGUMENT—SQUATTING AS AN OCCUPATION—THE CITY AND THE INTERIOR SQUATTER—TITLES IN DOUBT MANY YEARS—JURIES SIDE WITH SQUATTERS—SAN FRANCISCO A PUEBLO—THE LIMANTOUR CLAIM—THE LAND COMMISSION—POLITICAL CONDITIONS—NEGLECT OF CIVIC DUTY IN SAN FRANCISCO.. 147

CHAPTER XXI

THE LAYOUT AND BEGINNINGS OF A BIG CITY

NOT MANY PUBLIC IMPROVEMENTS AT FIRST—INDIVIDUAL EFFORT THE CHIEF FACTOR IN THE UPBUILDING OF THE EARLY CITY—PRACTICAL NEEDS ATTENDED TO BY PIONEERS—THE FIRST CITY HALL—CONFIDENCE IN FUTURE GROWTH OF THE CITY—YERBA BUENA COVE FILLED IN BY PIONEERS—HIGH RENTS—MERCHANTS ABLE TO PAY BIG RENTALS—EFFECTS OF EXCESSIVE SPECULATION IN 1853—OPPOSITION TO RECTANGULAR STREET SYSTEM—MUNICIPAL OWNERSHIP AND CARE OF STREETS—MISSION PLANKED ROAD—PROVIDING FACILITIES FOR SHIPPING—A WATER FRONT LINE—PERMANENT WATER FRONT LINE ESTABLISHED IN 1851—THE COUNTRY AND THE CITY—STEADY DEVELOPMENT OF THE CITY—EARLY WATER SUPPLY—A LAKE MERCED PHENOMENON.. 157

CHAPTER XXII

CLIMATIC AND OTHER PHENOMENA OF SAN FRANCISCO

SEISMIC TROUBLES DO NOT DETER IMMIGRATION—ADVANTAGES WEIGHED AGAINST DISADVANTAGES—THE VERIFIED PREDICTION OF A PIONEER—THE CLIMATE OF CALIFORNIA AND OF SAN FRANCISCO—VARIATIONS BUT NO CHANGES—CLIMATIC PECULIARITIES OF SAN FRANCISCO—THE JAPAN CURRENT—ABSENCE OF HUMIDITY MAKES HEAT ENDURABLE—SNOWFALLS SO RARE THEY BECOME HISTORICAL EVENTS—KILLING A MAN TO START A GRAVEYARD—MAN AND NATURE IN CALIFORNIA—PRACTICAL CHARACTERISTICS OF THE PIONEER—THE NAVIGABLE RIVERS OF CALIFORNIA—THE REGION ABOUT THE BAY.......................... 169

CHAPTER XXIII

TAXATION AND OTHER GOVERNMENTAL PROBLEMS OF THE PIONEER

NATIVE CALIFORNIANS SLIGHTLY TAXED—EXEMPTION FROM TAXATION NOT A BLESSING—ABUSE OF AN INHERITED SYSTEM—THE SPECULATIVE LURE—GENERAL KEARNY

AND THE ALCALDES—ALCALDE JUSTICE IN CALIFORNIA—FIRST ALCALDE UNDER THE AMERICAN FLAG—SAN FRANCISCO'S FIRST COUNCIL—THE RUSH TO THE GOLD DIGGINGS—PEACE EASILY KEPT—ORDINANCE AGAINST GAMBLING—COUNCILMEN DESERT THEIR POSTS TO DIG FOR GOLD—NATIONAL AND LOCAL POLITICS—FACTIONAL FEELING—THREE OPPOSING SETS OF COUNCILLORS—MILITARY INTERFERENCE IN CIVIL AFFAIRS—DELEGATES TO THE CONSTITUTIONAL CONVENTION—THE NEED OF REGULATION—A SHORT BALLOT EXPERIMENT IN 1849—VOTE ON ADOPTION OF THE CONSTITUTION—HORACE HAWES A WELL HATED REFORMER—A DEFIANT AYUNTAMIENTO—HAWES TURNED DOWN.. 177

CHAPTER XXIV

MANY EARLY EXPERIMENTS IN MUNICIPAL GOVERNMENT

CHARTER OF 1850 INSPIRES HOPES OF BETTER GOVERNMENT—SMALL REVENUES AND HIGH SALARIES—EARLY SALARY GRABBERS—CONDONATION OF OFFICIAL TURPITUDE—A SECOND CHARTER GRANTED IN 1851—DEBT CREATED AND CREDIT IMPAIRED—THE PETER SMITH JUDGMENTS—UNSUCCESSFUL ATTEMPTS TO REFUND—TAXATION BURDEN IN 1852—A CITY HALL SCANDAL—NEGLECT OF SANITARY PRECAUTIONS—ANOTHER NEW CHARTER IN 1853—THE CITY SUFFERS FROM SPECIAL LEGISLATION—A TAX ON GOODS CONSIGNED TO SAN FRANCISCO MERCHANTS—UNEQUAL TAXATION—WATER FRONT LINE SCANDAL—AN ABANDONED FREE PUBLIC DOCK SCHEME—HARRY MEIGG'S SPECTACULAR CAREER—HE FLIES THE COUNTRY, MAKES A BIG FORTUNE IN PERU AND WISHES TO RETURN TO CALIFORNIA—LEGISLATURE CONDONES HIS OFFENSES—DEATH OF MEIGGS............................ 189

CHAPTER XXV

THE PIONEERS AND THE CRIMINAL CLASS IN THE FIFTIES

CAUSE OF THE VIGILANTE UPRISING—THE "HOUNDS"—KNOW NOTHING TROUBLES ATTACKS ON FOREIGNERS—A TOWN WITHOUT POLICE—POLITICAL FRIENDS OF THE "HOUNDS"—THE VIGILANTE EPISODE OF 1851—COMPOSITION OF THE VIGILANCE COMMITTEE—HIGH HANDED METHODS—HANGING FOR STEALING—THE COURTS AND THE LAWS—THE READY REVOLVER—CIVIC DUTY DISREGARDED—INDIFFERENCE OF THE RESPECTABLE CITIZEN—CONDITIONS IN 1855-56—SHOOTING OF RICHARDSON BY CORA—THE BULLETIN'S ATTACK ON CASEY—INTEMPERATE JOURNALISM—EDITOR OF THE BULLETIN MURDERED—CORA AND CASEY HANGED BY THE VIGILANTES—LAW AND ORDER PARTY—CONSTITUTED AUTHORITIES DEFIED—CORRUPTION AT THE POLLS—NUMERICAL SUPERIORITY OF THE BETTER ELEMENT—DAVID S. TERRY—POLITICAL ASPECTS OF THE VIGILANTE UPRISING......................... 199

CHAPTER XXVI

POLITICAL AND OTHER RESULTS OF THE VIGILANTE UPRISING

VIGILANCE COMMITTEE REFORMS ITSELF—THE IDEA OF CIVIC DUTY BEGINS TO ASSERT ITSELF—THE RECALL METHOD IN 1856—ORGANIZATION OF THE PEOPLE'S PARTY—

PLATFORM OF THE NEW PARTY—RESULT OF ATTENTION TO CIVIC DUTY—A SECRET NOMINATING BODY—ONLY A HALF REFORM ACHIEVED—BRODERICK AND THE VIGILANTES—POLITICAL CAREER OF BRODERICK—BRODERICK'S MODE OF KEEPING UP THE ORGANIZATION—UNSETTLED OPINION CONCERNING SLAVERY—FOR OR AGAINST BRODERICK—COLLISION OF NATIONAL AND MUNICIPAL INTERESTS—POLITICAL JUDGMENT OF VIGILANTE LEADERS—DISSOLUTION OF THE VIGILANCE COMMITTEE—RETURN OF THE PROSCRIBED—THE QUESTION OF TITLES—VIGILANCE COMMITTEE RECEIVES A GOLD BRICK—STORIES OF CRIMINAL ASCENDENCY A MYTH—FEDERAL GOVERNMENT AND THE VIGILANTES—SHERMAN'S PART IN THE AFFAIR—SOLIDARITY OF THE VIGILANTES.. 211

CHAPTER XXVII

AFFAIRS AT LOOSE ENDS IN THE EARLY FIFTIES

THE PEOPLE NOT INTRACTABLE—BAD ELEMENTS NOT HARD TO CONTROL—VICES OF PIONEERS NOT OF THE HIDDEN SORT—HIGH LIGHTS ON SHORTCOMINGS—FIXING RESPONSIBILITY FOR EVIL PRACTICES—PUTTING THE BLAME ON FOREIGNERS—THE GOLD SEEKERS—GROWING COSMOPOLITANISM OF THE CITY—NEGLECT OF MUNICIPAL AFFAIRS—EVERYBODY BOARDED—PREVALENCE OF GAMBLING—THE GLITTERING BAR ROOMS—PORTSMOUTH SQUARE AND ITS SURROUNDINGS—GAMBLING HOUSE PROPRIETORS GROW RICH—REGULATING THE SOCIAL EVIL—A MIXED STATE OF AFFAIRS SOCIALLY—NO HOME RESTRAINTS—EARLY PHILOSOPHERS—PLENTY OF COLLEGE BRED MEN IN THE CITY—ATTEMPTS TO ERADICATE EVIL—PROGRESS TOWARDS ORDER.. 223

CHAPTER XXVIII

CONDITIONS IMPROVE SOCIALLY AND OTHERWISE IN THE CITY

A STRUGGLE FOR DECENCY—FRATERNAL ORGANIZATIONS—CHURCHES FOUNDED—ALL THE DENOMINATIONS REPRESENTED—A UNION OF PROTESTANT CONGREGATIONS—SUNDAY OBSERVANCE—FIRST PROTESTANT SERMON IN CALIFORNIA—THE CATHOLIC CHURCH—BISHOP ALEMANY ARRIVES—THE PIOUS FUND—SAN FRANCISCO'S FIRST CATHEDRAL—ATTEMPTS TO CHRISTIANIZE THE CHINESE—IMPROVED MANNERS AND MORALS—THANKSGIVING DAY—PIONEER DIVORCES—PASSAGE OF A SUNDAY LAW. 233

CHAPTER XXIX

LABOR CONDITIONS AND THE COST AND MODE OF LIVING

SAN FRANCISCO A VICTIM OF EXAGGERATION—SUMMARY MODES OF ABATING EVIL MISUNDERSTOOD—CONDITION OF THE WORKER IN SAN FRANCISCO—CHANGE IN LABOR CONDITIONS—PLENTY OF WORKERS WHEN THE GOLD RUSH WAS UNDER WAY—HURRY UP WAGES PAID—LABOR ORGANIZATIONS FORMED—RELATION OF EMPLOYER AND EMPLOYED—ENVIABLE CONDITION OF THE WORKER—INFLUX OF CHINESE—THE COST OF LIVING IN THE EARLY FIFTIES—IMPORTED FOOD STUFFS—EFFECT ON DOMESTIC PRODUCTION—PRICES FALL—THE LOW PRICE OF GOLD IN CALIFORNIA—

CONTENTS xvii

EFFECTS OF THE ABUNDANCE OF GOLD—EARLY EPICURIANISM—HOW MEN GREW RICH IN PIONEER DAYS—DRESS IN PIONEER DAYS—DISPOSITION TO CREATE IDOLS—EFFECT OF ISOLATION—FIRST ORPHAN ASYLUM AND HOSPITAL—EXCESSIVE MORTALITY FROM EXPOSURE—SAN FRANCISCO CHARITY—SISTERS OF MERCY....... 243

CHAPTER XXX

SOCIAL AND OTHER DIVERSIONS OF PIONEER DAYS

SAN FRANCISCAN ARDOR—FIREMEN THE ELITE OF THE CITY—FIRE PRECAUTIONS—FIRE ENGINE HOUSES CENTERS OF SOCIAL ACTIVITY—FIREMEN'S PARADES—THE MILITIA ORGANIZATIONS—CITIZEN SOLDIERY NOT DEPENDABLE—THE DRINK HABIT—BULL FIGHTS AND BEAR BAITING—HORSE RACING—PUGILISTIC CONTESTS—THE DUELLO IN PIONEER DAYS—EARLY CELEBRATIONS AND LOVE OF MUSIC—THE SPANISH ELEMENT—SPANISH LANGUAGE LOSES ITS HOLD IN SAN FRANCISCO—CHINESE QUARTER IN EARLY DAYS—"CHINA BOYS" IN PARADES—ROUTE OF THE PIONEER PARADES—RUSS GARDENS AND THE WILLOWS—JOYS OF THE CIRCUS—APPRECIATION OF THE DRAMA—STARS VISIT CALIFORNIA—CRITICAL AUDIENCES—CHURCH FAIRS AND PUBLIC BALLS—NO EXCLUSIVE SOCIAL SETS—OBTRUSIVE COURTESANS—THE UBIQUITOUS COLONEL—PREVALENCE OF MILITANCY................................. 255

CHAPTER XXXI

SAN FRANCISCO A BASE FOR FILIBUSTERING OPERATIONS

A RESTLESS PEOPLE—TWO DESIGNING FRENCHMEN—PLOTS AGAINST MEXICO—ATTEMPT TO CAPTURE SONORA—A FRENCH CONSUL IN THE GAME—WALKER'S DESIGNS ON SONORA—MEXICO AND THE AMERICAN MANIFEST DESTINY IDEA—SAN FRANCISCANS AID FILIBUSTERS—REMARKABLE CAREER OF WALKER—FATE OF THE FRENCH FILIBUSTERS—CRABB'S FUTILE EXPEDITION—RESTLESS MINERS—THE BLACK SAND SWINDLE—A RUSH TO AUSTRALIA—THE FRASER RIVER RUSH—STEADY GROWTH OF THE CITY—NUMEROUS HOTELS AND RESTAURANTS—POPULARITY OF TEMPERANCE RESTAURANTS—EVERYBODY BOARDED IN SAN FRANCISCO—THE GREGARIOUS TENDENCY—EARLY MEANS OF GETTING ABOUT—FASHIONABLE SECTIONS—CITY GROWS SOUTHWARD—NOT AMBITIOUS TO BECOME A CAPITAL—A BELIEVER IN MANIFEST DESTINY—SOUTHERN INFLUENCE—INCREASING IMMIGRATION.............. 267

CHAPTER XXXII

RESOURCES THAT PROMOTED THE GROWTH OF SAN FRANCISCO

CHARACTER OF CALIFORNIA LANDS—A BIGGER HOME MARKET FOR THEIR PRODUCTS NEEDED—PAST DEPENDENCE ON THE OUTSIDER—UNORGANIZED MERCANTILISM—EARLY TRADE DEPRESSIONS—THE PANIC OF 1855—BANKING TROUBLES—PLENTY OF GOLD BUT NO CURRENCY—PRIVATE COINAGE—BUYING AND SELLING GOLD DUST—GOVERNMENTAL METHODS OF DEALING WITH THE PEOPLE—MERCHANT PRINCES OF PIONEER PERIOD—PIONEER STOCKS OF MERCHANDISE—LITTLE ATTEMPT TO

DISPLAY GOODS—CREDIT SYSTEM AND COLLECTIONS—PIONEER IDEAS OF A TRANS-
CONTINENTAL RAILROAD—MUCH TALK OF CONNECTING EAST AND WEST—STATE
PRIDE DEVELOPS SLOWLY—WAGON ROADS—HIGH FARE AND FREIGHT RATES—SEA
AND RIVER NAVIGATION—CLIPPER SHIPS—PANAMA AND NICARAGUA ROUTES—THE
PANAMA RAILROAD—SHIPPING OF THE PAST—BUSINESS DRAWBACKS   279

CHAPTER XXXIII

JOURNALISM, LITERATURE, EDUCATION AND POLITICS OF PIONEER DAYS

NEWSPAPERS OF SAN FRANCISCO—PRESS AT TIME OF GOLD DISCOVERY—NEWS BEFORE
THE AMERICAN CAME TO CALIFORNIA—THE FIRST NEWSPAPER MERGER—VIOLENCE
OF EDITORIAL EXPRESSION—FREEDOM OF THE PRESS—EDITOR KILLED IN A DUEL—
JOURNALISM AN UNPROFITABLE CALLING—DRIVING RIVALS FROM THE FIELD—NOT
MUCH STRESS LAID ON NEWS—EDITORIAL WRITERS DURING THE FIFTIES—USE OF
THE TELEGRAPH—NEWS RECEIVED BY STEAMER—MAILS RECEIVED BY STAGE AND
PONY EXPRESS—JOURNALISM AND LITERATURE CLOSELY ALLIED—VARYING LITERARY
STANDARDS—POLITICS AND LITERATURE—EARLY LIBRARIES—FIRST PUBLISHED BOOK
—THE WEEKLY PAPERS—A WOMAN'S JOURNAL—GOLDEN ERA SCHOOL OF LITERA-
TURE—EDUCATIONAL FACILITIES—THE PUBLIC SCHOOLS AND THE HIGHER EDUCA-
TION—PAROCHIAL AND PRIVATE SCHOOLS—POLITICS AND THE SCHOOLS....... 295

CHAPTER XXXIV

POLITICAL CONDITIONS AFTER PASSAGE OF CONSOLIDATION ACT

SAN FRANCISCO'S SEAL—RESPECTABLE ELEMENT REFORMED—PURITY OF BALLOT BOX—
VIGILANTE'S DISCARD PRIMARY ELECTIONS—A SELF PERPETUATING NOMINATING
COMMITTEE—SECRET SELECTIONS PRODUCE GOOD RESULTS—THE CONSOLIDATION ACT
—MEASURES OF ECONOMY—MANY RESTRICTIONS—REFORMS EFFECTED—NATIONAL
PARTIES—BRODERICK THE CHAMPION OF FREEDOM—BRODERICK REFUSES TO OBEY
LEGISLATIVE INSTRUCTIONS—THE REPUBLICANS—TERRY KILLS BRODERICK IN A DUEL
—CAREER OF TERRY—BAKER'S ORATION AT BRODERICK'S FUNERAL—TERRY BECOMES
A CONFEDERATE GENERAL—OTHER POLITICAL DUELS—PACIFIC COAST REPUBLIC SUG-
GESTED—TALK ABOUT STATE DIVISION—POLITICAL REVOLUTION............. 309

CHAPTER XXXV

CONDITION OF THE CITY AT CLOSE OF THE PIONEER PERIOD

PUEBLO TITLES—VAN NESS ORDINANCE—VEXED QUESTIONS AFFECTING TITLES SETTLED
—CONTROL OF THE WATER FRONT—THE IMPENDING WAR—DOUBTS CONCERNING
CALIFORNIA'S AGRICULTURAL CAPABILITIES—MECHANIC'S INSTITUTE FAIRS—EXCES-
SIVE IMPORTS—SAN FRANCISCO AS A DISTRIBUTING POINT—MANUFACTURES IN 1860
—OBSTACLES TO GROWTH OF MANUFACTURING INDUSTRY—COMMERCE OF THE PORT
—EARLY DEPENDENCE ON WHEAT EXPORTS—FRUIT INDUSTRY IN ITS INFANCY—
MINERAL RESOURCES—EXHAUSTION OF PLACERS DISCUSSED—DISCOVERY OF THE
COMSTOCK LODE—OPTIMISM OF THE ARGONAUTS—APPEARANCE OF THE CITY IN
1861—GROWTH OF THRIFTY HABITS—DEPRESSION PRECEDING THE CIVIL WAR. 319

CONTENTS xix

CHAPTER XXXVI

SAN FRANCISCO'S ATTITUDE DURING THE CIVIL WAR

THE CITY LOYAL TO THE UNION—ATTEMPTS TO TURN OVER ITS DEFENSES TO THE CONFEDERATES—A MINISTER WHO UPHELD THE SOUTH—FIRE-EATING SOUTHERNERS—THE CALL FOR VOLUNTEERS—CONFEDERATE ATTEMPTS ON MEXICO CHECKED—DEPREDATIONS OF PRIVATEERS—HARBOR DEFENSES IN WRETCHED CONDITION—CONTRIBUTIONS TO THE SANITARY COMMISSION FUND—EAGERNESS FOR WAR NEWS—ATTEMPT TO CAPTURE A PACIFIC MAIL STEAMER—CONFEDERATE LAND PIRATES—A GREAT CHANGE OF SENTIMENT—MONUMENTS ERECTED TO HONOR BRODERICK AND BAKER—MONUMENT TO THOMAS STARR KING—THE NEGRO QUESTION—SENATORIAL ELECTION SCANDALS—MERCHANTS PROFIT THROUGH THE WAR........ 331

CHAPTER XXXVII

EFFECTS OF ADHERENCE TO GOLD MONEY DURING THE WAR

CHANGING COMMERCIAL CONDITIONS—THE PANIC OF 1857—INCREASING EXPORTS—TAXATION OF CONSIGNED GOODS—THE WAR TAX—EQUAL TAXATION DEMANDED—WAR INCREASES EMIGRATION TO CALIFORNIA—ADHERENCE TO THE USE OF GOLD MONEY—THE SPECIFIC CONTRACT ACT—MERCHANTS PROFIT THROUGH RETENTION OF GOLD MONEY SYSTEM—GREENBACKS NOT DISTRUSTED—SPECULATION IN GREENBACKS—HIGH RATES OF INTEREST—ILLIBERAL BANKING LAWS—LARGE GOLD PRODUCTION—RESULT OF BAD BANKING METHODS—FIRST SAVING AND LOAN SOCIETY—FEDERAL EMPLOYES ARE PAID IN DEPRECIATED CURRENCY—PAYING DEBTS IN GREENBACKS—ATTEMPTS TO INDUCE ABANDONMENT OF GOLD MONEY—MANUFACTURING DISCOURAGED BY SPECULATION IN MONEY—GREAT EXPECTATIONS OF THE PEOPLE—LOOKING FORWARD TO RAILROAD CONNECTION WITH THE EAST............. 343

CHAPTER XXXVIII

THE TRANSPORTATION PROBLEMS OF CALIFORNIA

EARLY FREIGHT AND FARE RATES—FIRST EXPERIENCES IN RAILROADING—PROPOSED TRANSCONTINENTAL RAILROADS—PROJECTORS OF THE FIRST OVERLAND RAILROAD—ORGANIZATION OF THE CENTRAL PACIFIC—CONGRESSIONAL AID TO OVERLAND RAILROADS—GRANTS OF LAND AND FINANCIAL AID TO THE CENTRAL PACIFIC—GREAT HOPES BASED ON OPENING OF COMMUNICATION WITH EASTERN STATES—EVERYBODY FRIENDLY TO THE PROMOTERS OF THE RAILROAD—FRIENDLINESS CONVERTED INTO HOSTILITY—GREED OF THE CENTRAL PACIFIC MANAGERS—CAUSES OF HOSTILITY—EFFORTS TO ESTABLISH A MONOPOLY—ATTEMPT TO GRAB MINERAL LANDS—SHUTTING OUT COMPETITION—CONTRACT AND FINANCE COMPANY—OAKLAND WATER FRONT GRAB—COMPLETION OF THE FIRST OVERLAND LINE................. 355

CONTENTS

CHAPTER XXXIX

LABOR CONDITIONS AND THE CHINESE QUESTION

ORGANIZATION OF A CENTRAL TRADES ASSEMBLY—STRIKE OF FOUNDRY EMPLOYES—LABOR AND POLITICS—ATTEMPT TO PASS AN EIGHT HOUR LAW—FORMATION OF AN EIGHT HOUR LEAGUE—TRADES UNIONS IN 1867—A WORKINGMEN'S CONVENTION—LABOR LEADERS FAVOR POLITICAL ACTION—WORKINGMEN WIN IN PRIMARY ELECTIONS—TRADE UNIONISM RECEIVES A BACKSET—WOMEN WORKERS—THE WORKINGMEN AND THE CHINESE—RACE PREJUDICE IN EARLY DAYS—LEGISLATIVE INVESTIGATION IN 1852—SAN FRANCISCANS TOLERANT OF CHINESE—OPPOSITION TO CHINESE IMMIGRATION—RAILROAD IMPORTS CHINESE LABORERS—FEW JAPANESE—ASSUMED NEED OF ORIENTAL LABOR—LAND MONOPOLY AND CHINESE LABOR..... 371

CHAPTER XL

THE MINING INDUSTRY AND MINING STOCK SPECULATION

SAN FRANCISCO AND THE MINING INDUSTRY—THE COMSTOCK LODE—DISCOVERY OF SILVER ORE—FOUNDATION OF SAN FRANCISCO'S FINANCIAL STRENGTH—CREATION OF A STOCK BOARD—PRIMITIVE DEALINGS IN STOCKS—MINING STOCK SPECULATION FROWNED UPON AT FIRST—THE SPECULATIVE FEVER TAKES HOLD—PROSPEROUS BROKERS—NEVADA STOCKS DEALT IN CHIEFLY—EXTENT OF THE MARKET—THE SUTRO TUNNEL SUGGESTED—THE ATTEMPT TO OVERREACH SUTRO PROVES UNSUCCESSFUL—MINERS STAND BY SUTRO AGAINST THE "BANK CROWD"—RELATIONS OF NEVADA AND SAN FRANCISCO—FAITH OF SAN FRANCISCANS IN MINING AS A SOURCE OF WEALTH—LEGITIMATE AND SPECULATIVE MINING...................... 381

CHAPTER XLI

COMMERCE, MANUFACTURES AND FINANCES OF SAN FRANCISCO

SAN FRANCISCANS VERY CONSERVATIVE—OPPOSITION TO CREATING A CLEARING HOUSE—OVERSHADOWING FINANCIAL IMPORTANCE OF THE CITY—EXPANSION OF SHIPPING INDUSTRY—CHANGE IN THE CHARACTER OF IMPORTS—SAN FRANCISCO A DISTRIBUTING CENTER—FISHERIES OF THE PACIFIC COAST—THE COD FISH INDUSTRY—THE ACQUISITION OF ALASKA—SEWARD'S GOOD BARGAIN—VALUE OF ALASKAN TRADE—TRADE WITH THE HAWAIIAN ISLANDS—COMMUNICATION WITH HAWAII—RECIPROCITY TREATY WITH THE ISLANDS—SAN FRANCISCO'S ATTITUDE TOWARD RECIPROCITY—PLANS FOR ANNEXATION—GROWING TRADE WITH THE ISLANDS—ORIENTAL TRADE—FIRST SHIP OF THE PACIFIC MAIL TO THE ORIENT—SAN FRANCISCO'S COASTWISE TRADE—RAPID GROWTH OF WHEAT EXPORTS—DIVERSIFICATION OF AGRICULTURE—WOOL INDUSTRY—WOOLEN AND OTHER MANUFACTURING INDUSTRIES—THE FUR SEAL CONTRACT—END OF CALIFORNIA'S ISOLATION.................... 389

CONTENTS xxi

CHAPTER XLII

NATIONAL, STATE AND MUNICIPAL POLITICS IN THE SIXTIES

THE LAST POLITICAL DUEL—CONTINUED SUCCESS OF THE PEOPLE'S PARTY—KEEPING DOWN TAXATION—PEOPLE'S PARTY SUFFERS DEFEAT—A LUKEWARM PERIOD—THE TAPE WORM TICKET AND BALLOT REFORM—LOCAL SELF GOVERNMENT DENIED—BUILDING A NEW CITY HALL ON THE INSTALLMENT PLAN—WATER SUPPLY—MOVEMENT TO SECURE MUNICIPAL CONTROL OF WATER SYSTEM—OPPOSITION TO CREATION OF DEBT—WIDENING OF KEARNY STREET—PROPOSAL TO CUT DOWN RINCON HILL—QUIETING OUTSIDE LAND TITLES—SECURING LAND FOR GOLDEN GATE PARK—THE LAND FOR PARK PURPOSES ORIGINALLY A DREARY WASTE OF SAND—WOODWARD'S GARDENS—ACTIVE BUILDING OPERATIONS—REAL ESTATE IN FAVOR—PRICES OF REAL ESTATE—MARKET STREET IN 1870—STREET CAR CONVENIENCES—CONGESTION OF POPULATION—BANKING AND BUSINESS CENTER—APPEARANCE OF CITY AT CLOSE OF SIXTIES.. 403

CHAPTER XLIII

THE HARBOR, THE RAILROADS AND THE LAND MONOPOLISTS

FERRY SERVICE—HARBOR COMMISSION CREATED—SEA WALL PROVIDED FOR—BAD MANAGEMENT DRIVES AWAY SHIPPING—THE BULKHEAD LINE DEFINED—HUNTERS' POINT DRY DOCK—BLOSSOM ROCK REMOVED—COMPLAINT ABOUT PILOT LAWS—SEA ROUTES FROM SAN FRANCISCO—LINES TO COAST PORTS—STATE INTERDEPENDENCE NOT MUCH THOUGHT ABOUT—RAILROAD PLANS OF MONOPOLIZING—ALL TRAFFIC RIVALS FORCED OUT BY THE CENTRAL PACIFIC—MORE LAND GRABBING—ATTEMPT TO MAKE GOAT ISLAND A TERMINUS—FEAR OF GOAT ISLAND RIVALRY—CALIFORNIA RAILROADS IN 1870-71—INCREASING HOSTILITY TO RAILROAD MANAGEMENT—THE RAILROADS AND THE LABORING CLASS—LAND MONOPOLY AND TAXATION QUESTIONS—WOMAN SUFFRAGE ADVOCATED—AGITATION OF QUESTION OF REVISING THE CONSTITUTION... 417

CHAPTER XLIV

SOCIAL SIDE OF LIFE IN SAN FRANCISCO IN THE SIXTIES

THE VACATION HABIT STILL UNDEVELOPED—NEAR-BY ATTRACTIONS—GOLDEN GATE PARK BEFORE IT WAS RECLAIMED—THE CLIFF HOUSE AND WOODWARD'S GARDENS FAVORITE RESORTS—GRAND OPERA GREATLY APPRECIATED—FAVORITE OPERAS OF EARLY DAYS—CONCERTS POPULAR—THE REIGN OF MINSTRELSY—ACTORS OF PIONEER DAYS—THE DRAMA DURING THE SIXTIES—VOGUE OF BENEFIT PERFORMANCES—BIG PRICES PAID TO HEAR EDWIN FORREST—HARRIGAN AND OTHER CALIFORNIA FAVORITES—EARLY VAUDEVILLE—LOCATION OF OLD TIME THEATERS—SAN FRANCISCO'S FIRST DRAMATIC PERFORMANCE—SOCIETY IN THE FORMATIVE STAGE—FIRE AND MILITARY ORGANIZATIONS—PUBLIC CELEBRATIONS—SPORTS—POLITICAL TURNOUTS. 431

CONTENTS

CHAPTER XLV

INCREASING INTEREST IN CIVICS AND A MORAL AWAKENING

PRECAUTIONS NEGLECTED IN PIONEER DAYS—RESTRAINT UPON EXTRAVAGANCE—THE INFLUENCE OF WOMEN—ABATEMENT OF THE DRINK HABIT—INCREASING RESPECT FOR LAW—BANDIT VASQUEZ—CRIME IN SAN FRANCISCO—KILLING OF CRITTENDEN BY LAURA D. FAIR—A MORAL AWAKENING FOLLOWS—THOMAS STARR KING'S CHURCH —ERECTION OF TEMPLE EL EMANUEL—GRACE CATHEDRAL—TEMPERANCE AND CHARITABLE ORGANIZATIONS—EDUCATIONAL WORK—GROWTH OF PUBLIC SCHOOL SYSTEM—MODE OF SELECTING TEACHERS—COURSE OF STUDIES—MODERN LANGUAGES TAUGHT—NIGHT SCHOOLS—PRIVATE AND PAROCHIAL SCHOOLS—THE HIGHER EDUCATION—THE STATE UNIVERSITY—LITERATURE—HIGHLY SEASONED WRITING— LITERATURE AS A CALLING—JOURNALISM IN THE SIXTIES—WOMEN REPORTERS— NEWS GATHERING IN THE SIXTIES—ART AND ARTISTS IN THE SIXTIES—INTERIOR DECORATION—HOTELS AND RESTAURANTS—THE HOME FEELING BEGINNING TO DEVELOP. 447

CHAPTER XLVI

DISASTERS OCCURRING DURING THE EIGHTEEN SIXTY DECADE

OPTIMISTIC TRAITS OF SAN FRANCISCANS—DISASTROUS FIRES FAILED TO DISCOURAGE THEM IN THE EARLY DAYS—THE FAILURE TO TAKE PROPER PRECAUTIONS AGAINST FIRES—BRET HARTE'S JESTING PROPHECY—THE EARTHQUAKE OF 1868—EFFECTS OF THE SHOCK—BADLY CONSTRUCTED BUILDINGS SUFFER—THE DISTURBANCE CAUSES NO APPREHENSION—WHY SAN FRANCISCANS ARE NOT APPREHENSIVE— INCIDENTS OF THE DISTURBANCE OF 1868—NEWSPAPERS STATE REAL ESTATE ONLY TEMPORARILY AFFECTED—NO ATTEMPT TO CONCEAL THE FACTS—A NITRO GLYCERINE EXPLOSION—OCEAN DISASTERS IN THE FIFTIES AND SIXTIES—NO INTERRUPTION OF PROGRESS—SIGNS OF AN IMPENDING DEPRESSION AT THE CLOSE OF THE DECADE SIXTY..467

CHAPTER XLVII

LABOR AND OTHER TROUBLES DURING THE SEVENTIES

TRANSCONTINENTAL RAILROAD BRINGS DISAPPOINTMENT—GROWTH OF THE ANTI MONOPOLY SENTIMENT—DEMANDS OF THE FARMERS—THE "DOLLY VARDEN" PARTY— BRYCE INVESTIGATES CALIFORNIA CONDITIONS—FRAUDULENT LAND GRANTS—THE PROGRESSIVE PLATFORM OF 1912 FORESHADOWED IN 1877—REVIVAL OF THE CHINESE QUESTION—THE FIRST APPEARANCE OF DENIS KEARNEY IN POLITICS—IRRIGATION AND SMALL LAND HOLDINGS—DIVERSIFICATION OF PRODUCTION—POLITICAL ACTIVITIES OF WORKINGMEN..477

CONTENTS xxiii

CHAPTER XLVIII

SAN FRANCISCO SURRENDERS TO THE SPIRIT OF SPECULATION

GROWTH OF COMMERCE OF THE PORT—UNHEALTHY URBAN EXPANSION—SAN FRANCISCO WITHOUT A RIVAL—CALIFORNIA PRODUCTS UNAPPRECIATED—GREAT CHANGES IN PRODUCTION—OIL PRODUCTION POSSIBILITIES SCOUTED BY CAPITAL—DISCOVERY OF THE BIG BONANZA—FAKE MINING PROPERTIES—CORRUPT MANAGEMENT OF MINES—EVERYBODY CRAZED BY SPECULATION—EXCITING SCENES IN THE EXCHANGES AND ON THE STREETS—VILE TRICKS OF MANIPULATORS—TREMENDOUS FLUCTUATIONS IN STOCKS—IRRATIONAL ACTIONS OF SPECULATORS—THE MANY FLEECED BY THE FEW—OUTPUT OF THE PRODUCTIVE MINES—THE ACCUMULATIONS OF A COMMUNITY ABSORBED BY SHARPERS—THE "MUD HENS" AND "PAUPER ALLEY"—THE COMSTOCK LODE—FLOOD, O'BRIEN, MACKAY AND FAIR—MANIPULATION OF BIG BONANZA STOCKS—STRUGGLES FOR CONTROL—THE BROKERS—SHEARING OF THE LAMBS AND THE RESULT..487

CHAPTER XLIX

THE BURSTING OF THE STOCK SPECULATION BUBBLE

EFFECTS OF CALIFORNIA'S ISOLATION—A SHORT LIVED BOOM—THE EASTERN PANIC OF 1873—FAILURE OF THE BANK OF CALIFORNIA—CAREER OF WILLIAM C. RALSTON—RISE OF RALSTON FROM THE RANKS—CAUSE OF THE FAILURE OF THE BANK OF CALIFORNIA—WILLIAM SHARON—RALSTON'S ENTERPRISE—AN EXHIBITION OF FICKLENESS AND INGRATITUDE—THE DEATH OF RALSTON—VICTIM OF A BAD SYSTEM OF BANKING—THE BANK CROWD AND FLOOD AND O'BRIEN—REHABILITATION OF BANK OF CALIFORNIA—FLOOD AND O'BRIEN START THE NEVADA BANK—THE DESIRE TO GET RICH QUICKLY—THE GREAT DIAMOND SWINDLE—THE BITERS BIT SPECULATION IMPEDED INDUSTRIAL DEVELOPMENT—MANUFACTURES IN 1876—LABOR'S SERIOUS MISTAKE—CROP FAILURE—UNEMPLOYED FLOCK TO THE CITY—BEGINNING OF SERIOUS LABOR TROUBLES—CONDITIONS ON EVE OF THE SAND LOT DISTURBANCES...503

CHAPTER L

CONDITIONS ON EVE OF ADOPTION OF THE CONSTITUTION OF 1879

CAUSES THAT LED TO "SAND LOT" DISTURBANCES—EVIL OF SPECIAL LEGISLATION CORRUPTION AND WASTE—THE NEW CITY HALL—CITY TREASURY LOOTED—STREETS AND SIDEWALKS IN A DILAPIDATED STATE—KEARNEY'S DENUNCIATION OF OFFICIALS—THE NEWSPAPERS AND THE SAND LOTTERS—BOSSISM IN THE SEVENTIES—BOGUS NON PARTISANISM—THE FEDERAL RING—THE SPECTACULAR CAREER OF GEORGE M. PINNEY—PINNEY BECOMES A BROKER AND A MILLIONAIRE—BECOMES INVOLVED AND FLEES THE COUNTRY—HIS RETURN RESULTS IN OVERTHROW OF REPUBLICAN PARTY—THE DESTRUCTION OF SEVERAL BANKS—BANK COMMISSION ACT OF 1878—ESTABLISHMENT OF CLEARING HOUSE—THE UNITED STATES MINT AND SUB-TREASURY—AVERSION FOR PAPER MONEY—INTRODUCTION OF SAEE DEPOSIT VAULTS........515

xxiv   CONTENTS

CHAPTER LI

THE SAND LOT TROUBLES AND THE NEW CONSTITUTION

STATE RIPE FOR REVOLT—THE LONG AGITATION FOR A NEW CONSTITUTION—THE LEGISLATURE OF 1877-78—A LONG LIST OF GOOD MEASURES TO ITS CREDIT—"PIECE" CLUBS—NUMEROUS REFORMS EFFECTED—THE MAIL DOCK RIOT AND THE PICK HANDLE BRIGADE—THE FIRST POLITICAL MEETINGS ON THE SAND LOT—THE WORKINGMAN'S PARTY—DENIS KEARNEY AS A LEADER—KEARNEY'S ATTAINMENTS—HISTORIAN BRYCE'S BLUNDER—THE MANIFESTO OF THE WORKINGMAN'S PARTY—FIRST W. P. C. TRIUMPH—SIMILARITY OF WORKINGMEN'S PLATFORM TO THAT OF 1912 PROGRESSIVES—CROCKER'S SPITE FENCE—KEARNEY SHOWS THE WHITE FEATHER—"WORK OR BREAD"—A GAG LAW PASSED—AN INADEQUATE POLICE FORCE—THE FIGHT FOR THE NEW CONSTITUTION AND ITS ADOPTION—THE NEW ORGANIC LAW NOT A SAND LOT PRODUCT—REFORMS EFFECTED—PROMINENT PART PLAYED BY "CHRONICLE" IN SECURING ADOPTION OF THE CONSTITUTION................529

CHAPTER LII

CONDITIONS AFTER THE ADOPTION OF THE NEW CONSTITUTION

PREDICTIONS OF DISASTER—THE LAST BIG STOCK DEAL—DEALING IN FUTURES PROHIBITED—NEW ORGANIC LAW IMPROPERLY DEALT WITH—WORKINGMEN CUT LOOSE FROM ALL ALLIES—KALLOCH ELECTED MAYOR OF SAN FRANCISCO—THE MURDER OF CHARLES DE YOUNG—THE ATTEMPT TO IMPEACH KALLOCH—JUDGES OVERAWED BY A "POPULAR" DEMONSTRATION—KALLOCH'S ADMINISTRATION HELD UP AS AN AWFUL EXAMPLE—JUDGE MADE LAW—RAILROAD TAXES SHIRKED—RAILROAD PROPOSES GROSS INCOME TAX OF $2\frac{1}{2}$ PER CENT—REPEATED FAILURES TO ADOPT A CHARTER—BRYCE REVISES SOME PREVIOUSLY EXPRESSED VIEWS—HENRY GEORGE'S SAN FRANCISCO CAREER—PREDICTIONS THAT CAME TO NAUGHT—SAN FRANCISCO'S BOSSES CHRIS BUCKLEY PREPARING FOR LEADERSHIP—THE BOSS REPAIRS THE FORTUNES OF THE SHATTERED DEMOCRATIC PARTY................................549

CHAPTER LIII

PUBLIC AND PRIVATE EFFORTS TO IMPROVE THE CITY

DEMAND FOR REFORM—COMMUNICATION OPENED WITH ALL PARTS OF THE STATE—STREETS AND SIDEWALKS IN BAD CONDITION—A GROWING SENTIMENT IN FAVOR OF GOOD PAVEMENTS—KEARNEY STREET WIDENED—DUPONT STREET CHANGED TO GRANT AVENUE—OBJECTION TO EXTENDING FIRE LIMITS—SUTRO'S INVESTMENTS IN REAL ESTATE—JAMES LICK AND HIS BEQUESTS—CITY HALL CONSTRUCTED ON THE INSTALLMENT PLAN—GETTING RID OF THE SAND DUNES—THE PALACE HOTEL OPENED—BALDWIN HOTEL—CONGESTION IN DOWN TOWN DISTRICTS—POPULATION SPREADING WESTWARD—"SOUTH OF THE SLOT"—DRIFTING AWAY FROM THE MISSION DISTRICT—CHANGES EFFECTED BY IMPROVED TRANSPORTATION FACILITIES—INVENTION OF THE CABLE TRACTION SYSTEM—THE FIRST CABLE ROAD—COAXING INVESTORS TO

CONTENTS xxv

BUILD STREET RAILWAYS—STREET CAR FARES REDUCED TO FIVE CENTS—GREAT DEMAND FOR STREET CAR FRANCHISES—WHOLESALE GRANT OF FRANCHISES—NOB HILL MANSIONS—ACTIVITY OF REAL ESTATE DEALERS—RECLAMATION OF GOLDEN GATE PARK—MULTIPLICATION OF URBAN CONVENIENCES—FIRST ELECTRIC LIGHT—TELEPHONE INTRODUCED—WATER SUPPLY—RAILWAY AND SEA TRANSPORTATION... 565

CHAPTER LIV

SOCIAL CONDITIONS AND THE UNREST DURING THE SEVENTIES

THE CHINESE QUESTION—FEDERAL COURTS AND CHINESE—THE CHINESE EXCLUSION ACT—VOTE ON CHINESE EXCLUSION IN 1879—CHINESE SERVANTS—SAN FRANCISCO HOTELS AND RESTAURANTS—THE WINE DRINKING HABIT—THE FREE LUNCH—SAN FRANCISCANS NOT GIVEN TO DISPLAY—VULGAR OSTENTATION NOT COMMON—RICH MEN WITH SMALL ESTABLISHMENTS—SOCIAL CHANGES—DECLINING INFLUENCE OF THE PIONEER—CENTENARY OF FOUNDING OF THE MISSION—SUNDAY OBSERVANCE—THE TREATING HABIT—MERCANTILE LIBRARY LOTTERY—SALMI MORSE'S PASSION PLAY—THE AUTHORS CARNIVAL—A LAW ABIDING PEOPLE—RECEPTION OF GENERAL GRANT—CELEBRATIONS AND PAGEANTS—AMUSEMENT—VOGUE OF OPERA BOUFFE—CHANGE IN TASTE OF THEATERGOERS—SPORTS—RACING ENCOURAGED—EVIDENT WANE OF NEGRO MINSTRELSY—FIRST PRODUCTION OF "PINAFORE" IN AMERICA—PROBABLE ORIGIN OF MOVING PICTURE IDEA—PRIZE FIGHTING—BASEBALL—WALKING CONTESTS—CHILDREN'S SPORTS—NEARBY RESORTS—GROWTH OF SUBURBS.... 595

CHAPTER LV

VARIED ACTIVITIES OF THE PEOPLE OF A GROWING CITY

SAN FRANCISCO POLICE FORCE IMPROVED—A GANG OF BANDITS EXTERMINATED—TWO NOTORIOUS CRIMINAL CASES—THE DELAYS OF THE LAW—A TWICE DISPOILED BANK—FIGHT FOR THE PROTECTION OF SAILORS—THE BARBARY COAST—THE BAR AND ATTEMPTS AT REFORM OF CRIMINAL PROCEDURE—COLONEL E. D. BAKER AND OTHER NOTED LAWYERS OF SAN FRANCISCO—JUSTICE FIELD OF THE SUPREME COURT—CALIFORNIA'S FIRST CHIEF JUSTICE—THE RAILROAD AND THE LEGAL PROFESSION—CORPORATION LAWYERS IN THE CONSTITUTIONAL CONVENTION—JOURNALISTIC INFLUENCE DURING THE PERIOD—GEORGE K. FITCH AND THE "BULLETIN"—THE "SAN FRANCISCO CHRONICLE"—THE "ARGONAUT" AND ITS FOUNDER—BEGINNINGS OF THE SUNDAY MAGAZINE IN DAILY PAPERS—WELL KNOWN WRITERS—ART IN THE SEVENTIES AND EARLY EIGHTIES—LIBRARIES—CALIFORNIA'S FREE LIBRARY SYSTEM—HENRY GEORGE'S LAND THEORIES AND HIS GREAT BOOK—JOHN F. SWIFT'S POLITICAL NOVEL—JOAQUIN MILLER—ROBERT LOUIS STEVENSON'S LIFE IN SAN FRANCISCO—BANCROFT'S PACIFIC COAST HISTORIES—MONT EAGLE UNIVERSITY—STANFORD'S FOUNDATION—EDUCATIONAL—PUBLIC AND PRIVATE SCHOOLS................ 619

CHAPTER LVI

TRANSPORTATION TROUBLES OF SAN FRANCISCO MERCHANTS

RAILROAD COMMISSIONERS CORRUPTED BY THE CORPORATION—EFFORTS TO REGULATE DEFEATED—CORPORATION COMPELLED TO PAY ITS BACK TAXES—THE FRESNO RATE

CASE—BUYING OFF SEA COMPETITORS—MERCHANTS SHOW SIGNS OF REVOLTING—FORMATION OF TRAFFIC ASSOCIATION—THE TRANSCONTINENTAL ASSOCIATION—NORTH AMERICAN NAVIGATION COMPANY—THE MOVEMENT TO BUILD A COMPETING RAILROAD—SUBSCRIPTIONS TO SAN JOAQUIN VALLEY RAILROAD—TERMINAL FACILITIES SECURED—THE ROAD TURNED OVER TO THE ATCHISON, TOPEKA AND SANTA FE—THE PEOPLE BETRAYED—PACIFIC COAST JOBBERS AND MANUFACTURERS' ASSOCIATION—GROWTH OF SOUTHERN PACIFIC SYSTEM—MONETARY TROUBLES OF 1893—BUSINESS DEPRESSION IN SAN FRANCISCO.................................. 649

CHAPTER LVII
MONETARY PECULIARITIES OF SAN FRANCISCO AND CALIFORNIA

THE USE OF GOLD COIN IN CALIFORNIA—WHY THE STATE WAS ABLE TO MAINTAIN SPECIE PAYMENTS—AN EXCESS OF SUBSIDIARY SILVER CAUSES TROUBLE IN SAN FRANCISCO—THE VARIABLE "BIT" AND THE HOSTILITY TO THE 5-CENT NICKEL—THE TRADE DOLLAR EXPERIMENT—IGNORANCE OF EFFECT OF SILVER DEMONETIZATION IN SAN FRANCISCO—THE TRADE DOLLAR REDEMPTION JOB—FALL IN SILVER PRICES INJURES MINING INDUSTRY—CAPITAL AND RATES OF INTEREST—BANK CLEARINGS—THE CRISIS OF 1893 AND THE SUBSEQUENT BUSINESS DEPRESSION—CALIFORNIA PRODUCERS SUFFER FROM FALLING PRICES—SAN FRANCISCO VEGETATES—HAWAIIAN TRADE—TEA MARKET SLIPS AWAY—IMPORTANCE OF ALASKAN TRADE—CUTTING UP BIG RANCHES—OPERATIONS OF MINT AND SUBTREASURY—OBSTACLES TO MANUFACTURING DEVELOPMENT—AGRICULTURE—IMMIGRATION..663

CHAPTER LVIII
NUMEROUS AND SERIOUS LABOR TROUBLES IN THE CITY

LABOR CONDITIONS IN 1883—CHANGED RELATIONS OF EMPLOYER AND EMPLOYED—DIMINISHING NUMBER OF CHINESE—AN ANARCHISTIC ASSOCIATION—THE INTERNATIONALS—CAREER OF BURNETT G. HASKELL, SOCIALIST AND AGITATOR—PROPAGANDA OF THE FEDERATED TRADES—STRIKE OF FOUNDRY WORKERS IN 1885—STRIKE OF THE BREWERS—SAILORS MAINTAIN A LONG STRIKE—TRADES UNIONS RECEIVE A SETBACK—FORMATION OF AN EMPLOYERS ASSOCIATION—TRADES UNIONS AGAIN ACTIVE—UNSKILLED LABOR ORGANIZED—UNIONS ENGAGE IN POLITICS—ENTER ABE RUEF—NUMEROUS STRIKES IN 1901—THE TEAMSTERS' STRIKE—THE ALLIANCE AND THE TEAMSTERS—POSITION OF THE EMPLOYERS—SCENES OF VIOLENCE—GOVERNOR GAGE INTERVENES—RUEF AND THE WORKINGMEN—FORMATION OF WORKINGMEN'S PARTY—PLATFORM OF WORKINGMEN—ELECTION OF SCHMITZ—CLAIM THAT HE MADE CITY PROSPEROUS—SCHMITZ REELECTED TWICE—RUEF'S METHODS—THE BOSS SUPERSEDED BY RUEF—CHRIS BUCKLEY................ 681

CHAPTER LIX
SAN FRANCISCO MAKES MANY EXPERIMENTS IN MUNICIPAL GOVERNMENT

REPEATED EFFORTS TO SECURE A NEW ORGANIC LAW—THE CONSOLIDATION ACT FINALLY DISCARDED—A CONTINUOUS STRUGGLE FOR REFORM—AUSTRALIAN BALLOT ADOPTED

CONTENTS xxvii

—OLD TIME PRIMARY FARCES—A GREATLY IMPROVED PRIMARY LAW—THE BOSSES AND THE STRATTON PRIMARY LAW—IT MERELY RESULTS IN GIVING THE CITY A NEW SET—BOSSES PROFIT BY DIVISION OF THE RESPECTABLE ELEMENT—THE RAILROAD POLITICIANS AND BOSSES WERE NOT INNOVATORS—SCANDALS ATTENDING ELECTION OF LELAND STANFORD—DOMINATION OF STATE AND MUNICIPAL POLITICS BY THE RAILROAD—INCREASED MUNICIPAL EXPENDITURES BUT FEW IMPROVEMENTS—CHANGES PRODUCED BY ADOPTION OF CHARTER OF 1898—NO ECONOMIES EFFECTED—A MORE EXPENSIVE FORM OF GOVERNMENT—CITY SECURES LOCAL AUTONOMY—THE CITY BEAUTIFUL MOVEMENT—MERCHANTS' ASSOCIATION AND ITS ACTIVITIES—IT FURNISHES MANY VALUABLE OBJECT LESSONS—DOLLAR LIMIT DEPARTED FROM—IMPROVEMENT CLUBS—CIVIL SERVICE LAW—COST OF CITY GOVERNMENT—VOTING MACHINES—WOMAN SUFFRAGE DEFEATED IN 1896—THE INITIATIVE IN SAN FRANCISCO—OWNERSHIP OF PUBLIC UTILITIES—GEARY STREET ROAD—TAXATION CHARGES. 701

CHAPTER LX

FREQUENT ALTERNATIONS OF ACTIVITY AND DEPRESSION

INDIVIDUAL ACTIVITY EFFECTIVE—PROGRESS IN SPITE OF POLITICAL DRAWBACKS—ADVERSITY AND PROSPERITY WELL BALANCED—GRIEVANCES SOON FORGOTTEN—GREAT INCREASE IN SAVINGS BANKS DEPOSITS—RESOURCES OF COMMERCIAL BANKS ENLARGED—ACTIVITY FOLLOWS SPANISH-AMERICAN WAR—THE MIDWINTER FAIR OF 1894—THE RAILROAD RIOTS OF 1894—TRANSMUTING CLIMATE INTO GOLD—SAN FRANCISCO HARSHLY CRITICIZED—THE KLONDIKE GOLD DISCOVERY AND THE RUSH TO ALASKA—A MILD REVIVAL OF MINING SPECULATION—HYDRAULIC MINING STOPPED BY COURTS—GOLD DREDGING—EXPANSION OF GENERAL MINING INDUSTRY—AGRICULTURE—RAPID URBAN DEVELOPMENT—IMPEDIMENTS TO MANUFACTURING GROWTH—FIGURES THAT DECEIVED—TRADES UNION RESTRICTIONS—MANUFACTURES IN 1904—IMPORTANCE OF HARBOR RECOGNIZED—HARBOR COMMISSION A POLITICAL MACHINE—CORRUPTION AND WASTE ON WATER FRONT—CITIZENS' COMMITTEE FORMULATE PLANS OF IMPROVEMENT—IMPROVED SHIPPING FACILITIES—HAWAIIAN AND ALASKAN TRADE—FAILURE OF A BIG WHEAT DEAL—LUMBER AND COAL TRADE—THE OIL INDUSTRY—DOMESTIC SHIPPING INDUSTRY—THE UNION IRON WORKS—WAR SHIPS BUILT—OTHER SHIPBUILDING CONCERNS......723

CHAPTER LXI

PEOPLE RISE SUPERIOR TO POLITICAL AND OTHER TROUBLES

INDIVIDUAL EFFORTS SCORES A TRIUMPH—UNBUSINESSLIKE METHODS IN CONDUCT OF MUNICIPAL AFFAIRS—LACK OF CONFIDENCE IN PUBLIC OFFICIALS—STREET IMPROVEMENT DUE TO INDIVIDUAL EFFORT—LACK OF IMAGINATION—SAN FRANCISCO'S FIRST STEEL FRAME STRUCTURE—IMPROVEMENT IN BUSINESS ARCHITECTURE—FIREPROOF STRUCTURES BEFORE 1906—RESIDENCE ARCHITECTURE—SITES THAT AFFORD MARINE VIEWS GROW IN FAVOR—APPRECIATIVE CRITICISM BY STRANGERS—SAN FRANCISCO'S PICTURESQUE APPEARANCE—GROWTH OF THE HOME INSTINCT

xxviii   CONTENTS

—REAL ESTATE AND REAL ESTATE DEALERS—OPENING OF NEW DISTRICTS—
"GRAFT" AND THE TIPPING HABIT—FRANCHISES NOT REGARDED AS VALUABLE—
THE DOOR LOCKED AFTER THE STEED WAS STOLEN—SCHEMES TO SHUT OUT COM-
PETITION—CABLE SYSTEM ADOPTED ON MARKET STREET LINES—AGITATION AGAINST
OVERHEAD TROLLEY—UNITED RAILROADS TAKE OVER CHIEF CITY STREET CAR
LINES—CONTROL EASILY SURRENDERED BY LOCAL CAPITALISTS—MUNICIPAL EF-
FORTS AT BUILDING A STREET RAILWAY—NO REAL OBSTACLE TO CREATION OF A
RIVAL STREET RAILWAY SYSTEM—BURNHAM PLANS FOR A CITY BEAUTIFUL—THE
PARKS—WATER SUPPLY—TELEGRAPHIC EXTENSION—CABLE TO THE PHILIPPINES
FROM SAN FRANCISCO 749

CHAPTER LXII

VARIED PHASES OF LIFE IN SAN FRANCISCO

THE AMERICAN PROTECTIVE ASSOCIATION—JAPANESE IN THE PUBLIC SCHOOLS—DOC-
TOR O'DONNELL AND THE CHINESE LEPERS—CHINESE QUARTER A SORE SPOT—THE
BUBONIC PLAGUE SCARE—COMMISSION INVESTIGATES AND FINDS NO CAUSE FOR
ALARM—HEALTH CONDITION GOOD—NEIGHBORHOOD SETTLEMENT AND OTHER UP-
LIFT WORK—THE ASSOCIATED CHARITIES—RISE OF WOMEN'S CLUBS AND THEIR
ACTIVITIES—SOCIAL CLUBS AND FRATERNAL ORGANIZATIONS—AMUSEMENTS—
SHIFTING OF AMUSEMENT CENTER—THE LAST LAY OF THE MINSTRELS—SUCCESSFUL
SEASONS OF GRAND OPERA—RESTAURANTS AND NIGHT LIFE IN SAN FRANCISCO—
ORIGIN OF MOVING PICTURES—NEWSPAPER SENDS OUT WEATHER WARNINGS—SAN
FRANCISCO METEOROLOGY—THE RACING GAME AND OTHER SPORTS—THE BICYCLE
CRAZE—AUTOMOBILES DISPLACE CARRIAGES—EDUCATION FACILITIES—PUBLIC AND
OTHER LIBRARIES—JOURNALISM—LITERATURE AND WRITERS—EASTERN CRITI-
CISMS OF SAN FRANCISCO SHORTCOMINGS—ABNORMAL FEATURES OF SOCIAL LIFE—
CONTRACT MARRIAGES—CELEBRATED CRIMINAL CASES—CHINESE CRIMINALS—
TECHNICALITIES AND THE ADMINISTRATION OF JUSTICE................... 777

CHAPTER LXIII

THE GREAT DISASTER AND CONFLAGRATION OF APRIL, 1906

CONDITION OF THE CITY ON THE EVE OF THE EARTHQUAKE—SAN FRANCISCO ON TOP
OF THE WAVE OF PROSPERITY—THE WORKINGMEN'S PARTY AND BOSS RUEF IN
POWER—COMMERCE AND MORALS MIXED—BUILDINGS BEFORE THE FIRE—OPPOSI-
TION TO EXTENSION OF FIRE LIMITS—LAST PERFORMANCE IN THE GRAND OPERA
HOUSE—NO WARNING OF IMPENDING DANGER—EFFECTS OF THE EARTHQUAKE—
THE THREE DAYS' CONFLAGRATION—MUCH PROPERTY UNNECESSARILY SACRIFICED
—EXPLOSIVES TIMIDLY AND UNSKILFULLY USED—ORGANIZATION OF CITIZENS COM-
MITTEE OF FIFTY—CIRCULATION OF WILD RUMORS—COMPOSITION OF THE COM-
MITTEE OF FIFTY—RIGID PRECAUTIONS ADOPTED BY THE MILITARY—FOOD IN GREAT
DEMAND—RELIEF POURS IN FROM ALL POINTS—THE UPLIFT WORK OF THE DAILY
PRESS—FILLMORE STREET BECOMES CENTER OF ACTIVITY—REJOICING OVER RE-
SUMPTION OF STREET CAR TRAVEL—OVERHEAD TROLLEY PERMIT FOR MARKET

CONTENTS   xxix

STREET GRANTED—CHIMNEY INSPECTION—AREA OF THE BURNED DISTRICT—NOTABLE ESCAPES FROM THE FLAMES—INVESTIGATION BY UNITED STATES GEOLOGICAL SURVEY—BUILDING TO GUARD AGAINST TREMORS—FAILURE OF WATER SUPPLY—THE EXODUS FROM THE CITY—RELIEF WORK OF THE SOUTHERN PACIFIC...........819

CHAPTER LXIV

PROMPT INAUGURATION OF THE WORK OF REHABILITATION

FIRST SPECK OF THE GRAFT TROUBLES—SCHMITZ AS THE PRESIDING OFFICER OF THE CITIZENS' COMMITTEE—ORDER PRESERVED WITHOUT DIFFICULTY—MARTIAL LAW NOT IN FORCE—A SUMMARY EXECUTION—GOOD SENSE DISPLAYED BY THE PEOPLE—WORK OF THE RELIEF COMMITTEE—EFFORTS TO RESUME TRADING—NEW BUSINESS CENTERS CREATED—RAPID GROWTH OF BUSINESS ON FILLMORE STREET—NEW SHOPPING DISTRICTS—VAN NESS AVENUE DEVOTED TO SHOPS—HASTILY CONSTRUCTED BUILDINGS—WAGES AND BUILDING MATERIALS HIGH—A SCENE OF HOPELESS CONFUSION—MAKING THE STREETS PASSABLE—STREETS DESTROYED BY THE FIRE—BACK TO OLD BUSINESS CENTER DOWN TOWN—PLANS OF BEAUTIFICATION DEFERRED—ACTIVE WORK BY UNITED RAILROADS—FITS OF PESSIMISM—EXHIBITIONS OF RIVALRY—FORTUNATE ESCAPE OF WATER FRONT PROPERTY—AMOUNT OF INSURANCE RECEIVED—BRISK BUSINESS—REFUGEE CAMPS—FINANCIAL EXPEDIENTS—ROBBER BAND RESUMES ITS SWAY............................857

CHAPTER LXV

GRAFT PROSECUTIONS AND OTHER TROUBLES AFTER THE FIRE

CHIMNEY INSPECTORS REAP A HARVEST—EXACTIONS OF LABOR DETER INVESTMENTS—A REIGN OF TERROR—THE "GAS PIPE" THUGS AND THEIR CRIMES—JAPANESE IN THE PUBLIC SCHOOLS—ROOSEVELT MENACES THE CITY—ATTITUDE OF THE PEOPLE ON THE SUBJECT OF JAPANESE IN THE SCHOOLS—CARMEN'S STRIKE OF 1902—TROUBLE RAISED BY THE CARMEN IN 1906—ATTITUDE OF PUBLIC TOWARD PATRICK CALHOUN—CARMEN'S TROUBLES ARBITRATED—STRIKE RENEWED IN 1907 AND MUCH VIOLENCE—A DIVIDED COMMUNITY—RUEF AND HIS UNSAVORY CREW—EXPOSURE OF SUPERVISORS BY DETECTIVE BURNS—INDICTMENTS BY THE HUNDRED—POLICY AND METHODS OF THE GRAFT PROSECUTION—PLENTY OF PRECEDENTS FOR GRAFT—RUEF IN THE ROLE OF ATTORNEY—THE SHARING OF THE LOOT—EXPLANATION MADE BY CALHOUN—ISSUES OF THE PROSECUTION GREATLY CONFUSED—FLUCTUATIONS OF PUBLIC SENTIMENT—MAKEUP OF THE PROSECUTION—SUSPICION THAT STRIKE OF 1907 WAS INCITED—RULING THE CITY BY THE GOOD DOG METHOD—SHOOTING OF HENEY AND SUICIDE OF HIS ASSAILANT—SUICIDE OF CHIEF OF POLICE BIGGY—BOMB EXPLODED IN GALLAGHER HOUSE—RUEF THE ONLY ONE OF THE GRAFTERS CONVICTED—CASES DISMISSED—ANOTHER TURN OF WHEEL OF POLITICS AND A WORKINGMAN ELECTED MAYOR..............................873

CONTENTS

CHAPTER LXVI

THE SUMMING UP OF THE ACHIEVEMENTS AFTER THE FIRE

NO INTERRUPTIONS OF THE PROGRESS OF THE CITY—THE PEOPLE MAKE HISTORY—GREATER SAN FRANCISCO MOVEMENT—A FREE MARKET EXPERIMENT FAILS—SAN FRANCISCO'S ORIENTAL POPULATION—REDISTRIBUTION OF THE POPULATION—TITLES NOT DISTURBED—APARTMENT HOUSES MULTIPLY—CHANGES ON NOB HILL—SOCIAL CLUBS REHOUSED—HOTELS AND RESTAURANTS IN INCREASED NUMBERS—CHANGES IN CAFÉ LIFE—THE SAN FRANCISCO ATMOSPHERE—THE OLD AND THE NEW VAN NESS AVENUE—THE NEW SHOPPING DISTRICTS—RETURN TO THE OLD AMUSEMENT CENTER—AMUSEMENTS AFTER THE FIRE—TETRAZZINI'S OPEN AIR CONCERT—VISIT OF BATTLESHIP FLEET—THE PORTOLA FESTIVAL—NEW YEAR'S EVE IN SAN FRANCISCO CONDITION OF STREETS—A NEW CITY HALL AND A CIVIC CENTER—ABOLITION OF CEMETERIES—THE STREET RAILWAY SITUATION—WATER SUPPLY—BONDED INDEBTEDNESS—THE CITY'S GROWING BUDGET—IMPROVED STEAM RAILWAY FACILITIES—THE PANAMA PACIFIC EXPOSITION—HARBOR IMPROVEMENTS—GROWTH OF COMMERCE—MANUFACTURING INDUSTRIES—MONEY EXPENDED FOR FIRE PRECAUTION AND PUBLIC IMPROVEMENTS—POPULATION GREATER THAN BEFORE THE FIRE—BRILLIANT FUTURE PREDICTED FOR PACIFIC COAST METROPOLIS........897

THE ANTE MISSION PERIOD
1513–1776

SAN FRANCISCO

CHAPTER I

THE SPANISH HUNT FOR A SHORT CUT TO THE INDIES

BALBOA SEES THE PACIFIC—THE SETTLEMENT OF PANAMA—SEEKING A SAFE HARBOR—SPANISH TREASURE FLEETS—SIR FRANCIS DRAKE AND HIS PURSUITS—THE SEARCH FOR ANIAN—SETTLEMENT OF CALIFORNIA ORDERED—THE HARBOR OF MONTEREY—SPANISH NEGLIGENCE OF OPPORTUNITIES—A HUNT FOR ISLANDS OF GOLD—REVIVAL OF INTEREST IN THE SHORT CUT.

HE history of San Francisco begins with the adventuresome march of Balboa across the Isthmus of Darien in the year 1513. It might even be maintained with some show of plausibility that it began when Columbus made his convincing exposition of the spheroidical character of the earth before Ferdinand and Isabella, for the object of that demonstration had as its underlying motive the discovery of a new route to the Indies, a quest which started in 1492 and never ceased until accumulating evidence in the piling up of which the Bay of San Francisco and what we know as California, figures largely, proved that there was no short cut.

Beginning of San Francisco's History

It is not probable that Balboa when he first caught a glimpse of the Pacific realized the full significance of his discovery, but it is evident from the promptitude with which plans were formed for cutting through the narrow neck of land separating North and South America that he, and those with him, comprehended that with the possibility of sailing into the new ocean would disappear the obstacle which stood in the way of accomplishing the desire of shortening the route to the riches of the Orient.

Panama was settled in 1517 and in that year a Spanish engineer named Saavedra, one of the followers of Balboa, mooted the project of a canal. He studied the subject many years, but in 1529, when his plans were nearly completed he died. Charles V became interested and ordered surveys, but the work was pronounced impracticable. His son, Philip II, subsequently gave the matter attention, submitting it to the consideration of the Dominican friars who found in the scriptural injunction, "What God hath joined together, let no man put asunder," and in his indisposition to exert himself, sufficient excuse for neglecting the recommendations of engineers and practical men.

Settlement of Panama in 1517

But while the Spanish crown refused to anticipate the accomplishment of what is to be the great achievement of the twentieth century there was no abatement of the desire to explore the unknown ocean. On the 28th of November, 1520, Ferdinand

Straits of Magellan Discovered

Magellan, who had bargained with Charles V to find for Spain a western passage to the Moluccas, sailed into the Pacific having passed through the strait which bears his name. The story of his adventuresome voyage is a familiar one, but the fact that his discovery of the Philippines was intimately associated with the Bay of San Francisco and resulted in its subsequent location is rarely dwelt upon by writers.

Discovery of the Philippines

The Philippines were discovered in 1521. Magellan and a number of his men were killed by the natives. Some of the survivors escaped and made their way to the Moluccas where they loaded one of their vessels with spices and set sail for Panama. But that port was never reached by the "Victoria." Instead she rounded the Cape of Good Hope, being the first vessel to circumnavigate the globe. Forty-four years later the Spaniards effected a settlement in the islands and from that time onward one of the chief objects of the navigators in the service of the King of Spain was the discovery of a safe port on the west coast of North America which would break the passage between the Philippines and Panama which by this time had become the half-way house for the voyagers between the distant spice isles of the Orient and the Pacific coast countries to the south of the isthmus.

Seeking a Safe Harbor

On the 31st of May, 1591, Luis de Velasco, the viceroy, wrote to Philip II, that the numerous disasters to the ships sailing between the Philippines and Mexico and Panama made it imperative to discover a safe harbor. The king ordered a survey to be made which was undertaken by Sebastian Rodriguez Cermeño, a Portuguese and an experienced navigator. The result of this exploration was disastrous. The "St. Augustin," the vessel sailed by Cermeño, after a visit to the Philippines set sail on July 5, 1595, from the port of Cavite and sighted New Spain at Cape Mendocino on the 4th of November. The diary of Cermeño which gives this information states that the "St. Augustin" subsequently entered a large bay in which the vessel was wrecked.

The description of Cermeño makes it apparent that the wreck occurred in the bay that had previously been entered by Drake, and that the Portuguese had already found the Bay of Monterey, which he named San Pedro. He described it as being fifteen leagues from point to point and in latitude 37° north, while the locality in which the wreck of the "St. Augustin" occurred is fixed by the statement that the islets in the mouth were in 38° 30', and that the distance between the two points forming it was about twenty-five leagues.

Wreck of the St. Augustin

The wreck of the "St. Augustin" occurred on the morning of December 8, 1595. It was not attended with great loss of life, only two perishing. The survivors managed to reach La Navidad, and later Mexico City. For many years there was a fiction based on the story of one Miguel Constanse that the party had made its way overland to Zacatecas, but recent researches of Richman establish that the journey was never made, but that the men, some seventy in all, had reached the port above mentioned in a small open vessel propelled by square sails and sweeps.

Spanish Treasure Fleets

The Spaniards had as early as 1556 a fleet of fourteen vessels devoted to the carriage of treasure and the transportation of supplies to the subjects of Spain established on the west coast of America. In 1564 Legazpi was commissioned by Luis de Velasco to subdue the Philippines and he accomplished his task, founding Manila in 1571. The purpose was to build up a trade with Mexico, but the islands did not contribute greatly to that result. But a tolerably brisk intercourse between

LIGHTHOUSE ON GOAT ISLAND, IN SAN FRANCISCO HARBOR

Molucca, Siam and China was brought about, the products of those countries being shipped in considerable quantity to New Spain.

The length of the passage was surprisingly great, many voyages consuming over two hundred days. It was the practice of the navigators to make their course from the Philippines to Cape Mendocino, after sighting which the coast was skirted to Cape San Lucas and Acapulco. It was to lessen the hazard of this long voyage by establishing a station between Mendocino and Mexico and Panama that such earnest efforts were made to find a safe anchorage as near to the former as practicable. There appeared to be no particular desire to explore with the view of effecting settlements. To the contrary there was something like a conviction that the region was uninviting, its chief drawback being its assumed inhospitable climate, the fogs of the coast having created the impression that the country was cold and desolate.

Long Passages

But while the Spaniard regarded California territory as a negligible quantity for purposes of development he was keenly alive to the usefulness of a port of call which would serve as a station whose function it would be to facilitate the trade intercourse established with the Orient. And to his perseverance in the search for the desired harbor, which finally culminated in the discovery of the Bay of San Francisco, may be traced all the causes which contributed to that long repose of two and a half centuries during which perhaps the most fertile region of the globe was withheld from development.

California Unappreciated

It may be idle but it is interesting to speculate on what might have happened, if Sir Francis Drake, who appeared on the scene about the time that the Spanish were so intent on making secure their intercourse with the Orient by navigating the ocean to which Magellan gave the name Pacific, had been animated by other motives than those of the bucaneer and the chaser of the will-o'-wisp of Anian.

Sir Francis Drake's Pursuits

Had Drake when he effected a landing on the shores of the bay which bears his name, like the Puritans who landed on Plymouth Rock, been a refugee from religious intolerance, and a searcher for a home, he would not have hastily decided that the country was too cold, a singular opinion to take possession of a man in search of a northwest passage from the Pacific to the Atlantic. It is not surprising that his search was so easily abandoned, and that so little came of his naming his discovery New Albion. Sir Francis was a good fighter, but a poor explorer. He had the qualities that go to make up the successful pirate, but was deficient in those calculated to reflect luster upon the country under whose flag he sailed, and absolutely none that confer real distinction.

Drake sailed through Magellan straits in 1578-9 and up the Pacific coast, accumulating in the hold of his ship, the "Golden Hind," a store of silver bars "the bigness of a brick bat eche," according to the chronicler of his adventures, and reached the comparatively sheltered body of water near the entrance to the harbor of San Francisco, which he passed without discerning its existence. When he abandoned his search for Anian, deterred by the cold, he simply effected a landing to make repairs, and concerned himself no further about his accomplishment.

Drake's Successful Piracies

The appearance of Drake in the North Pacific made the Spanish very uneasy. Although Drake was a buccaneer pure and simple, the kinsman of a piratical slaver who had made himself equally obnoxious, they suspected that his motives might be the same as their own. Maritime activity was very pronounced in England, and the desire to find a short cut to the Indies had taken possession of many minds and

Spanish Suspicion of Drake's Objects

it was naturally the subject of much discussion of a kind calculated to alarm the nation hugging the delusion that it could monopolize not alone the territory of the new world, but of the routes of communication. When Sir Francis sailed away from the coast, and after rounding the Cape of Good Hope reached Portsmouth with the news of his exploits there was no abatement of Spanish anxiety.

The Search for Anian

There was a renewal of the inquiry that had been made some years earlier when England threatened to become a rival. A memorial was presented to Philip II, which set forth in strong terms the danger to Spanish supremacy if the English or French heretics should find the strait which would enable them to enter the Pacific by sailing from Labrador. So fearsome of the consequences were some of the advisers of the Spanish king they recommended to him the conquest of China, probably assuming that possession of that country would remove the incentive to continued search for the mythical passage.

Death of Philip II in 1598

Philip was not enterprising enough to act on so bold a suggestion and he died in 1598 having done little to forward the ambitious projects of those of his subjects who sought to extend Spanish dominion in the new country. His successor, Philip III, displayed more active qualities. Shortly after his accession he found a memorial from Sebastian Vizcaino, who some years earlier had received a pearl fishing concession which had not proved very profitable, asking further favors from Philip II, and proposing to make a voyage of exploration with the view of taking possession of the coast of the Californias for the king. This proposal had received the indorsement of the Comde de Monterey, who had reminded Philip that since the wreck of the "St. Augustin" the exploration of the coast in connection with the object of establishing a station for the vessels in the Philippine trade had ceased.

Settlement of California Ordered

The examination of the document resulted in a cedula to the Comde de Monterey to undertake a discovery and settlement in California, and Vizcaino was commissioned to carry out his proposal. He sailed with four vessels from Acapulco on the 5th of May, 1602, encountering much stormy weather, landing November 10th in the harbor previously entered by Cabrillo which he named San Diego in honor of his flagship. Ten days later Vizcaino sailed from San Diego, and on December 16th he cast anchor in a harbor to which he gave the name of the Viceroy Monterey. On January 3d he continued his voyage northward reaching what is known as Drake's bay, which he called Puerto de los Reyes, finally attaining Mendocino from which he retreated, like Drake, deterred by the cold fogs of the coast from further investigation.

Harbor of Monterey

The net result of Vizcaino's voyage of exploration was the establishment of the fact that there were at least two suitable harbors on the coast of California, San Diego and Monterey. The latter had in all probability been discovered by Pedro de Unamuna, a navigator of Macao, who on his return from an exploring expedition in 1587 had reported finding a bay the description of which matched that of Monterey, but he never received credit for his discovery.

That Vizcaino, Drake, Cermeño and Unamuna should have all passed the entrance to the harbor of San Francisco without detecting it may seem singular to all but those who have sailed by the opening which even with the landmarks made familiar to mariners by the study of charts and observation, is not obtrusively noticeable. The configuration of the coast is such that the Golden Gate may be easily overlooked even by those searching for it. Only a survey of the sort not common in the sixteenth century would disclose it to those unaware of its existence. It is not

SAN FRANCISCO   7

strange therefore, despite the persistent search for a good harbor by navigators of undoubted courage, enterprise and some skill in their calling, that it should have been reserved for a land expedition to make the important discovery.

Spaniards Grow Negligent

The pressing object of the assiduous search for a safe port seems to have been lost sight of soon after Monterey was discovered. The political relations of Spain and England after the opening of the seventeenth century apparently removed the stimulus which moved the Spanish to exert themselves commercially and otherwise. There was something like a complete allayment of the proverbial distrust of the Dons, and from 1600 to 1700 there was not more than a single yearly visit to the coast of Alta California, and that took the form of sighting Mendocino by the galleon from the Philippines, which after having ascertained its bearings felt its way southward to the Mexican port of Acapulco.

Revived Interest in Short Cut

Thus it came to pass that the knowledge of the existence of the harbor of Monterey in the course of time became little more than a tradition scarcely kept alive by the cartographers whose imagination often outran their information. But the lively belief in Anian endured, and enterprising sailors still dreamed of finding the passage. Towards the close of the seventeenth century there was a decided revival of interest, the paramount desire being to find a route which would be shorter than that around Cape Horn, and perhaps divested of some of the perils that beset the navigator in rounding the southern extremity of the continent.

With the revival of the Anian fever there was a renewal and strengthening of the conviction that the region known as California was an island, a belief that was not discarded until explorations to the Colorado river in 1701, 1702 and 1706 by the Jesuit missionary, Eusabio Francisco Kino, disposed of the fiction. It can hardly be said that Kino's discoveries were the final word, for the subsequent explorations of the land expedition which started from the Gila toward the close of the eighteenth century were required to remove all doubt.

Absence of Initiative

The chief interest attaching to the search for the short route which occupied so much of the thought and time of the people of the centuries immediately following the discovery of America, so far as California, and particularly San Francisco are concerned centers in the remarkable attitude of the western world toward enterprise. The form it took was suggestive of that which governed during the crusades. There was an abundance of courage, and there was a not inconsiderable exercise of the faculties which help the solution of great problems. But there was a noteworthy absence of that highest form of initiative which devotes itself to the development of resources.

Spirit of the Explorers

The names of those writ largest in the history of the period are of men who were ready to devote their energies and lives, not to the creation of wealth, but to acquisition of riches already created. This spirit permeates all the accounts of the fruitless search for Anian. It begins with the temptation which caused Ferdinand and Isabella to succumb to the arguments of Columbus that great wealth could be secured from the Indies where it had already been accumulated if a short route could be found which would serve as a siphon to draw off the accumulations.

When the new world was discovered this attitude was but slightly changed. The opportunities presented by regions of illimitable fertility for profitable development, while not absolutely disregarded, were subordinated to the overweening desire to get rich, not by exertion, but by securing the fruits of the exertions of others. As a result we are called upon to note the persistence of the lure of the short cut, and the credulous acceptance of tales of isles of gold, and lands abounding in those things which contribute to the gratification of the love of ornamentation.

Islands of Gold
As early as 1543 there was a belief prevalent that there were islands of gold and silver somewhere in the North Pacific. These mythical isles at first known as "The Isles of the Armenian" were so firmly believed in that Pedro de Unamunu was sent to search for them in 1586. The stories concerning their existence probably had their origin in Japanese folk lore, but the credulous and eager Spaniard found nothing improbable in them, for the land in which they originated was rich in the things he coveted and what more natural than to associate beautiful objects with the abundance of the precious metals.

Crude Economic Ideas
They were crude economic ideas, characteristic of the times, and those imbued with them were not responsible for their existence. They were an inheritance from centuries of teachings that man's gainful instincts menaced his opportunities to enter into a future life of happiness, the result of which was to retard useful production, without, however, blunting his acquisitive desires. They were a survival from the darkest days of the middle ages, and their persistence explains the failure of the Spaniard to appreciate and make proper use of the resources at his command during the three centuries in which he had practical control over a region now recognized as the most productive on the globe. And the same explanation applies to the utter disregard of the advantages possessed by them in their position on the Bay of San Francisco for seventy years without in the slightest degree improving its facilities, which were no greater when they were replaced by a more virile people than when Mission Dolores was first established in 1776.

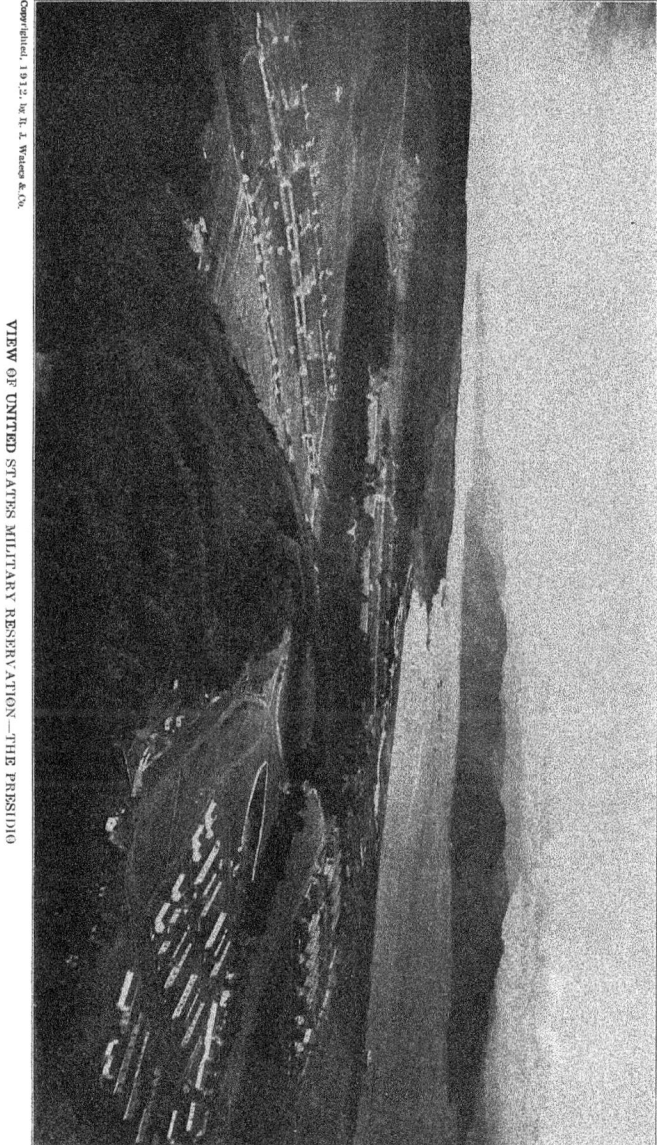

VIEW OF UNITED STATES MILITARY RESERVATION—THE PRESIDIO

CHAPTER II

SPAIN'S PURPOSE IN OCCUPYING CALIFORNIA

HALF WAY HOUSE FOR SHIPS IN THE PHILIPPINE TRADE—THE SANDWICH ISLANDS OVERLOOKED—RUSSIA COVETED CALIFORNIA—EFFECTS OF MISSIONARY ZEAL—THE BELIEF IN THE INSULARITY OF CALIFORNIA—INVESTIGATIONS OF FATHER KINO—SPANISH PROJECTS SLUMBER—THE FRANCISCAN ORDER—EXPULSION OF JESUITS—FATHER JUNIPERO SERRA—SEARCHING FOR MONTEREY—PORTOLA'S DISAPPOINTMENT—DISCOVERY OF SAN FRANCISCO BAY.

APTAIN COOK, the discoverer of the Sandwich islands, in his narrative threw out the suggestion that if they had been discovered at an earlier period by the Spaniards they would doubtless have availed themselves of so excellent a station, and would have made use of Atooi or some other island of the group as a place of refreshment for the ships that sailed annually between Acapulco and Manila. He noted that "they lie almost midway between the last mentioned place and Guam, which is at present (1777) their only port in traversing this vast ocean, and it would not have been a week's sail out of their ordinary route to have touched at them." *The Sandwich Islands*

It is perhaps idle to speculate on what might have occurred had the Spanish hit upon the islands. The possibility, however, is suggested of a complete change of the course of history, for despite the neglect during the seventeenth century of the matter of securing a desirable station on the coast of California it was not wholly lost sight of by the authorities, and to a large extent it engrossed the minds of missionaries who were working for the salvation of the Indians of Northern Mexico, and those of the regions we now know as New Mexico and Arizona. Their zeal did not hinder them from recognizing that their cause would be advanced by linking it with commercial affairs, and they exhibited a more intelligent appreciation of the material advantages which would flow from the possession of a safe port than the inefficient and almost supine representatives of the crown. *Missionary Work in Arizona and New Mexico*

It does no violence to the probability that the utilization of the Sandwich islands in the manner described by Cook would have indefinitely postponed the search for a harbor which resulted in the discovery of San Francisco. The activities of the Franciscans and Cook were nearly concurrent with those of the Russians. They were established in the regions north of California, and as early as 1788 we find a statement that they imported Chinese artisans, "because of their reputed hardiness, industry and ingenuity, simple manner of life and low wages," and they *Early Russian Establishments*

9

had well defined ideas of the desirability of developing the country to the south whose agricultural capacities appealed strongly to their enterprise.

Spain Relinquishes Territory

The facility with which the Spaniard abandoned his hold on the region lying north of San Francisco under British pressure indicates what might have happened had not the land expedition of Portola pushed north and established a settlement on the Bay of San Francisco. The steady eastward encroachment of the Russians, which led them across the vast deserts and through the gloomy forests of Siberia, defying its rigorous climate, and making light of the obstacles interposed by its mighty rivers until the shores of the Pacific were reached, compels us to believe that once well established on the American continent their march southward would have been irresistible had no political obstacles interposed.

Russia Covets California

The latter must have been greatly minimized if San Francisco harbor had not been discovered. The recent researches of the delvers among the musty archives of Russia disclose that the thought of the acquisition of California was still in the mind of the czar's advisers years after the missionaries had created their establishments. That they would have pushed their opportunities at an earlier period if Spain's indifference had been accentuated by the possession of an ideal station in the Pacific is hardly debatable. What sort of a civilization would have followed as the result of their occupation can only be conjectured. That it would have been more effective materially than that of the Spanish is suggested by the fact that Russians were able to comprehend possibilities of whose existence the Spaniard did not dream.

Effects of Missionary Zeal

But the Sandwich islands were not found by the Don, and, although the urgency for a station to serve the Manila trade was no longer so great a new promoter of desire had arisen. Zeal for the redemption of the Indian accomplished that which the navigator failed to achieve. This movement was by no means wholly dissociated from material considerations, but it was as nearly unselfish as any project devised by mortal man. On those points where the secular side was touched it is plainly apparent that nothing more than recognition of the necessity of cooperation governed.

As early as 1687 the Mission Nuestra Senora de las Dolores was founded by Father Kino about 120 miles south of the present Tucson. In 1690 Juan Maria de Salvatierra, who was sent to Sonora as visitador, called at Father Kino's mission and talked with him about "suspended California," and suggested that its fertile valleys might be made sufficiently productive to offset the barrenness of northern Mexico, and thus equalize conditions.

Insular Theory Refuted

At this time Salvatierra and Kino were both under the impression that California was an island, but subsequently while on a visit to the Mission San Xavier del Bac Kino told the Indians how the Spaniards had come over the sea from a distant land to Vera Cruz, and perhaps received some intimation of the untrustworthiness of the belief in the insular theory. In 1693 he pushed further into Arizona visiting the Sahos. Journeying about eight leagues from their land he saw from an eminence what he reckoned to be at least twenty-five continuous leagues of the land of California. In 1694 he again visited the shores of the sea of California, and had his doubts finally resolved.

Kino was now bent upon the project of extending the missions into California and visited the City of Mexico to secure assistance. But his requests were not favorably regarded, there being no fervor for missionary work at that moment, but in the ensuing year the new viceroy, the Comde de Montezuma, was inclined to lend ear to Kino's request and on February 5, 1697, he issued a license authorizing Kino and Salvatierra to undertake the reduction of the Californias, stipulating, however, that the work should be at their own expense and that if the reduction be effected it be in the name of the king.

In 1700 Kino descended the Gila to its junction with the Colorado, arriving there on the 7th of October. This achievement practically settled the doubts respecting the peninsular character of Lower California, but to silence all criticism Kino resolved to start an expedition which would leave Las Dolores and reach Loretto by land. It appears, however, that Salvatierra's faith in the insular belief still survived, for he wrote Kino that the rejoicings at Loretto were much greater "than he had means and desires to examine at close range what on distant view might be misleading." *Father Kino Reaches the Colorado*

To Kino the solution of the problem meant much. He, apparently, was profoundly convinced that California was a land of wondrous promise, and that its penetration would not merely result in the removal of pernicious errors and falsehoods concerning a crowned king, carried on a litter of gold, of a walled city with towns, and the destruction of the whole tissue of falsehoods which had been woven about the Anian idea, but that it would teach that the true way from Japan was by Cape Mendocino and whence might be brought to Sonora the goods of the very rich galleons from the Philippines. Salvatierra was less enthusiastic about the matter. The determination of peninsularity promised a safe means of moving supplies between the missions already established and he was satisfied to let it go at that. *Father Kino's Aims*

Father Kino died among the Pimas in 1711 without having penetrated the promised land, and in 1717 Salvatierra was also laid at rest. With their deaths the project of the extension of Spanish dominion northward slumbered until 1747 when a royal cedula sanctioned the reduction of the Californias on the exact plan of Kino, the main feature of which was the entrance of the land above the head of the Gulf of California by way of the desert of Arizona. Even at that late date the idea of Anian had not wholly disappeared, for Michael Venegas in some notes on California printed in 1757 is still found asking whether there was not a chance that a strait might be discovered by some Englishman. He also expressed apprehension of Russian designs and indorsed Kino's conception that the integrity of Spanish rule in America demanded that "the missions must be joined to the rest of New Mexico and extended from the latter beyond the rivers Gila and Colorado to the furtherest known coasts of California and the South Sea, to Puerto de San Diego, Puerto de Monterey, the Sierra Nevadas, Cape Mendocino, Cape Blanco or San Sebastian and to the river discovered by Aquillar in 43° north latitude." *Spanish Projects Slumber*

It was reserved for the Franciscan order of missionary friars to carry out the conception of Kino. The order had been established in Mexico since 1524, when its advance guard of twelve sandal shod and wide sackcloth gowned brethren presented themselves to Cortez and were graciously received by him. In 1761 the inspector general of the order, Jose de Galvez, was sent to the province, and at the same time Charles Francisco de Croix went as viceroy. Shortly after their arrival they united in a dispatch to the king in which the desirability of having Galvez visiting the Californias for the purpose of establishing in them pueblos, and *The Franciscan Order*

12   SAN FRANCISCO

to regulate their government, was urged on the ground that the remoteness of the peninsula from Sonora made it necessary to have a nearer source of supplies.

Jesuits Expelled by Portola

When Galvez reached Lower California he found the religious part of the establishment in charge of Serra and his Franciscans, while the temporalties were administered by Gasper de Portola, whose duty it had become on the 17th of December, 1767, to expel the Jesuits who had formerly been established there. The condition of affairs reflected discredit on the management of the secular arm. The licentious soldiery had spread disease among the natives, and the population, which had once numbered 12,000 souls, had dwindled to a few more than 7,000. Galvez sought to apply a remedy by restoring the temporalties to the Franciscans and a return to the system of the mission. By these means he hoped to wean the Indians from their nomadic habits and induce them to live in the pueblos.

Galvez Projects Settlements

Galvez's project embraced the idea of effecting settlements, but the difficulties attending the colonization of Spaniards were numerous. He sought to overcome them by offering crown lands and military rights. Perhaps his plans of native redemption could not have made progress without a resort to such concessions, but they afterward proved a source of trouble and did much to destroy the efforts of the padres to make good Christians of the Indians. It was through the offers of this kind made in August, 1768, that he was able to gather the necessary party to form the expedition to Monterey conceived by him, which received the prompt approval of the Viceroy de Croix, and which was enthusiastically embraced by Father Junípero Serra, who was made president of the California missions.

Father Junipero Serra

Father Serra is the most notable figure in the early history of California, and his character merits attentive study. He was a man of great piety, a firm believer in miracles and a wielder of the penitential scourge. He possessed in a preeminent degree all those qualities which are attributed to those who receive the honor of canonization from the Catholic church, but he was by no means deficient in shrewdness or practical ability. Had he been born in another age or had he been able to shake off the trammels of the medieval system, he might have succeeded in the task he set for himself of lifting up the wretched natives of the soil. The union of a pure mind and ability might under other circumstances have accomplished an aim which utterly failed because submerged by an idea which completely subordinated the only instinct which has ever contributed greatly to elevating a race in the scale of civilization.

Monterey an Objective

In 1768 Galvez de Croix and Serra met to discuss the method of attaining their object of reaching Monterey. The details of two expeditions were gone over—one by land and the other by sea. The latter, like most of the preceding maritime explorations having for their object the establishment of a station in Alta California, had an unfortunate experience. The vessels stored with supplies for the voyage and articles that would be needed in the new ports which were to be converted into missions sailed from La Paz on the 8th of January, 1769, Galvez accompanying the party as far as Cape San Lucas where he bade farewell. The little fleet did not reach San Diego until the following July, although the good padre had reported that its sailing qualities were admirable, one of the craft actually making six knots an hour in a moderate breeze.

The Search for Monterey

The plans of the expedition were completely disarranged by the appearance of scurvy on the ships, and it was recognized that if the purpose of occupying Monterey was to be realized it must be reached by land as the crews were no longer in condition to manipulate their craft. A party of 67 was formed which started from San Diego on the 14th of July leaving behind at that place, Serra, Vila, Vizcaino, some artisans and a number of sailors mostly ill. The work of establishing a mission was at once inaugurated by Serra, who laid the foundations of that of San Diego, the oldest in Alta California, on the 16th of July. The records show that the activities of the good padre were called into play at once, for the natives surrounding the new port who were under the influence of the warlike Yumas soon became troublesome, and on the 15th of August made an attack on the little establishment in which three of their number and a Spaniard were killed and Father Vizcaino was disabled by an arrow which pierced his hand.

The party which started overland was provided with notes of the results of the former explorations, but depended principally upon a reprint of a manual which placed the port of Monterey in 37° north latitude, and gave suggestions for finding it which would prove more valuable to an expedition approaching from the sea than to one seeking it by a land route. But as the explorers kept the ocean in sight it was inevitable that perseverance should reveal the object of their search. The itinerary of the party shows that it made its way past San Clementa; that the Catalina Islands were kept in sight and that Los Angeles was traversed. The San Fernando valley was passed through to the headwaters of the Santa Clara, and from thence the river valley was followed to the sea. Point Conception was touched, and from that the explorers made their way to the head of the Santa Barbara channel. Leaving San Luis Obispo they kept along the coast until the Sierra barred their way. They crossed the mountain and penetrated the Salinas valley which they pursued to the sea, following the shore of which they at length attained Point Pinos which their records told them was the determining landmark of Monterey harbor. *Route of the Explorers*

But viewed from that side Monterey did not answer the description of those who had eulogized it as a safe port. Portola, who headed the party, received the impression, which he recorded, that it was no better than an open roadstead. The rejoicings which the sight of the Point of Pines first occasioned were soon converted to despondency, and after a week's rest, on October 8th the explorers held a council which reached the resolution to again press forward. *Portola's Disappointment*

The party thus far had met with no serious adventures. They had seen numerous Indians, the males entirely naked, and they had noted with surprise and admiration the skill of those living along the Santa Barbara channel in handling their canoes, which were well constructed. They had killed some bears, a sort of game very abundant, and had felt some earthquake shocks which they set down in their records as "frightful," and had noted many things, the knowledge of which might prove useful to them in the future work of converting the Californias into a habitable country. The only evil results of their journey was the appearance of scurvy which attacked several members of the party.

This dread disease maintained its hold until the rains set in. When Portola and his party took up their toilsome march after their disappointment at Point Pinos the leader and Father Riviera were ill. The supply of food had run out, and some of the men had to be borne in litters. But they pressed on and on November 1st they reached Point San Pedro, and from an eminence saw the Farallones and the bay described by Cermeño, and recognized it as the locality in which the "St. Augustin" had been wrecked. *Portola's Party Attacked by Scurvy*

San Francisco Bay Discovered

On the day following, some soldiers of the party, headed by Ortega, while hunting for deer climbed the headland of Point Reyes and suddenly came in sight of a large body of water which he thought was an inland sea. The hunting party encountered some Indians who informed them that a ship was lying at anchor at the head of the newly discovered sea, and Ortega carried a report to that effect to Portola. A search for the ship was made, but in vain, and on November 11th the leader, convinced that Monterey had been passed in the fog, or that it had been overwhelmed with sand started southward with his command, now seriously short of rations.

Monterey Bay Unrecognized

He reached Point Pinos without identifying the bay as that described by Cermeño, and on December 10th he erected two great commemoration crosses, one on the shore of Carmello bay, and the other on the shore of the bay which he had found, but failed to recognize; and on the ensuing day began retracing his steps to San Diego which he reached on the 24th of January, 1770. In the ensuing month Portola and Crespi reported the results of their adventure to the Visitador. They were convinced that the belief in the existence of Monterey was an illusion, and felicitated themselves upon dispelling it; but Crespi put a bright side upon the fancied failure to discern the harbor of Cermeño by pointing out that they "had found an actuality" in the inland sea discovered by the hunters.

CHAPTER III

THE ESTABLISHMENT OF THE MISSION OF ST. FRANCIS

SEARCH FOR THE BAY OF MONTEREY CONTINUED—LIEUTENANT DE AYALA ENTERS THE GOLDEN GATE—THE EXPEDITION TO SAN FRANCISCO BAY—SELECTION OF A SITE ON MISSION BAY—THE PRESIDIO ESTABLISHED—FATHER SERRA REACHES MISSION DOLORES—SPANISH DRY ROT COMMUNICATES ITSELF TO THE NEW COUNTRY—SPAIN'S TRADE WITH THE PHILIPPINES—THE MISSION INDIANS—THE LIFE AND LABORS OF PADRE SERRA.

HE hunting party of 1769, and another which followed a year later, getting a glimpse of the Bay of San Francisco, were under the impression that the body of water seen by them was that which Cermeño had described. On a map which accompanied the diary of the Portola journey it is called Estero de S. Francisco, and the notes of Constanso treat it as an appurtenance of the Cermeño bay. It was not, however, deemed impracticable to found a mission on the shore of an estuary which might provide facilities for such intercourse as would arise out of the project of reduction if successfully carried out.

Mistaken for an Estuary

The idea of bringing colonists who would effect a settlement was adhered to, and the earlier suggestion of linking Monterey and Sonora was kept in mind, Portola's failure to positively locate the bay not having the effect of completely destroying faith in the existence of the "safe harbor," which had been named after the Viceroy Comde de Monterey. It was not until 1774 that all doubts respecting Monterey and the Bay of San Francisco were cleared away, and steps taken to carry out the cherished desire of Father Serra to honor the patron saint of his order by founding an establishment which was to take the name of St. Francis.

Doubts Cleared Away

On the 9th of March, 1774, a junta called by the viceroy decided that the port of San Francisco should be occupied by Juan Bautista de Anza, and that communication should be established between Sonora and the new foundation. Captain Anza had originally purposed bringing about a connection between Monterey and Sonora, and had started on January 8th from Tubac with that object in view, but in accordance with the plans of the junta he prepared to march to San Francisco.

Determination to Occupy Port of San Francisco

The expedition consisted of 40 soldiers and their families who were chosen from the poverty stricken districts of Northern Mexico. The appropriation made for the party was a slender one amounting to only 21,927 pesos and two reals. Only 10,000 pesos were to be called for at first, and they were to come out of the pious fund, a source of supply called into existence some time previously to provide

Expedition to the Bay

15

16   SAN FRANCISCO

the means for carrying on the work of converting the Indians in the countries occupied by the Spanish.

Indian Uprising at San Diego   Anza's journey was interrupted by a call for relief from San Diego which was menaced by an Indian uprising. Riviera, who had induced Anza to assist in. quieting the unruly natives, tried to persuade him to abandon his expedition to the north. He was very insistent that the "estuary" of San Francisco was not adapted to the purpose which the junta desired to effect, and doubtless he was convinced that the southern harbor would serve it much more admirably.

But Anza adhered to his instructions tenaciously and ended all discussion of the matter by announcing that he was determined to find a suitable place; if one could not be found at the mouth of the port he would go inland to where it seemed best to him even if he had to go several leagues from the shore. Anza was very confident that his efforts would be crowned with success and promised the doubting San Diegan that he would bring back a phial of the water of the river which had been seen by Fages in 1770, but which he did not follow to its mouth.

Lieutenant de Ayala Enters the Golden Gate   Anza, after a short illness which detained him at San Carlos mission, started on March 23d for the supposed estuary. On the 5th of August, 1775, Lieutenant Juan Manuel de Ayala of the royal navy had in the "San Carlos" passed through the Golden Gate and had cast anchor in the harbor near an island named by him Isla de Los Angeles, and in September the naval officer Bruno Heceta, who was under orders to cooperate with Anza, landed and made his way to Point Lobos, so it happened that when the captain finally arrived and on March 28, 1776, chose as a site for a fort the place where Fort Point is now situated the waters of the bay were not wholly uncharted.

Mission Dolores   On the day following he selected a place on what we know as Mission bay, for a mission. The calendar evidently suggested the name of Dolores which he gave it, and the story that it was inspired by the sight of a weeping Indian woman may be dismissed as one of the fantastic tales which the imaginative are always ready to supply as substitutes for actualities which have no color of romance or the unusual.

Riviera Changes his Mind   When Riviera received word at San Diego of the success of the exploration he changed his attitude and sent instructions which authorized the establishment of a presidio on a site selected by Anza, but he was slow about giving his sanction to the mission project. He had been in collision with the padres over an Indian who had sought sanctuary with the missionaries, and was strongly disposed to resent their interference with the administration of justice by the secular end of the San Diego establishment, and his hostility served for a time to interfere with the accomplishment of the desires of the zealous Franciscans.

Making the Presidio Habitable   Meanwhile, however, the party at San Francisco went on with the work of getting the presidio in habitable condition, and in June the padres Palou and Benito Cambon, with the help of Cazinares, and the crew of the "San Carlos," which arrived from Monterey in August, the spot named by Anza was provided with quarters, a chapel, commandantes' dwelling and a warehouse. These were constructed of palisades with roofs of earth and were in readiness by the 17th of September, and, despite the injunction of Riviera, who did not finally withdraw his opposition until the following November, after the establishment had been formally dedicated and named the Mission St. Francis de Asis.

SAN FRANCISCO

Riviera, whose opposition was attributed to jealousy of Anza, under viceroyal pressure gave his approval on the 9th of October to the new mission, which was the sixth founded in Alta California. The obstacles placed by him in the way of the foundation were a forerunner of the clashings which occurred at various times between the spiritual and temporal authorities in California, and which have been put forward by many writers in explanation of the failure to accomplish any really beneficial results, of either a religious or material character, while the Spaniards and their immediate successors ruled the destinies of the vast region which afterward came into the possession of the United States. The story when unfolded will disclose that while the conflicts often produced lack of harmony, the real cause of the absolute stagnation which endured during the years between 1776 and 1846 was the complete disregard of economic laws.

New Mission Approved by Riviera

It was not until the 10th of October, 1777, that Serra beheld the mission with which his name has been associated, and which to him seemed the key of the whole system he so laboriously sought to build up, and the establishment of which was followed by the creation of similar nuclei until Alta California had within its boundaries a chain of houses of the order of which he was president, numbering eighteen.

Serra Reaches Mission Dolores

They stretched from San Diego on the south, and in nearly every instance hugged the sea. They were named San Diego, Santa Barbara, San Juan Capistrano, San Buenaventura, Santa Cruz, San Luis Rey, La Purissima Concepcion, San Jose, San Carlos and San Francisco. The inland establishments were those of San Gabriel, San Fernando, San Luis Obispo, San Antonio, San Juan Bautista and Santa Clara, and they were near enough to salt water to be always reminded of its existence. Only two, those of Soledad and San Miguel were at all remote from the ocean, and they can only be said to have been so relatively.

A study of the inspiring causes leaves one in doubt as to the real desires of the authorities in Spain in countenancing the establishment of the missions, or whether they ever had any well defined aspirations. The extension of dominion appears to have been at the bottom of all the sanctions, but the absolute indifference to material advancement, so conspicuously displayed after settlements had been effected, indicate beyond the possibility of doubt that there was no conception of the results that might be achieved by the development of the resources of a region of extraordinary fertility, and there is reason to believe that very few in Madrid or in Mexico City had any real knowledge of what might be done in California by the exercise of industry, intelligently directed.

Objects of the Spanish

The dry rot of mediaevalism which had possession of Spain like a cancerous sore, promptly spread through Mexico into the virgin country, and even after the zealous missionaries had by their exertions succeeded in effecting what seemed like a fair start, its destructive progress was not arrested. Practically little more was accomplished between the seventy years of mission and mixed temporal and spiritual rule than had been achieved during the century when California lay wholly neglected by those who claimed it, but only thought of the vast region with its more than a thousand miles of sea coast, because in the indentations of the latter there might be found a harbor of refuge or station for the vessels engaged in a trade, which by comparison with that since developed in the disregarded territory was ridiculously insignificant.

Spanish Dry Rot

18   SAN FRANCISCO

Spain's Philippine Trade

There are days when more ships sail out of the port of San Francisco than would have made it their station in ten years when the Philippine trade of Spain was at its best. The proud galleons of which so much that is picturesque has been written made annual sailings, and the goods and treasures in their holds, if the statistics were attainable, would make a sorry showing by the side of the tables of exports and imports of the metropolis of the Pacific coast, and there is no reason for believing that the conditions which produced the frame of mind that led men to think that the main function of a great harbor on the northern coast of Alta California, had they endured, would have permitted any improvement of the results secured between 1776 and 1846.

Slow Growth of the Missions

Twenty years after the establishment of the Mission of St. Francis impatient critics declared that not in centuries would the Indians be fitted for the pursuits of civilization while remaining under the tutelage of the missionaries, and the results of the system justified the criticism. It was unquestionably founded on the erroneous assumption that the Indian is incapable of being lifted in the scale of civilization, but it was undoubtedly correct so far as it assumed that religious methods would not suffice to make the native an industrious member of society.

Mission Indians

Indians have been redeemed and made tolerable citizens in this country, and have acquired fair concepts of morals and religion, but the result has been achieved by indirection. Like more intelligent beings whose acquirements are the product of a long evolutionary period, the red man did not find it possible to industriously toil for a reward in the hereafter. This apparently was all that the good padres had to offer the Indians, who could not be made to believe that the privilege of toiling in the fields and praying in the churches was a desirable exchange for the liberty they had enjoyed before they were dragged into the fold.

But failure does not detract from the fact that Serra and his associates were animated by the highest of motives in the pursuit of their self-imposed mission of redemption. Their zeal, benevolence and integrity is unquestioned, and if instances can be cited which show that sometimes a padre subordinated the spiritual to the material, they must be taken as exceptions which prove the rule that they were a devoted band of men ready to sacrifice their lives to pluck brands from the burning.

Critics of the Missionaries

If their failure unduly impresses the reader, as it has some critics, animated by sectarian prejudice, they will be wise to modify their impression by attempting to measure against the performances of the padres the poor results achieved by some of their countrymen, who were inspired by more worldly motives. It must be remembered that the government had no other object in weakly supporting the Franciscans than to thwart the Russians, whose encroachments about the time of the establishment of San Francisco had become a source of alarm.

A Station no Longer Needed

The desire for a station had long since abated, the trade which gave birth to it having diminished to proportions that made it no longer an object for continued governmental concern. If it were not for the desire to maintain dominion, which had become a tradition rather than a vital policy the arguments brought against the establishment of missions in Upper California by the Jesuits must have prevailed. They urged that the distance of Monterey from the peninsula, the perils of navigation, the necessity of maintaining considerable bodies of soldiery at the presidios, the known bad character of the Indians, who, even Serra was compelled to admit, were great thieves, and the uncertainty concerning their docility, all pointed to the hopelessness of the task of reducing the country, unless God should interpose with a miracle.

These views were by no means confined to the followers of St. Ignatius; they were shared by not a few of the padres of the peninsula missions, who did not hesitate to voice them, but Serra was confident that the miracle would be worked, and he believed that it was his duty to act as the human instrument for its performance. He did not, however, expect the miraculous intervention to take the form of providing manna for the wanderers in the wilderness, and in all his actions subsequent to the conclusion reached at the conference he comported himself as a practical man and constantly kept in mind the fact that the blessings of Providence are only conferred upon those who exert themselves to obtain them. *Labors of Padre Serra*

In his subsequent administrations of the affairs of the missions he exhibited as much sagacity as he did patience of the kind which is only attained by those who set out to perform great undertakings filled with foreseen obstacles, which they think may be overcome by persevering in a lofty resolution which refused to recognize any other possibility than success.

It has been pointed out that in their zeal to win over the natives the padres made promises which they were not able to redeem, and that their desire to impress on the neophytes the grandeur and importance of the King of Spain aroused expectations of gifts that never materialized. There is no reason to discredit these representations. The imagery of religion finds expression in language easily misapprehended by the ignorant and untutored, who are too apt to take literally stories about golden streets and pearly gates. *Unredeemed Promises*

There is nothing surprising therefore in the recitals of discontent with which the comparatively brief annals of the mission days are filled, nor need we wonder that the neophytes, who at least were reasonably sure of getting enough to eat while they remained amenable, should envy the gentile Indians who roamed at will and preferred their liberty, even though it was often accompanied by hunger that not infrequently became starvation. What the Padres gave them in exchange for their days of toil could hardly have been regarded by them as an adequate compensation. The benefits on the material side were too slight to be accepted by people as low in the scale of civilization as the California Indian. *Neophytes Envy Gentile Indians*

THE MISSION PERIOD
1776–1846

CHAPTER IV

RESULT OF THE LABORS OF THE MISSIONARIES

DEATH OF PADRE SERRA AT MONTEREY—SPANIARDS POOR COLONISTS—MANAGEMENT OF THE MISSIONS—THE MISSION INDIANS—THE AIMS OF THE PADRES—CHARACTER OF CALIFORNIA INDIANS—INDIANS LOW IN THE HUMAN SCALE—WORKING ON UNPROMISING MATERIAL—INDIANS TAUGHT AGRICULTURE—PRACTICAL ENSLAVEMENT OF THE INDIAN—THE ABORIGINES MELT AWAY UNDER CIVILIZING INFLUENCES.

UNIPERO SERRA died at Monterey August 28, 1784, eight years after the foundation of the Mission of San Francisco. His last moments were spent on a bed of planks and he passed away mourned by all who knew him. When his body was carried to the grave it was covered with roses by Caballero and Indians, all of whom regarded him as a saint. His ministration was not without worries. There were rumors of the intended displacement of the Franciscans by the Dominicans forced on his attention, and while he was almost destitute of worldly mindedness he could not help being disturbed by intimations which appeared to discredit his work by reflecting on his order. <small>Death of Padre Serra</small>

The padre deserved something better than an exhibition of ingratitude of this sort, for within the limitations imposed upon him he had accomplished more than could reasonably be expected. The human material with which he had to deal was of the poorest. The aptitude of the Spanish for colonization was never of the highest order, and those of them who engaged in it were rarely the best of their race. The most of them were disposed to look to the world to furnish them a living without exertion, and the tendency was called into constant play when they came in contact with a race regarded by them as inferior. And their ignorance fully matched their inertness. <small>Accomplishments of Serra</small>

Whatever was produced within the limits of the mission establishments was due to the foresight and energy of the padres, who had to look after the physical as well as the moral welfare of the *gente de razon* and of the neophytes. The most of the former and all of the latter were incapable of taking care of themselves. Under such circumstances, and with such responsibilities devolving upon them, it would have been little short of miraculous if the padres, when some degree of prosperity attended their efforts, should not have assumed autocratic airs. There is no trace, however, of any such disposition in the conduct of Serra, under whose guidance the Mission of San Francisco, which at the time of foundation numbered a few more than eight hundred souls, including the converted Indians, had increased its population and fortunes considerably before his death. <small>Foresight of the Padres</small>

24   SAN FRANCISCO

Spaniards Poor Colonists

The despotic tendency came later and was not always in the ratio of the growth of prosperity which was not rapid. The soldiers of the presidios were not permitted to marry without the consent of the crown, and the policy of granting lands, which afterward became so liberal, was very restricted in the beginning. Doubtless both of these restrictions harmonized with the wishes of the padres, who, if they did not actually urge them, must have regarded them as facilitating their desires to bring into the fold the Indians, which was the main purpose of the establishment of the missions so far as they were concerned, although they worked in harmony with the higher authorities who more particularly had the aggrandizement of Spain and the preservation of the integrity of its territory in mind.

The pursuit of a policy almost wholly governed by considerations for the welfare of the souls of the Indians necessarily proved an obstacle to development. It must have done so, had it prevailed, even though the Spaniard had been endowed with the colonizing instinct; for its natural effect must have been to deter enterprise of an individual sort which could not possibly have succeeded in competition with the mission establishments, which were tolerably well equipped for the operations which they chose to engage in, and in addition were armed with the power to command the labor of the neophytes for the common good.

Management of the Missions

The possession of this power by the padres fully explains the failure of the territory in which they controlled to develop. There is no reason to question the judgment of early travelers who have recorded their opinion that the padres through experience soon became fairly competent business men, and managed the properties under their care in a fashion which, measured by individualistic standards, must have been regarded as satisfactory for thirty or forty years. That is to say, the inventories of the missions at succeeding periods showed what would be considered gratifying increases. The herds and flocks grew larger year by year, and the quantities of the cereals and other products of the soil were steadily being enlarged, but there was nothing even remotely resembling the expansion witnessed in other parts of the continent, where Nature had been much less generous than in California.

Status of the Indians

The assumption that the system adopted by the padres in dealing with the Indians was at the bottom of the total lack of progress is not far fetched. It is supported by the observed experiences of other countries in which the chief dependence was placed on servile labor for industrial development. Although the native Indians of California were not nominally slaves, they were so in fact. It was not the intention of the government to enslave them. Indeed the Spaniard may be credited with the intention to make good citizens of the natives, the theory evidently being that they could be educated sufficiently to realize the importance of citizenship and then be gathered into municipalities.

Missions only Temporary

This purpose implies that those highest in authority regarded the missions as temporary affairs to be supplanted by civil establishments when the suitable moment for the change arrived. It is not apparent, however, that the padres viewed their duties in this light. They were by no means disposed to subordinate the business of saving souls to the doubtful occupation of preparing very poor material for a future state in which religious restraint would be relaxed and the results of their zeal and energies be dissipated.

Aims of the Padres

The instructions of Jose de Galvez, under which the original missions were established, and various decrees of the Spanish government, clearly foreshadowed the policy of secularization which was later effected; but there is no evidence that

THE MISSION DOLORES AS IT APPEARED IN 1856
It survived the fire of 1906 and is still standing

the padres at any time sought to conform their work to the speedy realization of the idea. On the contrary, from the beginning, they persistently managed affairs so that, unless forcible interference were interposed, the system of elevating the care of the souls of their charges to the first place would be indefinitely perpetuated.

It was inevitable that the purpose of the missionaries, when combined with the power to carry it out, should have produced the result witnessed. The primary object being to save the soul of the Indian, he was regarded from the moment of his baptism as one who had taken a vow which was irrevocable. If after the ceremony he ran away, soldiers were sent in pursuit, and when he was brought back he was punished with lashes. Saving the Indian Soul

The testimony regarding the treatment of the Indians does not imply that they were cruelly dealt with as a rule by the padres. There is distinct evidence to the contrary furnished by impartial observers, and some from sources which might fairly be considered as prejudiced. Vancouver, for instance, spoke of the fathers as "mild and kind hearted, and never failing to attract the affections of the natives," but he noted with astonishment that they appeared to derive few advantages from their conversion. De Mofras, another observer, declared that the missionaries had accomplished magnificent results by the exercise of benevolence, and among the accomplishments he enumerated the teaching of the advantages of labor to the Indians. Treatment of Mission Indians

That the Englishman was the best judge of the two was developed in the fullness of time. The Indians of California never realized the benefits of labor, because the system did not permit them to obtain any just reward for their toil. They were serfs under the most benevolent of the padres and remained so after the Mexican revolution, the change made in their condition by the process of secularization being merely nominal. Indians not Benefitted

Reviewing all the evidence we have concerning the Indians of California, it does not seem so surprising that the Franciscans should have thought them capable of redemption, but it is astonishing that men of discernment and abundant opportunities to observe, should have believed in the possibility of their being evolved into suitable material for citizenship. The possession of such a belief indicates an optimism defiant of long experience.

While the earlier acquaintance of the Spaniard with the Indians of California was not entirely reassuring on the point of his docility, he exhibited some characteristics which to the observant padres seemed to promise tractability. The troubles in San Diego which occurred before the Mission of St. Francis was founded were easily traced to the inspiration of the warlike Yumas, and it was justly inferred that if the tribes immediately surrounding the Bay of San Diego had not been instigated to make trouble they would have cheerfully put up with the strangers who had invaded their country. Traits of California Indians

The experiences of the explorers when in search of Monterey amply confirmed this opinion. Few signs of hostility were displayed, and there were numerous instances of exhibitions of the opposite feeling. There was no evidence of the existence of intercommunication, nor of the qualities which the romancing recorder of the exploits of the buccaneer Sir Francis Drake discovered when he landed on the shores of the bay north of the entrance of San Francisco harbor.

If Portola and his party found any sceptered kings with crowns, who were accompanied by cabinet ministers who made displays of oratory, they maintained a discreet silence respecting them. They, and other parties of Spaniards who penetrated further into the interior than Drake, who appears to have had no desire to do more than effect a landing, found no natives with bags of tobacco, nor did they discover that "the country seemed to promise rich veins of gold and silver, some of the ore being constantly found in digging." From their relations there is no possibility of assuming otherwise than that the Indians throughout the length and breadth of the wide area over which they roamed were nearly all of one kind, and that the stage of their development was as low in the scale as could possibly be conceived.

California Indians Low in the Scale

Those who knew them best declare that they ranked lower in intelligence than Hottentots or the aborigines of Australia. They were as lazy as they were feeble minded and when pressed by famine easily fell into cannibalism. They had no religion, and even lacked imagination sufficient to form definite superstitions. It is related of the more virile Indians of other parts of the North American continent that they had some conception of a great spirit, but that they never even attained to the intellectual height of originating a creation myth. Some authorities have insisted that the Californian Indian reached that stage, but Father Ubach of San Diego, whose ministrations in that place were continued long after the occupation, and whose intercourse with Indians of that county was intimate, expressed the belief that there is no authenticated instance of a California Indian having formed a distinct religious concept without suggestion from the outside.

Destitute of Moral Concepts

Their sexual relations knew no restraint. They had no form of marriage. The missionaries found an instance of an Indian cohabiting with his mother and three sisters. They were without fixed abodes and roamed over a large territory in search of small game, which existed in great abundance, but they lacked the courage to attack bear or elk and the prevision to preserve meat, although throughout most parts of California that can be done by the simple process of drying. As a consequence they were visited by periodical famines which prevented their numbers enlarging.

Indians not Warlike

The Indians living near the Mission of St. Francis differed in no essential particular from those of other parts of Upper California, and there is no reason to believe that they had any warlike qualities, although they were frequently hunted down by the Spaniards living about the Bay of San Francisco, who professed to fear them. In a manuscript left by an American who lived near Ripon in San Joaquin county the statement is made that the Indians in that region never hunted any big game. The section abounded in large animals, but no bones of those of any size were ever seen in their mounds. They evidently subsisted almost entirely on pine nuts, manzanita and other berries, Indian turnips and a varied assortment of acorns which they ground in metates, or large stones hollowed so as to facilitate the operation of crushing with a rude pestle.

Wretched Condition of Gentiles

During inclement weather these Indians lived in caves in the neighborhood. The indications point to the probability of the group or tribe never exceeding thirty in number. When Dr. Marsh, who settled near them, arrived in 1835, they had dwindled to less than a dozen. At that time they had scarcely any covering for their bodies, and were still living in the caves, having no other habitation. They acknowledged or knew of no government other than their tribal head and had finally to be removed to the foothills of what is now Calaveras county, because they developed the habit of killing the cattle of settlers. Outside of this group or tribe the writer of the manuscript asserts there were no other Indians in all the section between Mount Diablo and the Sierra.

Teaching Indians Agriculture

It was this unpromising material that the missionaries were called upon to deal with, and it is less astonishing to learn that they had their labor for their pains than it would be to find evidence that they even remotely approached the accomplishment of their object. That they effected something which indulgent observers were inclined to praise must be conceded, but that it was in any wise commensurate with their hopes, or that their efforts could have succeeded, even if they had met with none of the obstacles which they severely deprecated because they regarded them as hindrances to the work of conversion, is not thinkable.

As already stated the underlying purpose of the padres, so far as the making of the Indian into a useful member of society was concerned, was to teach him to till the soil. Other nomads, by the evolutionary process, managed to attain the stage of civilization which cultivation represents, and in the process they acquired a knowledge of some of the other useful arts. It is not strange, therefore, that the California Indians, when induced by promises of presents and hopes of salvation to embrace Christianity, attained to some degree of aptitude in the pursuit of agriculture.

The lash Often Applied

The statistics of the missions, however, indicate that the proficiency was not of the sort dependable except when exercised under direction and the closest sort of supervision, which in accordance with the spirit of the age was usually accompanied by the use of the lash and other forms of punishment. Thus it happened that the exemplary regulations which were carefully devised for the government of the Indians in the Spanish dominion, although they expressly forbade slavery, easily lent themselves to a system which had all the vices of legal bondage and often evaded its obligations.

Rigid Rules for Indians

Thus it was prescribed that no Indian might live outside his village, and to preserve him from contamination, it was ordered that no lay Spaniard might live in an Indian village. The latter could not even tarry over night unless he were ill, and if he were a trader his stay was limited to three days or nights at the utmost. When these regulations were first established it was represented that the Indians would not work for wages, and that some expedient would have to be resorted to in order to keep them in touch with the Spaniard, so that the great object of converting them to Christianity might be achieved. As their Catholic majesties, Ferdinand and Isabella, and their successors would not countenance nominal slavery, a method was devised which had many of the features of the feudal system of the middle ages, and it is not remarkable that its application should have produced the same results as those witnessed in Europe between the sixth and fifteenth centuries, during which enterprise languished and population remained stationary.

A New World Feudal System

It would be interesting to trace the resemblances in this new world feudal system to that of the mediaeval period, but a history of San Francisco is more concerned with the results of its application by the missionaries than it is to trace its origins and describe its similarities. The modern reader, whose interest in the mission system is mainly confined to the ascertainment of the net results of the efforts of the padres, may relegate the solution of the problem whether it is wise to subordinate the spiritual to the material in the management of worldly affairs to the writers on sociology. There is plenty of suggestive matter in a mere recital of undisputed facts, and expending many words in the discussion of the causes would be a work of supererogation in this connection.

Natives Melt Away Before Whites

The chief thing we are concerned to know is, what did the padres succeed in doing with the laboring material at their command, which was almost wholly composed of natives, the Spanish colonists being even less favorably disposed to toil than the neophytes? The answer might easily be compressed into the statement that the benevolence of the padres was almost as fatal to the Indian as the grasping avarice of the settlers on the other side of the continent, who made little attempt at concealment of their design to take over the red man's heritage on their own terms.

In both cases the native melted away before the advance of the whites as the snow does when kissed by the ardent beams of the sun. But there was this essential difference in the two processes of the extinction of the native: In the region bordering on the Atlantic the extermination of the Indian might be attributed to the crowding-out process. The disappearance of the natives of the East made way for innumerable white successors who usurped their places; on the Pacific coast the Indian was displaced, and during the prevalence of the mission system the most fertile section of the continent scarcely maintained as many inhabitants as were contained in it before the advent of the missionaries.

CHAPTER V

THE UNPRACTICAL CHARACTER OF THE MISSIONARIES

THEIR FAILURE TO ENCOURAGE COMMUNICATION—THEY NEGLECT TRAVEL FACILITIES—PASTORAL PURSUITS IN CALIFORNIA—WRETCHED CONDITION OF SETTLERS—YANKEE TRADERS VISIT CALIFORNIA—LARGE NUMBERS OF HORSES AND HORNED STOCK RAISED—PRODUCT OF THE MISSIONS IN 1839—OCCASIONAL INDIAN UPRISINGS—ARCHITECTURE OF THE MISSIONS—INDOLENCE OF SETTLERS—LIFE ON THE RANCHES—PASTORAL PURSUITS TEND TO INDOLENCE—AGRICULTURE NEGLECTED AND MANUFACTURING IGNORED—NO TRADE EXCEPTING WITH SMUGGLERS.

ALTHOUGH the long search for a safe harbor on the northern coast of California in its inception was prompted by trade considerations, it is a singular fact that when the Bay of San Francisco was finally discovered, and after its discoverers had apparently awakened to a full realization of its value for commercial purposes, no effort was made by those who controlled its destinies to utilize its advantages. The only evidence of concern in this connection that we have is contained in actions and expressions showing the haunting fear of the Spaniard that some other nation might possibly attempt to make use of that which he neglected. *Bay of San Francisco Neglected*

As for the missionaries, their efforts were concentrated on the saving of souls, and such material affairs as engaged their attention almost excluded the idea of trade. The application of feudal methods was fatal to domestic trade, and such foreign commerce as was developed during the seventy years between the founding of the Mission St. Francis and the American occupation was in response to a demand for things which they recognized their inability to produce, rather than to the desire for gain. The exchange of hides and tallow for the articles brought to the coast by adventurous traders approached no nearer to true trade, profitable to both parties, than that of the Indian ready to swap a handful of gold dust for a few glass beads. *Work of the Missionaries*

The padres made no efforts to promote domestic intercourse with a view to encouraging trade, and the authorities, influenced by the jealousy of foreigners, placed every possible obstacle in the way of maritime communication for that purpose. Thus it happened that during the greater part of a century after 1776 the Bay of San Francisco, with all its superior advantages, remained as useless to mankind as though it had never been discovered. The missionaries devoted themselves exclusively, so far as physical effort was concerned, to the cultivation of the soil. That the results are not worthy of admiration is proved by the fact that in a country *Domestic Intercourse Neglected*

29

which has since been shown to have the capacity to feed millions the scant population of their period was sometimes compelled to endure the pangs of hunger.

Mission Statistics Statistical presentations of the conditions existing in the mission days, unless carefully analysed, are misleading. Unless they are studied by the light of the accomplishments of later days they must necessarily produce an erroneous impression. When we learn from the inventories of the missions that at such a time so many bushels of this, that or the other product was raised in their establishments, and that their flocks and herds were on many hills, visions of plenty arise, but they are disputed by the facts which show that the general condition of the sparse population was wretched and that even the forward ones lived lives which bordered closely on squalor.

Mission Live Stock As early as 1784 we are told that it had been found necessary to reduce by slaughter the surplus cattle at the San Francisco presidio. The number of horses became so great that some years later they were killed by tens of thousands. They roamed at large and many of them became the prey of wolves and bears, and others were mired in lagoons and marshes. Statements of this sort, accompanied by figures showing that there had been a gain in the production of live stock in all the missions of California between 1800 and 1810 of 162,882 head, and that the agricultural products had increased 113,625 bushels, convey the impression of great prosperity, but the secular authorities were under no illusions regarding the situation, and we find them expressing the opinion that the missions of Alta California were little better than expensive failures.

Excessive Indian Mortality They were not merely expensive failures; they were worse. The vital statistics with startling brevity express the true condition. At the end of 1800 the death rate of the natives had been 50 per cent of baptisms; in 1810 it was 72 per cent and a few years later 86 per cent. In 1810 President Payeras had declared that at Purisima nearly all Indian mothers gave birth to dead infants, and in 1815 it was reported throughout the province that the proportion of deaths to births had for many years been as three to two.

Settlers Not Well Provided For Governor Sola, in reviewing the condition of the Indians in the last named year pronounced them "indolent and disregardful of all authority, costing for half a century millions of pesos without having made at that time any recompense to the body politic." He declared that they had become spoiled by settling at the missions, and that though instructed in agriculture and other branches, "they are able to but cover half of their bodies." This summing up of results leaves us to infer that the Indian communities were actually in worse condition than when Serra first came in contact with the natives of San Diego and found their womankind "so honestly covered that we could take it in good part if greater nudities were never seen among the Christian women of the mission."

Naked Soldiers The Indians, however, were in no worse case than the soldiers of the garrison. In 1817 Commandante Luis Arguello at San Francisco begged Sola for clothing for his own family and a little later a Yankee trader, James Smith Wilcox, urged an excuse for smuggling that he had thereby served "to clothe the naked soldiers of the king of Spain," thus enabling them to attend mass which otherwise they could not do for lack of raiment. This apology for infractions of the revenue laws was frequently invoked, and apparently freely accepted by officials of the crown, who were aware that unless the stranger was permitted to provide, the subjects of the king would have to go unprovided.

It is difficult to conceive of such utter incapacity as these revelations disclose. **Incapacity Displayed** In 1825 an inventory of the property of the Mission Dolores was made which showed that there were 76,000 horned cattle, 950 horses, 2,000 mares, 84 steeds, 820 mules, 79,000 sheep, 2,000 hogs and 456 working oxen belonging to the establishment. It may be true as asserted that the quality of the wool supplied by the sheep was of an inferior character, and that the breeds of the animals were of the poorest, but that fact hardly explains the destitution commented upon. The poorest of wool may be spun and woven into garments, and the hides of the most wretched cattle may be tanned and made into good leather. But the processes of converting the raw materials into products suitable for apparel demanded exertion and some skill, neither of which were forthcoming, hence Indians, soldiers and all went naked or ragged.

When Dana visited California in 1835 he found that the people who were able to exchange their surplus products for articles brought by Yankee traders were ready to buy a bad wine made in Boston. The vagaries of the consumers of the juice of the grape might explain the purchase of a foreign kind of wine, but in this instance appreciation of the Massachusetts vintage is not urged. The idle and thriftless population made no wine although the country abounded in grapes and it was therefore Boston wine or none at all. **Wine Brought by Boston Traders**

That the padres produced some wine is undoubtedly true, but it was evidently retained for their own consumption. There does not appear at any time to have been a strong desire on their part to lessen the demand for the fiery alcoholic beverage known as aguardiente, by supplying a light and wholesome substitute by expressing the juice of the native grape or that of the variety introduced by them from Spain, and which has long been familiarly known as the California mission grape.

That the instructions given by the padres were not of a character to make good agriculturists of the neophytes may be inferred from the statements made by many observers. In preparing the soil for grain the earth was simply scratched with a heavy timber pointed with iron if the metal was obtainable. This wretched substitute for a plow was dragged by oxen who pulled against a yoke attached to their horns, the belief being that the strength of the animal lay in that part of its body. Later the Yankee trader came to their assistance with a share of more modern fashion, but even with this help the results were not of the sort to command admiration. **Crude Agricultural Methods**

In 1839, seventy years after the foundation of the San Diego mission, which enjoys the distinction of being the first establishment of the padres in Upper California, the total product of all the missions of California was hardly equal to that of a good sized American farm of the present day. Of wheat, maize, barley, beans and peas there was a total output of 14,438 quarters in the year mentioned. Of live stock, which took care of itself, there were over 400,000 head of all kinds, the number being made up of 216,727 black cattle, 32,201 horses, 2,844 mules, 153,455 sheep, the remainder being asses, goats and swine. **Products of Missions in 1839**

It is true that the operations of the missionaries had been interrupted before this date by the secularization of the establishments, but it would do violence to the probabilities to assume that any better showing would have been made had there been no interference with the methods of the padres. The tremendous inroads of disease, and the great falling off of the birth rate pointed to the speedy

32   SAN FRANCISCO

extinction of the supply of native labor, and indolence and incapacity of the colonists from Mexico, and the absolute refusal of the soldiery to engage in useful occupations precluded the idea of any substantial assistance from any other source.

Indian Uprisings Although the missionaries failed to transform the Indians into a dependable laboring element, their activities had an unlooked for effect which produced much subsequent trouble. The native Californian in appearance and manner encouraged the impression that he was made of docile stuff, but his frequent quarrels with his own kind should have suggested that the tractability which sometimes manifested itself was more apparent than real. Before the neophytes were gathered and kept within the mission precincts they had lived in small rancherias and there was no friendly contact between them. When associated together their attitude of hostility was awakened, and acquaintance soon developed something like organizing ability and a desire to act in common against the oppressor.

Indians Conspire How much this attitude affected their efficiency in the fields it would be difficult to decide, but it is evident that it must have militated against cheerful acceptance of the condition imposed upon them by the padres. The troubles which occurred after the missions were shorn of most of their privileges indicate that the exemption from uprisings was due more to the skillful management of the priests than the docility of the natives, or to their acceptance of the teachings of Christianity.

Zeal of the Missionaries That the missionaries could have succeeded in changing the habits of the native Californian by the swift process of religious conversion was believed by many, but it hardly admits of a doubt that the tendency to conspire which propinquity had developed among the Indians must have ultimately defeated the purposes of the missionaries no matter how zealously or intelligently they may have labored. About their zeal there can be no question. The most, if not all of the padres, had an earnest desire to recover the souls of the benighted natives, but that they went intelligently about their work is disproved by the meager results of their exertions.

Mission Architecture In addition to the poor showing of the inventories of the missions they left to California nothing to felicitate itself upon excepting a style of architecture which has many claims to distinctiveness. The remains of this talent have probably contributed more to the mistaken belief held by some that the padres were really efficient directors than any written record of their accomplishments or traditions concerning their doings. It is difficult to contemplate the ruins of the missions of California without investing them with a romantic interest. They are suggestive of a condition which never really existed. Their appearance, even in their present ruinous state, conveys an impression of peace and plenty that is no more truthful than the description of a baronial hall of the middle ages, in which the stress is laid on the barbarous feasting and rioting, while allusions to the poverty of the wretched serfs surrounding it is carefully suppressed.

The Mission Churches It might almost be inferred from the work expended in the construction of the mission buildings that the energies and talents of the monks were chiefly expended upon them. That the most of them would not have regarded this as an aspersion is undoubtedly true. They imagined that they were working for the glory of God, and strove in the manner which has always been considered most effective to accomplish their object. They were merely repeating in the new world the mistake made in the old during the Middle Ages, of subordinating the temporal to the spiritual. They fervently believed that the best thing that could be done for mankind was to wean it from the desire for worldly things, by concentrating thought on the future life, and deferring hope of reward until attained in an eternity of bliss.

Unfortunately man is too easily encouraged to exchange activity of a kind which accomplishes material results for the more peaceful and less troublesome occupation of laying up treasures in heaven. And unless the colonists of the mission period are greatly maligned their disposition was such that it naturally lent itself to easy acquiescence in the belief that it is not worth while to exert oneself here below to pile up riches. People in this frame of mind find no difficulty in accepting conditions that would be regarded as unendurable by those less inclined to religious domination. Hence we find that during the entire mission period individual exertion was at a minimum stage, and the only noteworthy accomplishments were those of the monks who were able to effect them cooperatively with the assistance of a system of labor that was slavery in everything but name.

Laying up Treasures in Heaven

Throughout the length and breadth of the vast territory comprised within the boundaries of Alta California there was not a single structure outside of the religious establishments, that any early traveler thought worth noting. We have plenty of accounts which enable us to picture the mode of life of the *gente de razon*, but the descriptions of their abodes is one which leaves an impression of simplicity which borders closely on actual squalor. What wealth there was did not lend itself to ostentation of the kind we are familiar with. A man of the period might have been rich in lands, and may have possessed great herds of cattle, and flocks of sheep and was looked up to on that account, but he lived little better, so far as mere housing was concerned, than his poorest neighbor.

Ranch Architecture

That this state of affairs was not wholly due to the friars, although it may be traced to the belief in the undesirability of mundane things which their predecessors had inculcated during centuries, and which they still taught, may be inferred from the fact that no more progress was made after secularization than before that event. Indeed, if anything, there was less energy displayed after the temporalities had displaced the spiritual than during most of the time between the founding of the Mission Dolores and the successful revolution in Mexico which reduced the influence of the padres to a negligible quantity. And it is a singular circumstance, worth noting in this connection, that the earlier settlers who found their way into the country and allied themselves with the native Californians, did not add greatly to the enterprising character of those with whom they took up their home. As a rule they were absorbed and speedily adopted the indolent habits and the acquiescent attitude of the colonists of Spanish extraction.

Life on the Ranch

It will not be difficult to understand why Englishmen, Scotchmen and Americans who found their way into California before 1846 adopted the unenterprising habits of the natives. The acceptance of mañana, or to-morrow, as a rule of life comes easy to most men, and when to the natural disposition to accept the plan of moving along the line of least resistance there was added the excuse that a fatuous system of trade restriction made enterprise almost impossible, it is not surprising that few escaped its seductive influence.

Pastoral Pursuits

Both by design and the acceptance of conditions, the inhabitants of California during the entire period of Spanish and Mexican rule were confined to agricultural and pastoral pursuits; and as the latter required the least exertion they were most favored. Agriculture of the kind which proves profitable to those engaging in it had few attractions for the *gente de razon* even when they could command Indian labor, and ceased to have any at all when serfdom was practically abolished. As for manufactures they were non existent, for at no time, even during the most flourishing days of the missions had the natives succeeded in developing enough skill to advance beyond the primitive stage.

Self-Sufficing Ranches

Necessarily a country in which agriculture was neglected, and manufacturing was confined to the production of things absolutely needed, and the fashioning of which required little or no art, could not develop a domestic trade. Consequently there was little or no intercourse such as that which the interchange of commodities brings about. Every ranch was self sufficing. If its owners were opulent enough to maintain a smith or a carpenter, the proprietor and his dependents were provided after a fashion with the articles produced by artisans of that sort, but most of the time they did without tools and things which an American frontiersman would regard as indispensable to the carrying on of farming operations of the simplest character.

Little Trading Done

The only approach to anything resembling real trade was that witnessed when a vessel from some foreign land touched at the ports which the jealous Spaniards and Mexicans permitted the stranger to visit. On those occasions the exchanges were made under such restrictions, and so many obstacles were placed in the way of freedom of intercourse that any considerable development was rendered impossible. This interference which might have stimulated a more energetic people than the native Californians, and the colonists, to exert themselves to provide by their own efforts that which a fatuous government prohibited them from buying from foreigners, did not result in the creation of a home industry of any kind. The doctrine of the beauty of contentment was ingrained, and resignation to deprivation was elevated into a virtue and ambition, except of the sort that manifested itself in aspiration for petty political favors was wholly extinguished.

CHAPTER VI

SPANISH DISCOURAGEMENT OF RELATIONS WITH OUTSIDERS

UNCOMMERCIAL METHODS OF SPAIN—THE PREDICTION OF A PADRE CONCERNING SAN FRANCISCO BAY—EARLY YANKEE AMBITIONS—SPANISH FEAR OF THE RUSSIANS—THE VISIT OF RAZENOFF AND HIS ADVICE TO THE CALIFORNIANS—NAVIGATION OF THE BAY DISCOURAGED BY GOVERNOR SOLA—EARLIEST TRAFFIC ON THE BAY OF SAN FRANCISCO—CAPTAIN MORRELL MAKES A SUGGESTION—UNCLE SAM SEEKS AN OUTLET—REPORT OF COLONEL BUTLER ON CALIFORNIA—MEXICO UNAPPRECIATIVE OF CALIFORNIA—ARGUELLO LAUDS POSSIBILITIES OF PROVINCE—THE EARLY IMMIGRANTS WELCOMED—SHIPS DROP INTO SAN FRANCISCO BAY—THE FOUNDATION OF YERBA BUENA.

The Uncommercial Spaniard

NOTHING could more plainly reveal the utterly uncommercial character of the Spanish than their mode of dealing with the port of San Francisco. For a couple of centuries a harbor was sought for with varying degrees of diligence and when it was finally found no more use was made of it than if it were non existent. It cannot be said that the discoverers were unacquainted with its advantages, or that they failed to make the authorities in Mexico and Spain acquainted with them, but there interest in the matter and desire terminated.

Jealousy of Foreigners

As early as 1772, four years before the foundation of the Mission Dolores, Verger wrote a letter in which he outlined the uses to which a good harbor could be put. He was under a misapprehension concerning the river which he described as flowing into the bay, and which he thought might be connected with the Colorado, but he was under no illusions regarding the possibility of establishing a port in which there could be ship yards and other facilities that would be easy to provide on account of the abundance of timber of a suitable sort for building boats and other vessels. He had an intimate knowledge of the foibles of his countrymen, which made him suspect that something more than a mere recital of advantages was necessary to stimulate them to exertion for he told Casafonda, to whom he sent his description, that "great prejudice to the crown of Spain must be feared should some foreign nation establish themselves in this port."

The Port Utterly Neglected

The suggestion that some one else might utilize the bay if the Spanish did not was heeded in a way. It was taken possession of by the crown, and interlopers were warned away, but during the seventy years while it was under the control of Spain and Mexico no Spaniard, Mexican or native Californian ever exerted himself to realize the expectations of those who predicted a great future for the unrivalled sheet of water which bears the name of the patron saint of the Franciscan order.

35

SAN FRANCISCO

A Padre's Prediction

It is related that one of the padres who assisted at the establishment of the Presido of San Francisco, after performing the ceremony of blessing the site of Fort Point, ascended to the slight eminence in its rear, where he found a very green and flowery table land abounding in wild violets and sloping gently towards the port. In a description which he subsequently wrote he pronounced the view "delicious." "There may be seen," he said, "not only a good part of the port with its islands, but the mouth of the bay and the sea where the prospect ranges even beyond the Farallones."

A man of his cloth might have stopped here but he went on indulging in practical comment, which probably reflected the belief and aspirations of the first settlers on the Bay of San Francisco. "I judged," he wrote, "that if this site could be well populated as in Europe, there would be nothing finer in the world, as it was in every way fitted for a most beautiful city—one of equal advantages, by either land or water, with that port so remarkable and capacious, wherein could be built ship yards, quays and whatever might be desired."

Fears of Viceroy Florez

A few years later, in 1788, Viceroy Manuel Antonio Florez, shortly after his arrival in Mexico, wrote to his home government that there would be no occasion for surprise if the American colonies of the British, "now that they are an independent republic, should carry out the design of finding a safe port on the Pacific and of attempting to sustain it by crossing the immense country of the continent above our possessions of Texas, New Mexico and California."

From these and similar observations made by representatives of the Spanish crown, and by early visitors to the Pacific coast of North America, we discover that there was no lack of appreciation of the importance of establishing a port of the sort described by Florez, nor of its desirability when viewed from the standpoint of the trader whose interest would lie in the development of a commerce between Alta California and the rest of the world. But there is an essential difference between recognition of possibilities and their realization.

A Period of Inertia

The crown, the viceroy of Mexico, the governors of California and the padres may have fully comprehended the importance of the Bay of San Francisco, but they never moved a hand to bring about the result which they desired to see achieved. Even the stimulus of fear, inspired by rivalry, was powerless to quicken them to action of any sort looking to the realization of their hopes. Their inertia was so marked during the entire period under review that a doubt arises whether the expressions of opinion by the optimistic were not merely words destitute of significance, and wholly devoid of that quality which spurs men to action.

Razenoff's Visit in 1806

In 1806 a Russian named Razenoff visited San Francisco for the purpose of obtaining supplies for his countrymen, who were taking pelts in Alaska. He was compelled to resort to extraordinary devices to escape the restrictions imposed by the distant authorities upon trade of all kinds with the Californians. Many of these obstacles were the result of fear of Russian encroachment, an not entirely unwarranted apprehension, but one which could hardly be removed by the pursuit of the policy of aloofness which involved complete abstention from effort to create the means by which aggression could be prevented.

This astute foreigner, who did not hesitate to spy out the land while attempting to persuade the commandante of the port of San Francisco, and the padres, that they would be committing no crime in disposing of some of their surplus products, appears to have lectured his hosts with vigor on their supineness, declaring with

SAN FRANCISCO

refreshing directness that they were negligent of their interests which required that they should develop their country, so that regions less favored by nature might obtain in exchange for their peculiar products needed supplies of food stuffs.

There is no evidence that his advice made any serious impression on his hearers. They may have regarded it as sensible, and were doubtless quite ready to admit that they would benefit by following his suggestions, but they failed to act. Eleven years later, while Arguello, who had been Razenoff's host, was still commandante, the magnificent body of water, about whose shores nearly a million people are now engaged in productive pursuits, was as little used by man as it had been before the first Spanish vessel entered through the Golden Gate.

The Russian's Advice Disregarded

Desiring to secure some timber necessary to effect some much needed repairs of the presidio buildings Arguello resorted to Corte de Madera to obtain what he required. The wood cutters who felled the trees and prepared them for use were compelled to cross the Carquinez straits on rafts and made their way to Corte de Madera by way of Sonoma, Petaluma and San Rafael, making a circuit of seventy leagues, while the actual distance between the forest and the presidio is less than four leagues. An English carpenter assisted in building a suitable craft to bring the timber to the presidio front and spent some days in teaching the soldiers how to sail it. Without this assistance, and that of an Indian named Marin, the cargo could hardly have been successfully brought across the bay; as it was the cumbersome craft was nearly wrecked in Racoon straits.

A Round-About Route

Unpromising as was this initial effort it met with the additional discouragement of the disapproval of Governor Solá, who was enraged that the launch should have been built without his authority. Commandante Arguello experienced great difficulty in convincing him that it was absolutely necessary to engage in the enterprise to save the presidio from falling into utter ruin. The explanation condoned the heinous offense of the commandante, but the sharp reproof he had received appears to have effectually cured any desire he may have felt to engage in further maritime activities.

Solá Discourages Navigation of Bay

It was not until several years after this episode that any serious effort was made to navigate the bay, and it soon developed monopolistic tendencies, which however, did not prompt attempts at regulation. William A. Richardson, who had first settled at Sausalito, in 1822, moved to San Francisco and not long after he began sailing a couple of schooners between points where settlements had been made, collecting produce from the missions and farms. His enterprise speedily developed into a monopoly, but the records do not show that he adopted any irregular methods to secure or maintain it; nor do they indicate dissatisfaction with his rates, which were 12 cents a piece for hides, $1 per bag of tallow weighing 500 pounds and 25 cents for two and a half bushels of wheat.

Richardson Starts a Schooner Line

The charges were not based on the length of the haul but appear to have been uniform for all distances, and the service performed in all cases was the transference of the products from various points on the bay to the Cove of Yerba Buena, where it was finally transferred to seagoing vessels. Later the Mission St. Francis, and those at San Jose, each maintained a thirty ton schooner, but it is noteworthy, as indicative of the utter inefficiency of the Spaniards and Mexicans, that they were built at Fort Ross by the Russians, no one connected with the religious foundations or any settler having the requisite skill to engage in such construction.

Transportation Charges

38   SAN FRANCISCO

Indifferent to Advantages of Harbor

Although the Californians were indifferent to the advantages of the magnificent harbor and allowed them to remain practically unutilized, that fact did not prevent the outside world gaining information which incited longings for an opportunity to compel a development which the Spaniards were disposed to neglect. In spite of a policy which sought to make the Bay of San Francisco as inaccessible as the interior of a monastery it was penetrated at intervals and usually the visiting strangers were prompted to speak in glowing terms of the disregarded possibilities. Captain Frederick M. Beechey of "H. M. S. Blossom" who entered the bay in 1826 subsequently wrote that "California must awaken from its lethargy, or fall into other hands. It was of too much importance to remain neglected."

Morrell's Description of California

In 1832 Captain Benjamin Morrell, a Yankee skipper who had traded on the coast, and had informed himself concerning its capabilities, wrote a book in which he echoed the words of Beechey and gave them point by suggesting that the young republic contained the people who would effect the redemption of the slumbering Californians. He said: "These beautiful regions (were they but the property of the United States) would not be permitted to remain neglected. The Eastern and Middle states would pour into them their thousands of emigrants until magnificent cities would arise on the shores of every inlet on the coast, while the wilderness of the interior would be made to blossom like the rose."

Growing Fame of the Bay

It is not clear that the Californians were acquainted with the growing interest that the outside world was taking in their affairs, and that other people were casting longing eyes upon their bay, which was becoming famous. They were not very literary and had small acquaintance with books, and it is not difficult to think of them as absolutely uninformed concerning the appearance of fresh publications. But such descriptions as those of Morrell made a vivid impression on the people of the Atlantic states which soon began to find expression in recommendations which did not go unheeded by those in authority.

Seeking an Outlet on the Pacific

The dominant note in all of these was the desirability of an outlet to the Pacific. The manifest destiny idea made suggestions of this sort welcome, and every bit of information was made to fit in with the popular desire. The difficulties with Mexico which culminated in the acquisition of the coveted territory were not of sudden origin; they may easily be traced back to a period many years anterior to the trouble on the Rio Grande. It would be far more reasonable to attribute to the desire for a station for American whalers in the harbor of San Francisco, which was strongly expressed during Jackson's administration, the war with Mexico than to charge it to the machinations of the pro slavery element.

Plans of the Slave Owners

That the advocates of slavery performed a conspicuous part in bringing about the result is undeniable, but the success which crowned their efforts was wholly due to the sentiment which found noisy expression in the "Fifty-four-forty or fight" slogan of the campaign which put Polk in the presidential chair. The American people were not particularly bent on sustaining the institution of slavery, but they were under the domination of an irresistible desire to extend the territory of the United States westward until it should reach the Pacific.

Butler's Report to Jackson

We find this longing outlined in the report of Colonel Anthony Butler, who was appointed *charge d'affaires* to Mexico by his friend President Jackson. In 1835 Butler went to Washington to press on the attention of the president a proposition to secure by treaties from Mexico the whole tract of territory "known as New Mexico and the higher and lower California." This region he declared

was "an empire in itself, a paradise in climate * * * rich in minerals, and affording a water route to the Pacific through the Arkansas and Colorado rivers."

Butler's information respecting the navigability of the two rivers mentioned by him was not accurate, but his desire for an outlet to the Pacific was plainly indicated. His opinion that the coveted territory, the acquisition of which would permit access to the great ocean whose waters lave the shores of the newest and most ancient of nations, was clearly expressed, however, and his view that it could be obtained by treaty found acceptance and in 1842 was urged upon Daniel Webster by Waddy Thompson, the American minister to Mexico, who was confident that the latter country could be persuaded to cede Texas and the Californias to the United States in payment of the claims of American merchants against the Mexican government. {Waddy Thompson Urges Acquisition}

The striking feature of Thompson's recommendation is the assumption running through it that Mexico thought so little of the territory whose acquisition he urged that it would part with it for less than a song. The minister was under no misapprehension concerning the value of the territory, but he evidently believed that the Mexicans regarded it as valueless, or, at least, that they realized that they were incapable of promoting its development. He said, in speaking of it: "As to Texas I regard it as of little value compared with California, the richest, most beautiful and the healthiest country in the world." But it was upon the value of the harbor of San Francisco that he laid the most stress, declaring that it was "capacious enough to receive the navies of the world." {Thompson's Appreciation of California}

Thompson's assumption that the occupants of California were unappreciative of its value was only partially true. The archives of the City of Mexico, and the records stored in San Francisco, and so liberally used in determining land title controversies at a later date, prove conclusively that there were Californians who had the capacity to judge and describe the resources of the territory although they were incapable of developing them. We have a report of Arguello, made in 1825 on the condition and prospects of California in which he spoke of the admirable physical characteristics of the country; its splendid forests; its soil of inconceivable fertility, and "its capacity of becoming one of the richest and happiest countries in the world." {Arguello's Valuation of the Country}

It is significant that Arguello's glowing description lays no stress upon the value of the harbor of San Francisco, and hardly suggests its existence. It is permeated throughout by the same feeling that the padres inherited from the feudalistic experiment of the middle ages, and which they managed to preserve and pass on down almost to our own times. It breathes the spirit of isolation, accompanied by that narrow conception of self sufficingness which was the most marked characteristic of the institution in the middle ages, and which in the midst of comparatively dense populations in Europe set up such barriers that intercourse between separated communities was almost wholly suspended. {Merits of Bay Overlooked}

It is not surprising that the productive faculties should have been atrophied, and the trading instinct weakened by the non intercourse predilections of the Californians, who did not apparently greatly resent the decrees and the legislation which threw them on their own feeble resources. Throughout the period while they were in control no efforts were made by the native Californians to open communication with outsiders. Such intercourse as they had with strangers was unsolicited by them, and often it was unwelcome. They were not merely content {Productive Faculty Atrophied} to refrain from efforts to create surpluses for exchange, they actually had to be coaxed to part with these which were created for them by their prolific herds.

Immigrants Welcomed

They were not inhospitable to strangers whose motives in visiting them were not open to suspicion, and even welcomed those who were ready to accept their habits and who assumed family relations which made them part of the community. But they did not go out of their way to invite immigration and promptly took alarm when it began to assume proportions which threatened to provide the labor needed to develop the neglected resources of the country.

Few Ships Visit the Harbor

This invasion, as we shall see later on, was not from the water. Despite the fact that the Bay of San Francisco was much discussed, and its advantages well apprehended, it was rarely visited by ships. Few merchantmen entered the harbor, their trading being more conveniently transacted at Monterey and other points along the coast where supplies of hides and tallow were stored. The records show that between 1816 and 1842 nine or ten war vessels entered the port, among them five flying the American flag. The first American war vessel to visit the bay came through the Golden Gate in 1841 and was followed in the same year by another, both being bent on surveying errands. A year later the "Yorktown," "Cyane and Dale" paid visits to the port that was to be, but which at that time gave few indications of its future greatness.

Foundation of Yerba Buena

Apart from these visits there was little to record of shipping activity in the harbor prior to 1842 but after that year the visits of war ships and merchantmen became more frequent. The laws of Mexico had reserved to the governor of the province the disposal of lands within a certain number of feet below high water mark, but the power was not made use of until 1835, and then only in a negative fashion, Figueroa framing an ordinance in that year forbidding the presidial authorities making any grants of land about the Yerba Buena cove nearer than 200 varas from the beach without his special order.

Land Granted to Settlers

From this order may be said to date the foundation of Yerba Buena, the village that has since developed into a great city. The purpose of Figueroa in making the reservation was to preserve it for government use. Applications had been made before that date by individuals who desired to secure the land about the cove for farming purposes, and he desired to prevent it falling into private hands. He also contemplated something in the way of creating a settlement; but he died before the town he proposed could be laid out; and nothing was done until 1839 when Alvarado, the then governor, dispatched an order to survey the plain and cove of Yerba Buena, which was executed by Alcalde Francisco Haro with the assistance of Captain John Virget who ran the lines.

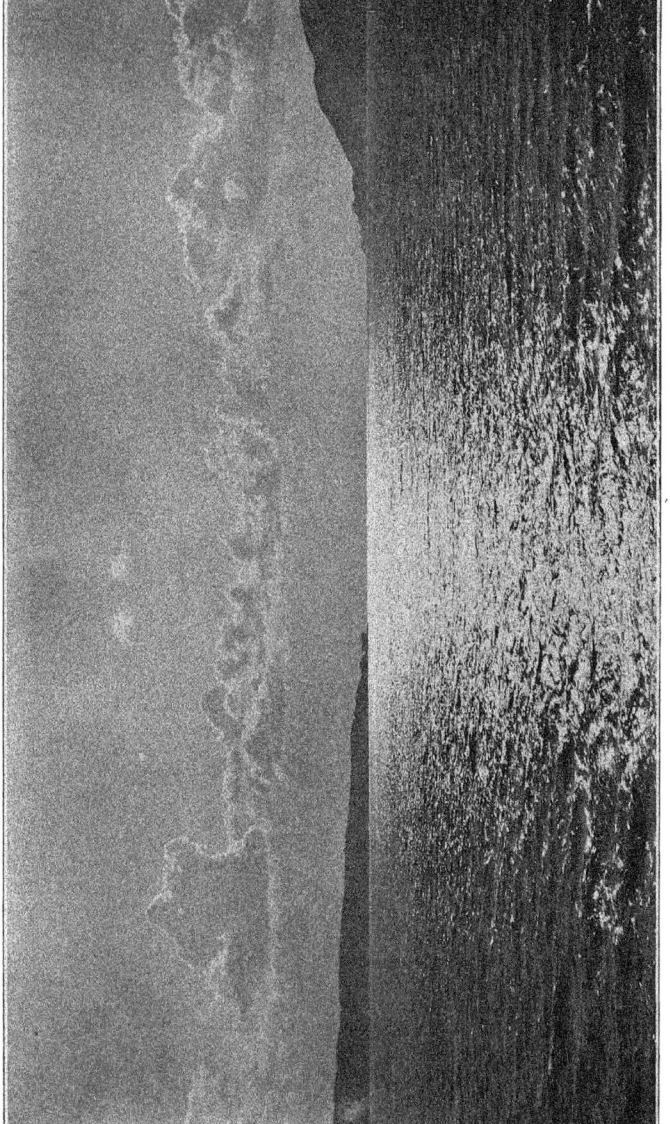

THE GOLDEN GATE

CHAPTER VII

FOUNDATION OF THE VILLAGE OF YERBA BUENA

YERBA BUENA IN 1839—THE FIRST HOUSE ERECTED IN YERBA BUENA—DEDICATION OF THE MISSION OF ST. FRANCIS—REZANOFF'S VISIT TO SAN FRANCISCO BAY IN 1806—THE RUSSIAN IS WELCOMED—A ROMANCE OF YERBA BUENA—REZANOFF SECURES SUPPLIES FOR THE ESTABLISHMENT OF THE RUSSIANS IN SITKA—DEATH OF REZANOFF IN SIBERIA—RUSSIAN METHODS IN CALIFORNIA—FEW BOOKS IN CALIFORNIA BEFORE ARRIVAL OF AMERICANS—DANCING FORBIDDEN BY THE PADRES—PATERNAL RULE ON THE RANCHES—THE INFLUENCE OF THE CHURCH.

HE boundaries of the town laid out under the order of Alvarado would make but a small dot on the map of the San Francisco of 1912, and to the person unfamiliar with the fact that much of the land in what is now the business section of the City was recovered from the bay, it would appear that no special effort was made to get near the water front. The ambitions of the founders were satisfied by setting off a space which had Pacific street for its northern and Sacramento for its southern boundary, while its western limit was described by Dupont street and its eastern by Montgomery, the waters of the cove reaching the latter street in 1839, the year in which the survey was made.

Yerba Buena in 1839

This district, known as Yerba Buena until 1847 when the name was changed to San Francisco, was described by the early comers as being about the most unlovely part of the region surrounding the bay. It was barren and in the immediate vicinity were low sand hills covered with coarse shrubbery and patches of grass. Yerba Buena derived its appellation from the village of that name which stood on the spot surveyed in 1839, but it was only known locally by that designation, its true name being given on the map as San Francisco.

Name Changed in 1847

Yerba Buena is the Spanish name of a vine found in the underwood of the region about the bay which has some claims to fragrance. Literally translated it means good herb, and the earliest annalists state that it was held in some estimation by the settlers of Spanish extraction who brewed a tea from its leaves.

The first house in Yerba Buena appears to have been erected in 1835 by Captain W. A. Richardson who anticipated the survey. It was not a very substantial construction, being merely a ship's foresail stretched over four redwood posts. Richardson was in charge of the two schooners mentioned as belonging to the missions of St. Francis and Santa Clara. His connection with the padres secured for him the privilege of planting the tent-like structure on the spot mentioned. Later he built an adobe house on what is now Dupont street west of Portsmouth square.

First House Erected

41

42 SAN FRANCISCO

Yerba Buena in 1841

That was in 1841 and there were then thirty families living in the village. In addition to the adobe house of Richardson, Juana Briones, a widow, had erected another one on the corner of Powell and Filbert streets, and there was an establishment of the Russians which was built of wooden slabs and covered with tarpaulin. Three years later Yerba Buena had about a dozen houses and in 1846 the number had increased to fifty. The expansion of the two last years was caused by the impending change in the administration of Californian affairs foreshadowed by the collision between the United States and Mexico, the outcome of which held no riddle for active minded Americans.

Establishment of Dolores

In addition to this small settlement there was the establishment at Dolores and the garrison at the presidio. Although the site selected by the padres for their operations does not suggest extensive tilling of the soil, a century ago it presented an entirely different aspect and as the records attest it was capable of producing on a liberal scale. At no time after its foundation was the importance of the mission inferior to that of the military or the commercial part of the community, and throughout the somewhat tense periods when the spiritual and temporal powers were in conflict the padres retained their hold upon the respect and affections of the little society.

Dedication of Mission St. Francis

It is not in the doings of so small a community as Yerba Buena was in the years immediately following the establishment of the mission that we can find the materials for a picture of the social life of the people who first displaced the native Indians of California. There were other and large establishments which outranked that of St. Francis in wealth, but the latter from the day that it was dedicated with firing of muskets, which greatly scared the poor Indians who were drawn to the scene by the ceremony, and by a display of such banners, vestments and other articles of ceremonial display as the padres could provide, always occupied a position of importance in the minds of the authorities, and perhaps that of the people generally because it was the northern outpost of the mission establishments and in a way the only barrier that had been set up to guard against Russian encroachment.

Monterey the Social Center

Monterey down to the time of the American occupation was the social center of Northern California, as it was also of the political activities of the region. But while the foundation on Monterey bay outshone that of St. Francis the latter appears to have had attractions at an early date for foreigners, especially the Russians, who exhibited a decided inclination for the locality and in one way and another proved a source of uneasiness to Spain and the people planted by that country in Northern California.

Mention has already been made of a Russian named Rezanoff who in 1806 visited the harbor of San Francisco in quest of supplies for the hunter's station established by Russia in Alaska, the occupants of which were in a condition bordering on starvation. The adventure of Rezanoff is interesting as it discloses the desires of Russia, but more particularly because it affords us a glimpse of the mode of life in the little community made up of the garrison of the presidio and their families, and the fathers and the servants and workers of the mission.

Rezanoff's Designs

Rezanoff was chamberlain of the czar in 1803 and conceived the design of securing trade concessions for Russia from the Japanese, but proving unsuccessful in his effort he crossed over to the Aleutian islands bearing with him credentials as inspector of the Northwestern establishments of the Russian crown. He found the condition of the station at Unalaska deplorable when he reached there in 1805, the employes of the Russian-American Company being in a state bordering on starvation.

Rezanoff at once resolved to relieve their distress by obtaining supplies from California. His expedition for that purpose was attended with many hazards. It started at a season of the year when terrific gales were likely to be encountered, and he realized that in the event of weathering the storms which menaced his voyage that he might meet a hostile reception at the hands of the Californians. But he stated in a communication to the home office that it was merely a question of taking the risks or of remaining in Alaska and starving. Russians Seek Supplies

In this same correspondence traces of other objects than the obtaining of relief are found. In it he discussed the unenterprising character of the Spaniards who made scarcely any use of their fertile lands, and he also animadverted upon the Bostonians who were trading to a limited extent with the Californians, and proposed supplanting them if possible, remarking that there was no reason why factories in Siberia should not supply to the Spaniards cloth, ironware, linen and such things in exchange for breadstuffs and other produce.

If Rezanoff had any expectation of the strict regulations made by the Spaniards for the port of San Francisco being enforced he must have been surprised when he sailed into the harbor on the 5th of April. There was a reasonable prospect of his being fired upon by the battery of San Joaquin as he ran by without asking permission to enter, but he met with no such reception probably because advices had been received from Madrid, not long before that date, to the effect that a better understanding between Spain and Russia had been reached, and that a Russian vessel would shortly visit the coast. Regulations Disregarded

Instead of the expected rebuff which Rezanoff was prepared to encounter, trusting to his ability to smooth things over after effecting an entrance, a confidence which was by no means misplaced, he was received with pleasure, and he and those on board his ship the "Juno," were overwhelmed with civilities by the son of the commandante of the port Luis Arguello, whose father Jose happened to be absent at the time at Monterey, where he was visiting the governor. Rezanoff Welcomed

Rezanoff took advantage of the situation created by the misapprehension. He at once wrote to the governor, Arrillaga, proposing to visit him at Monterey, but that official, who was not altogether satisfied as to the regularity of the proceeding, answered that he would do himself the honor of receiving his guest at San Francisco which he did, and there met the Russian. On the day following the official meeting Rezanoff and the governor were invited to dine with the commandante and there the Russian encountered his fate in the shape of the daughter of Jose Arguello whose accomplishments, lovely disposition and beauty were celebrated throughout the Californias. An Early San Francisco Romance

Concepcion was only 14 years old and was romantic and highly impressionable and longed for adventure. Rezanoff promptly surrendered to her charms and the youthful senorita reciprocated his advances. It does not appear that this first San Franciscan romance suffered interruption in its earliest stages, but later on when it had fully developed, and the Russian formally offered his hand, the padres and the whole community protested against the match, regarding the difference of religion of the lovers as an insuperable obstacle to their union. Rezanoff Falls in Love

Objections to Rezanoff

Rezanoff and his sweetheart looked upon the matter differently, probably feeling that verbal distinctions made by disputing religionists should not be permitted to interfere with their happiness, and vowed eternal constancy to each other. The Russian, however, did not allow the love affair to interfere with the accomplishment of his main purpose. If it were not for information derived from the archives of Russia years after the affair had become merely a memory it might even be supposed that he made use of Cupid to forward his objects.

Supplies Secured by Rezanoff

At any rate he continued his negotiations for supplies and eventually succeeded in breaking down the scruples of the governor whose instructions on the subject were rather precise, and did not contemplate trading with Russians under circumstances suggestive of lending aid and comfort to a power whose intentions were suspected by the Spanish. But the padres were quite willing to trade and the commandante offered no opposition and the hold of the "Juno" was well filled with flour, maize, beans and peas when the Russian sailed away for Alaska. As she passed down the harbor the battery on San Joaquin thundered out a parting salute; the people on shore waved good-bys and many of them hoped for a speedy return of the engaging Russian and his agreeable entourage.

Rezanoff's efforts were by no means confined to securing a cargo of needed supplies for the Alaskan station. He discussed with the padres his scheme of trade relations between Siberia and California, and convinced them of its desirability. He even tried to persuade Arrillaga to make representations to the court of Spain which would pave the way to the consummation of a commercial treaty, but the governor was indisposed to meddle with the project.

Plans for Future Trade Relations

When Rezanoff sailed away from San Francisco he was filled with the idea of closer trade relations and his correspondence recently unearthed by Richman shows that he meant to push it with vigor, and it also discloses that the pledge he made to Dona Concepcion was sincere, and that when he had succeeded in his purpose of effecting a treaty between Russia and Spain he meant to return to California by way of Mexico and marry her.

But fate willed otherwise and perhaps his inability to carry out his plan changed the destiny of California. Rezanoff reached Sitka in safety and relieved the suffering employes of the fur company and in September, 1806, he crossed over to Kamtchatka and from thence he started overland to St. Petersburg. He was ill when he began the long and arduous journey and had the misfortune of falling from his horse while in that condition. A fever took hold of him and became so bad that he died at Krasnoyarsk on the 1st of March, 1807, and was buried there and a monument was erected to his memory.

Death of Rezanoff in Siberia

But those who accompanied him failed to take the trouble to apprise the little Californian beauty of his death and she remained in ignorance of the fact for many years, but always maintained an abiding faith in the constancy of her lover. It may help to a realization of the isolation of California to know that Concepcion did not learn of the circumstances attending the demise of Rezanoff until they were related to her in 1842 by Sir George Simpson at Santa Barbara. She had assumed the duties of the Third Order of Franciscans some years before, and in 1851 as Sister Maria Dominica she entered the Dominican Convent of St. Catarina at Monterey, and in 1854 she followed the institution to Benicia where she died December 23, 1857, at the age of 63.

SAN FRANCISCO 45

The romance was not completely rounded out until three or four years ago when an indefatigable searcher found in certain records the correspondence of Rezanoff which indisputably settled the honesty of his professions of devotion, respecting which there was for a time some doubt in California although it was never shared by the faithful Concepcion.

^{Faithful to the Last}

The story deserves a place in the history of San Francisco because it reveals facts which explain the methods by which the Russians subsequently gained a foothold in California... The visit of Rezanoff paved the way for the planting of the establishment at Ross which continued down almost to the time of the American occupation, and it has its value also because it throws some sidelights on the methods of the padres in dealing with their charges, and to some extent reveals the extent of their domination over those who lived outside of the immediate precincts of the mission.

Prelude to Russian Foothold

The case of Rezanoff makes it perfectly plain that whenever religion was concerned, and especially if the matter touched women, the priests had no difficulty in controlling the people. It is true that Concepcion's mother was antagonistic to the union of her daughter with the Russian, because she believed that it meant separation, but she realized that the ardent attachment of the two would not yield to her wishes so she invoked the assistance of the church which was promptly rendered, and would have prevailed unless Rezanoff had abjured the Greek church.

The Padres and the People

That he had any intention of doing so seems improbable. He undoubtedly designed returning to California but the tenor of his correspondence indicates that his mind was too thoroughly saturated with ambitious projects for the advancement of the fortunes of Russia to permit him to easily renounce the established church of that country. He was a resourceful man, and the padres would have had trouble with him had he come back to claim his bride; but their threats of ex-communication had sufficient power to postpone the union of the two until death finally separated them.

There are not many recorded instances of recalcitrancy of a gravity sufficient to call for the use of this formidable weapon of the church, but those of which we have knowledge suggest that, except in the case of exceptional men, there was no disposition on the part of the native Californians to question the right of the padres to regulate their lives so far as spiritual affairs were concerned; and that they continued to keep the boundary line between the temporal and spiritual so indeterminate that it was always easy to make the latter overlap the former.

Weapon of Excommunication

In the matter of education the padres were especially jealous and unremitting in their effort to preserve the people from the contamination of bad books. There was a great scarcity of literature of any sort in California when the padres were in control, and the supply was not augmented until the Americans began to make their appearance. The extent of the mission library in San Francisco was a geographical dictionary, the laws of the Indies and a copy of Chateaubriand. At San Juan the monks regaled themselves with "Gil Blas." San Luis Obispo boasted twenty volumes of Buffon's "Natural History," and at San Gabriel a "Life of Cicero" was treasured together with an edition of the lives of celebrated Spaniards, "Goldsmith's Greece," "Venega's California," "Exposures of the Private Life of Napoleon" and Rousseau's "Julie."

Few Books in California

In 1834 Dr. Alva brought from Mexico several boxes of miscellaneous and scientific books, but they were promptly seized and burned by the missionaries, and while Alvarado was governor they attempted to control his taste in the matter of reading, which had inquisitive features not agreeable to the fathers. His disposition, however, was not of the yielding sort, and he disregarded threats which would easily have scared a less independent character. There may be some connection between the fact that Arguello read what he pleased and the reputation for efficiency which was freely accorded him by the people but not always by his superiors who sometimes found him troublesome.

Padre Interdicts Dancing

It is almost unthinkable considering the later reputation of the Californians that there should have been a time in their history when the pastime of dancing was interdicted, or perhaps it would be more precise to say when an effort was made to taboo the waltz. That form of terpsichorean art had been introduced by foreigners during the administration of Governor Arguello and at once became very popular. Father Sarria regarded the innovation with much displeasure and procured from the bishop of Sonora an edict forbidding the waltz. It was posted on all the church doors and created great consternation, but the governor who had taken kindly to the new fangled dance when appealed to encouraged the ungodly to persist in their whirling practice by remarking that he was neither a bishop nor an archbishop, but if he felt an inclination to dance he would do so, whereupon Father Sarria prudently withdrew his objections.

Arbitrary Exercise of Authority

It may be unwise, however, to attach too much importance to these interferences, or to assume that they were dictated by religious intolerance or sacerdotal arrogance. There are stories of the existence of a domineering spirit which make it reasonable to suppose that much of the effort to restrain may have been due to the propensity of the period to exert authority in an arbitrary and overbearing manner. Thus it is related of Sola, the first governor of California under Mexican rule, that having ordered Luis Antonio Arguello to Monterey to explain the building of a vessel without his order the latter entered his presence with a sword which he carried at his side, using it in lieu of a cane, having injured his leg on the ride from San Francisco to Monterey. As soon as Sola perceived the weapon he began upbraiding Arguello and was about to use his cane upon him when the latter straightened up and prepared to answer in kind. This brought Sola to his senses and he apologized to Arguello by saying that his cane was reserved for the pusillanimous.

Rule of Head of the Family

This well authenticated case of the attempted exercise of arbitrary power fits in with the knowledge we have of the almost despotic rule of the head of the family whose authority, especially among what might be called the better classes, was little less than that accorded to the father in Ancient Rome. When the Californian father entered the room where the family were assembled for meals or any other purpose all arose and respectfully greeted him, and the ceremony was repeated when he departed. The custom may present a refreshing contrast to the almost absence of respect paid by children to their parents in these days, but it undeniably points to a condition of dependence unfavorable to initiative; and the results it produced were somewhat like those witnessed in China where the dead hand stretched from the grave to clutch the skirts of progress holding her back for centuries.

Parents and Children

The deference of children to their parents was more than matched by that shown by the dependents of the household. It was exhibited in a manner which had many peculiarities distinguishing it from the elaborated exactions of the grandees of Spain, and observance of these misled many observers who failed to get back of the veil of familiarity which had its rigid requirements. The Southerner hailing from the slave states could understand the Californian, but the New Englander and Americans from other parts of the Union where involuntary servitude was unknown, rarely perceived the striking resemblance to the mode of life so common south of Mason and Dixon's line before the war, and attributed the shortcomings of the people to the interference of the priests, when in fact it was due to the survival of the feudal spirit, under whose thraldom the church was as securely held as the other members of the community.

CHAPTER VIII

LIFE OF NATIVE CALIFORNIANS ON THEIR RANCHES

HOSPITALITY OF THE NATIVE CALIFORNIANS—NATIVE CALIFORNIANS AND THEIR HORSES—THE FEASTING AND MERRYMAKING OF THE PEOPLE—DANCING AND MUSIC AT FIESTAS—LOVE OF FINERY—SOCIAL DISTINCTIONS—INDOLENCE A BESETTING SIN—AN EASILY CONTENTED PEOPLE—A GREAT LACK OF CREATURE COMFORTS—SOAP SPARINGLY USED—SIMPLE DIET OF THE NATIVE CALIFORNIAN—HE DID NOT EXERT HIMSELF TO PROVIDE FOR THE TABLE.

IR WALTER SCOTT and other writers of romances who have dealt with the lives of the people who lived under the feudal institution have given us pictures of a state of society the reverse of unpleasant. If we divest ourselves of the feeling that has had possession of the world since the Renaissance, and ignore what amounts to a passion for material progress it is by no means difficult to find much to admire in the manners and entire mode of life of the people of the middle ages. California during the period 1776-1846, if considered in the same spirit, creates the frame of mind obtained by the impressionable reader of "Ivanhoe," and is very apt to produce a judgment which easily passes over the defects and only sees the virtues of the actors and the system.

Amiable, Qualities of Native Californians

Foremost among the amiable qualities of the Californians, those who occupied the land before the gringo came, was that of hospitality. It was dispensed in a fashion calculated to suggest that the phrases framed by the Spanish in which the courteous host turned over all of his possessions to the visitor or guest were not wholly insincere. The native who made a person at home by saying my house and all within it is yours, came near meaning what he said, and it might be added without greatly departing from the truth that the one to whom the tender was made usually accepted it very literally.

Hospitality Freely Exercised

It was said in another connection that the lack of intercourse between the different sections of California in the days before the American occupation was a barrier to progress. The facilities for communication were so utterly inadequate that the development of domestic trade was impossible. A people whose ingenuity and industry were unable to produce anything better than the caretta with its clumsy wheels made of discs of wood, and who were outclassed as boat builders and navigators by the Indians they found fishing in the Santa Barbara channel, could hardly be expected to promote that sort of intercourse prompted by desire for gain.

Communication Difficult

Horsemanship of Californians

But while the facilities for moving articles were wretched, being confined on the land to the slow moving cart drawn by a yoke of oxen, and to practically no means of getting about on the water, the natives found no obstacles to free intercourse when hospitality, or the desire for the amusements which its exercise brought about, were in question. Then they rose equal to the occasion. The horse, which for some inexplicable reason never served conspicuously as a draught animal, was then brought into requisition and surprising results in the way of traveling were achieved.

Mention has been made of the great number of horses bred at the missions, and on the ranches. No especial care was taken to keep up the strains which might have been fine in the beginning, but had greatly deteriorated through neglect. Quantity and not quality characterized the stock; still the result was not entirely bad, for out of the great herds choice specimens could be picked, and as the number to be drawn upon was practically illimitable there were plenty of fairly good animals at the command of all classes.

Everybody Rode Horseback

As a result of this abundance everybody rode, and riding became the chief accomplishment of the ranchowner, his wife and daughters and his sons and dependents. It was the custom in the morning to catch a horse and to saddle and bridle it ready for the use of the person who had selected the animal, which, on occasion might stand for hours waiting to be used. The supply of horses was so great that they were practically valueless, and it never occurred to the owner to bother about the return of an animal borrowed from him provided the borrower sent back the saddle and bridle.

Long Distances Traveled

Thus it happened that distance formed no obstacle to the assemblage of a large number of guests at the various feasts and merry makings in which the people indulged themselves. If the means of the ranchers permitted weddings were always made great affairs, and it was not unusual, if the contracting couple belonged to a well known family, for the celebration of their union to draw friends hundreds of miles. The San Francisco beaus and belles made little of riding to Monterey or Santa Barbara; and if the actors were sufficiently distinguished or particularly well liked Los Angeles was not too distant to draw them.

Fiestas

Naturally feasts thus attended were not the ephemeral affairs moderns indulge in, which are usually limited to a few hours. The Californian when he went forth to enjoy himself meant to protract the enjoyment as long as possible; and as he found others were of his way of thinking, and had like desires, days were spent in merrymaking. There were ill natured critics who declared that the gatherings never dispersed until all things eatable and drinkable were consumed, but be that as it may the testimony is uniform that while supplies held out the guests were welcome.

No Invitations Sent Out

The attendants at Californian merrymakings were not always formally invited. Relatives to the remotest degree considered themselves as on the expected list, and unfailingly availed themselves of the opportunity to feast at the expense of their more fortunate connections. A rich rancher usually had an astonishingly large number ready to assert their relationship on the slightest pretext, and they rarely shrunk from the obligation imposed by custom of sharing their good fortune with those who had claims upon them. The claims were sometimes more imaginary than real, but the spirit of the times and their peculiar environment made the owners of broad lands and cattle on many hills welcome the implied dependence.

The favorite recreation at festal gatherings was dancing. Before the advent of the waltz, and even after its general introduction into the province, individual exhibitions of the terpsichorean art were common. If the dancers borrowed their steps from Spain the loan must have been effected long before the styles made familiar during recent years by professionals were in vogue. It is possible that some of the Californian belles may have displayed the same vigor and poetry of motion of the highly accomplished modern Spanish danseuse, but most of them comported themselves with modesty and without any suggestion of abandonment.

<small>Dancing a Favorite Recreation</small>

The amusement was by no means confined to the younger members of the community. It was no uncommon thing for a mother who could boast a half score of children to display her agility and grace of movement. Nothing was more calculated to arouse the enthusiasm of all present than when a grandmother took the floor and revived the memory of her youthful days by showing how they danced when she was a girl. Perhaps she executed a double shuffle bearing on her head a tumbler filled with water, not a drop of which was spilled while she danced; and when she had finished, for a while she was the heroine of the room, and over her head were broken more *cascarones* filled with bright colored confetti than were expended on her vivacious granddaughters.

Not infrequently the head of the family, though his life may have been filled with years and wisdom, cut a pigeon wing to demonstrate that he was still to be reckoned with, and he too, like his dame received his round of applause. But as a rule the people of mature age surrendered the floor, which oftener than otherwise was well tamped adobe, to the youngsters whose favorite dance, until it was superseded by the waltz, was the fandango which they executed with a degree of skill which called for frequent rounds of applause from their elders, who reposed in the seats of honor against the wall of the room; and from the servants and dependents of all kinds who crowded every opening that commanded a view of the dancers.

<small>Old and Young Dance</small>

The music on these occasions would scarcely command the admiration of modern devotees of the waltz or other dances. Sometimes a violin was available, but not often. The instrument most used was the guitar upon which many performed with a skill more suggestive of a natural talent than an acquired art. Some of the early visitors make mention of the use of the mandolin, but there could not have been many in the province for long after the gringo came it was still an unfamiliar instrument. It is possible that there were performers who could extract from the guitar sweet sounds, but the semi-professionals who gave their services at dances without scorning a consideration only succeeded in producing a monotonous twang which, however, had the merit of being good time and that is all the dancers asked.

<small>Music at the Fiestas</small>

There was one other feature of the fiesta which deserves mention. It afforded the members of both sexes an opportunity to display their finery. Dana says the women were excessively fond of dress, and intimates that the sex had a monopoly of the vanity which finds outward expression in rich and beautiful garments, but the Californian caballero attached as much importance to dress as his sister. When arrayed in all his glory with slashed pantaloons of velveteen or broadcloth, profusely trimmed with gold or silver lace and buttons of those metals, a black silk

<small>Displays of Finery</small>

handkerchief about his neck, a vest of brilliant scarlet and a silk sash and a gaily decorated broad sombrero, he was a very gorgeous affair and was fully conscious of the fact.

<small>Dress of the Natives</small>

The dress of the native Californian of both sexes had distinctive features but they can hardly be regarded as a peculiar product of the taste of the people for nearly all that appeared characteristic was borrowed from the outside. The calzonera or slashed pantaloons were derived from Mexico and so was the stiff brimmed hat which was sometimes loaded with ornaments of silver, and in the case of the more opulent occasionally with braid fashioned from the more precious metal. The serape which the men wore over their shoulders, and the rebosa which the women threw over their heads were also of Mexican or New Mexican origin. Indeed everything in the way of finery worn by the people of the province came from foreign lands, and for the most of the articles of every day wear they were likewise indebted to the outside world.

<small>Social Gradations</small>

The gradations of society were not many and the line of demarcation between classes was so faint as to be almost indistinguishable. The only sharp division was that which separated Indians from all others who were called *gente de razon*, or people of reason. The latter embraced negroes, mulattoes, Sandwich islanders, in fact all except aborigines. The admixture of blood was very obvious, and all who could establish the slightest claim to being white traced their origin to Castile.

It cannot be said that the commingling of blood had the effect witnessed in some countries where the admixture resulted in a decided improvement as in the case of the blend which produced what we call the Anglo-Saxon. There is a consensus of opinion that with the exception of a few favored by fortune, and who by courtesy were designated as the upper classes by visiting foreigners, the great majority of the California colonists were lazy, ignorant and addicted to the consumption of aguardiente.

<small>Indolence of the Natives</small>

The indolence of the people so conspicuously exhibited has been attributed to various causes. The fact that most of the Californians who found their way into the province after the establishment of the missions were of the military class is held responsible for the general aversion for work. It is assumed that the children of these colonists inherited the disdain for useful occupation from their military ancestors, but this view disregards the undoubted fact that it did not take long for those settlers who found their way into the country from various lands, and whose occupations were usually of a peaceful nature, to fall into the easy going ways of the natives.

<small>Early Immigrants</small>

It is not in evidence that the adventurous few who made their homes in California, and took unto themselves wives of the country, ever developed the idea that work is degrading, but they soon adapted their lives to the plan of moving along the line of least resistance, and at the time of the occupation there was a not inconsiderable number who regarded that event as the passing of the golden age.

<small>The Simple Life</small>

It is not difficult to account for this condition of mind. It was an outcome of what may be regarded as a modified form of the simple life. The latter very often was involuntary, and had some features which sharply differentiated it from voluntary asceticism but the result was nearly alike in both instances. When the number of things used by man is limited the necessity for exertion to reach his wants is diminished. If he chooses to roam about with no other covering than a breech clout he has no occasion to bother himself about the manufacture of textiles, and secures immunity from a multitude of troubles, big and little, which constitute the penalty that man pays for the satisfaction of achieving a higher civilization.

Californians did not strive consciously or unconsciously to achieve this latter condition. Even those in whom a certain degree of prosperity had engendered longings which were perhaps fostered by tradition never succeeded in attaining to that restlessness of desire for more which is the mainspring of progress. The conception of wealth and its uses was of the narrowest. Even the possession of land failed to carry with it the same importance that attached to it in older countries. The chief value of a ranch was in the stock that roamed over it, and a man was rich in proportion to the number of cattle, horses and sheep owned by him.

<small>Spirit of Contentment</small>

This primitive concept of wealth produced incongruous results. It was no uncommon thing, we are informed, "to see a man of fine figure and courtly manner, dressed in broadcloth and velvet, and seated on a horse, covered with trappings, without a real in his pocket and absolutely suffering for the want of something to eat." If that was true of men whose outward appearance suggested comfort, what must have been the condition of those who in the struggle for existence were not able to secure enough clothes to cover their nakedness?

<small>Queer Contrasts</small>

But it is unwise to base a judgment on the exceptional. In spite of the records which show that at various times the people who inhabited California between 1776 and 1846 were in severe straits there is good reason for believing that extreme want was by no means a continuous experience. There were doubtless times when the people generally were on short commons, and it may even be true that there were occasions when the scourge of famine afflicted them; but so far as mere meat and bread were concerned, it is not likely that the deficiency ever extended over a long period, or that it was so great that it carried with it the menace of starvation.

<small>Exceptional Dearth</small>

Man, however, does not live by bread alone, and if we are to judge the lives of a people correctly we must not confine our observations to the mere matter of subsistence. Whether properly or improperly we base our estimates of those who have gone before us upon their achievements of a material sort. We may blunder in doing so. Our inferences drawn from a beautiful Gothic cathedral may be all wrong; or we might be accused of overrating the accomplishments of the ancient Greeks and Romans if we tried to read the story of their lives in the ruins of their buildings, but we cannot go far astray if we study the self-imposed limitations of a population.

We lack no evidence on that score. The native Californians placed in a region where flowers grow spontaneously never exhibited any fondness for them. Father Serra, it is related, was filled with joyous enthusiasm when he found wild roses which reminded him of Castile, but his admiration for them did not communicate itself to his flock. The Californians did not have gardens nor did they plant trees. With the example continuously before them of the padres, who with the aid of the Indians succeeded in growing fruit of good quality, they never thought of securing like results. When the American came the only garden and orchards were those under the care of the missionaries which were not always well kept. Vancouver records that the vineyards were not properly cultivated and consequently were not in good condition. At Santa Clara apple, peach, pear and fig trees were growing, but none were seen about the ranches.

<small>Neglect of Graces of Life</small>

54 SAN FRANCISCO

Unkempt and Unlovely Surroundings

Very often, if not invariably, the ranch buildings of the Californians were placed in positions which seemed to have been selected with regard to availability for defense, and without any consideration for the possibility of making them attractive. More frequently than otherwise the site chosen was barren and incapable of cultivation had the desire to cultivate been present. No trees or gardens surrounded them, and the practice of having the corral convenient was productive of discomforts in the shape of dust when the weather was dry, and of mud in the vicinity of the home when it rained. The condition sometimes was suggestive of that met with in Ireland and some other countries where poverty compels the inhabitants to live more intimately with the lower order of animals than is the case in regions where space is abundant and the inclination to use it more general.

Soap not Freely Used

One observer, Wilkes, noted that there was little good soap to be had in California and set down the fact as an indication of a general disinclination to use it; but it is not impossible that the indifference he spoke of was due to the feeling that its use involved an expenditure of energy which could not accomplish the object that caused it to be put forth, as the dirt floors of the houses and the general untidiness of the surroundings of the home must have demanded an incessant application to secure results.

The limited use of soap is more interesting viewed from the standpoint of the economist than from that of the sanitarian because it calls attention to the fact that the Californians were in the habit of shipping out of the country great quantities of raw material which with the expenditure of a little energy could have been converted into the best of cleansing agents. That it was not so employed can only be attributed to the operation of a system which stifled ambition by narrowing the field of human desire.

Habit of Dependence

This contradiction was witnessed on every hand. It exhibited itself in the case with which the relation of dependent was accepted, and in the cheerful acquiescence of those who with a little exertion might have provided themselves with many luxuries of which they deprived themselves. It would be a mistake, however, to attribute this deprivation to the spirit of voluntary self denial. The ascetic tendency was by no means prevalent. It did not even have as a basis the philosophic thought that the most things men use are superfluities and can be dispensed with. Californians were contented because their training, and that of their ancestors had been along lines which permitted them to think leniently of the shiftless and incompetent members of society.

Simple Diet of the People

There is no contradiction involved in this assumption. It exhibited itself in the fact that the most of the Californians were almost childlike in their eagerness to secure and enjoy things which they were incapable of making themselves. Although their habitual diet was as plain as that of a Kentucky frontiersman in the days of Daniel Boone they craved luxuries and were always ready to purchase them when the adventurous trader brought them to their doors. Even in the best households, where as a rule there was plenty to eat the bill of fare was of the shortest and was scarcely ever varied. Fresh beef and frijoles with tortillas appeared on the table day after day. The beef was usually roasted on the coals, but sometimes boiled. Vegetables were scarce and fruit was almost unknown outside the missions. There was a little chocolate and sugar brought from Mexico consumed by the very well to do, but no other beverages such as other people take at their meals were common.

The cooking was as wretched as the bill of fare was limited. The tortillas which served as bread were thin cakes of maize flour which was ground on metates. They were baked before the fire or like griddle cakes on sheets of heated iron. An inordinate fondness for hogs' lard was a trait not suggestive of epicurianism. A favorite dish was boiled beans afterwards fried in hogs' fat which was used without stint when it could be commanded. The use of olive oil appears to have been very limited. Outside of the mission at San Diego which contained a grove there were few olive trees planted, a singular circumstance considering the marked predilection for this vegetable oil in Spain, and all the more remarkable as the olive once it begins to produce continues to bear indefinitely. The trees in the mission orchard in the oldest mission, which were set out nearly a century and a half ago are still producing.

CHAPTER IX

LIFE IN CALIFORNIA BEFORE THE AMERICAN OCCUPATION

SOME SQUALID FEATURES—DRINKING AND GAMBLING—VICES ADOPTED BY NEW COMERS —THE CALIFORNIA BULL RING—EXTRAVAGANT HABITS EASILY ACQUIRED—TRADING INSTINCT NOT HIGHLY DEVELOPED—EXCESSIVE FEAR OF LUXURIOUS HABITS—THE TROUBLESOME RUSSIANS—CAUSES OF CALIFORNIAN BACKWARDNESS—YANKEE TRADERS ON THE COAST—SMUGGLING A FINE ART—CELEBRATIONS AT THE MISSION ST. FRANCIS—AN UNCONVENTIONAL PEOPLE—SEXUAL MORALITY.

 N AMERICAN writer reviewing the conditions existing in California before the occupation declares that the nearest approach to Arcadian life was that reached by the people during its pastoral age. His assumption is somewhat at variance with the facts as he presents them, and hardly accords with the ideas of simplicity which permeate the sixteenth century romances. The lives of the Californians were by no means idyllic. The military taint, and imported urban vices, divested them of the characteristics pertaining to purely rural communities.

Not an Arcadia

The rural side of life in mission days was the most pronounced, and in many parts the pastoral was most in evidence, but there is less suggestion of Arcadia than of Homeric days. While not deserving the appellation of quarrelsome, the Californians were by no means Quakers. Their padres may have taught them that peace was desirable, but they often were at outs with each other and their brief history is filled with tales of conflicts which might have made their story a tragic one if it were not for the disposition to act very much as the modern French duelist is charged with doing when he enters upon an affair of "honor."

Natives were not Quakers

It is not of these idiosyncrasies, however, that we are thinking when we reject the Arcadian assumption to accept which we must believe that a spirit of real contentment existed and accounted for a condition approximating primitiveness. There is nothing admirable in the "simple life" of the early Californians, because on occasion they displayed that it was not voluntarily assumed, and as a rule they exhibited a readiness to accept urban vices without offering the excuses which are tendered by the dwellers in cities when charged with laxity.

Primitive Conditions

The domestic merry makings and their brighter side were dwelt on in another chapter, but no reference was made to the well established fact that they were oftener than otherwise attended by exhibitions of drunkenness, the result of an indulgence in the fiery spirituous liquor known as aguardiente. This was a vice to which the Mexicans were addicted and was imported into the province by the colonists, many of whom were not of irreproachable character.

Drunkenness and Gambling

57

58   SAN FRANCISCO

Herod Outheroded

Another vice freely indulged in was that of gambling, which likewise formed a leading attraction of all gatherings, the purely domestic as well as the public. Weddings, christenings, and occasions unconnected with religious ceremonies were alike enlivened by the presence of the gamester, who not infrequently was a "professional" if that word may be properly applied to a practice like gambling.

It is not in a spirit of pharisaism that an American writer should approach this subject, as many have done, but rather as an investigator seeking an explanation of phenomena whose outward manifestations are calculated to deceive; and it may as well be said at the outset, in order to divest the assertions here made of unfairness, that after the occupation the gringo who dispossessed the native Californian out-Heroded Herod, and that he furnished a more striking example of the lengths to which man may go in his endeavor to secure something without working for it than any other people on the globe.

An Excuse for the Pioneer

It may be justly claimed as a mild sort of extenuation for the excesses of the first few years after the American occupation that they were to some extent the result of an existing condition. Had the gold hunters found their way into an environment of another kind, one in which gambling was vigorously deprecated, even when practiced, there would have been no such flagrant exhibitions of disregard for morality and the conventions of an advanced civilization as were witnessed in pioneer days in this City.

Gambling Unchecked

It cannot be urged that the vice of gambling was inherited, but it is true that the propensity to do as Romans do when in Rome had a liberal exemplification in the closing years of the "Forties" of the last century and in the first years of the ensuing decade. Before our flag floated over Monterey gambling was interdicted nowhere in California. Professional gamesters were on hand wherever the people were gathered together for any purpose and they plied their vocation openly, and all classes risked their money in the hope of winning.

Betting at Horse Races

Betting was carried to excess at horse racing, and no Californian ever thought of urging that the sport he was so fond of had for its purpose the improvement of the breed of horses. He was not temperamentally truthful, but he would have scorned to make believe that he had any other object in view in attending a race than securing the pleasure he derived from witnessing the contest, and the opportunity it afforded him to bet his money on the result, which he did with an amazing disregard of the consequences to himself and family. There were few Californians who wholly escaped the vice, and there were many who did not hesitate to stake their last peso, or the saddle on the back of their horse, and even the clothes on their own backs, when other money or property were unavailable for the purpose.

The Bull Ring

The taste for the bull ring was not indigenous; it came into the country through Mexico, but the sport as displayed in California had modifications which were the outcome of the general proficiency in horsemanship which asserted itself rather in showing skill in handling the beast to be attacked than in efforts to elude its fury, or to show superiority by slaying it for the gratification of the onlookers. The strict rules of the game as it was played in Spain were sometimes adhered to but oftener than otherwise the effort of the bull baiter was confined to dexterously throwing down the animal by a peculiar twist of the tail, and to keeping out of its way until this feat was achieved. On great occasions, however, such as the Mexican national holiday of September 16th, the baited brute would be stuck full of skewers adorned with ribbons and a real feast of blood would be afforded. Most amusement was derived from turning a bull and bear into an enclosure to fight for the mastery. It was less hazardous watching them than encountering an enraged bull even when the latter had its horns sawed off as a measure of safety for the bold matador.

It would be hard to establish a theory of Arcadian simplicity out of the material which the annals of early California furnish, or indeed of simplicity of any sort excepting that of a dense general ignorance. The "simple life" of the Californians did not stand for self abnegation, as we shall see later on when we examine the records and find disclosed the fact that there was an eager desire to share in luxuries, an echo of the enjoyment of which came to them from the outside world when a traveler penetrated their country, or which were hinted at in the stocks carried in the trading vessels visiting the coast for the purpose of obtaining cargoes of hides and tallow. Simplicity of Dense Ignorance

When such opportunities presented themselves they were eagerly seized by all classes able to buy; and it was to this propensity that many of them owed their undoing. Long after American was substituted for Mexican rule the Californians continued to bewail the facility with which the outsider was able to strip them of their possessions in a perfectly legitimate manner. Their plaint amounted to a virtual admission that they were as incompetent as children to take care of themselves, and that like children they were ready to pay the price for anything that caught their fancy. Eager for Luxuries

It was to this shortcoming that many of the foreigners who entered the province and engaged in business owed their prosperity. In the arena of trade the native Californian exhibited no more skill than he did in the workshop or in the field. The Spaniard and his descendants stood idly by while Frenchmen, Englishmen and Americans conducted thriving businesses. They did not hold aloof because they despised trade; the Spanish grandee in his home might have had a genuine contempt for such dealings, but his new world offshoots did not refrain from trading on that account. Their lack of energy and incapacity for initiative of any kind were the real obstacles to their engaging in commerce and not Castillian pride. No Aptitude for Trade

If the native Californians had possessed any of those qualities which make great trading peoples they would have soon disposed of the restraints placed upon them by Spain and later by Mexico. The American colonists when the mother country sought to bring them into harmony with her commercial system by taxing tea without previously obtaining their consent, boarded the ships bringing it and threw their cargoes overboard. The Spanish settlers in California, from the beginning, quietly acquiesced in a system which made them dependent upon the Crown for supplies of foreign things, and they were only heard in feeble protest when through neglect the galleons which were supposed to put in an appearance at stated intervals failed to do so, and threw them wholly on their own resources, or compelled them to resort to illicit trade to eke out their wants which, under such circumstances necessarily were limited. Spanish Restraint not Resented

In describing the long quest for a passage to India mention was made of the trade with the Philippines and the efforts made to retain it exclusively in Spanish hands. The transports engaged in this business were not permitted to pursue it after the fashion of men bent upon securing all the profit which the traffic might bring. In the beginning they were placed under restrictions which indicated a paternal solicitude for the consumer, and also some of that spirit which signalizes Trade with the Philippines

60   SAN FRANCISCO

modern times, and which has for its object the prevention of great riches being acquired by traders. The king was insistent that the vessels in the Philippine trade which had formerly made Cape San Lucas their port of call should continue to make regular visits to the coast of California, and in 1782 had made an order that they should put in at San Francisco or Monterey, but as the interdictions of trade remained in force, there was little or no disposition on the part of the colonists to accumulate for the purpose of making exchanges.

Abatement of Trade Restrictions

The necessities of the missions and the colonists in 1786 caused the Crown to remove restrictions for a period of five years, during which transports were permitted to trade more freely, and this permit was further extended in 1794, but it is significant of the spirit of the times and the attitude of the people that Governor Fages in 1791 expressed apprehension that the relaxation would prove conducive to luxury. His warning voice must have been heeded in Madrid for in 1797 pleas for more commercial privileges urged by Borica and Manuel Carcaba received no attention, and the same inattention to colonial needs was manifested as during the years prior to the temporary removal of restrictions.

Dread of Luxury

If the Spanish, in attempting to hold the trade for themselves, had imitated the examples of the English, and vigorously sought to cultivate their opportunities for commercial profit, the outcome would have been different. But their jealousy accomplished nothing more than to prevent anyone deriving advantage and kept the people of California in a condition bordering on absolute stagnation. This jealousy exhibited itself in many forms, sometimes, as in the case of Fages, who was perhaps inspired by the missionary idea that the people might become corrupted by luxury, it was based on considerations for the moral welfare of the inbahitants of the coast; but in most instances it was due to the apprehension that if the foreigner was permitted to trade with Californians he might pave the way to seizing the country.

Proposal to Acquire Hawaii

In 1788 Martinez actually recommended to the viceroy a plan for the acquisition of Hawaii and the planting thereon of an establishment, and the reduction of the islanders so that the possibility of the island being used as a port of refuge by foreigners would be destroyed. He urged in support of his recommendation that the facilitation of commerce which would follow the use of Hawaii as a port of refuge must prove a menace to California, and while his suggestion was not acted upon there is every reason to believe that his arguments were sound. Nothing was done in the premises, for long before Martinez sounded his warning Spain had dropped out of the habit of doing things.

Encroachments not Resisted

The failure to take steps to prevent encroachments were wholly due to the cause last mentioned and not to any feeling of security. That was non existent, but the apprehension, which seemed to be a pervading state of mind in Madrid, Mexico and in California, was not of the kind calculated to interpose obstacles to the accomplishment of the dreaded result. The attempts of the Russians to secure a foothold in California, to all appearances, were regarded with alarm, and there are documents in which may be found vigorous instructions imposing upon someone the necessity of getting rid of them; but for a long period, comparatively speaking, they were allowed to do pretty much as they pleased in the vicinity of San Francisco bay; probably because there was no force adequate to the carrying out the recommendations made by superiors located at the seats of government.

SAN FRANCISCO

The inaction in the case of the Russians affords another illustration of the ineptitude of the Californians which was scarcely disguised by professions of fear for the integrity of the Spanish territory on the Pacific coast, or by moral considerations such as those put forward by Fages. The suppression of trade had no effect in repressing desire; it simply made it difficult or impossible to obtain things eagerly longed for by all classes, even the padres sharing in the longing.

<small>Russian Advances</small>

When the "Juno" entered the harbor of San Francisco in 1806 on her errand of securing supplies for the employes of the Russian establishment in Alaska, she brought many articles which Langsdorff, the chronicler of the voyage, says the missionaries were well pleased with. Among them were linen cloths, Russian ticking and English woolen cloth. But the things inquired for which the "Juno" was unable to supply, when enumerated give a better idea of the combined results of restriction and inefficiency. There was a demand for tools for the mechanical trades, implements of husbandry, household utensils, shears for shearing sheep, axes, large saws for sawing out planks, iron cooking vessels, casks, bottles, glasses, fine pocket handkerchiefs, leather, particularly calf skins and sole leather, and the ladies at the presidio sought cotton fabrics, shawls, striped ribbons and other articles of adornment.

There is a suggestion in the not unnatural demand of the women for articles of finery of the decided formation of habits of luxury, but in the long list of almost indispensable things we discover evidence of needs, the failure to meet which must be held responsible for the backwardness of the province. In it we also have presented a picture, the details of which may easily be filled in, of a community living in the midst of a region of plenty, yet unable to command the simplest articles of common use, such as are found in the household of the least rewarded mechanic or laborer of the present day. And it must be borne in mind that this deprivation was not merely felt by the poor; it was also suffered in common by all the inhabitants from highest to lowest.

<small>Cause of Backwardness</small>

It is from the study of such demands and the inadequate fashion in which they were met that we may obtain the best knowledge of the actual conditions existing in California during mission days, and not from loose statements suggestive of Arcadian simplicity. And the inquiry will not be made in vain if it serves to make clear the fact, which is too often lost sight of, that the theories respecting the difficulties of an increasing population gaining a livelihood are untenable. The accuracy of the Malthusian assumption that population must ultimately press on the limit of subsistence may be demonstrated mathematically, but it is far easier to prove that people invite suffering and want by their failure to guard against them.

Had the early Californians made use of their opportunities they could have provided themselves with most of the things which they so eagerly demanded, and which they were only permitted to obtain under suffrance. After the year of the arrival of the "Juno," and even before that date, the enterprising Yankee had gained a knowledge of their needs, and what they had to offer in order to obtain the things necessary to satisfy them. The cargoes brought by these enterprising purveyors tell a story of their own which is very interesting and throws valuable side lights on the mode of life and even affords some illuminating hints respecting religious usages and the attitude of the people towards those managing their spiritual affairs.

<small>Yankee Traders Visit the Coast</small>

62 SAN FRANCISCO

Customs Evaded

It has been mentioned by the chronicler of the "Juno's" voyage that the padres were well pleased to obtain certain articles brought by that vessel from Sitka, but the privilege was reserved for a Boston skipper to make a plea in extenuation of an infraction of the custom's laws, that he was actually making it possible to properly perform the ceremonies of the church by smuggling into the country many things imperatively required.

A Yankee Smuggler

This man fertile in excuses was Captain George Washington Eayrs, whose vessel, the "Mercury," was seized for smuggling in 1813. When caught in the act Eayrs did not bother the United States government to help him out of his difficulty, but set up the plea that he was not conscious of having done anything wrong. On the contrary he asserted that he should be regarded as a benefactor rather than as a malefactor as he had "provided the priests with what they required for instructing the natives and for the ceremonies of religion." He added, "they have paid me with provisions and some few otter skins. I have clothed many naked, and they have given me in return products of the soil, as the officers of this district can inform your excellency."

Padres Encourage Smuggling

The padres and the officers appealed to were quite ready to back up Captain Eayrs, but when we examine the list of the articles brought to the coast for trading purposes by the "Mercury" we discover that it embraced many things not usually regarded as the necessaries of life, nor as essentials of Arcadian simplicity. Among them we find mention of hardware, crockery, fish hooks, gunpowder, cotton cloth and blankets, camelshair shawls, Chinese silks of various colors, and a particularly admired rose shade, white lady's cloth, fine kerchiefs, decorated water jars, gilded crystal stands, flowered cups for broth, porcelain plates, platters with red and green flowers upon them, shaving basins, black mantillas, etc., etc.

Helping the Church

We fail to discern in the long list any articles particularly devoted to church uses, but there is no doubt that the claim was justified, and that the kindly intervention of Captain Eayrs helped the padres to make their churches more attractive in appearance, and their ceremonials impressive. These were the chief diversions on the religious side of the Californians, every feast day being signalized by processions in which the most magnificent vestments attainable were brought into requisition, together with silken banners and other religious insignia.

In the accounts we have of the equipment of the expeditions formed for the purpose of reducing Upper California, there is frequent mention of the provision of vestments, altar utensils, and other articles demanded by the elaborate ceremonial of the Catholic church; and occasionally there are intimations that the supply was not as great as desired. It is not improbable that the silks and some of the other articles brought by the "Mercury" were employed to replenish the store which must have become depleted by years of wear. The powder, too, we may assume, was requisitioned for the church feasts, in which musketry discharges as well as music played a part.

Morality Plays

The population of the locality in which the Mission of St. Francisco was situated was not sufficiently large to afford the necessary actors for the morality plays which are described by some of the early visitors, but the old church still standing in the mission had its share of celebrations, which were probably as instructive to the neophytes as the religious spectacle of "Holy Night," which we are told was produced in San Diego with great splendor and much realistic effect. This drama was enacted after the midnight mass and was participated in by several persons,

San Francisco Water Front.

Pacific Ocean, from the Land's End.

The Golden Gate, from Boulevard.

male and female, who took the parts of Lucifer, the Archangel Gabriel, a hermit, a lazy vagabond and shepherdesses. The action represented a conflict of Satan with the angel, in which the champion of the heavenly hosts always won.

The music in the mission chapels was of a somewhat better order than that produced at the dances. The padres taught the Indians to play on several instruments and helped out themselves. It is related of Pius X, that he took serious exceptions to the use of airs derived from operatic scores by Catholic church choirs, but the missionaries were not so particular. If we may accept the assurance of Duflat de Mofras he heard the Marseillaise played as an accompaniment to a mass at the Mission Santa Cruz. He did not mention the fact censoriously but rather as a curious matter; perhaps because the sentiment back of the French revolutionary hymn was so much at variance with the extreme conservatism of the padres. <small>Indians Taught Music</small>

There were other practices of the native Californians which gave them a reputation for unconventionalism, but most of them may be set down to ignorance of the usages of polite society rather than any desire to adhere to the tenets of the simple life. The desire to make a display was sufficiently pronounced, but the equipment was defective. The etiquette of the table varies greatly in different lands and what is good manners in one place may easily be regarded as bad form in another. Therefore it is unnecessary to dwell with too much emphasis on such stories as that related of a visitor on board one of the trading ships who was much disappointed in not obtaining the same aromatic result from grating the end of his thumb nail into a glass of punch as his neighbor who used a spicy nutmeg; or that of the other ranchero who found the sauce of the pudding so much to his liking that he consumed the contents of the sauce dish and asked for more. <small>Ignorance of Polite Usages</small>

It is idle to discuss the question of the morality of the sexes; and certainly it is unwise to make sweeping assertions. Dana spoke slightingly of the women, but he was contradicted point blank by other writers, who had better opportunities for observation and whose knowledge of Spanish and of Californian manners made them better qualified to pass judgment. The duena system prevailed, but more as a tradition than because its necessity was recognized. Perhaps the earlier writers are not entitled to as much consideration in determining the matter as observers who came much later. It may be affirmed with positiveness, that unless twenty years of American rule in California vastly changed the character of the native women the standard of morality was as high among them as in any other modern nation. <small>Sexual Relations</small>

There is no doubt that after the secularization of the missions, and when the padres had completely parted with their powers, there was a marked change in the devotion to religious observances which in many cases, especially when unions were formed with Protestants, approached close to the border of absolute indifference, but native California women were not singular in that regard, and their indifferentism did not appear to undermine their morals; as for the men, religion never was their strong point, and the padres had to be content with their outward observances of its forms, and a more or less lukewarm compliance with the demands of the church. <small>Religious Sentiment Relaxed</small>

CHAPTER X

BEGINNING OF THE AMERICAN INVASION OF CALIFORNIA

THE FIRST SETTLERS OF SAN FRANCISCO—MEXICAN OPINION OF CALIFORNIA—AMERICAN CRITICISM OF SPANISH METHODS—RESTRICTIONS ON IMMIGRATION—FOREIGNERS WELCOMED BY CALIFORNIA WOMEN—THE FIRST AMERICAN INTRUDERS—RUMORED SEIZURE OF THE PORT OF SAN FRANCISCO—FRICTION WITH FOREIGNERS—INTRIGUING AMERICANS—TRADE WITH NEW MEXICO—ADVANCE GUARD OF THE AMERICAN INVASION—AGGRESSIVENESS OF AMERICAN IMMIGRANTS.

HE composition of the population during the mission period has been indirectly alluded to in the preceding chapters, but its changing complexion at various intervals, especially after the successful Mexican revolution, makes it more fitting to attempt to describe its source and peculiarities by including the immigrants whose presence in the country anticipated and to a considerable extent promoted the scheme of American occupation.

<small>First Settlers of San Francisco</small>

It is quite clear that the animating purpose of the Franciscans who assisted in the work of reducing the province was the conversion of the Indians and not the opening of the lands to settlement. Whatever may have been the views of the Spanish authorities in the premises they were completely subordinated to the exigencies of the situation which compelled the acceptance of such settlers as offered themselves, and they were as a rule of an inferior character and sometimes very disreputable.

<small>Prime Object of Missionaries</small>

The first expeditions were military rather than industrial, and those composing them had no stomach for work, and they soon fell into the habit of shifting everything like exertion onto the Indians who accepted Christianity and by so doing placed upon their necks the yoke of slavery. Perhaps had they been formed of better material the men composing the garrison of the presidio might have assisted in forwarding the work of development in spite of their disinclination for work, but unfortunately for the country they were in large part, in the beginning, members of the poverty stricken region of Northern Mexico, the backward condition of which was due to the general incapacity of the inhabitants who were in a constant state of pauperism.

<small>Soldiers Disinclined to Work</small>

It may be inferred from a publicly expressed opinion of one of the governors of Upper California that it was a place too good for convicts but not inviting enough for decent people to make their home in it, that it had a bad reputation in Mexico and perhaps a worse one in Spain. Those who have paid any attention to the subject will recall that for a time after the discovery of gold a like impres-

<small>California Traduced</small>

Vol. I—5

sion prevailed in the Eastern states of the Union, derived from the statements of those who misjudged the capabilities of the country because it did not present the same characteristics as the regions with which they were acquainted, and whose absence they assumed would offer insuperable obstacles to agricultural productivity.

Mistaken Opinions of Mexicans

The Spaniards and the Mexicans had little excuse for making such a blunder, for in its general aspects Upper California closely resembled many parts of Spain, and did not essentially differ from a good deal of Mexico except in one particular. In both of the countries named successful efforts had been made to bring under cultivation land which, however uninviting it may appear before the application of water, after it is applied surpasses all other kinds in productivity. As the earliest settlers could not have been unaware of this fact it must be assumed that it was an unconquerable aversion for work of any sort which caused the neglect that occasioned the bad reputation which they perhaps welcomed because it afforded them immunity from adverse criticism.

Habits Easily Acquired

It is quite certain that they enjoyed such immunity during the entire period from the establishment of the first mission in San Diego until four or five years after the American occupation. The first Americans who entered the country neither by word nor example rebuked the Californians. Unless the records are very misleading they promptly fell in with the customs of the country, and soon learned to adopt the fallacies of the inhabitants among which were embraced the settled conviction that its chief if not its only value was for grazing purposes.

Early Comers Sharp Critics

When criticism began it was of the sharpest. The Americans regarded with scorn the inefficiency of the earlier occupants of the land and sweepingly asserted that the soldiers at the presidios were of no value as settlers and even of less account as warriors. They declared that they were utterly without discipline, were wretchedly underpaid and that they were riotous and indolent and gave the mission fathers more trouble than the Indians. They were commonly, they asserted, the refuse of the Mexican army, or deserters, mutineers or men guilty of military offense who were sent to California as a place of penal banishment. Not infrequently convicted felons were sent to the presidios and their presence was not calculated to elevate the general tone of the society.

Views of Americans

These were the views entertained by the Americans who thronged into the country after the discovery of gold, and they might properly be suspected of exaggeration if they were not amply corroborated by the testimony of the padres, Mexican officials and others whose disinterestedness is not open to question. They, perhaps, more nearly described the condition existing after the Mexican revolution, but with some modification they apply equally to the whole period of Spanish and Mexican rule.

Restrictions Upon Immigration

In the Fifties when the municipal troubles of San Francisco assumed such proportions that drastic measures had to be taken to suppress them the condition was attributed to the mixed character of the population, but no such excuse could be offered by the Spaniards or Mexicans for their shortcomings. Jealousy of foreigners had always characterized the Spanish and the feeling was inherited by their Mexican successors. There were laws which permitted immigration, but there were so many restrictions accompanying them they were practically without effect. As a consequence there never was any considerable number attempting to enter the country, and the few who did would not be regarded as the flower of the lands to which they owed their origin.

Outside of the Russians who penetrated California in the early part of the nineteenth century, and who were not absorbed in the general society, the first foreigners to make their homes in the province were deserters and shipwrecked sailors. The earliest of these was a young Briton who in 1814 reached the coast in a British vessel and found it sufficiently to his liking to remain. The town of Gilroy is named after him. He became a Catholic, married and was admitted to citizenship a few years later. About the same time an American carpenter and an Irish weaver took up their abode and assumed Spanish names, a practice very generally resorted to by the settlers of this period.

The Early Settlers

A nominal acceptance of the Catholic faith was a prerequisite to toleration, and if the conversion was complete, and accompanied by marriage to a Californian girl there was an approach to something like a welcome at least by the women who showed a decided inclination for the strangers, while the males of the family usually regarded them with distrust until their superior energy won for them a place in the community. It is a matter of record that the most of these marriages turned out fortunate, probably because the foreign husbands had a keener appreciation of the necessity of providing for their wives and offspring, with the result that they became forehanded, often converting the land poverty of the girl and her relatives into comparative affluence.

Settlers Easily Assimilated

In 1826 a law was passed by the Mexican congress prohibiting foreigners from entering the country without a proper passport. It was not called for by any great influx of outsiders, for as late as 1829 there were only 44 foreigners in Monterey. Its probable inspiration was the arrival in the first named year of a party of Americans who came into the country overland. It was headed by Jedediah Smith, who had been authorized by the United States executive authorities to hunt and trade west of the Rocky Mountains. They entered the desert country near the Colorado river and were in grave straits because of the failure of their supplies. They managed, however, to reach San Gabriel in Los Angeles county where they encountered trouble owing to the suspicions of the native Californians, which were only appeased by the representations of the captains of foreign vessels who certified to the honesty of their intentions. Subsequently they made their way to San Francisco in search of supplies and were summoned before Governor Echeandia at Monterey, and again were delivered from surveillance by the interposition of sea captains. Smith and his party left San Francisco and pushed toward the Columbia. Later he was killed by Indians.

Mexican Laws Prohibited Immigration

The presence of Smith and his party caused a rumor to become current that the United States had seized the port of San Francisco. Echeandia took occasion to deny it, and in doing so intimated pretty broadly that the disposition to do so undoubtedly existed, as it was by far the best harbor belonging to the Mexican republic, and he cited in support of his belief that the Americans did not hesitate to take the Floridas from Spain, and added that he had no doubt that they would cheerfully round out their possessions by seizing California.

American Immigrants

These foreigners who entered the country in a more regular fashion than the deserters from ships were chiefly attracted by the colonization laws already referred to which provided for the disposition of vacant lands. The provisions were very liberal and would undoubtedly soon have resulted in adding a considerable number to the sparse population of the province if it were not for the interposi-

Liberal Land Grants

68   SAN FRANCISCO

tion of obstacles which were not lessened when the fear of an American influx took possession of the authorities.

Mexican Colonization Laws 1824-28
The laws dealing with colonization were passed in 1824 and in 1828. That first enacted provided for the disposition of the public lands. Preference was given to Mexicans, but foreigners who proposed to establish themselves in the country were to enjoy certain immunities and were to share in the privilege of taking up lands. These grants were not to exceed one square league of irrigable land, four square leagues which depended upon the seasons and six square leagues suitable for grazing. Colonists were, however, prevented from transferring their property in mortmain, nor were they permitted to retain the granted lands in the event of their leaving California.

Antipathy to Foreigners
While the law extended these privileges to foreigners, Californian sentiment was not favorable to the law, and the dislike to see it executed was made manifest in many ways. Manuel Victoria in a report charged that Abel Stearn's only object in becoming a citizen was to acquire land. He also accused John B. R. Cooper with being animated by the same purpose, and he pretty broadly intimated that the padres whose hostility to the new government was pronounced were aiding them in their attempts to secure large tracts. There is little doubt concerning the correctness of Victoria's accusations. The event justified the charge as they both succeeded in getting immense grants.

Foreigners Self-Reliant
In 1829 Alphonso Robinson, who came to the coast after hides and tallow, heard rumors of the intention of the Californians to seize the property of foreigners. The country was filled with convicts and an uprising was actually planned by them but they never attempted to carry it out. Robinson furnishes an explanation of their inaction in his statement that the foreigners were perfectly able to take care of themselves. The ostentatious placing of a bell on the top of his store room in Monterey probably served to warn the desperate characters of the reception they might receive if it was tapped to bring Americans together to defend themselves.

Intrigues Against Foreigners
Although the better sort of Californians had no connection with these contemplated uprisings they were by no means pleased at the prospect of being driven out by the foreigners, and a faction at the head of which was Pico charged that their rivals were being assisted by them. The accusation was made by them that Zamorano, with whom they were at loggerheads, had no other support than that afforded by a company made up of deserters from ships, some of whom had been prosecuted for bad conduct.

Tense Situation in 1833
In 1833 the situation was quite tense. Jose Figueroa, the governor, was particularly concerned about the presence of Americans and Russians, and his uneasiness was shared by Father Guitierez of San Francisco who said the foreigners "made his soul sick." He declared that the Russians on the one side and the Americans on the other were possessing themselves of the fertile lands of the frontier "which he said should be reserved for Californians." He specifically charged that a party of some forty Americans, English and French was corrupting the Indians and teaching them how to steal, and urged that they should be expelled on that account. He also objected to their presence on the ground that some of them were heretics.

Russians Excite Apprehension
Figueroa took up these charges and directed M. G. Vallejo to give particular attention to the actions of the Russians. Vallejo apparently did not sympathize with Guitierez for he retorted in a report that the missionaries were the cause of the hostility of the Indians on the northern side of the bay, and that there was

little to fear from the Russians, as Fort Ross was a post of traders rather than of soldiers. The difference between Figueroa and the Californians in Sonoma, and around the bay generally, became so acute and he became so unpopular that he was finally expelled. That the American contingent took an active part in the movement that led to this result is evident; and that Figueroa greatly resented their interference in California affairs may be inferred from his bitter tirade against Stearns on an occasion when he denounced him as a despicable foreigner, unfit to associate with honorable gentlemen.

That the Americans who entered the country were sometimes of the sort calculated to disturb the equanimity of a people less jealous of foreigners than the Spaniard the records show. Isaac Graham certainly came in this category. He was a trapper who had gathered about him a number of men engaged in the same pursuit. In addition to hunting for furs he carried on the business of illicitly distilling aguardiente which he sold in defiance of the authorities who were unable to prevent the trade although it was by no means clandestine. Graham, perhaps for the purpose of self protection, organized those about him into a military company whose services were commanded by the highest bidder. *Americans Feared*

In one of the quarrels between the factions Graham and his followers were engaged to take part against Alvarado and the latter, acting on information which caused him to believe that a revolution was contemplated, ordered Jose Castro to arrest them. Castro succeeded in surprising and capturing the entire gang who were loaded on a vessel and shipped to Mexico to be tried. The impending troubles with the United States saved them from the fate which they doubtless deserved, even though the charge of revolutionary intent may have been groundless. There were other offenses committed by them which would only have been tolerated by a government conscious of its weakness. *Graham's Party Sent to Mexico*

In addition to the trappers who found the region about the Bay of San Francisco more favorable to their pursuit than the country further south, that section was receiving some accessions to its population through a trade with New Mexico which sprung up in 1833. As already related the inefficiency of the Californians rendered them absolutely dependent upon the outside world for nearly everything but the barest necessaries of life. Particularly were they in need of clothing, and this want was in large part supplied by New Mexicans who brought blankets and serapes to California and exchanged them for mules. Every expedition of the enterprising New Mexicans resulted in leaving some of its members behind, and the route over which they traveled pointed out the way to American Southerners who even at that time had set covetous eyes on the promised land. *Trappers Around the Bay of San Francisco*

But the true advance guard of the American invasion was composed of Missourians who left Independence in May, 1841, entering the country through Walker's pass. There were about sixty in this party which contained several members whose names were prominently identified later with California affairs. Among them were John Bidwell, Joseph B. Chiles, Josiah Belden, Charles M. Weber, Charles Happer, Henry Huber, Talbot H. Green, Robert Rykman, Charles W. Flügge, Benjamin Kelsey, Andrew Kelsey, Grove C. Cook and Elias Barnett. *Advance Guard of American Invasion*

There was no question about the purpose of these men. They were in search of land on which to make homes, and probably had the conditions been different they would have become good Mexican citizens. But the jealousy so frequently alluded to, and which was kept alive by knowledge of the fact that there were societies in the East, especially organized to promote emigration to the Columbia river region, and to California, naturally made it impossible for the authorities to view the advent of the strangers with pleasure, or to welcome them; and it is not surprising that a disposition was shown to put up exclusion bars.

Feebleness of Mexican Government

But the feebleness of the Mexican government prevented a resort to an extreme course. In the affair with Graham, Governor Alvarado had acted with resolution and promptitude, but he received no support from the authorities in Mexico. A few days after Castro had sailed for Mexico with his prisoners, Captain Forrest of the corvette "St. Louis" arrived in Monterey and immediately took a hand in the affair. He addressed a letter to Alvarado in which he denounced the capture of Graham and his gang as an outrage, and demanded the arrest of those who had committed the indignity of seizing American citizens engaged in extensive commercial business. Alvarado replied justifying his action and said there was no disposition on the part of the government to interfere with foreigners engaged in honest industry. The Mexican governor's attitude was dignified throughout, and he was able to show that Graham and his company were not strictly honest, but Mexico in 1842 deemed it prudent to release and indemnify the arrested men.

Graham Released and Indemnified

It is hardly to be wondered at that after such experiences the Americans were emboldened to act pretty much as they pleased. But even before the arrest and deportation of Graham and his release and indemnification, they assumed an aggressive attitude and virtually denied the right of the Mexicans to exclude them or place obstacles in their way of occupying the land. In 1839 quite a number of Americans came into the country and in the succeeding year were followed by parties from Oregon. These Vallejo sought to prevent landing, but they went to the American consul and demanded passports, declaring that they would only wait fifteen days to get them, and that if they were not received in that time they would resort to arms to establish their rights. Their determined attitude had its effect and no further attempt was made to disturb them.

CHAPTER XI

COVETOUS EYES CAST ON THE BAY OF SAN FRANCISCO

SEVERAL NATIONS ENVIOUS OF SPAIN—THE SPANISH FAILURE TO MAKE USE OF THE PORT OF SAN FRANCISCO—THE PADRES AND THE MILITARY—THE FATHERS OPPOSED TO REPUBLICAN GOVERNMENT—POLITICAL SQUABBLES IN CALIFORNIA—OFFICIAL LIFE UNDER SPANISH AND MEXICAN RULE—MEXICO UNCONCERNED ABOUT THE FATE OF CALIFORNIA—CONCILIATORY AMERICANS—FRENCH AND BRITISH INTRIGUES—STIMULATING DISLIKE OF AMERICANS—FREMONT APPEARS ON THE SCENE—THE "PATHFINDERS" ACTIONS EXCITE SUSPICION.

HERE would be no excuse for presenting so much of what may with propriety be regarded as California and not San Francisco history, if it were not for the fact that the real object of American desire was the bay, the value of which was perfectly comprehended by the people of all civilized countries, and which the leading nations of the world were anxious to wrest from Spain. While most of the scenes of the drama were enacted at a distance from its shores the actors knew what the prize was, and in the struggle which was carried on over a large area they never lost sight of the fact that San Francisco was the key of the situation.

San Francisco Bay Coveted

The almost absolute indifference of the natives to the advantages of the magnificent harbor, and the fact that they preferred to plant their capital at Monterey, and that what little energy they displayed in developing the country was mostly exerted at missions at a distance from San Francisco, may seem to contradict this assumption, but the records clearly established that the Spanish, the Mexicans and the people of California generally, appreciated the value of their jewel even while they neglected to put it to use.

A Neglected Jewel

They were like the finder of a diamond in the rough, cut off from that part of the world where gems are valued, and without any prospect of a market for his treasure, which could only have value attached to it by cutting and exposing its beauties and making them an object of desire. They, however, realized the possibilities, and while totally lacking in the capacity to develop them, they were quite ready to defend their prize and do everything in their power to prevent it falling into the hands of those who might make use of it for their own profit.

But the incapacity which operated to prevent their developing the commercial possibilities of the Bay of San Francisco, and the imperial region surrounding it, asserted itself in every direction, and rendered them as incapable of defense as they were industrially. Just how much of this benumbment was due to the mission system it would be difficult to tell. The attentive reader of history may not be ready to acquiesce in the assumption that the inculcation of the doctrine of

Results of Incapacity

71

"turning the other cheek" is always productive of humility and pusillanimity. There were monks in Spain too, but it will be recalled that there were plenty of adventuresome and brave men sent forth by that country, who gave good accounts of themselves on the field of battle, on the ocean and wherever danger might be encountered.

Warlike Spirit Unsubdued by Religion

Religious teachings may have been the primary cause of the general decline of prosperity in the middle ages, and the consequent arrestment of population; but it would be idle in the face of the evidence concerning the combativeness of the period to assume that it greatly diminished the warlike spirit of the people. The story of feudalism is a long recital of feats of arms, and struggles for supremacy, in which personal valor, never surpassed under other systems, was constantly exhibited.

The examples of the priests and the lives of the monks were powerless to extinguish the contentious spirit, but they were potent enough to bank the fires of economic energy during centuries in the old world, and they accomplished a like result on a smaller scale in that portion of the new world whose fortunes we are describing. Thus it happened that in California between 1769 and 1846 a condition was created which had all the characteristics of mediaevalism in an accentuated form, owing to the racial admixture which under any circumstances, no matter how favorable, must have produced bad results.

Native Californian Political Wrangles

There was much wrangling throughout the whole period, and contests for supremacy which failed to reach the dignity of real conflicts, and never resulted in the spilling of any considerable quantity of blood. The wretched administration of affairs contributed to this condition. Petty restrictions and regulations were numerous and exasperating but there was an entire absence of the firm hand. From the beginning the Spanish government practiced a policy of practical non-interference in temporal affairs; no effort was made to keep up the civil establishments in a fashion calculated to insure respect for the laws, the enforcement of which for a time was assumed by the missionaries. A commandante general was appointed by the crown to command the garrisons of the presidios, but he confined himself almost wholly to the business of protecting the missions from the depredations of Indians and left the priests to pass laws affecting property and even life and death.

Secular Authorities and the Indians

Up to the time of the overthrow of Spanish rule in Mexico there was comparatively little friction between the peons and the secular authorities. The differences that arose usually had their origin in the attempts to protect their charges from aggression. The strict regulations designed for the purpose of keeping the soldiers apart from the Indians occasionally precipitated trouble, and some instances are recorded of demands for the punishment of sentries failing to respect the rights of the cloth, but nothing of a serious character grew out of these trifling collisions, and on the whole the relations of the padres and the military functionary were pleasant.

Spanish Rule Overthrown in Mexico

The Spanish power in Mexico was overthrown in 1822 and two years later a Republican constitution was framed. Under this new government Upper California became a Mexican territory under the title of "New California" and was accorded a delegate in the congress of Mexico which met in the city of that name. No attempt was at first made to curtail the powers or privileges of the missionaries. The commandantes had a privy council, selected by the people and called a deputation imposed upon them, but its functions were very limited and no particular desire to exercise them was displayed.

But with the growth of the spirit of republicanism new ambitions were created which resulted in formidable breaches, and finally in the overthrow of the mission system. The influence of the missionaries was exerted against the new government, and it was some time before they accepted the constitution. In 1818, when Monterey was attacked by insurgents from Buenos Ayres, Arguello had hastened by forced marches to the assistance of Governor Sola. He favored the continuance of the Spanish government, and was not disposed to contribute to the success of the revolt.

Padres Hostile to Republic

His attitude was not generally approved; there were some who strongly favored the revolutionary movement, but that fact did not stimulate the Californians to activity, and they contributed little to the cause of independence. Perhaps the remoteness of the country from the capital contributed to that result; but the belief was prevalent that it was the hostility of the missionaries which prevented action which might have helped the cause; and when the new government was firmly established it took pains to frame a test oath which was as effective in its way in bringing about an emigration of the padres as the decree framed in 1827 which forbade any person of Spanish birth holding office in Mexico.

By this time the Californians had become so completely reconciled to the new government that a proposal made to change the name of the territory to Montezuma met with ready acceptance. The territorial assembly which dealt with the matter had at the same time under consideration a suggestion made by Echeandia, the Mexican governor, to fasten on Los Angeles a designation which would have greatly embarrassed the present population if it had been adopted, but the resolutions were never heard of after being sent to the capitol for action.

Californians Accept New Government

It would be profitless to enumerate all the squabbles that ensued after the acceptance of the Mexican constitution. They must have been regarded as family rows by the people at the capital, as no steps were taken to interfere; or perhaps they had too many troubles of their own in Mexico to think of worrying about those of remote California. They did not even take a hand when movements were started which had for their object the expulsion of governors appointed by the central authority. There was such an uprising in 1832, and in 1835 there was one fomented by the padres which was suppressed by Figueroa.

Numerous Political Squabbles

A prolific source of trouble was the location of the capital which had been at Monterey from the earliest days of Spanish occupation. A decree had been secured from the superior government in 1835 to transfer it to Los Angeles. The measure was attributed to the intrigues of Pico who persisted in his efforts to make the change down to the day of occupation. His zeal in the premises was so ardent that in the assembly which convened in August, 1844, to deliberate upon the impending trouble with the United States he sought to subordinate the main question, that of removal, and succeeded in having that body compromise on Santa Inez, until word could be received from the city of Mexico.

Quarrels Over Location of Capital

The prizes of office in California during the period were not great, but such as they were they were eagerly sought after. In 1843 the aggregate amount of salaries paid to officials was a little over $171,000 and this expenditure was cut down to $132,000. A little incident which occurred during the incumbency of the governorship by Alvarado throws a side light on the administration of financial affairs. A treasurer who had been provided with $1,785 to be expended for a certain purpose only used $215 of the amount. Alvarado was so surprised that such honesty should

Meager Official Salaries

exist he offered to put the honest treasurer in charge of the custom house, but he declined the position on the ground that he did not desire public employment of any sort because of its precariousness.

Work of Conquest Made Easy
This rapid survey of differences will enable the reader to form a judgment whether the Californians were by training, experience or natural ability, capable of successfully resisting the aggressions of a vigorous neighbor; but when to the information is added the fact that there was the strongest kind of feeling against the centralization of power in Mexico, which constantly manifested itself, and on one occasion resulted in an effort to separate from Mexico and erect California into an independent state, we cease to wonder that the work of American conquest was so easily accomplished.

Mexican Indifference
No help whatever was extended by the superior government to the authorities in California and it might be supposed if it were not for occasional orders sent out from Mexico that there was complete indifference to the fate of the territory. There were sporadic exhibitions of wrath which had the effect of arousing such Californians as were completely reconciled to the republican idea, but the people generally were so apathetic that Americans who made it their business to inquire into the situation were led to believe that when the crucial moment arrived there would be no difficulty whatever in persuading Californians that they would be so greatly benefited by a change that they would welcome the stars and stripes.

Undiplomatic Americans
This expectation was not realized, but it might have been had matters been managed more diplomatically, and with greater consideration for the feelings of the Californians whose sensibilities were totally disregarded by Fremont and a portion of his adherents who were contemptuous of the prowess of the native, and were disposed to look upon any one who did not speak English as an inferior sort of person, a propensity exhibited most freely by those least entitled by education or any other qualification to pass judgment.

Efforts to Placate Frustrated
Had the desires of the more successful Americans who had managed to gain the good will of their neighbors prevailed, the attempt to pave the way to an entirely peaceful occupation would have succeeded. While there were sporadic displays of dislike against foreigners, and especially against Americans, there is not the slightest doubt that some of the latter were held in great esteem and possessed much influence. The material success of this class, while it inspired jealousy in the breasts of some, convinced the more thoughtful of the better classes that their best interest would be promoted by encouraging their enterprise even if all the rewards from it did not come to them.

The Yankee Traders
While the Americans who devoted themselves chiefly to the acquisition of land as a rule fell easily into the slouchy habits of the Californians, and were too often content to accept the conditions of life which the unenterprising natives had imposed on themselves, the Yankees who engaged in mercantile pursuits betrayed no such shortcomings. They were not affected by the *dolce far niente* disposition of those with whom they came in contact, and almost wholly escaped the prevailing tendency to postpone until to-morrow. Their houses and other buildings were of better construction than those of the natives and in other ways they set an example which was not without some effect.

If this contingent had been allowed to assert its influence without interference, there must have been some such result as that witnessed in Texas, which might have been accomplished without any serious conflict, owing to the remoteness of Califor-

SAN FRANCISCO 75

nia from Mexico and to the impoverished condition of the Mexican exchequer which would not have permitted the formation of an expedition of sufficient strength to go several hundred miles to force an unwilling people to keep up a nominal allegiance to a state which had shown its incapacity to govern and its indifference to the needs of California.

It was at one time assumed that dislike of Americans was excessive, and there is considerable evidence that the British sought to profit by what they considered an insuperable obstacle to a peaceful adhesion of Californians to the American system. Great Britain and France were both apprehensive that the power of the United States would be too greatly augmented by territorial accessions that would give them an area of continental dimensions, stretching from ocean to ocean, and containing on the Pacific a harbor which was by universal consent conceded to be one of the finest in the world, and by reason of its situation was destined to be of commanding importance. French and British Intrigues

The desire of Britain took a preventive rather than an acquisitive form. Although there is some testimony which points to plans for the acquirement of California, the preponderance of evidence favors the belief that the British merely hoped to see it erected into an independent state, whose authority might be guaranteed and thus prevent it falling into the hands of the United States.

Something like an active intrigue to produce that result was begun during the vice consulship of James A. Forbes, who had been appointed to represent the British government at Monterey. In 1842 Forbes began an inquisition into the feelings of the Californians with a view of ascertaining how they would regard the extension of a protectorate over them by Great Britain. Forbes seems to have shared the opinion expressed by Eugene de Mofras, who in 1841 had predicted that it would be the fate of California to be conquered by Great Britain or the United States unless she placed herself under the benevolent protection of some European monarchy, preferably that of France. But he must have been compelled to modify it to conform to the more reasonable plans of his superiors, who made use of California as a club to beat down the American demand of extension to the line of fifty-four-forty on the north. Unavailing Efforts of a Briton

Both de Mofras and Forbes were convinced that the Californians were antipathetic to Americans, but they differed in regard to their attitude toward the British. De Mofras said that all the people of California were by religion, manners, language and origin out of sympathy with Americans and English; Forbes had reason to believe that the feeling against his own countrymen was not general, but on the contrary that they were well liked. He was certainly justified in thinking that there were many Englishmen who were appreciated and who stood high in the esteem of the Californians, while it is not so certain that the points of resemblance indicated by the Frenchman predisposed the Californians to an alliance with a country like France. Stimulating Dislike of Americans

As a matter of fact both of these foreign critics were wrong. They did not understand the situation, and but imperfectly comprehended the workings of the Californian mind. They misinterpreted the indisposition shown at an earlier date to sever relations with Spain and wholly failed to recognize the import of the opposition to centralization, which was an exhibition of extreme republican sentiment rather than antagonism to Mexico. In short, they overlooked the fact that Californians, like the Mexicans, and the other Latin American peoples who estab- Mistakes of Foreign Observers lished republics after the destruction of Spanish rule, were admirers of the institutions of the republic of the United States and that it would be difficult to persuade them to any step which would oblige them to relinquish the desire to model upon that country.

Larkin Starts a Back Fire

Larkin, the American consul, who was well informed concerning the efforts of Forbes, who made no serious effort to conceal them, apparently had no doubt about his ability to head off British and French intrigue. With or without authority he at once started to back fire the work of the British consul, and fortunately for his efforts the influence gained by the commercially inclined Americans proved sufficient to nullify the advantage Forbes might have gained had all immigrants from the United States been of the kind who made it their business to stir up animosity by plainly betraying their contempt for Californians of every degree.

There were several, however, who contrived to remove, or at least modify the bad impression made by the intemperate criticism of native shortcomings. They were usually men of substance and had married women of the country. These few without attempting to disguise their object persuaded some of the more influential Californians that they would be wise to retain their original predilection for republicanism, and that their best chance of achieving their desire for material prosperity would be to cast in their fortunes with the nation which had pioneered the path of liberty in America and had announced its determination to prevent the introduction or restoration of monarchial institutions in the western world.

Fremont's Marplot Actions

The accounts all agree that these considerations and the arguments of Larkin would have prevailed had it not been for the precipitate action of John C. Fremont who, from the time of his first advent in California, had caused considerable friction. It seems inconceivable that he should have planned to thwart a programme of peaceful acquisition, but many of his actions point to something of that sort. That he was not in complete accord with the authorities in Washington is shown by the fact that he and Commodore Sloat worked at cross purposes. The latter was acting under instructions which assumed that Americans would be received with open arms; Fremont on the other hand was pursuing a course which has been characterized as a deliberate attempt to promote hostilities, and some of his critics did not hesitate to assert that his object in so doing was to further his personal ambitions.

Efforts to Preserve Harmony

That was the opinion entertained by many who had hoped to see California accept the inevitable without protest, and who believed that the interests of natives, and of Americans who were expected to seek homes in the country then so sparsely settled, would be best served by maintaining harmonious relations. It should be kept in mind that during the years immediately preceding the Mexican war the outlook to Americans in California must have presented itself in a manner quite different from that which shapes itself in our minds when dealing with the subject retrospectively. There was then no thought of a rapid influx and swift growth of population such as followed the gold discovery at Sutter's fort.

The probabilities must have formed the belief that the work of settlement would proceed slowly, and there was reasonable ground for the fear that the creation of unnecessary enmities would retard development, and thus frustrate the hopes which those familiar with the resources of the region had formed and which furnished the excuse some of them desired to offer for violating an obligation they had assumed when they sought Mexican citizenship.

CHAPTER XII

LABOR PROBLEM BEFORE AMERICAN OCCUPATION

CALIFORNIA AND THE SLAVEHOLDERS OF THE UNITED STATES—CHINESE LABOR SUGGESTED AS EARLY AS 1806—INDIANS AS SLAVES—THE INDIAN AN OBJECT OF DREAD—THE ATTEMPT TO ELEVATE THE INDIAN—ENSLAVEMENT OF INDIAN CHILDREN—INDIANS CRUELLY TREATED—NO REWARDS FOR THE INDIAN LABORER—OPPOSITION TO INDIAN PUEBLOS—INDIAN PUEBLOS NOT A SUCCESS—RELIGIOUS TRAINING OF MISSION INDIANS—UNSATISFACTORY RESULTS.

IT MAY be interesting to conjecture how two difficult problems would have been solved by the people of California had they been permitted to work out their solution slowly. What would have happened if the reasonable anticipation that population would necessarily grow slowly had been realized, and instead of mining proving the dominating factor, the cultivation of the soil had been the main occupation of the inhabitants?   *California and Slavery*

The subject is usually approached from a standpoint which obscures the probability that California would have become a slave state had gold not been discovered in sufficient quantities in 1848 to draw to it people from all quarters of the earth, the majority of whom were opposed to the extension of the evil on American soil. In that event it is not unlikely that the agricultural community which would have grown up slowly would have been made up chiefly of recruits from the Southern states and they might have succeeded in carrying out the purpose which was at the bottom of the aggressions upon Mexico of extending slavery to the coast.

The labor question in the province of California and later under Mexican rule had never been very acute, because the inhabitants were indifferent to their advantages, and by inherited disuse of the faculty which prompts enterprise they had almost ceased to desire improvement of any kind. They were like children and desired the good things of earth, but when they did not see them they were contented and put up with what they had.   *Labor Question in Early Days*

It does not appear that at any time the Californians showed a disposition to use the Indians they were able to command for any other purpose than to relieve themselves from the drudgery of work. There was slavery of a genuine sort, but it was wholly different from that which existed in the South before the Civil war, and it was never employed, as it was in many parts of Latin America, for objects of gain, such as the increase of productivity with the view of creating a surplus for sale, or to extract gold from the soil.

The Russian, Rezanoff, who visited California in 1806, was so impressed by the failure of the Californians to make use of their fertile soil that he could not refrain from comment and suggestion. In a letter to his government in which he outlined the possibilities of trade between Siberia and California, and somewhat significantly hinted that if the Californians did not make use of their opportunities some other people should step in and show them how, he discussed the labor question in a fashion which indicates that he must have considered the possibility of making the Indians useful, but that he had dismissed the idea as impracticable.

Indian Labor Undependable As for the natives he was under no illusions regarding them. He left them completely out of the reckoning, summing up their deficiencies in a general statement which virtually indicted them as a people too lazy to do hard work, and too incapable to successfully engage in any occupation requiring skill. So thoroughly was he impressed with their deficiencies, and so little importance did he attach to the possibility of converting the Indians into a dependable labor supply, he proposed to introduce Chinese, whose industry and skill he extolled as only second to their tractability.

This judgment was formed after thirty-six years of experimentation by missionaries and rancheros, and is probably a far more accurate estimate of the value of the Indian as a laborer than any made by later travelers, some of whom, misled by the achievements in the immediate vicinity of the missions, overlooked the general condition of the country, which was very much down at the heel because of the incapacity of the rancheros and the absence of a reliable supply of labor.

Attempts to Enslave Indians The Southerners had attempted in some sections of the Union to make slaves of the Indians but without success, but the material they dealt with was not of the same sort as that found in California. They might easily have been induced to believe that they could achieve success where the missionaries and the native Californians had failed. The testimony that many thought along these lines is abundant and there is no reason to doubt, had the gold rush not interfered to mar their plans, that slavery would have been introduced into California and that the Indian would have formed part of the institution.

The California Aborigine Had that turned out to be the case it is doubtful whether the attempt would have proved successful. The aborigine in California was not made of the same stuff as the Seminoles and Creeks, but he was by no means the docile creature which his acceptance of the yoke imposed upon him by the padres implied. As already observed his propensity to relapse into the ways of the gentiles could hardly be restrained, and as the process of creating neophytes advanced, and he was thrown more and more in contact with his own kind he began to develop an organizing ability which was unknown to him when he was a member of an isolated family or tribe.

Fruitless Struggle for Existence When he was a nomad the California Indian expended his energies in an almost fruitless struggle for existence. He showed little disposition to cultivate relations with his own kind, and, although not made of fighting stuff easily collided with other tribes or bands when they approached his neighborhood too closely. This antagonism was practically wiped out by the mission policy, which assembled considerable numbers of Indians closely together, and enabled them to compare notes, with the result that on several occasions they were able to combine in uprisings which, although they never proved successful, sufficed to keep the Californians uneasy and made the Indian an object of dread rather than the useful draught creature into which they sought to convert him.

That the California Indian was so regarded after the years of effort made by the missionaries will be gathered from an expression in the "Annals of San Francisco," which seems to have epitomized the general opinion. The writer, after extolling the goodness of heart of those who sought to make a good citizen of the Indian, summed up the situation by saying: "Therefore it may be concluded that * * * the sooner the aborigines of California are altogether quickly weeded out, the better for humanity. Yet the fathers would retain them: then sweep away the fathers too." *Pioneer Opinion of the Indian*

This language breathes a spirit of intolerance which owed much of its bitterness to the prevalent "know-nothingism" of the period, but it distinctly indicates the line of cleavage in the efforts for the uplift of the California Indian. The religious motive which prompted the missionaries to engage in the work of the redemption of the Indian, and the political object of making him a good citizen were always conflicting, and by some the conflict is held responsible for the poor results achieved; but candor compels the admission that they were no worse than those attained by Americans in dealing with the aborigines; and that the Anglo Saxons never made as serious an effort to help them as the Latins of California. *Intolerant Attitude of Pioneers*

Some years before the successful revolution of Mexico the Spanish Cortes laid the foundations for the later attempts to secularize the missions. It had been the design from the beginning that these establishments should, when the fitting time arrived, be converted into civil or municipal corporations. In various documents the object of their creation was stated to be the civilization and education of the Indians so as to prepare them for citizenship. In 1813 the Cortes declared that the missions ought to be converted into ordinary parish churches, but as often happened in the dealings of the mother country Spain with her colonies, the Cortes proposed and the missions disposed. *Missions Secularized*

The revolt of the Mexicans once successfully accomplished the new government began to interest itself actively in the condition of the Indians, a natural consequence of the fact that the success of the revolution was largely due to that race which produced some leaders, and not a few who afterward participated in the administration of Mexican affairs. In 1827, evidently acting under this inspiration, a territorial deputation which met at Monterey proposed to emancipate from mission tutelage all Indians within certain jurisdictions who were qualified to become Mexican citizens. At this same deputation a resolution was adopted which limited the right to inflict corporal punishment on the neophytes to fifteen lashes. *Mexican Interest in the Indian*

It is quite clear that the body which passed these resolutions had no definite idea concerning the qualifications necessary for good citizenship. The Mexican opinion on this point was extremely liberal, and it may be said without greatly straining the truth that it excluded all limitations. But while the deputation may have been somewhat hazy so far as the eligibility of the Indian to citizenship was concerned, it seems to have had well defined views on the subject of the desirability of not driving him forth to join the gentiles by a resort to harsh measures, hence the restriction on the use of the lash.

It is noteworthy that this deputation confined its attention to the treatment of the Indians by the missionaries. It was reserved for Governor Echeandia to attempt to put a period to a practice which resulted in the practical enslavement of the Indians by the rancheros. In 1829 he ordered that no more Indian children should be seized under the pretense of teaching them Christian manners. The children *Missionaries and Indians* thus seized were made use of as domestic servants, and were sometimes badly treated. Echeandia's order was aimed not only at future abuses, but was retroactive as it compelled the restoration of the children held at the time to their parents.

Indian Uprising in 1829
It is not impossible that the attempted application of remedies was responsible for an uprising which occurred in 1829, and which resulted in an exhibition of ferocity rarely surpassed by any people. In that year the Indians at the Mission San Jose were induced to desert and join a number of gentiles in the San Joaquin valley. They were pursued by troops from San Francisco, but the latter were repulsed in a thicket and compelled to retreat. Subsequently the defeated Californians were reinforced by a body of men under the command of Vallejo who descended on the camp of the recalcitrant neophytes, killing many of them and taking a number of prisoners. A cruel vengeance was inflicted on those supposed to have been responsible for the desertion. They were tortured in various ways, and the instruments selected to inflict the punishment were Indians, who, as was often the case with negro slaves in the South, delighted in the exercise of barbarity.

Cruelty to Indians
One of the padres protested against the cruelties, but nothing came of the protest except recrimination. As in former cases when priests were charged with gross abuses of Indians the testimony of the latter was disregarded, or the witnesses were charged with having perjured themselves. The Californians were not unlike the settlers in the regions east of the Rocky Mountains still infested with Indians. Their prejudice was so great that a charge against a white man was sufficient to array all the whites on his side. They honestly entertained the belief that any attempt to repair an injustice would create the impression in the minds of the Indians that it was inspired by fear. Hence a solidarity which put the poor neophyte at a great disadvantage and doubtless encouraged the naturally cruel who were in positions of command over them to commit acts of cruelty.

Indians Ungrateful
But acts of cruelty do not explain the undoubted fact that the Indians were quite as ready to assail the padres who were really kind to them as the major domos who freely employed the lash to secure obedience from their charges, or to compel them to perform their tasks in the field or elsewhere. In the uprisings of which we have knowledge there is every reason to believe that in the event of success they would have sacrificed the most benevolent missionary as ruthlessly as the cruelest overseer who made their lot so bitter.

Perhaps such an attitude is inseparable from a system which does not recognize the right of the toiler to more than a bare existence. That was the condition of the California Indian who received absolutely no pecuniary advantage from his connection with the mission. He was a slave in all particulars except one. While he could be worked to death he could not be sold, although it was not impossible to transfer his services. That indeed was as common as the practice of making domestic servants under the pretense that they were to be taught Christian manners.

Indian Labor Unrewarded
The failure to recognize that the Indian after he assumed the duties of Christianity had any rights which his superiors were bound to respect was in large degree responsible for the facility with which conspirators could enlist him in enterprises against the authorities, or of men engaged in personal feuds to use him to accomplish their wicked ends. The California Indian could hardly be likened to a Hessian, for he was not a trained soldier, but his actions were as easily controlled as those of the men whose services were sold by princelings to fight against a cause

SAN FRANCISCO IN 1849
From an old drawing

in which they had no interest, and whose success or failure could not affect them in the slightest degree.

It was remarked that the Indians derived absolutely no advantage of a pecuniary sort from their connection with the missions, and this statement might be supplemented by the assertion that their condition was not greatly improved in this regard after the authority of the padres was wholly destroyed and the property of their establishments was dissipated among the eager crew who only awaited their dissolution to grab the wreckage. But it is true that something like an effort was made by the successful revolutionaries to carry out the declared purpose of the Spanish Cortes of fitting the tractable Indians for the duties of citizenship, and to that end an attempt was made to put into practice a municipal system which in a measure imposed the work of self government upon those participating in its expected benefits. <small>The Indians Hopeless Life</small>

Manuel Victoria, the fourth Mexican governor, sought to effect the betterment of the Indians by other methods than those embraced in the plan of placing them in pueblos. He asserted that the project of Echeandia was not in their interest, and that it meditated a scheme of spoliation, the result of which would be the division among a few favorites of the property of the missions and the consequent waste of the labors of the padres and the neophytes who had built them up and made them worth plundering. His antagonism sufficed to temporarily block the scheme of secularization, but nothing ever came of his suggestion to select likely Indian youths with a view of sending them to Mexico to be educated so that they might in turn help in the uplift of their brethren. <small>Efforts to Improve the Indian</small>

Governor Alvarado, whose general course exhibited a greater desire for reform than was displayed by most Californians in 1839 appointed an Englishman named E. P. Hartwell, who had carried on a merchandizing business at Monterey since 1822, as "Visitador General of Missions." His duties embraced the investigation of complaints with the view of remedying the troubles of the Indians. Few of them remained at the missions and those who did were in a miserable condition and contemplated desertion. Hartwell was much in earnest, but the communities in which he worked were indifferent to the sufferings or needs of the Indians, regarding them only as material for labor. The Indians on the other hand were bitterly hostile to the old families and could not be persuaded that any interest taken in their affairs was called forth by the desire to benefit them. <small>A Mexican Investigation</small>

Hartwell's investigations caused a great deal of talk which sounded well. There were many propositions looking to giving the Indians complete liberty and of organizing them into pueblos as was contemplated in the Mexican act of secularization. At this time the Indians in San Francisco were so few in number, and their condition was so wretched that Hartwell recommended that they should be assembled at San Mateo and formed into a pueblo at that place; and it is probable that if he had retained his position something of the kind would have been done; but he resigned on September 7, 1840, disgusted with the opposition of the Vallejo and Pico factions and with the interference he met with in the appointment of majordomos. <small>Proposals to Liberate Indians</small>

The net result of the efforts of Hartwell and of the movement to help the Indian was the creation of a pueblo at San Juan Capistrano which maintained a sickly sort of existence. Two years after its establishment the records showed that of one hundred and fifty persons to whom lots had been given sixty-four, including forty-six Indians, had forfeited their grants.

Indians Turned Adrift

It is not necessary to question the sincerity of the efforts of the Mexican governors to improve the condition of the Indians, and it is idle to assume that the failure of the pueblo plan was due to the avarice of men eager to secure possession of the property of the missions. Doubtless this desire existed, and the sequel shows that it prevailed; but all the evidence points to the utter inability of the wretched aborigines to do for themselves. After years of tutelage they were as inefficient and helpless as they were when the Spaniards first invaded the country, and had the latter turned over every rood of land in the vast territory to them, and left them to their own devices they inevitably must have reverted to their original nomadic habits.

Why no Improvement was Effected

In the year 1779 one of the Franciscans who was displeased with the slow progress made in gathering the Indians into the fold made a plea for them which when taken in connection with the final result exhibits clearly the illusions under which the most earnest of the missionaries were concerning the capacity of their charges for improvement. This critic who signed himself "The Most Unworthy Minister of the Order of St. Francis" declared that the innumerable apostacies, already common at that time, were not due to "the natural inconsistency of the Indians or to their impatience of subordination to labor," but to the failure to impart to them proper religious instruction when gathered in widely separated missions.

A Padre's Explanation

He enumerated other causes which to a later generation furnish a more rational explanation of the propensity of the aborigines to take to the mountains, such as the application of the lash for the punishment of trivial faults, the levying of contributions by curates, and the utter disregard of regulations designed for the benefit of the neophytes who were to be gathered in pueblos. These would seem to have proved sufficient to provoke recalcitrancy but he adds one more that is not usually considered in this connection, namely "the keeping of lands in common, whence it results that the most powerful appropriate them in order to form haciendas fifteen, twenty or thirty leagues in extent." At first this may suggest that the good padre was under the impression that these liberal appropriations of land tended to deprive the Indians of a means of subsistence, but another cause assigned by him under a different heading shows that he regarded individual enterprise as the chief obstacle to the elevation and redemption of the Indians for he tells us that "the maintenance of dispersed ranchos of Spaniards, mulattoes, and other castes by their isolation became a prey to the gentile Indians," hence the temptation to the neophyte to desert his work for the missionaries and the frustration of the efforts of the latter to lift him in the scale of civilization or to effect the salvation of his soul.

Plans of Doubtful Merit

We may doubt the efficiency of the plan which the good padre evidently had in mind to bring about the results he desired. Had it been acted upon it must have resulted very much as the later efforts of Americans to save the Indian from contamination by herding him in reservations. No one now contends that any real good was ever accomplished by the system of keeping Indians apart. They never derived any real benefit from the white man until they were absorbed in the whole body of the people and educated to believe that like other men they had responsibilities, chief among which was the hard necessity imposed on the whole of mankind of earning a subsistence within a comparatively limited space, a stern law fatal to the nomadic propensity and before which the nomadic instinct must disappear as does the winter's snow when the spring thaw comes.

CHAPTER XIII

THE SPANISH LAND GRANT SYSTEM IN CALIFORNIA

FIRST LAND GRANTS IN 1773—LIBERAL ALLOTMENTS DID NOT ATTRACT SETTLERS—LARGE RANCHES PRODUCTIVE OF INDOLENCE—THE NEGLECTED STOCK OF THE NATIVE CALIFORNIANS—PARALYZING EFFECTS OF THE BAD LAND LAWS—SUPPLIES RECEIVED FROM ALASKA—NO MANUFACTURING SKILL DEVELOPED—EARLY CONSERVATION SUGGESTIONS—LUMBER SCARCE—CALIFORNIANS NOT LOVERS OF THE SEA—MONTEREY OVERSHADOWS SAN FRANCISCO IN IMPORTANCE.

A Liberal Land Grant System

WHILE the isolation of the ranchero may have been responsible for the straying habits of the neophytes who were enticed by the gentiles to join them in their mode of life, which was rendered somewhat less precarious by their ability to prey upon the herds and flocks of the *gente de razon*, that evil was light by comparison with the greater one inflicted on the country by a policy which made it impossible for California to become the home of a thrifty farming population.

The conferring of enormous grants of land on individuals was the main factor in keeping California in the condition of a pastoral community down to the time of the American occupation, and its blighting influence was felt long after the discovery of gold brought on the scene a people who by instinct and from force of example were disposed toward the diversification of industry. The reader will be enabled to judge of the drawbacks imposed upon the earlier population by studying the troubles encountered by a more energetic community when the story of the retardment caused by the indisposition of the holders of large grants of land to dispose of their holdings is told in future pages.

Origins of an Abuse

In this chapter the effort of the writer will be confined to showing the workings of the system under Spanish and Mexican rule, and to tracing the connection between it and the stationary stage in the development of California during the early part of the nineteenth century, a condition which must have prevailed indefinitely had not men with other ideals and ambitions than those of the early occupants broken into the territory, and by the force of their example, and their success in operating on a small scale, shown the futility and profitlessness of methods that were characteristic of the feudal period and utterly out of harmony with the aspirations of the present age.

The land grant system of California dates back to August 17, 1773, when authority was given by the Viceroy Bucareli y Ursuas in instructions to Fernando Rivera y Moncada on the occasion of his appointment as commandante of the new establishment at San Diego and Monterey, and the first grant was made to a soldier who had married an Indian girl who had accepted Christianity and was duly baptized. No pains whatever were taken to describe the permanent landmarks, and in the course of time the grant which was in the San Carlos mission failed of confirmation on account of the uncertainty regarding boundaries.

Earliest Land Grants

A few years later the commandante general of the jurisdiction, Jacobo Ugarte y Loyola, then residing at Chihuahua, directed that four square leagues be allotted to new pueblos in California, and in 1789 he ordered that an allotment be made to a retired corporal at San Luis Obispo mission. This soldier had also married a Christianized Indian belonging to the establishment named. Prior to these grants of a public character Governor Fages had in 1784 granted to Manuel Nieto a place called Santa Getrudis, and to Jose Maria Verdugo another known as San Rafael. Both of these were in Los Angeles county. The first named contained over 300,000 acres and the latter 34,000 acres. In 1795 Patricio and Miguel Pico received grants aggregating 100,000 acres in Santa Barbara, and an indefinite tract between San Pedro and Point Año Nuevo was granted Jose D'Arguello.

Mexico Follows Spanish Policy

These Spanish grants were all subsequently confirmed, and after the revolution the Mexicans entered upon a liberal policy of land bestowal. Laws were enacted in 1824 and 1828 by which the governor or political chief was authorized to make grants for the purpose of inducing colonization. Under this authority heads of families, leaders of colonies or private individuals could have lands conferred upon them, which grants had to be confirmed by the supreme government. There were numerous restrictions upon the granting power of the governors. They were not permitted to grant lands within 30 leagues of the boundary of a foreign power nor nearer the sea coast than 10 leagues. The grants were limited to one square league of irrigable land, 4 square leagues of ordinary land and 6 square leagues of grazing land. The grantee was not permitted to transfer his land in mortmain nor retain it if he resided out of the territory of the Mexican republic.

Lands did not Attract

These laws, liberal though they were, did not greatly promote the desired colonization. There were some grants made under them but it was not until the secularization of the missions in 1833 that numerous demands were made for the valuable tracts to which the missionaries laid claim and which were regarded as the most fertile lands in the country. The number of grants made which complied with the requirements of the laws and were afterward pronounced valid by the United States Land Commission, established after the occupation, was 514. In addition there were nearly three hundred claims rejected, some of which, on review by the United States supreme court were finally confirmed. It was estimated that the total acreage of the grants with which the commission dealt was 12,000,000, nearly one seventh of the area of the state.

Land Poor Settlers

This reckless disposition of the public lands did not accomplish the purpose which prompted it. It failed to people the vast territory with a population of workers or of colonists of any sort. It was not alone disappointing in that particular, it also failed to realize the expectations of the grantees who experienced all the embarrassments attendant upon "land poorness." There were owners of thousands of acres of land who were so wretchedly poor that no well paid laborer of to-day would envy their condition. The brothers Andreas and Pio Pico who had vast tracts confirmed to them were always on the ragged edge of real want, although they were among the grandees of the land, and the last named of the two enjoyed the distinction of being the last Mexican governor of California.

As may well be imagined the lack of care exercised by the authorities in granting the lands of Upper California was productive of great trouble when the property became valuable. No regular surveys were made by the Spaniards or Mexicans. The grantees usually received juridical possession, and in most cases the nearest alcalde with suitable land marks designated the boundaries of the grant. The title, however, was supposed to be complete without the juridical possession. Naturally this loose method resulted in disputes as it lent itself to fraudulent claims based on forgeries and misstatements of various sorts. In a letter written to President Buchanan in 1860 by United States Attorney General Black he stated that the value of lands claimed in California under fradulent grants was not less than $150,000,000, and that the most of the rejected claims were based on absolute forgeries.

<small>Land Titles</small>

But it is not with the troubles after the occupation that we are here dealing, but rather the evil results which were experienced by the recipients of the extravagant bounty of the Spanish and Mexican governments. The padre who referred to the temptation presented by isolated ranches to marauding gentiles indicated one source of mischief, but it was small by comparison with the result produced by the invitation to a naturally indolent people to shirk exertion of all kinds. A virile people such as those who pioneered Kentucky, and the other states of the American Union, which at that time were on the outskirts of civilization, would have made short work of the Indians and secured the peace necessary to successfully carry on farming operations, and perhaps they might have created an environment for themselves which would have enabled them to overcome the limitations of a pastoral life. But the Californians were not made of that stuff, and consequently they easily accepted conditions little better than those of the aborigines they dispossessed.

<small>Incitement to Indolence</small>

The only superiority of the *gente de razon* over the nomadic Indians was their practical attachment to the soil which enabled them to apply some of their inherited knowledge to the business of maintaining life. They devoted themselves chiefly to pastoral pursuits, or rather it should be said they permitted their herds and flocks to multiply and thus obtained a means of existence. To speak of them as raisers of stock would mislead, for the term stock raising implies attention to the improvement of the breed of the animals, and they gave no thought to anything of the kind.

<small>Social Distinctions</small>

It is asserted that the Spanish jealousy of competition was responsible for the inferior quality of the wool produced on the California ranches, but there is no evidence whatever that the natives ever made any effort to prevent deterioration of their stock. The sheep, as was the case with horses, horned cattle and hogs, were utterly neglected, and the inevitable consequence was the multiplication of their kind after a fashion, the most of which were worthless for any other purpose than to kill. The scant supplies of wool obtained scarcely sufficed to provide the not exacting demand for clothes; the "razor back" hogs were deficient in the fat which the Californian taste craved, the oxen were miserable creatures hardly able to perform the work imposed on them by their lazy owners, and the other horned cattle were valueless except for their hides, and the tallow which was extracted from their bodies when they were in fit condition for killing. As for horses they roamed over the land in vast numbers, and from them enough good mounts could be selected

<small>Uncared for Live Stock</small>

86   SAN FRANCISCO

to satisfy the requirements of the rancheros, but the great majority were valueless for any purpose.

Estates as Large as Principalities The men who permitted these conditions were incapable of advancement, but it is doubtful whether any better result could have been achieved under the system which created estates as large as small principalities. The benumbing influence of the big ranch was not confined to the Californian. There are plenty of instances of men who, in another environment would have been enterprising, but who could not resist the enervation induced by their surroundings, which, however, they were prone to blame on the climate. They easily adopted the indolent habits of the people contemptuously called "greasers" by the later comers, and to all intents and purposes were as worthless, and did as little to promote the progress of their adopted country as those they affected to despise.

Native Shortcomings It would be idle to assume the possibility of any rapid change in the condition of a people thus situated, and it may be a work of supererogation to even describe their shortcomings which were not due to racial deficiencies. The difficulties to be surmounted by them were of the same sort that brought about the institution of feudalism in Europe, which has to its discredit not merely the arrestment of progress during the middle ages, but is chargeable with the destruction of policies through which a civilization was effected that brought great material prosperity in its train, no matter what may be said about its defects on the moral side.

Paralyzing Effects of Band Land System California offered no opportunity for the exercise of the destructive effects of a bad laud system, but it was an admirable field in which to exhibit its paralyzing influence. There was nothing to destroy for it was a virgin country into which it was introduced, but it kept the land and the people in precisely the same condition to which Europe was reduced after the decline of the Roman empire, and in which it remained until the Renaissance, when commercialism burst the fetters of restraint and showed the world that the true road to improvement, and the betterment of human conditions generally, was that which was paved by enterprise and industry, and not by good intentions.

Example Wasted Example was wasted in a country destitute of means of communication, and of the instinct for gain, which is at the bottom of commercialism, and is responsible for human progress, and the higher civilization on which it is based. The missionaries planted vines and set out orchards, but the rancheros did not imitate them. William Wolfskill, one of the early settlers, turned his attention to fruit raising and showed what could be done in that line, but although he began his operations as early as 1830, when the gringo overran the country, the acres of the big ranches were as barren of fruit trees as they were when Padre Junipero Serra first saw the land and gloried over its possibilities. About the same time a Frenchman named Vignes set out some vines, and showed that the soil was excellently adapted to the growth of grapes, but for many years afterward those who could command the price were still eagerly purchasing the products of the brick vineyards of Boston or consuming the fiery aguardiente.

Want in Midst of Plenty Notwithstanding the fact that the hills of California were overrun with cattle the Californians rarely made any butter or cheese and were too indolent even to milk their cows. They lived on a monotonous diet at which the inmates of our reformatory institutions and those of our almshouses would revolt. In the midst of the plenty implied by the existence of untold numbers of cattle we learn that there were periods during which the problem of existence in California was one of subsistence, and that in 1814 "from San Diego to Monterey there was for the Spaniard the need of manufactured goods."

Eight years earlier the Russian Rezanoff learned of this condition and proposed to remedy it. He did not live to carry out his projects, but those who were on the ground in Alaska after his death took the hint, and in that remote and desolate region was produced a large part of the not very great quantity of manufactured articles consumed by the Californians. It was from the ship yard of Sitka that many of the cumbersome hoes and crude plows used in California were derived, as were also a number of household utensils of the commoner kind, pots, pans and the like. In the foundries of the Alaska ship yard were also cast a considerable number of the bells used by the mission establishments to call the faithful to prayer and the neophyte to work. *Supplies from Alaska*

It cannot be said that no attempt was made in the mission days to manufacture for the padres did make essays in that direction. But their efforts if they were consciously directed towards building up an industry, which is doubtful, were unavailing because their methods tended to produce the same result as that which was witnessed during that period of the middle ages when intercourse between men was reduced to a minimum, and the only evidences of manufacturing activity were those of the household. *Feeble Efforts at Manufacturing*

In a report of Governor Victoria made in 1831 we are told that there were no manufactures carried on except in the mission where wool was worked up by the neophytes into blankets and coarse cloths. On the ranches there was an inconsiderable amount of blacksmithing, carpentering, tanning and shoemaking, but absolutely nothing was produced for export. In 1824 there appears to have been no more than a single source of lumber supply, which was provided by a man named David A. Hill, who together with an Irishman operated a rip saw in a pit. At San Luis Obispo there was a water mill for grinding grain, but the most of the meal was produced by a process which showed very little advancement over the metate and pestle of the Indians, and indeed the latter was oftener found doing duty than the arrastra, composed of two stones, the upper of which was made to revolve by mule power.

The missionaries imported or brought with them a few artisans from Mexico who were to teach the neophytes their crafts, but the latter except in rare cases never attained to any proficiency even measured by the standard of the time and place. Father Viader of the Santa Clara mission had built for him by his Indian mechanics a wonderful vehicle which was drawn by a mule. It is described as having a long narrow body, the entire framework of which was covered with brown cotton, and was furnished with a seat made of lambs wool. The good padre was usually accompanied on his outings by vaqueros, who assisted the mule to pull the carriage up steep places. It appears, however, that the contrivance was frowned upon as an object tending to luxury and there was no disposition to imitate it manifested by the rancheros, who depended upon their horses to get them about, and upon the oxcart for moving freight. *Artisans Brought from Mexico*

The allusion to brown cotton cloth calls attention to the fact that a small quantity of cotton yarn was imported at different times from Mexico, and that some of the Indians were taught to weave and spin, but the industry, which was confined to one or two missions, never made any progress and was abandoned despite the great need for clothing, which seemed to be a chronic affliction shared by soldiers, *Indians Weave and Spin*

88   SAN FRANCISCO

neophytes, the padres and rancheros, and one that was not wholly removed even when enterprising Yankee traders sought to supply the deficiency.

The First Saw Mill We have seen that as late as 1824 a single rip saw provided all the lumber demanded by the Californians. Not much progress was made by the industry after that year until 1843, when Stephen Smith, who visited the East after sojourning some years in California, on his return brought a complete outfit for a steam grist and saw mill which he located at Bodega. Between the two dates nothing calculated to create alarm occurred, yet in 1839 a paper was issued by Romero, the Mexican minister of the interior, who sounded a warning note on the subject of the necessity of conservation. He said the republic had suffered in some years from droughts which caused the harvests to fail and the cattle to die. Reason, tradition and experience, he declared, pointed to the devastation of the forests and the denudation of the hills and mountains as the chief cause of these troubles. Consequently he proposed to restrict the cutting of trees with the view of preserving the health of the people and to protect agriculture and the industries dependent upon it, and he even suggested the planting of trees along public roads and such places as could not otherwise be made useful.

First Vessel Built in California The warnings were hardly needed in California as no disposition was exhibited there to denude the land of its timber. Although the Bay of San Francisco invited navigation, and years before when the presidio was first located men peering into the future saw ship yards springing up along its shores in which the excellent timber of the surrounding forests could be utilized, it is recorded that the first vessel of any sort built in the province was a launch, the timbers of which were hewn at San Gabriel and put together in 1831. This, however, was not a product of native Californians for it was constructed by Englishmen and Yankees.

Use of the Sea Discouraged It is difficult at times to distinguish between cause and effect, but no extraordinary penetration is required to divine the reasons of the failure of California to make progress in any direction during the period under review. It is said of the ancient Romans that their roads played a more important part in building up their great empire than the soldiers who marched over them. Undoubtedly the multiplication of facilities for close intercourse is a powerful agency in the development of commerce and in promoting the growth of civilization, but the Californians disregarded this valuable experience and actually adopted a policy which had for its object the discouragement of the use of the ocean as a means of communication.

Settlers Amid the Coast The pains taken in the land grant laws of the Mexicans to prevent development along the sea coast by compelling grantees to take up tracts at a considerable distance from the shore; the display of temper exhibited by the governor who censured the commandante of the presidio of San Francisco for daring to engage in such an enterprise as the building of a rude craft to bring lumber from the opposite shore to repair the ruined quarters of the soldiers, and the vexatious and utterly unreasonable methods adopted to preserve the integrity of the territory, and which practically shut off all intercourse with the outside world except that of a clandestine character, all point to the utter incapacity of those who occupied the land before the Americans poured in upon them to realize the value of their possession or to develop its resources.

Their obtuseness and indifference to the benefits of communication by land and sea also explain the singular fact that although nearly two centuries were

SAN FRANCISCO

spent in finding a safe harbor in about the locality where San Francisco bay was finally discovered it was sixty years after the establishment of a ranch on its shores before a beginning was made towards the creation of a port. That event practically dates from the laying out of a single street along the cove which was first utilized by shipping. In August, 1834, Governor Figueroa put into effect the law of August, 1831, which decreed the secularization of the missions and provided for the establishment of pueblos, which were to be organized in conformity with its provisions. In October, 1835, Francisco de Haro, who was residing at the Mission Dolores, received orders to lay out Yerba Buena, which he did by marking on the ground a single street to which the high sounding name of Street of the Foundation was given.

It was a feeble beginning from which good results commercially might have followed in later years even if the uncommercial Californians had remained in possession of the territory, but such an outcome would hardly be inferred from its excessively slow development and its utter subordination to Monterey, which remained the place of most importance until the gold rush made it imperative for the shipping which was finding its way to the coast to seek a more convenient and safer harbor. Monterey served the purposes of the traders who visited California to obtain cargoes of hides and tallow. In many respects it suited them better than Yerba Buena. The latter might have superior attractions for captains who laid stress on security, but even they were ready to subordinate that consideration in order to get nearer to the source of supply of the merchandize they were seeking, and closer to the population which was ready to exchange its rude products for the manufactured articles and the luxuries brought to the coast by the trading ships.

Monterey the Chief Port

CHAPTER XIV

EARLY TRADING TROUBLES OF THE CALIFORNIANS

SPANISH AND MEXICAN ATTEMPTS TO REPRESS TRADING—SMUGGLING POPULARLY APPROVED—THE FUR TRADE—SPAIN SURRENDERS NORTHWEST COAST—VISITS OF YANKEE SHIPS TO CALIFORNIA—THE FORT ROSS ESTABLISHMENT—AN AMICABLE ARRANGEMENT WITH THE RUSSIANS—SUTTER AND VALLEJO QUARREL—THE TRADE IN HIDES AND TALLOW—THE WHALERS AND THE WHALING INDUSTRY—HONOLULU A RIVAL OF SAN FRANCISCO—FIRST MERCANTILE ESTABLISHMENT IN YERBA BUENA—CONTINUED IMPORTANCE OF MONTEREY—SAN FRANCISCO'S FIRST PUBLIC IMPROVEMENT—SEVENTY YEARS OF INACTIVITY.

Trading Instinct Repressed

N THESE days of intense commercialism when every opportunity to engage in enterprise is eagerly seized, and when men devote their thoughts to creating opportunities to extend the field of their energies, it is almost impossible to comprehend the temperament which shrunk from exertion and actually placed obstacles in the way of development. The inertia of the occupants of the territory, which is now one of the most prosperous states of the American Union, was a bad thing in its way, but its consequences would not have been so fatal to advancement as they proved to be, if the active factor of direct interference had not supplemented the enervating effects of a system which succeeded in crushing out ambition in every country in which it was tried.

Tariffs Fail to Promote Industry

The story of trade repression in California during the first half of the nineteenth century is interesting, amusing and instructive. It is amusing because it illustrates to the fullest extent the futility of attempts to interfere with the gratification of the desires of a people when the necessary force to compel compliance with regulations is lacking. It is instructive because when properly viewed it brings out plainly the fact that high tariffs, and even prohibitions of intercourse do not promote a domestic industry unless the desire for its creation is existent. The Californians enjoyed all the advantages natural and artificial that are considered the chief factors in the promotion of production. They had raw materials in abundance for manufacturing purposes, and the natural protection which distance from established manufacturing and producing centers affords, and in addition they had tariffs which, had the disposition existed to make them so, would have proved prohibitory to the introduction of foreign products.

Foreign Goods Acceptable

But the desire to exclude did not exist. On the contrary there was a decided propensity to encourage the foreigner to bring his wares, which brought about a condition that can be best described by the paradoxical assertion that the Califor-

92   SAN FRANCISCO

nians succeeded in legalizing illegality. They did not merely elevate smuggling into a fine art, they acutally accomplished the extraordinary feat of converting the officials whose duty it was to exercise repressive and restrictive authority into active supporters and defenders of a trade which, although contraband, was carried on without attempts at secrecy, and which was supported by public sentiment, not excluding that of officials.

No Objection to Foreign Traders

Perhaps this is less surprising than the fact already alluded to that the native Californians made no opposition to the establishment of foreigners in their midst as traders. They may have felt some slight pangs of jealousy when they observed Captain N. A. Richardson erecting a house in Yerba Buena, the first put up in that place, but they were assuaged by the feeling that after all he was useful to them, as he operated two schooners for their benefit, and thus enabled them to get their hides and tallow to a place where they could be sold to the skippers of the trading ships.

Richardson's advent may not have been complacently regarded by the missionaries but they were not able to overlook the fact that he filled a want which they were unable to supply by becoming a common carrier on the bay, and that he helped to facilitate that trade with the outside world by which they obtained articles that contributed to their comfort, and other things absolutely indispensable, if agriculture was to be pursued even in the rudest fashion.

Hide and Tallow Trade

But years before Richardson came on the scene enterprising traders had found their way to the coast and were buying the hides and tallow which were the only articles of consequence exported by the Californians. Some valuable furs were obtained by the exertions of intruders who were not unwilling to do the work necessary to secure them. Spain did not entirely disregard this valuable trade. The desire to secure its benefits was sufficiently pronounced, but the same causes which induced the Spanish explorers to shun the coast north of San Francisco harbor on account of its fogs and their assumed discomforts prevented its development. If the seals and other fur bearing creatures had presented themselves for capture, or had it been possible to take them as easily as cattle running on the hills of California, there might have been as lively a trade in furs as in hides and tallow.

The Fur Trade

The fur trade of the coast, even that of parts remote from San Francisco bay, has been linked with the destinies of the Pacific coast metropolis from the time that Captain Cook's men in 1778 obtained from the natives at Nootka a number of skins of the sea otter which they carried to Canton and sold at the high price of $120 a piece. The Russians and British had been taking skins for years, but it remained for the publication of the account of Cook's voyages in 1784 to create an almost universal interest in the fur trade. Spain awakened to the possibility of profit being derived from her American possessions through this industry and in 1786 a monopoly was projected which, however, was soon abandoned.

Russian Activity on Coast

In 1788 Martinez, who had just made a supply trip to the coast, wrote from Monterey describing the intentions of the Russians, and urging Spain to extend her claims to Nootka. By doing so, he asserted, Spain would establish herself on the coast from Nootka to the port of San Francisco. The Viceroy Florez sent him to Nootka, where he arrived in May, 1789, and discovered that an American vessel, the "Columbia," and an English brig, the "Iphigenia," sailing under Portuguese colors were ahead of him. He made no attempt to molest the American, but seized the "Iphigenia" and her consort as poachers on Spanish possessions. There was

SAN FRANCISCO IN 1849
From a sketch

SAN FRANCISCO IN 1846, AT THE TIME OF THE OCCUPATION. IT WAS THEN
KNOWN AS YERBA BUENA

much bluster over the seizure but in the end Spain made restitution and a treaty was concluded October 28, 1790, by which Spain yielded claim of exclusive sovereignty to the northwest coast, but obtained from her adversary an agreement not to navigate or fish within ten leagues of any part of the coast occupied by Spain.

Despite this agreement, which implied the determination of Spain to exclude foreigners from the privilege of fishing on the coast, Americans and Russians engaged in otter hunting expeditions from Trinidad bay to Todas Santos islands and even ventured within the estuary of San Francisco. In these adventures the Russians furnished the hunters and Americans the equipment of the vessels. The officials of the Russian American Company viewed these arrangements with displeasure, and one of the objects of Rezanoff's visit to California in 1806 was to investigate the possibility of ousting the Bostonians from what was already regarded as a profitable trade. In a report made by him to the government he advised the building of a war brig to drive the Americans from California waters unless they procured their supplies from the factories in Siberia. He had learned that the Spanish were ready to trade surreptitiously with the Yankees, and that the latter were receiving in exchange for what he characterized as trifles valuable otter skins. Jealous of the Yankees

The first Boston captain to visit the coast was Ebenezer Dow in a vessel called the "Otter." He touched at Monterey October 29, 1796, but does not appear to have visited California with the intention of engaging in unlawful trade, although other American vessels did, and very soon they beset the padres, whose necessities were numerous, with great temptations. The commandante on the occasion of these visits interposed few obstacles. If he was disposed to be captious his attitude was soon changed by a bribe; the padres usually succumbed to the desire for useful articles which they were able to pay for with otter skins, for which they had no conceivable use in a climate like that of California. First Boston Trader

Rezanoff's efforts to head off the Bostonians proved unavailing, but out of his visit to California came an understanding between the Russians and Spain which resulted in gaining for the former a foothold near the port of San Francisco from which they were not dislodged for many years. The anxiety of the Spaniards to prevent Americans effecting a settlement on the "Columbia" caused them to receive with favor a proposition from the Russian American Company to assist in frustrating such a purpose, and thus began the advance southward toward San Francisco, which point Rezanoff had advocated as the boundary line between the Russian and Spanish possessions on the Pacific coast. Efforts to Head Off Americans

The encroachment was not completed in a day. Kuskoff did not reach Bodega bay until March, 1811. A year later he repeated his visit, this time in force, and on September 10th, at a point 18 miles north of Bodega, on a bluff 100 feet above sea level, Ross was established. It was fortified with a battery of ten guns, and manned by 95 Russians, and a party of Aleuts who were probably brought along to assist in otter taking rather than to help defend the position which was never seriously endangered by the supine Californians. Russian Encroachments

Meanwhile, despite the proximity of the Russians, and their desire to shut out the Yankees, one of the latter appears to have been able to do a brisk business with the Californians and perhaps there were others. That will be inferred from the fact that Jose Sevilla, who was made coast guard of California, alleged in a report that it was the custom of English vessels to anchor at Santa Catarina islands, A Shrewd Yankee Skipper

ten leagues from the coast, and there exchange China and East Indian goods for otter skins and cattle. Sevilla appears to have been in error so far as the nationality of the vessels was concerned, and was probably deceived by the fact that their crews spoke English; but he made no mistake when he asserted that the officials connived at this illicit trade, for all he said was amply supported by statements made in a letter by Captain George Washington Eayrs, of the "Mercury" of Boston, written on the 7th of February, 1814. In that document the captain tells of the arrangements made with the head people and the "Pardres" who entreated him to bring them many articles which they sorely needed, and could not obtain from the continent. As the letter was accompanied by several orders of the padres making the requests, the captain's statement must be accepted as fully corroborated.

Trading with the Padres
About the time that Eayrs was dealing with the padres and driving successful trades with the rancheros, the Spanish home government was directing Viceroy Calleja to take steps to get rid of the Russians whose proximity was creating great uneasiness. The viceroy did not deem precipitancy prudent, but he passed on his orders to Governor Jose Arguello, who in the early part of 1815 notified Kuskoff that the Russian post at Fort Ross must be abandoned. Kuskoff visited San Francisco and tried to convince the Spanish authorities that the presence of his countrymen in the neighborhood did not menace their possessions, and that Russia made no claim to territory south of the Strait of Fuca. There was considerable palavering during three or four ensuing years and finally in 1820 the Russian American Company through its representative announced that it would abandon the settlement which caused the Spaniards so much apprehension, and dismiss all ideas of obtaining another site if by this sacrifice the privilege of a permanent trade with California could be gained.

Russians Permitted to Hunt
This proposal, like other negotiations of the Spanish at this particular period does not appear to have been formally acted upon, but a few years later under the Mexican Governor Arguello an agreement was entered into by which the Russian American Company was permitted to hunt otter on shares with Californians, probably a euphemistic wording of an arrangement by which the fact that an improper payment by the Russians for the privilege was concealed. Arguello, however, held unusually liberal views on the subject of trade, and it is not improbable that he acted in violation of tradition because he believed the result would be beneficial to California. His complacency toward the Russians did not prevent his entering into a contract with an English house in December, 1823, by which the company was obligated to take all the hides and tallow produced in the province, at a stipulated price, during a period of three years.

Englishmen Secure a Monopoly
This arrangement between McCulloch, Hartwell & Co., the English firm referred to and the toleration accorded to the Hudson Bay Company, whose relations with the Californians were always friendly, probably explains the belief entertained by the British in the province, and the people in Downing street, that in certain contingencies California would gladly have placed herself under the protection of Great Britain. Certainly color was lent to the impression by a privilege accorded to the Hudson Bay Company in 1841 by Alvarado, by which its hunters were permitted to operate along the Sacramento. This concession called forth an angry letter from Sutter, a foreigner, who had established himself in the region where the British proposed to operate after assuming citizenship which enabled him to secure a large tract of land.

SAN FRANCISCO

Sutter's letter fell into the hands of Vallejo, who used it to injure the writer, whom he charged with having assumed a title which did not belong to him, and also accused him of having made war on Indians in his neighborhood, and of selling into servitude the children who were made orphans by the killing of their parents. Sutter's name appears very frequently in California history, and not always in a manner reflecting luster upon it. His operations, however, did not closely touch San Francisco. The nearest they came to doing so grew out of his attempt to secure the property of the Russian establishment at Fort Ross, which Vallejo in a letter to Mexico dated December 12, 1841, said was sold to Sutter, a transaction which, had it stood, would have greatly increased his prestige and perhaps might have materially influenced the course of affairs which subsequently resulted in American occupation.

Sutter Quarrels with Vallejo

The hide and tallow business which under Spanish rule had been wholly confined to government vessels excepting that which was illicitly carried on, when the Mexicans administered the affairs of the country was distributed more generally and was shared by Americans. After the exclusive contract with McCulloch, Hartwell & Co. had expired, several Boston concerns came on the scene and were permitted to buy freely. The trade was of considerable consequence. In 1826 there were at least 200,000 head of cattle in California. At the private ranches there was an annual slaughter, but the missionaries did their killing weekly. The hides when not sold in their green state were dried. The tallow was tried out and run into bags of bullock skin, which held twenty-five pounds each. No very exact figures of the extent of the exports of these two commodities, hides and tallow, exist, but after secularization became a certainty, large numbers of cattle were killed for their hides. Twenty thousand dollars worth were sold by the San Luis Obispo mission, and the money was used to purchase goods which were distributed among the Indians. At San Gabriel, whose herds numbered 100,000 head, the cattle were killed where found, and some of the valleys were covered with putrescent masses, no effort being made to secure the tallow.

Importance of Hide and Tallow Trade

The wholesale slaughtering which followed the disestablishment of the missions was exceptional, but as early as 1784 it had been found necessary to reduce the number of cattle at the San Francisco presidio. Between 1805 and 1810, as already stated, the devastation resulting from horses running at large was so great that a campaign was carried on which got rid of them by tens of thousands. Usually after the rodeos, the annual rounding up of stock for the purpose of branding and separating and distributing the cattle among their owners, there was a slaughter the extent of which was determined by agreement. It necessarily caused a great deal of offal, for the consumption of which scores of dogs were kept by the rancheros. It was no unusual thing for one of the lords of the soil to be attended by a train of dogs half a mile long. How they were fed at other times than at these annual killings we have no specific records, but in a country where when the horses became too numerous they were driven over cliffs to kill them the canine probably never suffered even if his owner at times experienced privations because he was too lazy to adjust matters so that he might have a steady supply of meat.

Wholesale Slaughter After Secularization

One of the first things to attract the attention of Americans to the importance of the harbor of San Francisco was the practice of the whalers of wintering in the Hawaiian islands. The latter prospered greatly in consequence of these visits and the whalers were able to secure the supplies they needed from there much

Whaling and Whalers

more advantageously than they could have obtained them in California. At that time, however, the manifest destiny idea was fermenting in the American mind, and it took a form which differed greatly from that which held possession in later years. The whalers were convinced that their interests would be subserved, and those of the country as well, by securing possession of a port like San Francisco, and they so managed to impress the authorities in Washington, that official coguizance was taken of the matter. Whaling was then an industry of great importance, and those engaged in it by reason of their wealth and enterprise commanded a great deal of influence and by their efforts some of the sentiment which later resulted in acquisition was created, and helped to divert attention from the true motives of those who were bent on seizing California.

No Interest in Fisheries

Although the people of remote New Bedford were alive to the value of the whaling trade the Californians gave it no thought. After the time that one of the Spanish navigators had pointed out the desirability of occupying the Sandwich islands to prevent any foreigner from doing so no one in Spain or Mexico bothered about the matter and the predicted came to pass. In 1820 the foreigner in the shape of seven missionaries from New England planted himself in the islands, and in the fullness of time they were attached to the United States. The missionaries were followed by enterprising men whose energies soon accomplished what the Spaniard who settled on the shores of the Bay of San Francisco only talked of doing. In 1827 a ship yard was started in Honolulu by Americans, and in 1836 a newspaper was published by them called "The Sandwich Island Gazette," and from that time on despite guarantees of autonomy and various governmental experiments the group was practically American.

Rivalry of Hawaii

While the enterprising Yankees were creating a rival port in the tropic seas the Californians were pursuing a course calculated to make trade impossible. Instead of welcoming the whalers, they actually placed restrictions on the quantity of provisions that might be sold to them. Despite the fact that they were in sore need of many manufactured articles which the whalers would gladly have brought to them they limited the amount that a ship might sell to $400. At Honolulu, of course, the whaler was permitted to buy all that the islanders had to sell, and in 1844 the annual trade of that port with the adventurous fishermen was fully $250,000.

Leese Starts Store in Yerba Buena

This condition of affairs was not changed until after the American occupation. In 1836 when Jacob Primer Leese started the first mercantile establishment in Yerba Buena he may have had some foreshadowing of the possibilities of trade with shipping, but there was no active interest taken in Hawaii, or for that matter in anything or any place outside of California. Leese had been doing business in Monterey in partnership with Nathan Spear and W. S. Hinckley, and was evidently gifted with prescience, for he recognized possibilities of development in the new pueblo which were disregarded by most others. When he first made application to the alcalde and commandante for a location on the beach he was confronted with the order directing the setting aside of reservations, but was offered a choice of two other places, one at the mouth of Mission creek and the other near the entrance of the bay, close to the presidio. Subsequently letters given him by Governor Chico procured for him an allotment within the reservation limits, and on the 1st of July, 1836, he took possession of a hundred vara lot, distant about 250 yards from the beach, the spot selected being near to what is now the corner of Clay and Dupont streets.

Leese's establishment was a considerable one for the locality and the stock of goods and its character indicates that he expected a patronage somewhat greater than the insignificant village and the ranches in the immediate vicinity afforded. He was well patronized and the city began to take on an air of business it had not known before his arrival. Captain Richardson had pioneered the way in this vicinity with his two schooners, which, as already stated, gathered hides and tallow and wheat from points about the bay accessible to the rancheros who brought their products to the landings in their rude ox carts and sometimes utilized the Indians as porters. *[Progress of Yerba Buena]*

But Monterey continued to be the most important place in the North several years after Leese had established himself in San Francisco. But the wisdom of his choice was made apparent even before the Americans took possession. The town grew slowly and gradually began to divide the honors with its neighbors to the south. Leese had married a sister of Vallejo who became the mother of the first child born in Yerba Buena. This event occurred April 15, 1838, and was made the occasion for great festivities in which all classes participated. Leese's relations with the Californians were of a friendly nature and his American proclivities were not reckoued against him. When he celebrated the completion of his store by a house warming in 1836, on the 4th of July of that year, the American and Mexican flags floated side by side over the new structure, and the stars and stripes were hailed with as many *vivas* as the green, red and white colors of the sister republic. At the banquet, which all the old Spanish families that could reach Yerba Buena attended, the best of feeling prevailed, and no sign of impending trouble made its appearance. *[Importance of Monterey]*

While Yerba Buena made some little progress commercially after the establishment of Leese's store its anomolous political condition put it at a disadvantage, even though there was nothing like real rivalry throughout the length and breadth of the province. There was no place in California before 1846 where any consideration was given to such matters as public improvements. The open spaces set aside as plazas were in no instance made attractive by shrubbery. If anything, their dedication to public use caused them to be more unlovely than they were when unfrequented. But enterprising men, with a bit of the civic instinct, might have done something in the way of adding to their convenience had they been furnished with the machinery to bring about such a result. *[No Public Improvements]*

They were not, however. The mixed condition of the law relating to the missions and pueblos created such uncertainties that had Leese and a few others who made their way into Yerba Buena before 1846 been possessed by the spirit of the modern boomer, they could have done nothing. The abolition of the mission system, and the attempt to convert the missions into Indian pueblos which had proved unsuccessful, resulted in complete disorganization. Strictly speaking, there was no pueblo in the sense of an organized municipality. The control had passed into the hands of the political government which responded to pressing needs slowly, and never anticipated them. In 1839, the prefect, Jose Castro, when urged by the inhabitants of Dolores, made application to the government to establish a pueblo, which brought forth a permit to grant building lots, but the place failed to receive the same authoritative sanction as Los Angeles, Los Flores and other pueblos. *[Political Conditions]*

It is not surprising, therefore, that no improvements were made and that the settlement remained pretty much in the same condition down to the time of occupation, and for that matter until a few years after the Americans had taken possession *[Yerba Buena Slumbers]* and caused the name of Yerba Buena to be changed to San Francisco. A few scattered houses, without any well defined streets, gave it the appearance of an illy regulated village. In 1844, William Sturges Hinckley, who had arrived in 1840, was elected the first alcalde of Yerba Buena, and he distinguished himself by inaugurating a public improvement.

First Yerba Buena Public Improvement

In 1844, in the locality now bounded by Montgomery, Washington, Kearny and Jackson streets, there was a salt water lagoon or lake connected with the bay by a creek or slough. The tide ebbed and flowed through this slough which at all times contained water separating the original village of Yerba Buena and Telegraph hill. For years those who wished to pass in a direct line between the then harbor and the eastern point of the hill were obliged to jump or wade across the slough. The enterprising alcalde caused a rude bridge to be thrown across the watery obstacle and his action was regarded as so extraordinary that the rancheros came from considerable distances to view the marvelous structure that apparently excited more interest and admiration than the erection now-a-days of a bridge costing millions of dollars.

A Solitary Instance of Enterprise

This important improvement, the achievement of eleven years of the close intercourse of village life and the commercialism of the day, appears to be the only recorded instance of what might be termed public activity if it were not for the suspicion that the bridge was built at the personal expense of Hinckley, and not by the people in their collective capacity. The relation of the fact will serve to impress on the reader the utter absence of enterprise existing in California before the occupation and will, perhaps, enable him to form a judgment of the obstacles to growth which would have been encountered had the Mexicans retained their hold on the territory.

Seventy Years of Rest and Quiet

This solitary instance of municipal enterprise, a few straggling houses and the mission establishment at Dolores were the net product of seventy years of effort on the shores of the bay which was found after centuries of vain search for a short cut to the wealth of the Indies. The absurdly inadequate results achieved can fairly be attributed to one primary cause. Had not the spirit of industrialism been almost extinguished by the feudal system of the middle ages which was transplanted to California, and all the vices of which were inherited by Californians, they would have found a way to produce wealth in quantities that would have paled into insignificance even the fabulous hoards of the isles of gold and silver which the Spanish explorers so eagerly sought.

Spanish Occupation a Failure

They and their successors failed to achieve the object of their desires. They did not discover the passage to Anian, but they found a country abounding in untold possibilities. It is true that they did not recognize them, and never appreciated California at its real value, but there must have been something resembling an instinctive recognition that the land they regarded as so unpromising would eventually demonstrate its worth. Some such feeling may account for the zealous effort to preserve the territory from encroachment, but while adherence to so narrow a sentiment must be set down as something far from admirable, Americans have no reason to find fault with it, as it preserved for them in almost virgin state a vast region with illimitable resources, which are being intelligently developed, and in such a way that the whole of mankind, and not merely those engaged in their exploitation, will be benefited.

CHAPTER XV

THE EVE OF THE OCCUPATION BY AMERICANS

SPANISH FAILURE TO DISCOVER GOLD IN QUANTITY—A FEW OUNCES FOUND IN LOS ANGELES BEFORE THE SUTTER FORT DISCOVERY—HOPES OF THE AMERICAN SETTLERS—SOUTHERNERS HOODWINK THE NORTHERN PEOPLE—THE PLOTS OF THE SLAVEHOLDERS—JACKSON'S OFFER TO PURCHASE SAN FRANCISCO BAY—THE WAR WITH MEXICO—FREMONT'S EXPEDITION—FREMONT'S POLICY OF PROVOCATION—WASHINGTON AUTHORITIES MISLED—FREMONT AND IDE—THE BEAR FLAG EPISODE—WHAT MIGHT HAVE HAPPENED.

 HE irony of fate was never exhibited in a more striking fashion than in the failure of the Spanish to discover that the El Dorado they were seeking lay concealed beneath the soil of California. From the day that Columbus blundered upon the island of San Salvador, when trying to reach India, down almost to the time that the Spaniards were driven from Continental America they were constantly in quest of the precious metals. No stories concerning their existence seemed too improbable for belief, and to some extent their credulousness was justified, for the most rapacious of the adventurers sent forth by them secured gold and silver in such quantities that the supply of them must have seemed really inexhaustible to the people of the old world, who, for centuries preceding 1492, had been suffering from their scarcity.

Spaniards Find no Gold

The early successes of the adventurers, like Pizarro and Cortez, were partly responsible for the failure of the Spanish to discover the metallic riches of the territory which came to be known as the Golden State. They had obtained the supplies of gold accumulated by the Indians with such surprising ease that they fancied it could be picked up from the ground without exertion. This self deception, combined with an indolence bred in their bones, prevented them, when they finally reached the field in which the object of their desires might be gratified, from making use of their opportunities. And thus it came to pass that they sojourned in the country for nearly eighty years unconscious of the fact that they were living in a land of gold, and that diligent search would have rewarded them beyond the dreams of avarice.

Why no Gold was Found

They did not wholly neglect the search; that would have been impossible while the eager desire for the metals was the animating purpose of so many who made their way into the new country. They did hunt for gold after a fashion, but their success was so meager and the reward so scant that the search was not persistent. In a report made by Manuel Victoria in 1831 he declared that no mines worth working had been discovered in the occupied portions of the territory and it was generally believed by those who gave the matter a thought that there were no valua-

A Perfunctory Search

100   SAN FRANCISCO

ble minerals in the country. There were reports that Jedediah S. Smith, the first American who reached California by traveling overland, had found gold in the Sierra Nevada about 1826, but they have not been authenticated and the story, in view of his later exploits and his failure to make further search, seems improbable. The accounts given by Drake's party that the Indians seen by them when they landed had gold in their possession are utterly discredited by the fact that none of the aborigines later encountered by the Spanish had any of the metal. Investigators who have given the subject attention regard the statement concerning gold, and also that which represents the Indians as possessing tobacco, as an interpolation.

Traces of Gold in 1841
It was not until 1841, during the incumbency of Alvarado that Andreas Castilero, the man who afterward discovered the quicksilver mines at New Almaden, saw a number of water-worn pebbles which he said were always found in the vicinity of gold, that interest was excited. A ranchero named Francisco Lopez, who had heard this statement, while pulling up some wild onions at San Francisquito, about thirty-five miles north of Los Angeles, found similar pebbles and immediately began a search for the precious metal and was rewarded by finding some. The news of the discovery soon spread, but the gold hunters were not very lucky and the diggings never were important. But there is no question respecting the genuineness of the discovery, for in 1842 a package containing eighteen ounces was sent East to be assayed at Philadelphia where it was found to be worth $344.

Discovery Causes no Excitement
The discovery created scarce a ripple on the surface of the even life of the missions and on the ranches, and was no factor in the promotion of the interest in California which developed rapidly after 1842. Unlike the Spaniards, whose search for the golden fleece led them to the acquisition of new territory, the Americans appeared to give the possibility of mining little or no consideration. Their thoughts were directed into the broader channel of the creation of wealth by the practice of industry and the pursuit of commerce. If the first Americans who entered the territory heard of the discovery of gold at Los Angeles attached any importance to it, there is no evidence of the fact. The lure of gold was a force that operated later, but its story does not begin until a couple of years after the American flag was floating over Portsmouth square in San Francisco and over the custom house at Monterey.

What Might Have Happened
Those whose arrival anticipated that event had an opportunity to study the question of development uninfluenced by the excitement which attends the extraction of gold and the sudden acquirement of wealth by lucky finds. The problem they were creating for themselves, as it appeared to them, was uncomplicated by questions of rapid transit. They looked forward to the settlement of the country by Americans, but they imagined that the invasion of immigrants would be chiefly by land, and not a few hoped that it would be of the kind that would clear the way for the introduction of slavery and thus settle a question which was continually threatening the destruction of the Union.

Aims of First American Settlers
Men engrossed by ideas of that sort were less inclined to adversely criticize the shortcomings of the people whose places they hoped to usurp, than those who arrived later filled with the lust for gold, and with all the intolerance which consciousness of a wrong done invariably begets. The early Californians who had received large land grants, and who lived upon them in a style which showed that they were strangers to exertion, were not as incomprehensible to the man who hoped to share the land with them as they were to the Yankees and other Eastern men

who had been in the scramble for existence, and who had flocked to the coast with no other purpose than to "make their pile" and return home.

The Missourians and others familiar with the institution of slavery could regard with a lenient eye habits that were not entirely foreign to communities in which servile labor was depended upon almost exclusively, and there is reason to believe that there were many wholly disconnected from the movement for acquisition who would welcome any class of workers who would make it possible to develop the broad lands which the finger of destiny pointed out to them as being intended for their countrymen.

<small>The Missourians</small>

It was the presence of this advance guard in California that facilitated the easy acquisition of the territory. Had the men who were on the ground before Wilkes surveyed the Bay of San Francisco, or who were present when the premature attempt of Thomas Catesby Ap Jones to seize the port of Monterey was made, been of a different material, it is not impossible that they might have dissuaded by their advice and action the projectors from carrying out their purpose which at that time was generally understood to be the addition of more territory to the American Union to permit the expansion of slavery.

<small>Advance Guard of Americans</small>

It is not improbable, however, that other motives were mixed with the predominating one, and it is even susceptible of demonstration that in its inception the desire to secure California was as much felt in the North as in the South. The manifest destiny idea had a strong hold on the popular imagination. It prevailed to such an extent that cunning politicians had no difficulty in making use of it to carry out purposes which were not always apparent on the surface.

The facility with which the dispute on the northern boundary question was turned to the advantage of the advocates of slavery illustrates the ease with which the popular mind could be diverted from the real object of the slave oligarchy, and induced to start in full cry after something else when put on a wrong scent. When the democratic convention which nominated Polk in 1844 demanded "the occupation of Oregon up to fifty-four degrees forty minutes regardless of consequences," such a manifest destiny dust was kicked up that the North was completely blinded. "Fifty-four forty or fight" was the slogan which elected the man who within nine months after his inauguration recommended the speedy settlement of the Oregon boundary question, not by a resort to arms, but by peaceful diplomacy.

<small>Northern Boundary Question</small>

It is not very creditable to the perception of the North that it could be so easily fooled as the events immediately preceding and following the Ashburton treaty imply. When Webster effected the convention there was as much rejoicing over the event as though he had accomplished a remarkable diplomatic feat and saved the country from the consequences of a disastrous war. It is possible that England might have been ready to proceed to extremes if the United States had persisted in its demand that the boundary should be fixed at 54° 40″ North, but it is absolutely certain that Polk had no intention of forcing a war.

<small>Northern People Hoodwinked</small>

The pro-slavery element had other fish to fry at that particular moment. They were too acute to think it possible that the United States could successfully carry on a war on its northern and southern boundaries at the same time, and it had been decided by them that one should be waged against Mexico. Not only were the Southerners determined upon attacking the republic, they were equally determined that their proposed addition of territory on the south and west should

<small>The "54-40 or Fight" Fizzle</small>

102 SAN FRANCISCO

not be balanced by acquisitions on the north which would permit the creation of more free states.

Plotting Slave Owners

These are facts of history and must be related, as they are linked up with the events which led to the occupation of California and its subsequent annexation by conquest. If the warlike cry of "Fifty-four forty or fight" had been a genuine national demand, and had it been backed by force, there might have been a wholly different story to tell. There might, in that event, have been a Pacific coast metropolis at some future day, but its history probably would have been wholly different from that which it has made for itself under American auspices.

Early Efforts to Secure California

It has already been told how Jackson as early as 1839 began his intrigues to secure Mexican territory, and how, in that year, he offered the republic $5,000,000 for Texas, as his overtures to purchase the Bay of San Francisco made in 1835 have also been related. Reference has been made likewise to Waddy Thompson's eulogy of the resources of California, and his suggestion that Mexico might be induced to part with it in settlement of the claims of American citizens. These movements were made with little or no attempt at concealment. Some of them were freely discussed by the American people who read without resenting the suggestions contained in such books as that of Captain Benjamin Morrell of the schooner "Tartar," whose smuggling experiences on the coast had qualified him to speak understandingly, that if the United States had possession of the harbor of San Francisco commerce would be quickly developed and that the resources of the region about the bay, which he described in a fashion calculated to appeal to the manifest destinarian, would be exploited with benefit to the people of California and of the whole world.

Offer Made by President Jackson

The necessities of the whalers and Morrell's description and persuasive arguments probably had a good deal to do with the offer made by Jackson to purchase the Bay of San Francisco, which was accompanied by the proposal that a line should be run northward along the east bank of the Rio del Norte to the 37th parallel and then west to the Pacific. It was diplomatically suggested that Monterey might be excluded, as there was no wish to interfere with the actual settlements of Mexico on the Pacific coast, which implied that the president had ample knowledge of the fact that nothing had been accomplished in the way of development of the shores of the body of water which he sought to gain possession of for the United States.

Question of Acquisition

After 1835, the question of acquisition appears to have been little considered from the commercial side. From that time forward the matter engaged the attention of the Southerners more particularly, and they regarded it solely from the standpoint of the needs of the institution of slavery. The struggle which ensued is part of the history of the nation, and to attempt to describe it would necessitate the relation of the events which led up to the Civil war. San Francisco and California were merely pawns on the political chessboard of the period, but they were often moved with such dexterity that the bigger pieces were endangered, and at no time after the slave-holding element had set its covetous eyes on the territory so glowingly described by Butler, Thompson and others were they wholly negligible quantities.

War Declared Against Mexico

War was declared against Mexico by the United States on the 13th of May, 1846, but hostilities were looked for much earlier by those not behind the scenes, and the result was occasional exhibitions of precipitate action. In 1842 Commodore Jones, on the strength of rumors related to him by the American consul at

Mazatlan, to the effect that the British were negotiating with the Mexicans for the cession of California, set sail for Monterey to head off the supposed intended occupation. The story ran that Great Britain had agreed to take over the province in satisfaction for debts aggregating $50,000,000 owed by Mexicans to British subjects, and it was accompanied by rumors that the expected war between the United States and Mexico had begun.

Jones crowded on sail in order to reach the coast of California first. British war vessels had been cruising off Mexico when the consul reported the alleged negotiations between England and that country and Commodore Jones thought he was engaging in a race for possession. When he arrived at Monterey he promptly summoned Governor Alvarado to surrender, and as the Californian was powerless to resist, he did so, not, however, without demurring to what he regarded as a breach of the rules of war. The American flag was hoisted over the fort or castle and the bloodless victory was celebrated by the victors and those in sympathy with the desire to place California under the protection of the United States. Subsequently, Jones, upon learning of his error, struck his colors, apologized and saluted the Mexican flag. *Commodore Jones' Precipitate Action*

Meanwhile events were occurring in the interior, the significance of which may be as easily understood by the reader as by the Californians who were observing with jealous suspicion the action of certain unwelcome intruders on their soil. In 1842 John C. Fremont made a scientific expedition to the Rocky Mountains and a year later he started on a second trip, his objective this time being Oregon and California. In February, 1844, he crossed the Sierra near Tahoe and descended to the plains, reaching the Sacramento at Sutter's place, New Helvetia, in March. His presence caused a great stir among the defenceless Californians who disbelieved his profession that his mission was purely scientific. *Fremont's Expedition in 1842*

It is not impossible that Fremont was technically within the limits of truth. His mission was undoubtedly scientific in the same sense that an engineer's movements in running lines before a beleaguered fort with the intention of springing a mine under it are scientific. He was undoubtedly performing work of a sort which in certain contingencies might prove very useful and which were curiously linked up with the persistent and oft-expressed desire of Americans to secure the harbor of San Francisco.

In the early Forties the most of the country west of the Missouri river was a *terra incognito*. Land now recognized as the most fertile in the United States was then supposed to be desert. Among the numerous fictions there was one which Fremont had apparently decided upon investigating, because it might prove useful knowledge which could be made to contribute to the success of his enterprise. It was supposed up to the time of Fremont's expedition that there was a river which flowed from the Rocky Mountains to the Bay of San Francisco. This imaginary river was called the San Buenaventura, and had it existed it would have afforded facilities for penetrating the coveted land which an engineer could not afford to overlook. *An Imaginary River*

When he discovered that the San Buenaventura was a myth Fremont made his way to the Sacramento valley and in 1844 he and his party began to be a source of worry to the Californians. About the same time Thomas O. Larkin, acting under instructions, was actively corresponding with Americans supposed to be friendly to the project of occupation. Larkin wrote to Jacob P. Leese at Sonoma, to John *San Buenaventura River a Myth*

Warner at San Diego and Abel Stearns at Los Angeles, all Mexican citizens who, however, despite their relations to Mexico were well disposed towards the United States. The purpose of Larkin was to induce them to engage in the work of bringing about a favorable disposition towards the United States. Conviction and interest prompted them to make the attempt, but as the sequel shows they were not very successful, although they undoubtedly were under the illusion that they were and so reported to the consul, who in turn communicated his information to Washington, producing there an impression that subsequently caused the issuance of some contradictory orders which caused the actors in the absorption drama to play at cross purposes.

Winning Favor for Americans

If at any time Leese and the others succeeded in cultivating the desired favorable impression it was speedily converted into the opposite feeling by Fremont, whose course was the reverse of conciliatory and from the beginning seemed to have been adopted with the view of provoking the Californians to the commission of some act which would afford him an excuse to engage in hostilities. There was no such demonstration during the year 1844, but early in 1846, after a visit to the East, he again made his appearance on the coast with a party of sixty-two. His presence this time created great alarm, for the rumors of impending war were numerous, and the Californians could not help regarding him as an enemy.

Fremont and the Castros

Shortly after his arrival in California Fremont visited Castro at Monterey and attempted to allay the fear created by the presence of the small band of Americans by giving the Californians to understand that they were on their way to Oregon. Castro professed to accept these assurances but it is quite evident that he placed no faith in them, for a few days afterward while Fremont and his men were encamped in the Gabilan Mountains, about thirty miles east of Monterey, they were ordered to leave the country. These orders, which were accompanied by threats that if they were not complied with forcible means would be used to expel the Americans, were sent by Manuel Castro, the prefect, and Jose Castro, the commandante of Monterey, who were acting in conformity with instructions sent from Mexico, which also embraced directions to get rid of the families of Americans who had established themselves on the frontiers.

Collision with the Natives

Fremont's only reply to the Castros was to retire to a ridge of the Gabilans, where he posted his men in full view of the Californians at San Juan Bautista and hoisted the American flag. Nothing came of the "defy." The Californians did not attack, and Fremont in a little while retired from his position "growling," as he subsequently wrote in describing the affair. He evidently did not feel warranted in bringing on a collision unless he could put the onus of it upon the Californians, and as they failed to attack, he withdrew, marching leisurely towards the Sacramento, keeping along its banks in the direction of Oregon, no one attempting to follow or molest him.

Fremont's Provocative Policy

Just what influenced his movements, after what can only be regarded as a feint, is a matter of surmise rather than accurate knowledge. It is supposed, however, that Lieutenant Gillespie, who arrived on the "Cyane," April 16, 1846, brought dispatches to Fremont from his father-in-law, Senator Benton, or the war department. These were delivered to him at Sutter's fort and after their receipt there was no further pretense of continuing the march to Oregon.

After receiving the dispatches Fremont evidently resumed his policy of provoking an attack while keeping appearances in his favor. But events were rapidly shaping which were to have the effect of spoiling his plans and to deprive him of the glory which he was seeking. The Bear Flag movement, which has been attributed to Fremont, had begun. The Americans living in the Sacramento valley, alarmed by the prospect of being attacked if they did not take precautions for their safety, banded together for defense under the leadership of William B. Ide. To the latter, and not to Fremont, belongs the honor, if any attaches to the Bear Flag uprising or its accomplishments, for it is quite clear from the evidence that the plan of the Missourian did not contemplate a declaration of independence, or the pursuit of tactics such as had been resorted to by the Americans in Texas.

Fremont desired to enlist the assistance of American settlers to carry out a scheme which he thought would provoke an attack from Castro. This plan was undoubtedly not in harmony with the ideas of the authorities in Washington, who had been led to believe by the letters of Larkin, and from other information, that the people were quite ready to accept American rule, and that no serious opposition to taking possession of the country would be offered by the native Californians. Evidently the Americans headed by Ide and Fremont did not share this confidence. They were perhaps in a better position to judge than Larkin and those with whom he advised, for with them the wish was father to the thought, while the isolated American settlers, who, perhaps, had good reason to fear for themselves, knew that a bitter animosity existed against the gringo which could not be allayed by a bit of diplomacy. Washington Authorities Misled

In joining the names of Fremont and Ide it is necessary to point out that the association was not entirely voluntary so far as the former was concerned. Fremont had planned to compel the Californians to attack him, always keeping in mind his object of making it appear that the natives were the aggressors. To that end he caused a band of horses belonging to Castro to be seized by a party of his men under the command of Lieutenant King. The latter, before making the capture, had asked Ide and the other Americans with him what they would do in event of the seizure. Their answer was that there would be nothing left for them to do but to make a rush on Sonoma. The question put by King was merely in the nature of preparation and was not framed with the view of eliciting advice, for while the discussion was under way the horses were being stolen by the lieutenant's men, who shortly rode up to the party with the captured animals. They related that they had sent word to Castro that if he wanted them back to come and take them. Fremont and Ide

There was then no other course left for the Americans than to act promptly, and they did so. They agreed that if things went wrong, and the expected war did not break out, that they would be put in the position of horse thieves, and that it might go hard with them. Accordingly the rush on Sonoma, which made some slight pretense of being a stronghold, having nine brass cannon and a provision of muskets, followed and the place was captured. The victory was a bloodless one and was celebrated indifferently by captors and captives, but not by the adherents of Fremont, a few of whom were in the attacking force. There was an attempt made by a man named Grigsby, while the men under Ide were awaiting the dawn to make the advance on Vallejo's house, the most important on the Plaza, in which the defenders had assembled, to persuade the Americans to abandon their purpose. Grigsby was accused of being inspired by Fremont, who had shown his disapproval of the project. His arguments, however, were not sufficiently strong to allay the fear of Ide's men that unless a warlike act were committed they would be put in a dangerous position, from which they might find it difficult to extricate themselves. Capture of Sonoma

SAN FRANCISCO

Ide's Declaration of Independence

This fear shaped the policy of Ide, who as soon as Sonoma had surrendered began the preparation of a declaration of independence which set forth the grievances of the settlers. In it the charge was made that they had been invited to settle, but that they were denied the right to buy or rent lands; that they were oppressed by a military government and were threatened with extermination. The government was arraigned for its shortcomings and maladministration, and it was asserted that the property of the missions had been seized for the aggrandizement of individuals. From beginning to end the document contained evidence of a desire to include the native Californian in the protest; and that the latter, who were assembled in Sonoma, for the time being, regarded it as much an affair of their own as of the Americans is attested by the fact that all present joined in its acceptance with enthusiasm, which may have been helped along by copious libations of the freely dispensed aguardiente.

Independent Republic Proposed

The declaration of independence was plainly the preliminary to the establishment of an independent republic. In part it was directly addressed to the native Californians, who were urged to join Ide in his undertaking, which he declared was as much intended for their benefit as to assert the rights of American settlers. But Ide was not in a position to push any plan he may have conceived or wished to carry out. Fremont disapproved of the movement and when Ide suggested that a hundred muskets be provided to arm men on the south side of the bay who were ready to rise he flatly refused.

Hoisting of the Bear Flag

The declaration of independence prepared by Ide was preceded by the hoisting of the Bear Flag, a rudely designed emblem, the execution of which scarcely matched the conception, as the animal depicted by the painter has been criticized as bearing a closer resemblance to a pig than the formidable grizzly it was meant to portray. As soon as Fremont heard of what had been done he hastened to Sonoma from Sutter's fort, where he was during the time of the attack. When he met Ide he began to upbraid him, but he soon realized the impolicy of such a course, and took steps which resulted in effecting something like a satisfactory arrangement. A convention of all the Americans was called to meet at Sonoma on July 5th, and when assembled Fremont explained that as a representative of the United States he could not interfere in California politics, but he urged that it was desirable for all to stand together. Ide and his associates still retained their fear and insisted that unless they put themselves in the position of revolutionaries they might be regarded and treated as bandits in the event of the failure of Fremont's enterprise.

Elimination of Ide by Fremont

It required manipulation to accomplish Fremont's object of eliminating Ide, but he succeeded in his efforts. A pledge drawn up by Ide, which required all signing it to stick together until the object of attaining a full degree of rational liberty was achieved, did not prove satisfactory to Fremont, who managed to have the committee dealing with it increased to three, which formulated a document to his liking, but he could not prevent Ide putting forward a minority report in which he presented his views. Two days after the adoption of the majority report the Bear Flag, with its single star and grizzly, with the words "California Republic" beneath it, was hauled down and the American flag was hoisted in its place.

Whether Ide's plan if it had not been interfered with could have been carried out no one can tell. It is not impossible that owing to the distance from the central authority that a revolution might have proved successful, in which event the same process which effected the acquisition of Texas would have been resorted to, for California, like the vast state north of the Rio Grande, was predestined to fall into American hands. The only question of interest connected with the different methods of procedure is that raised by the subsequent hostilities which undoubtedly were responsible for a great deal of bad feeling that might have been overcome by following a plan which would have seemed to give the Californians a voice in the disposition of the territory they had so long occupied.

That the authorities in Washington hoped that the acquisition of California could be effected without bloodshed is reasonably certain. When Commodore Sloat arrived on the second of July, apparently acting under instructions, he issued a proclamation saying that he had come as a friend of California, and up to the day of the transfer of his command to Commodore Stockton he persisted in his efforts to smooth over matters, Stockton on the other hand fell in with the views of Fremont, and issued a proclamation in which he took the absurd stand that he was present in California to protect the natives against such men as Castro. Sloat subsequently wrote to the secretary of the navy to inform him that Stockton did not truly present his (Sloat's) reasons for taking possession of the country. These he said were to be found in his proclamation of July 7, 1846, at the hoisting of the flag, in which he promised the inhabitants that they should enjoy the same rights and privileges they were then in possession of; that they should choose their own magistrates and other officers for the administration of justice among themselves, and that the same protection would be accorded to them as to the other parts of the Union. He also predicted the rapid advancement of agriculture and commerce and a career of prosperity. *No Bloodshed Anticipated*

These promises and predictions might have produced a different result had Fremont and Stockton cooperated to bring it about, but they adopted a course which prevented a graceful acceptance of conditions by the Californians, and precipitated a war in which neither side covered itself with glory, but which was speedily terminated by the superior force and resources of the Americans. The story of the conflict is not part of the history of San Francisco. It was wholly confined to the South, to which the leaders of the native Californians with their followers had fled. *Unfulfilled Promises*

At its conclusion, and even before the signing of the treaty of peace, a disposition to adapt themselves to the new conditions was shown by the Californians. They gave no signs of being enthusiastic over the promise of material improvement which the occupation held forth, their attitude was simply one of acquiescence in results. Whether they really believed that Commodore Sloat's predictions would be realized it would be hard to tell, but it is permissible to say that they showed no signs of desire to contribute to the result. What was accomplished was wholly due to American effort. After the raising of the flag at Monterey and over Portsmouth square in San Francisco the native Californian ceased to be a factor in the history of the state or City. *Californians Adapt Themselves to the Change*

THE PIONEERING PERIOD
1846 1861

CHAPTER XVI

ACQUISITION OF CALIFORNIA BY THE UNITED STATES

THE CONQUEST OF CALIFORNIA—YERBA BUENA—EARLY INHABITANTS OF THE VILLAGE—ARRIVAL OF MORMONS—THE DONNER PARTY—YERBA BUENA GROWING—OCCUPATIONS OF THE FIRST SETTLERS—COMMERCE OF THE PORT IN 1847—TEMPTING THE WHALERS—TRADE WITH NEW MEXICO—THE MISSION DOLORES—MISSION ARCHITECTURE—YERBA BUENA CHANGED TO SAN FRANCISCO—FIRST REAL ESTATE TRANSACTIONS—THE ORIGINAL STREETS OF YERBA BUENA.

NEARLY eighty years had elapsed between the date of the establishment of the first mission in San Diego and the occupation of California by the Americans and at the end of that interval the white population of the territory was still so insignificant that a handful of strangers found no difficulty in wresting it from its possessors.

Conquest of California

The Greeks vaunted the march of the 10,000 and the conquerors of England have had the story of their exploit told by a score of historians; the piratical excursion of Pizarro and his overturning of the Inca civilization, and the performance of Cortez in Mexico have all been duly recounted by writers who found themselves unable to divest their narratives of something like admiration for the conquerors even while denouncing the motives of the invaders whose feats of arms they recorded. But no Xenophon or Prescott has yet arisen to tell the story of the invasion of California as it will be told when the impression produced upon the world by what the awakening conscience of the period could not help regarding as an unscrupulous act of land grabbing has faded away.

Some day when kindly time has softened the asperities of criticism, and when results are regarded as of more importance than the mode of achieving them, some one will set the happenings in California in the years immediately preceding 1846 in such a form that only the brilliant fact will stand forth that a handful of men achieved the conquest of what in the fullness of time is destined to be the Empire state of the American Union.

The Verdict of Time

When the time for writing the story arrives the author will tell that in 1803 Humboldt, in an essay, estimated that the entire population of California did not exceed nine thousand, and that this small number had only increased to ten or twelve thousand when the covetous American laid hands on the neglected territory and put it to the uses which Nature had designed it for; and if he is given to making startling comparisons he will relate how in less than four years after that act of depredation had been committed, the 12,000 had multiplied more than twenty-fold.

He will also describe the wonderful metamorphosis of the village of Yerba

112   SAN FRANCISCO

Buena, which in the midsummer of 1846 contained only two hundred people, indifferently accommodated in forty or fifty houses, but which eight years later had grown to be a city of 50,000 inhabitants, whose name was known to the whole world and was on the lips of all men. He will not, however, lightly pass over the few years in which this extraordinary growth was effected, for they were filled with events, some of them serious and tragic enough to have a place in history, and others not so grave but equally interesting because the actors in them were unlike any ever before gathered together in so short a time, unless perhaps the motley throng which rushed to Colchis in search of the "Golden Fleece" may have formed such an assemblage.

Yerba Buena in 1847

Descending to minute particulars we find that in the first year after the occupation there were 459 residents of Yerba Buena, the place that is now San Francisco; and that of this number 375 were whites, the remainder being Sandwich islanders, Indians and negroes. Of the whites 268 were adults. The 107 children were made up of 51 under 5 years of age, 32 who were between 5 and 10 and 24 between 15 and 20. Of Indians there were only 34, and they like the 10 negroes, were chiefly in domestic service. The 40 Sandwich islanders were almost all sailors, Captain Richardson, and the few others engaged in transportation, finding them the only material available for that purpose, the native Californian having no liking for the water, and still less for the work attendant upon the navigation and the loading and unloading of the few craft on the bay.

A Cosmopolitan Population

The composition of the population of Yerba Buena in 1847 foreshadowed the cosmopolitanism which later became so marked a characteristic of San Francisco. As might have been expected the largest part of the addition during the first year of occupation was made up of whites born in the United States. There were 228 who called themselves Americans, 38 Californians, 2 from other Mexican departments, 5 Canadians, 2 Chileans, 22 Englishmen, 3 Frenchmen, 27 Germans, 14 Irish, 14 Scotch, 6 Swiss, 4 born at sea and Peru, Poland, Russia, Sweden, the West Indies, Denmark, New Holland and New Zealand had one representative each.

Occupations of the Villagers

There is scant information concerning the occupations of these first settlers of the future metropolis of the Pacific, but we know that among them were numbered a fair proportion of adventurers, who had come to spy out the land. A regiment formed in New York, which Colonel Jonathan Stevenson commanded, had the reputation of being made up of men especially selected with reference to their habits, the idea being that at the conclusion of the war they would settle in California, but how many of them remained in San Francisco after the disbandment of the command is not accurately known. During 1846 and 1847 a large number of immigrants journeyed over the Rockies. These latter were chiefly from what would now be called the middle west and the most of them were farmers, and their purpose was to settle on the land. That was also the object of a colony of Mormons, formed in the Eastern states, which was among the first considerable bodies of men to enter the port of San Francisco.

Prospective Agriculturists

These prospective agriculturists contributed something to the growth of the new town. They arrived from New York on a vessel called the "Brooklyn," on July 31, 1846. Before reaching California they had quarreled among themselves. They were headed by Samuel Brannan, who had joined them in 1842 and published a newspaper for the cult. He is credited with having conceived the idea of settling on the Bay of San Francisco, but the party which left on the "Brooklyn" in Feb-

SAN FRANCISCO 113

ruary of 1846 gave out that their destination was to be Oregon. Their undoubted purpose, however, was to establish a tabernacle on the shores of the bay, and to accomplish that end they expected to secure a concession from the Mexican government.

The changed condition of affairs frustrated their plans. The occupation of California cut off all hopes of negotiating with Mexico but it did not deter the colonists from attempting to effect a settlement. They had been driven from the East by public sentiment, but they probably hoped that in the new and sparsely settled country there would be less antagonism, and this emboldened them to make the attempt to remain on the shores of the bay, and accordingly they made a camp in the sand hills near Yerba Buena. The Mormon colonists numbered 238, and they were provided with many of the essentials of a modern town. Among these was a printing plant, which produced the "California Star," a weekly paper, the first number of which was issued January 9, 1847. *Mormon Colonists*

Their neighbors at Yerba Buena apparently made no objections to their presence, and it is among the possibilities that these Mormons, had not the gold rush which took place in 1848 completely submerged them, might have succeeded in creating a mart of commerce as successfully as members of their peculiar sect subsequently created a prosperous agricultural community in the region about the Great Salt Lake of Utah. The discovery of the precious metals brought them good fortune, but it also resulted in serious dissensions, which finally disrupted the colony. Brannan, who was the high priest of the church, had assumed the right to collect tithes, but the prospects of securing wealth independently had weakened the ties which bound the brethren together, and his privilege was challenged. One of their number, William S. Clarke, refused to pay, and when the others saw that Brannan lacked the power to enforce they imitated his example. Brannan, who had already collected sufficient to lay the ground work of a fortune when his tithes were cut off, refused to recognize the claims of the church and the association dissolved. *Gold Discovery Disrupts Mormon Plans*

There is little to record of commercial or social activity in Yerba Buena until the discovery of gold at Sutter's mill in 1848. Emigrants were leaving the East in considerable numbers during 1847 and their movements occupied the minds of the settlers on the bay, who evidently looked upon them as the agency which would result in promoting the realization of their expectation, that their little village would develop into a seaport of consequence. Occasionally they were called upon to render assistance to emigrants who had miscalculated the demands that would be made upon them in their hazardous journey from civilization to the promised land of California. *Social Activities*

The "California Star" of April 10, 1847, relates the doings of a relief meeting, at which $1,500 were subscribed for fitting out an expedition to go to the relief of the Donner party in the Sierra. Of some eighty persons who composed the original company, thirty-six perished. Horrible stories of the condition to which the emigrants were reduced were told, and one of them named Kingsbury was charged with cannibalism. The accused man denied the charge, but evidence that he had taken the precaution to salt down parts of several bodies, induced the relief party to believe that he had committed a number of murders and it was with difficulty that they were dissuaded from hanging him. Kingsbury lived several years in Brighton, near Sacramento, with two idiotic children, and protested his innocence *The Donner Party*

Vol. I—8

to the last. That his life was spared was wholly owing to the impression created by the horrible sufferings to which the party was reduced by starvation.

Signs of Improvement

Despite the lack of recorded information of the social and other happenings of the little community in 1847, we can form some sort of an idea of what occurred. In the absence of any mention of serious trouble we may assume that the residents of Yerba Buena occupied themselves pretty much as a similar number of people gathered in any small village would. But, even in this early stage of the career of the place, they took account of the callings and the accomplishments of the inhabitants and from the recital we may gather that the new society differed in a marked fashion from any that had previously existed in California.

Mechanic Arts and Professions

In the days of Spanish and Mexican rule there was absolutely no disposition on the part of the better element to engage in professional work, the mechanical arts were almost wholly neglected, commerce was at an exceedingly low ebb and there was a close approach to general illiterateness. One year after American occupation Yerba Buena in its population of nearly five hundred boasted 273 who could read and write, and 13 who could read but not write. It acknowledged to 89 who could do neither, but they were children under ten years of age. We have no account of what they read and wrote, excepting that they had an opportunity to peruse the weekly "California Star," but we may be assured that the new settlers had brought with them more books than California had gathered in all the years before the gringo began to rule.

Occupations of First Residents

The list of occupations of the inhabitants of the settlement is in striking contrast to that which could have been made up for any other town in California at that date. It embraced 1 minister, 3 doctors, 3 lawyers, 2 surveyors, 1 school teacher, 11 agriculturists, 2 gunsmiths, 4 masons, 7 bakers, 6 blacksmiths, 1 brewer, 6 brickmakers, 7 butchers, 2 cabinet makers, 3 hotel keepers, 11 merchants, 26 carpenters, 1 cigar maker, 13 clerks, 3 coopers, 1 gardener, 5 grocers, 20 laborers, 1 miner, 1 morocco case maker, 6 inland navigators, 1 ocean navigator, 1 painter, 6 printers, 1 saddler, 4 shoemakers, 1 silversmith, 4 tailors, 2 tanners, 1 watchmaker and 1 weaver.

Men Doing for Themselves

This represented a diversification of callings that must have seemed astonishing to the most enterprising of native Californians, whose desires were never strong enough to advance them beyond the stage of attempting to gratify any but primary needs. We may be sure that the work of some of these new comers must have proved as surprising a revelation to the earlier occupants of the soil as Hinckley's effort at bridging a slough had been a few years earlier. That men should do for themselves seemed queer to those who had been accustomed to letting nature do for them; and, perhaps, like the Indians, they regarded with contempt a people so silly as to exert themselves merely for the purpose of producing things which they had found themselves able to dispense with.

Gambling in Yerba Buena

There was one feature of early California life which was promptly grafted onto the transplanted industrial stock of Yerba Buena, and that was the love of social diversion. It has already been related how Jacob Leese launched his new house, the first in the place, with a banquet, at which all the people of consequence who could get to it were assembled. Necessarily a feast at that time was followed by a dance and this custom appears to have been liberally imitated by Leese's neighbors, who neglected no opportunity that would afford an excuse for a ball.

SAN FRANCISCO   115

It is said that the Americans exhibited as marked an inclination for dancing as the
natives, even if they did not so readily acquire as much proficiency in the art.

With this harmless amusement there had long been associated the gambling <small>Attempts to Check Gambling</small>
vice. No fiesta was ever celebrated by the native Californians at which the pro-
fessional gamester was not in evidence. The Americans seem to have taken kindly
to the peculiar games of the Spanish speaking people, and they introduced a few
of their own. The practice of gaming must have grown rapidly and assumed a
form distasteful to the new community, for at the opening of the year 1848 the
authorities ordered that "all moneys found on a gambling table where cards are
played" should be seized. The spasm of virtue was a short one, however, as the
order was repealed at the next meeting of the council. The recital of this little incident suggests the necessity of accepting with caution the assumption of those
writers who later attempted to account for the deliquencies of early San Francisco
by attributing them to the riff-raff who came in with the "gold rush."

In the list of occupations above quoted there was no mention of servants, but <small>Servant Problem</small>
the 500 inhabitants of Yerba Buena had that problem to deal with as well as those
who came after them. There does not seem to have been any scarcity of domestic
help, but it was of a nondescript sort, made up chiefly of Indians, Sandwich islanders and negroes who formed about one-fifth of the population. Respecting the
qualifications of these servants, who were chiefly males, we have little information,
perhaps because the love of the cuisine and other creature comforts which developed so speedily after the placers began yielding their nuggets and dust had not
yet begun to manifest itself.

The surprisingly small number set down in the list of occupations as navigators <small>Few Seafar- ing Men</small>
indicates that the new port had not as yet begun to realize the expectations of those
who had predicted a great future for the harbor of San Francisco. The six inland
navigators mentioned probably comprised the crews of the two schooners operated
by Captain Richardson, and the ocean navigator was doubtless the captain himself,
who sought to distinguish between a mere sailor on the bay and one who had earned
his rank serving on deep sea ships. The statistics of the commerce of the port
for the year 1847 bear out the assumption that the maritime activity of the port
in that year was not calculated to greatly alarm its rival at Monterey.

The value of the exports of Yerba Buena in 1847 was $49,597.53 and of the <small>Commerce of Yerba Buena in 1847</small>
imports $53,589.73. Care was taken by the statistician to note that $30,353.35 of
the amount exported represented California products, of which $21,448 went to
the Sandwich islands and Peru; $560 to Mazatlan; $7,285 to Sitka and $700 to
Tahiti. The imports were chiefly from the United States, Chile, Oregon and the
Sandwich islands, aggregating $31,740. Sitka, Bremen and Mexico also figured in
the table of imports, which did not distinguish very clearly between foreign and
coastwise trade.

The chief part of the California produce exported to the Sandwich islands was <small>Whalers Not En- couraged</small>
destined for the use of whalers, who by this time had fallen into the habit of win-
tering in the ports of the group. The policy of the Spanish and their successors,
the Mexicans, had effectually succeeded in depriving the inhabitants of California
of this valuable trade, the importance of which may be inferred from the fact that
in 1855 there were as many as 500 vessels engaged in the whale taking industry
of the North Pacific, and that they were all compelled to resort to ports in temperate
regions during the winter months. As early as 1826 Captain Beechey reported

116   SAN FRANCISCO

that he found seven whalers anchored at Sausalito, where they were enabled to obtain fresh water, supplies of fire wood being cut on near-by Angel island.

Whalers Praise California

The whalers found the Bay of San Francisco greatly to their liking, and, as already related, it was their glowing accounts of the surrounding country (concerning whose soil they seemed to have formed a better judgment than the Americans who rushed to California to search for gold) that directed the attention of the people of the East toward the desirability of acquisition. Perhaps these suggestive reports were in part responsible for the policy of trade restriction which drove the whalers to the islands to secure the supplies which were begrudged them by the short-sighted rulers of California.

Americans Offer Inducements

The Americans after their establishment in Yerba Buena immediately began considering a complete reversal of the Mexican policy. There were discussions of the value of the trade and a disposition to offer inducements was shown which had they been extended, must ultimately have had the effect of greatly increasing the business of the port. The value of the fisheries, and the trade incident to the pursuit of the whaling industry were well understood, and it is not improbable, had not attention been diverted to other sources of wealth, that the development of the salmon and cod fisheries, which began several years later would have been anticipated.

Hudson Bay Company

The Russian American Company had abandoned Fort Ross before the close of Mexican rule, but it was not until 1846 that the Hudson Bay Company, which had preserved amicable relations with the Californians and had been accorded hunting privileges, disposed of its property in Yerba Buena and retired from the scene. This left the region about the Bay of San Francisco to American trappers and hunters, who made good use of their opportunities and contributed to the growing importance of the port; but the principal business of the latter remained the same as during the regime of the Mexicans, the chief surplus products available for export being hides and tallow. These were gathered from the ranches about the bay, and with such assiduity that with the assistance of the padres, who had been compelled to abandon stock raising and had disposed of their herds, the country, which had formerly been overrun with cattle, promised to go to the other extreme of disregard of what was once its main dependence for subsistence.

Trade With New Mexico

Some fifteen or sixteen years before the American occupation a trade of some importance had sprung up between New Mexico and California but it was mainly confined to the southern part of the territory. The New Mexicans produced a blanket, which met the approval of the Californians, and a well woven serape. These articles were brought to Los Angeles by caravans, which traveled by the route that afterward became the chosen one of emigrants moving from the southwestern states into California, and were exchanged for mules. A more energetic people than those living in Los Angeles at that time would have built up a distributing trade, but it does not appear that efforts were made by the merchants in that part of California to supply the rest of the territory with New Mexican blankets and serapes, and the commercial intercourse between New Mexico and California, which was considerable in 1839-40, had ceased entirely before the outbreak of hostilities.

Newcomers Enterprising

One of the earliest exhibitions of enterprise of the newcomers in Yerba Buena was an attempt to supply the blanket and serape requirements of the Californians by a substitute which would be as acceptable as the New Mexican product had formerly been to the natives. The merchants were not under the illusion that a change

that he found seven whalers anchored at Sausalito, where they were enabled to obtain fresh water, supplies of fire wood being cut on near-by Angel island.

Whalers Praise California   The whalers found the Bay of San Francisco greatly to their liking, and, as already related, it was their glowing accounts of the surrounding country (concerning whose soil they seemed to have formed a better judgment than the Americans who rushed to California to search for gold) that directed the attention of the people of the East toward the desirability of acquisition. Perhaps these suggestive reports were in part responsible for the policy of trade restriction which drove the whalers to the islands to secure the supplies which were begrudged them by the short-sighted rulers of California.

Americans Offer Inducements   The Americans after their establishment in Yerba Buena immediately began considering a complete reversal of the Mexican policy. There were discussions of the value of the trade and a disposition to offer inducements was shown which had they been extended, must ultimately have had the effect of greatly increasing the business of the port. The value of the fisheries, and the trade incident to the pursuit of the whaling industry were well understood, and it is not improbable, had not attention been diverted to other sources of wealth, that the development of the salmon and cod fisheries, which began several years later would have been anticipated.

Hudson Bay Company   The Russian American Company had abandoned Fort Ross before the close of Mexican rule, but it was not until 1846 that the Hudson Bay Company, which had preserved amicable relations with the Californians and had been accorded hunting privileges, disposed of its property in Yerba Buena and retired from the scene. This left the region about the Bay of San Francisco to American trappers and hunters, who made good use of their opportunities and contributed to the growing importance of the port; but the principal business of the latter remained the same as during the regime of the Mexicans, the chief surplus products available for export being hides and tallow. These were gathered from the ranches about the bay, and with such assiduity that with the assistance of the padres, who had been compelled to abandon stock raising and had disposed of their herds, the country, which had formerly been overrun with cattle, promised to go to the other extreme of disregard of what was once its main dependence for subsistence.

Trade With New Mexico   Some fifteen or sixteen years before the American occupation a trade of some importance had sprung up between New Mexico and California but it was mainly confined to the southern part of the territory. The New Mexicans produced a blanket, which met the approval of the Californians, and a well woven serape. These articles were brought to Los Angeles by caravans, which traveled by the route that afterward became the chosen one of emigrants moving from the southwestern states into California, and were exchanged for mules. A more energetic people than those living in Los Angeles at that time would have built up a distributing trade, but it does not appear that efforts were made by the merchants in that part of California to supply the rest of the territory with New Mexican blankets and serapes, and the commercial intercourse between New Mexico and California, which was considerable in 1839-40, had ceased entirely before the outbreak of hostilities.

Newcomers Enterprising   One of the earliest exhibitions of enterprise of the newcomers in Yerba Buena was an attempt to supply the blanket and serape requirements of the Californians by a substitute which would be as acceptable as the New Mexican product had formerly been to the natives. The merchants were not under the illusion that a change

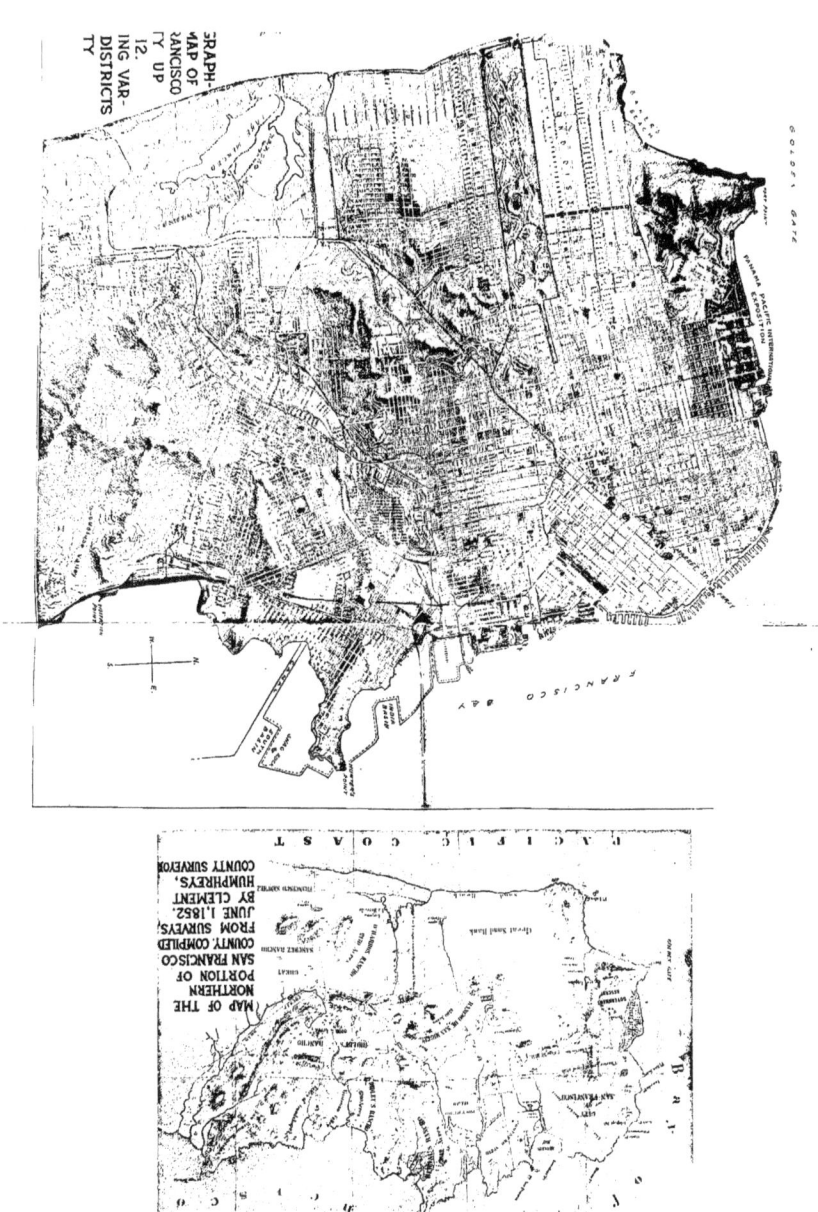

of flag would effect a revolution in Californian habits and dress. Perhaps they regarded the latter as more picturesque than that of the Americans. At any rate, it is a well attested fact that the serape retained its hold on the Californian affection for many years after the occupation. It distinguished the native from the American down to very recent times, and may still be seen in some of the southern counties of the state from which the language of the Spaniard and his habits have not been wholly banished.

The final extinction of the missions was accomplished under the decree of May 28, 1845, and a supplementary one of September 10th, but two years before that date the Mission Dolores, the near neighbor of Yerba Buena, had fallen into a deplorable state. In 1843 the Indians of that establishment numbered only eight, the remnant of the once large congregation. They were plunged in the depths of indigence, nakedness and hunger was their lot, and they were utterly destitute of property of any kind. This little band was composed of aged people, who had worked all their lives, but had nothing to show for their toil. They were probably too feeble to do more than protest, and what their ultimate fate may have been is not recorded. On October 28, 1845, Pio Pico had issued an order directing the sale of San Rafael, Dolores and other missions, and in the proclamation the doubtful privilege was accorded the Indians of doing for themselves.

Deplorable State of Mission Dolores

In accordance with this proclamation Dolores was sold at auction and passed into private ownership. The newcomers in Yerba Buena had little opportunity, therefore, to judge of the missionary system from the evidence presented by disestablished Dolores. What they knew about it was gained from earlier observers who recorded their impressions. Even if Dolores had survived without impairment down to the date of occupation, it would hardly have furnished a fair sample of the more prosperous establishments in other parts of the territory, for it lacked many of the features which had made an impression on several visitors who have recorded what they saw in books or letters.

Mission Dolores Sold at Auction

The mission buildings of California were generally of one type, but in some more attention was paid to architectural effect than in others. The description of San Luis Rey, so far as its practical features were concerned, would nearly fit that of all the establishments. The buildings of that mission enclosed an area of about 80 or 90 square yards, in the center of which was a fountain of pure water. The buildings around the courtyard were divided into separate apartments for the missionaries and the major domos, and with store rooms, work shops, hospitals and rooms for unmarried males and females.

Mission Buildings

Near at hand was the home of the superintendent and a guard house, usually occupied by ten or twelve soldiers. In the rear were granaries and store houses for maize, beans, peas and other products, and near them were corrals, in which carts and such other vehicles as the missions owned were kept. In the vicinity of these were two gardens, in which vegetables were grown, and some fruit trees. The ranches worked by the Indians were a few lengths distant.

Arrangement of Mission Buildings

San Luis Rey, however, was more attractive architecturally than many of the other missions. Its front was ornamented with a long corridor supported by 32 arches, and inclosed by latticed railings, which afforded protection from the inclement weather to the padres in winter and from the hot sun in summer. The church at the end of the corridor gave the whole an aspect which made a distinctly favorable impression on travelers. The church of San Luis Rey was built of stone, and

118   SAN FRANCISCO

its interior was decorated with numerous pictures, very highly colored, some of which, however, were not without merit.

Modest Buildings in San Francisco — The mission buildings at San Francisco or Dolores were much more modest. The church was built of adobe, as were the other structures used for residential purposes and storehouses. There was nothing striking about them, and they would never have served as an inspiration to succeeding architects. Already, in 1854, all the buildings but the church were little better than a confused heap of dried mud, a condition to which the adobe is speedily reduced when neglected. The old church, however, is still preserved and is the only remaining monument in San Francisco of the days of the missions. The castillo or fort at the presidio had fallen into decay before the occupation. A few guns of small caliber were still mounted, but neglect and rust had overtaken them, and they were of no value except to serve as hitching posts, a use to which they were put later.

Development of Mission Architecture — It has been suggested that mission construction had its inspiration from a combination of causes, among them a recognition of the fact that California was subject to earthquakes, and to the fear of the incursions of Indians, but it is more than probable that the character of the material employed in building compelled the main feature, that of thick fortress-like walls. The adobe did not lend itself to a light or graceful style of construction, and there was nothing left to the builders but to depend upon mass and line for effect. Perhaps they did not give the subject half as much thought as the modern critic, who has found beauties where the original builders only aimed at securing results.

The Presidio — The mission and presidio were widely separated in San Francisco. The latter was at first constructed of palisades, but these were replaced by adobe walls in 1778. It is quite certain when the presidio buildings were erected there was no longer any fear of Indian uprisings, but the original style of single story, white-washed adobes, with roofs of red tiles, seen in other parts of the province, was adhered to by the builders and sixty years later the same style of construction was still pursued. Richardson built an adobe house on what is now Dupont street, west of Portsmouth square and a widow named Juana Briones caused another to be erected on the spot that is now the corner of Powell and Filbert streets.

Russian Establishment in Yerba Buena — The Russians had an establishment, the building of which was constructed of slabs covered with tarpaulin. This and the store of Leese, which presented some peculiarities, were the only structures that distinguished Yerba Buena from other Mexican villages in 1846, but in the early part of that year the annalist tells us there began to be an improvement. It is doubtful, however, whether the lumber substitutes for adobe, which the Americans provided for themselves, had any real advantage over the style they displaced. The flimsy wooden structures were certainly not as warm as the adobes, although hygienically they marked a distinct step in advance as they were sometimes provided with floors, which could be cleansed.

Name of Yerba Buena Changed to San Francisco — Perhaps the most important event of the two years preceding the gold discovery was the official act of Alcalde Washington A. Bartlett, who on the 30th of January, 1847, issued an ordinance which was published in the "California Star" of that date to the effect that as the use of the name Yerba Buena was liable to lead to confusion, owing to the fact that the town was designated on the public map as San Francisco, he ordered that thereafter it should be so called in all official documents.

Back of Bartlett's action, however, was an attempt, which proved successful,

SAN FRANCISCO 119

to head off an ambitious rival. On the 15th of September, 1846, Mariano G. Vallejo, of Sonoma, and Robert Semple, of Monterey, formed a project of creating a town on the Straits of Carquinez, which they purposed naming the City of Francisca, after one of the Christian names of Vallejo's wife. This document was presented to Alcalde Bartlett for record on January 19, 1847, and he objected to the similarity of the designation and refused to accede to the request. Vallejo, Semple, and Thomas O. Larkin protested, but Bartlett remained firm and they accepted the situation, choosing another of Señora Vallejo's Christian names, that of Benicia. From that date the title Yerba Buena was dropped, and the town, including the mission, came to be known as San Francisco.

In all the years intervening between the promulgation of the ordinance by Governor Figueroa, which prohibited the granting of lands around Yerba Buena cove nearer than 200 varas from the beach, which was followed by the laying out of the "Street of the Foundation," there appears to have been no movement in real estate until the Americans took charge of affairs. As already stated, a survey was made in 1839, under the direction of Alcalde Haro, but it was not followed by any active demand for lots. A sudden change in this attitude of indifference took place in 1847, when the principal part of the town was laid out in fifty vara lots. Seven hundred and fifty of these were surveyed, and 450 that had been applied for were sold by the alcalde at a nominal price. The amount demanded for fifty varas was $12, to which were added the charges for deed and recording, making the cost to the purchaser $16.   *Earliest Real Estate Transactions*

The buyers of these lots were required to inclose them with fences and to build upon them within a year, under penalty of reversion in case of failure to comply with the regulation. In addition to the 750 fifty vara lots there were also sold lots 100 varas square, six of which formed a block bounded by streets on the four sides. The price established for these lots was $25 each, plus the cost of the deed and recording which, as in the case of the 50 vara lots, was $4.   *Restrictions on Buyers of Lots*

The streets as originally laid out in Yerba Buena were only 60 feet wide, but in the new survey none was less than 70 feet in width, and one broad thoroughfare of 110 feet was provided. The expectation that San Francisco would develop into a maritime city of importance stimulated the desire for water front lots, and the far seeing and speculatively inclined caused measures to be taken as early as 1847 to extend the town over the shoal places of the cove.   *The First Streets*

Water front lots were sold in pursuance of an order made by the military governor, General Kearny, on the 10th of March, 1847, between Fort Montgomery and the Rincon, but the work of filling in did not begin until a year later. The eagerness with which this sort of property was sought in 1847 indicates that there was little doubt in the minds of the would-be purchasers that the port of San Francisco would have a rapid growth.   *Water Front Lots*

CHAPTER XVII

THE BAY OF SAN FRANCISCO AND ITS GREAT IMPORTANCE

SURROUNDED BY A WILDERNESS—THE "GOLDEN GATE" NAMED BY FREMONT—THE NAME "CALIFORNIA"—THE ENTRANCE TO THE HARBOR—THE SHORES OF THE BAY OF SAN FRANCISCO—A NATURAL BASIN FILLED IN BY THE PIONEERS—CONTOUR OF THE BAY NOT GREATLY CHANGED—FIRST STEAM VESSEL ON THE BAY—RUSSIANS IN ALASKA—ALASKA A SOURCE OF SUPPLIES—COMMERCE OF THE PORT IN 1848—HUNDREDS OF SHIPS IN THE HARBOR—THE DAWN OF COMMERCIAL GREATNESS.

HE port so eagerly sought by the Spaniards and so jealously guarded by them from intrusion; the body of water whose magnificent opportunities had excited the cupidity of rival nations, until the Americans took possession and permanently settled its ownership, was as nearly neglected up to that time as during the centuries preceding the year when Drake sailed past its mouth without discovering it, and anchored in a roadstead when he might have enjoyed the shelter of a land-locked harbor. It cannot be said, however, that there was lack of interest. That was kept alive by frequent descriptions given to the outside world by navigators, who could not refrain from extolling its advantages, and who appeared more keenly alive to the possibilities of the development of the region surrounding it than those who occupied the soil and should have some knowledge of its resources.

Ignorance Concerning the Bay

The ignorance concerning the Bay of San Francisco among those who lived on its shores in the first years of the nineteenth century was of the densest. The maritime instinct was wholly lacking in the small community made up of the inmates of the mission and the garrison of the presidio. Its members were apparently as unfamiliar with the surroundings of the inland body of water and the opportunities it presented of opening a vast expanse of territory by its superior facilities for communication as they were with the discoveries made after they had entered the country.

Maritime Instinct Lacking

In November, 1826, when the British ship "Blossom" entered the harbor of San Francisco, its captain compared notes with the observations of Vancouver, who had been in the bay 33 years earlier. The only change observed by Captain Beechey was that everything presented an appearance of decay. The dilapidated condition of the fort particularly impressed him, but not more than the uncompromising ignorance of the missionaries, who still believed the lying account of Maldonado, who professed to have sailed through the center of the continent, and who would not believe his statement that the Tahatian group of islands had been discovered, because they could not find them laid down on charts made in 1782.

Few Changes in Thirty-three Years

122 SAN FRANCISCO

Bay Surrounded by a Howling Wilderness

No wonder that Captain Beechey was moved to write that the Bay of San Francisco was in the hands of people who made no use of it, and who were not merely ignorant of its value but were unwilling to learn. Alfred Robinson, who anchored in the cove three years later than Beechey's visit, was equally unfavorably impressed. He landed at North Point with a small party, purposing to make a visit to the mission. Horses were provided for them and they rode through a dense thicket, occasionally running across cayotes and seeing plenty of bear tracks. After a circuitous ride of several miles over a narrow trail through brush whose overhanging branches endangered their heads, they reached Dolores, whose dark and tiled roofs they thought compared with "the black and cheerless scenery" surrounding the establishment.

Missionaries Make no Use of Bay

In the more than fifty years from the establishment of the mission this trail through underbrush, with its accompaniment of cayotes, howling wolves and bear tracks was all that had been accomplished in the way of providing facilities for communication with the port or cove. It is possible that the missionaries knew the latitude and longitude of the entrance to the bay, but there was absolutely no use of the knowledge made by them or those who accepted their direction spiritually and otherwise. Up to 1842, as already noted, several foreign war ships had entered the bay, and they all apparently did something in the way of surveying. The "Blossom," commanded by Beechey, went about the work with some system, and the rock, which was in later years removed by the United States government because it had become an obstacle to navigation, was named after that vessel.

American War Vessels Enter Port

In 1841 two American war vessels, the "San Luis," and the "Vincennes," entered the harbor and made surveys, and in the year following the "Yorktown," "Cyane" and the "Dale" did a little in the same line. French war ships, the frigate "Artemesia" in 1827 and the "Brilliante" in 1842, anchored in the bay and the observations of their officers added something to the common knowledge, but we have no information of any serious effort by the Spanish or the Mexicans to enlighten the world concerning the harbor which they did not use themselves, and were unwilling to have others make use of even though benefit might accrue to them by stimulating its use.

Vessels in the Bay in 1847

In 1847 there were six square rigged vessels in the harbor, the names of which have been preserved for us by the annalist. They were the U. S. ship "Cyane," the ships "Moscow," "Vandalia," "Barnstable," ."Thomas H. Perkins" and the brig "Euphemia." They enjoyed the benefits of the more precise surveys of the "Wilkes," made on the eve of the occupation, but had not yet learned to make use of the name "Golden Gate," which was applied to the entrance by John C. Fremont a year later. On his map of California and Oregon, published in 1848, he used the Greek word *Chrysopylae*. The title was not suggested to Fremont by the discovery of gold, but as he explains in a geographical memoir, published at the same time the map appeared, it was inspired by reasons similar to those which gave to the entrance to the harbor of Byzantium, now Constantinople, the appellation *Chrysoceros* or Golden Horn.

Appositeness of Name "Golden Gate"

The closely concurring discovery of gold gave to the name bestowed by Fremont a double significance, but the luster of the first conception has not been diminished by time or circumstance. As the years roll on the appositeness of the title is more clearly recognized, and in the fullness of time San Francisco's portal opening out upon the ocean destined to become the greatest highway of commerce will attain to a fame surpassing that of antiquity's most celebrated port.

It is fortunate that Fremont deemed it wise to explain his reason for the bestowal of the name so happily appropriate. Had he not done so another fruitful subject of discussion would have been opened, and, as in the case of "California," there would have been endless speculation and innumerable attempts to solve an unsolvable riddle. After a century of more or less brilliant guessing and patient research the world is still in doubt respecting the origin of the word California. The once easily accepted explanation that it was taken from a work of fiction has been dismissed, and it is now attributed to the borrowing propensity of the Spanish adventurers, who were not indisposed to retain phrases of a descriptive character derived from Indians. Thus we are told that the Indians of Lower California were accustomed to designating a high hill or sandy coast as "Kali forno." Alvarado, Vallejo and other native Californians leaned to this view, and Bancroft asserts that an old Indian of Sinaloa called the peninsula, in 1878, Tchal ifalni-al—the sandy land beyond the water. The supporters of the theory that the name was derived from *Calida fornax* (hot furnace) point to the method of classification of the Mexican regions, into tierra fria, tierra templada and tierra caliente, and a writer in the "Chronicle," in an extended examination of all the claims, concluded that Cal y forno was a name given by Indians who recognized in the white hills of the lower part of the state a resemblance to lime kilns which he had seen.

<small>Origin of Name of California</small>

There is some point to the inquiry instituted by Shakespeare concerning the importance of a name, but while we may agree with him that "a rose by any other name would smell as sweet," it is reasonably certain that "Hot furnace" would not be regarded as aptly descriptive when applied to California. The designation may have suited the Colorado desert, but it would have been rejected as inapplicable to the other parts of the province. Certainly those Spanish navigators who later became familiar with the region about the Bay of San Francisco, would not have persisted in the use of so obvious a misnomer, unless perhaps they were of the same mind as one of the governors of the Mexican period, who did not hesitate to stigmatize California as too poor a place to attract decent people and a little too good for convicts.

<small>Something in a Name</small>

There was something loose about the method of naming places adopted by the Spaniards who settled California. The padres were very careful to register the baptisms of the neophytes, and always gave them a Christian name, but the soldiers, it would seem, when the duty devolved upon them of picking out a designation for a site, sometimes became fanciful, and abandoned the sentimental habit of translating an old world name to the new, or the equally convenient one of selecting that of a saint from the calendar, and sought to commemorate an event by an apt word or phrase. According to Palou, Mission bay came by its name in that manner; but the critics assert that Las Dolores was more probably bestowed by the padres to honor "the mother of Sorrows," than to commemorate the discovery by Aguirre of three Indians weeping on its shores.

<small>Little Care Exercised in Naming Places</small>

California nomenclature has been the subject of much discussion and not a little adverse criticism, but the fact that there was no disposition to substitute commonplace names for those already bestowed has not been much dwelt upon. The "Red Dogs," "Hangtowns," "Sandy Bars," "Yuba Dams" and like titles have been cited as instances of lack of fancy, but the retention of the Spanish appellations

<small>California Nomenclature</small>

indicates a keep appreciation on the part of the argonauts of mellifluous titles. The accounts unite in the assertion that much trouble was experienced in dealing with the names of individuals and of towns, but the struggle proved successful and only in rare instances was there an attempt made to translate; hence the retention of designations which still worry the visitor from the East, but present no difficulties to Californians.

A Greek Word "Englished"
But while the first comers were ready to incorporate Spanish words, and took kindly to Yerba Buena, Dolores, Sacramento and San Francisco, and were even prepared to wrestle with Moquelumne and other words of Indian origin, they would not accept the scholarly imposition of *Chrysopylae* of Fremont, but insisted on converting it into English so that it might be understood by that part of mankind with which they were identified, and which they felt was most interested in their fortunes. It is not probable that the matter was given much thought in the hurly burly of the first years of the gold rush, but the promptness with which "Golden Gate" was accepted and transferred to maps, following that made by "The Pathfinder" exhibits a lively appreciation of the value of a significant title.

Entrance to the Harbor
If names did not occupy a very large share of the early public mind there is evidence that the things and places they designated or described were carefully considered. *Chrysopylae*, in the first years after the occupation, may have been little discussed even by those who lay much stress on origins, but the entrance to the harbor was a matter of profound concern, and there was an earnest effort made to let all mankind know that the gate was one through which the commerce of the world might ebb and flow without hindrance. The very earliest descriptions indicate that not long after the occupation the facts concerning the portal and its approaches and the bay itself were as well known as they are today.

Early Accounts of the Bay
An account of the ease with which entrance to the harbor is effected, published when San Francisco occupied the center of the stage, describes it as perfectly as the latest chart. Speaking of the ports to the north and south, Columbia river and San Diego, the writer said: "The available depth on the San Francisco bar is considerably more than is found at either of the ports named, being fully five fathoms at the lowest stage of the tide over much the greater length of the bar, which, measured along the crest of its crescent from shore to shore, is fifteen miles. Over about four miles of this distance the depth is a little more than four fathoms, leaving eleven miles over which it is not less than five fathoms. Inside of the four fathom bank and lying close under the north head, known as Point Bonita, there is a channel half a mile wide, through which more than seven fathoms can be carried at the lowest stage of tide, the rise of which varies from three to seven feet, giving an additional depth at periods of high water."

Survey of the Golden Gate
Later surveys describe the Golden Gate as being nearly three miles in length, nearly a mile wide in its narrowest part, and having a maximum depth of 360 feet. The shores of the gate are bold and rocky. The North or Bonita channel is a third of a mile wide, according to these measurements and has a depth of 54 feet. When the first description was written it was not considered necessary to explain that ships would have no difficulty in entering the harbor, but a commission which had under consideration methods of improvement of the harbor, in 1907 deemed it expedient to explain that "no matter how great the draft of the ship of the future it will always be able to enter the port of San Francisco with safety."

SAN FRANCISCO IN 1851

YERBA BUENA COVE IN 1851

SAN FRANCISCO 125

San Francisco bay, with its northern extension, San Pablo bay, has an area of 420 square miles. The shore line of the main body of water, excluding its numerous navigable inlets, measures 100 miles in length. This body of water, presenting such remarkable facilities for commercial purposes, has since its discovery occupied the minds of physiographists, who are nearly agreed that its entrance was originally the outlet for the combined waters of the Sacramento and San Joaquin rivers, and that some time in the remote past there was a subsidence of their beds, with the result that the waters of the sea were admitted through the Golden Gate, thus forming San Francisco bay. It is asserted that the Indians had a tradition of a great cataclysm that accounted for the creation of the bay, but the story may be set down as one of the cases in which the framer of an ingenious theory seeks to obtain support by dubious methods for a view which is plausible in itself.

Area of Bay of San Francisco

The uses to which the Bay of San Francisco may be put at some future day will be described later, when the period in which harbor improvement became a dominating consideration is under review. Here the conditions existing on the eve of the gold rush will be chiefly dealt with so that the progress of development may be followed. In 1848, and the years immediately following, the question of port facilities was a burning one, but it assumed a different form from that which it presents at present, and it may be said that the unwisdom shown in dealing with it was responsible for many of the problems which later brought so much vexation.

Conditions on Eve of Gold Rush

The appearance of the shores of San Francisco bay has been changed in some particulars by the hand of man, but his artificial additions have not greatly altered the general aspect. If Portola, Beechey, Robinson, Dana and others who have left descriptions were to return they would find more that was familiar than strange to them. They would miss the solitary group of tall redwoods on the summit of the mountains on the northern side of the Golden Gate, which the writer of the "Annals" tells us made a striking land mark for the mariner at sea; and Dana would be unable to find any traces of the herds of red deer which he saw "under a high and beautifully sloping hill" near the mouth of the bay, and Beechey would hunt in vain for the dense growth of wood which he had to pass through to reach the mission when he landed at North Point. But the main features which impelled Dana to remark in his "Two Years Before the Mast": "If California ever becomes a prosperous country this bay will be the center of its prosperity," still exist. The bay still affords "the best anchoring grounds in the whole coast of America," and the region about it retains the climate which he said "is as near being perfect as any in the world."

Appearance of Shores of the Bay

The modern facilities for the speedy docking of vessels have caused navigators to think less of good anchorage grounds, but when Dana wrote they were uppermost in the sailor's mind when he thought of harbors. Dana visited the bay in 1835. Thirteen years later the enterprising Americans, who were determined on removing the "if" which the author interposed when talking of the future of California, began to revolutionize the ancient trend of thought by resolving to dispense with anchorage except as a temporary expedient. The revolution and the way it has worked out helped make a great deal of the history of San Francisco in the first few years of occupation, some of it very unsavory, but all of it interesting and significant.

Good Anchorage Grounds

SAN FRANCISCO

The Cove of Yerba Buena

The cove so frequently mentioned in the descriptions of those who left their impressions of the San Francisco before the occupation was early doomed to obliteration. In 1847 the work of filling in began and it was continued until the place which had once been the snug harbor of all the craft visiting the port was converted into something that might be likened to an untidy Venice. The nearby sand hills formed the chief part of the material used in converting what was water into land, but the rubbish of the growing town was freely employed for the same purpose. These operations, which were begun before the influx of gold hunters commenced were pushed with vigor as soon as funds and labor were available for the purpose.

Filling of the Cove a Mistake

The primary object of filling in the cove was to get as near to deep water as possible, but the sand dunes and steep hills in the rear had their influence in determining the pioneers of San Francisco to make for themselves an artificial water front. It was believed in 1848, and for some years afterward, that the nature of the land surrounding the semicircular beach enclosing the cove would prevent the town extending westward and the desire for concentration suggested the accomplishment of a double stroke, that of creating more room for building purposes on a level, and the facilitation of the unloading and loading of ships by providing berths for them in which they might lie securely while the process was in progress.

Speculation and the Water Front

There was also another object to be served and that was perhaps more influential in hastening results than the immediate necessity of providing wharves. The speculator had a great deal to do with the shaping of affairs in the port of San Francisco. His prescience was responsible for much of the activity before which the semicircular beach of the cove disappeared to allow its place to be taken by a straight line of buildings extending across what had once been the anchoring ground of deep sea ships. The locality may yet be recognized by surviving land marks, describing its boundaries, some of which, however, are being removed, and others are destined to share that fate. The writer of the "Annals of San Francisco" mentions one hill which it would be difficult to identify, probably because it was leveled, and Rincon hill, another point which he felt sure would always be recognized, is now on the eve of demolition. Telegraph hill alone seems destined to endure, because it has been made an object of sentimental consideration, and even it may have to go when the demands of commerce become more urgent.

Slight Changes in Contour of Bay

The changes necessitated by the growth of San Francisco are the only ones which have seriously altered the appearance of the hundred miles or so of the shore line of the bay. The numerous other towns surrounding it have made but slight alterations in its contour, although they furnish abundant evidence of human activity which would certainly astonish any surviving pessimist of the ante occupation period, and would perhaps fill with surprise the optimists, who predicted the great future of the harbor. The inhabitants of Yerba Buena, who in 1847 saw what they called "the steamboat" making an experimental trip about the harbor, could not have imagined the possibility of the bay being navigated by so many vessels propelled by what was then a comparatively strange force, that it would be necessary to establish fairways and to resort to the strictest sort of regulation in order to guard against accident.

First Steam Vessel on the Bay

The vessel referred to as "the steamboat" was brought from Sitka in the year named. It never proved a success and its fate is a matter involved in doubt. The writer of the "Annals" declares that the launch, for it was really nothing more, perished in a norther in 1848, but more recent researches indicate that after making a trip up the Sacramento river, in which it was outdistanced by an ox team, which left San Francisco after its departure, the engines of the steamboat were taken out and put to what was deemed a better use, and the hull was converted into a sloop.

<small>Steam Vessels in South Pacific</small>

The steamboat was by no means the first vessel on the Pacific to be propelled by steam. In 1840 two steamships were brought out from England and plied between South American ports and Europe. The fact is interesting because it calls attention to the advances made by some of the countries on the west coast of South America, while Mexico and its great territory of California were at a standstill. That the first steam craft on San Francisco bay came from Alaska also suggests a degree of energy in the North difficult to reconcile with the subsequent policy of Russia in dealing with its possessions on the American continent.

<small>Russian Comprehension of Value of California</small>

As shown in a previous chapter the resources of the region comprising Alta California and the territory above it, since occupied by the United States and Great Britain, were apparently better comprehended by the Russians than any other people, and they made more use of the part of North America controlled by them in some respects, during the time they were in possession of Alaska, than the United States did until after the gold discoveries in the Klondyke. We are accustomed to thinking of that event as the practical starting point in the industrial history of Alaska, but long before the rush from the United States to the Dominion province, and the subsequent development of the American territory, the Russians were energetically engaged in prosecuting various industries in Sitka, and were hopeful of becoming the source of supply of manufactured articles for the Californians.

<small>Russians in Alaska</small>

The Russians operating in Alaska continued prosperous down to 1821. In that year the Russian American Company declared good round dividends. Some impression of its enterprise may be gained from the statement that it sought to establish a market for Alaskan coal in San Francisco. Several hundred thousand dollars were expended in attempting to accomplish that object but the enterprise proved a failure because of the poor steaming qualities of the coal. The people engaged in this undertaking derived some profit from shipping ice to the rising town, but the business could not be successfully carried on after it was found impossible to create a market for Alaskan coal in California. The various activities of the Russians on the coast necessitated a considerable fleet. At one period there were 500 persons in the employ of the Russian American Company, who were served by a number of brigs and a regular line of supply ships between St. Petersburg and the American colonies was maintained.

<small>Sitka Ship Yards</small>

It was in the shipyards at Sitka, called into existence primarily for repairing purposes, that various auxiliary manufacturing establishments were created which continued to produce numerous articles in great demand by the Californians, and a profitable trade in these was carried on down to the time of the American occupation. When the discovery of gold was made at Sutter's fort many cargoes of shop worn and hitherto almost unsaleable goods were shipped to San Francisco and found ready purchasers, who paid big prices for them. These transactions, however, appeared to have ended the profitable connection of the Russians in Alaska with California. On the 18th of October, 1867, the territory, in pursuance of a treaty of purchase arranged by Secretary of State William H. Seward, passed into the possession of the United States, and from that time forward it began to be an important factor in the commerce of the port of San Francisco, as will be related in the proper connection.

128   SAN FRANCISCO

Commerce of San Francisco 1848

The official reports inform us that the tonnage of ocean arrivals in the port of San Francisco in the year 1848 aggregated 50,000 tons, of which 1,000 only were steam. The foreign tonnage was 23,000 and the domestic 27,000, the latter including the 1,000 steam tonnage. A better idea of the shipping industry at this period and in the years following is derived from the statement in the "Annals," that in the first half of 1849 there were two hundred square rigged vessels in the harbor at one time, and that before the close of the year between three and four hundred were in port, many of them unable to leave on account of the desertion of the sailors, and not infrequently of the officers.

Wharves in 1850

At this time there was one wharf known as the Broadway and another, the Central, was projected and completed early in 1850. There were several small landing places which scarcely deserved to be dignified by the title wharf. These were constructed by private parties, and extended but a little distance across the mud flats and were of no use at low tide, but they afforded facilities for landing passengers and goods in open boats and were a source of profit to their owners. The Central wharf was built by an association and cost $180,000. It extended to deep water and large vessels could lay alongside and discharge at any stage of the tide.

The year 1850 was marked by great activity in wharf building, the longest of which was that at the foot of Clay street. Its original length was 900 feet, but the demand for berth space was so great than in the month following its completion it was extended to 1,800 feet. In addition to the wharves already mentioned there were in 1850 similar accommodations for shipping, some of which were not so long. Market, California, Sacramento, Washington, Jackson, Pacific, Clay and Broadway all terminated in structures whose lengths varied from 250 feet to that of Clay street, which, as already recited, was nearly a third of a mile long.

The Bay Full of Vessels in 1850

On the 1st of June, 1850, there were 526 vessels of various kinds lying in the harbor, the greater number of which were ships and barks, the remainder being brigs and schooners. In addition to these there were at least a hundred large square rigged vessels lying at Benicia and in other well sheltered parts of the bay, where they were secure from the occasional northers which swept over its waters. The records indicate that considerable damage resulted from these visitations in the first few years after occupation, but before 1853 the facilities provided for protection were such that it was stated no further injury was experienced from them.

Activities of the Pioneers

It is not marvelous that the argonauts should have dwelt with great satisfaction upon their achievements in wharf building, and the provision they made for the expeditious transaction of the great commerce which had grown up in so short a period after the occupation. When the Americans hoisted their flag over Portsmouth square in 1846, Yerba Buena cove was as innocent of pretensions to activity in maritime matters as it was when a few native Californian soldiers marched around the head of the bay to procure lumber for the decaying presidio buildings, which they brought from the opposite shore in a rude lumber drogher built under the direction of a foreigner. This was the chief nautical achievement of the men who had dreamed and talked of a great city on the shores of the Bay of San Francisco.

In four years the Americans had at a cost of more than a million and a half provided artificial thoroughfares over two miles in length along a water front of considerable extent to serve vessels numbered by the hundred bringing passengers and merchandise from every country on the globe for the consumption of a population which had sprung up like a mushroom, and which felt so assured of its future that it promptly set to work to convert the sea into dry land in order that business might be done with convenience and dispatch; for all these early constructions in another four years had ceased to perform their original functions and had been converted into public streets.

CHAPTER XVIII

THE DISCOVERY OF GOLD AT SUTTER'S MILL IN 1848

EFFECTS OF THE DISCOVERY—THE CAREER OF SUTTER—A POORLY KEPT SECRET—BEGINNING OF THE RUSH TO CALIFORNIA—MILITARY GOVERNOR RICHARD B. MASON—PROPOSAL TO CONSERVE THE GOLD—MARSHALL'S LIFE THREATENED—SAN FRANCISCO BECOMES THE MINER'S MECCA—MINING AND TEMPERAMENT—EEFECTS OF THE GOLD LURE—THE GOLD HUNTERS—THE RUSH IN 1849—POPULATION IN 1849—IMMIGRANTS POURING INTO CALIFORNIA—UNSTABLE CHARACTER OF THE NEW POPULATION—DEPENDENCE ON MINING.

Effects of the Gold Discovery

IT WOULD be idle to ascribe the wonderful metamorphosis described in the previous chapter to the unassisted energy of the Americans who settled in Yerba Buena when the territory of California passed under the flag of the United States. There is every reason for believing that there would have been progress, which would have presented a brilliant contrast to the inactivity of the dispossessed Californians, but in the nature of things the work of building up a great city must have proceeded slowly, removed as Yerba Buena was from the great centers which could have contributed the population necessary to effect its upbuilding if it were not for the adventitious circumstance of the discovery of gold.

Mineral Resources Not Considered

The first Americans who settled in Yerba Buena and those who found their way into California when it became the property of the United States did not place mineral products high in the list of its resources. If they gave the subject of mineralogy any consideration in this connection, they did not lay much stress upon it. There is little or no reference to gold made in most of the early descriptions of the State of California. As already related gold had been discovered in the vicinity of Los Angeles by native Californians and a few ounces were gathered and sent to Philadelphia to be refined, but the discovery attracted little more than local attention, and even there it did not stimulate extensive prospecting, and in a very short time the find was a closed incident.

First Settlers Not After Gold

It may be asserted in a general way that Californians and the newcomers prior to 1848 never thought of the territory as a possible gold producer. The small but growing town of Yerba Buena was engrossed with entirely different matters, and if the minds of the more enterprising inhabitants of the place ever harbored thoughts of gold they gave no expression to them. When the discovery was finally made at Sutter's mill by accident, the intelligence of the fact brought to the people of Yerba Buena as much surprise as it did to the outside world, which knew little about California resources, and did not bother itself much about them until it

131

SAN FRANCISCO

The Discovery at Sutter's Mill

awakened to the knowledge that the placers of the newly occupied country were yielding gold nuggets and dust in abundance.

The discovery which caused the adventurous spirits of the civilized world, and some from countries that had not attained the stage implied by the term enlightened, was made in January, 1848, by a man named James W. Marshall who had contracted with John A. Sutter, the owner of a large tract of land granted to him by the Mexican government in the Sacramento valley, and which he entered upon in 1839 and practically took possession of the surrounding country which he called New Helvetia. In the summer of that year he established himself at a place afterward called Sutter's fort and built a road to the point on the Sacramento river, where the city of that name subsequently had its beginning. Sutter was born in Baden, Germany, in 1803, and had a wandering career before finally settling in California, and in the course of his peregrinations had become a citizen of Switzerland. Later he swore devotion to Mexico. Before he moved to California he had pursued farming in Missouri and it was from thence that he made his way to the Far West accompanying a party under the command of Captain Tripp, known as the American Fur Company, to the Wind river country. He left Tripp there and made his way to Oregon and from there to the Sandwich islands. His objective was California, but before reaching the territory he found his way to Sitka and it was not until 1839 that he achieved his aim, arriving in Yerba Buena on the 2d day of July in that year.

Sutter's Characteristics

Sutter was a man of varied acquirements and undoubted enterprise. He also enjoyed the reputation of being a brave man, and it was chiefly to that fact that he owed his large grant and the consideratble latitude accorded him in the administration of affairs about his place. His so-called fort was regarded as an outpost against the Indians and he was not infrequently called upon to take action against them, albeit he was charged with deliberately provoking collisions in order to secure captives who were reduced to a condition little better than slavery.

Marshall Finds Gold

In order to secure power for the saw mill he had contracted to build, Marshall admitted the water from the south fork of the American river, a feeder of the Sacramento, into the tail race for the purpose of widening and deepening it by the force of the current. The rush of water brought with it considerable gravel, mud and sand which was deposited in a heap at the foot of the race. In this deposit Marshall noticed a number of glittering objects. He carefully examined them and soon concluded that the shining particles were gold. He gathered about an ounce of the dust and, greatly excited over his find, he repaired with it to the fort where he exhibited it to Sutter, who thought Marshall had gone mad when he first told him that he had found gold.

A Secret That Could Not be Kept

Tests of the dust soon satisfied Sutter of the genuineness of the discovery and it was arranged between the two that they should keep their find a secret but a woman employed about the place who had overheard them divulged it and in a very short time everybody in or near the fort was discussing the discovery and in an incredibly brief period all the neighborhood was hunting gold. Everybody in the vicinity abandoned his regular employment and hurried to Sutter's mill to hunt for gold, and in a few days over 1200 persons were on the ground, from which they spread to other places where the prospects seemed good.

On June 1, 1848, Thomas O. Larkin wrote to James Buchanan, then secretary of state, an account of the discovery. He followed this letter with another from Monterey, dated June 28, 1848, in which he spoke in glowing terms of the importance of the newly found placers, saying he was inclined to believe that a few thousand men in a hundred miles square of the Sacramento valley would yearly turn out the whole price of all the territory newly acquired from Mexico. As the amount paid to the republic for all the region embracing New Mexico, Arizona and California, in conformity with the terms of the Gadsen treaty, was only $15,000,000, Larkin cannot be accused of having overestimated the possibilities. Since he made the modest statement quoted no year has passed in California in which the yield of gold has not equalled that amount, and during many years the product has been four times as great as the cost of the acquired territory.

In the closing years of the decade 1840-9, information traveled slowly. There were no enterprising newspapers in those days to disseminate intelligence, but letter writing was an art more in favor than at present and it was not many months after the discovery before the enterprising began to turn their steps Californiaward. The Baltimore "Sun" on Sept. 20, 1848, took notice of the discovery but there were parties on the way from the East to the new diggings earlier than that date. They had gained their information from private letters which had been received before the discovery was noticed by a newspaper. *News Disseminated Slowly*

The appearance of the article in the "Sun" and the dispatch of Larkin's letter to Buchanan had been preceded by a visit to the diggings made by Governor Mason, accompanied by Lieutenant William T. Sherman, afterward general of the United States army. They started from Monterey on the 17th of June, 1848, visiting San Francisco en route, finding it almost deserted. They made their way to Sutter's fort by passing through Bodega and Sonoma, reaching there on the 2d of July. They found the neighborhood a scene of great activity. From Sutter's fort they traveled up the American river about twenty-five miles to the lower mines which were known as the Mormon diggings, and thence to Coloma, where they spent several days with Marshall and Weber. At this place they found over 4,000 employed in mining. *Larkin on Sherman Report*

Richard B. Mason was the military governor who took charge of the affairs of the territory in the absence of General Kearny. He was colonel of First United States Dragoons and had the bureaucratic notions of the arm of the service to which he belonged, and had some thoughts of putting into execution an idea which suggested itself to him, which to some extent foreshadowed the recently developed conservation policy of the government. As the result of his observations he concluded that the total yield of the mines he had visited was from $30,000 to $50,000 a day. As the gold was all derived from public land he seriously deliberated a method of securing to the government "a reasonable rent or fee for extracting it." He was dissuaded from adopting such a course by consideration of the fact that the country was too big and the people of the wrong sort to be managed by the force at his command. *Suggested Gold Conservation*

It was fortunate for California and the rest of the world that Mason abandoned all idea of interference and permitted the work of extracting the gold from the soil to proceed freely. Had he attempted to put his plan in force there would have been a collision which in any event must have proved disastrous. Had he succeeded in exacting fees, and in otherwise hampering the prospectors, the inevitable result would have been a restriction of production; but it is more than probable that the course he proposed would have aroused an antagonism or a *The Conservation Idea Abandoned*

134   SAN FRANCISCO

rebellion which would not have been as easily quelled as the uprising of the Californians after the hoisting of the flag at Monterey. Mason must, however, be credited with good judgment. He displayed it when he wrote to Commodore James on his return to Monterey that the destiny of California was settled by the gold discovery, treaty or no treaty, but the latter was consummated before the missive reached its destination.

Early Manifestation of Intolerance
Mason was not alone in his view respecting the conservation of gold. It was shared by General Persifer Smith who, while on his way in January, 1849, to join the American forces in California, announced at Panama that he intended to treat every man not a citizen of the United States, who entered upon the public land to dig for gold, as a trespasser; and he proposed, if possible, to drive all foreigners from the diggings. It is probable that Smith was inspired more by the "know nothing" spirit of the times than by a desire to save the gold for posterity, but he, too, was obliged to abandon his views and assent to the free-for-all policy which had established itself in the gold fields. Such decided benefits were derived by those who hunted for, and found the precious metal, and the world's commerce was so greatly stimulated by its abundance, that conservation went out of fashion and was not heard of again for over a half a century.

Marshall and the Miners
An idea of what might have occurred had Mason or Smith attempted to enforce their views may be gained from the experiences of Sutter and Marshall who took the ground that the gold of the Coloma fields was theirs by right of discovery. As soon as the rush to the placers began, Sutter attempted to exact a toll of 10% upon all the gold found. This exaction was not submitted to by the miners, who moved away. Later Sutter sold his claim in Coloma for $6,000 and Marshall disposed of his interest in the mill for one-third that amount, but he still claimed to be owner of the ground and involved himself in many quarrels by so doing, and by his propensity to boast of making big finds. His professions in this regard were believed by some and he acquired the reputation of withholding the secret of his discoveries out of pure contrariness. This exasperated the miners to such an extent that they threatened to lynch him and he fled for his life. The animosity he excited was so great that his enemies wreaked vengeance on his mill and as a result it became impossible to locate the spot where it had stood.

The State and the City
The personal fortunes of the miners and the methods they adopted to secure the gold they sought only indirectly concern San Francisco. Books have been written describing the characteristics of the miners and their performances but they are part of the history of California rather than that of its metropolis. But it is impossible to draw the line between what pertains to the state at large and that which directly affected the city which at once became the mecca of the fortunate seeker after gold and the refuge of the unfortunate prospector who, in the slang of the time, "went bust." It is safe, therefore, to assume that for many years after 1848 nothing of consequence occurred anywhere in California which did not in some manner touch San Francisco interests.

Gold the Attraction
It was the gold the miners extracted from the soil that brought a ceaseless procession of ships to the port of San Francisco; and it was the bad luck or failure of the searcher after the golden fleece to achieve his desire that sent him back to the new mart of commerce to attempt to earn the living there which the auriferous soil begrudged him. To supply the demands of the miners who thronged the hills and built up numerous towns in the mining districts, mercantile establishments

SAN FRANCISCO

of consequence were started in the city, whose imports in some cases in a single year exceeded in volume and value all the merchandise brought into California during the entire period of Spanish and Mexican possession of the soil. And soon it became the business of the same bustling community to find a market for the surplus agricultural products of a region which the argonauts, at first, unmindful of the differing peculiarities of agricultural countries, had set down as unfertile and only adapted to the uses to which it had been put by the unenterprising inhabitants who were there before they came.

Because all these interests are linked up so closely the historian must draw on them and he may use them in the full assurance that their bearing will be perceived without taxing the reader with explanations. There may be no apparent connection at first between the statement that for many years the miner who carried his "outfit" on his back and was always ready to move on to where he thought he could do better, typified the restlessness of the inhabitants of San Francisco until the rushes which sometimes nearly depopulated the City are described. It will then be seen how greatly the occupation of the gold seeker affected the temperament of San Franciscans, and how, until mining became only a part of the industrial activity of the state, it developed tendencies which would not have exhibited themselves so conspicuously if the process of growth could have been as devoid of the elements of chance as in other communities.

Mining and Temperament

At no time after the discovery of gold were the stages of development the same as those in other countries. The growth was never normal. It began with a rush and was interrupted by rushes. From the day that the merchant abandoned his store, the printer his case, the minister his pulpit and the teacher his desk to dig for gold down to the days when the discovery of the precious metal in the Klondyke drew away from the City a goodly proportion of its floating population, and not a few of those who in other localities would be regarded as settled inhabitants, San Francisco was subject to waves of excitement which sometimes materially retarded its growth, but despite the drawbacks of this nature due to the lure of the "golden fleece" the City steadily increased in numbers and wealth.

Growth Abnormal

When Constantine removed the capitol of the Roman Empire to Byzantium there may have been some such transformations effected in incredibly short periods as were witnessed in San Francisco when the news spread throughout the civilized world that El Dorado had at last been found or that at least there was sufficient gold in California to permit slaves of savage kings to bathe in its glittering dust and parade in gilded splendor if they so desired. And when with this intelligence the word was passed on that in this new land all were free to dig, the exodus of the enterprising from the older settled communities was sufficiently great to make inroads on the population statistics of ambitious American towns that had already acquired the "boosting" habit.

Rapid Transformations

Something like a chronological arrangement of the national features of the invasion of the gold seekers has been attempted but the attempt did not prove very successful. The accounts agree that a large proportion of those who were first on the ground were Mexicans, the Sonoranians being particularly numerous. They were followed by contingents from Oregon on the north and soon the Sandwich islanders made their appearance. Then ships began to arrive with Peruvians and Chileans. The Orient was not far behind in contributing its quota, for in 1848 the world was on a nearly even footing in the matter of the transmission of intelligence,

Nationality of the Gold Seekers

and the ambitious Chinese were as quick in resorting to the feast as their Caucasion competitors. Among the latter was a not inconsiderable number from the Australian colonies; men with shady records and some perhaps who were reckoned as such, who merely suffered from the taint that long attached to the antipodean continental possession of the British, because it had been a penal settlement.

The Rush to California in 1849

When the year 1849 opened wagon trains were slowly moving by various routes to the region whose wealth in the popular imagination immeasurably surpassed that of the famed Indian Golconda. Ships were sailing around the Horn in fleets with thousands of passengers all animated by the same desire as the other thousands who were moving in caravans through the passes of the Rocky Mountains to the promised land. In this motley throng the good and the bad were inextricably mingled, but there is no foundation for the assumption, which later events seemed to warrant, that the latter element predominated.

The Wicked in Evidence

It is well to bear in mind in considering the composition of the population built up out of the adventurers of all sorts who found their way into California from all quarters of the globe that assertiveness is a propensity of the wicked. The good, until aroused, play their part in the world without attracting any attention to themselves; but the criminal, even when he works in secrecy, shrinking from the publicity which might invite the halter or a prison cell, engages in performances which force notice even when they are not wholly spectacular. Nobody sets down the number of good acts performed, but more or less accurate statistics of criminality are easily accessible.

Good Mixed With the Bad

There were many unscrupulous and utterly reckless men among the first comers in the gold rush, and they continued to be followed by others as the stream of immigration broadened and increased in volume. These added to the criminal class imposed on the unfortunate province of the Mexicans, who for a long time had used California as a place of exile and penal servitude, made a powerful impress on the new community and gave it a reputation not wholly deserved, and which was in a measure confirmed by the extra legal methods later adopted to repress crime and get rid of the criminals. As will be seen later on the experiences of San Francisco in 1851 and 1856 merely exemplify the truth at the bottom of the ancient lines in which the assertion is made that "the fame of the youth who fired the Ephesian dome outlasts that of the pious fool who reared it." Had the pyromaniac not indulged his predilection we might never have known that there was an Ephesian dome, and had not a few wicked men provoked an outraged community to action the world would never have learned the sort of stuff the pioneers were made of, and how, when aroused, they could straighten out matters.

Population in 1850

It is estimated that during 1849 over 40,000 immigrants were landed in San Francisco, but at the end of the year the population of the town did not number more than 25,000. The major part of those arriving only stayed long enough to secure an "outfit" for the mines and to add to what they had brought. During 1850 the arrivals numbered upwards of 36,000, of whom fully one-half were from foreign countries. At the end of this year the population of San Francisco showed no noteworthy increase, the number not exceeding 30,000. As in 1849 all or nearly all who arrived by sea hastened to the mines.

At the same time that immigrants from all quarters of the globe were pouring into California through its chief port, daily accessions to the population were received by the various land routes. The major part of this immigration was of

American origin, and no inconsiderable portion of it was from southern and southwestern states, a circumstance which influenced the course of events in San Francisco in succeeding years, and not always favorably. In 1852 a census was taken by authority of the legislature and the number of inhabitants of the state was ascertained to be 264,435, while that of the City and county of San Francisco was 36,751. It was asserted, however, that the enumeration was very imperfect owing to the shifting character of the population and that at the close of the year named San Francisco had fully 42,000 inhabitants.

The secretary of state in a report in which he abstracted the census returns noted that the population had increased at the annual rate of 30% during the two years preceding 1852, and indulged in some conjecture regarding the future. He assumed that it was reasonable to expect that the increase during the ensuing ten years would be at the rate of ten per cent annually, and that the population would be quadrupled within that period. His anticipations, however, were not fully realized, for at the time of the outbreak of the Civil war the number was not greatly in excess of 400,000. The census of 1860 only showed 379,994. *Population Predictions Not Realized*

It is possible that the census made by direction of the state legislature was accurate, but the figures obtained by the general government in 1860 above given, cast a doubt upon the veracity of the enumerators. It is true that the year 1853 made no large additions to the total of 1852. If any such rate of increase as that witnessed between 1900 and 1910 had been maintained in the Fifties, the population of the state should have been greater in 1860 than the federal census marshals assigned to it, but the probabilities favor the belief that the tide of immigration receded greatly during the later Fifties, and that California suffered a considerable diminution of inhabitants throughout the decade owing to the propensity of those who had struck it rich to return "home." *Immigration During the Fifties*

Home to the pioneers, for several years after 1849, meant to most of them the states on the other side of the Rocky Mountains. An approximation of the number of Americans in the 326,000 estimated population of 1853 was 204,000, or nearly two-thirds of the inhabitants of California. Very few, comparatively speaking, of the Americans, prior to that year, thought of California as a place of permanent abode. Their families in many cases, and their relations and other ties were in the region they had abandoned, and they yearned to return to them. It was many years after the discovery of gold before the generality of Californians thought of the state as home, and the habit of applying that appellation to the East and other sections of the Union did not wholly cease until a new generation came on the scene. *California Not Regarded as Home*

In the estimate or approximation referred to the number of people of non-American origin in the state in 1853 was about 100,000, of which 30,000 were Germans, 28,000, French, 20,000 Latin Americans, and 17,000 Chinese. In addition there were 20,000 Indians and 2,000 negroes, the most of the latter from south and southwestern states. At the close of the year, probably owing to the practice ever since maintained of large numbers of persons who while working in the interior in summer resorting to the City in winter, San Francisco had at least 50,000 people. *Numerous Foreigners*

There was not an undue proportion of foreigners in the City at this time, considering the sources from which the population was derived, the whole world having contributed to the result. Of English speaking peoples there were nearly 32,000. The Germans numbered 5,500; the French with 5,000 had a relatively greater representation than later; the Spanish Americans numbered 3,000 and there were 3,000 Chinese. *Foreigners in San Francisco*

The remaining 1,500 was composed of representatives of every nationality on the globe, a large proportion of this special contingent being made up of deserters from the ships in the harbor, which in many instances, when bereft of their crews, were abandoned, and subsequently made to do duty as warehouses, hotels and in one case as a prison.

<small>Mining the Chief Resource</small>

This not inconsiderable population in the first years after the occupation was almost wholly dependent upon the output of the placers, in which perhaps a hundred thousand men were seeking for the precious metal during the summer of 1853. The other resources of the state were as yet scarcely touched by the eager gold hunters, the most of whom were unfitted by previous training or knowledge of agricultural possibilities to recognize that there were other greater and more enduring sources of wealth at their doors. Even those few specialties which the indolent natives had made their own were neglected, and for a period no one thought of any other means of gaining worldly substance than through the direct agency of the nuggets and dust extracted from the soil.

<small>Abnormal Conditions</small>

It requires little imagination to realize that the conditions produced by this complete absorption in the quest for gold must have been abnormal, and the results flowing from it had to be wholly different from those witnessed in communities where the process of upbuilding was more orderly and where the diversification of industry introduces complexities which by their attrition speedily wear off the rough edges of extreme individuality and put on the veneer of conventional civilization. It will be interesting to trace the effects of this practical confinement to a single field of endeavor with the view of ascertaining the part it played in bringing about the serious troubles San Francisco had to deal with in the beginning of her career, but which were happily overcome by vigor of action, which often had to be called into play to repair the damage done by carelessness and neglect.

CHAPTER XIX

MANY VICISSITUDES EXPERIENCED BY THE PIONEERS

A FLIMSILY CONSTRUCTED CITY—SAN FRANCISCO IN 1848—THE BIG FIRES OF EARLY DAYS—LACK OF PRECAUTIONS AGAINST FIRE—FIVE CONFLAGRATIONS—METHODS OF CONSTRUCTION IMPROVING—FIRST STORE BUILDING IN SAN FRANCISCO—GOOD ARCHITECTS—EXPENSIVE BUILDING MATERIALS AND HIGH COST OF LABOR—MISSION STYLE NOT FAVORED BY THE PIONEERS—JERRY BUILDING—NUMEROUS BRICK STRUCTURES—APPEARANCE OF THE CITY IN 1854—EARLY LAND GRABBING—LAYING UP TROUBLE FOR THE FUTURE.

A STRANGER visiting a city of normal growth, if he is not statistically wise concerning its standing, soon forms an impression of its wealth and resources by observing how its people are housed, the character of its public and quasi public buildings, its warehouses and stores and its streets and parks. These are the outward signs which tell the informed the story of its status as unerringly as the figures of the assessor and the tax gatherer. But the keenest observer landing in San Francisco any time within five or six years of the gold discovery at Sutter's fort would have been at loss to form a judgment of possibilities or probabilities, for the visible manifestations were entirely dissimilar from anything he could have witnessed in the older communities.

A Flimsily Constructed City

It is only from something like a detailed description that an idea can be gained of the impression that the nondescript collection of devices made to do sheltering duty must have made on the stranger as late as 1854, and to understand the cause of the great vicissitudes to which the population was repeatedly subjected by fire, it will be necessary to trace the course of building operations during several years. In the architecture of the growing City, if the term architecture may be applied to that in which so little art was exhibited, we can discern the attitude of the inhabitants toward the land in which most of them imagined that they were merely temporary dwellers; and in it we may find an explanation of the restlessness which more than anything else, contributed to the instability that was so marked a characteristic of early days, and which was responsible for an indifference that tolerated lawlessness until it became unendurable, and defied the danger of conflagration which was recognized and feared but which men were too busy to guard against.

Appearance of the City in 1854

For several years after 1848 San Francisco was not a city of homes; it was merely a place where men lived, and some few women. The great preponderance of males produced this result, and its effects were visible in the temporary and makeshift construction or rather, it should be said, expedients resorted to for the

Not a City of Homes

purpose of housing a population almost nomadic and always ready to move on. It was not until the home instinct began to assert itself that an improvement was visible. Until that was developed the metropolis of the Pacific coast presented the appearance of a great circus in winter quarters, ready to resume its wanderings on short notice.

San Francisco in 1848   At the end of April, 1848, when the gold rush began, the town contained about 200 buildings; 135 of these were used as dwellings and 12 were devoted to the sale and storage of goods. The statistician furnishing these figures also enumerates 35 shanties, which implies that those set down as dwellings were of better construction, but the testimony does not encourage the view that they were at all pretentious, the most of them being frame and rudely put together. The first brick house erected in San Francisco was put up by a firm named Mellus & Howard, on the corner of Montgomery and Clay streets. It was the second brick structure in California, one having previously been built of that material in Monterey.

No Public Buildings   In an address delivered by John W. Geary, the alcalde, in August, 1849, he mentioned that there was not a single public building in the town, not even a jail. The failure to provide a place of detention was remedied before the close of the year, not, however, by building but by utilizing the brig "Euphemia," which was bought by the council and converted into a prison. The "Euphemia" was moored in the cove of Yerba Buena, and doubtless the fact that she was surrounded by water added to the belief that prisoners were kept in greater security on that account, but her isolation was only temporary. In a very short time after the establishment of the floating prison it began to be surrounded by houses, and soon it had for a neighbor the "Apollo," which was converted into a saloon.

Big Fires of Pioneer Days   There were five great fires in the first four years after occupation, to which the term conflagration may be applied. The first of these occurred in December, 1849. It broke out in a place called Dennison's Exchange on the east side of the plaza, now known as Portsmouth square, and consumed nearly all the buildings on that side and destroyed a line of structures on the south side of Washington street, between Montgomery and Kearny. Its progress was finally arrested by blowing up a building with gunpowder. The loss was estimated at a million dollars.

The First Conflagration   This was the first pronounced warning of danger, the only two previously recorded fires being the destruction of a hotel in the preceding January and the burning of the ship "Philadelphia." But there are no indications that the warning made any serious impression, for tents and shanties were made to take the place of the destroyed buildings, and the invitation to disaster they held out was accepted very promptly. On the 4th of May, 1850, a fire started in a building on the east side of the plaza, known as the U. S. Exchange, and three blocks were consumed before it was arrested. The district burned over was that between Jackson and Washington and Montgomery and Dupont streets, and the block between Montgomery and Kearny. There were suspicions of incendiarism, and arrests were made, but the accused were released, there being no evidence against them. The probability favors the belief that the charges were wholly unfounded.

Inadequate Precautions   Although the loss occasioned by this fire was nearly four million dollars, there appears to have been no serious effort to prevent a recurrence of the disaster. The new buildings that took the place of those destroyed were flimsier than those that had been swept away. A few unavailing precautions were adopted by the council, which ordered the digging of artesian wells and the immediate construction of cisterns. An ordinance was also passed compelling every available person to assist in extinguishing a fire when called upon, a penalty ranging from $5 to $100 being imposed in case of refusal, and all householders were required to keep water buckets filled with water in readiness for an emergency.

The inefficiency of these simple measures was soon exhibited. Forty days after the second fire what the early annalists designated as the third great fire occurred, and it is chargeable with the destruction of five millions' worth of property, the space between Clay, Kearny and California, down to the water's edge, being swept by the devastating flames. The Third Great Fire

Once again the damage was repaired and numerous hook and ladder, engine and hose companies were formed, more wells were dug and the number of reservoirs was added to, but they proved unavailing to entirely ward off a danger which was becoming a menace to prosperity. On the 17th of September, about 4 o'clock in the morning, a fire started in the Philadelphia house on the north side of Jackson street near Washington, and the flames swept through the district bounded by Dupont, Montgomery, Washington and Pacific streets. The structures destroyed were chiefly one story affairs, but the damage was estimated at between a quarter to half a million dollars. On this occasion, which the pioneers ranked as the fourth great fire, the newly organized fire companies did work which brought forth a great deal of commendation, but the critics were loud in their denunciation of the shortage of water in the cisterns, which prevented their getting the best possible service out of their new apparatus. Fire Companies Formed

The fifth and last great fire of pioneer days occurred on the anniversary of the second fire. On the night of May 3d, 1851, flames were seen issuing from a paint or upholstery store on the south side of the Plaza. The planking in the street facilitated their spread and the fire extended from block to block. In ten hours 1,500 to 2,000 houses were destroyed, eighteen blocks being burned over. The brick buildings on Montgomery street and ten or twelve in other localities escaped, but all the remaining structures in an area three quarters of a mile north to south and a third of a mile east to west were wiped out. In this conflagration a number of old ships that had been abandoned in 1848 or 1849 were burned, among them the "Niantic" at Clay and Sansome streets, the "Apollo," which had been converted into a saloon and the "General Harrison." By breaking up the wharves the spread of the fire was arrested and the shipping was thus saved. The loss occasioned by this calamity was estimated at from ten to twelve million dollars, but the depression it created was short lived, nothing apparently being capable of downing the indomitable spirit of the inhabitants or extinguishing their confidence in the future of the City. The Fifth Great Fire

These repeated disasters, and the growing desire for something better, at length produced a change in construction. Many new buildings in the business quarter, erected after the fourth fire, were built of more enduring materials. Solidity was aimed at by the owners of property, and we are told that many of the structures erected at this time were "remarkable for their size and beauty." Tents and shanties had disappeared from the center of the town, but a few of the latter still survived on its outskirts at the close of the year 1850. The price of building material, which had been abnormally high during the preceding year, was now much lower, some things costing scarcely one sixth to one fourth as much as formerly. The reduction gave a big impulse to building during 1851 and 1852, which resulted in Improved Methods of Construction materially improving the appearance of the City. At the close of the latter year California, Sansome and Battery streets contained many brick houses, and granite was beginning to be employed in the lower stories.

First Store Building

It was during this year that the granite building at the northwest corner of Montgomery and California streets was erected. It enjoys the double distinction of being the first stone building put up in San Francisco and of passing through the great conflagration of 1906. The granite was cut and dressed in China and put in place by Chinese workmen. It was regarded as a handsome edifice in its time, and was still standing when this paragraph was penned, but is not likely to be preserved as a memorial, although its retention might admirably serve the purpose of illustrating for future generations the architectural standards of the period in which it was erected. The vicissitudes through which it has passed give assurance that it would prove an enduring monument.

Substantial Structures Erected

The erection of the Parrot granite building was speedily followed by the construction of a number of others of the same material, all of which were regarded as fireproof. Many of these survived down to the day of the great disaster, and they all had the same external appearance imparted to them by their shutters of wrought iron and doors of that metal. There was nothing distinctive about their architecture, but the precautions taken to guard against fire gave the business part of the town a fortress-like appearance totally unlike that of any other American city, and confirmed the impression of the beholder that at length effective steps had been taken against the "fire fiend."

Great Building Activity

The succeeding year was one of great building activity and there was evidence on every hand of attempts to escape from the severely plain models of 1852. The improvement must have been marked, for we find an enthusiastic critic declaring that "in a few years more, if she be not changed into marble like Augustan Rome, she may be turned into as beautiful and enduring a substance—into Chinese or rather California granite." In 1853 there was completed the largest edifice up to that time erected in California. It had a frontage of 122 feet on the west side of Montgomery from Washington to Merchant and extending 138 feet along the latter street.

Good Architecture

This burst of enthusiasm and the statement that "the distant reader can hardly form a conception of the magnificence of some of these new buildings," so different from those constructed in the cities of the Atlantic states in the early stages of their career, was not wholly unwarranted. Competent critics of a later period, who had an opportunity to study the productions of 1853, 4 and 5 unite in the assertion that some of the constructions in the business district were both exotic and interesting and "retained under American surroundings a certain propriety and positive charm."

Early Architects

This artistic turn was due to the presence in California in the early days of a number of foreign trained architects, whose quest for the golden fleece was not rewarded by an abundance of nuggets taken from the soil and who sought to repair their fortunes by applying their talents. Among those whose names have been preserved as worthy of mention were Thomas Boyd, Henry Kenitzer, Victor Hoffman, Peter Portois, Stephen H. Williams, Prosper Huerne, Reuben Clarke and Gordon Cummings. These men were graduates of the best French and English schools, and their work, some of which survived the fire of 1906, testifies to the

PANORAMIC VIEW OF SAN FRANCISCO IN 1851
From an autotype

justness of the appreciative remarks of the annalist of 1856, and the later summing up of their accomplishments.

That the disposition to encourage art should have existed under the unfavorable circumstances which attended the growth of the City in the early Fifties is astonishing. Costly materials are not employed as a rule in the construction of buildings in small towns. Their use is reserved for later periods when those making the expenditures see the possibility of direct returns for their enterprise from the competition which always results from the concentration of a great number of people in the contracted precincts of a city. But the unique conditions in San Francisco prompted men to discount the future, and the result merited the tribute paid, that on the whole the business structures erected between 1850 and 1860 were better designed and better looking than those used for like purposes anywhere else in the United States at that time. *Pretentious Business Structures*

Most of the new houses erected in the first half of the decade fifty were of brick, but even this material was as costly as it was unsatisfactory. The owner of a building constructed in 1850 paid $140 a thousand for bricks, and they were of a very poor quality, being burnt at the San Quentin prison kiln, where care was not always taken to use fresh water in mixing the clay. The wages of bricklayers and hod carriers were fabulously high. When the brick fort at the Golden Gate was erected the contractor paid bricklayers $25 a day and the hod carriers $17.50. Carpenters and masons not infrequently were paid $20 a day. *Costly Building Materials*

The Parrott block, which has been referred to as still standing, cost its owner $117,000 to erect. It was constructed by Chinese labor, but the expenditure it involved does not suggest cheapness. The owner of the second brick house erected in San Francisco paid $140 a thousand for his brick and $20 a day to masons. Henry M. Naglee had been burned out four times before he formed the resolution to provide for himself a fireproof structure. The building did not meet the modern architects' definition of indestructibility, but it passed through the fires of 1851 unscathed, and survived down to the day of the great conflagration as the oldest brick structure in San Francisco. It was situated on the corner of Montgomery and Merchant streets and underwent many external disfigurements before its final obliteration, but architects recognized under these disguises that "it must have been a very respectable piece of mid century Parisian design." *Cost of Labor*

The largest of the early buildings, the Montgomery block, was planned by Gordon Cummings, and betrayed the inspiration of London construction of the Forties. At the time of its erection in 1853 it was an object of great attention, the declared purpose of its projectors being to secure an absolutely fireproof structure. The precautions taken were not wholly responsible for the fact, but the Montgomery block escaped the flames of 1906, and the building still stands as a monument of the abiding faith of the pioneers in the future of the City of San Francisco. *Montgomery Block*

It should be added in speaking of the architecture of the early Fifties that the high cost of labor, as too often happens, was not coupled up with incompetency. The stone carving and wrought iron work on some of the best buildings show conclusively that the architects were able to obtain the assistance of well trained mechanics, who were not over numerous in the United States at that time; and the flattering tribute paid to the workers of this period, that they built well and better *Good Artisans* during the Fifties than they have until the rehabilitation of the City after the great fire, was fully deserved.

Mission Architecture Not Favored

There is no trace in the architectural movement of the early Fifties of appreciation of the work of the missionaries. Contemptuous allusions to mouldering piles of adobes are met with, but not the slightest hint of a disposition to imitate or adopt. That came later. It may have been unconscious prejudice formed by men of action against what they considered an institution that clogged progress, and prevented recognition of the possibilities in the arched corridors, the patio, the tiled roofs, domed towers and pierced belfries of establishing a style; but it is far more likely that the complete failure during the entire period to accept a suggestion from the buildings of the missions was due to the alien architects, who had brought with them the traditions of the schools in which they were educated, and who preferred to work along the lines to which they had been accustomed. The pioneer owners exercised little choice, preferring to trust to the guidance of their trained advisers.

Instances of "Jerry" Building

The fact that architects found good mechanics at hand did not entirely save investing owners from loss through inferior construction. The haste with which work was done under the pressure of urgent demand resulted in some "jerry" building. On the 12th of April, 1854, a portion of the United States bonded warehouse fell, and it was only one of a number of similar accidents, due to the use of inferior materials and to the frail character of apparently solid walls. The settling of walls began to be a common affair, and for a while militated against the construction of solid buildings on the made ground in the cove. The uncertainties concerning the water front also played their part in arresting progress in the business section, but it was by no means wholly checked, for the year was marked by the erection of some lofty buildings, notable among them being that of Samuel Brannan, known as "The Express," which was put up at a cost of $180,000, exclusive of the value of the land, which was appraised at $100,000. It was situated on the northeast corner of California and Montgomery streets, directly opposite the Parrott building, and the lower part was occupied by Wells Fargo & Co.'s express and by a real estate agency and brokerage.

The City at the Close of 1853

At the close of 1853 there were 626 brick or stone buildings, 154 of them three stories high; 350 of two stories and 83 of one story. In addition to these there were 38 exceeding three stories, 1 of six, 34 of four and 3 of five stories. Fully half of these were built in 1853. The section in favor for residential purposes at this time was north and west of the business district. The majority of these dwellings were frame, but occasionally preference was given to brick. While on the other hand, in what might be termed the hotel and business district, there were few departures from the strict rule of solidity. Any deviation from the determination to avoid the mistakes of the past was checked by the destruction of the Rosette house, a five story frame structure on the corner of Bush and Sansome streets, the burning of which would have caused another conflagration, as a high wind was blowing at the time, had not the neighboring houses been built of brick.

Appearance of City in 1854

Speaking of the appearance of the City in 1854 the writer of the "Annals" said: "Over all the space, some eight or nine square miles in extent, on the heights and in the hollows are spread a variety of detached buildings, built partly of stone and brick, though principally of wood. The heart and strength and wealth of the City," he added, "is contained within the little level space lying between the hills or

PICTURE OF SAN FRANCISCO, DRAWN AFTER NATURE, 1852, SHOWING THE WATERS OF THE BAY REACHING NEARLY TO MONTGOMERY STREET

rising grounds (back of what was Yerba Buena cove) and the narrow waters of what remained of that harbor." The nominal limits of San Francisco, as actually surveyed and mapped out, extended from the west side of North Beach to the side of Mission creek, a distance of nearly four miles, and from Rincon Point to the mission church, a distance exceeding three miles.

Already in 1854 the idea that the hills immediately back of the cove would offer an insuperable obstacle to the growth of the City in a westerly direction was being abandoned. Although the town was building along the line of least resistance there were numerous persons with a predilection for sea or water views, who chose the side hills for sites, but the movement was by no means general and there were many who still believed that the future city would be on the level expanse to the south, which would require very little preparation or clearing to convert it into excellent building sites.

The Hills Back of the City

Much hard work had to be done to bring the City to the condition it had attained in 1854 and it was attended with exciting events of various kinds, not least among which were the struggles growing out of the desire to get hold of the desirable lands under the control of the local authorities. The methods of the grabbers have rarely been matched in any country, and the public, which hears much about modern "grafting" tendencies will not be apt to maintain that we are worse than our predecessors after reading about them. It is an unsavory story, but the truth of history demands that it be told without reservation, even though the telling may raise a doubt concerning the strict accuracy of writers who, in extolling the merits of the argonauts, have manifested a tendency to gloss over their delinquencies.

Grabbing the City Lands

But the struggle for land, despite its fierceness, cannot obscure the fact that the men who grabbed, and those who obtained it in a manner only remotely suggesting irregularity, accomplished results which might not have been achieved in a century by the people acting in their collective capacity. Private ownership, when the title is acquired by dubious means, is not an admirable thing to contemplate, but it has this to say for it, that the unregenerate grabber is apt to put it to better, or at least more prompt use than a community holding land in common. Much of what is now the most valuable real estate in San Francisco was acquired by methods which reflected discredit on the persons obtaining it, but it would be idle to conceal that it was owing to the energy of this acquisitive class that the growth of San Francisco was enormously stimulated, and that they caused it to become a real city almost before its inhabitants realized that they had emerged from the village state.

Enterprise of the Grabbers

CHAPTER XX

LAND TITLES AND TROUBLES OF PIONEER DAYS

BIG DEMAND FOR TOWN LOTS—WATER FRONT LOTS EAGERLY BOUGHT—ATTEMPT TO VALIDATE FRAUDULENT LAND GRANTS—COLTON GRANTS DECLARED FRAUDULENT—TROUBLESOME SQUATTERS—FEDERAL DETERMINATION OF TITLES—CONFUSION CONCERNING PUEBLOS—AMERICAN ALCALDES IMITATE THEIR PREDECESSORS—OFFICIALS CONNIVE WITH SPECULATORS—THE SQUATTERS' ARGUMENT—SQUATTING AS AN OCCUPATION—THE CITY AND THE INTERIOR SQUATTER—TITLES IN DOUBT MANY YEARS—JURIES SIDE WITH SQUATTERS—SAN FRANCISCO A PUEBLO—THE LIMANTOUR CLAIM—THE LAND COMMISSION—POLITICAL CONDITIONS—NEGLECT OF CIVIC DUTY IN SAN FRANCISCO.

HE plain bordering on Yerba Buena cove was surveyed in 1839 but, as already related, there was little effort made to secure the lots within the boundaries of the survey. These latter were not very extensive, embracing only the blocks between Pacific on the north, Sacramento on the south, Dupont on the west and Montgomery on the east, the latter at that date being the shore line of the cove. This neglect was amply offset by the eagerness displayed as soon as American rule was established. General Kearny, in compliance with an active demand made by newcomers anxious to provide commercial facilities ordered a sale of lots between Fort Montgomery and the Rincon, which was carried into effect.

The Demand for Town Lots

This was in March, 1847. In June of the following year the Alcalde Bryant, in pursuance of this order of the military governor, directed another sale, the announced terms of which were one fourth cash, one fourth six months, one fourth twelve months and the balance in eighteen months, with interest at the rate of ten per cent per annum. By this time the gold hunger had taken hold of the people and the alcalde found it necessary to stimulate interest in the sale by proclaiming the merits of the site and making a few predictions. He reminded the people that "the site of the town was known to all navigators and mercantile men acquainted with the subject to be the most commanding commercial position on the Pacific ocean," and he declared that "the town itself is no doubt destined to become the commercial emporium of the western side of the American continent."

Sale of Town Lots

This bit of promotion literature was issued on March 16, 1848, and the date of sale was fixed for June 29th, but a postponement became necessary and it did not take place until July 20th, when it was conducted under the auspices of Alcalde Hyde, lasting three days. The lots sold were all between high and low water mark, and four-fifths of them were covered with water. The right, title

Promotion Literature

and interest of the government in this property had been conveyed by General Kearny to San Francisco, and although the validity of his action was early called into question, the officials of the municipality did not hesitate to act on the authority granted, and long before the question was finally determined a large part of the lands had been disposed of to meet the financial requirements of the city.

The Spanish Vara
Under the original decree of March 10, 1847, a portion of the property had been laid out in lots of 45 feet 10 inches frontage, and 137½ feet in depth. These irregular sizes were due to the conservatism which caused the acceptance of the Spanish vara of 33 1/3 inches as the unit of measurement, a practice which is still maintained in the older sections of the City, and occasionally causes surprise to the stranger unaware of the circumstances responsible for the apparent oddity. There were 444 lots in the first batch of land sold, and they went at prices ranging from fifty to one hundred dollars each. Deeds were given to the purchasers by George Hyde, alcalde and chief magistrate. In the latter part of 1849 there was another survey of beach and water-front property, which was divided into 328 lots of the same size as those sold in the previous year, and the greater part of these was disposed of on January 3, 1850, at public auction by the Alcalde John W. Geary, who executed the deeds for them on behalf of the City.

Water Front Lot Titles
The purchasers of these water front lots were apparently undisturbed by the question raised concerning Kearny's authority to make the grant. Their confidence that the sales would be held valid was justified by the subsequent action of courts and the legislature of California. It had been the settled law of the United States that land situated as was that disposed of under the Kearny grant belonged to the sovereign power by virtue of its sovereignty, and as California when admitted to the Union became a sovereign state, the ownership of the water-front lands, not otherwise legally disposed of, passed from the United States to the state as an attribute of its sovereignty. In view of these facts, and assuming that those who had purchased the water front lots at the public auctions in good faith, the legislature of the state, on March 26, 1851, passed an act which granted the use and occupation of the lands in question to the City of San Francisco for ninety-nine years, providing, however, that "all lots sold in accordance with the terms of Kearny's grant, and all lots sold or granted by any alcalde and confirmed by the ayuntamiento should be granted and relinquished to the purchaser for a term of ninety-nine years."

Legislature Confirms Titles
This action of the legislature, while it settled the question so far as the water-front lots were concerned, was productive of trouble in another direction, as it apparently encouraged the effort made to secure confirmation for titles about which there was no pretense of legality or good faith on the part of the purchasers who held them. In May, 1851, the legislature passed an act relinquishing the right of the state to the City conditional upon the latter confirming the grants of all lots within certain specified limits originally established by justices of the peace. This would have covered the Colton grants, about the fraudulent character of which there was not the slightest doubt. Colton was appointed to assist in the administration of justice during the time when Horace Hawes was acting as prefect. He abused his position by making grants to anyone applying for them of lots at $100 a piece, which were easily worth five times that amount when the grants were made. He was a bold swindler, who did not hesitate to appropriate every dollar he re-

ceived to his personal use, promptly shipping it to the Atlantic states, to which he fled to enjoy his ill gotten wealth.

The ayuntamiento caused legal proceedings to be adopted against Colton and on December 24, 1849, declared all the grants made by him were void because they were unauthorized. Some fifty-three beach and water-front lots were sold by Colton, and the purchasers although the affair was obviously a job, and not a dollar had accrued to the treasury from the transaction, had the effrontery to appeal to the common council four years later to have their fraudulent purchases confirmed. They succeeded in having an ordinance passed by the council accepting the conditions of the legislative act of May, 1851, but the mayor, Stephen R. Harris, interposed his veto. The statute was subsequently repealed on the 12th of March, 1853, the jobbers failing to induce the City to accept its conditions. *Fraudulent Colton Grants*

The uncertainties produced by these and other irregularities greatly stimulated a propensity which began to exhibit itself very shortly after the occupation. The right of Hawes to authorize the sale of lands was not merely contested by the court, which issued an injunction to restrain Colton, but there were many in the community who planted themselves on the proposition that no one had any right to sell because, as they claimed, they belonged to anyone who chose to take possession of them. Before Colton began selling a number of persons had squatted upon the land of the Rincon, which was held as a government reserve and was leased to Theodore Shillaber. When Shillaber attempted to make use of the property he found it occupied by several men, chiefly from Sydney, who refused to abandon the land. He was enabled to take possession by the aid of a party of U. S. soldiers under the command of Captain Keyes, who was afterward sued by one of the ejected squatters but was sustained in his course. *Squatter Troubles*

The uncertainty respecting titles was increased by the known attitude of Mason who, while disposed to recognize the practice of alcaldes to sell lots within the limits of their towns, because it was the custom of the country before occupation, held to the opinion that all grants made by such officials should have the confirmation of the federal government when it became the owner of the soil by treaty. In his view the alcaldes were not authorities of the United States, but merely of the military government of California, and as such subject to removal by the military governor. His position was recognized as sound, and the government later took steps to secure all the information possible respecting the earlier grants. Captain Henry N. Halleck was directed by the secretary of state to collect and examine all of the archives of the old government of California. He was very successful in this work and the documents secured by him were the chief reliance of the commission, which was subsequently appointed to determine the merits of the many claims put forward by real or fraudulent grantees. *Views of Mason*

The necessity of this precaution will be realized when the confusion attending the status of the lands later embraced in the city limits is studied. As already related there were originally two settlements, which were afterward practically merged when the City expanded. These were the mission and the presidio. The former, by the operation of the Mexican secularization laws, had in 1834 become an Indian pueblo and was known as Pueblo Dolores. According to the plan as originally devised Dolores should have had a regular ayuntamiento, but the territorial body known as the deputation ordered the establishment of the ayuntamiento at the presidio, of which Francisco de Haro was the alcalde or first magistrate. *Status of Public Lands*

SAN FRANCISCO

The deputation, while failing to accord an ayuntamiento to the Indian pueblo, recognized its existence in various ways, among these recognitions accorded to the ayuntamiento being the right to grant building lots, provided they were not within two hundred varas of the beach. Immediately after the exercise of this right by the presidial authority a grant was made by the deputation of the rancho Laguna de la Merced, in which it was recited that the grant should not prejudice the common lands of the Pueblo de Dolores.

Confusion Concerning Pueblos

Out of this mixed state of affairs grew uncertainties which were eagerly seized upon by the unscrupulous. Up to July, 1846, nearly eighty grants had been made by alcaldes or justices of the peace for hundred vara and fifty vara lots, many of which were subsequently held to be invalid because they were granted on the supposition that Dolores was a pueblo. In addition to these grants there were others made by the governor or prefect, within what was subsequently the territory of San Francisco, which in no wise recognized the pueblo and without reference to its existence. Among these were the Laguna de la Merced, of about half a square league, one of four hundred varas square in the level ground northwest of the Mission Dolores made in 1836 to Francisca Guerrero, one of a hundred varas square near the presidio to Appolinaris Miranda in 1838, a hundred vara lot in Yerba Buena to Salvador Vallejo and Jacob P. Leese in 1839, one to Cornelio Bernal of about a square league on the bay shore, including Hunter's Point, made in the same year, one of the depression southeast of the Mission Dolores, known as the Willows, to Jose Jesus Noe in 1840, another of two square leagues in extent south of the Bernal rancho to Jacob Leese in 1841, and another to Noe of the rancho San Miguel in 1845.

Liberality of Mexicans Imitated

These liberal disposals were freely imitated by the American alcaldes, who, in pursuance of the idea of adhering to the customs of the country until a new system of government was provided, not only assumed the title of their predecessors under Mexican rule but exercised their functions and were not slow to avail themselves of every precedent which they could make fit in with their desires or forward the interests of the new settlers. The sale of town lots by auction was a novelty, but apart from the method of disposal there was little difference between the system of conveyance after the occupation and that in vogue under Mexican law. The American alcaldes followed the course of their predecessors and did not ask for confirmation of their grants, until the adoption of the resolution of the ayuntamiento in August, 1849, which prohibited alcaldes selling without the special order of that body.

No Effort to Save Land for Municipal Use

It is doubtful whether this restraint would have been imposed had not the growing demands for money forced the authorities to cast about for sources of revenue. There does not appear to have been any concern for the conservation of the land for future municipal uses, for the council showed a great eagerness to get rid of all the property under their control. There was something like an exhibition of desire to prevent monopolization but it was only a temporary manifestation. There had been in existence a regulation prohibiting a purchaser from obtaining and holding more than a single fifty or hundred vara lot, but the first town council elected September 13, 1847, removed all restrictions upon the sale of lots, thus throwing open wide the door for speculators who were not slow to accept the invitation.

TWO VIEWS OF SAN FRANCISCO HARBOR, DURING THE GOLD CRAZE, SHOWING THE DESERTED SHIPS

Before March, 1848, all the choice lots, or those so regarded at the time, had been snapped up by the astute buyers, who were assisted by complaisant or conniving authorities to get them on their own terms. Once in the possession of private owners the lots in desirable locations speedily rose in value, but their appreciation did not seem to stimulate the price of the property still remaining to be sold, as was displayed by the fact that at a sale of fifty-two lots in the month mentioned the prices paid for them only ranged between $16 and $50 a lot, averaging about $25. *Authorities Connive with Speculators*

It is not surprising that the looseness attending the disposal of the lands subsequently embraced within the limits of the City, both before and after the occupation, should have added to the already existing sentiment that non occupants had no just claim upon the soil. The method of the general government in disposing of its property, and the opinions expressed by Mason and others, encouraged the belief that the theory of first come first served would be adhered to, and that the squatter who took up a piece of land and planted himself upon it in the City would be as much entitled to hold it as the locater on farm lands. This feeling was responsible for the freedom of action afterward extended to gold seekers, not, however, without some fruitless opposition interposed by the military authorities. *Looseness of Methods*

But the conservatism of the period was too pronounced to permit the successful prevalence of loose notions of rights in landed property. The current of opinion ran in one direction in the middle of the nineteenth century. The desirability of settling up the country was generally recognized, but it was felt that vested rights must be respected, and that the fabric of society would be endangered if the title to land was not secure. There were no refinements indulged in by those who adhered to the sacredness of the vested rights idea. They were newcomers in a practically new country and for that reason refused to cumber their theory with time limitations. They could not show title extending back through a long period, and therefore rested their claims upon the deeds which they had secured, and denounced as land thieves those who sought to deprive them of what they considered as their property. *Respect for Vested Rights*

They denied the right of squatters to go behind the returns and assume the functions of a court, and the result was considerable bloodshed. The beginning of the trouble in San Francisco, as already related, was the attempted seizure of a reservation made by the government, which had been leased to a man named Theodore Shillaber. *Arguments of the Squatters*

The practice thus inaugurated in 1850 was subsequently elaborated into a regular system. Men not only engaged in squatting for themselves, but there were plenty who were quite ready to engage in the business for those willing to employ and pay them. Except in the built up parts of the city for many years squatting was a common method of acquiring and holding land. It was no unusual circumstance for rough characters to hire themselves out to hold possession of a piece of property, and the same men were equally ready for pay to assist in dispossessing for a claimant squatters who had entered on their land. *Squatting an Occupation*

The evil was by no means confined to San Francisco. It extended throughout the state and assumed a political aspect. An organization was formed to promote the movement, which had for its underlying theory the belief that the land of California belonged to the people. The squatters contributed to a fund designed to protect them in what they conceived to be their rights, and there was much bad blood and a readiness to contest for possession with arms. One prominent leader *An Evil General Throughout the State* of the squatters in the course of a debate growing out of an alleged misuse of the funds collected, said openly that he would rather fight than palaver or collect subscriptions. "If the speculators wish to fight," he said, "I am for giving them battle. Let us put up all the fences pulled down," he added, "and also put up all the men who pulled them down."

The Interior and the City Squatter

There was far more warrant for the attitude assumed by the interior squatters than for that taken by those who sought to get possession of the land within what were known as the pueblo limits of San Francisco. It was justly suspected that grants had been made to such an extent that the whole country would be absorbed by the wily schemers, who were obtaining them from the original grantees, and in many instances concocting claims absolutely fraudulent, as was later disclosed by the researches of the commission which investigated the subject. The differences of opinion respecting the pueblo of San Francisco hardly warranted grabbing, for in any event it had been the recognized practice to pass title to the lands in some authoritative manner, and in no case was mere entry regarded as a warrant for possession. The argument put forward by the squatters, that the grants were invalid and that, therefore, they were open to anyone who chose to enter upon them, was not of the sort calculated to appeal to people who had views respecting the regularity of proceedings, and who were disposed to relegate the settlement of vexed questions of title to the courts, and the outcome was necessarily a triumph for what might, with more propriety, be termed law and order than some later performances which were carried on under the aegis of those two great factors in promoting and preserving civilization.

Titles in Doubt Many Years

The triumph was not achieved in a day, for the validity of the pueblo titles occupied the attention of the courts for many years, and the disputes concerning them were not finally settled until the so-called pueblo decisions were rendered in 1864 and 1866, by which the government relinquished and granted to the City all the lands included in such pueblos. Meanwhile until public sentiment proved strong enough to finally carry the day, there were cases of squatting in all parts of the City, and occasionally they were attended with serious consequences. In 1853 something like a pitched battle occurred between a squatter and a deputy sheriff, who sought to eject him and the official was killed. There were several other encounters during this year and these were not always between persons holding alcalde titles and squatters, but between the squatters themselves, who were quite as ready to dispute possession with each other for the lands to which they held no title whatever, owing to the disposition manifested to carry to its logical conclusion the theory that ownership did not vest in anyone who could not or did not occupy and hold the premises.

Squatters and the Jury System

In the settlement of these controversies juries ceased to be of value. If a man was killed in defending a piece of property claimed by him, no matter how clear his title, it was impossible to obtain a conviction. There were always plenty who, influenced by the belief that the Spanish and Mexican grants were all tainted with fraud, and that all the sales made on the authority of the military governors were corruptly conducted, were ready to stand by the squatter, or at least would not lend their aid to maintain the claims of men they believed to be unconscionable speculators and grabbers. This feeling in a measure abated as the years wore on. A decision rendered by the state supreme court in October, 1853, confirming the alcalde grants, contributed greatly to allaying the passions growing out of the grabbing propensities of the period, but there were repeated disturbances of the security of owners between that year and the final adjudication of the matter by the supreme court of the United States.

The decision of the state supreme court in substance was that by the laws of Mexico towns were invested with the ownership of lands; that by the law, usage and custom of Mexico alcaldes were the heads of ayuntamientos or town councils, and as executive officers of the towns they rightly exercised the power of granting lots within the towns, which were the property of the towns; that before the military occupation of California by the army of the United States San Francisco was a Mexican pueblo or municipal corporation and entitled to the lands within her boundaries, and finally that a grant of a lot in San Francisco made by an alcalde, whether a Mexican or of any other nation, raises the presumption that the alcalde was a properly qualified officer, that he had the authority to make the grant and that the land was within the boundaries of the pueblo. The effect of this decision was to legalize many fraudulent alcalde grants and it was severely criticized on that account, but it had the merit of practically settling a question which was causing much friction, and it soon was accepted as the best mode of bridging over a serious trouble. San Francisco a Mexican Pueblo

While it effectually disposed of the doubts concerning the alcalde titles it did not give complete security to owners. Disturbance arose in another quarter, which at first was not regarded as serious, but soon occasioned great concern. A Frenchman named Jose J. Limantour was the cause of disquiet. He claimed that he had advanced to the Mexican governor in 1843 the sum of $4,000, and had received for the same a grant of land in the neighborhood of Yerba Buena, which had it been held valid would have covered the site of the City like a blanket. At first the people were disposed to regard Limantour's pretensions lightly, but they soon perceived that they were backed by a great deal of what seemed like important evidence. The land contained in the alleged grant to Limantour was embraced in several parcels. One conveyed a tract running from the line of the pueblo of Yerba Buena, distant 400 varas from the settlement house of Richardson, to the southeast, beginning at the beach on the northeast and following it along its edge, turning round the point of Rincon on the southeast and following the bay as far as the mouth of the estuary of the mission, including the salt water and following the valley to the southwest, where the fresh water runs, passing to the northwest side about 200 varas from the mission, to where it completed two leagues northeast and southwest to the Rincon. The Fraudulent Limantour Claim

The second granted two leagues beginning at the beach at the ancient anchorage of the port of San Francisco, below the castle, following to the southeast, passing the presidio and following the road to the mission and the line to the southwest as far as the beach, which ran to the south from the port, taking the beach to the northwest, turning round Point Lobos and following to the northeast along the beach of the castle for 200 varas, and continuing as far as the estacada, the place of beginning. Trying to Grab the Whole City

In addition to these tracts comprising four square leagues Limantour also claimed the islands of Alcatraz, Yerba Buena, the Farallones and a square league on the island of Los Angeles opposite Racoon straits and other tracts throughout the state, all of which were apparently conferred upon him for the sum of $4,000. The boundaries as laid down in the alleged grant were of the vaguest sort and

154 SAN FRANCISCO

suggested fraud, but it required several years to rid the City of the incubus. It was not until April 22, 1858, that a decision was given which finally disposed of Limantour's claim, which the United States Attorney General Jeremiah S. Black declared was the most stupendous fraud, the greatest in atrocity and magnitude the world had even seen perpetrated.

The Land Commission

The land commission which passed upon the Limantour claim, and numerous others equally fraudulent, but representing more modesty than was displayed by the Frenchman in his effort to grab nearly the whole of San Francisco, was greatly assisted in its labors by the intelligent work of Edwin M. Stanton, afterwards war secretary, during the war of secession, who succeeded in making such use of the material in the archives assembled under the direction of Captain Halleck, that the City began to breathe more freely, but the period of uncertainty endured during the whole of the decade, and all the claims were not finally disposed of until the closing years of the nineteenth century.

Title Uncertainties is Obstacle to Growth

But uncertainties attending land titles did not impede the growth of the City. Owners were subjected to annoyances, and breaches of the peace were of frequent occurrence because of the unsettled condition of affairs, but clouds on titles did not seem to affect values very seriously, for the optimism of the people made them confident that matters would come out all right in the end. It would be possible to fill volumes with the details of the conflicts in the courts over claims growing out of the vicious system prevalent under Mexican rule of disposing of lands without adopting anything remotely resembling careful registration, or attempting to properly define the boundaries of the grants made. Absolute neglect, failure to survey and a total absence of system produced many complications for a people who, by their energy, made the lands of California valuable, but the Spaniards and their successors, the Mexican administrators, might claim that they were troubles we brought on ourselves, and that if they had not been disturbed in their possession of the soil there would have been none, for it would never have been made valuable enough to quarrel about.

Big Interior Land Holdings

The assertion that the complications brought about by the loose land grant system did not retard development applies only to the City, and must be qualified by the observation that its growth was indirectly affected by the retardment of interior progress through the retention of immense tracts of farming land in the hands of men who showed little disposition to make any better use of them than the original grantees from whom they had obtained them by one method or another, and not always in a fashion to reflect credit on Americans. During a considerable period California was menaced by the possibility of having fixed upon it a system of land monopoly or large holdings which, had it been perpetuated, must have permanently arrested the diversification of industry, and made the state lag in the work of developing its resources, and of creating homes for a happy and prosperous people.

Thriving on Disorder

It would be difficult to trace the origin of all the evil effects described as resulting during the earlier period of San Francisco's development under American rule. During the Fifties adversity, crime, bad government, insecure titles, shameless grafting, all were powerless to prevent the town going ahead. For a while it seemed to thrive on disorder, and in spite of the contradictory evidence there is no reason to believe that even the best sentiment of the period was well disposed to carry through any thorough measures of reform. The drastic means adopted to put a stop to rampant criminality are quoted to support the assumption that the so-called better elements in the community had the matter of bringing about good government much at heart, but there are too many attending circumstances connected with their efforts to permit the claim to pass unchallenged. Men with property to protect may always be relied upon to act as the bulwark of social order when emergencies arise, but it is unfortunately true that they are often, through negligence or indifference, the direct cause of the disorders and criminality which they, in wrathful moments, seek to suppress.

San Francisco's history abundantly illustrates this propensity, and in their proper place will be found descriptions of events which will amply support the charge of contributory negligence on the part of those whose duty it was, by the exercise of vigilance and attention to civic duty, to make it impossible for the worst elements of society to control. The mere relation of certain proclivities, and what they tended to, will show that in most instances the spectacular displays of civic house cleaning would have been wholly unnecessary had the decent inhabitants, the members of the class whose personal interests are directly subserved by the preservation of order, and who are the chief sufferers when disorder reigns, always set a good example, one calculated to inspire the belief in the evil minded that they cannot profit by defying the conventions prescribed by civilized societies.

_{Contributory Negligence of Good Citizens}

It is with the view of making clear and emphasizing the fact that absorption in the struggle for wealth was indirectly responsible for the troubles of the years which brought the Vigilantes on the scene, that the conditions of growth in population and wealth will be described in advance of the political shortcomings of the inhabitants of San Francisco during the years preceding the overturn of law and order in 1856. It is only by contemplating the processes of accretion that a just estimate of the performances of that year and of 1851 can be obtained. The study of the events preceding and accompanying these ebullitions of popular wrath will reveal the fact that the pioneers were men of extraordinary energy and intelligently enterprising, but it will also disclose that they were the victims of a laxity due to the shaking off of the restraints imposed by an older civilization, which, while they may not always be sincerely regarded as desirable by those who accept them nevertheless exercise a powerful influence and tend to the elevation of society.

_{Absorbed in the Struggle for Wealth}

CHAPTER XXI

THE LAYOUT AND BEGINNINGS OF A BIG CITY

NOT MANY PUBLIC IMPROVEMENTS AT FIRST—INDIVIDUAL EFFORT THE CHIEF FACTOR IN THE UPBUILDING OF THE EARLY CITY—PRACTICAL NEEDS ATTENDED TO BY PIONEERS—THE FIRST CITY HALL—CONFIDENCE IN FUTURE GROWTH OF THE CITY—YERBA BUENA COVE FILLED IN BY PIONEERS—HIGH RENTS—MERCHANTS ABLE TO PAY BIG RENTALS—EFFECTS OF EXCESSIVE SPECULATION IN 1853—OPPOSITION TO RECTANGULAR STREET SYSTEM—MUNICIPAL OWNERSHIP AND CARE OF STREETS—MISSION PLANKED ROAD—PROVIDING FACILITIES FOR SHIPPING—A WATER FRONT LINE—PERMANENT WATER FRONT LINE ESTABLISHED IN 1851—THE COUNTRY AND THE CITY—STEADY DEVELOPMENT OF THE CITY—EARLY WATER SUPPLY—A LAKE MERCED PHENOMENON.

HE writer of the "Annals of San Francisco," in surveying the condition of the City in 1854, pessimistically remarked that there were no parks, nothing but Portsmouth and two or three other squares, none of which had any green grass. He spoke of contemplated thoroughfares, and other projects having for their object the improvement of the municipality, but he mourned the fact that there was not foresight enough to provide future "breathing holes" for a population which he predicted would be numbered by hundreds of thousands. He stigmatized the failure to make provision for future needs as a serious oversight and attributed it to avarice. *Few Public Improvements*

Avarice and ignorance, allied with indifference, were justly chargeable with the omission he denounced, as was also the unfortunate disregard of the topographical requirements exhibited in laying out the City. He declared that "the eye was wearied and the imagination stupefied in looking over the numberless squares—all square—building blocks, and mathematically straight lines of streets, miles long, and every one crossing a host of others at right angles, stretching over sandy hills and plains and chasms. Not only is there no public park or garden," he added, "there is no oval, circus or anything ornamental, nothing but the four squares alluded to," which he already had evidence told us were utterly destitute of grass, and no better than the dusty plazas bequeathed to them by the indolent native Californians. *Avarice and Ignorance Denounced*

It has been shown that some of the pioneers were not wholly regardless of the graces and comforts of civilization, and that there was an early display of good taste in architecture, but all the evidence we have of development along esthetic lines indicates the narrowest sort of individualism. There were numerous excellently constructed buildings, which would have been an ornament in a much more populous city, but they were erected for the personal gratification and profit of the *A Narrow Individualism*

157

owner. Public buildings there were none until the middle of 1851, when a theater known as the Jenny Lind was purchased for $200,000 to serve as a city hall. It was wholly unsuited for the use to which it was put, and was destitute of external attraction. The council responsible for the acquisition was accused of jobbery and David Broderick, who at a public meeting spoke in favor of the purchase, was severely criticized.

Practical Needs Receive Attention

But while parks and plazas and green grass received scant consideration it cannot be said that the pioneers were backward in the matter of making the City habitable. They proceeded with vigor in the work of creating streets and grading in order to make communication easy and succeeded in an incredibly brief space of time in accomplishing results that were a tribute to their enterprise and a substantial benefit to the community. Perhaps men confronted with such a task as that which San Franciscans took upon themselves in the early Fifties may be exonerated from the charge of civic indifference because they disregarded the superfluous, and posterity would doubtless readily excuse them on that ground if it were not for the fact that the disposition to ignore the public needs while struggling for private gain was manifested during many years subsequent to the period when good judgment and common sense demanded that the practical needs of the community should first receive attention.

Labor Conditions

The essentials received attention as soon as the labor conditions were such as to permit the carrying out of projects of improvement. During the rush to the mines, when the City was practically deserted by its inhabitants, who had joined the searchers for gold, and while every successive installment of immigrants remained in San Francisco only long enough to fit out for the work of digging the precious metal, it was simply impossible to make any considerable progress. In 1849 streets were still ungraded and their condition was so bad that miring was no unusual occurrence on the best thoroughfare. No sanitary regulations were imposed and people deposited rubbish where they pleased. For a while it was found more expedient to use bags of coffee, cases of tobacco and barrels of spoiled provisions to make crossings or fill up holes than to cart the nearby earth or rock to the places where needed.

Rush to Mines Continues

There was no appreciable abatement of the rush to the mines during the two or three years immediately following the discovery at Sutter's fort, but the tide ceased to flow only in one direction long before the attraction of the placers diminished. Not everyone who went to dig for gold succeeded in finding what he was after, and many soon abandoned the quest and repaired to the City, where they thought they could mend their own fortunes by serving the more fortunate hunters, who resorted to San Francisco whenever they struck it rich to enjoy themselves and were more frequently than otherwise, parted from their hard earned nuggets and dust and obliged to return to the diggings to procure more or were reduced to the necessity of abiding in the town and getting a livelihood as best they could.

Extension of City Limits

The working element available from this source, reinforced by constant arrivals, to whom the temptation of the large wages offered proved more alluring than the chances of the diggings, soon began to produce an impression on the ragged surface of the town site, the habitable limits of which were daily being extended to meet the requirements of the increasing population. The charter framed by the legislature April 15, 1850, fixed the southern boundary or the city limits at a distance of two miles from Portsmouth square, making its line run parallel with

SAN FRANCISCO

that of Clay street on the north. The western line was one and a half miles distant from the center of the square and paralleled Kearny street on the east, and the northern and eastern boundaries were made the same as those of the county of San Francisco.

These lines indicated confidence in the future growth of the City and the area prescribed seemed to furnish abundant room for expansion. The original survey, made by O'Farrell, had long before 1850 proved insufficient in that regard, and habitations of all kinds had spread far beyond the district in which the streets were laid down. But the principal operations carried on by individuals and by the authorities in that year were confined to seventeen or eighteen streets in the section between Battery and Taylor and Bush and Francisco. Within this district the thoroughfares were all graded and planked, and in several blocks sewers were laid. The longest improved street running north and south was Battery, which extended from California to Market. Sansome was only put in condition between Bush and Broadway. Montgomery and Kearny extended only from California to Broadway, and Dupont was passable between Sacramento and Broadway. The work on the east and west streets was not as extensive as on those running north and south, the hills offering formidable obstacles to the young community. Bush street was graded and planked between Battery and Montgomery, and California started at the bulkhead and stopped short at Montgomery. Washington and Jackson stopped at Dupont and Pacific reached to Kearny.

<small>Confidence in Future Growth</small>

Simultaneously with these grading operations there was carried on the work of recovering from the waters of the cove of Yerba Buena more level space on which to erect business structures. The early annalist of San Francisco likened the City at this stage to "those other queens of the sea Venice and Amsterdam," but pointed out that "where the latter had canals for streets and solid earth beneath their first pile founded buildings," San Francisco over a great part of its most valuable business district "had still only a vast body of tidal water beneath the plank covered streets and beneath the pile founded houses themselves." It took some years to change this feature, but by degrees all the spaces between the wharves and under the buildings were filled, the sand and the earth removed from the hills brought to grade contributing to that result.

<small>Filling in Yerba Buena Cove</small>

The energetic work during the summer greatly improved the condition of the streets, which were pronounced measurably passable toward the close of 1850. In 1851 the legislature reincorporated the City, extending its boundaries in a southerly direction and the work of grading and planking the streets was prosecuted with increased vigor. But there was as yet no serious encroachment on spots outside of the business district, which lay within the boundaries of the tract or space traversed by the seventeen or eighteen streets before referred to when the grading operations were mentioned. In 1851 there was still a valley in the locality that is now Second and Mission streets, and it was made attractive by a grove of evergreens. Telegraph hill was used for residence purposes to a limited extent but the disposition to keep to the improved section was pronounced and this stimulated the owners of property to reserve and make habitable the region further south. Market street, which at that period was a sand dune of no mean proportions, was cut through from Battery to Kearny streets in the year following. A machine known as the steam paddy was employed and did excellent work in

<small>Energetic Work Improves Conditions</small>

removing and leveling the sand hills and effected speedy transformations which the satisfied denizens of the growing City were inclined to speak of as "magical."

Making a City Site

They were certainly entitled to be characterized as wonderful for they completely altered the aspect of the site as viewed from the water three of four years earlier and made it nearly unrecognizable to those who returned to it after a sojourn of a year or so in the mining region. These visitors found in place of the quagmires they were familiar with, well planked streets which were tolerably free from mud and dust, and many of them provided with sewers. The thoroughfares were lined with buildings of various sorts, some of them of impressive dimensions with attractive exteriors. There were shops where luxuries and necessaries of all kind could be found, and plenty of good hotels and restaurants, and the complacent opinion freely expressed by those enjoying the benefits of these exertions was that San Francisco was rapidly attaining the dignity of a metropolis.

High Rents

To this belief the active real estate dealer and speculator freely contributed by word and action. The latter took the form of putting up rents to rates which sound fabulous, but were apparently freely paid. In 1853 we are told the commonest shop rented at from $200 to $400 a month and that stores of any size brought $1,000 for the same period. The demand for quarters played its part in fixing the valuation of real property with the result that enormous prices were demanded and paid for choice lots which had been purchased by the original owners only a short time before for a song. By this time the City was deriving some benefit from the increased appreciation and demand for its property. On the day after Christmas of 1853 there was a sale of water front lots, 120 in all, which realized $1,193,500. Four small blocks extending from Davis street eastward, and between Sacramento and Clay, divided into lots 25x59.9 sold from $8,000 to $9,000 a lot, the corners commanding $15,000 to $16,000. A few larger lots brought from $20,000 to $27,000.

Values Purely Speculative

This enhancement was out of all proportion to the value at the time, and was based wholly on the speculative assumption that the abnormal conditions created by the enormous production of gold would continue indefinitely. It disregarded the fact that the opportunities for extension were not restricted, and ignored the experience of the two years following the gold discovery during which there was a tremendous modification of the demands of landlords. In 1849 the Parker house, a two story frame structure, was rented for $120,000 a year, and there were several mercantile concerns that paid from $30,000 to $70,000 in the year mentioned. One building with less than thirty feet frontage brought $36,000 a year.

Effects of a Gold Plethora

Only conditions produced by a plethora of gold would warrant such rents in a town of less than 50,000 inhabitants. The storekeeper who took gold dust for his goods from men who were not particular about the quantity of metal they gave in exchange for the articles they desired, and on occasion dispensed with the use of scales entirely, could well afford to pay any amount demanded for a suitable location. The saloon keeper who charged extortionate prices for the liquors dispensed by him, and took an additional toll from the careless miner when weighing his dust, and the gambling house did not need to bargain closely; they could depend upon coming out ahead of the game no matter what they paid.

But the demand for the gold increased much faster than it could be taken out, a fact apparently not well considered by those who believed that every one who

had obtained possession of lots at the ridiculously low prices prevailing when the first sales were made by the alcaldes would become millionaires. It would seem when a piece of property which may have originally cost not more than $12 brought in an annual rental of thousands of dollars that the process of millionaire making would be a rapid one, and that a great number of them would be produced. But the result did not justify the expectation. In the end it developed that fewer millionaires were made in San Francisco by the great output of gold, and the abnormal conditions created by it, than were subsequently produced by the more dependable growth of agriculture and manufacturing industries and the pursuit of commerce in an orderly and less speculative manner than that which marked all transactions and occupations in pioneer days.

In 1854 there began to be something like an appreciation of the uncertainties produced by excessive speculation. In the fall of 1853 and the spring of 1854 there was a reaction in business due to the overstocking of the markets. Goods had been rushed into the new town from all parts of the world without reference to the needs of the community. The prices obtained in previous years had infected the universe with the idea that California could absorb all the goods sent to it, and as a result every mercantile house in San Francisco was deluged with consignments which could not be disposed of and bankruptcies were numerous. Empty stores were seen on every hand and reduction of rentals proved no temptation to open them. The trade depression soon communicated itself to real estate speculators and many of them failed. The decreased rates of rent and the depreciation of property, however, did not have the effect of destroying confidence in the future of the City. On the contrary, predictions were made that values would greatly exceed those which had been attained; but they were not realized as speedily as the sanguine men of 1854 believed they would be.

Result of Excessive Speculation

In 1854, on March 9th, there was another sale of town lots on what was called the government reserve which realized $241,000, but the prices obtained were much lower than those eagerly bid the preceding year. Meanwhile building activity was not seriously interrupted. Although rents were falling the unbounded confidence of owners of property stimulated them to increased exertion. Their opinion respecting the value of real estate was shared by the squatter element whose activities became very pronounced, no unoccupied lot being safe from intrusion. There were numerous riots due to the determination of owners to protect their property, which they did by hiring watchers who were prepared to resist with arms any invasion of what they considered the rights of their employers. The authorities made no efforts to check the evil. Perhaps they recognized their inability to preserve order with the inadequate force at their command, but the popular impression was that they were indifferent—or worse still, that they were catering to the lawless element, for the squatters had begun to assert themselves in politics in the city and throughout the state.

Town Lots at Low Prices

It is not surprising that in the hurly burly of this eager game of grab that suggestions concerning gradients when made by "scientific gentlemen," should have gone unheeded. The grade established by a surveyor named Hoadley was strongly protested against by men who combined with their knowledge of civil engineering some taste, and were at the same time gifted with the ability to peer into the future and divine its needs. They urged the abandonment of Hoadley's grades which demanded a great deal of costly excavation to carry out the scheme of

Rectangular Street System Opposed

rectangular streets but their efforts proved wholly unavailing. The reason assigned for the persistence in a system so unsuited to a city topographically situated as San Francisco is was an overweening desire for profit by individuals who were determined to make their property valuable even though the general welfare was sacrificed; but the true cause was the indifference of the people generally due to the utter absence of civic spirit of the sort which impels a community to act together for the common good.

The Care of Streets

Very early in the history of the City of San Francisco the question of municipal ownership was brought up, but it failed to receive the attention it deserved. It is mentioned in this connection because it has a direct bearing on the subject of street improvement, and the ideas respecting it which prevailed at the time. The Mission, which had a small settlement in 1850, was some $2\frac{1}{4}$ miles distant from the Plaza or Portsmouth square. An ordinance was adopted by the council to connect it with a plankroad from Kearny street, but a proposal was made by Charles L. Wilson to construct and maintain a toll road for a period of seven years. There was some opposition on the ground that the profits which it was thought might be derived from the undertaking should be enjoyed by the City, but the discussion of the question did not take a wide range and at no time was consideration given to the policy of the maintenance of absolutely free roads which was then receiving considerable attention in other parts of the world.

Mission Street Planked Road

The construction of the planked road along Mission street to the Mission had the effect of carrying building operations in the direction of that settlement which was within municipal bounds but not included in the city limits until later. In 1853 there were so many houses on the line of the road that it presented the appearance of a continuous street. It was much traveled, for there were numerous drinking houses in the Mission which for a time was the sporting and amusement resort of the City.

Cutting Through Sand Hills

In 1853 and during some years later the difficulties attending the construction of the road were impressed on the people but in course of time the transformation effected was so great that the community could hardly be persuaded that the made ground was not as solid as that of other localities, and the Federal government was induced to select as a site for its general postoffice a number of lots which had formerly been a quagmire. In constructing the road several sand ridges crossing Kearny south of California street had to be cut through. One particularly large one near Post street caused a heavy expenditure for its reduction. It was near this point that a toll gate was established, the surrounding dunes compelling vehicles to pass through the cut at that place. This gate was maintained for a number of years.

A Difficult Piece of Roadway

The sand dunes were a less formidable obstruction than the soft places in the two and a quarter miles of road. The steam paddy performed its service efficiently and with comparative cheapness, but the quagmires taxed the ingenuity of the road builders. At the place already mentioned an attempt was first made to construct a bridge, but when piles were driven they disappeared, a couple of blows of the hammer of the pile driver sufficing to produce that result. The idea of bridging was then abandoned and heavy planks were laid platform-wise. This served the purpose for a while, but the traffic finally caused the platform to sink several feet, and considerable expense was incurred in keeping it in a state of passibility. This first road was built at a cost of $150,000 and the tolls charged were 25 cents for a single horse and rider, 50 cents for a horse and buggy, 75 cents for two horses and a vehicle and $1 for a four-horse team. A second road was built later at a cost of $96,000. It superseded the earlier construction and was maintained down to the date of the expiration of the franchise. The undertaking was a profitable one, it being estimated that its projectors realized at least 3 per cent. a month on the amount they had invested during the period they were in control.

The movement to convert the cove of Yerba Buena into dry land was one of·those undertakings marked by concert of action produced by the desire of individuals for gain which often produce results nearly impossible of attainment through organization. It is unthinkable that the recovery of what is now a large part of the most important business section of the City could have been accomplished at the time by public effort. No one has ever attempted to estimate the enormous cost of this improvement, but from first to last it was so great that to even attempt to approximate the probable expenditure would have appalled the young community. But what the people in their collective capacity would have shrunk from attempting, had any one been so preposterously deficient in knowledge of practical affairs as to propose it, was achieved with comparative ease by individual effort. Filling in Yerba Buena Cove

Doubtless had the argonauts been advised in the last years of the Forties by a L'Enfant, and at the same time been assured that the national government would ultimately carry out a far-seeing plan of improvement, they would have listened to him; or had some person gifted with as much foresight as modern harbor commissioners are with hindsight, a plan would have been devised for the settlement of San Francisco's water front, which would have saved much subsequent annoyance to their successors by giving them a thoroughly worked out system. In that event the pioneers might have made provision for the monster ocean carriers of today which were undreamed of then. But lacking the prophetic gift and means they did the best they could. The Water Front Problem

A community with the certainty that its development would be along the lines of orderly growth might have done something of the sort, although wisdom and order do not always walk hand in hand. If there had been no gold, the inhabitants of the little town on the shores of Yerba Buena in the course of a hundred years or so might have begun to feel rich enough to improve their harbor, in which event they would in all likelihood have imitated the example of Liverpool and resorted to closed docks. Instead of filling in they would have scooped out and in the long run perhaps the scooping process would have proved the best. Not an Orderly Growth

But the pioneers, after the gold discovery, were confronted with a different problem. Their harbor was suddenly filled with hundreds of ships of all kinds, whose owners were demanding speedy discharge of their cargoes. With such a condition existing the natural thing to do was to provide wharves alongside which the ships and other vessels might lay while unloading. To have created docks would have been out of the question; the labor, the material and the money were not available for such expensive works, and the urgency of the demand for facilities forbade the thought of engaging in the construction of basins which would have been years in building. The Need of Wharves

Under the circumstances the rational thing to do was to utilize the timber of the forests surrounding the bay, and this was promptly done, but not by the people in their collective capacity. Each individual was too intent on making his own fortune to concern himself about the general welfare, but, as is usual when individualism is allowed free play and hopes of great reward are held out, that which the community refused to do for itself, or to put it more truthfully that which it was unable to do was done for it by men eager for gain. Their motives were wholly selfish, and in almost every instance they were unscrupulous, or not overscrupulous respecting the means they adopted to carry out their projects. But the outcome was a substantial gain for the City, even though the unsystematic way in which they went about the work of recovery entailed some annoyances and later procured for them some criticism from those wise after the event.

Encroaching on Waters of the Bay

The eagerness to bring ship and landing place close together necessitated the establishment of a water front line. Had no prohibition been interposed there is no telling how far the land would have been made to encroach on the waters of the bay. But the much-abused principle of vested rights promptly asserted itself and in an incredibly brief period, as historical periods go, brought something like order out of chaos, for the struggle for vantage points was near to bringing about that result. Public authority had to be invoked to effect regulation, and sometimes it is assumed by superficial critics that because it became necessary to do so it would have been wiser for the public to have commenced at the beginning. But an assumption of this sort ignores the lesson of the fable of the monkey called upon to make the decision of the piece of cheese between the quarrelling cats. The cats found the cheese but the monkey took it all in his efforts to divide fairly and the cats were permitted to go hunt for more.

Centralized Authority

Something of the sort happened when the individuals who had built the wharves invoked public protection. In those days the appeal could not be made to the community directly interested, for that was the era in which there was much talk about the hatefulness and the danger of centralization. The opposition was merely theoretical, for that really exercised was considerably overlooked. San Francisco's water front more directly concerned the people of that City than those of Los Angeles, or the mining regions, but it was the state's province at that time to regulate and legislate specially for municipalities, and other political subdivisions, and it had to be invoked and permitted to take its share of the cheese. Later it took the whole of the cheese.

Water Front Line Established

By an act of March 26, 1851, a permanent water front was established for the City, and maps were ordered to be made and deposited in various public offices delineating the prescribed boundary by a red line. In after years this map became familiarly known by the title red line, because it had to be frequently invoked. The water front established by it would have been satisfactory to the owners, and perhaps the act of the legislature would have been wholly beneficial if it had stopped at reserving the right of the state to regulate the construction of wharves so that they should not interfere with navigation. But the interference did not stop there. On May 1st of the same year the legislature passed another act which empowered the City to construct wharves at the ends of all the streets connecting with the bay by extending such streets 200 yards beyond the water front, or red line, and authorizing the City to prescribe wharfage rates. In the same act the legislature relinquished the right of the state to the beach and water lot property, but on the express condition that all the titles to such within the limits of the Kearny grant that had been conferred by justices of the peace should be confirmed. The obvious purpose of this proviso was to validate a great

fraud and should have had no place in a statute which was assumedly devised
for the regulation of the water front. It would not have been inserted had it not
been for the machinations of a class of politicians who became very active in the
promotion of schemes which had for their object the security of holders of property
obtained with the connivance of rascally or the carelessness of incompetent officials.

This venal interference with an affair which should have been wholly con- *Interference*
trolled by San Francisco was followed not long after by an attempt to make the *of the*
commerce of the port help pay the running expenses of the state government. *Legislature*
In April, 1853, Governor Bigler sent a message to the legislature in which he
recommended that the limits of the City be extended toward the water front and
that the space thus gained should be leased or sold. California was heavily indebted at the time and the legislative financiers conceived the idea of replenishing
a depleted treasury by extending the City front six hundred feet beyond the line
established by the act of 1851. The campaign to accomplish that object was conducted chiefly by interior members, nothing but remonstrance coming from San
Franciscans who might reasonably have been supposed to have a knowledge of
the present and future requirements of the port, equal at least to that of the
legislators living in the interior at distances remote from the harbor whose interests they assumed to defend.

These self-constituted champions of the navigation interests of San Francisco *Legislature*
argued that the water front limits embraced by the line of 1851 were too restricted *Helps the*
and that this enabled the owners of water front property to charge extortionate *Jobbers*
rents for their wharves thus precluding people of moderate means from the benefit of their use. This antimonopoly plea was accompanied by statements that the
proposed extension would enable larger vessels to be berthed conveniently and
would also permit the free ebb and flow of the tide in the channel, thus increasing
its scouring capacity and keeping it clean. The arguments presented seemed plausible enough and would have prevailed had it not been for the uproar raised in
San Francisco where the charge was openly made that Bigler and the legislature
were in league with real estate speculators who had acquired for a song the lots
to be made valuable at what were called "Peter Smith Sales," a name used to
characterize the most outrageous fraud ever devised by the rogues who infested
San Francisco.

The Peter Smith rascality will be described in another place when the subject *The Peter*
of municipal mismanagement and grafting is dealt with; here it is alluded to only *Smith Sales*
to emphasize the fact that the men who were vigorously at work seeking to make
a convenient port of San Francisco received no aid in their efforts from the people whose representatives, when they were not engaged in schemes of spoliation,
were studying out methods of embarrassing those seeking to promote facilities of
the sort calculated to encourage the growth of commerce and the development of
the interior.

Despite these drawbacks the work of improving the water front of San Fran- *Improvement*
cisco proceeded steadily and the result must be set down as one of the greatest *of Water*
achievements of undirected energy of which we have a record. Had there been *Front*
no other accomplishment to place to the credit of the pioneers they might have
rested their fame upon their successful conversion of what under the most favorable
circumstances would have been only a relatively advantageous place for discharg-
ing and loading ships into a district which affords every convenience for the trans-

action of a large part of the business of the leading port of the state. Its creation very greatly facilitated the handling of freight and passengers, the primary object of those who seek to develop and improve natural harbors.

The City's Water Supply in 1851

As in the case of the creation of facilities for shipping, individual exertion was depended upon by the people in the early Fifties for the introduction of a supply of drinking water. In 1851 the privilege was granted to Argo D. Merrifield to introduce fresh water into the City. Previous to that date the dependence had been wholly upon wells, but the failure of the reservoirs at crucial moments, due to the fact that the water obtained was required for immediate consumption, made it necessary to turn to some other source for an adequate quantity to meet the demands of the growing population.

The Mountain Lake Water Company

Merrifield proposed to obtain a sufficient supply from a small lagoon called mountain lake which was situated about four miles west of the Plaza. He was to receive a franchise for a period of twenty-five years at the expiration of which the plant was to be turned over to the City. In the ensuing year, on July 14th, the term of the franchise was reduced to twenty years and a board for rate-making purposes was created consisting of three members of the council and two representatives of the Mountain Lake Co., the name of the concern. It was also provided that at least $50,000 should be expended by the company during the ensuing six months, and a like sum before Jan. 1, 1854; and that a million gallons should be provided daily. This company had a great deal of trouble with the authorities and finally failed in 1862. Before that year the increasing necessities of the town called into existence another company known as the San Francisco Water Works which began operations in 1857, by bringing the waters of Lobos creek around the shores of the Golden Gate, by tunnel through Fort Point and a flume to Black Point, where it was pumped to suitable elevations. Like its predecessors the new company was frequently in collision with the authorities, a fact responsible for the passage by the legislature of 1858 of a law designed to encourage private enterprise in the development of water for cities and towns. Under its provisions the Spring Valley Company was inaugurated and succeeded in meeting public requirements for some years, not, however, without creating considerable friction between itself and the public it served.

Lake Merced Violently Disturbed

A notable occurrence connected with the water supply of the City is mentioned in the "Annals." On the night of November 22, 1852, the few persons living in the vicinity of Lake Merced felt what they thought was an earthquake shock. On the following morning they discovered that the waters of the lake had fallen thirty feet during the night. Various conjectures were advanced to account for the phenomenon. It was suggested that it was due to a volcanic disturbance which had permitted the waters to subside through the bottom of the lake, but opinion finally settled on the heavy rains as an explanation. They had increased the body of water to such an extent that the pressure became great enough to force an outlet to the sea through the banked up sand on its shores.

This singular incident, and the talk it created, suggests that the early San Franciscans may have been impressionable and ready to draw conclusions which careful investigation would not justify. It also illustrates the indisposition of the

KEARNY STREET, LOOKING TOWARD TELEGRAPH HILL.

newcomers to be deterred by phenomena of any sort from carrying through their self-appointed task of settling the country and making the best of its resources, and it furnishes evidence that the pioneers were not ready to accept the theories later advanced by a distinguished English author, who laid down the proposition that regions in which the manifestations of Nature are sometimes over-vigorous is sure to be the habitat of a people deficient in energy and given over to superstitions.

CHAPTER XXII

CLIMATIC AND OTHER PHENOMENA OF SAN FRANCISCO

SEISMIC TROUBLES DO NOT DETER IMMIGRATION—ADVANTAGES WEIGHED AGAINST DISADVANTAGES—THE VERIFIED PREDICTION OF A PIONEER—THE CLIMATE OF CALIFORNIA AND OF SAN FRANCISCO—VARIATIONS BUT NO CHANGES—CLIMATIC PECULIARITIES OF SAN FRANCISCO—THE JAPAN CURRENT—ABSENCE OF HUMIDITY MAKES HEAT ENDURABLE—SNOWFALLS SO RARE THEY BECOME HISTORICAL EVENTS—KILLING A MAN TO START A GRAVEYARD—MAN AND NATURE IN CALIFORNIA—PRACTICAL CHARACTERISTICS OF THE PIONEER—THE NAVIGABLE RIVERS OF CALIFORNIA—THE REGION ABOUT THE BAY.

HOMAS BUCKLE did not write his "History of Civilization in England" until 1857. Had it appeared ten years earlier it might have created a state of mind adverse to the speedy settlement of California. The qualifying word "might" is advisedly employed, for despite the learned disquisitions of the eminent Englishman expericuce has demonstrated that men will go anywhere that a prospect of earning a livelihood offers itself. The most terrifying exhibitions of Nature's unrest will not drive them away permanently from regions where opportunities are presented.

Seismic Disturbances

It is not probable that the knowledge that California occasionally experiences geological disturbances would have stayed the movement from the farms of the southwest and south to the coast, which set in before the discovery of gold and it is absolutely certain that it would have had no deterring influence upon the adventurous men who flocked to the new El Dorado from all parts of the world as soon as the news of the find was heard. They were made of the stuff that would seek gold on the rim of an active crater. Seismic convulsions had less terror for them than the possibility that they might be compelled to reproach themselves with poverty if they neglected the chance to mend their fortunes which the discovery seemed to offer.

The Gold Hunters

But while it is certain that men would have rushed to California with as little fear of consequences as the man who plants a vineyard on the slopes of Vesuvius, it is not impossible that the manifestations may have played some part in shaping the characters of those who encountered them without an accumulation of previons experience calculated to give them confidence of the kind which persuades the sailor who goes down to the sea in ships that his vocation is less hazardous than that of the landsman who is constantly subjected to unexpected dangers far more numerous than those who brave the deep have to contend with.

Balancing of Chances

169

170   SAN FRANCISCO

Advantages Outweigh Disadvantages

The pioneer may not have felt like assuming the role of Ajax defying the lightning, but he promptly began to weigh advantages and disadvantages and to balance them against each other and the result was an early conclusion that the former so greatly exceeded the latter that it was hardly worth while to borrow trouble. The processes of mind by which the conclusion was reached were not those of the sort suggesting indifference; they were efforts in which pure reason played an important part, and they were based on observations which were probably more trustworthy than those of the insurance actuary who calculates the chances of life.

The Pioneer and the Temblor

It was not likely that men who considered earthquakes from the standpoint of the pioneer would ever become victims of superstition. They may not have elaborated seismic theories as highly as they have been during recent years but they were under no illusions concerning the origin of earthquakes and would have laughed at the suggestion that the agency which produced them was supernatural. They may have believed that Nature had its mysteries, but they were ready to pit against them the law of chance. If it proved adverse to them they felt they would be able to repair the damage inflicted by the exercise of energy aided by wit and ingenuity.

A Verified Prediction

A spirit of this sort, which we find expressed in some comments on the subject in the "Annals," was generally prevalent. The writer remarked that almost every year slight shocks and occasionally smarter ones had been felt, and he speculated on what might happen to "the huge granite and brick palaces of four, five and six stories" if a great shock occurred, but he was sure that if they came down with a prodigious crash or if even half of the town should be half destroyed "like another Quito or Carracas" the damage would "speedily be remedied by the indomitable energy and persevering character" of its American builders.

Italy as an Example

Having delivered himself of this prediction, which was more than verified in 1906, the annalist goes on to tell why earthquakes could have no discouraging results and pointed out that Italy, although it had endured and emerged from many calamities of that sort, had never impressed men as an undesirable place to live in, but to the contrary had always proved a powerful magnet to draw people from all parts of the world to enjoy its varied attractions.

Precautions in Building

There were no serious shocks experienced in San Francisco between 1839 and 1854 and for many years after the latter date the solidity of the construction of the "huge granite and brick palaces" was not tested. Perhaps it was not altogether fortunate that the test was deferred for so many years. Had it come earlier, when the City was smaller and less populous a lesson might have been learned which would have tended to minimize the disaster when it finally came. It is advisable to qualify with the word "perhaps," for there is no evidence that the people of San Francisco, at any time prior to 1906, were impressed by the danger of covering large areas with inflammable wooden structures. Indeed when the subject of seismic disturbances was connected with that of construction it was usual to assume that the safest buildings in an earthquake country are those built of wood.

There was undoubtedly a decided disinclination to discuss the subject of earthquake in the early days, but it was by no means due to fear or to apprehension of injurious results to property from such disturbances. It was owing wholly to the feeling that those who were unacquainted with seismic phenomena would be sure to magnify the danger and thus, by causing the country to be misunderstood, impede the settlement of the state. The desire to see this accomplished was general, and with many amounted to something like a passion. It began to assert itself as soon as the feeling that "home" was the region east of the Rocky Mountains weakened, and when those who had merely come for gold made up their minds that the state was a good place in which to abide.

When this stage was reached the Californian began to count up the advantages possessed by California over the older states of the Union, and he found so many to enumerate that he felt a natural reluctance to spoil the picture by inserting in it anything that would detract from his claim that it was "the land of the blest." He did not wish to be forced to explain or to contrast. He deemed it wiser and easier to pass over the matter than to attempt to show cyclones are infinitely more destructive than earthquakes, that more people are killed by excessive heat and cold every year than are taken off in a century by temblors in California. In short, he believed that his new home came as near to realizing the idea of an earthly paradise as possible, and he was not disposed to weaken his belief by dwelling on possibilities that he chose to consider remote. {Californian Advantages}

This reluctance extended down to a very late period, as periods are measured in California. In a history of the state, written in the early Eighties, the subject of earthquakes is scantily treated. Several of those recorded were enumerated by the author, but the barest facts only were related, and no attempt whatever was made to study the phenomena; perhaps because of the absence of data, but more probably for the reason above mentioned, and the additional one that as nothing could be done to avert them there was little benefit to be derived from giving much thought to them. {Earthquake Subject Avoided}

In marked contrast to this avoidance was the very pronounced disposition to expatiate on the charms of the climate. Long before the American occupation travelers had dwelt in glowing terms on the equable temperature of California. Dana, Morrell, Robertson and others had told how over a great part of the long stretch from San Francisco to San Diego snow never fell; and navigators who had visited every country said there was no place that surpassed in delightfulness this neglected part of the world. But it was reserved for the pioneers to appraise the climate at its real worth. Their valuation of this physical feature was never under the mark, but it never was made on a strictly commercial basis as in later years when it began to be perceived that sunshine could be made as valuable an asset as an unfailing gold mine. {Charms of California Climate}

The account given to Eastern people of the resources and attractions of the country rarely omitted mention of the climatic features, which distinguished California so greatly from the states on the Atlantic seaboard, and those of the Middle West and Southwest, which had contributed a large proportion of the immigrants. These descriptions were not always made in the language of the meteorologist, and they often lacked exactness, but on the whole they were sufficiently accurate to convey a correct impression if they had been attentively considered. Their principal interest for us now consists in the fact that they refute the assumption which frequently finds expression, that the climate of California is changing. {California Climate Unchanged}

The records show the same uncertainties regarding the weather as those experienced in the twentieth century. There were alternations of wet and dry seasons in the Fifties just as there are at present, and the fluctuations in the volume of precipitation were as great then as now. There was one mistake made by the pioneers in their descriptions that has resulted in a misconception, which explanations seem powerless to correct. They were accustomed to speaking of the rainy and the dry season, thus conveying the idea that at one period of the year there is incessant rainfall, while during the other there is no precipitation at all. This misstates the fact. If they had spoken of "the season when it rains" instead of "the rainy season," and had added that in certain months it scarcely rains at all, it is possible that the very common error that California is alternately drenched and desiccated would not be made.

Inexact Weather Records

It may be said in defense of the inexactness of the early reporters of weather conditions in California that there was a series of winters after that of 1850-51, in which the rainfall was copious, ranging in San Francisco from 18.55 inches in 1851-52 to 35.26 in the following year, and not falling below the first named quantity in any year until 1862-63, when there was something like a repetition of the exceedingly dry season of 1850-51, when the precipitation was only 7.42 inches. Ten years of such experience would naturally suggest the division into rainy and dry seasons, but the terms, when not qualified by the information that the rains are frequently punctuated by intervals of cloudless weather, naturally convey the false impression that Californians constantly seek to remove.

Many Brands of Climate

The climate of California can be best comprehended by actual experience, which must be extensive, for the area of the state is great, stretching through many degrees of latitude, and having a longitudinal breadth which, while not great, has two ranges of mountains running through it, whose elevations result in producing climatic conditions in parts closely resembling those of the older states of the Union. In fact there are many sorts of climate in California and they are not determined by latitude or longitude, but by physical peculiarities, which produce striking variations that prevent a description that accurately fits one locality being correctly applied to another section only a few miles distant.

Climate of San Francisco

The climate of San Francisco enjoys the distinction of differing from that of most other parts of the state. It has peculiarities which cause it to be misunderstood by the casual visitor. These peculiarities can be best understood by attentive study of the records. Before the discovery of gold several pioneers appreciated the value of careful observation, and as a result the professional meteorologists have data extending back fully sixty years. Among the careful citizens who engaged in this work were Dr. G. H. Gibbons, Dr. T. M. Logan and Thomas Tennant, and from their tables the present weather bureau officials have been able to extract information which has greatly assisted them in their important duties.

Weather Bureau Records

The records of the weather bureau only date back to February 2, 1871, but as its operations deal with the past and the future as much as with the present, its accounts of climate conditions are more dependable than those made by empirical observers, whose observations only extend over limited periods. This being the case it will be wise to disregard the exactions of chronological presentation in order that a comprehensive idea of the conditions existing in the past and which are likely to endure may be gained by the reader. Such a view may be derived from the data specially prepared for this history by Professor A. G. McAdie, the head of the weather bureau in San Francisco in 1912, and during many years prior to that date.

In order to understand the climatic peculiarities of San Francisco it is necessary to give consideration to the general climatic conditions of the Pacific coast,

SAN FRANCISCO 173

which are controlled by four factors. The first of these is the location of the
areas of high and low pressures, which within recent years have been known as
the great centers of atmospheric action. These have been carefully observed and
the meteorologist is aware of certain conditions corresponding with the departures
of those centers of action from their normal location. The second factor in determining the climate of California is the prevailing drift of the surface air from
west to east in temperate latitudes. The west, northwest winds so characteristic
of the California coast north of Point Conception, have often been miscalled the
trades, which, properly speaking, are the northeast and southeast winds of lower
latitudes. The correct designation of the California coast winds is "prevailing
westerlies."

Much has been written about the influence of the Japan current in controlling The Japanese
Current
the temperature, but as a matter of fact it plays a small part in moderating climatic conditions. The Japan and Bering sea currents have their greatest strength
at the end of winter, or in the early spring, while for the equatorial current the
conditions are reversed. Coming from the south the equatorial current is most
marked in the end of summer or early in the fall.

A third factor is the proximity of the Pacific ocean, the great natural conser- Influence of
Pacific Ocean
vator of heat. Both because of the great mass of water with its high specific heat,
and the water vapor carried by the prevailing wind, the range of temperature is
small along the coast from Puget Sound to San Diego bay. It is because of this
blanket of vapor that the isotherms run nearly north and south instead of east
and west as they do in other parts of the United States. Topography is the
fourth factor. The state has an extremely diversified surface. In one county,
Inyo, is situated Death valley, wherein lies the lowest land in the United States,
some 273 feet below sea level. Seventy-five miles west of this locality is the eastern range of the great Western Divide. The high Sierra culminates in this section. Mount Whitney, the highest point in the United States (excluding Alaska),
has an elevation of 14,502 feet above sea level. On the other hand near the northern part of the state, where the coast range and the Sierra come together, we find
Shasta 14,380 feet. Along the coast line there are several remarkable bays, and
within short distances marked differences in the surface air drainage exist, and
finally, perhaps, the greatest of the natural features is the extensive inland valley
of California.

Within the limits described the highest temperature in the United States occurs. Highest
Temperature
The shade temperatures of the Colorado desert frequently reach 130° F., while the
most noticeable climatic features of the coast are the moderate temperatures, frequent fogs and high winds. The latter, however, rarely attain a high velocity;
their continuance during the season of the year when the atmosphere is usually
undisturbed in sections is what produces the unusual summer climate of San Francisco.

The weather bureau has seen fit to comment on the difficulties which beset the Climatic
Peculiarities
Misunderstood
stranger in his endeavor to understand the climatic conditions existing in San Fran-
cisco and furnishes this explanation, which contains facts that even residents who
have lived in the City for some time are apt to overlook unless specially observant.
Professor McAdie says: "The climate of San Francisco is so unusual that it has
attracted universal attention. When a native of that city is asked which is the
coldest month he is apt to say that July is. If asked which is the warmest month

he may say December. His confusion arises from the comparatively small range of temperature. The mean annual is 56°. May and November have practically the same temperature, and are about ten degrees warmer than the mean. The warmest month is September, when the temperature rises to 61°, and the coldest is January, when the mean is slightly above 50°. The highest temperature recorded in San Francisco was on September 8, 1904, when 101° was observed, and the lowest 29° on January 15, 1888. The next warmest day was June 29, 1891, when the temperature reached 100°. Temperatures above 90° occur very rarely. Warm days are most likely in September and October. A warm period seldom exceeds three days, and as a rule is brought to a close by strong and dense fog and temperature ranging from 50° to 55°."

<small>Heat Without Discomfort</small>

These observations may be supplemented by the statement that the 101° recorded on the 8th of September, 1904, did not prevent the Knights Templar marching in procession, enveloped in their black velvet cloaks, on the occasion of their triennial gathering in that year; nor did the lofty flight of the mercury cause any interruption of ordinary avocations. There were no strokes, although the Knights marched in the blazing sun along an unshaded street; nor were there any prostrations. The explanation of this extraordinary exemption is the total absence of humidity, which is so marked a feature of California heat and makes it endurable even when it is uncomfortable.

<small>Rarity of Snow Falls</small>

Snow falls so rarely in San Francisco that when it does the occurrence attains the dignity of an unusual if not an historical event. The heaviest snowfall ever recorded in San Francisco was that of December, 1882, when over three inches fell. In February, 1887, there was another fall, the quantity being about the same in the lower levels of the City, but a depth of fully seven inches was measured in some places. On the 20th of January, 1854, the annalist of San Francisco records that ice an inch thick was formed in the streets, and that within doors water in pitchers was generally frozen. At two P. M. icicles hung from the roofs of houses in the City, on which the sun had been shining all day. Small ponds in the vicinity were frozen over and there was excellent skating in the mission. The weather was so extraordinary that the native Californians declared that the Yankees had bewitched the climate. It may be added that there is no record of any repetition of the phenomenal occurrences mentioned since 1854.

<small>Vital Statistics Defective</small>

The pioneers were convinced that the climate of San Francisco was conducive to health and the general conditions supported their view. There are, however, no vital statistics available, and if they existed they would have small comparative value because of the peculiar composition of the population, in which males of an age which offers resistance to disease largely predominated. Inferences may, however, be drawn from current jokes, which, under the circumstances, are perhaps as reliable as mortality tables. One of these was to the effect that a man had to be killed to start a grave yard.

<small>Few Visitations</small>

The only serious visitation to which the City was subjected was in 1852. In the fall of that year there were numerous cases of cholera, but the disease's ravages were not nearly so great as in other places in the United States. The pioneers were under no illusion regarding the cause. The utter disregard of sanitary precautions, and the rapid extension of the City into the waters of the bay were held responsible for the trouble, and the authorities were roundly denounced for their failure to perform the duty of compelling cleanliness; but it does not appear that any disposition existed to provide funds for that purpose.

The seismic and climatic phenomena described above may have had some influence in shaping the character of the community in the early Fifties, but it would have been difficult to establish the fact, and it would have been equally troublesome to trace a connection between the other physical peculiarities which theorists assume play an important part in moulding the dispositions of a people and determining whether they shall be indolent or industrious. There is no proof that lofty mountains and wide spaces were awesome, and that their proximity had a deterent effect on energy. If the pioneers gave them much thought it was not of the kind calculated to breed superstition, for, from the beginning, those who did not admire the grandeur of California mountains, and the beauty of its scenery, devoted themselves to the task of bending Nature to their own purposes.

Only as the latter were affected can it be said that Nature had much to do with California temperament, or the creation of that which a later generation, with the poetic instinct high developed, has been pleased to call "atmosphere." The physical peculiarities of California influenced the population indirectly, but the operating cause was usually economic. In no wise was it traceable to fear or a feeling of insecurity. The general attitude toward natural phenomena of a disturbing kind was one of careless indifference, and sometimes it was even jocular, as was the case when Bret Harte wrote his condensed novel in 1867, in which he pictured the total destruction of San Francisco in a fashion that amused the residents of the City more than it did outsiders, because the latter could not understand the subtle allusions to the aspirations of a neighboring city.

The pioneers of 1849-56 would have enjoyed the paragraph referred to quite as much as the people of San Francisco did ten or eleven years later, although Oakland had as yet made no progress towards urban greatness. They would have accepted it in the same spirit that they did the more seriously expressed conviction of the annalist, that the indomitable American spirit would rise superior to any untoward manifestations of Nature, because they were matter-of-fact men trained by experience to count chances, which they did with deliberation, and having done so they were firmly convinced that Nature's smiles so greatly outnumbered its frowns in California that it would be idle to take the latter seriously.

These practical men were more disposed to think of rivers and mountains and great plains from the standpoint of possible utilization, and gave only a passing thought to geological phenomena, and that usually was confined to speculation concerning the part they played in assisting man to secure the much desired precious metals, and in fashioning the water courses, which might be made to bear to the mart they were establishing the products of the region they drained. They were prosaic, a fact which stirring events have not been able to obscure. They looked at everything from the standpoint of utility.

The Sierra Nevada on the east and the Coast range on the west were interesting to them because they were the mountains inclosing a great plain, which those gifted with the ability to peer into the future realized would one day become a vast agricultural region. It cannot be said that this perception was very general in the Fifties. To the contrary, there was a very prevalent belief which was retained during nearly a generation, that what is now recognized as the greatest body of fertile land in California, and perhaps in the whole world, was chiefly desert.

Some Far Seeing Men

There are traces, however, of the fact that there were far-seeing men who realized that the Sacramento and the San Joaquin valleys inclosed by the Sierra and Coast range were destined to be something else than mere pasturing grounds for herds of cattle and flocks of sheep, and business acumen very early divined that the region we now know as the Great valley, a plain some 400 miles long and from fifty to sixty miles in width, almost unbroken throughout its length and breadth except in the northern half, where its even surface is varied by the Marysville Buttes, would one day be the chief contributor to the commercial greatness of the port of San Francisco.

Navigable Rivers

It was appreciation of this fact that caused a lively interest to be taken in the rivers which drained this great plain. The Sacramento in the northern half, and the San Joaquin in the southern half of the enormous valley, it was thought would develop in their vicinity a large quantity of agricultural land, the products of which would be borne on their waters to the Bay of San Francisco, into which they discharged, and to the port of that name, whence they would be sent to all parts of the world. As these two rivers are the only navigable streams in California, and as in the period when the development of the resources of the state began in earnest, water transportation still held its place in the esteem of men as the most feasible and cheapest way of moving products, it is not surprising that the importance attached to them was very great.

The Great Valley

But while this great valley appealed to the imaginative and tempted the practical to speculate on its possibilities, nearby resources were not overlooked. The great Santa Clara valley and other regions close to the bay were perhaps earlier objects of consideration than the vast tract whose settlement was long delayed, a fact attested by the efforts made at a very early date to provide rail transportation for the thriving region. The land on the peninsula side of the bay, intervening between the City and San Jose, and the valleys south of that city, was also favorably regarded and that of the transbay country, comprising the county of Alameda, and the timbered regions were all held in esteem, and the day was looked forward to when they would make urgent demands upon the facilities of the port, which were daily being added to, and which those concerned in the City's development believed would soon rival those of the greatest harbors of the world.

CHAPTER XXIII

TAXATION AND OTHER GOVERNMENTAL PROBLEMS OF THE PIONEER

NATIVE CALIFORNIANS SLIGHTLY TAXED—EXEMPTION FROM TAXATION NOT A BLESSING—ABUSE OF AN INHERITED SYSTEM—THE SPECULATIVE LURE—GENERAL KEARNY AND THE ALCALDES—ALCALDE JUSTICE IN CALIFORNIA—FIRST ALCALDE UNDER THE AMERICAN FLAG—SAN FRANCISCO'S FIRST COUNCIL—THE RUSH TO THE GOLD DIGGINGS—PEACE EASILY KEPT—ORDINANCE AGAINST GAMBLING—COUNCILMEN DESERT THEIR POSTS TO DIG FOR GOLD—NATIONAL AND LOCAL POLITICS—FACTIONAL FEELING—THREE OPPOSING SETS OF COUNCILLORS—MILITARY INTERFERENCE IN CIVIL AFFAIRS—DELEGATES TO THE CONSTITUTIONAL CONVENTION—THE NEED OF REGULATION—A SHORT BALLOT EXPERIMENT IN 1849—VOTE ON ADOPTION OF THE CONSTITUTION—HORACE HAWES A WELL HATED REFORMER—A DEFIANT AYUNTAMIENTO—HAWES TURNED DOWN.

Production and Taxation

HE adoption of a form of government whose theories commend themselves as sound does not always assure the people that they will be well governed. Imperfect laws, administered by able and honest men are likely to produce better results than can be derived from a perfect legal system executed by venal and incompetent officials. The Spanish and Mexican inhabitants of California had their affairs conducted for them by officials, during nearly three quarters of a century, without obtaining any special benefits from their services; but on the other hand they were never seriously victimized by the rapacity of those who were placed over them by others, or by men whom they chose to serve them.

Taxation Light Under Spanish Rule

It would not be safe to assume, however, that because the Californians nearly escaped taxation that their exemption was due to the wisdom of their rulers or to the excellence of their system and the integrity of those who administered the law. The evidence points to a wholly different cause, namely the failure to produce on a scale calculated to afford a field in which the ingenious and unscrupulous elements of society could successfully and profitably operate. The cynical observation of Governor Alvarado concerning the return of certain moneys to the treasury, which it was supposed had been expended, but through prudent expenditure had been saved, indicates that occurrences of that sort must have been extremely rare for he virtually declared that the case was so exceptional that it deserved comment and reward.

Spanish Rule Terminated

The Spanish rule in California terminated in 1823 and the last governor under the crown was made the first Mexican governor. His administration did not give perfect satisfaction nor did that of his successors. There were frequent squabbles of a factional sort, the accounts of which sometimes suggest the absurdities of the court of the Duchy of Gerolstein, made famous by Offenbach, but there are no accounts of uprisings on account of excessive taxation or oppression. If the native Californians were oppressed they were unaware of the fact until Ide told them that such was the case in his Bear Flag declaration of independence, the preamble of which recited a formidable list of grievances regarding the nature of which there must have been serious doubts in their minds.

A Cheaply Administered Government

The government of California before the occupation was carried on for a ridiculously small sum of money, so insignificant indeed that the figures cast a doubt on their own accuracy. It seems incredible that any sort of an establishment could have been maintained upon the revenues of the territory, which are given at $32,000 in the year 1831. The cost of presidial garrisons, and the salary of the commandante general and the pay of a few auxiliary troops were the chief charges and they amounted to considerably more than the revenue, aggregating $131,000, or pesos, in the year mentioned, but only $32,000 appears to have been directly drawn from the people; the deficit was made up by borrowing from the fathers, who up to that date reckoned the central government in Mexico as debtor to the amount of $450,000.

Ridiculously Small Revenues

A review of the administrative methods of the Spanish and their successors disclosed why the revenues were so ridiculously small. The native Californians, from highest to lowest, were systematic nullifiers of regulations and paid no respect to tariffs. By common consent disregard of the laws relating to taxation was counted a virtue, and evasion was more honored than disposition to pay. Smuggling was conducted with such openness that it was impossible to corrupt an official. When a whole community joins in a practice offenders cannot be singled out for punishment. In such cases it is the part of wisdom to ignore what cannot be prevented, and this was a policy adhered to by both Spanish and Mexicans with sufficient closeness to make the exceptions stand out as acts of oppression, which the people, who had become unaccustomed to contributing anything to the support of government, really believed they were.

Exemption from Taxation not a Blessing

If exemption from taxation could be considered a blessing the native Californians would be regarded as a blessed people, but modern enlightened opinion holds to quite another view, and justly considers that to be the best government which can extract the largest revenue and expend it for the benefit of those from whom it is drawn. It is not apparent, however, that the pioneers entertained this advanced opinion. They appear to have been influenced very largely by the prevalent belief of the period, that the best governed community is the one that is taxed the least, and doubtless adherence to that idea played its part in causing the ready acceptance of the suggestion that the existing system should be continued without any material modification or change until the necessity for it should arise.

Adherence to Ancient Customs

As a result, during the first years after the occupation of California, Americans living in Yerba Buena were content to adhere to the ancient customs. They were not, however, voluntarily adopted, but were imposed upon them by the military authorities who, after a conquest, never display celerity in the matter of acceptance of popular rule. It was deemed wise by those in command that the institutions of the country should be maintained so far as possible until the central government should put machinery in motion that would give the people something better.

NORTH BEACH AS IT APPEARED IN 1851

SAN FRANCISCO

The project seemed to be in accord with those conservative instincts usually justified by the assumption that the slow course is the safest; but in this instance the belief did not work out in practice. It is hardly conceivable that any system adopted by a sane body of Americans could have produced as much mischief as was entailed by the retention of the alcaldes whose powers, when they came to be exercised by men animated by the desire for gain, were abused in some cases and in others injudiciously asserted under the mistaken impression that the community would be benefited.

Abuse of an Inherited System

The early critics of the system assert that under the Mexican law the entire control of municipal affairs was intrusted to the alcalde, and that he administered justice according to his own ideas, the only limitation on his power being his ability to carry his decrees into effect. It was perfectly safe to intrust the average Spaniard or Mexican with extensive authority, for they lacked the energy, even though they may have possessed the inclination, to abuse their power. It has been related that during the long interval between the successful Mexican revolution and the American occupation of California very few lots were asked for and granted in the pueblos, and that in some cases after grants had been made and accepted by individuals they abandoned them.

Town Lots not in Demand by Natives

There was a very speedy change when the "gringo" took hold of affairs. The results have hitherto been variously regarded, but no matter what success may have attended the vigorous efforts to energize a dormant community and start it on the road to progress it will never be contended that the means adopted to effect the purpose were scrupulously conceived or carried out. Nothing is plainer in the history of San Francisco than the fact that the Americans and other people first on the ground were convinced that Yerba Buena should be speedily settled, and that the best way to accomplish that object was to put the land in possession of people who would occupy or make use of it, and thus promote the public good. The theory was sound, but the absence of effort to compel those who were permitted to buy land for a song to make use of their purchases opened wide the door to speculation and the grossest forms of fraud.

The New Settlers Eager for Real Estate

One of the first acts of Commodore Sloat was to issue a proclamation promising the people that they should be governed by officials of their own choosing. It was accompanied by a prediction which seems to point to the existence of a strong speenlative spirit, which he desired to make use of to attract native Californians to the new government. He said that the undoubted effect of the change would be to enhance the value of real estate. His opinion was certainly shared by all Americans, who knew by experience that land is valueless until it is made use of and a demand for it created. The native, however, profited little by his advice, which practically amounted to an admonition to get land, and they seemed to be even less concerned to exercise the privilege of choosing their alcaldes.

Commodore Sloat's Prediction

Sloat's proclamation was issued on the 7th of July, 1846, and in August an election for alcalde was ordered for September 15th. There were several candidates in Monterey, but the total vote cast was 338, and the successful man received only 68, which gave him a plurality over his competitors. But while the naval branch thus liberally accorded the people the right to choose their own rulers, the army was not disposed to relinquish any authority. General Kearny very soon intervened, doubtless influenced by the belief that the alcaldes had too many powers conferred upon them. The author of a history of California has told us what

The Proclamation of July 7, 1846

they were at the time. He says that "the office of the alcalde of Monterey involved jurisdiction over every breach of the peace, every crime, every business obligation and every disputed land title within a space of 300 miles. To his court was an appeal from every other alcalde's court in the district, but there was none from it to any other tribunal." The alcalde was in effect supreme, and "there was not a judge on any bench in the United States or England whose power was so absolute as that of the alcalde of Monterey."

<small>Arbitrary Acts of General Kearny</small>

These extraordinary powers must have resulted in working an injury to the commonwealth had they been permitted to endure for any considerable period, and therefore the critic hesitates to characterize as an act of unjustifiable usurpation the arbitrary performance of General Kearny, who promptly assumed control over the magistrates and removed them at his pleasure. He did not always proceed with that respect for civil authority now demanded and occasionally took a course which would in these days cause a flame of indignation throughout the land. His method of dealing with John H. Nash, the alcalde of Sonoma, illustrates his arbitrary propensities. When he apprised Nash that he was dismissed the latter resented the dismissal and threatened to invoke the assistance of his friends among the Bear Flag party. The general settled the question by kidnaping Nash, Lieutenant W. T. Sherman, afterward the general of the armies of the United States, acting as kidnaper and carrying him to San Francisco, from whence he was removed to Monterey to prevent his giving further trouble.

<small>The Alcaldes Regulated</small>

Not only did Kearny thus effectively regulate the alcaldes, he also exercised the functions which from the beginning must have been regarded as more important than the administration of justice. As already related he attempted to make grants of land on the water front of San Francisco. On March 10, 1846, he issued a decree, in which he granted to the people of San Francisco by virtue of his authority as governor of California, all the right, title and interest of the government to the beach and water front lots on the east front of the town between Rincon Point and Fort Montgomery, except such as should be selected for the use of the United States.

<small>Alcalde Justice</small>

The first settlers of Yerba Buena were perhaps justified in thinking lightly of the judicial side of the alcalde's administrative duties. Law and justice was dispensed by them very much after the manner of the Oriental cadi until after the Americans came. That this mode was perfectly satisfactory to most of the native Californians is proved by the tenacity with which they clung to alcalde law in the lower part of the state down to very recent times. It is related of a major domo of the estate of Don Juan Foster in San Diego county, who was repeatedly elected as justice of the peace in San Juan Capistrano, that he invariably gave the natives who came before him to have their disputes settled the choice of statutory law or his own, and that they always chose his, which, in their minds, stood for common sense, and was not complicated with intricacies they could not comprehend.

<small>First American Alcalde</small>

But the complexities introduced by the newcomers would not permit the continuance of this simple method of dispensing justice. Washington A. Bartlett, the first alcalde under the American flag, was able to get along with the system, but one of his immediate successors, George Hyde, was compelled to call for the assistance of an ayuntamiento. He selected six persons to act in that capacity, but his action did not meet the approval of Mason, who issued an ordinance in which the necessity of providing an efficient town government was dwelt upon. Among the reasons assigned was the rapid growth of the town and the fact that the expected advent of the whaling fleet would make its policing necessary.

In accordance with Mason's ordinance an election was held on the 13th of September, 1847, and William Glover, William D. Howard, William A. Leidersdorff, E. P. Jones, Robert A. Parker and William S. Clarke were elected. Hyde attempted to have his selections endorsed and an opposition ticket was put in the field for that purpose but only two of his appointees, Leidersdorff and Parker, were elected. The highest vote received by any of the six successful candidates was that of Glover, for whom 126 ballots were cast. William S. Clarke received only 72 votes. Leidersdorff was chosen treasurer.

San Francisco's First Council

There are no signs of increased efficiency in the records of this first council, one of whose earliest acts was the rescinding of the regulation restricting the sale of lands. While the bars were thus thrown down to speculation no harm ensued directly, because the speculative element was too small at the time to be very mischievous. The administration of Hyde was attended with much dissatisfaction and he resigned on that account, not, however, until complaints were made against him which caused Governor Mason to institute a formal inquiry, the result of which did not disclose anything sufficiently grave to warrant his removal. Hyde's place was filled by Dr. J. Townsend, who was sworn in on the 3d of April, 1848, and was in office when the gold rush began.

Throwing Down the Bars

The second election took place on October 3, 1848, when Dr. T. M. Leavenworth, who had been elected on the 29th of August as first alcalde, was again chosen. At the same time B. R. Buckalew and Barton Mowrey were chosen councilors. There were 158 votes polled at this election, a number suggestive of indifference to public duty, but the smallness of the vote is accounted for by the fact that there had been an exodus to the newly discovered placers. Its extent may be measured by the fact that in May the "Californian" was obliged to issue a fly sheet instead of its regular publication in order to announce that it would be necessary to suspend as the printers had gone to the diggings, an example which was promptly followed by its rival the "Star."

A Small Number of Voters

It is not surprising that under such circumstances the councilors abandoned the duties they had been elected to perform. The temptation of enormous rewards to be obtained in the gold field proved irresistible, and for several months no meeting was held by them. The result was unfortunate for the prestige of civil authority, for it involved the necessity of the governor making a direct appeal to the people to assist in the apprehension of deserters from the army and navy who were abandoning their commands and ships. The request, however, bore no fruit. Nobody seemed to think that he was called upon to keep men from participating in the opportunity to get rich quickly even if obligations were violated and the public interests thereby jeopardized.

Authorities Desert their Posts

Up to the time of the gold discovery the course of events in San Francisco had not been attended by much excitement of any sort except that growing out of the possibility of getting hold of desirable property cheaply. As already noted the citizens seemed so engrossed in their personal affairs that Governor Mason was impelled to remind them that an efficient government was required in order to insure the policing of the town. The possibility of an influx of whalers suggested that something of the kind would be necessary to keep the sailors in order while in port, but there was no apprehension of trouble from any other quarter.

A Vegetating Community

182　SAN FRANCISCO

Police Protection

If the whalers proved a troublesome element the fact has not been recorded. There is evidence that they were not difficult to deal with, for we find that in 1849, when the population had increased to fully 5,000, the only police protection was that afforded by six constables, utterly undisciplined, and no more effective than a like number of men performing the duties of peace officer in an interior village. If the sailors or other classes in the growing seaport were turbulent no special effort was made to keep them within bounds. There were very few disturbances during 1847 requiring the active intervention of the authorities, and that probably excused the failure to make ample provision for maintaining the peace, when the necessity arose in 1848, as it did soon after the gold rush began. There was as much indifference on this point then as during the interval when the most serious troubles were those which grew out of over-indulgence in aguardienti, and the disputes of the gamblers and their patrons.

Council Attempts to Stop Gambling

On January 11, 1848, the council had passed an ordinance in relation to gambling, but it was less designed to repress the evil than to create a source of revenue for the town. It provided that all the money found on gambling tables should be seized and turned into the treasury. Its effect was to indirectly license the practice of public gambling, which had been so prevalent in California before its occupation by the Americans. It proved absolutely ineffective so far as restraining it was concerned, but it did produce a feeling of irritation among the considerable class who regarded interference with the monte table as an infringement of personal liberty.

The City Limits

At the time of the election of Leavenworth as first alcalde, the limits of the town for judicial purposes embraced a small area. They were within boundaries described by a line commencing at the mouth of Guadalupe creek, following its course to where it emptied into the bay, and from thence west to the Pacific, thence north along the coast to the entrance to the harbor, thence eastwardly through the middle of that inlet to the bay, including the whole of the anchorage ground. Marked out on the map of the City of to-day this seems but a comparatively small space, but it soon taxed the abilities of the newly created authorities to keep peace within its limits.

Prevalence of Crime

Perhaps had the councilmen remained at their posts the troubles which speedily arose might have been averted, but disorder gained ground rapidly and dissatisfaction manifested itself. Public meetings were held to urge the necessity of establishing a provisional government because of the growing prevalence of crime. As is usual in all such public movements the system rather than the administrators was held responsible, and it was believed that a speedy remedy would be found in abandoning the Spanish-Mexican methods and resorting to those to which the dissentients had been accustomed in their old homes. Much stress was laid upon the neglect of congress and resolutions were passed by gatherings in December, urging the holding of a general convention in the following March. Meetings were held in other parts of the state, at which resolutions of like tenor were adopted.

National and Local Affairs

At the period we are speaking of it was the fashion to subordinate everything political to what was conceived to be the most important issue. National, state and municipal affairs were inextricably bound together, and the determination of inconsequential as well as important local matters was dependent on the attitude of the people of the various communities towards the institution of slavery. It was not always possible to distinguish the effects of the injection of partisan prejudice into local affairs, but a searching analysis of the moving causes that produced dissension almost invariably discloses that no dispute, however trivial, was wholly dissociated from national politics.

California was more afflicted in this regard than any other part of the country during the decade preceding the Civil war, and in the early Fifties it was a battle ground on which the advocates of the extension of slavery, and those opposed to the institution fought with varying success. The adoption of a constitution, in which the part of freedom was boldly taken and maintained, by no means settled the dispute. California unequivocally declared against slavery and took its position as one of the free states, but the Southerners, who had entered the country in large numbers, refused to abide by the decision of the constitutional convention. *A Political Battle Ground*

It is due to this incessant conflict that there was so much division of opinion on local matters in San Francisco, and to the evil influence of the overshadowing importance of the national issue may be traced many of the troubles to account for which contradictory explanations have been given. It is improbable that the men who on two occasions exhibited their ability to absolutely control the lawless elements of San Francisco would have found it difficult to preserve the peace if they had not been divided by the burning question of the day. It was solely owing to this division that extra legal methods had to be resorted to in order to save the City from the rule of the mob. The ordinary machinery of government had been taken possession of by men engrossed by one idea, and who could not find a point of contact which would permit them to act in unison with others on questions purely local, while the control of the ballot box, the courts and the legislature was necessary to carry out their larger aims. *Local Matters Subordinated*

It will be seen that men who were utterly unable to come together to use the machinery provided for the purpose of giving effect to American theories of government, could strike hands and work shoulder to shoulder for a common cause when that machinery was discarded. But until they did so every question of municipal government was directly or indirectly influenced by national politics. To the complications thus introduced are attributable the difficulties growing out of the selection of bad men for municipal positions; men who usually owed their success in securing office to the division of the forces of those who would naturally stand for good government and the indifference of those who were too busily engaged in trying to advance their own fortunes to concern themselves very much about the methods adopted by others to achieve their purposes. *Municipal Government Weak*

There were other causes of division than those produced by national politics, but in some manner they were always linked up with the latter. The connection may not have been obtrusively apparent, but it existed nevertheless, and had its effect in aligning men against each other who would have naturally been found in the same group if the disturbing influence had not kept them apart. In the elections of January, 1849, evidence of the disturbing element may be easily traced. On the surface it appeared to be a contest to decide which were the best men to carry out local policies, but the squabbles which resulted in three sets of claimants to the town councilship, all of them attempting to exercise authority simultaneously, would not have engendered so much bitterness if there had not been back of them the factional feeling which divided the City into hostile camps. *Causes of Division*

In April, 1849, the military still assumed to have charge of civil affairs. Brigadier General Bennett Riley on the 13th of that month announced that in addition to commanding the tenth military department, he would also attend to "the administration of civil affairs in California." A district legislature had been elected on the 21st of February, 1849, which ordered the abolition of the office of alcalde and the substitution of justices of the peace in their stead, but Leavenworth, when ordered to deliver the documents in his possession refused to do so, being instigated to take that stand by General Persifer Smith. The legislative assembly also ordered an election for the purpose of choosing a sheriff, who was to take steps to oust Leavenworth from office, but the latter contrived to resurrect the council of 1848, which gave its sanction to his proceedings. Riley finally ended the dispute by declaring the legislative assembly to be an illegal body, and issued the proclamation directing the election of certain specified municipal and district provisional officers, to which reference has already been made.

Military Usurpation Denounced
The issuance of this proclamation by General Riley was denounced at a large public meeting as a gross usurpation, and an interference with the right of the people to organize a government for their own protection, but it ended in accepting his order for the holding of an election to choose delegates to attend a convention to be held at Monterey. But the committee chosen by the meeting, while making this concession, let it be known that they regarded Riley's proclamation as "discourteous and disrespectful," and the legislative assemblymen announced their intention to hold until deprived of their offices by the people who had chosen them. With the view of securing an expression of opinion on the subject an election was held on the 9th of July, at which 167 voted for their continuance and only seven against. The main body of the electorate having declined to take the trouble to vote, the assembly, regarded the indorsement as unsatisfactory and dissolved itself, and Leavenworth was reinstated.

Election Under Military Auspices
On the 1st of August another election was held under the auspices of the military. It succeeded in bringing out a larger number of the electorate, the vote for the successful candidates ranging from 1,516 for John W. Geary, to 691 for Gabriel B. Post. At this election Peter H. Burnett was chosen judge of the supreme court; Horace Hawes, prefect; John W. Geary, first alcalde; Frank Turk, second alcalde; Francis Guerrero and James R. Curtiss, sub-prefects. A town council designated as the ayuntamiento was also chosen. It consisted of Talbot H. Green, Henry A. Harrison, Alfred J. Ellis, Stephen C. Harris, Theodore B. Winton, John Townsend, Rodman M. Price, William H. Davis, Bezer Simmons, Samuel Brannan, William M. Stewart, and Gabriel B. Post.

Delegates to Monterey Convention
At this election delegates to the convention to be held at Monterey were chosen. There were several tickets in the field and the vote was much split up. Edward Gilbert, Myron Norton, William M. Gwin, Joseph Hobson, William M. Stewart, William D. M. Howard, Francis J. Lippett, Alfred J. Ellis, Francisco Sanchez and Rodman M. Price were elected. The convention, which met at Monterey on the first of September, completed its organization on the 4th. Its deliberations were continued during the month and extended well into October, the constitution framed by it being finished and signed on the 13th of that month. Its adoption affected the future growth of San Francisco in many important particulars, but, as will be seen, as the story unfolds, hardly in the way that the sanguine believer in the efficacy of forms imagined it would.

The deliberations of the convention clearly indicate that the dominating idea of the majority of the framers of the constitution was to prevent the introduction

SAN FRANCISCO   185

of slavery into California. San Francisco had been particularly insistent that every "honorable means" should be used to frustrate the attempt that would be made to foist the institution upon the people of the territory, and resolutions were adopted at mass meetings to instruct the delegates elected by the voters of the town to that effect. Apart from the absorbing interest in the slavery question the general public, and for that matter the delegates themselves when assembled in convention, had no such well defined ideas respecting the relations of municipalities to the state government as those now existing. As a result the instrument contained no innovations of consequence, the delegates being content to accept and copy the methods of the states of the Union which assumed that the sort of local autonomy which guarantees to the people the right to conduct their own immediate affairs was a dangerous privilege to confer.

The experiences through which the City had passed, and the condition in which it was while the convention was sitting certainly were not of a nature to create the impression that municipalities do not require guidance and excessive regulation by an authorty only indirectly affected by the prosperity or adversity of the regulated community. John W. Geary, who had been elected at the same time that the delegates to the convention were chosen, gave some information on this point. In his capacity of first alcalde he addressed the ayuntamiento on its assemblage and told them that affairs were in very bad shape. He dwelt particularly on the necessity of taking precautions to preserve order and insure security, and emphasized the desirability of economy, giving point to this part of his address by declaring that there was not a dollar in the treasury and that the City was greatly in debt. Municipal Affairs in Bad Shape

"You are without a single police officer," he said, "and have not the means of confining a prisoner for an hour. There is no place to shelter sick strangers or bury them when dead. In short, you are without a single requisite for the promotion of prosperity or for the maintenance of order." Having made perfectly clear the deficiencies of the City the chief magistrate recommended the addition of a license tax to supplement that on real estate, which he claimed, should not bear all the burden of government. He indicated among the classes of business that should pay a license tax that of auctioning, which was very prevalent at the time, and urged that drays and lighters should be licensed. Deficiencies Pointed out by Geary

Another part of his address disclosed the fact that the Public documents were in the custody of private individuals, probably because the City had no place to keep them. The failure to provide a place of detention for criminals was not the only instance of neglect; it appears that there was no building or office in the town, which the people could call their own, and that there was no attempt made to keep the records together. The omission to make provision for the detention of criminals was promptly repaired, the first money appropriated by the ayuntamiento being for the purchase of a deserted brig lying in the harbor, which was used as a jail for some months by the City. No Public Building or Office

It is worth noting that the system thus temporarily resorted to by the pioneers was essentially the same as that now extolled as a novelty. When the ayuntamiento met on the 6th of August, 1849, it organized and immediately proceeded to appoint a list of officials now selected by popular vote. The tax collector, city attorney, sheriff and treasurer were all designated by the governing body. The practical effect of this method was to reduce the number of elective officers to a minimum and to repose all power in the legislative body. It was a nearer approach to Appointive Officials

186 SAN FRANCISCO

the short ballot than is likely to be again attained, despite the growing distrust of the popular judgment, which the advocacy of a limited number of elective officers implies.

Vote on Adoption of Constitution

The first state or general election under the constitution was held November 13, 1849. The vote for the instrument was 12,064 and 811 against. In San Francisco 2,051 votes were cast for adoption and only 5 against. Considering the eagerness of the demand for an organic law, and the liveliness of the campaign for the selection of delegates the ballotting was very light. Heavy rains, however, served to keep people from the polls in the interior, and certain defects in the tickets caused a large number of ballots to be thrown out, but the small vote was not wholly due to those causes. The indifference to public affairs, which later caused so much trouble, was in part responsible, and was the subject of adverse comment.

Partisan Politics in 1850

On January 8, 1850, there was an election at which John W. Geary was reelected first alcalde, receiving 3,425 votes. At this same election David C. Broderick, whose name appears so conspicuously in the annals of the City, state and nation, was elected to the state senate. The annalist of San Francisco tells us that in this election partisan politics began to play their part, but this ignores the fact already noted by him, that the slavery question exercised a great influence during the preceding year, which manifested itself in many other places than at the polls. The expression "began" refers more particularly to the disposition shown to separate on party lines, and also directs attention to the significant signs that the scandals growing out of the sales of the water front and other lands of the City were to be participated in by the people of the state and not confined as theretofore to San Francisco.

Official Turpitude

These scandals indicated a degree of official turpitude never exceeded in this or any other country. The worst feature disclosed by them is the fact that the attempts at reform met with little encouragement and brought the principal advocate of a searching investigation more kicks than honors. Horace Hawes, who entered upon the work of cleaning the municipal stables, lacked the quality known as magnetic, but there is no question regarding his knowledge and ability. His disposition was not an engaging one, and he had complicated the situation by putting those whom he assailed in a position to retort by "calling him another" because he was the owner of city lands, which had also been acquired, if not irregularly, at least in such a manner that his purse was not seriously depleted through their acquisition.

A Well Hated Reformer

Hawes was what is called a self made man. He was born in New York in 1813 and when he reached a suitable age learned the trade of carpenter, which he abandoned to try house painting and later cabinet making. He also did some farming and read law. In 1837 he left New York and adopted the profession of teaching, to which he adhered until he received the appointment of consul to the Society islands. He came to California from Tahiti in 1848 and, after the discovery of gold, which resulted in the rapid growth of population and prospective clients, he resumed the practice of law. In July, 1849, he was selected by the people to prosecute the "hounds," a band of criminals who were terrorizing San Francisco, and at the election of August 1st of that year he was elected to fill the office of prefect, whose importance he never lost sight of, nor did he permit the community to do so, as he insisted on exercising its powers to the fullest extent.

On the 10th of September he vetoed an appropriation of the ayuntamiento on the ground that it would raise more revenue than would be required, but Henry W. Halleck, as secretary of state, representing General Riley, denied his authority to interfere, and the council thus supported refused to pay any attention to Hawes and after holding a large sale of the city lands on January 3, 1850, they refused to make an accounting. Hawes laid the matter before Governor Burnett, and on February 15 that official issued a proclamation suspending all further sales until the legislature should act in the premises. The order of the governor was brought to the attention of the ayuntamiento several times, but no account was forthcoming from them.

<small>A Bad Lot of Officials</small>

Hawes again appealed to the governor and in a letter addressed to him on the 27th of February, 1850, he declared that it evidently was the determination of the ayuntamiento to proceed with the sale of municipal lands until all the property of the City was disposed of, and that its members were not going to render an accounting, plainly intimating that their reason for acting in this fashion was disinclination to expose that they had criminally taken advantage of their official positions. The ayuntamiento by formal resolution declared that the governor had no right to interfere with the sale of town lands, and another sale was announced for March 15, 1850.

<small>Getting Rid of all the Public Lands</small>

Before this sale took place, the attorney general, E. J. C. Kewen, advised the governor that the transfer of sovereignty over California to the United States divested Mexican law of all power to alienate American soil, and that his proper course was to issue a quo warranto, requiring the ayuntamiento to show by what authority it presumed to act. On the day fixed for the sale the ayuntamiento received a letter from Kewen, advising them of his intention to resort to quo warranto proceedings. It is doubtful, however, whether Kewen's intimation had as much to do with the abandonment of the sale as Hawes' threats of exposure. He had transmitted to the ayuntamiento on March 13th, and caused to be recorded in the archives, a long list of sales made in November and December of 1849, and on January 3, 1850, in which members of the ayuntamiento figured as purchasers. The names of some of this delectable lot are still perpetuated and honored by the people of San Francisco. Among the councilors who figured in the role of grabbers were Samuel Brannan, J. W. Osborn, his business partner, Osborn and Brannan as a firm, Wm. H. Davis, Gabriel B. Post, Talbot H. Green and Rodman Price.

<small>A Respectable Lot of Grabbers</small>

The grabbers, enraged at their exposure, or rather because Hawes attempted to make their actions appear odious, turned upon him, and charged him with having advised the Colton grants, with having corruptly granted lands and with the acceptance of illegal fees. All of these accusations were specifically denied by Hawes. His most malignant accusers were Brannan and Green, alias Geddes, who, like many others of the period, had a past which he sought to obliterate by the simple process of changing his name. These charges were taken up by the governor, and without investigation, or giving the accused man a chance to present his evidence he suspended Hawes, alleging as a reason for so doing that he had received a report of the finances from the ayuntamiento, covering the period from December 6, 1849, to March 4, 1850, and that it showed that additional revenues would be required to carry out certain projected improvements, for which funds could not be raised through the ordinary channels of taxation and that further sales of town lots would therefore be necessary.

<small>Exposure of the Grabbers</small>

Hawes Demands Impeachment of Governor

This action of the executive greatly exasperated Hawes and he demanded the impeachment of the governor for suspending him without cause. In his demand Hawes repeated his charges of improper purchases of town lots by members of the ayuntamiento, and added that an appropriation of $150,000, for the purpose of purchasing the Graham house, had been corruptly made, and that in receiving a report of the council, which had not passed through the regular channels, the governor was guilty of malfeasance. The attempt of Hawes to defend himself by this method was treated with scant courtesy by the legislature. On the 4th of April Speaker John Bigler, in presenting the charges to the assembly, moved that they be laid on the table. The motion prevailed and that was the last ever heard of them.

CHAPTER XXIV

MANY EARLY EXPERIMENTS IN MUNICIPAL GOVERNMENT

CHARTER OF 1850 INSPIRES HOPES OF BETTER GOVERNMENT—SMALL REVENUES AND HIGH SALARIES—EARLY SALARY GRABBERS—CONDONATION OF OFFICIAL TURPITUDE—A SECOND CHARTER GRANTED IN 1851—DEBT CREATED AND CREDIT IMPAIRED—THE PETER SMITH JUDGMENTS—UNSUCCESSFUL ATTEMPTS TO REFUND—TAXATION BURDEN IN 1852—A CITY HALL SCANDAL—NEGLECT OF SANITARY PRECAUTIONS—ANOTHER NEW CHARTER IN 1853—THE CITY SUFFERS FROM SPECIAL LEGISLATION—A TAX ON GOODS CONSIGNED TO SAN FRANCISCO MERCHANTS—UNEQUAL TAXATION—WATER FRONT LINE SCANDAL—AN ABANDONED FREE PUBLIC DOCK SCHEME—HARRY MEIGG'S SPECTACULAR CAREER—HE FLIES THE COUNTRY, MAKES A BIG FORTUNE IN PERU AND WISHES TO RETURN TO CALIFORNIA—LEGISLATURE CONDONES HIS OFFENSES—DEATH OF MEIGGS.

The Charter of 1850

F THE people hoped that a change for the better would be effected by depriving their municipal government of one or two of the features inherited from the Mexicans, they were doomed to disappointment. Unless they imagined that the names of political or governmental bodies exercised some mysterious and potent influence it is impossible to divine, why they should have thought that the new charter given them on the 15th of April, 1850, would work a revolution in conditions. This new measure of government provided for the division of the City into eight wards and prescribed that there should be a mayor and recorder and a board of aldermen and a board of assistant aldermen, which were to be styled the common council, the two bodies consisting of a member from each ward. A city treasurer, a comptroller, street commissioner, tax collector, city marshal, city attorney and two assessors for each ward were also prescribed.

Illusions Soon Dissipated

Any illusions that may have existed concerning the efficiency of the new system to effect reforms were speedily dissipated. The financial condition was not of the brightest when the officials under the charter entered on their duties. When they took stock they found that the receipts from the three installments of the payment for the water front lots sold would aggregate $238,253, and that the liabilities, including the purchase of a city hall were $199,174.19, a surplus of $39,078.81 over immediate demands. But as the source of revenue furnished by the sale of town lots was practically dried up for the time being by the disposal of all the immediately marketable property of the City, by their predecessors of the ayuntamiento, the new council had to study up other methods of procuring funds for running the town government, which appeared to require considerable expenditures

190   SAN FRANCISCO

for its maintenance, despite the fact that it was unable to make any showing in the way of public improvements.

Extravagant Officials

Although the outlook was not encouraging the officials elected acted as if they were convinced that an Occidental pactolus was to discharge itself into their treasury. The excitement over the gold discoveries still ran high, and the almost fabulous quantities of the metal taken from the placers may have justified optimism of an exaggerated kind, but the community was too much infected with the democratic idea that official life should be simple, and the rewards of the servants of the people moderate to patiently endure the attempt made by the aldermen within a couple of months of their installation, to raise salaries to an extravagant height.

Small Revenues and High Salaries

By resolution the council voted that its members should receive $6,000 per annum, and that the mayor, recorder and some of the other officials, should be paid $10,000 a year. Public indignation flamed high and an immense mass meeting was held, at which resolutions were adopted denouncing in scathing terms the greed of the salary grabbers. A committee was appointed to wait on the extravagant officials, but the resolutions presented by the representative of the meeting were promptly laid upon the table with such a show of insolence that the protestant, Captain J. L. Folsom, was obliged to report to his fellow citizens that something stronger than mere expressions of disapproval would be required to dislodge them from their position. A second meeting was held, which dealt with the matter even more vigorously than the first, and created a committee of 500, which was to have waited on the council on the 14th of June. This plan, which had something of a menace in it, was interrupted by one of the big fires, which at recurring intervals afflicted the town, but the council took the hint and subsequently made a big reduction in stipends, which touched the entire city government.

A Salary Grab

Salary grabs have occurred in so many other parts of the United States since 1850, even congress succumbing to the changed ideas respecting the simple life, it would hardly be fair to charge the first city council of San Francisco with venality on that account. Perhaps if the grabbers had subsequently demonstrated by their devotion to duty that the laborer is worthy his hire, the community in reaching a verdict might have even gone the length of agreeing that an alderman, or a mayor, performs services as important as those rendered by carpenters, blacksmiths and plasterers who, only a few months previously, had been earning as much as the councilors proposed to pay themselves.

A Gold Medal Scandal

But these councilors did not stop at appraising their services at a high figure; they went a great deal further and singled themselves out for special honors, which their fellow citizens, who had given them a vote of confidence only a few months earlier, were unwilling to bestow upon them or permit them to appropriate to themselves. The great event of the year 1850 was the admission of California into the Union and its celebration was on a scale adequate to its importance. San Francisco made extraordinary preparations to render it memorable. The councilors appear to have been duly impressed with the importance of the occasion and their own importance, and to contribute to the latter they voted that gold medals, to cost $150 a piece, should be prepared for their use, to be worn by them in the parade, and to be retained by them as souvenirs. The medals were to be decorated with a star on one side, surrounded by the letters E U R E K A, and on the other with the date of admission, September 9, 1850, and were to be inscribed "Presented to . . . . . ., Member of Board of Aldermen, by the City of San Francisco, October

VIEW FROM STOCKTON STREET IN 1856

19, 1850." The affair raised such a hubbub that the originators of the scheme of self laudation relinquished it, and the matter was turned into a joke. Some of the members, however, secured the coveted honor by paying for the medals out of their own pockets, and one so obtained is now available for the inspection of the curious in the Midwinter Memorial museum in Golden Gate Park. The others, presumably, went into the metal pot.

It would be a serious mistake to assume that this council and the other members of the city government in 1850 were hopelessly corrupt, or that their actions caused them to lose the confidence of the community. It will be seen as the narrative progresses, that when the day of purification came, men who were conspicuous as members of the ayuntamiento in 1849, which displayed extraordinary eagerness to save the City the trouble of taking care of a lot of property, were foremost in demanding that the ordinary forms of law should be dispensed with in dealing with criminals, and that summary punishment should be inflicted on all accused persons believed to be guilty of crime, even if the evidence necessary to convict them was not always attainable. Condemnation of Rascality

The names of the ayuntamiento of 1849 have been given, and to complete the record those of the members of the first city government under American methods are here presented: Mayor, John W. Geary; recorder, Frank Tilford; marshal, Malachai Fallon; city attorney, Thomas H. Holt; treasurer, Charles G. Scott; comptroller, Benjamin L. Berry; tax collector, Wm. M. Irwin, and street commissioner, Dennis McCarthy. The aldermen were Charles Minturn, A. A. Selover, Wm. M. Burgoyne, F. W. Macondray, William Green, M. L. Mott, D. Gillespie and C. W. Stuart. The assistant aldermen were A. Bartol, John Maynard, L. T. Wilson, C. T. Botts, John P. Van Ness, A. Morris, William Corbett and William Sharon. The list of assessors embraced Robert B. Hampton, John H. Gibon, John P. Hoff, Halsey Brown, Francis C. Bennett, Beverly Miller, Lewis B. Coffin and John Garvey. First City Government

It is difficult to reconcile the sweeping verdict of the annalist and other historians of this period that these two administrations were hopelessly inefficient with the subsequent tributes paid to some of the members composing them. The assertion has been made that, while they were in control "the City was fleeced and preyed upon in every quarter," and that it had to pay "for nearly everything it purchased two or three times more than ordinary prices." We can only assume that in pioneer days, as at a later period, the opinion was prevalent that in dealing with the community it was not necessary to apply the rigid rules governing personal relations, and that the people in their collective capacity are incapable of being robbed. In no other way can the tolerance accorded public men, who abused their trust, be accounted for by the historian, who would hesitate to accept the explanation if the practices of his own time did not afford abundant evidence of the existence of this vicious opinion. Hopeless Inefficiency

The unsatisfactory working of the first scheme of municipal government under American auspices pure and simple suggested another experiment and the legislature was appealed to, with the result that the first charter was repealed and a new one granted April 15, 1851. In the act of reincorporation the limits of the City were considerably extended, but no changes in the direction of amplification or restriction of the powers or duties of the governing body were made. Perhaps the result would not have been different if some of the modern reformatory meth- A Second Charter Secured in 1851

SAN FRANCISCO

ods had been applied, but they were not and the City went on in the same old way, expending the money of the taxpayer without getting proper returns, and piling up debt without making provision for its payment.

Debt of City in 1851
On May 1, 1851, the indebtedness of the City was over a million and a half, and there does not appear to have been much to show for the expenditure implied. Some of these obligations may have been incurred properly, but the most of the debt represented mismanagement and extravagance. Between August 1, 1849, and November 30, 1850, the amount disbursed was $1,450,122.57, and in the three months following $562,617.53, making a total expenditure in nineteen months of over $2,000,000, an enormous sum, considering the size of the City and the undoubted fact that scarcely any improvements of a permanent character for the public good were made during the period.

No Adequate Provision for Payment of Debt
The failure to make adequate provision for the payment of the city debt necessarily greatly impaired its credit and called into existence a group of speculators, who bought up the scrip of the municipality, which bore the enormous interest rate of 3% a month. A great deal of this paper fell into the hands of an unscrupulous manipulator, who subsequently used it to consummate a scheme to get possession of a large part of the land still in the ownership of the City. The projector of this daring job was one Peter Smith. His method was to buy the City's paper, which had greatly depreciated, and to obtain judgments. There is reason to suspect that a ring existed, formed in part of municipal officials, which helped Smith to carry out his operations. Their actions certainly facilitated them, the tax collector refusing to receive the scrip in payment of taxes, and the comptroller upholding him in his refusal.

The Peter Smith Judgments
The judgments obtained by Smith and those who profited by the nefarious transaction were usually for small amounts and bore interest at the rate of ten per cent per annum. They were not secured for the purpose of recovering the amounts represented by the scrip, but to afford the requisite excuse for obtaining possession of the remaining city lands, sales of which were ordered to satisfy the judgments. At the sales under these executions the lots were sold for a trifle. Perhaps all who bought were not in the conspiracy to rob the City, but they were under grave suspicion. The wretched transaction caused a great scandal, which involved numerous citizens of repute, among them David C. Broderick, afterward United States senator. He was the purchaser of sixteen beach and water lots, two south beach blocks and a hundred vara lot. The fact that he did so must not be counted too strongly against him, as the iniquity of the transaction, if it was iniquitous to do what every one sought to do, was shared by others, against whose names no word of criticism has been directed, and was practically condoned by the community.

Beach and Water Front Lots
It is true that the transaction created a great scandal and that an attempt was made to defeat the purposes of the jobbers, but the fact remains that after several years of litigation it was decided that the Peter Smith sales carried the title to all the beach and water lots, wharves and city property below high water mark that had been sold and not otherwise previously disposed of by the City; and that an attempted redemption which followed the protests against the job was invalid for the reason that the commissioners of the funded debt were not authorized to redeem. Thus in the case of the property indicated it was in effect held that the people, when acting in their collective capacity, may not recover stolen goods, pro-

vided the robbery was accomplished with some semblance of adherence to the forms of law.

The funding commission appointed after the Peter Smith grab sold most of what was left of the city property conveyed to them for the purposes of extinguishing the debt, but the proceeds did not go far towards the accomplishment of that object. The operations of the commission continued through a long period, but at the expiration of ten years only one-sixth of the bonds issued were redeemed. It was not until 1871, when the bonds matured that these old bonds were paid in full. They originally bore ten per cent interest, and were given in exchange for the scrip obtained by the speculators for absurdly small considerations.

An Unsatisfactory Funding Experiment

In 1852 the people of San Francisco were called upon for $769,887.22 to support the government. Of this amount $275,873.14 was derived from licenses and $262,665.23 from taxation of real and personal property. In addition they contributed $231,348.85 in the shape of state and county taxes. The burden, according to an estimate made by a statistician of the period, amounted to $35 per capita for the support of the City, and $10 for the state. The demands made on the taxpayer, according to this showing, were nearly double those which he was called upon to meet during many years in which public improvements of some importance were made, but the administrators of 1852 did not accomplish much with the sum placed at their disposal.

Municipal Expenditures in 1852

Out of this amount they expended little or nothing for the improvement of streets. That work was a direct charge upon the property owner, who had to pay for grading and planking the street or roadway on which his holdings were situated. He was also called upon to make large payments for a special police service, that furnished by the municipality being ridiculously inadequate and inefficient. There were plenty of means, however, for getting rid of the money of the taxpayer and the latter had no doubt in his mind that they were largely corrupt and did not hesitate to charge that they were by resolutions passed in mass meetings and through the medium of the press, which was becoming aggressive in its criticisms.

No Returns for Money Expended

One of the scandals of the year 1852 was caused by the purchase of a theater for the use of the municipality. The city hall had been destroyed in the fire of June 22, 1851, and a place had to be provided for housing the municipal government. Although there were contractors who stood ready to erect a suitable building for the sum paid for the Jenny Lind theater the council disregarded their offers and purchased that structure. It had to be entirely remodeled to adapt it to the needs of the city officials, and a considerable sum for that purpose had to be added to the purchase price of $200,000. The transaction excited great indignation. Mass meetings were called and the councilmen were accused of jobbery, but they were undeterred by the clamor directed against them. Legal steps were taken to prevent the consummation of the bargain, but the supreme court finally decided that the council had the right to make the purchase. Less than two years after its purchase, despite the expensive change made in order to make it at all useful, the building had become too small for the accommodation of the city officials.

The Jenny Lind Theater Purchase

If the records are at all dependable the authorities gave the people absolutely nothing in return for their money. The writer of the "Annals of San Francisco," speaking of the causes responsible for the cholera visitation in 1852, said the condition of the streets was bad. They were covered with black, rotten mud, and were

No Concern for Public Health

the receptacles for rubbish and sweepings of all kinds. Rats, huge, lazy, fat things, infested them and pedestrians abroad at night would tread on them. They were of all varieties, black, grey and white. A sickening stench pervaded every quarter. Hollows made by raising grades were filled with anything that came to hand.

Unsatisfactory Government

Some of these evils appear to have been the direct result of the feverish haste which marked the effort to convert the waters of Yerba Buena cove into land available for business structures. Often beneath the houses there remained pools of stagnating water, into which putrid substances were thrown in order to save the trouble and the expense of removing them. This practice was not interfered with, and unless the chronicles are wholly unveracious there was no attention whatever given to sanitation. Altogether it was a wretched state of affairs and it is not surprising that good men should have despaired of the future of the City. One such tells us that: "It was confessed on all sides that almost everyone who had a chance of preying upon the corporation means unhesitatingly and shamelessly took advantage of his position. His brother harpies kept him in countenance. This gave rise to a general opinion that the City never could possibly obtain a pure government until the bone of contention among rivals for office—its property, to wit —was all exhausted. Had the affairs of San Francisco been prudently managed," he added, "the City might have been the richest of its size in the world."

A Third Attempt at Charter Making

The people were by no means patient under their afflictions. They sought a remedy, and as before they turned to law making to correct the evils of bad government. On February 16, 1853, delegates to frame a new charter were elected. They were chosen from the various wards of the City and the list embraces the names of one or two who afterward achieved an unenviable notoriety, but on the whole the body was an eminently respectable one. Despite the fact that so much was expected of the new instrument very little interest was displayed by the citizens generally. Its provisions relating to the establishment of titles excited the antagonism of the squatters, but the discussion of the instrument by no means indicated a hearty desire for reform. In six of the eight wards of the City, when submitted for adoption, it met with an adverse vote, but a majority of the voters of the City cast their ballots in favor of its adoption.

Neglect of Civic Duty

It is not improper to suggest that the fact that only 1,367 persons voted at the election of September 7, 1853, although the population of the City at the time was not less than 50,000, and the City's misgovernment were closely connected. It was not, however, because lack of interest was shown that the legislature rejected the instrument. Its rejection was due chiefly to the energetic action of some of its adversaries, whose influence at the capital was greater than that of the people of San Francisco. There may have been no real ground for the belief prevalent at the time, that anything desired by the City was certain to be antagonized by the representatives of the people, but many years had to pass away before the principle of local self government was well enough established in California to induce the legislature to abandon its propensity to engage in special legislation.

Legislature Interference with City Affairs

San Francisco suffered greatly from this cause in the early Fifties, and it was not always the malevolence of the outsider that induced interference with the management of the City's purely municipal affairs by the members from interior counties. More frequently the troubles growing out of the system arose from the machinations of interested San Franciscans, who could depend upon the active assistance of a part of the legislature, and the indifference of the remainder to carry out their schemes. It is true, however, that from a very early date there was a disposition to regard San Francisco as a toll gatherer by the sea and to utterly ignore the services it rendered the interior.

The prevalence of this feeling led to numerous experiments in taxation, which seemed to have for their object the extraction of a relatively larger proportion of the sum required by the state for carrying on the government from San Francisco than from other parts of California. An instance of this sort was the revenue act of 1853 imposing a license of $1,000 on auctioneers, a license tax of 10 cents on every $100 of business done by bankers or dealers in exchange, stocks or gold dust or bullion, and an imposition of .60 cents on every one hundred dollars of consigned goods sold, not the property of persons domiciled in the state. San Francisco refused to submit to these extortions even after the supreme court had decided that they were not unconstitutional. Numerous meetings were held denouncing the act, which fell into desuetude, not because of its manifestly one-sided character, but because it was systematically and successfully evaded, the state having no machinery to enforce the law.

The inspiration of this legislation came from San Francisco. It was plainly instigated by merchants, who were importing on their own account, and who objected to the rivalry created by large consignments sold for the benefit of eastern and foreign exporters. This practice had attained large proportions and later precipitated disaster by glutting the market. It was an undoubted evil, but one which could not be properly corrected by the state converting the practice into a source of revenue. Had the measure been completely dissociated from those provisions of the act which were added for no other purpose than to increase the state's sources of revenue by singling out the City as the object of a method of taxation, which would not directly touch any other part of the state, San Francisco would have submitted to the unjust exaction as cheerfully as it did in subsequent years, during which it bore, because it could afford to do so, more than its proportion of the public school tax.

The inequality of the early taxation methods were a frequent cause of disagreement between City and country, and between the sections devoted to mining and those in which grazing was still the leading pursuit. In a message of Governor McDougal the fact was dwelt upon that the southern grazing counties, with a population of 6,367, had been called upon to pay taxes on real and personal property to the amount of nearly $42,000, while the twelve mining counties, with 119,000 inhabitants, paid only about $21,000. The latter, he pointed out, had a representation in the legislature of forty-four, while the counties in the southern part of the state had only twelve members. Taking all the agricultural counties together their population aggregated only 79,778, and they were called upon to pay taxes to the amount of $246,000, while 119,000 living in the mining counties only contributed $21,000 to the support of the state.

The poll tax was also a source of vexation. A few years later it was charged in the legislature that Butte, El Dorado, Nevada, Placer, Sacramento, Siskiyou and Tuolomne paid more than half of all the pool taxes received by the state, and that San Francisco, with 6,000 more voters than Siskiyou, contributed $3,000 less to the amount derived from poll taxes than the mining county. A similar inequality of distribution was noted by McDougal, who asserted that there was a per capita tax of $51.495 levied in the mining counties as against $7.205 in the grazing counties, but that the amount actually collected in the mining region was only $3.580, while $3.918 was contributed by sections devoted to grazing.

Making the City Pay Dearly

Perhaps these inequalities may be set down as being due to inexpertness and inefficient machinery for the proper collection of the taxes levied rather than to deliberate purpose to impose a greater burden upon one section of the state than on another, but the debt-making proclivities of the early administrators of the state created a pressing demand for funds, which had to be met in some way, and the idea that the City could more easily respond to the tax collector than the country undoubtedly influenced the legislature in 1853 to take a course which seriously affected San Francisco. Here again, however, the manipulations of a San Francisco contingent played as important a part as the alleged "cinching" disposition of the interior.

Water Front Line Scandal

The attempt of the legislature to extend the water front line of San Francisco harbor 600 feet further in to the bay than the red line, and to dispose of the property thus gained, was inspired by unscrupulous grabbers, who had bought lots at the Peter Smith swindling scrip sales, to which the City could give no title, because it had no proprietary interest beyond the red line. These purchasers, if they did not instigate, easily entered into the scheme which, had it been successfully consummated, would have shut in all the owners who had bought at other than the Peter Smith scrip sales, while at the same time adding something to the revenues of the state, which claimed the land outside of the red line.

The State and the Water Front

On the 17th of March, 1853, an assemblyman from Tuolomne county introduced a bill to carry out the proposed extension, and to dispose of the property that would be gained thereby, the proceeds of which were to be divided, one third to go to the state and the remainder to the purchasers at the Peter Smith sales and their grantees. It was expected that the sale would realize a couple of millions for the state, as the property embraced in the extension was valued at six million dollars. The flagrant iniquity of the transaction, which proposed to violate the terms of the act of March 26, 1851, which fixed the water front of the City permanently, did not deter the assembly from voting for the bill and passing it in that body by 31 to 27. The action of the San Franciscans in the lower house caused so much resentment, and the protests were so vigorous, that the members who had abused the confidence of their constituents resigned. The project, however, was persevered in by Governor Bigler, and his attorney general attempted to allay apprehension and divert attention from its real purpose by stating that its object was to save the City from itself by preventing it from thereafter extending its water front. The measure, however, received its quietus in the Senate where on the 26th of April, Samuel Purdy, lieutenant governor and presiding officer, by his casting vote against it, earned the approbation of the City, which was nearly a unit against the proposed change.

Pessimistic Views of an Annalist

The legislature was not alone in its assaults upon the integrity of the water front. The city council of 1853 exhibited equal disregard of the public interest and helped to give point to the declaration of the writer of the "Annals" that there would be no more pure government in San Francisco while anything remained to be stolen. By the act of March 26, 1851, four blocks lying along Commercial street wharf, and extending from Sacramento on one side to Clay on the other, between Davis and East streets, were given to the City and by an ordinance of the council of November 4, 1852, they were reserved as a free public dock for shipping. Originally these blocks had been covered with deep water, but the nearby wharves in the course of their extension eastward had rendered them useless for the purpose designed by the ordinance. The council of 1853 decided that the free public dock scheme would be impracticable and by ordinance of December 5th ordered the lots to be sold. The sale was made but was afterward declared void, but not until the City had lost considerable money through the transaction. An idea of the rapidly increasing estimation in which water front property was held may be gained from the fact that purchasers were willing to pay ten thousand dollars a piece for lots not equal in value to those formerly sold for a few dollars.

But the experiences already described were eclipsed in 1854, when an event occurred which disclosed a degree of municipal rottenness compared with which the worst exhibitions of recent misgovernment will seem venial. In 1850 there arrived in San Francisco from New York a man named Henry Meiggs. He had an engaging personality and was a typical boomer. He early conceived the idea that the North Beach section of the City had a great future because it was nearer to the Golden Gate than the region about the cove and must, therefore, he argued, be superior for business purposes. He was a man of action and backed up his belief by causing a level road to be built above high water mark, around the base of Telegraph hill to Clarke's Point from the beach, where he had invested considerable money, together with friends he had persuaded of the soundness of his views. Harry Meiggs and His Schemes

The construction of the road was followed by that of a long wharf which, beginning at a point near the foot of Powell street, extended 2,000 feet into the Bay in the direction of Alcatraz island. Meiggs' personality and his enterprise caused him to become extremely popular. He was "Harry" to everybody and no man in the community was better liked or more highly esteemed. In 1853 he was elected a delegate to the convention which framed the charter rejected by the legislature after its adoption by the people; and later in the same year he became a member of the board of aldermen. He made the best possible use of his connection with the council to push along his North Beach projects. Through his efforts the burying grounds of the North Beach section were closed and the bodies they contained were removed to Yerba Buena cemetery, which later became the site of the city hall destroyed in the fire of 1906. The Long Wharf

Meiggs' principal energies were directed to overcoming the natural obstacles interposed by the hills, which were numerous in the section he was booming. Through his efforts many streets, among them portions of Stockton, Powell street from Clay to North Beach, and Francisco through to the northern end of Telegraph hill, were graded, but his activities were not convincing enough to induce outsiders to invest in North Beach property. Having loaded himself with obligations his financial condition became precarious, and when the commercial and general depression of 1854 set in he tried to save himself by resorting to a daringly criminal expedient. Meiggs's Energy in Opening Streets

At that time street work was paid for by warrants drawn on the city treasury. These warrants required the signature of the mayor and the comptroller to render them valid. It was also required that they should have the name of the creditor. In order to save trouble the comptroller was in the habit of signing a number of blanks, which were bound in books, and he appears to have had no difficulty in inducing the mayor to also attach his signature. These were left in the care of the Making Rascality Easy clerk of the comptroller, a particular friend of Meiggs, who, when occasion arose, filled in the blanks intrusted to his care. In some way Meiggs became possessed of one of these books of blanks, which he applied to his own use. He had no difficulty in doing so, as there was no money in the street fund at the time, a fact which made the offer of the scrip as collateral seem perfectly natural. The extent of his borrowings upon this fraudulent security is not known, but it is said that he was called upon to meet interest payments aggregating $30,000 a month.

"Honest" Harry Meiggs in Trouble

The singular feature of the transaction is the failure of his borrowings, which were sometimes effected at the rate of ten per cent per month, to excite suspicion. Perhaps the appellation which he had in some manner earned of "Honest Harry" helped to blindfold his victims, who were numerous. In addition to using the scrip as collateral Meiggs, driven by his necessities, entered on a career of forgery, the indorsement of promissory notes being his specialty. He continued his practices for some time, being fertile in expedients, but in the autumn of 1854 he was called upon to make payment to the banking house of Lucas, Turner & Co., of which W. T. Sherman was then manager, and who insisted upon the reduction of his obligation to $25,000. He managed to procure an indorsement or acceptance from a house, whose headquarters were in Hamburg, which was duly accepted by the bank which held a mortgage on Meiggs' home on the northeast corner of Montgomery and Broadway streets and some $10,000 of the fraudulent warrants to secure the $25,000 balance. The securities given to the Hamburg concern were soon discovered to be worthless and the firm failed.

Flight of Meiggs

It was impossible to conceal the facts any longer, and on October 6, 1854, with the assistance of his brother, John G. Meiggs, who only a month earlier had been elected comptroller, he escaped on a vessel ostensibly engaged for a cruise about the bay and made his way to Chile. His liabilities were about $800,000, and for a long time it was generally supposed that he had carried away with him about a quarter of a million dollars, but he subsequently asserted that when he arrived in Valparaiso he had only $8,000 and that before he got a fresh start in life he was reduced to the extremity of pawning his watch.

Legislature Condones Meiggs' Crimes

Meiggs was a versatile man, and demonstrated his ability by engaging in railroad building in Peru. He obtained contracts for the construction of some 800 miles of road in that country, from which he netted an enormous sum, his wealth being estimated at fully a hundred million. With the return of prosperity a great yearning to revisit California took possession of him, and he induced his friends to put through the legislature a bill ordering that all indictments against him should be dismissed, and that future grand juries should refrain from reopening the cases against him. This extraordinary proceeding, which took place in 1873-74, called forth very little protest from the people, but the scandalous attempt was frustrated by the interposition of the veto of Governor Booth, and the state was saved the disgrace of openly condoning crime out of deference to wealth.

CHAPTER XXV

THE PIONEERS AND THE CRIMINAL CLASS IN THE FIFTIES

CAUSE OF THE VIGILANTE UPRISING—THE "HOUNDS"—KNOW NOTHING TROUBLES—ATTACKS ON FOREIGNERS—A TOWN WITHOUT POLICE—POLITICAL FRIENDS OF THE "HOUNDS"—THE VIGILANTE EPISODE OF 1851—COMPOSITION OF THE VIGILANCE COMMITTEE—HIGH HANDED METHODS—HANGING FOR STEALING—THE COURTS AND THE LAWS—THE READY REVOLVER—CIVIC DUTY DISREGARDED—INDIFFERENCE OF THE RESPECTABLE CITIZEN—CONDITIONS IN 1855-56—SHOOTING OF RICHARDSON BY CORA—THE BULLETIN'S ATTACK ON CASEY—INTEMPERATE JOURNALISM—EDITOR OF THE BULLETIN MURDERED—CORA AND CASEY HANGED BY THE VIGILANTES—LAW AND ORDER PARTY—CONSTITUTED ANTHORITIES DEFIED—CORRUPTION AT THE POLLS—NUMERICAL SUPERIORITY OF THE BETTER ELEMENT—DAVID S. TERRY—POLITICAL ASPECTS OF THE VIGILANTE UPRISING.

Crime in Pioneer Days

HE intimate connection between the municipal mismanagement of San Francisco during the six or seven years following the discovery of gold, and certain events which stand out prominently in the early history of the City, has been obscured by the assumption that those drawn to California by the hope of mending their fortunes were largely composed of the criminal classes. There were undoubtedly many with shady records, and more whose adventuresome disposition tended to recklessness and crime, but it does not appear that at any time this element was too large to have been easily kept under control by the decent and orderly portion of the community, had not the latter been completely absorbed in the effort to get rich quick.

Neglect of Civic Duty

It was for the purpose of bringing out this fact clearly that the sequence of the narrative was interrupted and the recital of the doings of the so-called Vigilance Committees was reserved for this chapter. It will be seen as the narrative proceeds that crime and disorder were rampant between 1849 and 1856 because the "good" citizens utterly neglected their civic duties, and that they would not have been forced to resort to extra legal methods had they not permitted themselves to become engrossed in the struggle for wealth. That the well disposed always had the power to preserve order by the exercise of ordinary methods is proved by the celerity with which it was restored when a serious effort was made to do so, and the ease with which it was maintained when the citizens had their eyes opened to the fact that their practical acquiescence in a policy of indifference to official turpitude was responsible for the mischiefs inflicted upon the community.

A historian who has devoted many words to describing the performances of the

200   SAN FRANCISCO

Vigilance Committees tells us that the creation of what was known as the People's Party after the affair of 1856 resulted in making San Francisco the best governed city in America for several years, and that this change for the better was due "to carrying into the legitimate administration of municipal affairs the same pure and well intentioned spirit which had characterized the proceedings of the Vigilance Committee." He apparently was unable to perceive that the same degree of interest in civic affairs exhibited during several years after 1856 must have produced a like result had it been shown between 1849 and 1856.

<small>The Hounds</small>

The earliest trouble recorded was that growing out of the formation of a band of bad characters said to have been made up largely of ex-Australian convicts and disreputable members of the regiment of New York Volunteers, who came to California to assist the regulars in the work of conquest. By others we have been told that this regiment was composed of picked men, selected with especial reference to the settlement of the new territory by a class, whose help in the upbuilding of the new commonwealth would prove of the greatest value; but unless the "Annals" are misleading, they contributed a large quota to the organization known as "The Hounds," which was formed in 1848 and which, in its inception at least, seemed to have for its object the persecution of foreigners.

<small>"Know Nothing" Troubles</small>

In considering the depredations of this body it must not be forgotten that the gold discovery in California, synchronized with what was known as the "Know Nothing" movement in the East, and which during a considerable period took on large political proportions, and exhibited itself in a particularly aggressive form in California, where a governor and supreme court judges were elected by the native Americans. The bad feeling engendered by this anti foreign movement manifested itself in various ways. In the early rush of adventurers to California efforts were made to prevent others than Americans securing passage on vessels sailing from the isthmus for San Francisco, and at least one prominent army officer, General Persifer Smith, openly advocated the exclusion of all but Americans from the gold fields.

<small>Attacks on Foreigners</small>

The Hounds in the beginning devoted themselves to assailing the people of Latin American origin in the City. There was at the time a considerable number of Chileans, Mexicans and Peruvians, many of whom were fresh arrivals. It was charged by the Hounds that the women of these people were grossly immoral, and that the colony lived in a disorderly and riotous fashion, but the methods of purification adopted by the reformers were not calculated to produce any desirable result. The Hounds were accustomed to parading the streets with banners flying and drums beating, and the annalist tells us that these parades, which often ended with attacks on foreigners, were not discountenanced, "but were openly approved by good citizens."

<small>Hounds Became "Regulators"</small>

Had the Hounds confined their outrages to foreigners they might probably have gone on unchecked for a longer period, but they broadened their operations and began to enter taverns, whose proprietors they robbed on occasion, but oftener made them become involuntary hosts of the gang. This met with disapprobation, but did not sufficiently arouse the people to the gravity of the situation, nor did they realize it until, as the result of an assault on the Latin American settlement a bystander, who it is said was not "properly" one of their number was shot and fatally wounded by one of the "greasers," the name applied to the Spanish speaking people by the ruffians, and for that matter by the community generally. The

Hounds took summary vengeance on this occasion, and followed up their riotous proceedings by changing their name to that of the "Regulators" and on the following Sunday, July 15, 1849, they made a daylight attack on the Chileans in their tents, seriously maltreating many of them.

At last the town was aroused. Demands were made upon Alcalde Leavenworth for the suppression of disorder, but the fact that he had no police at his service rendered him impotent. A mass meeting was called on July 16th and held in Portsmouth square, the leading spirit being Samuel Brannan. It resulted in the formation of a special police of 230, the command of which was given to W. E. Spofford. This body made short work of the matter. They apprehended twenty of the Hounds and placed them aboard the U. S. ship "Warren." Another meeting was held on the same day, at which Dr. Wm. M. Gwin and James C. Ward were unanimously elected associate justices to relieve the alcalde from the excessive responsibility imposed upon him, and Horace Hawes was appointed district attorney and Hall McAllister associate counsel. The arrested Hounds and their alleged leader, named Roberts, were tried on the charges of conspiracy, riot, robbery and assault with intent to kill, and were fined and sentenced to ten years at hard labor. *A City Without Police*

The charge was made at the time that the Hounds were instigated to their excesses by influential men who profited by the disorder they created, but the accusation was not accompanied by specifications. That the disorderly band in many particulars resembled the gangs common in eastern cities at the time, and who usually made their headquarters in the houses of the volunteer fire companies, and were available for carrying out the purposes of unscrupulous politicians there is no doubt. That the Hounds caused greater disorders, and were more disposed to viciousness than their Eastern prototypes, was due undoubtedly to the negligence of the people of San Francisco, who from the time when the gold rush began, lost sight of the necessity of adhering to recognized methods, and instead embraced the curious belief that irregular manifestations of wrath would prove more impressive and a greater deterrent of crime than systematic repression. *Political Friends of the Hounds*

The example made of the Hounds did not produce results which conformed to the idea that spasmodic effort was more efficacious than persistent watchfulness and zeal in compelling the enforcement of the laws, for the criminal element contintued its depradations throughout the winter of 1849 and during 1850, and the early part of 1851. No additions of consequence were made to the police force, and the few men employed were poorly paid. The prisons provided were small and insecure, but they were not in much demand, as bail was accepted in the most serious cases; and when there were trials they failed to result in conviction. Up to 1851 no criminal had been executed for murder, although there were several who deserved hanging. *Useless Spasmodic Efforts*

It can hardly be said that these results justified confidence in the efficacy of Vigilante methods. Those with criminal instincts were not deterred by the knowledge that a body of men met at intervals to receive complaints, and that good citizens were ready to respond when called upon to assist in suppressing lawlessness. There were frequent crimes but the committee was not aroused to action until an exceptionally bold thief, named John Jenkins, entered a store on Long Wharf and stole a safe, which he threw overboard from a boat when pursued. He was captured and the safe was recovered, and he was promptly tried by a jury of the *Brannan as a Public Prosecutor*

Vigilance Committee, which had assembled when summoned by the tolling of the bell of the Monumental Engine Company. There were about eighty of the Vigilantes present, and their deliberations lasted about two hours, at the expiration of which he was condemned to death. The prisoner denied his guilt but the evidence against him was conclusive. The bell was tolled a second time and the assembled crowd was addressed by Samuel Brannan, who stated that Jenkins had been found guilty and had been sentenced to die within the hour on the Plaza. He asked if the committee's action was approved and great shouts of "aye" went up; only a few noes were heard.

Hanging of Jenkins

A procession was then formed and the mob proceeded to the Plaza. Up to this time there was no show of interference on the part of the authorities, and when they did finally interpose an objection it was ineffective, because, as subsequent events suggested, they were not entirely assured of their own safety. Jenkins was undoubtedly an ex-convict or what was called a "Sydney cove," and the committee believed that he was one of an organized gang of robbers responsible for numerous depredations. A coroner's inquest was held and it found that Jenkins had died by the violent means of strangulation "at the hands of and in pursuance of a preconcerted action on the part of an association of citizens styling themselves a Committee of Vigilance, of whom the following members were implicated by direct testimony: Captain Edgar Wakeman, William H. Jones, James C. Ward, Edward A. King, T. K. Battelle, Benjamin Reynolds, John S. Eagan, J. C. Derby and Samuel Brannan.

Stand Taken by Vigilance Committee

The verdict was never followed up by the authorities and the committee paid no further attention to it than to publish a full list of its members as a significant intimation that they were ready to assume responsibility for the act and to show that the methods of the extra legal body were approved by the most influential citizens of San Francisco. On this point there could not be much doubt, and that every member of the committee was proud of the part he took, and of his association with the organization, which had avowed its purpose of putting a period to the reign of crime. Their firm stand resulted in greatly scaring the rogues infesting the town and many of them fled to the interior. Those under suspicion, who failed to fly were haled before the committee, which had conveniently resurrected a Mexican law forbidding the entrance of criminals. When contumacy was shown the committee imprisoned the defiant until arrangements could be made for their deportation.

High Handed Methods of Vigilantes

The methods of the Vigilance Committee were as high handed as they were temporarily effective. They assumed the right to enter any person's premises in which they claimed to have good reason for suspecting that they would be able to secure evidence, which would substantiate their charges and help them to carry out their object. The authorities protested against the irregularity of the proceedings of the committee. The grand jury for the July term, when it made its reports animadverted upon the inefficiency of the law authorities, charging that the trials of criminals were unnecessarily protracted by postponements and otherwise, and ended up with a declaration that, while the acts of the committee were to be deplored, they were undoubtedly influenced by the best of motives and that on the whole what had occurred was for the public good.

It is almost superfluous to state that the qualified disapproval of the committee's irregularities had no influence, and that it was shortly afterward followed by more

FORT GUNNYBAGS, HEADQUARTERS OF THE VIGILANCE COMMITTEE OF 1856

action of a vigorous character. Two men, named Whittaker and McKenzie, charged with burglary and arson, were arrested by the committee on the 20th of August and were promptly sentenced to death. This action brought forth a proclamation from Governor McDougal, who called upon all good citizens to unite for the purpose of maintaining the law. He was not a forceful man and his efforts were turned into ridicule by the publication of an anonymous circular, which quoted him as saying that he approved of the acts of the committee and that much good had resulted from them. The sheriff of the county, however, undertook to give effect to the proclamation by serving a writ of *habeas corpus* on the members of the committee, who had Whittaker and McKenzie in their custody, and they were surprised into delivering their prisoners to him. But the engine bell was promptly sounded, and as soon as a sufficient number of the Vigilantes could be assembled they recaptured the accused men, who were hanged within seventeen minutes in the presence of the crowd which had assembled in the square when the usual alarm was sounded. The coroner's jury, as in the case of Jenkins, voiced a feeble objection to the irregularity of the proceedings and there the matter ended for the present so far as San Francisco was concerned.

These exhibitions of mob violence were not confined to San Francisco. Like summary methods had been adopted in dealing with interior criminals. The first recorded lynching in the state took place in Santa Barbara, in 1848, where two men, who had killed a couple of miners in Tuolomne, and stolen their gold, were overtaken by a party organized to pursue them, and hanged by the sea. These lynchings were attributed to the gold discoveries, but a writer, Jeremiah Lynch, who made a careful investigation of the circumstances attending the killing of David C. Broderick by David Terry, commenting on the propensity of the Californians of pioneer days to take the law in their hands, emphatically dissents from the commonly accepted view that violence and disorder is a necessary attendant of what may be called "gold rushes," and to support his position points to the fact that Australia escaped the infliction, and that the comparatively recent opening of the Klondyke mining country in British Columbia did not result in breaking down the laws. He attributed their immunity from this particular form of violence to avoidance of the tendency to permit courts to override the laws. "We have the same laws," he said, "but with us the tribunals are superior to them; with the British the tribunals obey the laws and do not override them." <small>Hanging for Stealing</small>

Theorizing respecting causes is a profitless occupation when for guesses we may substitute actual facts. We know that one of the vices of the time was the carrying of fire arms. Every man went "heeled." It is related that at one of the first sessions of the legislature it was the habit of the members to take off their pistols and lay them on the desks before them. The practice was so common it attracted no attention. The weapons were ostensibly carried for defensive purposes, but the fact that a pistol may be used offensively as well as defensively was lost sight of by those who assumed that it was necessary to go armed in order to cope with bad men. This fashion has been held responsible by some for the contempt into which the law fell during the early Fifties, but it is an insufficient explanation. Besides we have the recent example just quoted of the Klondyke, where fire arms were as common as they were in California in pioneer days without producing the same evil results. <small>Carrying of Fire Arms</small>

204 SAN FRANCISCO

The Courts and the Laws

The true reason for the breaking down of the law is the one already pointed out. It was owing wholly to the utter disregard of civic duty by the so-called respectable element of society. This is freely admitted by historians, who have inconsistently defended the extra legal methods of the Vigilance Committee and assumed that the necessity of going outside the law was imposed upon good men. The ablest historian of California in dealing with the subject has told us that "in the unsettled condition of business and society, and the feverish rush for gold, few or none of the respectable classes of the community took sufficient interest in public matters to go to the polls, or to sit on juries." And he adds that as a consequence "the management of municipal affairs, and for that matter of national affairs also, in so far as they depended upon municipal representation fell into the hands of men of the vilest character, who had served an apprenticeship in New York and other hotbeds of political corruption."

Indifference of Respectable Citizens

The author who thus expressed himself lived near to the times of which he wrote and took part in some of its activities. His opportunities for learning the exact facts were unsurpassed, and his sympathies were wholly with the class that resorted to the extraordinary methods of the Vigilance Committee. It may be assumed, therefore, that he did not carelessly charge his fellow citizens with dereliction of duty; but while thus holding the respectable classes responsible for the existing condition he does not escape the error of putting the blame for the trouble on "the last straw that broke the camel's back," nor does he avoid the blunder of excusing a resort to violence, which might have been averted by the simple process of respectable citizens performing their civic duties.

Swift Punishment not a Deterrent

The prevalent assumption that examples of swift punishment would have a deterrent effect was not justified by experience. The criminal element was undoubtedly cowed for a short time when the respectable citizens rose in their wrath, but it speedily forgot the lesson. In the first ten months of 1855 there were 489 murders committed in California, and there were only six legal hangings. On the other hand there were forty-six cases of summary punishment by the mob, and there was always a possibility of the machinery of the Vigilance Committee (for the interior in places had modeled itself on San Francisco and maintained like organizations) being put in motion. But thieves and violent men continued their practices, and politics remained as corrupt as they had been.

Conditions in 1855-56

It is not astonishing that there should have been a recurrence to the methods of 1849 and 1852, when the business depression of 1855 came. The flight of Harry Meiggs and the disreputable failures of a couple of important banking concerns created a state of frenzied apprehension, which was kept at white heat by the vigorous attacks of the press on municipal corruption. The journals of the early Fifties had not acquired the modern habit of sparing the past lives of officials, and confining their criticisms to the shortcomings of the immediate present. California was filled with men who had a past, and when one of that sort, and there were plenty of the kind in San Francisco, came up for public honors, or managed to creep into office, he was unsparingly dealt with.

Richardson Shot by Cora

It was this journalistic propensity and not an overly sensitive public conscience that precipitated the activities of the Vigilance Committee of 1856. On the 18th of November, 1855, two men, named Cora and Richardson, met in a saloon. They had not previously been acquainted, but the familiarities of the bar room soon put them on an easy footing. They had several drinks together and quarreled, but separated on that occasion without coming to blows. The next day they met again, quarreled and in a scuffle Cora shot and instantly killed Richardson. Cora was a professional gambler and openly consorted with the keeper of a bagnio; Richardson was a United States marshal, but it does not appear that he came in contact with Cora in his official capacity.

The trial of Cora took place two months later. Despite his bad character he had many friends and some influential defenders. Colonel E. D. Baker, afterward United States senator, was one of his counselors and used all his art to save the accused man from the gallows and succeeded in bringing about a disagreement of the jury, which after forty-one hours' deliberation reported that it was unable to find a verdict. The failure to convict caused great dissatisfaction and the charge was freely made by the press that the jury had been packed, and intimations were thrown out that the outcome would be a resort to lynching. The long roll of un-convicted murderers was frequently referred to, and the blame was placed upon the lax enforcement of the laws.

The Trial of Cora

Cora was remanded to prison after the mistrial, and he and his friends hoped that the excitement would subside, when their plans could be more safely resumed. But such expectations were disappointed by the vigorous attacks made by the "Evening Bulletin" upon the criminal element which, it asserted, was shielded by politicians. The owner and editor of the paper was James King of William, who, before engaging in its publication had been in the banking business. King's assaults were largely directed against the so-called "Federal brigade," the employes of the government in San Francisco, whom he charged with being in alliance with the blackguards of the City. The federal officials found a champion in James P. Casey, the editor of a weekly paper, who printed an anonymous communication, in which the assertion was made that King's brother had sought the position filled by Richardson, but had been repulsed. The alleged office seeker repaired to Casey's office and denied the statement and demanded the name of the writer of the anonymous letter, but Casey refused to disclose its authorship.

Bulletin's Crusade Against Crime

A day or two later Casey, learning that King purposed attacking him, repaired to the "Bulletin" office to remonstrate against the expected publication. His visit did not dissuade the editor, who on the same evening that he had received Casey published a slashing article, in which this paragraph occurred:

The Bulletin's Attack on Casey

"The fact that Casey has been an inmate of Sing Sing prison in New York is not an offense against the laws of the state; nor is the fact of his having stuffed himself through the ballot box, as elected to the board of supervisors from a district where, it is said, he was not even a candidate, any justification why Mr. Bagley should shoot Casey, however richly the latter may deserve having his neck stretched for such fraud upon the people."

The publication of this paragraph on May 14th, was by no means the first time that the statement had appeared in print. On November 2, 1855, Casey had testified in a case growing out of an election brawl, which occurred on the corner of Pine and Kearny streets, on the preceding 21st of August, that he had been convicted of larceny in New York, and that he had served eighteen months in Sing Sing prison. His admission was published on the following day by all the papers, and one of them, the "California Chronicle," contained a strong denunciatory editorial of the methods by which Casey's election as supervisor had been secured, and reference was made to his criminal record in New York. This por-

Casey's Career Exposed

tion of the "California Chronicle's" editorial was reproduced by the "Bulletin" on November 5, 1855, and at the time provoked no mischief, nor does it appear that Casey very greatly resented the assaults made upon him by the other papers.

Casey Shoots Editor of Bulletin

Bad blood had been created in the meantime, and Casey was unable to control himself when he was confronted with a rehearsal of his past misdeeds, the inspiration of which he attributed to his political enemies. He did not repair directly to the "Bulletin" office to wreak his vengeance, but lurked in its vicinity awaiting King's departure for his home. When the editor appeared he opened fire upon him and shot him down. There was an instantaneous uprising but the authorities succeeded in saving Casey from the crowd, which was fiercely demanding that he be hanged. For security he was removed to the jail on Broadway, where a guard of three hundred was maintained to protect him from the thousands who surged around the building. The mayor begged that the law be observed, but was interrupted by fierce cries reminding him of the delays in dealing with Cora.

Death of the Editor

King did not die at once, although the wounds he had received were fatal. The shooting occurred on May 14th and he passed away six days later. During this period daily bulletins of the condition of Casey's victim were posted, the excitement rising and falling as changes showing improvement or the reverse were noted. On the morning after the shooting a call appeared in the press for a meeting of citizens, which took place in the quarters occupied by the "Know Nothings" prior to the event. Over a thousand persons signed the roll, subscribing to the constitution of the committee, which was the same as that adopted by the members in 1851.

The City an Armed Camp

During the time that King's life was in the balance the City resembled an armed camp. The Vigilance Committee had secured all the stock in the gun shops; guards were stationed about the jail to prevent the removal of Casey and Cora by the authorities, and there were other evidences of intention to defy the latter. The governor, J. Neely Johnson, visited the City and had a conference with the executive committee of the Vigilantes, and accorded them permission to place a small body within the walls of the prison in order that there might be complete assurance against attempted removal of the prisoners. The sheriff on the other hand summoned a posse of one hundred, obtaining only fifty, for the purpose of frustrating any effort that might be made to take the prisoners from his custody.

Authorities Inefficient

The futility of the efforts of the authorities was plainly apparent, but the advocates of "law and order" were not deterred by that fact from attempting to save the prisoners from summary vengeance. While the sheriff was making his puny preparations the Vigilance Committee was at work organizing its forces. King's condition was growing worse and his death was momentarily expected. On Saturday night the alarm bell summoned the Vigilantes to headquarters to receive instructions, and on the ensuing morning twenty-six hundred of them assembled and were formed into companies of artillery, cavalry and infantry. William T. Coleman, the president of the committee, directed the operations of this armed force. Cannon were taken to the jail and planted in front of its gates, and Coleman demanded an interview with the sheriff, in which he insisted upon the prisoners being placed in the custody of the Vigilantes.

Cora and Casey Lynched

The sheriff, thus overpowered, surrendered Cora and Casey. James King of William died on Tuesday, May 20th, and his death was the signal for the expiation of the crimes of the two murderers. The mayor and the other officials of the City made no effort whatever to prevent the carrying out of the plans of the committee and the state authorities were no more active, and it was stated that the governor, after his interview with Coleman, had tacitly acquiesced in the irregular proceedings. The funeral of the murdered journalist was attended by the whole community, and was made doubly impressive and significant by causing the cortege to pass the hanging bodies of Cora and Casey.

The labors of the Vigilance Committee did not end with the removal of Cora and Casey. It plainly exhibited a determination to put affairs on a new footing. Its avowed purpose was to stamp out crime and to bring about the purification of the municipal offices. The necessity for such a course may have been apparent at the time, but it was never clearly explained why the overwhelming majority adhering to the cause of the Vigilantes found itself unable to accomplish its objects by methods more in harmony with modern ideas of popular government than those to which it resorted.

Operations of the Vigilance Committee

Whatever may be said in condonation of the summary act of the committee in executing Cora and Casey, cannot apply to its subsequent proceedings, which took on the shape of settled defiance of constituted authority. All the testimony points to the complete cowing of the criminal element. Murders ceased and for a period the City was as orderly as could be desired. It was assumed that this condition of affairs was wholly due to the continued activity of the Vigilance Committee, and that its assumption of the functions of public prosecutor and of the administration of criminal justice were positively necessary to the preservation of peace; but those who were opposed, although an insignificant minority, boldly charged that the object was to secure possession of offices, and that the movement was inspired solely by political objects.

Constituted Authority Disregarded

That this latter allegation was well founded there is no doubt, but it is impossible to believe that the leaders and the great majority siding with the Vigilance Committee were actuated by improper motives or that they had any other object in view than the reformation of conditions which, as has been shown, were indescribably bad. The only question that is debatable is whether the Vigilante method of cleaning the augean stables was the proper one to adopt, and that there were many good men in San Francisco who thought it was not is clearly established by the evidence. These men, who called themselves advocates of "law and order" had the misfortune, however, of seeming to defend crime and disorder. It is unthinkable that men of the caliber of William T. Sherman and some others, who vigorously opposed the committee, were influenced by any other desire than the maintenance of established institutions, or to doubt that they sincerely believed that the methods of the Vigilantes menaced their existence.

Advocates of Law and Order

But it is equally undeniable that the office holders, and a considerable number of their adherents, hated and feared the Vigilance Committee because its activity threatened the perpetuation of their rule. Their fears were well grounded, for it only needed the awakening of the community to the necessity of actively interesting itself in civic affairs to dislodge from their position a gang of political cormorants and inefficients. And the fears of this class were shared by all those with criminal instincts, who hoped to profit by municipal corruption, and who to accomplish that end were always ready to contribute their support at the polls to the men who promised to be their friends in the hour of need.

Political Features of Movement

It was because the circumstances made the disreputable elements of the City the allies of the law and order advocates that the term "law and order" became

The Slavery Question

almost a stench in the nostrils of those who had reached the conclusion that the only way to secure the object they aimed to achieve was to act outside the law. There was another factor, which played its part, but has never been given the consideration it deserved. Although the attitude of the Vigilance Committee was apparently based on hostility to municipal misgovernment, it was found necessary to give assurances to its own members that there were no ulterior objects in view. On the 14th of June a resolution was adopted expressing confidence in the constitution and laws of the United States and the state of California, and deprecating all action at that time looking to constitutional changes or reform. National questions were at the time almost inextricably mixed up with state, municipal and even ward politics, and while there was probably no reason to suspect that there was any serious thought of converting California into an independent republic, the matter was freely discussed, and the politicians who were supporting the administration at Washington were undoubtedly apprehensive that the feeling which inspired the threats, would crystallize into a sentiment which would weaken the hold of the pro-slavery party on California.

The National Unrest

It is impossible to dissociate the Vigilance Committee's actions from the national unrest of the period. Whatever the purposes of the directing spirits may have been, and no matter how sound the reasons for believing that they were of the purest, it was inevitable that active politicians of the class to which David S. Terry belonged should regard with apprehension the creation of a machine which might wrest power from them. They did not love corruption for its own sake, but they were educated in a political school, which lived up to the motto that the end justified the means, and they had no squeamishness about employing the devices by which small men reached out and obtained small places, because they went on the assumption that it was absolutely essential to obtain and retain control, in order to preserve the institution of slavery.

Corruption at the Polls

We have, in many sections of the Union, attained so near to the ideal of a fair election that it is almost impossible to realize how general the disregard of honesty at the polls was in the years preceding the Civil war. The public conscience, which voices itself so forcibly now in such matters, was nearly dormant in the Fifties in San Francisco, but it flared up quickly when touched on the raw, as it was a little later when the determination of the respectable element to mend its ways and attend to its duties began to assert itself. It will be seen that one of the first effects of the awakening was a movement to put an end to vote-stuffing, and that the most potent argument in favor of a new deal and better government in the future was the public exhibition by the committee of a captured ballot box, so arranged that those manipulating it could insure as many votes for their candidates as might be necessary to secure their election.

Numerical Superiority of Better Element

The ease with which good results were achieved after the hanging of Cora and Casey was the subject of felicitation in the ranks of the Vigilantes, who never perceived the inconsistency of their position, even after a practical demonstration had been afforded of their numerical superiority and therefore of their ability to win at the polls had they worked as earnestly together with peaceful methods as they did when they took up arms to assist in the purifying process. When those adhering to the law and order party attempted to oppose the Vigilance Committee with a show of numbers they could scarcely secure a corporal's guard. Governor Johnson, who is credited with having expressed approval of the action of the committee,

VIEW OF CALIFORNIA STREET IN 1856

was persuaded to set in motion the machinery of the state for the suppression of lawlessness and disorder. He attempted to use the national guard to overcome the Vigilantes and appointed W. T. Sherman, whose military experience gained at West Point qualified him for the work to command the troops, but only seventy-five responded to the call, an insignificant force to oppose to the 5,000 Vigilantes, who were well armed and were in possession of two field pieces. Sherman was given the rank of major general of national guard, and there is no doubt but that he would have given a good account of himself if he had had at his back a firm executive. But there was no firmness in Johnson's composition. He was weak and vacillating, and before a week had passed Sherman threw up his command in disgust.

The literature dealing with this event was extremely voluminous, and every phase of the affair has been discussed in all its bearings, but all the descriptions are easily condensed into the statement that, after a brief period, the office holders recognizing the futility of their attempts to withstand the will of the community, as expressed by the Vigilance Committee, gave up the struggle. The superior organization and zeal of the Vigilantes checkmated the Law and Order people and won every move in the game. There were some encounters between the opposing forces, growing out of the attempt of the Law and Order forces to secure arms. In one of these affairs David S. Terry, who formed one of the rear guard of a party of the Law and Order adherents stabbed an official of the Vigilantes, who sought to prevent it entering the armory.

A Flood of Vigilante Literature

Terry was subsequently arrested. A strong force of the Vigilantes, which was promptly summoned to the scene when the Law and Order party offered resistance, surrounded the armory, opened its gates and compelled all the inmates to surrender their arms, after which they were all, with the exception of Terry, released. He was charged with resisting the officers of the committee, and with this offense were coupled others, some of which it was alleged had been committed by him several years earlier. Whether the charges against Terry were true or false it is not necessary to inquire, but in a written commuincation to the committee he made a statement which is interesting because it professes to describe the motives which prompted him to array himself on the side of the Law and Order party. He said:

Arrest of David S. Terry

"You doubtless feel that you are engaged in a praiseworthy undertaking. This question I will not attempt to discuss, for whilst I cannot reconcile your acts with my ideas of right and justice, candor forces me to confess that the evils you arose to repress were glaring and palpable, and the end you seek to attain a noble one. The question on which we differ is, as to whether the end justifies the means by which you have sought its accomplishment; and as this is a question on which men equally pure, upright and honest might differ, a discussion would result in nothing profitable."

Terry's Position

From these expressions the inference might be fairly drawn that Terry and the other men who sided with the Law and Order party were of the same way of thinking as the Vigilance Committee so far as the presence of a great evil was concerned, and that they differed merely as to the methods to be adopted to bring about a better condition of affairs; but the facts forbid this assumption. They show conclusively that the majority of the Vigilantes and the bulk of the Law and Order advocates were as wide apart as the poles. The Vigilance Committee, no matter how much the civic indifference of its members in the past had contributed to the bad state of affairs which they sought to repress, were earnestly desirous of clean-

Object of Law and Order Party

ing out the bad lot, who infested the public offices, while the Law and Order party were struggling to retain control, some merely for the purpose of plundering the community, and others for what they considered the most important of political considerations, namely to safely hold the state for their party.

Personal Character of Terry

The personal fortunes of Terry, and the other actors in the Vigilante drama, are only a part of the history of the period, and not the whole of it as many writers have assumed. Biography is always interesting, but it may easily be made to usurp the place of more important matters. If Terry, who conducted his own defense in the hearing, which was entirely secret, had been convicted, which might easily have happened had the man he stabbed died, he would doubtless have been hanged, in which event his fate would have been linked up with that of Cora and Casey, and his name might have passed down to posterity as that of a mere brawler, who suffered the consequences of being in too close touch with those who made a business of politics and who after the manner of business men, sought to profit through the pursuit to which their energies were devoted.

Political Game not Understood

But Terry's survival and his subsequent actions are worth tracing, because they bring into bold relief the fact that the Vigilante upheaval of 1856 was not merely a movement for the purification of the municipal offices, but was also a part of the game of national politics, the stakes in which were the perpetuation of the Federal Union. The connection between the two is not always perfectly clear, but that is due to the fact that the actors were not always conscious that they were pawns in the game. Had they realized what was in the minds of those who were making the moves on the national chess board the alignment would have been different. That they did not appreciate all the intricacies of the situation is shown by the line of cleavage afterwards so sharply drawn, which separated men who had stood together in what they regarded as a great municipal emergency, but could not have been persuaded to act in unison had they realized that their efforts were destined to completely alienate California from the Democratic party and put it in line with the states opposed to the perpetuation of the institution of slavery.

CHAPTER XXVI

POLITICAL AND OTHER RESULTS OF THE VIGILANTE UPRISING

VIGILANCE COMMITTEE REFORMS ITSELF—THE IDEA OF CIVIC DUTY BEGINS TO ASSERT ITSELF—THE RECALL METHOD IN 1856—ORGANIZATION OF THE PEOPLE'S PARTY—PLATFORM OF THE NEW PARTY—RESULT OF ATTENTION TO CIVIC DUTY—A SECRET NOMINATING BODY—ONLY A HALF REFORM ACHIEVED—BRODERICK AND THE VIGILANTES—POLITICAL CAREER OF BRODERICK—BRODERICK'S MODE OF KEEPING UP THE ORGANIZATION—UNSETTLED OPINION CONCERNING SLAVERY—FOR OR AGAINST BRODERICK—COLLISION OF NATIONAL AND MUNICIPAL INTERESTS—POLITICAL JUDGMENT OF VIGILANTE LEADERS—DISSOLUTION OF THE VIGILANCE COMMITTEE—RETURN OF THE PROSCRIBED—THE QUESTION OF TITLES—VIGILANCE COMMITTEE RECEIVES A GOLD BRICK—STORIES OF CRIMINAL ASCENDENCY A MYTH—FEDERAL GOVERNMENT AND THE VIGILANTES—SHERMAN'S PART IN THE AFFAIR—SOLIDARITY OF THE VIGILANTES.

HE immediate political results of the Vigilante movement of 1856 were purely local. The attack on the criminal element was salutary. It was noted that the bad characters who had not fled the town were completely cowed. Brawls almost entirely ceased, and during a couple of months after the hanging of Cora and Casey there were no murders in the City. The jocular reference to "a man for breakfast" was beginning to lose its point, and San Francisco was entering on a career which subsequently permitted good citizens to boast that it was as orderly a community as any in the country. The ability to make this claim was by no means due to the flight of criminals from the City. Some had fled when the Vigilantes were dangling the noose before their eyes, but there was no place in California where they could depend upon receiving a hospitable reception, for Vigilance Committees had become as popular in the interior as in San Francisco.

Effects of Vigilante Uprising

There were several deportations of notorious characters, and there was a proscribed list, the knowledge of which had a marked restraining influence, and it operated so powerfully on the minds of some that they deemed it prudent to absent themselves until matters quieted down. That they had reason to expect that the storm would soon blow over may be inferred from what happened after the previous popular uprisings, but the precedents of 1849 and 1852 were not to be followed in 1856. The Vigilance Committee, in its attempt to drive out criminals and reform municipal politics had reformed itself and was ready to adopt a course which proved more efficacious in keeping down corruption and repressing crimes of violence than irregular intimidation could possibly effect.

Vigilance Committee Reforms Itself

212   SAN FRANCISCO

A Sense of   In short, the upheaval had resulted in creating civic sentiment of the sort that
Civic Duty   can be relied upon to prevent municipal corruption. Those arrayed against that
Created   sort of crime soon gave practical effect to their beliefs by demanding the resignation of the entire city government. A mass meeting was held on June 14, 1856,
at which William Sharon, afterwards a conspicuous figure in San Francisco life,
was the moving spirit. He introduced a set of resolutions, the purport of which
was "turn the rascals out." The meeting adjourned without putting them to a
vote, but on July 12th the suggestion embodied in them was acted upon. A petition
reciting the most flagrant abuses of the administration was circulated and numerously signed, demanding that the men responsible for them resign their offices and
was published in the press.

Recall   The thugs and thieves had been completely intimidated but the same effect had
Methods of   not been produced on the city officials. This early attempt to put the recall into
1856   effect met with no success. Its outcome was the reverse of what those who urged
the demand for resignations expected. Instead of resigning the officials turned upon
those who made the demand and charged that the object of the Vigilantes was to
secure the offices, and that their resort to violence and irregular methods was solely
for that purpose. County Judge Thomas Freelon; sheriff, David Scannell; district
attorney, Henry H. Byrne; mayor, James Van Ness; clerk, Thomas Hayes; recorder, Frederick D. Kohler; assessor, James W. Stillman; surveyor, James J.
Gardener; coroner, J. Horace Kent, flatly refused to comply with the behest of the
petitioners, while some of the minor officials ignored it entirely.

Purifying   Prior to this failure the Vigilance Committee had caused a list of eligibles for
the Jury   jury service, whose characters made them undesirable, to be made, which was ac-
Lists   companied by the request that any member of the committee, or others who knew
of cause why anyone should not be permitted to serve on juries, should make known
the facts. This list was posted in conspicuous places. The suggestion of the committee to add to it was liberally acted upon and caused great indignation and considerable flutter in the breasts of numerous persons, whose past reputations were
not of the best, but the movement undoubtedly had an excellent effect.

Organization   The refusal to accept the recall was perhaps the best thing that could have
of People's   happened for the cause of municipal reform, because it resulted in action of the
Party   sort which must be exhibited in a conspicuous fashion if good government is to be
maintained under a system which calls for manhood suffrage. A People's party
was organized, which was something more than a mere name, for it embraced all
classes of citizens anxious to assist in putting an end to political corruption. Men
who had formerly, for various reasons, refrained from going to the polls, now
displayed a lively interest in the movement to "get out the vote." There were no
excuses of the kind covered by the expression "what is the use?" nor was there
anyone found ready to suggest important business as an explanation of failure to
act. There was a complete revolution. Incivicism of the worst type had been replaced by devotion to the public interest, and the community, for the time being,
experienced a complete political regeneration.

Platform of   The platform of the new party was something more than a promise. It con-
New Party   tained an indictment of past conduct of those who framed it. It demanded that the
administration of justice should be in the hands of pure minded men, and that
good men should devote at least a few weeks of their time to public affairs. There
were numerous other reforms asked for, but they may have appeared in previous

party professions. The chief reform, however, was contained in the pledge to devote a few weeks' time to the public interest, for on it depended the whole situation. If it were lived up to all the rest would come easy, for when good men make up their minds to have things done properly, and give their attention to bringing about the results they aim to achieve, they usually succeed in their endeavors, because the actively and passively good element in any community always greatly outnumbers the corruptly inclined.

The People's party elected their candidates to office at the election in November, 1856, without any difficulty and the good citizens of San Francisco could have done the same thing during the previous years had they stood together. There has been much stress laid on the number of "Sydney coves," who were lured to the coast by the hope of finding gold, and the fact that there were numerous bad men among the adventurers who flocked to San Francisco between 1849 and 1856, but a fair survey of the composition of the immigrants does not warrant the conclusion that the community as a whole, at any time during the period, had a much larger proportion of the viciously inclined than any other seaport. We are told by a historian in a review of the character of the immigrants who made their way to San Francisco, that they were composed of three classes. A tenth of the number, he estimated, were politicians who had outlived their period of usefulness in their old homes; another tenth were idle loungers around gambling saloons, men who had come to San Francisco with the idea that they could pick up gold without working for it; "but much the largest class, comprising at least four-fifths of the American immigrants, who seemed to outnumber all others twenty to one, and perhaps a large share of the immigrants from other lands, were honest and industrious workers."

People's Party Elects its Candidates

The story of the Vigilance Committee is not completed by the relation of its triumphs at the polls. That triumph secured something like decency in the administration of local affairs, but the overshadowing national political questions had so divided good citizens that corrupt practices at the polls were still the order of the day where the legislature was concerned. At the same election, which resulted in the return of men to whom it seemed safe to confide the administration of municipal affairs, a politician who was past master of all the tricks known to Tammany, and resorted to by it for the preservation of power, so manipulated affairs that he was able to control the legislature.

Corrupt Political Practices

One of the unfortunate features of the campaign made under the auspices of the Vigilance Committee in 1856, was the introduction of the undemocratic method of selecting candidates by a secret body. The resort to this plan indicated a distrust of the organization which it hardly deserved. A resolution was framed and adopted after some opposition to appoint a committee of twenty-one to name a ticket. This committee's deliberations were entirely secret, but its members appear to have been earnest in the determination to name first class men, and to that end thoroughly canvassed the names of all eligible candidates. On September 11th it completed its labors and presented a ticket for city and county officials, and members of the legislature. This was formally given the name of the People's Reform party, and this appellation was retained several years.

A Secret Nominating Body

The ticket had arrayed against it candidates of the Democratic and Know Nothing parties. The Republican party, then a newcomer in the field of politics, endorsed the ticket of the People's party. The Vigilance Committee in the election

The Opposition

did not depend on the efficacy of putting forward good names. Before the election stirring addresses were made urging upon good citizens the necessity of going to the polls, and assurances were given that the old time practices would be completely suppressed and that the election would be honestly conducted. To secure that object the City was districted and a Vigilante police force was created to preserve order at the polls, and to see that there was no stuffing of ballot boxes or cheating in the count.

Broderick's Plans not Interfered with

The close scrutiny which resulted in an election, the honesty of which was a subject of felicitation, while it undoubtedly gave the City a purer and better administration, failed to interfere with the machinations of Broderick, who had secured absolute control of the legislature. Writers whose criticisms in general were favorable to the Vigilance Committee movement were disposed to regard this as "the fly in the ointment;" perhaps because Broderick had not heartily entered into the campaign for purification, or because they knew that he was opposed to the attempt of the Vigilantes to control municipal affairs.

Broderick and the Vigilantes

The only definite knowledge of Broderick's position toward the Vigilance Committee is that disclosed by a statement made by him some three years later, that during Terry's incarceration by the Vigilance Committee he had paid $200 a week to a newspaper to print articles in his defense. The journal alluded to was the "Herald," probably the most ably conducted daily paper in 1856, and the most prosperous. Because of its attitude towards the Vigilantes it was destroyed by the business men of the City, who withdrew their advertisements in a body.

Broderick's Political Career

It would have been extraordinary had Broderick sympathized with the efforts to purify municipal government, for he, more than any other man in San Francisco, was responsible for the wretched condition of affairs. Broderick's subsequent career has cast a glamour over his life, but the truth of history demands the statement that for a long period his methods were utterly vicious, and that he shrunk from no infamy which would promote his objects. He had been in politics for several years, having been elected state senator in 1849, and his political career in California was a stormy one. He had come to the state a year earlier from New York, where he had learned all the arts of the political rogue of the period, and was soon recognized as a past master.

His Successful Bossism

It may be necessary to relate his career more fully later, when the causes of his tragic death are examined; here it is merely desired to make clear the fact that the undoubted "boss" in municipal politics concurrently with a vigorous and aggressive effort to effect the reform of municipal government was able to secure control of the legislature, a body which had the power, and often chose to exercise it, of nullifying the efforts of the better elements of San Francisco to manage their affairs for the benefit of the community rather than for the comfort of extravagant politicians.

Methods of Broderick

The methods of Broderick differed in no essential particular from those of his numerous successors. When he arrived in San Francisco there was no party system and he applied his undoubted organizing talent to create one modeled on that of New York. He professed to stand aloof from local affairs, interfering in them only to the extent of making them pay for keeping up the organization, but his professions do not relieve him from responsibility for all the evil practices which resulted in the misgovernment of the City, for his attitude was that of the boss who sells offices to the highest bidder with permission to recoup themselves at the expense of the taxpayer. He was virtually the dictator of the municipality, and his dictatorship was secured by stimulating the belief that it was of the highest importance to keep up the national party organization, even though the methods employed directly promoted the corrupt conduct of municipal affairs.

One of the sources of his popularity was his early identification with the volunteer fire department. In 1852 he organized a company, and soon introduced the idea that firemen should be an important factor in politics. No opportunity to popularize himself was neglected, and it was not long before he was in a position which permitted him to say to the candidate ambitious for the shrievalty, "this office is worth $50,000 a year; keep half of the amount, and turn over the other half to me for the use of the organization." The biographers of Broderick acquit him of personal jobbery, and say that he never descended to vulgar venality, but this verdict hardly accords with the notorious fact that he participated in numerous grabbing schemes, and that the foundation of his wealth was the purchase of water front lots sold at Peter Smith scrip sales.

Broderick and the Firemen

Whether Broderick used any of the money ostensibly collected to advance the purposes of the organization to increase his store of wealth, or devoted it wholly to securing the election of men adhering to the party to which he belonged matters little, for so far as the public was concerned the results were the same. The Broderick plan permitted unscrupulous men to gain local office and fleece the taxpayer, and the success of the organization inured to the advancement of the personal ambitions of the boss. That his political eminence and practices were not seriously regarded at the time by the majority of those who contributed to the success of the municipal ticket nominated by the Vigilance Committee seems evident, for they voted for the men put forward by Broderick, and perhaps in the full knowledge that he was their sponsor.

Funds for the Organization

It has been remarked that in the election which gave Broderick control of the legislature that no sectional lines were drawn. That assumption rests largely upon the fact that Broderick was warmly supported by many ardent Southerners, and that he was bitterly antagonized by some Northerners, some of them from his own state. But that establishes nothing; it simply recalls that in 1856 the opinions of men on the subject of slavery were in an unsettled condition, and that there were almost as many men living north of the line, which was drawn to prevent the encroachments of the institution, who actively advocated its perpetuation, as there were in the states where slavery actually existed. It was sometime later before views became fixed. In 1856 Northerners were still ashamed to be regarded as abolitionists. They were still unable to perceive what a great statesman later pointed out, that slavery and freedom could not exist side by side, and that the conflict between them would continue until one or the other was destroyed.

Unsettled Opinions Concerning Slavery

This indecision of the masses, however, was not shared by the men who were guiding the destinies of the country. They had well defined views respecting the desirability of maintaining the institution at all hazards, and they did not intend to permit its expansion to be interfered with by those who were beginning to fear the effects of its encroachments upon free labor. These pro-slaveryites, however, found it necessary to proceed with caution in a state which had adopted a constitution emphatically inimical to the extension of slavery; they recognized that there was even less probability of a successful attempt to convert California by open methods to the idea that the institution should be permitted to expand than in the

California Support Sought

216   SAN FRANCISCO

Northern states east of the Rocky Mountains, whose close business relations with the South made them ready to accept political domination rather than provoke trouble.

"For or Against Broderick"
It was owing to the indecision described that Southerners were found supporting Broderick and not the absence of sectional feeling. That already found a harbor in many Southern bosoms in San Francisco, as is well attested by the sympathy extended at various times to men actively engaged in attempts to extend the area in which slavery might be maintained. The strength of "Know Nothingism" in California also furnishes evidence that Southern sentiment was very strong, for the movement undoubtedly had its stanchest supporters in those who feared that a great influx of foreign immigrants, by providing the country with an abundance of free labor, would menace the "institution" and the political supremacy of the South. But while conflicting views were causing a ferment which was producing a line of cleavage that created some antagonisms for Broderick his personal popularity in a measure overcame them. In short, the campaign on the surface was for or against Broderick, and did not concern itself much with principles.

National and Municipal Interests Collide
And to the personal popularity of Broderick we may look for an explanation of the fact that despite his record he was not openly antagonized by men who were fighting against the evils produced by the methods of the boss. They probably accepted his view that it was necessary in order to carry on the organization to obtain money from candidates, and did not seriously inquire to what obtaining funds by this plan tended; or it is not impossible that they were so engrossed by their purpose of purifying the municipal offices that they would not run the risk of defeating their own aims by engaging in a contest which might easily have distracted attention from their main object by converting the fight into a partisan struggle in which the local must have been subordinate to the national issue.

Political Judgment of Vigilante Leaders
This may suggest a compromise on the part of the Vigilantes with the powers of evil, of the kind the present generation is perfectly familiar with, and the possibility that it may have been made, while it may not be defended, can at least be set down to their credit as an act of good political judgment, for it resulted in the achievement of the main purpose of the Vigilance Committee. The election of the ticket nominated and supported by the committee gave the City good government. It practically put an end to corruption, and extravagances, an assertion eloquently backed up by the statement that whereas the expenditures for municipal purposes in 1855 had aggregated $2,646,000 in 1857 they were only $353,000. That this great reduction of expenditures testifies to the honesty of the city officials elected under the auspices of the Vigilance Committee is undeniable; that it furnishes evidence of their sagacity in the conduct of municipal affairs is open to grave doubt. It is true that the large sum expended by the deposed city government in 1855 was chiefly squandered on inefficient officials, and that much of it was corruptly made away with, but under the new regime a policy of do nothing was entered upon which endured for several years, during which the City added nothing to its attractiveness. Although the cost of administration after a while steadily increased there were no improvements to show for what was expended.

Suits Brought Against Vigilantes
After the success in the election of 1856 the Vigilance Committee did not cease its activities entirely. It was obliged to maintain its existence as a measure of defense for lawsuits of various kinds were brought against its members in the United States courts. These, however, all came to naught; although they were

MINERS EXCHANGE BANK BUILDING, ON MONTGOMERY STREET BETWEEN WASHINGTON AND PACIFIC, AS IT APPEARED IN 1856

provocative of much ill feeling and charges of bias and prejudice were freely made against the judge and the grand jury which brought the indictments. These suits were not confined to San Francisco; the federal courts were invoked in other states, but the suitors there were no more successful than in the City where the damages sued for were alleged to have been incurred.

On the 21st of August, 1857, the executive committee and board of delegates of the Vigilance Committee, which still held joint meetings, adopted a resolution to the effect that order and perfect security had been established through the efforts of the People's party, which had complete control of municipal affairs and had established a modern government; and that the conditions were such that the committee might with propriety terminate its existence. This action was subsequently made the subject of criticism, the preamble of the resolutions being particularly objected to by the critics who succeeded in causing the subject to be taken up again at a meeting on October 12, 1857, when the original preamble and resolutions were adopted. Termination of Committee's Labors

Within a year of this action many of the proscribed had returned to San Francisco, and some of them brought suits for damages. There were two cases of recovery, those of Charles P. Duane who secured a decree in the United States circuit court against the owners of the steamer "John L. Stephens" for the sum of $4,000, and by the Greens who had earned some notoriety in disturbing titles. They asked for $50,000 and were awarded $150. This latter case was decided in 1860, and its connection with the Vigilante uprising directs attention to the committee's concern with other matters than the repression of the criminal classes, and the purification of municipal politics. It points to an alignment not much dwelt upon in the criticisms of the actions of the Vigilance Committee, but which was perfectly natural under the circumstances. The fraudulent land grants, and the irregularities attending the sale of water front and other city properties, together with the attempt of a part of the population to carry into effect the theory that the land belongs to the man who occupies it had greatly disturbed titles, and the Vigilance Committee attempted to assist in the work of straightening out those that were most tangled. Return of Proscribed

In the case of the Greens they sought to effect this object by compromise. The family in question had been troublesome squatters, harder to deal with than some of the others who merely depended upon possession to hold their claims, for they professed to have valuable documents bearing on the moot question of pueblo lands. The alleged existence of these papers, which were said to have been derived from one Tiburcio Vasquez, were a cause of disquiet to property owners, and the Vigilance Committee determined to allay the apprehension by bringing the Greens before them with the view of making them produce the disturbing evidence. They were accordingly arrested and subjected to a searching inquisition which was at one stage converted into a negotiation, Alfred, one of the family, inducing the committee to consider a proposition for the purchase of the papers in their possession. Title Disturbers Bought off

Whether these documents were of any value is not of as much interest in this connection as the fact that the Vigilance Committee regarded it as part of its duties to make an investigation, and that it endeavored to gain possession of the Green papers by purchasing them from the family. Alfred, who apparently was not its representative, soon realized that recalcitrancy might prove destructive, and The Green Family's Secrets instead of being defiant, he offered to sell. Although the Vigilance Committee had numerous lawyers on its roster they were evidently unable to agree as to the value of the documents. The question whether there had ever been a pueblo at San Francisco was an intricate one and the committee as a whole felt itself unable to cope with it, and took the short cut of attempting to buy off the possibly disturbing elements.

Green Papers a "Gold Brick"

Accordingly they offered Alfred $12,500 for the papers, the sum he had demanded, but he refused to give the papers up until his brothers who were held by the committee on their parole should be tried, and their cases disposed of by the inquisitors. They were subsequently examined by the executive committee on August 10th, and all were released excepting Alfred. The charges against them were probably baseless, not to use the harsher word "trumped up," as they were dismissed on the ground that they had not been substantiated. Later the committee reached the conclusion that Alfred had fooled them with worthless papers, but they had paid him the $12,500 he had demanded. The documents were subsequently turned over to the United States district court. It is doubtful, however, whether that disposition would have been made of them had their tenor been different. If they had been of a character calculated to establish that there had been no pueblo, it is reasonably certain that the committee would have taken measures to prevent their proving a further disturbing element in the community.

Lynch Law Justified

The actions of the Vigilance Committee of 1856 have rarely been considered from the same standpoint as other departures from established methods of administering the law common in the United States almost from the foundation of the government. It has often been quoted as the one defensible instance of lynch law. It was so regarded at the time by a vast majority of the people of San Francisco and California, and also by a very considerable proportion of the American people. The latter did not always understand the causes which had brought the Vigilance Committee into existence, but the belief was general that it was fighting criminals, and corruption of all kinds, and Americans were ready to applaud even if the methods adopted were not those which should suffice in a civilized community.

The Critic's of Vigilante Methods

There was no disposition at any time on the part of those who championed Vigilante methods to go behind the returns and attempt to discover the causes which made them necessary. It was assumed without question that the conditions existing in San Francisco were wholly different from those which might be found in other American cities, and that they were entirely without precedent. The discovery of gold, and the rush of adventurers to the coast, was supposed to have inflicted upon San Francisco an overwhelming horde of criminals who could only be restrained by summary processes, and the safety of society and the preservation of civilization, it was urged, demanded that they should be put forth.

Criminal Ascendancy a Myth

And yet the evidence is indisputable that this fancied criminal ascendancy was a myth, and that the trouble was due to the failure of the better elements in the community to use the peaceful means at their command to exercise restraint. Instead of decency and respectability asserting itself it quickly submitted to the introduction of the worst vices of Eastern municipal politicians. An overwhelming majority of voters who were interested in maintaining good government, instead of exerting themselves to that end, allowed the Brodericks, and the broken down politicians of the Atlantic states and the South to conduct their affairs for them, and the result was precisely the same, so far as misgovernment was concerned; as was witnessed in other sections of the Union where less fuss was made about such matters than in California, where love of the spectacular has been something like a passion ever since the discovery of gold.

Red shirts were worn in other cities, and disreputable rowdyism had flourished in places where the veneer of civilization was a little thicker than in San Francisco, but no one thought of indicting the whole community on that account. Probably the mistake of making a target of the Pacific Coast city would not have been made had there not been shown, from the beginning, a disposition to regard as picturesque what was merely vulgar, and to assume that because a place is new that its population, no matter what its previous training, may safely disregard the conventions of established societies and revert to primitive conditions. *San Francisco Atmosphere*

The critics East, West, North and South, had no hestitation whatever in 1856 about accepting San Franciscans at their own valuation. Then, as now, they were quite ready to believe that the community was out of the ordinary and might therefore be a law unto itself. The word "atmosphere" had not yet been applied to conditions produced by relaxation of the rules which obtain in older communities, but San Francisco was universally considered as a queer town, peculiar in many respects, but on the whole very likeable, and not entirely bad even though its people sometimes did things that set the whole world talking, and shocked a great many who regard departure from the beaten track as a serious matter. *Acceptance of California Verdict*

It was largely due to this estimate of San Francisco that the federal government refused at any stage of the Vigilante uprising to directly interfere with its operations. The authorities at Washington were asked by the Law and Order people to intervene, and the governor set the machinery in motion to bring about that result, but the Washington politicians managed by one means or another to evade action. During the administration of Governor Downey in 1860 a bill was passed by the legislature, and approved by him to pay R. A. Thompson and Ferris Forman, who were sent to Washington to invoke assistance in putting down the Vigilance Committee. In the course of the debate over the matter statements were made which clearly established that it was not uncertainty concerning the propriety of intervening which held back the administration, but inability to decide whether intervention would interfere or help the cause which those at the head of affairs had most at heart. *Federal Authorities Hold Aloof*

But while the federal authorities on one pretense and another evaded their duty, there was no lack of sympathy for the advocates of law and order among the military and naval officers of rank on the coast. But they acted with circumspection, and were evidently restrained by orders from Washington which tied their hands. Thus General John S. Wood, commanding the Pacific division of the U. S. army, when applied to by Governor Johnson on the 4th of June, 1856, for arms, answered that such a request could be granted only upon the authorization of the president. In the meantime, however, one of his subordinates at the presidio, Lieutenant J. H. Gibson, although ordered by Wood to remain perfectly neutral had, on the requisition of Mayor Van Ness, promptly issued a quantity of ammunition. His indiscretion nearly caused him to lose his position, an active effort to have him cashiered being defeated with some difficulty. *Erosion of a Duty*

The part played by Sherman in the days of the Vigilance Committee of 1856 illustrates the peculiarities of the situation. A long time subsequent to the upris- *Sherman's Position* ing he expressed the opinion that if he had been properly supported by the governor he would have been able through the instrumentality of the committee of citizens favoring law and order to bring the operation of the Vigilance Committee to a standstill, or that he could at least have succeeded in placing the movement in such a light that it would have lost the support of many who remained identified with the organization to the last. The point on which Sherman laid stress was the misleading of Johnson by such men as Terry, Howard and some others, who made him believe that the committee was weak and ready to give in, and that the proper method to pursue was to demand an unconditional surrender. The ex-lieutenant, it appears, was a believer in pacific methods, and advocated a compromise. It is perhaps significant that Volney E. Howard, who was appointed to succeed Sherman, when the latter resigned the command of the militia in disgust, because he was not supported, and David S. Terry, later developed into pronounced secessionists and cast in their fortunes with the South at the outbreak of the Civil war.

Efforts to Effect a Compromise

The effort to bring about the compromise to which Sherman referred was instituted by a group of citizens at the head of whom were such men as Joseph B. Crockett, Frederick W. Macondray, Henry S. Foote, Martin R. Roberts, John Sime, James D. Thornton, James Donohue, John J. Williams and Bailey Peyton. This committee asked and obtained an interview with the Vigilance Committee and preferred among other demands that the writ of *habeas corpus* should be respected, and that all exhibitions of force should be dispensed with. This was on June 3, 1856, but nothing came of the meeting, the Vigilance Committee planting itself on the proposition that the Law and Order party should disband their forces, whereupon the governor withdrew his proclamation. Sherman after this interview accompanied the citizens committee to Benecia, where they met the governor, but the latter was by that time so completely under the influence of the men mentioned that the moderate measures suggested were rejected and force was resolved upon to compel an unconditional surrender.

Solidarity of Vigilance Committee

The Vigilance Committee to all appearances acted as a unit, but there were occasional dissensions within the ranks. There was objection at times to the secrecy of proceedings, and the black list. The former was assailed as dangerous because it might lead to the same excesses which followed the exercise of arbitrary authority by the tribunals during the French Revolution, and the singling out of individuals for proscription on mere suspicion without giving them a trial, it was feared, might result in injury to innocent persons. But on the whole the Vigilance Committee was a harmonious body, and the majority of its members were profoundly convinced that the method to which they had resorted was the only one which could be depended upon to cure the troubles of San Francisco. There may have been some members whose motives were ulterior, but they were a small minority, but candor compels the statement that they were not the least influential members of the committee.

Failure of Majority to Exercise its Power

The objects of the committee were stated in an address of the executive committee of the Vigilantes which after reciting various abuses, and dwelling with great particularity upon election frauds and ballot box stuffing, declared that "embodied in the principles of republican government are the truths that the majority shall rule, and that when corrupt officials fraudulently seize the reins of authority and designedly prevent the execution of the laws of punishment upon the notoriously guilty, then the power reverts back to the people from whom it was wrested."

The declaration carries with it the admission that the majority had been negligent in its duties. Had it not been the minority could not have wrested power from the majority for it could have controlled at the polls as easily before 1856 as it did afterward, had there been half as much zeal displayed as there was when the People's party came to be a factor in politics.   *Negligence of the Majority*

CHAPTER XXVII

AFFAIRS AT LOOSE ENDS IN THE EARLY FIFTIES

THE PEOPLE NOT INTRACTABLE—BAD ELEMENTS NOT HARD TO CONTROL—VICES OF PIONEERS NOT OF THE HIDDEN SORT—HIGH LIGHTS ON SHORTCOMINGS—FIXING RESPONSIBILITY FOR EVIL PRACTICES—PUTTING THE BLAME ON FOREIGNERS—THE GOLD SEEKERS—GROWING COSMOPOLITANISM OF THE CITY—NEGLECT OF MUNICIPAL AFFAIRS—EVERYBODY BOARDED—PREVALENCE OF GAMBLING—THE GLITTERING BAR ROOMS—PORTSMOUTH SQUARE AND ITS SURROUNDINGS—GAMBLING HOUSE PROPRIETORS GROW RICH—REGULATING THE SOCIAL EVIL—A MIXED STATE OF AFFAIRS SOCIALLY—NO HOME RESTRAINTS—EARLY PHILOSOPHERS—PLENTY OF COLLEGE BRED MEN IN THE CITY—ATTEMPTS TO ERADICATE EVIL—PROGRESS TOWARDS ORDER.

ONCENTRATION of attention on the early political history of San Francisco is apt to produce the impression that the inhabitants of the City were a particularly intractable people who required the application of extraordinary measures to keep them within bounds. Much of the evidence concerning this point is presented in a manner calculated to emphasize this view, but the impartial investigator, ready to consider all the facts, is forced to conclude that great exaggeration has been indulged in by witnesses in order to justify their assumption that the resort to unusual methods to preserve order was necessary.

Not an Intractable People

Some of the contradictions in the testimony have been pointed out in the chapters dealing with the Vigilance Committee and its operations. The testimony of one historian that four-fifths of the population was made up of honest and industrious Americans has been cited, and his implied and expressed opinion that this better element could at all times have controlled the disorderly classes had they performed their civic duties with half the zeal with which they pursued their personal interests has been dwelt upon. The expression of such an opinion, while it seemed called for by the extraordinary exaggeration of the bad features of early California life, to the logical thinker will always appear superfluous in the face of the attested fact, that in every instance when the better elements took the trouble to assert themselves, the criminally inclined, and the predatory politicians, were easily kept in check.

Bad Elements Easily Controlled

But the precise thinker is not in the majority. The most of those who have read of the Vigilante episodes of San Francisco have reached the conclusion that they were a necessary accompaniment of the development of a country whose first vigorous inhabitants were adventurous men who had cut loose from the ties of

Misleading Circumstances

settled communities and were disposed to be a law unto themselves. That there were many such is undeniable, and that they and their doings were much more in evidence than that of the majority who were not disposed to break away from the conventions of the world they left behind them is equally true; but their presence and actions did not prove that the whole society was any more reckless than a procession of red-shirted firemen at about the same period in New York proved that all the people in that city were "Bowery Boys."

Only a Brief Episode

The annalist of San Francisco in telling of the first rush to California describes a condition of affairs in 1848 which has been taken as typical of a period, but which really endured but a short time. Telling of the desertion of the town when the news of the gold discovery at Sutter's fort reached it, and of the speedy growth which followed the great influx from the East, he says: "Everybody made money and was suddenly growing rich; nobody had leisure to think for a moment of his occupation; all classes gambled, the starched, white neck clothed professor of religion and the bootblack." The description fitted San Francisco for a short period only. From the pages of the "Annals" and other sources we can easily extract the evidence that despite some staring external manifestations San Francisco rapidly put on the garb of the older sections of the country, adopting most of their virtues, and neglecting none of the things which contributed to the advancement of civilization.

Vices not Hidden by Pioneers

The men who made San Francisco their home also brought with them some of the vices of an older civilization, and these were accentuated in appearance by their refusal to conceal them. They disdained the hypocrisy which takes the form of hiding evils from the public gaze, and openly practiced vices that were equally common in other places, but were discreetly hidden behind doors. No one now seriously urges that this attitude was either admirable or desirable, and few will deny that the glittering saloons and their wide open doors, and easily accessible gaming tables, converted many a man into a loafer who might have been a good citizen, had the temptations to stray from the path of sobriety and industry not been so numerous; but it must be borne in mind that in the early Fifties, in most sections of the Union, puritanical notions concerning gambling and drinking were not prevalent, and that San Francisco's distinctiveness in this regard was chiefly due to ostentatious disregard of appearances.

High Lights on Shortcomings

We have been too prone in thinking of early San Francisco to place in the foreground of our mental picture the gilded gin shops, and the painted harlots, while we have relegated to the rear the churches and schools and other outward evidences of modern progress. The meretricious desire to find a peculiar atmosphere is responsible for the fact that the El Dorado and other gambling places in the City were talked about at home and described in letters to the East, while little or no mention was made of the soberer side of life. But the omission is repaired by the testimony of the daguerreotypes reproduced in this volume, in which structures devoted to religion and learning are conspicuous in the landscape.

Serious Side of Life not Neglected

At the risk of imperiling the picturesqueness of the narrative it must be told at the outset that the serious side of life was not wholly subordinated, and that the churches and schools had their earnest supporters, and that they were the saving salt of a community, undoubtedly over much given to struggling for wealth. The part they played, as is fitting, will be described later on. They were the instruments which imperceptibly, but nevertheless efficaciously worked toward the regeneration of the City, and to appreciate their work at its real value it is necessary to first portray as faithfully as possible the difficulties with which they had to contend.

One of the causes assigned by historians when endeavoring to account for the corruption of Rome in the days of the Empire was the lure of gain its wealth held out to foreigners. The assumption predicates a state of purity in the Romans which never existed. It implies that the natives were spoiled by the people who flocked in upon them from the whole of the known world of the period when in reality they merely exchanged their uncouth habits and brutal customs for refined vices. Had they been what the historians assume, a really moral people, they would not so easily have adopted the vices of the foreigner; they would have assimilated his good qualities and rejected the bad ones which he brought with him. It has been the custom during the ages to put the blame for shortcomings on the stranger. It was not departed from by the early Californians; if anything the propensity was exhibited by them in a more marked fashion than usual. There were several reasons for this. The first was that inspired by the uneasy feeling of the interloper determined to maintain his position against all comers; and strongly cooperating with this was the jealousy inspired by the discovery of gold which gave birth to the apprehension that in the flood of immigration the owners of the soil through conquest would completely be submerged, and that the treasures of the new El Dorado would be absorbed by the outlander. But the most potent factor in the creation of adverse sentiment against foreigners was the transplanted "Know Nothingism" which flourished luxuriantly in California soil.

<small>Responsibility for Evil Practices</small>

San Francisco was not at first disposed to boast of its cosmopolitanism. The Americans were inclined rather to regard with distrust and suspicion all who could not speak English. They did not seek to ingratiate themselves with the native Californians, and were very apt to apply contemptuous names to them, and to think of them as inferior beings, making few distinctions between the classes and regarding none of them as entitled to much consideration. There was a disposition to be aggressive, or at least to be tolerant of the aggressions of the vicious, and what is more discreditable than anything else to hold foreigners, as a class, responsible for outrages in which disreputable Americans figured as freely, and much more numerously than those of other countries. The Sydney "coves" would not have been emboldened to act as they did in the affair of the Hounds in 1849 if they had not been well supported by a strong contingent of rowdies and black legs from the states east of the mountains.

<small>Putting the Blame on Foreigners</small>

All races were mingled in the influx. There were Chinese and Malays, Abyssinians and negroes, Kanakas and New Zealanders, Feejee Islanders, and even Japanese, described as "short, thick, clumsy, ever bowing jacketed fellows," Hindoos, Russians and a few Turks. The Latin American peoples were well represented, the number of Chileans, Peruvians and Mexicans being especially noticeable. Germany and Great Britain had large contingents, by far the largest proportion from the latter country being Irish. The French were not absent from the throng and there were a few who claimed the distinction of being real Spaniards. And in greater number than any other nation could boast were the Americans who, however, were as much strangers in a strange land as those whom at first they were disposed to regard as interlopers. Happily the intolerant spirit did not last long, and, except in rare instances, it was unproductive of mischief. In an incredibly

<small>The Gold Seekers</small>

brief period there was an astonishing assimilation of all the respectable elements, only occasionally disturbed by the political manifestations of the "Know Nothings," which, however, usually expended their force at the polls. The friction produced by native Americanism after 1849 was never very great, even though the party proved victorious in elections and succeeded in putting its candidates into the gubernatorial chair and on the supreme bench.

Foreigners Gain Respect

It soon came to pass that foreigners were as much esteemed by Americans generally as though they were citizens, which indeed they took pains to become as speedily as possible when eligible for the honor. Among the names of the prominent business men of the Fifties will be found a large proportion whose origin may be easily detected, and the roll of the Vigilance Committee has its share of members who were born under other flags than the stars and stripes. Even the Chinese at that period shared in the general indulgence, and were familiarly known as "China boys." They were invited to take part in public functions and treated on terms of perfect equality in San Francisco at a time when they were being discriminated against in other parts of the world.

Growing Cosmopolitanism of City

With the perception of the fact that foreigners were an advantage rather than a hindrance to the prosperity of the community San Franciscans became proud of the cosmopolitan character of their City, and long before the Know Nothing fever had spent its strength they were wont to dwell upon the varied costumes and peculiar habits of the people who lived in their midst and made the life of San Francisco interesting. There are many interesting descriptions of street scenes in the early Fifties in which the picturesque features receive ample recognition. The native Californian on his prancing steed or slouching around with serape over his shoulders was much in evidence. There were a few Indians who roamed the streets half naked, and Chinese trudged along with baskets suspended from bamboo poles which rested on their shoulders. Red shirted men were numerous, but they could hardly be regarded as distinctive, for that garment was much affected at the time by firemen and others in Eastern cities. An occasional woman was sometimes seen parading her rich attire, for the purpose of advertising her calling.

Apologies for Streets

The condition of the streets used by this motley gathering from all parts of the world received as much attention from the critics as the people. It was indescribably bad. The thoroughfares could hardly have tempted pedestrians to extraordinary effort. At first there were mere pathways of boards, and later there were walks which were illy divided from the planked roadways. They were unclean by day and unlighted by night, rendering them dangerous, as in many places they crossed swamps in which one might easily pay a serious penalty for carelessness. There was a plague of rats of all sorts, many of them doubtless introduced into the new country by the ships which brought the immigrants. There are old prints depicting the consternation they created in the female breast, which amusingly illustrate the extent of the evil and at the same time call attention to the almost total neglect of sanitary precautions.

Every Body Boarded

The buildings which housed the people were not much better than the streets. Small rough board shanties were numerous, and tents were freely used for shelter until successive disastrous fires to which the City was a victim compelled the abandonment of such flimsy structures. In the first year after the gold rush home life was almost unknown. At the close of 1849 nearly everybody lived in boarding houses, or at restaurants, which were numerous, but with rare exceptions were

JENNY LIND THEATER, LATER CONVERTED INTO A CITY HALL, ON EAST SIDE
OF KEARNY STREET, OPPOSITE PORTSMOUTH SQUARE
The saloon on the left was the famous El Dorado

MASONIC TEMPLE, MONTGOMERY AND POST STREETS, ERECTED IN
1860 AND DESTROYED BY FIRE OF 1906

wretchedly deficient in anything contributing to human comfort, although those who conducted them exacted enormous prices for the miserable accommodations and fare provided by them.

It would have been amazing if under such circumstances a population composed almost wholly of men could have escaped the allurements of the saloon and the gambling table. The lack of opportunity for unobjectionable recreation, and the disposition to squander easily gained wealth combined, greatly stimulated the inherent tendency of men to indulge in games of chance, and there were plenty ready to provide the means to gratify the propensity. As a result, when gambling is unrestrained, it became a passion for the many, and a mere matter of business for the cold and calculating professionals who lived by preying upon the unwary. It cannot be said that the vice was introduced into the country by those who made their way to California when gold was discovered, for the natives were inveterate gamblers; but the newcomers brought with them many strange methods of parting the fool from his money, which were formerly unknown, and which became fully as popular as the Spanish game known as monte which had up to 1849 been the chief diversion of the people. Preponderance of Males

The games mostly played in the big saloons were monte, faro, roulette, *rouge et noir* and *vingt-un*. Poker, which later vied in attractiveness with the games mentioned is not often referred to among the fascinations held out by the dens clustered about Portsmouth square, although it must have been played, as it was well known in the South, and on the Mississippi years before 1849, and long before Bret Harte wrote his stirring verses on the celebrated encounter between Ah Sin and the haughty Caucasian. The stakes played for were often high. The annalist tells of a single wager in which $16,000 was risked, and his testimony is amply corroborated by others who assert that it was no uncommon thing for men to come in from the mines and get rid in a single night of all the gold gathered by them during months of toil. Gambling Games

We may trust the descriptions of the gambling saloons (they can hardly be called dens, their aggressive openness would make the term a misnomer) up to a certain point, but unless we keep in mind the changed significance of adjectives we may easily be misled by the free use of such words as glitter and magnificent. Things are usually judged relatively, and measured by their surroundings the appellation "palace" may have seemed appropriate, but there is reason to believe that the showiest were tawdry affairs despite the almost uniform testimony of the argonauts to the contrary. A woman, writing under the *nom de plume* of "Shirley," in a sketch in which she entered into details, conveys the impression that a bar room trimmed with red calico, from the midst of which gleamed a mirror flanked by decanters and jars of brandied fruit, was regarded in the mining country as something luxurious. We may assume that the saloons of the metropolis were provided with better adornments than this description implies, but specimens of what were once known as "gorgeous" affairs survived down to a comparatively recent period and permitted the more discerning critic to decide that the impression of grandeur was produced largely by a display of glittering glass, mirrors, and a little gilt, and that if reproduced today they would hardly be considered an attractive addition to the water front of a sea port. Glittering Bar Rooms

Until very recently the alert traveler, anxious to see novel sights, might have obtained a fair impression of San Francisco's bustling center in 1849 by examining Portsmouth Square

any of the open places so common in towns of considerable size along the transcontinental railroads. Portsmouth square, like these more recent examples of pioneer life, was flanked by saloons. The whole eastern side was devoted to them, and a not inconsiderable portion of the street on the south. The latter was particularly affected by gamblers, and many of the saloons whose names were almost household words in California for years were situated there. Gambling, however, was by no means confined to these places whose owners used every device to bring the man with money to their tables; it was pursued in all the hotels of consequence, the practice being to set aside rooms where "gentlemen" could find a quiet game, from which we may infer that, while everyone may have gambled, there were some who did not care to openly advertise the fact that they were gamblers.

Women in Gambling Places

In all the big saloons women dealt cards and turned the roulette wheels. It goes without saying that they were of the lower world, and that they owed their positions to that fact. In some of the larger saloons there were as many as a dozen tables, and it was usual to make large displays of gold upon them, the spectacle being arranged with especial reference to exciting the cupidity of the visitors. The policing of the town was notoriously bad for the first few years after the discovery at Sutter's fort, but it is one of the anomalies of the period, that although the men entrusted with the rule of the community could not preserve order the saloonkeepers succeeded in doing so in their places, their motto being "no interference with the progress of the game." Brawlers and fault-finders were summarily ejected, and the sentiment of the visitors usually approved the methods of securing peace even when they were accompanied by a display of force.

Gambling House Proprietors Flourish

It is not of record that the argonauts generally succeeded in amassing wealth, although the opportunities for thrifty persons to do so were abundant; but the proprietors of the saloons were, as a rule, forehanded, and many of those conducting the popular places made big fortunes. Their patrons were cast in a different mould, and with them it was "easy come, easy go." No one has attempted to reduce to terms of percentage the proportion of the first comers who were heedful enough of the future to save a competence, but it was not large. It was not the miner who made a lucky strike who loomed up as an important figure in the community. He too often realized the adage concerning "a fool and his money," and when he parted with his "dust" or "nuggets," not infrequently it was to the man who ran the gambling tables and to dissolute women.

Plenty of Fast Women

Of the latter the community soon had more than its share. Among the earliest to appear on the scene were numerous Mexicans and Chileans, and it was their presence which formed one of the excuses for the depradations on the Latin Americans by the Hounds, who alleged that they aided their paramours in robbing the indiscreet visitors to their quarter. They were probably no worse than their sisters of evil repute from other countries, who surpassed in audacity the Mexican and Chilean women, who were not unaware of the fact that they were especial objects of that peculiar resentment which is often manifested against the conquered by the conquering class, and were less obtrusive on that account than their rivals. It was noted in 1853 that there was a small and steady increase of female immigrants, and that among them were some "beautiful and modest women," but the preponderance of the disreputable class was such that the annalist feelingly remarks that "there are common prostitutes enough to bring disgrace on the place." He also adds that many men openly maintained mistresses. Perhaps the severest indictment against the looseness of the period was the flagrant disregard of the decencies of life which attended this practice. It was no uncommon thing for men of standing in the community to parade their mistresses in public, and to obtrude them on women having claims to respectability. But not infrequently men who thus defied the conventionalities later repaired their error by accepting to the fullest extent the obligations imposed by the relation, and clothed their mistresses with the title of wife without the intervention of minister, priest or justice.

The social evil and gambling were a source of trouble to the authorities, who resorted to various devices to check them but with little success. Very early an ordinance was adopted, and promptly repealed, authorizing the seizure of money openly displayed on gaming tables. The sentiment of the period did not sustain the effort, and in 1854, when the common council passed a stringent ordinance against houses of ill fame, and penalizing the inmates, it was soon permitted to fall into desuetude. At first it was rigidly enforced against the cheap brothels of the Mexicans and Chileans, but when it was sought to extend its operation to "the fashionable white Cyprians," it was promptly discovered that it was "intrinsically illegal and tyrannous in some of its provisions." A commentator of the period tells us that it was soon found out "that impurity hid by walls could not be put down by mere legislation."

Regulating the Social Evil

This attitude was not changed for many years, and while the evils ran their course "society" in San Francisco can only be described as very mixed. General Sherman in his "Memoirs" gives us a glimpse of the state of affairs in a story he tells about a chance encounter on the ship which brought him to California in 1853. It appears that the general, who was then a young officer, was obliging enough to help two "ladies" to secure a change of the stateroom assigned to them, and as a result of his courtesy he not only lost his own berth, but was recorded as being their escort, the passenger list reading "Captain Sherman and ladies." "At every meal," he tells us, "the steward would come to him and say 'Captain will you bring your ladies to the table?'" The "ladies" were the most modest and best behaved on the ship, but sometime after San Francisco was reached a fellow passenger asked the captain if he personally knew Mrs. D., who had so sweetly sang for them, and who had come out under his special escort. He told the inquiring individual that she was a chance acquaintance of the voyage, and that she expected to meet her husband, who lived near Mokelumne hill. He was then informed that Mrs. D. was "a woman of the town." "Society was decidedly mixed in California in those days," was the general's comment on the incident.

A Very Mixed Society

The fact that very few of the gold seekers were in the country with a view of making it their home was more largely than anything else responsible for the loose conditions described. In 1852 many who had made their "pile" were leaving, and usually they made it very clear that they had no desire to return. While many of the earliest American settlers had abundant faith in the future development of California and clearly perceived that San Francisco was destined to become a great sea port, not a few of those who rushed into the country in search of gold, deceived by unfamiliar conditions, quickly reached the conclusion that the land was not fit to live in, and that about the only thing it was good for was to extract the precious metal from its soil. Their brief experience inclined them to share the belief of the Mexican governor, who reported to his government that California was too good for convicts, but not exactly a desirable place for decent people.

No Home Restraints

Effects of Home Sickness

Nostalgia, sometimes in its acute and again in its milder form, was productive of extremely pessimistic views. The morbidly homesick man always looks at the dark side of things, and San Francisco in the first year of the fifty decade was filled with adventurers thus afflicted. The distractions of the bar room and other dissipations were resorted to by some to quell their pangs; it was not always the mere love of excitement that turned men from the straight path in pioneer days; too frequently it was the desire to escape mental torments that drove them to excesses, which, under other conditions, would not have appealed to them. The adventurous class may be entitled to all the encomiums bestowed upon it by writers who admire the microbe of unrest; it may have more than its share of the spirit of enterprise; its stock in trade may embrace courage and intelligence, but it does not possess stability of character in an unusual degree. The mass of the argonauts were singularly deficient in this latter respect. It was a long time before they began to show a disposition to look upon San Francisco as a desirable town in which to abide permanently. As late as March, 1855, we find Governor Bigler extolling as one of the advantages of San Francisco the facilities offered by the port for shipping "home" the oil and bone taken by the whalers in the North Pacific, who by that time had begun to use the harbor as a place for wintering.

Early Philosophers

There were some, however, who amid the excitement and the discomforts incident to existence in a town which had sprung up like a mushroom, were able to philosophize and make the best of circumstances. One such was the writer of the "Annals," who, after telling us that "San Francisco was in a state of moral ferment;" that "the scum and froth of its strange mixture, of its many scoundrels, rowdies, and great men, loose women, sharpers and few honest folk" was about all that was visible in the current of the daily life of the City, was still able to exclaim: "Happy the man who can tell of those things which he saw, and perhaps himself did at San Francisco at that time. He shall be an oracle to his admiring neighbors." The prediction has been amply fulfilled, and as might be expected the oracle has not always approached his narrative in a critical mood. He may at one time have longed as ardently as a boarding school girl for "home," and may have loathed his surroundings even though he contributed to making them what they were, but when the change came, when San Francisco became habitable by a process of elimination, repression and addition, he became as ardently attached to the City as though its early history were without a blemish. Forgotten were the vicissitudes and the hardships, the incessant drinking and gambling, and the daily calendar of crime. The only memory that has survived is that of achievement and in that all the argonauts share, even he who remarks with complacency that he might once have bought the lot on Market street, now worth a million dollars or more, for a pair of old boots if he had been thoughtful enough of the future to have done so, or if he had the old boots to spare to make the purchase.

Plenty of College Bred Men

All the adventurers who thronged to California in the early days did not make fortunes, and all the fortunes that were made were not accumulated in the mines. Many a respectable citizen of later days commenced his career in San Francisco by accepting a menial position. We hear a great deal now-a-days of college students earning sufficient money to procure an education by waiting on the table; in pioneer days the job of "waiter" was sought by many college graduates who had been more proficient in earning educational honors than they were in the work of finding gold or in the pursuit of the more prosaic occupations. It is said that in

1850 there were more collegians in San Francisco than any other city in the country, and unless the chroniclers of the period grossly misrepresent the facts they found more difficulty in adapting themselves to their new environment than the mass of gold hunters and other adventurers less equipped with learning.

It would be a mistake to assume that the conditions described required the drastic performances of the Vigilantes to bring about their elimination. Something better than the inspiration of fear was steadily undermining the powers of darkness. The introduction of those agencies of civilization which have lifted man to the high plane he now occupies followed close upon the heels of the adventurer. It may have seemed a correct judgment to the annalist when he summed up the situation by asserting "that nearly all come to the City as devout worshippers of Mammon." The facts, however, do not bear out his view, for the evidence of the working of the leaven of good clearly indicates that there were plenty of earnest men who labored hard to eradicate evil in the early Fifties, and that while their fight was an uphill one it never seemed hopeless to them. Nor did it seem so to the writer of the "Annals," whose alternations between pessimism and hopefulness testify to the sincerity of his narrative, for he was able to record in 1854 that "for the honest, industrious and peaceful man San Francisco is now as safe a residence as can be found in any other large city. For the rowdy and shoulder striker, the drunkard, the insolent, foul-mouthed speaker, the quarrelsome, desperate politician and calumnious writer, the gambler, the daring speculator in strange ways of business, it is a dangerous place to dwell in. There are many such here, and it is their excesses and quarrels that make our sad daily record of murders, duels, etc."

Attempts to Eradicate Evil

The admission that there were still plenty of rogues in San Francisco, and that they engaged in excesses does not impair the force of the statement that the City had become a safe place of residence for the peaceable and industrious. While the City had not yet reached the stage of orderliness attained in the older communities it was fast marching in that direction. The conspicuously vicious features had by no means disappeared, but there were daily additions being made to the agencies calculated to counteract their harmfulness. There was still much open flaunting of vice, too much gambling and a great deal of drinking; but schools, churches, charities and social organizations were multiplying rapidly, and what was of much more consequence the number of homes was increasing. It may be necessary to again recur to the darker side of San Francisco life in dealing with this period, but before doing so, lest the impression be conveyed that it was once like the city abandoned by Lot, it is desirable to present the facts which show that the struggle toward the light began early, and that while it did not eventuate in creating a community of the sort found in many parts of the East, that the efforts, on the whole, were successful in making the metropolis of the Pacific coast a desirable place in which to live and work out the problems of modern civilization.

Progress Towards Order

CHAPTER XXVIII

CONDITIONS IMPROVE SOCIALLY AND OTHERWISE IN THE CITY

STRUGGLE FOR DECENCY—FRATERNAL ORGANIZATIONS—CHURCHES FOUNDED—ALL THE DENOMINATIONS REPRESENTED—A UNION OF PROTESTANT CONGREGATIONS—SUNDAY OBSERVANCE—FIRST PROTESTANT SERMON IN CALIFORNIA—THE CATHOLIC CHURCH—BISHOP ALEMANY ARRIVES—THE PIOUS FUND—SAN FRANCISCO'S FIRST CATHEDRAL—ATTEMPTS TO CHRISTIANIZE THE CHINESE—IMPROVED MANNERS AND MORALS—THANKSGIVING DAY—PIONEER DIVORCES—PASSAGE OF A SUNDAY LAW.

ACH passing year brought an improvement to San Francisco, we are told by the annalist, and we may credit his statement even though at times he despairingly exclaimed that the City was going to the dogs. Among the changes for the better noted by him in 1850 was the fact that some of the immigrants were sending "home" for their families.

Changing Social Conditions

The most of the inhabitants were still living simply to heap up dollars, but the churches and a few good people were establishing sociable and charitable organizations. The prisons were full, but they could not hold a tithe of the offenders and there was a good deal of talk about lynch law. There was some disquiet caused by fear of incendiarism, and gambling was common; the drink habit was dreadfully prevalent. Treating was carried to extremes and carouses were indulged in by many. From the gambling dens increasingly came the cry "the ace! the ace! the ace! a $100 to him who will tell the ace! Who will name the ace of spades? A $100 to anyone who will tell the ace!" The play went on by day and night. Through the twenty-four hours foolish men were getting rid of their hard-earned dust or nuggets, and the adventurers of the Cora stamp untiringly devoted themselves to the task of relieving the silly ones of the money they were anxious to get rid of, although the most of them professed to believe that they were striving to augment their store. But decency entered into competition with blackguardism, and while its advocates had an uphill fight before them they never lost courage and always felt sure of victory in the end.

It is interesting to follow the contest. It began early in 1849. Against the revelries of the bar room were placed the attractions of the lodge. Instead of men spending all their time and money in a society in which each sought to drag the other down the more sober minded were organizing for rational enjoyment and mutual benefit. In 1849 a lodge of Masons was formed under a charter granted by the District of Columbia and named the California Lodge. It was small in numbers at first and held its meetings in a room in the third story of a house on Montgomery street. In less than six months, on the 17th of April, 1850, a grand

Fraternal Organizations

lodge was organized and in 1852 there were as many as thirteen lodges in the City. Organizations of Odd Fellows were effected with equal promptitude. California Lodge No. 1 was started in 1849 and in 1853 a grand lodge was formed, and by 1854 there were five more or less flourishing lodges in the city. In 1849 there was also organized by the Rev. T. D. Hunt a temperance society which waged war on the saloon and did its part in the work of regeneration.

First Protestant Church

After the occupation by the Americans the new members of the community were quick to introduce their religion. The Mission church at Dolores had met the needs of the Catholics up to that time, and there were few of any other denomination until the gringo came. In 1847, on the 6th of May, a public meeting was held in the City to consider the question of erecting a Protestant church and a committee was appointed to that end. There is some dispute as to which denomination is entitled to the honor of priority. The claim is made for the Baptists that they erected in 1849, in the month of July, a structure, which was the first Protestant edifice on the coast with the exception of a small chapel built in Washington county, Oregon, by Rev. Victor Snelling in 1843. The San Francisco church was not very imposing in appearance, having Oregon pine boards for walls and ship's sails spread over scantlings serving as a roof. The major part of the cost of construction was borne by one person, Charles L. Ross, but he was stimulated and encouraged in his work by the American Baptist Home Missionary Society of New York. Its first pastor was the Rev. Osgood C. Wheeler, who arrived in San Francisco in February, 1849. On March 18th services were held by him in the new church, and it is recorded that in closing an address on the 17th of June in that year he predicted the great commercial future of the City, and urged upon his hearers the importance of the Baptist church effecting a thorough organization so that its religious work could develop with the City and become a part of its future greatness. In August, 1850, the second Baptist church in San Francisco was organized with twelve members. This congregation held its services in a rented building on the north side of Pine street, not far from the site of the present California Market, but the organization only continued a few months. Its members after the disbandment of the congregation united with the first church. The first pastor, Rev. Mr. Wheeler, resigned his pastorate in November, 1851, and for an interval the pulpit of the First Baptist church was filled regularly by ministers of other denominations. It appears that the worldliness and the bustle and excitement of the City in the first two years after the discovery of gold made San Francisco seem a profitless field for religious work, and there was some difficulty in getting a successor, but the place was finally filled by Rev. Benjamin Brierly, who began his ministrations on September 29, 1852. It is interesting to note that his salary was fixed at $3,000 a year.

A New Brick Church Building

In July, 1853, the membership of the church had increased to seventy-five. In the meantime the building on Washington street had been enlarged, but the increasing attendance demanded more commodious quarters and the building of a brick edifice was resolved upon by the congregation. The new church was 52x85 in size and had a seating capacity of 450 when finally completed in 1857. Its construction was delayed by various causes, but the congregation had the forethought to retain the old building, which they removed to the rear of their lot and used it as their place of worship until they were installed in their new quarters. Mr. Brierly's ministrations lasted six years. There was an interval between his departure in May, 1858, in which the pulpit was not filled. In June, 1859, Rev. Dr. Cheney, of Philadelphia, accepted a call and within a year after he commenced his labors the congregation was nearly doubled.

In the "Annals" we are told that in 1852 it was noted that the number of women immigrants were increasing, and that many of them were of a better class than the earlier arrivals. This testimony is amply corroborated by the statement that on the day after Christmas, 1849, John C. Pelton and his wife opened a school with three pupils in the First Baptist church building, the free use of which was granted to him by resolution of the trustees. In April, 1850, the number of pupils had increased to 130, and the care of the school was assumed by the city council, and Pelton and his wife were paid $500 a month for their services. The pioneer school continued to occupy the church building, rent free, until its destruction in the fire of June 22, 1851, and at one time it had close to 300 scholars enrolled. The significance of this increase, and the further statement that there was a flourishing Sunday school maintained, will be realized by those who carefully trace the connection between it and the steady improvement of the condition of the community. *Women Immigrants Increasing*

The first Presbyterian church of San Francisco was due to the Presbyterian Board of Home Missions, which sent the Rev. Albert Williams to this City in 1849. He arrived on April 1st, and in accordance with instructions he opened a school in a small tent on Portsmouth square, near its northwestern corner, but he said subsequently: "I had no more children than if I had opened it on the Desert of Sahara, and for the same reason—there were no children in either place." In the course of a couple of weeks, however, he succeeded in securing four pupils, but he only retained them for a few days as their parents abandoned the City for the mines and took their progeny with them. Mr. Williams commenced preaching at once after his arrival, but owing to insufficient housing accommodations he was compelled to move from place to place for several Sundays, but finally, on May 20th, he secured a location for a good sized tent and organized the First Presbyterian church of San Francisco. A writer who has traced the fortunes of the church since its establishment tells us that "although the Baptists, under the ministerial charge of Reverend O. C. Wheeler, had been holding Sunday services in the private house of Charles L. Ross for several weeks, they had not formally organized as a church, so the First Presbyterian church," he says, "stands as the first Protestant church organization inaugurated in San Francisco." *First Presbyterian Church*

When the First Presbyterian church was organized the only Protestant ministers in San Francisco were Rev. Albert Williams, Presbyterian; Rev. O. C. Wheeler, Baptist; Rev. T. Dwight Hunt, Congregationalist; Rev. Wm. Taylor, Methodist, and Revs. F. S. Mines and J. L. Ver Mehr, Episcopalian. On August 19, 1849, a lot was secured by the Presbyterians on Dupont between Pacific and Broadway, and a large tent, the property of a disbanded miners' association, was bought and pitched. At the very first meeting under the canvas the small congregation was gratified by the announcement that a church building had been bought in New York and was being shipped around the Horn. It arrived in due season and was duly set up on Stockton street between Pacific and Broadway and "thirty-two ladies were present at the dedication," a notable fact, as it was the largest number of women ever gathered in a place of worship (excluding the Mission Dolores) in San Francisco up to that time. This building was destroyed in one of the fires of 1851. A new church was planned to take the place of that which had been burned. *Protestant Ministers in 1849*

It was to be of brick, but its construction, owing to the vicissitudes of the times, proceeded slowly and it was not entirely completed for several years, the services being meanwhile held under a temporary roof. With the rapid increase of population between 1850 and 1860 other Presbyterian churches were organized. In 1851 Howard church was formed with Rev. S. H. Willey as pastor. It was located on Mission street near Third. In June, 1854, a number of members of the First church were granted letters to form a new congregation and Calvary Presbyterian church was ushered into existence. The first pastor was Rev. W. A. Scott, and he filled its pulpit until 1863, when he was succeeded by Rev. William Wadsworth, who in turn was followed by the Rev. John Hemphill. The first Calvary church was built on the north side of Bush street between Montgomery and Sansome.

Union of Protestant Congregations

Although the first Presbyterian church, as already stated, was organized under the auspices of the Presbyterian Board of Home Missions by the Reverend Albert Wheeler in 1849, the Rev. T. Dwight Hunt, a minister of that denomination, had arrived in San Francisco a year earlier from the Hawaiian islands with a view of establishing a church. In the "Californian" an announcement of his arrival was printed, and the statement was made that a fund had been raised by a number of citizens to maintain a Protestant chaplain, which office had been unanimously tendered to Mr. Hunt and by him accepted. A popular meeting was held in the Institute on Portsmouth square on November 1, 1848, which was presided over by Edward E. Harrison, and James Creighton acted as secretary. Addresses were made by several present and five trustees were elected: C. E. Wetmore, Joseph Banden, C. V. Gillespie, C. L. Ross and E. H. Harrison. Mr. Hunt was chosen chaplain for one year and an appropriation of $2,000 was made for his support. This was distinctly a union of various prominent denominations, and Mr. Hunt had agreed to make no effort to found a church of his own preference during his incumbency of the chaplainship. The ministrations of Mr. Hunt signalized the advent of Protestantism in San Francisco and he is regarded by the members of the various denominations as the pioneer preacher of the City. It is related that Mr. Hunt's exhortations were effectively employed against conducting business on Sunday, a practice almost universal at the time in California. Whatever he may have accomplished in that regard, however, was not enduring, for Sunday closing remained a vexed question for many years. Efforts were made at various times to restrict the practice by law, but the sentiment of the people did not favor restraint, although the closing habit finally became established by general consent, which was by no means accorded through consideration for religion but rather through the growing recognition of the necessity of a day of rest.

First Protestant Sermon

The first sermon preached by a Methodist minister was heard in an adobe building opposite Portsmouth square on the 24th of April, 1847. It was not the first time Methodist doctrine was expounded in the City, for before the arrival of the Rev. William Roberts, missionary superintendent of Oregon and California, a layman named Anthony at different times talked to the few Protestants in the community, and tradition asserts that he spoke with great fervor. It is also stated that sea captains were sometimes moved to speak "the word," and that they did so convincingly, but to very small congregations. It was not, however, until August, 1848, that the first Methodist congregation was regularly organized, and its first church was not dedicated until October 8, 1849. It was a very humble edifice,

25x40. feet, rudely built, and its first pastor was William Taylor, afterwards ordained bishop.

In the following year steps were taken to found the University of the Pacific, now the College of the Pacific. This institution takes rank as the premier in the field of the higher learning in California, a claim which Methodists love to dwell upon, as they also do upon the fact that in 1851 they founded the "Christian Advocate," the first religious paper published in the new state. In this year the Howard Street church was organized with Rev. M. C. Briggs as its first pastor. Dr. Briggs, like the Rev. Starr King, was an eloquent advocate of the preservation of the Union and shares with him the honor of crystallizing the sentiment which proved powerful enough to thwart the plans of Southerners who hoped to bring about the secession of California.

<small>A University Founded</small>

In a sketch prepared for the author the claim is urged on behalf of the Congregationalists that the honor of establishing the first Protestant church in San Francisco belongs to them. The writer states "that out of the union service presided over by Mr. Hunt in November, 1848, emerged the First Congregational church, and that Mr. Hunt, though a Presbyterian, was called to be its pastor." He adds that by "what was regarded as a bit of innocent and amusing, but rather sharp practice the First Presbyterian church, led by Rev. Mr. Williams, hastened its formal organization and perfected it three or four days in advance of the others." For this reason the writer of the reminiscence believes that the order of priority should be Congregational, Methodist and Baptist. The zeal displayed thus early by the different church organizations unmistakably indicates that the workers in the religious field had no doubt about the outcome of their labors, and that they divined the real condition of affairs and understood the temperament of the people of San Francisco far better than those who pessimistically declared that the City was utterly without saving salt.

<small>Disputed Question of Priority</small>

Although the Catholic church, by reason of its long establishment in the province, should have been firmly intrenched in San Francisco at the time of the occupation, that does not appear to have been actually the case. The "Annals" tell us that the condition of St. Francis church was not inviting, that its attendance was very small, and that the congregation was usually composed of women. It was built of adobes, was very plain externally and had a comfortless interior, but was the possessor of some fine bells, which were probably cast in the Russian foundry at Sitka. The apathy, however, was soon changed into activity when the adventurers began to pour into the City from the Eastern states, and other parts of the world, for among them was a considerable number of Catholics of the sort who believed that works were a necessary accompaniment of faith.

<small>The Catholic Church</small>

There were several Irish colonists in California before the gold rush, who had crossed the plains, and they had been preceded by others who had made their way into the territory by other routes. The influential among these were quick to discern the possibilities of the future and they wrote to Bishop Hughes of New York, describing the condition of affairs and urging him to interest himself in organizing the church. The needs of the people were brought to the attention of Rome and a young Spanish provincial, Joseph Sadoc Alemany, who had labored for ten years in the missions of Kentucky and Tennessee, was settled upon as the one best adapted to meet the difficulties of the change of rule in California and to harmonize the old with the new regime. Alemany numbered among his friends and admirers ex-

<small>Irish Colonists Ask for Bishop</small>

President Andrew Jackson, and this with his Spanish affiliations, it was properly assumed would lessen friction should any occur. Alemany was consecrated in the Dominican church of the Minerva in Rome in June, 1850, and arrived in San Francisco on December 7th of that year and was given a reception in the school room of St. Francis church built by Father Langlois, on which occasion a purse of $1,350 was raised to help pay his expenses in visiting at least a part of his vast diocese, which extended from the Pacific to the Rocky Mountains.

Division of the Pious Fund
The necessity of resorting to this early collection was imposed upon the Catholics by the Mexicans, who diverted to political uses what was called the Pious Fund, which was started as early as 1697 in New Spain, by Father Salvatierra. The Church of Nuestra Señora de los Dolores of Mexico, and private individuals, contributed sums to this fund ranging from $10,000 to $20,000, the money to be applied to missionary work, each new mission to receive a donation of at least $10,000 for its maintenance. The original contributions were judiciously invested by the Jesuits and when the income of the fund was transferred to the Dominicans and Franciscans in Upper and Lower California it amouted to $50,000 a year. From 1811 to 1818 and afterwards to 1828 the church in California received nothing from the fund; instead the missions were often subjected to enforced contributions. In 1832 the Mexican congress ordered the properties belonging to the Pious Fund to be rented for a term not to exceed seven years, the proceeds to be deposited in the mint for the benefit of the California missions. In the ensuing year the Mexican governor, Figueroa took the ground that owing to the law of secularization the missions no longer existed and in 1834 a congressional decree was issued that all missions of the republic should be secularized and converted into curacies, their limits to be designated by the governors of the different states.

The Sequestered Fund Regained
Many years afterward the fund thus sequestered was regained for the church by the activity of Archbishop Riordan, but when Bishop Alemany came on the scene in 1850, despite the labors of the missionaries and their accumulations, the Catholic faithful of San Francisco were as poor as the founders of the Christian religion. Besides the Mission Dolores, which was some three miles from the new town, there was the little adobe church of St. Francis, and only two priests, Fathers Langlois and Croke. The former's congregation had been made the victim of an imposter in 1849, who had obtained a considerable sum by misrepresentations, and he was determined that there should be no repetition of the offense, and it is related as an amusing incident that he asked Bishop Alemany to exhibit his credentials before giving him his confidence.

Growth of Church Under Bishop Alemany
Soon after the advent of Bishop Alemany the activities of the church were greatly increased. In 1851 a new parish was organized in a hall on the corner of Third and Jesse streets and by a vote of the congregation it was named St. Patricks. About the same time a pioneer who had been on the ground long before the forty-niners arrived, donated the land where the Palace hotel now stands for a church, orphanage and school. This orphanage was the first refuge of the kind established in California, it having been the custom of the native Californians to adopt into families the unfortunate children deprived of their parents. The institution was well supported from the date of its foundation. It was the precursor of many other charitable institutions founded by the Catholics all of which flourished under their care. In 1852 San Francisco was made a diocese and an archdiocese at the same time, the formal translation of Archbishop Alemany to the

PLATT'S HALL, CORNER OF MONTGOMERY AND BUSH STREETS, OPENED IN 1860

SAN FRANCISCO 239

Metropolitan See of San Francisco taking place on July 29, 1853. The jurisdiction of the new archdiocese extended from Santa Cruz to Oregon and from the Pacific to the Great Divide, an area almost half as large again as France.

The first cathedral in San Francisco was that of St. Marys on the corner of California and Dupont streets. Its corner stone was laid on the 17th of July, 1853. The site was donated by Mrs. Catherine Sullivan, and the edifice erected was for a long period the most notable in San Francisco. It was destroyed in the great conflagration of 1906, only the walls surviving, but was restored without any change being made in its appearance, and stands today as a reminder of the fact that there was some good designing done in the early Fifties. The cost of the original structure was $175,000, and there is a tradition that its erection contributed largely to the quieting of the pretensions of Benicia which for a time exhibited a disposition to engage in rivalry with San Francisco for supremacy of the bay. "Old St. Marys," as it came to be called, remained the cathedral until 1891 when the structure on Van Ness avenue was completed.

San Francisco's First Cathedral

On the 9th of April, 1856, the French Catholics bought for $15,000 the Baptist church on Bush street between Dupont and Stockton streets and converted it to their own use. Gustave Touchard made the purchase. The French government at this time was much interested in San Francisco and made an appropriation of 450 francs annually for its maintenance. Even with this munificent help the church did not flourish. It was badly administered and was seized for a debt of $30,000. Two years earlier the Germans of San Francisco established a congregation in an iron building which had been used as a store on Montgomery street by Tucker the pioneer jeweler. Mr. Tucker had prospered and built a new place for his business and generously presented the iron building to the Germans, a graceful and courageous act considering the fact that he was a Protestant and that Know Nothingism was rampant at the time. The building was removed to a lot on the north side of Sutter, between Kearny and Montgomery streets, where it was used by the German Catholics until 1869, when they procured a fifty vara lot on Golden Gate avenue, then Tyler street, between Jones and Leavenworth streets.

Other Catholic Churches Built

The Italians in the early days, although later they became very numerous, the colony numbering fully 20,000, had no church of their own prior to 1884. They were looked after spiritually by Old St. Marys, which for a period was a polyglot congregation, the priests ministering at different masses to Italians, Spaniards, French and German and preaching in those languages. In old St. Francis, which had the distinction of being the first Catholic cathedral of San Francisco, there were sermons in English, Spanish, French and Italian. By 1857 the congregation of St. Francis had so enlarged that the construction of a new church in the Gothic style was begun by Father Magagnotte. St. Patrick's on Market street also increased its membership rapidly, and was obliged as early as 1854 to erect a new church to take the place of the modest frame structure which had served the parish during three or four years, and which was converted into a school house and used as such until 1872 when church and school moved to Mission street between Third and Fourth.

Latin American Catholics

Very early efforts were made by the Catholics to effect conversions among the Chinese, but the time was not ripe for labor in that field. In 1853 a Chinese student was brought to San Francisco and made his headquarters in St. Francis

Efforts to Convert Chinese

church. His name was Father Cain, and he strove very earnestly with his countrymen to win them from heathenism, but after ten years of unsuccessful work he returned to Naples where he became the head of the seminary for Chinese missions, dying in Italy in 1868. Father Valentine from Hong Kong and Father Antonucci, met with no better results. Later a Chinese school was started and fostered by the Paulist fathers. The Protestants also devoted themselves to the conversion of Chinese and later of Japanese, and established schools which were provided with substantial buildings. The results of their efforts are variously viewed. The hopeful being inclined to regard them with satisfaction while the skeptical assert that the apparent success in recent years is chiefly due to perception of the value of the English education imparted in the mission schools.

Improved Manners and Morals

It is impossible to sum up the results of these religious efforts with precision, or to apportion the shares of the various social activities of an uplifting kind in contributing to the steady diminution of license in San Francisco after they were well introduced, but it is not hard to trace an improvement in manners and morals. The advance of the community was rapid, although a different impression may have been created by the recital of the story of the Vigilance Committees. In 1849 the mayor, John W. Geary, saw no other way of dealing with the gamblers than by licensing and regulating them. In an address he presented a picture of the disordered condition of the community and despairingly urged as a remedy for the evil its sanction by law, but four years later it was voted that gambling was losing its attractions. In 1854 there were still numerous gambling saloons. On the Plaza the El Dorado flourished, and on Commercial street the Arcade and the Polka continued to exhibit on their walls lascivious pictures, and women were dealing cards, but the stakes were no longer abnormally high even within their precincts, and the bankers in other houses did not disdain a dollar stake. The annalist still speaks of the people of San Francisco as "an excitement craving, money seeking, luxurious living, reckless, and heaven, earth and hell daring," but the attractions of the bar room were being pitted against many agencies and the professional gambler was compelled to meet new sorts of rivalry every day, and no longer had things all his own way. The Salvation Army was foreshadowed by street preachers who planted themselves before the saloons, and their words and singing blended with the rattle of the chips. "The Chariot! The Chariot! Its Wheels Roll in Fire," and other hymns often drowned the cries of the monte dealers and the words of these itinerant religionists although they fell on the ears of "loafers" often made an impression.

First Thanksgiving Proclamation

Governor Burnett's proclamation appointing November 29, 1849, as a day of thanksgiving and prayer may have fallen on few attentive ears, but at the close of 1853, when there were eighteen churches with 8,000 members, many schools, and numerous charitable and other social organizations, the impression produced by such a call must have been vastly different. The leaven was at work and while it did not suffice to leaven the whole mass it produced some striking results. In 1852 a bill was introduced in the state senate for the suppression of gambling which was only defeated by the casting vote of the presiding officer Purdy, thirteen senators voting for and as many against the reformatory measure.

Smoking and Chewing Prohibited

A year earlier bad manners were attacked in the same body with more success. On the 17th of April, 1851, the senate by resolution ordered that no more smoking or chewing be allowed within its bar. Prior to that date the free and easy manners of the pot house prevailed in the chamber, and as might be inferred they were not conducive to orderly proceedings. About the same time that the attempt was made in the legislature to put a stop to gambling the Annalist noted "the advent of a better class of women," and he happily brackets their arrival with the increase of churches, teachers, schools and charities. He does not tell us that they should be connected as cause and effect, but the inference was plain.

But the presence of good women while wholesome did not wholly abate; it merely modified the evils of loose living. The divorce habit early asserted itself. In 1853 there were public complaints that divorces were becoming shamefully numerous, and in 1856 the governor of the state urged in a message that testimony be taken in open court in all divorce cases so that as many obstacles as possible might be placed in the way of separations. His theory that publicity would tend to interfere with the spread of the divorce habit may have been faulty, but the fact that he thought that it would have a discouraging effect indicates his belief in the existence of an active public opinion which might be depended upon to preserve respect for the marriage relation. <small>Numerous Divorces</small>

Another bit of evidence testifying to the remarkable change in the habits of the people was the persistence of the demand for the enforcement of a Sunday law which finally prevailed in the legislature of 1858 which passed an act requiring every store, shop and house of every description devoted to business purposes, excepting taverns and eating houses, to close on Sundays. It was declared unconstitutional on the ground that the legislature had no right to restrain a citizen in the lawful pursuit of a lawful occupation. Subsequently another law was passed which survived the test of the courts, but could not be enforced. Public opinion was not unfavorable to observance, and in time there came a complete cessation of Sunday business through voluntary action. The temperament of the people of California, and especially those of San Francisco, made it impossible to bring about the result in any other manner. In 1883 that fact was recognized and the Sunday closing law of 1861 was repealed. <small>Passage of a Sunday Law</small>

CHAPTER XXIX

LABOR CONDITIONS AND THE COST AND MODE OF LIVING

SAN FRANCISCO A VICTIM OF EXAGGERATION—SUMMARY MODES OF ABATING EVIL MIS-
UNDERSTOOD—CONDITION OF THE WORKER IN SAN FRANCISCO—CHANGE IN LABOR
CONDITIONS—PLENTY OF WORKERS WHEN THE GOLD RUSH WAS UNDER WAY—
HURRY UP WAGES PAID—LABOR ORGANIZATIONS FORMED—RELATION OF EMPLOYER
AND EMPLOYED—ENVIABLE CONDITION OF THE WORKER—INFLUX OF CHINESE—
THE COST OF LIVING IN THE EARLY FIFTIES—IMPORTED FOOD STUFFS—EFFECT ON
DOMESTIC PRODUCTION—PRICES FALL—THE LOW PRICE OF GOLD IN CALIFORNIA—
EFFECTS OF THE ABUNDANCE OF GOLD—EARLY EPICURIANISM—HOW MEN GREW
RICH IN PIONEER DAYS—DRESS IN PIONEER DAYS—DISPOSITION TO CREATE IDOLS—
EFFECT OF ISOLATION—FIRST ORPHAN ASYLUM AND HOSPITAL—EXCESSIVE MOR-
TALITY FROM EXPOSURE—SAN FRANCISCO CHARITY—SISTERS OF MERCY.

San Francisco Much Misrepresented

T IS now time to review the activities other than religious which assisted in evolving from the disorders of the early Fifties a community whose respect for law, and for most of the conventionalities of life, has not merely equalled but has surpassed that of most of the older cities of the Union. Without deserving or desiring it San Francisco has achieved a reputation which has procured for it sometimes sympathy and at other times detestation. The latter has been incurred partly through misrepresentation, but oftener through misunderstanding. As the story of San Francisco's upbuilding progresses much of the latter will be removed by evidence which will conclusively demonstrate that sins which the outsider has been pleased to regard with much horror have been venial by comparison with those of cities more favorably situated for the practice of all the virtues, and that they seem particularly black in the case of the Pacific coast metropolis because the spirit of reform at recurring intervals induced spectacular exhibitions of self deprecation which can be properly likened only to those self abasements produced at revival meetings when the mourners' bench is filled with sinners whose imaginations transform them, for the time being, into wretched creatures unfit to remain on the footstool.

A Victim of Exaggeration

San Francisco throughout her career has neither been so black nor so gay as she has been painted. All of her actions have been seen through distorted lenses. From the days when the significance of the discovery at Sutter's fort was first realized by the outside world, down to the present a disposition to exaggerate has been manifest. Little offenses have been magnified and big ones have been minimized. There has been a continual straining to discover something unusual in ordinary men, and to treat as exceptional conduct which differs in no essential from the performances of other peoples who escape censure by being prosaic, and are happy because they have no annals.

Summary Methods of Dealing with Evil

The Vigilante uprising stands out as a startling manifestation, but the experience which produced it was by no means peculiar to San Francisco. At the time when it occurred there were other corrupt communities, in which venal politicians did pretty much as they liked, and where crime was dealt with no more severely than in San Francisco. The only thing that distinguished San Francisco from them was the summary method adopted to end the trouble when it became unbearable. The latter was indefensible because a decent regard for civic duty would have averted the necessity of resorting to extra legal methods, yet it was better to have cured the evil in that way than to have gone on winking at it, as the nation persists in doing to this day, an assertion which will not be disputed by those who study the homicidal record of the United States and who read the diatribes of statesmen and publicists directed against the laxity of our courts and the failure of juries to perform their sworn duty.

The Exceptional and the Humdrum

A simple recital of the efforts of good citizens to make their environment endurable, and avoidance of the propensity to throw high lights on the exceptional, will effectually dispose of the romances and give the reader a truthful idea of conditions as they existed in the Fifties. There was much that was exceptional, but there was more that was humdrum, and sometimes even the exceptional became humdrum, as for instance when the artisan or laborer who received fabulous wages found that the price level of the period made his earnings and his expenditures harmonize in nearly the same fashion that they do or did in countries where the scale of compensation was lower.

Labor Troubles

All things are relative, and especially is the saying true when the economic aspects of the labor problem are considered, but the generality is inclined to disregard the fact. Because of this latter propensity a tremendous impression was created by the stories which were told of the labor situation in California in the first few years after the discovery of gold. It would have been astonishing had the result been otherwise, for it should be remembered that when there was talk of mechanics and artisans receiving $20 a day in California, the people of the East were verging toward a condition that culminated in a political campaign in which the charge was made that the success of one of the candidates would result in wages of ten cents a day, while the triumph of his opponent would insure to the worker "a dollar a day and roast beef."

Condition of the Worker

In the last analysis of the labor question it always will be found that the getting of the roast beef rather than dollars is of most importance for the worker, and it is more interesting to inquire how much of it the San Francisco worker got than to learn how many dollars a day he earned. The information on this point is abundant and varied, and such as it is it indicates that for a short time at least the man who worked with his hands prospered because of the plethora of gold. The labor question was not troublesome in California before the discovery of gold. During the Spanish and Mexican regimes the disinclination to work was so general that a condition of repose was produced which militated against productivity and permitted decay, but it had its compensations. There was little or nothing done, but there were no strikes or quarrels respecting rates of wages. Occasionally a protest was heard against the enslavement of Indians, but it was never seriously enough urged to discommode those who engaged in the practice, probably because the condition of the involuntary worker was a great deal better than it would have been had he been allowed to roam at large. As for the other workers, many of whom by courtesy were called white, money of any kind was so scarce in the country that a wage scale was unnecessary. Those willing to work were usually glad to get subsistence for their efforts, and those who refused to labor managed to subsist somehow.

This situation was not materially changed between the day of the hoisting of the flag over Portsmouth square and the announcement of the find at Sutter's mill, but immediately after that event a revolution in labor conditions occurred. When the rush to the diggings took place it was impossible for a while to procure labor of any sort. The few artisans who were often their own bosses deserted their ocenpations to search for gold, and they were joined by every one who felt able to wash out the precious metal and was willing to undergo the hardship which the trip to the diggings and work in the mines involved. The result of the exodus was to bring the town to a complete standstill for a few months, a condition which endured until the influx of immigrants from the East, and other parts of the world, made some men see that there was as much money to be made by ministering to the comfort and needs of the gold hunters as there was in searching for the metal. *Changed Labor Conditions*

With the rush came a plentiful supply of workers. Perhaps the most of the first immigrants designed going directly to the placers to pick up big nuggets, but not a few of them found that they had miscalculated the expenses of the undertaking and elected to stay in the town where wages were good; and a fair proportion had intended to make their home in San Francisco because they believed that the City would grow and that it would offer better rewards to the toiler than could be obtained at the East, where in every other industry than agriculture the compensation was wretchedly small and the opportunity to obtain jobs very slender. To these supplies of labor constant additions were being made by men returning from the mines, whose bad luck forced them to cease their search for gold and take refuge in the City where they could earn some sort of a living. *Plenty of Workers*

The conditions produced by the great output of gold, and the pressing necessities of the people crowding into the small town were abnormal. There was no scarcity of workers but the means to pay them were temporarily so abundant, and the desire of men to put themselves in a position to trade or otherwise employ their talents to get their share of the gold being extracted from the placers was so great, that for the time being those able to do things could name their own terms. At first, those with capital to invest, accustomed to the insignificant wages of the East and Europe hesitated, but hesitation was soon swept aside, and the man who wished to put up a store, a saloon or a house, or to have a ship unloaded and the goods put under cover, paid what was asked. In 1849 the average daily wage of mechanics was roughly estimated at $20, and the commonest kind of labor was paid for at the rate of $10 a day. Carpenters who at first received $12 a day demanded $16 before the year was over and when refused they "struck." They were not idle long, the employers seeing that it would pay better to push their enterprises than to stand out. Apparently this first strike, although successful, was not an organized affair, but it was speedily followed by efforts in that direction which seem to have been very effective. In the ensuing year sailors, bricklayers and musicians conducted strikes, and in 1851 the printers went out. In 1853 *Hurry up Wages* there was an epidemic of dissatisfaction with wages, and a resort to methods on the part of the workers which called forth vigorous protests from the press. The "Alta" in August of that year remonstrated against the action of the striking firemen and coal passers who insisted on making passengers on the steamers show their tickets to prove that they were not strike breakers.

Labor Organizations Formed

Before the close of 1856 there were labor organizations, not always called unions, which embraced teamsters, draymen, lightermen, riggers and stevedores, bricklayers, bakers, blacksmiths, plasterers, masons, shipwrights, caulkers and musicians. The latter struck for the enforcement of the union scale in 1856. The bands that held these associations together were, however, by no means as strong as those of later years. The printers who had formed a union in 1850 with 8 members, which number had increased to 147 in 1852, fell to pieces in that year, was reorganized in 1855 and repeated the experience, but came into the national organization in 1859. The ship carpenters' union was so prosperous during this period that it had to cast about for methods to get rid of accumulating funds, and it became an association for social enjoyment rather than an aggressive agency to secure the rights of its members.

Relations of Employer and Employe

On the whole the Fifties may be characterized as a period of comparative amity between employer and employed. The writer of the "Annals" is moved to remark of the condition in 1850 that "labor of any description was highly paid, and all branches of the community had reason to be satisfied with the profits." He also in 1852 contrasted the wages in Australia, where gold had been discovered, and was being taken out in great quantities, with those of California, saying that they were only about half as much in the English colony as in San Francisco, and gave his comparison point by remarking: "Let interested people say what they will, there is no land so well fitted for the comfortable residence of the poor and industrions man as California." And what may seem more surprising in view of his repeated assertions in other places, and the excuses made for the resort to extra legal methods by the Vigilance Committee, he added: "Soil, climate, wages and political, religious and domestic institutions here make his position more ennobling and agreeable than he can expect or possibly find in any other country."

Enviable Condition of the Worker

The figures of compensation in 1853 bear out the claim that the worker's condition in California was enviable, compared with that of the countries from which he had emigrated. Bricklayers, stone cutters, ship carpenters and caulkers received $10 a day; plasterers $9; house carpenters $8; blacksmiths $8; watchmakers and jewelers $8; tinsmiths $7; hatters $7; painters and glaziers $6; longshoremen $6; tailors $4; shoemakers $100 a month without board; teamsters $100 to $120 a month and feed themselves; firemen on steamers $100 a month; coal passers $75; farm hands $50. These wages were at least five times as high as those paid in the Atlantic states, and fully double those of Australia, where large quantities of gold were also being taken from the soil.

Influx of Chinese

In the early Fifties the influx of Chinese was on a scale to cause alarm, but their presence in San Francisco did not occasion much trouble. In the mines, however, they were a constant menace to the peace of the white workers who regarded them as rivals, and resorted to all sorts of aggressions to make their presence uncomfortable. In the City they were regarded as thrifty, but "feeble in body and mind." They were credited with the virtue of perseverance and "from their union into laboring companies capable of great feats." It was this propensity which excited much of the hostility of the miners to the Chinese, and caused repeated aggressions upon them; but these can in no sense be attributed to trades unionism, for the associations in the mining communities were chiefly composed of men working on their own account and who were almost invariably their own bosses.

The cost of living in the early Fifties must have presented more problems for the solution of the worker than it has at any time since in California. He was not only called upon to pay high prices for the things he consumed, he was also confronted with variations which must at times have made him wonder whether low wages and a reasonably steady source of supply were not preferable to high wages and recurring scarcities of the things he was in the habit of consuming. In 1848 a brig arrived in the port of San Francisco from New York and discharged her cargo at Broadway wharf. The result was a general fall in prices. On December 1st of that year a barrel of flour sold at $27 in San Francisco; two weeks later flour was selling at $12 a barrel and other commodities experienced the same drop in price. {Cost of Living in Early Fifties}

Although cattle in great numbers roamed the hills of California in 1848 salt beef was brought to San Francisco and was sold at $20 a barrel; salt pork cost three times as much, and butter and cheese were respectively 90 and 70 cents per pound. Brandy which was in moderate demand brought $8 a gallon. Four years later prices were still subject to great fluctuations. Flour which was sold in March, 1852, at $8 a barrel rose to $40 in November of that year. This five fold advance was due to a delay in the arrival of a fleet of clipper ships which did not make its appearance in the harbor until the stocks of the merchants were nearly exhausted. A year later there was a great fall in prices due to excessive imports, but it does not appear that any portion of the community was benefited as the general stagnation in trade, due to the miscalculations of importers who overstocked the markets, caused many failures and made it difficult for workers to obtain employment. {Food Stuffs Imported}

The exceptionally high prices of 1849 have been dwelt upon so much that attention has been diverted from the comparatively speedy change to a better condition of affairs. The fact that in 1849 potatoes and brown sugar were sold at 37½ cents a pound; that a small loaf of bread which usually retailed for six cents in the Atlantic states demanded fifty cents in San Francisco; that a pair of coarse boots cost from $30 to $40 and a fine pair $100, and that the services of the launderer were only procured by paying from $12 to $20 a dozen for articles large and small has been made use of to such an extent that a distorted idea of the true condition has been conveyed. A very little reflection would save anyone from committing the blunder of supposing that these soaring prices continued for any length of time, or that they told a true story of the pioneers' struggle for existence. {Speedy Decline of Prices}

California was a country of relatively high prices for several years after 1849, for labor reluctantly accommodated itself to changing conditions, but all things were not dear. When the placer mines were producing millions worth of gold monthly, the most of which was freely exchanged for commodities, luxuries were in great demand and men were willing to pay handsomely for them, but the staples of life were soon provided by domestic industry and in an incredibly brief period they were as easily obtainable as in the older communities. The abnormalities which many have accepted as typical of pioneer days were soon corrected. Stores {Result of Domestic Production} that rented for $3,000 a month in 1849 a very few months after could be obtained at reasonable rates, and long before the gold excitement had completely worn itself out there were many owners vainly seeking tenants for their premises.

Things Reasonably Cheap

But figures of this sort impart no intelligent idea of conditions. Rentals in some quarters of the modern San Francisco range much higher than they did in the "days of old, the days of gold, the days of '49," without exciting comment, and there is nothing startling in the statement that some dwelling houses in 1854 rented for $500 a month, when it is accompanied by the information that people of modest desires could be accommodated at the rate of $15 to $20 a month. It must be apparent to the most superficial that if the writer of the "Annals" could truthfully declare that San Francisco was a desirable place for the honest, industrious and peaceable man to make his home that the bulk of the things consumed by those in that category were reasonably cheap. The price list of San Francisco in 1854 may have appalled the people living in the Atlantic states at that time, but it may be studied by them now without exciting consternation. Some of the quotations may strike one as indicating an excessive cost of living as for instance fresh eggs, which sold at $1.25 per dozen, while their rivals, known as "Boston Eggs" cost only 75 cents. Best cuts of beef were 37½ cents a pound, and venison 31 cents, prices which compare not unfavorably with those of 1912. Turkeys are spoken of as selling at from $6 to $10 a piece, but buyers about Christmas time in 1911 find no call for the plentiful use of exclamation marks accompanying the 1854 quotation, and the butter prices of the early period ranging from seventy-five cents to a dollar a pound are not apt to startle the person familiar with the demands of the modern dairymen.

Low Price of Gold

Observations of the effect of the abundance or scarcity of the precious metals when confined to a limited area are not always illuminating, but the comparative isolation of San Francisco in the early Fifties produced a condition which to some extent bore out the theory that the quantity of money governs prices. The value of gold in the first years after the discovery in California was directly affected, the amount allowed for it in exchange for commodities being considerably less than the ruling rate at the world's money centers, and very much lower than was obtained for the few ounces found in Los Angeles several years earlier, and sent to the mint in Philadelphia to be refined. This discrepancy in the selling price of gold dust was partially explained by the cost of moving it to regions where it could be absorbed, but it is undeniable that the effect of its plentifulness operated directly to force up the price of goods, and the wages of labor, in such a fashion that they presented a marked contrast to those obtaining at the East where, until a large part of the output of the California placers was transferred by trade operations, the precious metals were scarce and prices were low in consequence.

Effects of Abundance of Gold

While the output of the California mines remained relatively large this depreciation of the value of gold was very marked. But as soon as the mechanism of trade was called into play, bringing improved means of communication, and offering in exchange for the metal great quantities of products of all sorts, the adjustment began, and conditions soon became at least not strikingly different from those in the Atlantic states. The change was not effected without abberations, for the early dealings of the mercantile world with the gold diggers were of a highly speculative character, and the result was an alternation of abundance and scarcity of goods which made itself apparent in price lists. The irregularities noted were responsible for the spectacular price of $40 a barrel for flour, and for some other manifestations which made a profound impression on chroniclers and lost nothing in the telling. It was much more picturesque to speak of the fabulous sum paid for such a necessary of life as flour, than to tell of the adequate supply which subsequently brought down the price to $8 a barrel; and it was natural to dwell upon the epicureanism of Sam Ward rather than refer to the sober life of honest and industrious workers.

In that respect the annalists of the days of gold resembled those of Rome who emphasized the gastronomic performances of the actors who provided such dishes as the brains of talking birds for their guests, and delighted to tell about the splendors of the feasts of Lucullus. That tradition has handed down to us the fact that Ward, who afterward passed much of his time in Washington and became more famous gastronomically at the national capital than he was in San Francisco in 1853 and 1854, suggests that he was by no means representative of a type. The description of Ward derived from a deposition pictures him as a man of lively wit, with a knowledge of languages and great culinary skill, and "a rotund, expansive appreciation of good wine," which the deponent avers was oftener obtained by the subtle art of flattery than by the expenditure of money earned by himself. Ward's mode of living, and that of his few imitators, was no more illustrative of the real life of San Francisco at this time than that of the man who caused the dancer in a fashionable New York restaurant to divert his guests by pirouetting on the dinner table.

Early Epicureanism

It has been remarked that a single swallow does not make a summer, and it may be observed with equal force that isolated instances are not to be depended upon to illustrate general tendencies. There are authenticated cases of men climbing the ladder of fame in the early days of California without putting their feet on the lower rounds. We are told that Niles Searles, who afterward became a justice of the supreme court, took his first case while waiting on the table, and we have a circumstantial relation of the mode by which Lloyd Tevis and his partner, John B. Haggin, laid the foundations of their great fortunes, which is interesting but does not detract from the fact that the most of the lawyers of pioneer days who practiced in San Francisco in the Fifties attained prominence in a humdrum manner, and that the rich men of the City built up their wealth as they did in other communities by taking advantage of circumstances or by making circumstances that they might take advantage of them.

How Men Grew Rich

As Lloyd Tevis later became a conspicuous figure in San Francisco affairs it is not amiss to relate that like many others he reached San Francisco in a condition of impecuniosity which compelled a prompt search for work. He wrote a fine hand, and succeeded in persuading the recorder that he would find in him an efficient copyist. At first he merely received what might be termed the overflow of the office, but presently he made a proposition to the recorder that he would do the work performed by two clerks for the salary paid to one of them. As civil service reform and the merit system had not been introduced the recorder was able to make the experiment. Tevis was equal to his profession of ability, kept the job, earned a couple of thousand dollars and joined forces with Haggin and by judiciously loaning their united capital at ten per cent a month they soon had enough to engage in broader enterprises.

Building up a Fortune

250   SAN FRANCISCO

Dress in San Francisco

Keeping in mind the adage about the swallow and the summer, and by ignoring the desire to find an "atmosphere" for San Francisco, we may be able to form a more correct impression of San Francisco life in the early Fifties than is conveyed by dwelling upon the exceptional. There were plenty of red shirts in evidence upon the streets of the City in the early Fifties, but garments of that color were as familiar a sight in the big towns of the Atlantic states as on the coast, being much affected by the volunteer firemen of that day and were copied by their admirers. The Bowery boy of New York found their vivid hue particularly appealing. The wearers of the red shirts also were given to sticking their trousers into the longlegged boots which were worn at the time, but it is a matter of record that the men who wore this striking costume were from the mines, and that as a rule, when their luck permitted them to gratify their desire they promptly arrayed themselves in "boiled shirts" and even ventured upon "plug hats."

Overdressed Pioneers

Charles Warren Stoddard, whose boyhood days were spent in San Francisco, in one of his delightful papers describing the conditions and scenes of pioneer days tells us that one of the features which impressed him greatly was the propensity to over dressing. This hardly harmonizes with the idea usually conveyed, that uncouthness and disregard of the conventionalities endured for a long period, a view which ought not to have survived the statement of the annalist that as early as 1852, "the day of the blouse, the colored shirt and shocking bad hat had fled never to return." We may overlook the tendency to exaggeration displayed in the further statement that "superb public carriages plied the streets, and beautiful private equipages glittered and glided smoothly along," but we shall make a mistake if we fail to draw the inference that a vast change had occurred between 1849 and 1852, and that San Francisco in three brief years had progressed so rapidly that it was taking on the airs of a metropolis. Not every man in San Francisco had become a dandy but there were plenty who aimed to dress well and succeeded. The pains taken to describe the peculiarities of the few persons who attained the distinction of being regarded as dandies indicates that they were rare. The governor who succeeded Burnett, McDougal of San Francisco, undoubtedly earned the appellation. He was accustomed to wearing elaborately ruffled shirts. His pantaloons and vest were buff, and over them he wore a blue coat with shining brass buttons. His resplendant attire in no wise diminished his popularity, perhaps it helped to secure for him the overwhelming majority by which he was elected lieutenant governor, thus putting him in the line of succession which made him governor of the commonwealth of California when Burnett resigned.

Disposition to Create Idols

The town in its early days boasted another character whose mysterious source of livelihood was perhaps more responsible for his fame or notoriety than his fastidiousness in the matter of dress. His name was William F. Hamilton. That, and the fact that he made it his solemn business to parade the streets whenever the weather permitted in irreproachable clothes, were well known to all, but no one knew his occupation until after his death, when it was discovered that he secretly engaged in upholstering and that his specialty was stuffing cushions for church pews and carriages, for which he was well paid, and the proceeds of which he devoted to adorning himself with shiny hats, patent leathers, and the other insignia of an effete civilization. His crowning glory was his dyed hair, which he thought concealed his advancing years. But no one was deceived, and almost as much was made of his eccentricities as of those of the shrewd individual who lived at the expense of the community by making believe that he was under the hallucination that he was a mighty potentate, or of Lilly Coit, the daughter of a well known physician named Hitchcock, whose desire for notoriety led her to "run with the machine." San Francisco in the pioneer days, and well on toward the Eighties was in the habit of making for herself idols. She refused to be unconventional but dearly loved to exploit someone or something out of the usual. Hamilton was her Beau Brummel during the Fifties and Emperor Norton, who bore some likeness to Napoleon III, gave distinction to her streets during a couple of decades, arrayed in a once gorgeous uniform, with massive epaulets whose brilliancy was tarnished by the weather until their color and general appearance harmonized with that of the coat which carelessness at the lunch counter had rendered almost undistinguishable. Norton was welcome in many of the eating houses of the City and could always command the price of a dinner from a host of admirers, and he shared with two dogs, "Bummer and Lazarus," about whom tradition has woven many remarkable stories, the affections of a people, who, despite the exciting events of the Vigilante period, and some other experiences were often hard pressed for diversions exactly suited to their tastes.

It is possible that there were other communities in this work-a-day world a half a century or so ago that could make as much out of little, and as little out of much, as San Francisco, but it is doubtful. If they existed they had no one to throw the glamour of romance over their inconsequential doings, and make an epic out of material that as often as otherwise was commonplace. There were few places on the footstool where the disposition existed to make a heroine out of a hoyden who derived amusement from running to fires with the boys, or who were ready to expend their admiration upon a man who preferred to live like a crab in a shell rather than pay $32 a day for treatment in a hospital. This disposition to admire at random was an amiable weakness due to isolation rather than to peculiarity of temperament. It disappeared rapidly when San Francisco came into close touch with the rest of the world. But the period of isolation was not wholly given up to red shirts, gambling and amusements of a doubtful character. San Francisco in 1849 and in the Fifties had its serious as well as its excitable and happy-go-lucky sides. As already pointed out it promptly arrayed the forces of religion against those of vice, and opposed to the selfishness engendered by the eager desire for gold the ameliorating sentiment of consideration for the unfortunate. The man "down on his luck" had little difficulty in finding a friend in San Francisco in the days of gold, and those who helped were not always over zealous in their efforts to ascertain whether the one asking aid deserved to be helped; it sufficed to know that he needed a helping hand. It is not surprising that where such feelings prevailed charity should quickly take on an organized form in order to make it more effective and the "Annals" and other sources of information inform us that such was the case.

Effects of Isolation

All great cities draw the unfortunate. The adage about God making the country and man making the town conveys an impression that it is only in the former that we need look for goodness and its accompaniments, but actual experience contradicts the assumption and discloses that it is in the places where men congregate in large numbers that the virtues are most actively displayed. The opposite qualities may be rampant; crime and immorality may be painfully conspicuous; but they cannot repress the nobler instincts in a people in whom the germs of a better life have been implanted. The Sydney coves and the transplanted rowdies may

Amelioration of Suffering

have been cruel and unscrupulous, but the mass of those who crowded into San Francisco in the earlier days were made of the right stuff, an assertion well supported by the record of the promptitude with which it provided itself with all the instrumentalities for the amelioration of suffering, and of the spontaneity it displayed in extending sympathy and help to those in need.

First Orphan Asylum and Hospital

The fact that before the occupation no such institution as an orphan asylum existed in California has been mentioned, but it will do no harm to repeat it and add that for quite a time the most conspicuous edifice in San Francisco was the Roman Catholic orphanage, which stood on the spot where the Palace hotel now stands, and was built with funds largely subscribed by men who were not of the Catholic faith, but belonged to the universal brotherhood which easily unites when a demand for help is made. Not only were the little ones who were left alone carefully looked after, the sick also received attention from the various benevolent societies which multiplied rapidly, and in 1853 the state established a hospital in San Francisco which was to be the sole general state hospital in California. The revenues for its support were to be derived from taxes levied upon persons arriving in the port and from fines imposed for infractions of harbor regulations. Half of the amount obtained from these sources, not to exceed $100,000 annually, was to go to the maintenance of the hospital, and if the sum collected fell short the deficit was to be made up by the state treasury. The hospital was at first located on Stockton street in what had formerly been a hotel, but later a substantial brick building was constructed on Rincon hill.

Mortality From Exposure

This action of the legislature was prompted by recognition of the tendency already commented upon of the sick and the needy to make their way to the port when in distress. San Francisco, then as at present, was a magnet, and the result was productive of singular aberrations in the mortality reports. It is related that in 1849 and 1850 there were so many unfortunates who found their way to the City that it often happened that men died on the streets or in the bushes without a soul near them. The annalist states that the majority of those who died in 1850 were actual paupers. They had made their way from the mines to the City, hoping for relief which they failed to receive in the burly-burly of the same excitement that had taken them to the mining regions where they contracted the diseases which destroyed their lives. Between 1850 and 1854 the total number of interments in the three cemeteries, Yerba Buena, Mission Dolores and the Jewish, was 5,770. A large proportion of this relatively great mortality was due to hardships incurred in crossing the plains, and to the wretched accommodations of some of the ships which brought the immigrants, but the greatest part by far was set down to the exposure and unaccustomed work of the gold hunter. The indifference to the needs of the poverty stricken who had fled to San Francisco for refuge did not endure for any great length of time. Very soon an active sympathy was manifested, which did not confine itself to the precincts of the City, but responded to calls from remote places. The awful plight of the Donner party of immigrants caused the formation of a body of men who volunteered to go to their relief at their own expense, and they would have done so had not an equally generous spirit manifested itself in settlements closer to the scene of the awful tragedy. Subsequently when there were calls for help from settlers threatened by Indians the response was equally prompt.

These were manifestations of the spirit which at a later day, when wealth was more abundant, and society better organized, impelled California and particularly San Francisco to go to the aid of the Sanitary Commission and evoked from its head the effusive tribute "Noble! tender, faithful San Francisco; City of the heart; commercial and moral capital of the most humane and generous state in the world." The praise may sound exaggerated, but San Francisco had long been trying to live up to its reputation for liberality and hospitality and deserved all the good things said about her people by generous outsiders who just as often were censorious critics of actions and habits they could not understand. In the story of San Francisco charity there is one episode which San Franciscans would like to forget. In 1856 there was an exhibition of intolerance growing out of the Know Nothing antagonism to foreigners. The Sisters of Mercy, who had been brought to the City in 1854, and who had braved the cholera epidemic, nursing patients deserted by all others, had contracted with the municipality to take care of the indigent sick. They were at once made the objects of calumnious attacks by a portion of the press, the "Bulletin" being particularly virulent. Charges were made which were resented by the Mother Superior, who demanded an investigation by the grand jury, which developed the fact that the Sisters had given their services without compensation during seven months of a most trying period. The disturbed condition of municipal affairs prevented the recognition of their claims, and in 1857 they cancelled their contract with the City because it refused to pay its bills. But this was only a temporary wave of intolerance which soon subsided, and enables the historian to say with an approach to accuracy of statement that San Francisco was less disturbed than other sections of the Union by the illiberal uprising, even though the state enjoyed the unfortunate distinction of electing a Know Nothing governor and supreme justices, whose careers did not add luster to the reputation of California.

Pioneer Charities

CHAPTER XXX

SOCIAL AND OTHER DIVERSIONS OF PIONEER DAYS

SAN FRANCISCAN ARDOR—FIREMEN THE ELITE OF THE CITY—FIRE PRECAUTIONS—FIRE ENGINE HOUSES CENTERS OF SOCIAL ACTIVITY—FIREMEN'S PARADES—THE MILITIA ORGANIZATIONS—CITIZEN SOLDIERY NOT DEPENDABLE—THE .DRINK HABIT—BULL FIGHTS AND BEAR BAITING—HORSE RACING—PUGILISTIC CONTESTS—THE DUELLO IN PIONEER DAYS—EARLY CELEBRATIONS AND LOVE OF MUSIC—THE SPANISH ELEMENT—SPANISH LANGUAGE LOSES ITS HOLD IN SAN FRANCISCO—CHINESE QUARTER IN EARLY DAYS—"CHINA BOYS" IN PARADES—ROUTE OF THE PIONEER PARADES—RUSS GARDENS AND THE WILLOWS—JOYS OF THE CIRCUS—APPRECIATION OF THE DRAMA—STARS VISIT CALIFORNIA—CRITICAL AUDIENCES—CHURCH FAIRS AND PUBLIC BALLS—NO EXCLUSIVE SOCIAL SETS—OBTRUSIVE COURTESANS—THE UBIQUITOUS COLONEL—PREVALENCE OF MILITANCY.

T IS not difficult to invest with singularity customs which were prevalent in the early days of San Francisco, but which, upon investigation turn out to have been nothing of the sort, but were merely imitations and sometimes exaggerations of practices common in other cities of the period. San Francisco in a way epitomized all the vices and follies as well as many of the virtues of the times in which it had its commercial beginnings. During many years it was conspicuously devoted to militarism and to fire fighting, but it was not peculiar in this regard. Throughout the Fifties military companies were common in all the cities of the East. Volunteer fire fighting organizations were relatively as numerous as in the City by the Golden Gate, although the people of the latter were perhaps more disposed to appreciate the importance of a good fire department because of the disasters through which the town had passed than those of some other more fortunate cities. Ardor of San Franciscans

The enthusiastic praise of the writer of the "Annals" was doubtless deserved by the fire brigade which, he informs us, was regarded as "the right arm of San Francisco." He tells us the members of the various organizations were as proud of the leathern caps they wore as if they were bedecked with finery. They were the elite of the City and considered it an honor to belong to a company. The first fire company was organized Christmas day, 1849, and in its membership roll we discover several names of men who afterward became prominent, among them that of David C. Broderick. In the beginning of 1850 the number of engines had increased to three which, after the fashion of the times, were given names. They were the San Francisco, Empire and Protection. They were not well provided with hose and this drawback was held responsible for the ineffective work of the department Firemen the Elite of the City in the fire of September, 1850. The trouble was remedied by the council, which made appropriations for additional equipment and for cisterns, also some new apparatus. At the close of the year there were in addition to the companies named the Eureka, Howard, Monumental and California engine companies. There were also three hook and ladder companies: the St. Francis, Howard and Sansome.

Fire Precautions in 1854

This equipment was increased from year to year and in 1854, in summing up the fire fighting resources of the City, the annalist tells us there were fifty cisterns already constructed and others in course of construction. It is a curious commentary on the inadequacy of human foresight that in 1912 the City has provided itself anew with cisterns to replace those abandoned when the introduction of a water system was supposed to have rendered them unnecessary. The most of the cisterns constructed in the Fifties had fallen into disuse and their existence was almost unknown to the firemen in April, 1906. In one or two places the oldest inhabitant knew where they were and their almost forgotten stores of water were drawn upon to check the flames. In 1854 there were thirteen engines, which were described as powerful and well equipped and three hook and ladder companies. This apparatus was wholly manned by volunteers, there being 950 certified members who were exempted from jury duty in recognition of their public service. Five years of active membership secured exemption from a duty which seemed to have even less attractions for citizens in those days than it possesses at present. The engines were all built in the East and were generally of the type known as side lever, and were usually provided with hose carts which were reels mounted on wheels. The cost of the engines ranged from $3,250 to more than $5,000. They were handsomely decorated, and there was much rivalry between the different companies, each seeking to outdo the other in the matter of effectiveness and the appearance of their machines.

Centers of Social Activity

The engines and other apparatus were well housed in substantial and in some cases pretentious structures, which were the centers of the social activities for quite a period. The Sansome Company's building cost its members $24,000 and was furnished as well as any residence in the City. It boasted "a large library." In a few cases the engines were provided by public spirited citizens, but in most instances they were procured by united effort. The members contributed their services gratuitously, but the companies properly organized received appropriations from the council for maintenance. There were frequent contests to determine which was the most powerful engine and to test which company was most effective at the pumps, which were worked with brakes which made heavy draughts on the energy and skill of those who manned them. The chief glory of the department may have been the readiness of its members to respond to the call of duty, but its activities and usefulness were not confined to fighting fires. The "Fifties" were remarkable for the interest taken by the people in parades and public celebrations of all sorts and in no American city was there a greater desire shown for such diversions than in San Francisco. No event or anniversary of consequence was allowed to pass without a demonstration, and in these outpourings the firemen with their apparatus were the most conspicuous feature, rivaling in popularity the military companies, whose members were arrayed in "uniforms" that were not uniform, no two organizations being garbed alike.

Firemen's Parades

On these festive occasions the engines were drawn through the streets by hand by their members arrayed in their leathern hats. At the head of each company

ST FRANCIS ENGINE HOUSE, 1856   KNICKERBOCKER ENGINE
                                  HOUSE, 1856

MONUMENTAL VOLUNTEER ENGINE COMPANY'S HOUSE ON THE PLAZA, 1856.

Great attention was paid to architectural effect by the members of the Volunteer Fire Department, and some of the best of the early buildings were erected under their auspices

was the foreman or engineer, who carried a horn, usually of silver, handsomely chased, and his assistant was also provided with one, only less splendid than that of his chief. The rope by which the machine was drawn was immaculately white, and distended to about the width of the engine or hose, and the firemen marched two and sometimes four abreast, the intervals between ranks being properly spaced. The apparatus itself, as brilliant as paint and varnish could make it, with all its metal parts glittering, was as much an object of admiration as the men who drew it, and the relative beauties and "squirting" capacity of the fire extinguishers, and of the hook and ladders and hose carts were as much discussed as the abilities of the men who operated them.

In the numerous parades the militia companies were only less conspicuous than the firemen. Immediately after the affair of the Hounds a company was organized called the First California Guard. Its officers were prominent men, whose names frequently figure in the "Annals" and in the later history of the City. The captain was Henry M. Naglee; there were two first lieutenants, W. D. M. Howard and Myron Norton; and two second lieutenants, Hall McAllister and David T. Bagley. Subsequently other companies were formed, and on the Fourth of July, 1853, five companies in addition to the Sutter Rifles were reviewed by Sutter, and a handsome flag was presented by Mrs. Catherine Sinclair in Russ' Gardens, where the birth of American liberty was celebrated by reading the Declaration of Independence and by listening to patriotic addresses. The militia companies did more than parade and enjoy themselves in the first years of the Fifties. They were always ready to respond to calls, and in 1851 the San Francisco and Aldrich Rangers when summoned to repress a threatened Indian uprising, hastily adopted a uniform more adapted to the field than the one used on parade, and was about to proceed to the scene of the disturbance when the news was brought that the disorderly aborigines had taken alarm and dispersed. In the beginning the fire and military companies were often closely identified, part of the membership of the former hearing arms, while the remainder more particularly occupied themselves with the operation of the apparatus. The status of these early militia companies was a trifle indeterminate. At first they were supported by voluntary contributions, but in the fall of 1853 an appropriation of $500 a month was made by the City for the rent of the fourth floor of a building on the northeast corner of Sacramento and Montgomery streets, which was used as an armory in common by all the companies.

In the latter part of 1850 the Washington Guards was formed, the company which in 1851 responded to the call of the municipal authorities and prevented the lynching of Burdue and Windred by the Vigilantes. The organization only lasted a few months. In 1856, when William T. Sherman attempted to support the state authorities in suppressing the Vigilance Committee, the militia of San Francisco was slow to respond and he threw up his commission in disgust. It was not astonishing that support was refused by the militia for many of its prominent members were identified with the Vigilance movement, but the defects of the system were also largely responsible for the inaction. The law called upon every white male citizen to perform militia duty and penalized refusal by a tax of $3, but the statute received no attention and became a dead letter.

The social side of militia and firemen's life implied by the creation of libraries and well furnished rooms, and the giving of frequent balls, did not keep politics out of the organizations and later we hear of them, under the manipulation of men ambitious for national preferment, forming a part of the municipal machine responsible for so much of the corruption witnessed in the early Fifties. The militia was never a serious offender in this regard. The citizen soldiery may have been more accessible to the blandishments of politicians than if they had not been connected with militia companies, but they were never made use of as freely as were the firemen by the cunning men who had learned their politics in the Atlantic cities. Many of the firemen were easily manipulated by clever and ambitious politicians of the Broderick stamp, but the militia were less vulnerable. For a while at least firemen and militiamen were as important factors in the development of San Francisco as the schools and churches. They helped to make life endurable in a city whose remoteness from the populous centers of the nation threw its inhabitants on their own resources and compelled them to work out their social problems in a different fashion from that prevalent in the sections from which they had emigrated.

The Drinking Habit

It would be a mistake, however, to assume that this isolation always resulted in spectacular manifestations. Occasionally there were departures from sanity, such as that which marked the celebration of the admission of the state to the Union, when a large company assembled in one of the big drinking places and formed itself into squads, and successfully essayed the feat of consuming all the champagne in the place by each squad regularly advancing to the bar in military style, drinking and falling back to let another squad take its place and repeating the performance until all were drunk. But the drink habit had a powerful hold on the pioneers, and those who viewed its excesses with disapproval declared that the practice of treating was responsible for the greater part of the evil. It may have played its part, but the unsociable drinker was likewise much in evidence in 1849 and 1850, and men of talents and ability often fell victims to the "spreeing" propensity, which was much more common in San Francisco at the time than in any place in America because there was no restraining public opinion. That did not begin to assert itself in real earnest until men began to bring their wives and families in increasing numbers. With their advent the coarse and often brutal habits of a population in which males were unduly preponderant held sway, how generally may be inferred from the fact that it seemed necessary to caution the priests of the diocese from lending the sanction of their presence to bull fights and bear baiting.

Bull Fights and Bear Baiting

These latter were amusements of an indigenous character, but the gold seekers took to them with astonishing facility. These contests were usually held near the Mission church in an enclosure of adobe walls which was entered through an iron gate. It is not recorded that the priests were witnesses of these spectacles, but there was for years an official prohibition against attending the *concorsus taurorum in cemeteris*. This may have deterred the clergy from attending, but it had no effect on the Americans, who thronged the sides of the bull ring in great numbers whenever a fight was advertised, or when bull and bear were pitted against each other. These exhibitions may have lacked some of the accessories which make the bull fights of Spain and Mexico so attractive to the peoples of these countries, but a much traveled pioneer, who has enjoyed opportunities to make comparisons, declares that the spectacles presented to San Franciscans in 1849 and the early Fifties were up to the standard so far as cruelty to animals was concerned.

Horse Racing

Bull fighting and bear baiting shared popularity with horse racing in the Fifties. Running races were in vogue but there were no planned meetings as in later days when the amusement was converted into a pursuit whose principal object was to separate foolish men and women from their money. The races in the period we are describing were usually attended with betting, but the bookmaker was almost unknown. Those who frequented the track, which was situated in the Mission district, were mostly men in search of diversion, with a sprinkling of followers of the turf, and a few who believed that the sport tended to improve the breed of horses, a matter of much more consequence in those days when automobiles were undreamed of, and when "2:40 on the turnpike road" was still a phrase with a meaning for those who heard it, and thought it represented the highest possible achievement of a trotting nag. There were many native Californians whose accomplishments rivaled those of the circus rider, and they were easily tempted to exhibit their dexterity in the management of their steeds. They were not, however, permitted to enjoy supremacy without a contest. There were plenty of Americans ready at any time to attempt any feat which appeared extra hazardous and as a result there was plenty of dare-devil riding added to the major attractions of the somewhat informal meets which drew the crowds Missionwards on Sundays and other days of the week.

Pugilism during the Fifty decade was in much favor. The noted characters of the ring, John C. Heenan, nicknamed the Benicia Boy, Yankee Sullivan, Tommy Chandler and other pugilistic celebrities, gave exhibitions of boxing which were conducted under London prize ring rules, no attempt being made to conceal the object of the contests by prescribing gloves. The fights were always with bare knuckles, and when the "pugs" succeeded in drawing blood the onlookers were as much delighted as a modern crowd is when a like result is produced in a regulated ring, which suggests that there may be something amiss in the assumption that the growth of wealth and luxury tends to brutalize people. Some of these notable exponents of the "manly art" conducted themselves in a fashion that brought them under the observation of the Vigilance Committee. Their associates were usually of the vilest character and their presence was regarded as a menace to the community, hence some of them were politely invited to deport themselves, and one of them, "Yankee Sullivan," narrowly escaped having his neck stretched.

Pugilistic Contests

Meetings on "the field of honor" were quite common during the Fifties. They differed essentially from the affairs which have made the duel ridiculous, for the combatants usually shot to kill. They were not lacking in the formalities with which the French are pleased to invest their encounters. There were seconds and rigid requirements of various sorts, but the outcome was never ludicrous. Navy revolvers and rifles were the favorite weapons, and as those who used them, as a rule, knew how to shoot, the consequences were almost invariably serious. There was no privacy surrounding these meetings. Announcements were sometimes made in the newspapers a day or two in advance of a duel and a crowd would turn out to witness the spectacle. Benicia was a favorite resort for duelists, and when a particularly interesting affair took place the steamboats would carry loads of passengers to the scene of the conflict. Political quarrels were chiefly responsible for these meetings, the politicians of the period laboring under the delusion that a stain upon their honor could be wiped out by killing somebody. In some cases there was ground for the suspicion that quarrels were deliberately provoked by bullies for the purpose of getting rid of persons obnoxious to them, or to the group with which they trained. Newspaper men seem to have been frequent victims of

"The Field of Honor."

260   SAN FRANCISCO

the curious idea that a statement could be clinched by shooting the person resenting it; and the aggrieved individual, oftener than otherwise a politician, labored under the hallucination that his reputation would be repaired by killing his alleged calumniator.

Numerous Celebrations There were other diversions far less exciting and demoralizing than bull fights, bear baiting, horse racing and the duello. The foreigners, who formed a large proportion of the early population of San Francisco, by the introduction of their habits contributed considerably to the modification of the desire for the more violent forms of amusements, and helped to introduce the taste for music and the kindred arts. The Turner Gesang Verein, an organization of the Germans, who were estimated to number at least 6,000 in 1854, gave frequent entertainments, and its annual celebration on May Day, at a local resort known as Russ' Gardens, generally drew out the entire population. May Day was also marked by the festivities of the school children. On the 1st of May one thousand pupils of the schools, of both sexes, marched through the streets to the schoolhouse in Broadway, receiving the plaudits of the admiring crowds who watched the progress of the tastefully dressed children in the train of their queen for a day.

Foreign Residents The Germans, unlike the Latin peoples who made their homes in San Francisco in the early days, were not disposed to clannishness and did not seek to keep in touch with each other by establishing themselves in a particular residential district. At no time was there anything like a German quarter, although there were as many of that nationality in the City as of any other kind of foreigners. On the other hand the French and Spanish exhibited a decided inclination for social intercourse with their own kind and failed to mingle as freely with the population generally as the Germans. There were about 5,000 French in the City in 1854, and already at that time they had a theater of their own, in which plays and operas were acted and sung in their own language. They showed little inclination to become citizens, few of them becoming naturalized, but they admittedly made a distinct impression on the manners of the people, and had a decided influence in the moulding of the taste of the women, who eagerly copied the styles of dress which they introduced from France. The annalist, in his enumeration of the occupations of the French residents, leaves it to be inferred that they were chiefly engaged as hairdressers, cooks, wine importers and shoe blacks and fails to dwell on their activities in commerce, but the colony was fairly well represented in all the walks of trade and a little later, although there was a large relative diminution of the importance of the French element in the City, that nationality boasted several prominent merchants noted for their enterprise.

Latin American Population The Spanish speaking population of San Francisco was not as great as the fact that the state had been occupied by people who had owed allegiance to Spain and Mexico would suggest. About the middle of the Fifties there were probably 3,000 who could be described as of Spanish extraction and they were made up of Mexicans, Chileans, Peruvians and a slight sprinkling of natives of Spain. The colony in those days was located chiefly on Dupont, Kearny and Pacific streets. It was not regarded with admiration by the chroniclers of the period, who doubtless imparted some of their prejudice to their statement that on the whole the Spanish speaking people were illiterate, and that the most of them were only fitted for "menial and servile" pursuits. One writer unhesitatingly classes them with the Chinese and Africans. Unlike the French they had no paper of their own, but were content with a page in a tri-weekly issued by a Frenchman. Many unsavory crimes were committed in the quarter and then, as now, dance houses were a conspicuous feature of the locality.

In other countries in which the Spanish planted themselves their language gained and maintained a firm hold, but its tenure was short in California after the American occupation. There was a disposition on the part of the earliest legislators to recognize Spanish, and some documents were printed for the benefit of people who did not understand English, notably the inaugural message of Governor McDougal, of which 1,000 copies in Spanish were authorized by the assembly. The senate, however, had refused to sanction the publication of 3,000 copies of the statutes in that language, and the attempt to perpetuate the practice begun in the lower house was soon abandoned.

Spanish Language Loses its Hold

The Chinese quarter became a conspicuous feature of San Francisco as early as 1850, and after that date the number inhabiting it increased rapidly. The earliest immigrants from China, as a rule, made their way to the mines as speedily as possible, but very soon the commercial instinct asserted itself and Oriental merchants established themselves in the City who acted as intermediaries for their countrymen, and a growing number found their way into households as servants. The latter very generally had their lodgings in the district which, almost from the beginning, was known as Chinatown. In 1852 it was estimated that 20,000 Chinese arrived in the port of San Francisco and the population of that race in the state numbered at least 27,000. The propensity of the race to crowd together exhibited itself from the first. The theory that congestion in cities is due to the rapacity of land owners receives no support from a study of the life of the Chinese in San Francisco. They lived together because they liked to, and not because circumstances compelled them to herd. Even when they might have spread themselves over the entire landscape they preferred to huddle, and Chinatown in 1854, and during the rest of the decade, presented all of the characteristics which has given it its undesirable notoriety. In a description of the quarter at this time we are told by the writer that basements were used by barbers, and that "in apartments not more than fifteen feet square three or four different professions" were often represented, "and these afforded employment to ten or a dozen men." Then, as during many years after, "no corner was too cramped for the squatting street cobbler," and the venders of sweetmeats and conserves infested the sidewalks or "crouched under overhanging windows" or in dark doorways.

Chinese Quarter

The Chinese of "the Fifties" were not regarded as particularly picturesque. The squalor of the quarter seemed to be more resented then than later. Although there was no sign of active opposition to their presence in San Francisco there were frequent expressions of disapprobation of the constantly increasing flood of the yellow immigrants, and predictions were made in which possibilities of disaster largely figured. In the interior there were numerous collisions between the Chinese miners and those of other races, but in the City the bustle and activity attending the constant expansion of business and population, and the troubles growing out of bad municipal government occupied the people too fully to permit them to give much attention to what subsequently was conceded to be a great menace.

Too Busy to Bother About Chinese

For a while the "China Boys," with their dragons and gaudy banners were welcome additions to the parades which celebrated every event of importance, and sometimes their prominent men were asked to take part in demonstrations that were

The "China Boys"

not altogether disconnected from politics. An occasion of this sort was the funeral solemnities commemorative of Henry Clay, when all business was suspended, and the whole town was draped in mourning. The resolutions of condolence were participated in by the Chinese merchants, who wore the outward signs of grief even though they may not have deeply felt the loss of the statesman. In pioneer days great men were not allowed to pass away without recognition. The funeral of Clay testified to the affection of San Franciscans for the Kentuckian. Bells were tolled and many citizens wore mourning, not only while in the procession, which was headed by bands playing funeral dirges, but for days afterward. Not every great statesman was thus honored. When Daniel Webster's death occurred a few months after that of Clay, a proposal to pay his memory equal honor was rejected. The necessity of practicing economy was given as an excuse, but the fact that the former was from Massachusetts probably influenced the decision against public mourning.

Route of Early Parades

The route of the parades on national holidays as late as 1856 was not so long as that laid out for more recent demonstrations. The weary wanderers who cover several miles in a modern procession, marching from some place of formation near the foot of Market street, to a point far north on Van Ness, will be interested in the statement that the participants in the great celebration which was held to signalize the successful consummation of the work of the Vigilance Committee formed at Third and Market streets, marching from thence to Montgomery, turning up Clay to Stockton, along Stockton to Vallejo, then to Powell, traversing that street to Washington as far as Kearny, along which they proceeded to California, thence to Sansome, to Clay, to Front and Sacramento to headquarters, the Fort Gunnybags alluded to in the account of the Vigilante trouble. Within these boundaries were situated all the shops of importance, and they also embraced the hotel district of the period. Plainly the object of the projectors was to give an opportunity to all to witness the spectacle and considerations of a straightaway march were not entertained.

Russ' Gardens and the Willows

Mention has been made of the attractions of Russ' Gardens, which was a favorite place of resort during the Fifties and was quite out of town and boasted some trees which were not always refreshingly green. The visitors, in addition to discussing the refreshments provided, were entertained with performances of various kinds. The celebrated Blondin gave an exhibition which the critics agreed was very wonderful, of his ability to climb a tight rope, ascending from the ground to the peak of a pavilion trundling a wheelbarrow before him. The Willows was another sylvan retreat. Its proprietors maintained a small menagerie, but the drawing card of the resort was the singing and dancing. It was chiefly patronized by the French colony and its "air" was in direct contrast to that of the Russ place, which was as decidedly Germanic as the Willows was French.

Popularity of the Circus

The writer of the "Annals" in deprecating the indisposition of the municipal authorities to anticipate the future by providing breathing places for the people, and scolding them for failing to make the Plaza attractive mournfully remarked that there was not even a circus oval. The oval may have been lacking but not the circuses, for during 1849 and 1850 there were two rival organizations entertaining the public. One of the tents was pitched at Kearny above Clay and the other on Montgomery below California. The taste for this form of amusement was so pronounced that a third company entered the lists, being operated on the west side of

Portsmouth square. The prices of admission ranged from $3 in the pit to $5 for a private stall. The performances only dimly foreshadowed the "marvels" of the modern circus "under three tents," but the patronage accorded indicates as great a degree of appreciation of this mode of entertainment as that displayed in 1912 when the circus comes to town.

The statistical presentation of the amusement business in the early Fifties furnishes conclusive evidence that San Francisco was entitled to the reputation she achieved of being "a good show town." In 1853 there were five American theaters, a music hall for concerts, a French theater and a theater in which German and Spanish performances were made a specialty. Occasionally one of these houses was closed, but as a rule three or four were running. These theaters were not ramshackle affairs by any means, and the professionals who appeared on their boards ranked with the best then playing in the country, the actors being lured by high rewards offered by the flush miners. The first professional performance given in the City was in Washington hall, which was situated in the second story of a building on Washington street. This was in January, 1850, and it is recorded that, although the attendance was good, the actors were poor and not worth the price of admission. "The Wife" and "Charles II" were played on this occasion. This essay was soon followed by another in a house on Kearny, between Clay and Sacramento, in which an English company exhibited its ability. Then a French vaudeville troupe came on the scene, its talents being exhibited in a building on Washington street near Montgomery. The Jenny Lind theater was first opened over Maguire's Parker House saloon. After its destruction in the fire of 1851, Maguire built the new Jenny Lind theater, which was afterward converted into a city hall.

Amusements in the Early Fifties

The advent of so many theaters soon undermined the popularity of the circus. The fickle populace transferred its affections to the more serious drama and gave it a strong support. It is noted that "The Hunchback" was played twenty-one nights during February, 1852, to crowded houses. The company that gave this performance made a tour of the mining regions and the management realized a profit of $30,000 in a nine months' engagement. The "Julia" was a Mrs. Baker, a great favorite. She was supported by her husband, Lewis Baker, who shared her popularity. Some interesting facts are related in connection with this engagement, which apparently revived a waning interest in the drama. The people were out of conceit with the bad actors who at first inflicted themselves upon the amusement-loving public, but the Bakers changed this feeling to one of lively appreciation, as may be inferred from the fact that shortly after their advent there were three theaters running simultaneously.

Appreciation of the Drama

The Metropolitan theater, an excellently constructed building of brick was opened on the night of December 24, 1853, with a stock company, but the management soon made a feature of introducing stars. Many of the most prominent actors of the day trod its boards. A list of them amply justifies the assertion made in the "Annals" that "stars of the first magnitude appeared." Some of the names are not familiar to the modern theater-goer, but their reputation was national during the Fifties and for years afterward. It is not surprising that great artists were tempted to visit California. Crowded houses usually greeted them, and as the rates of admission were $3 for dress circle and parquet; $2 for the second circle

Stars Visit California

and $1 for the place allotted to the "gods," the management was usually enabled to offer terms which much larger cities on the Atlantic seaboard could not rival.

Love of Music

The love of music manifested itself in as marked a fashion as did approbation of good drama. A music hall was erected by Harry Meiggs in 1849 on Bush near Montgomery streets, in which concerts and oratorios were given. In 1854 opera was presented in Italian, English and French at the Metropolitan and Union theaters. Four prima donnas gratified audiences with their notes, and the seasons were represented to be profitable. Among the more noted singers were Mesdames Anna Bishop and Biscaccianti, who achieved great local reputations. Among the actors who pleased the theater-goers of the Fifties in San Francisco were some whose names were American household words. There was Lola Montez, J. B. Booth, Jr., Edwin Booth, Samuel Murdock, Matilda Heron, Oceana Fisher, Laura Keene, and a large number of less notable people whom the San Franciscans persisted in liking as well as some who came to them heralded by fame.

Critical Audiences

The audiences of the period counted themselves excellent judges of a performance and some of the early visitors were disposed to concede the claim. The large pecuniary rewards received by some of the admittedly good actors tempted many of inferior talent to try their fortune on the San Francisco stage, but the pioneers boasted that only merit was recognized, and the fact that they extended a liberal support to stock companies of acknowledged ability, while turning a cold shoulder to stars lacking brilliancy, supports their claim. An attempt to introduce the claque, we are told, proved unsuccessful, the reason assigned for its failure was the general intelligence of the theater-going public and its disposition "to reward the meritorious and to condemn the upstart." The miscellaneous character of the population of early San Francisco was perhaps responsible for the fact that in the infancy of the local drama the actors at times had their feelings hurt by undeserved criticism, but on the other hand they not infrequently received substantial tokens of approbation in the shape of presents of nuggets thrown over the footlights. But this sort of demonstrativeness did not endure long. "The peanut eaters of the upper circles and the gentlemanly loafers in the parquet were speedily subdued into gentility, and the quiet decorum of the parlor soon superseded the noisy bustle of the circus."

Church Fairs and Public Balls

The milder diversion of the church fair was not unknown to the pioneers, and its lottery accompaniment, and the propensity of those who conducted such entertainments to "brazenly exact unreasonable prices for worthless goods" was censured, but in their way these gatherings were fully as popular as the public balls, the religious and irreligious alike patronizing them. Not infrequently the public dances under the auspices of foreign societies drew larger crowds than the balls promoted by Americans, who were not indisposed to admit that there were some things that foreigners could do better than Yankees.

No Exclusive Society

The decade of the Fifties had nearly closed before any sign was witnessed of a tendency to form social groups. The pioneers very early exhibited a desire to erect themselves into an exclusive cult, entrance into which was based solely on priority of arrival. Only those who arrived in California earlier than the close of 1850 were admitted to membership, and while the organization exhibited social desires and distinctly proclaimed its purpose of benefiting those who belonged to it, there was no affectation of superiority; that came later when the reputation of the state had become so well established that it was regarded as a distinction to have been identified with its beginnings. In that particular the pioneers did not differ essentially from other aristocracies, whose claims are based on the fact that their ancestors were earliest in spying out the land and getting it into their possession.

Otherwise the pioneers were very democratic, as indeed everybody who lived in San Francisco in the Fifties had to be unless disposed to flock by himself. There was no trace of exclusiveness in San Francisco for many years; that feature of life only became apparent, or at least did not make itself conspicuous until men by perseverance or good fortune had accumulated or become possessed of wealth. Before 1856 all sorts of people mingled in public affairs without asking questions about their neighbors, which would have been a superfluity. People knew all about the present mode of life of those they met, and whatever ambiguity there may have been about their past they did not seek to clear up, perhaps because of an instinctive dislike for disillusionment. *The Democratic Pioneer*

It was not unusual for courtesans to intrude themselves into perfectly respectable gatherings. Their presence for a time called forth no strong protest, and one may venture to suspect that the reason for refraining was the very natural one that it was felt to be unkind in an unsettled community to inquire narrowly into antecedents or to seriously scrutinize the mode of life of anyone not actually under the ban. There is no doubt that this peculiar laxity, or liberality, was chiefly due to the disregard of the necessity of sanctioning sexual relations shown by men who attained prominence through their abilities, and that it did not meet the approval of women whose status was well determined, but they were helpless. It was also in a measure promoted by the presence of a not inconsiderable number of enterprising individuals who were trying to redeem the errors of early life under new names, and were therefore disinclined to be censorious, or to insist upon too close a scrutiny of credentials. *Obtrusive Courtesans*

While there was no "society" of the sort whose doings fill the modern press, the pioneer community had a mode of singling out some of its members for distinctions which, despite the simplicity of its workings, was fully as effective as that adopted by kings in conferring titles. It is related of a well known general of the ante bellum period that he obtained his dignified appellation by means of an introduction at a banquet, and there must have been many others who obtained their titles in the same easy manner, for the town was full of colonels. Lieutenant John Derby, in his "Phoenixiana," tells us that when he sailed from San Francisco for San Diego every passenger but himself seemed to have friends to bid them goodbye, and that it made him feel lonesome and of small consequence. But he remedied the latter shortcoming by a happy device. As the steamer cast loose he lifted his hat and called out "Good-bye, Colonel!" and every man on the wharf responded by raising his tile and shouting "Good-bye!" *The Ubiquitous Colonel*

It would be a mistake, however, to attribute this title-conferring propensity solely to a disposition to bestow unusual distinctions, or to suppose that it was peculiar to San Francisco. It reflected the spirit of the times, which was decidedly militant. The atmosphere of early San Francisco was remarkably congenial to militancy, and for some years it was a hotbed of intrigue against the peace of other countries. The war which resulted in the acquisition of California was not altogether responsible for these breaches of international comity. It did inspire the idea that the institution of slavery might be extended at the expense of the integrity of Mexican territory, and efforts were made by Americans to accomplish this ob- *The Militant Spirit* ject; but the most serious assault on the sister republic was that planned and carried far in the direction of success by Frenchmen, who made San Francisco the base of their operations. The story of these affairs is part of the history of the City because it illustrates in a very pertinent fashion the restless disposition of the people, and the ease with which schemes, no matter how visionary, were eagerly supported by the men who made their way to San Francisco in search of gold or adventure.

CHAPTER XXXI

SAN FRANCISCO A BASE FOR FILIBUSTERING OPERATIONS

A RESTLESS PEOPLE—TWO DESIGNING FRENCHMEN—PLOTS AGAINST MEXICO—ATTEMPT TO CAPTURE SONORA—A FRENCH CONSUL IN THE GAME—WALKER'S DESIGNS ON SONORA—MEXICO AND THE AMERICAN MANIFEST DESTINY IDEA—SAN FRANCISCANS AID FILIBUSTERS—REMARKABLE CAREER OF WALKER—FATE OF THE FRENCH FILIBUSTERS—CRABB'S FUTILE EXPEDITION—RESTLESS MINERS—THE BLACK SAND SWINDLE—A RUSH TO AUSTRALIA—THE FRASER RIVER RUSH—STEADY GROWTH OF THE CITY—NUMEROUS HOTELS AND RESTAURANTS—POPULARITY OF TEMPERANCE RESTAURANTS—EVERYBODY BOARDED IN SAN FRANCISCO—THE GREGARIOUS TENDENCY—EARLY MEANS OF GETTING ABOUT—FASHIONABLE SECTIONS—CITY GROWS SOUTHWARD—NOT AMBITIOUS TO BECOME A CAPITAL—A BELIEVER IN MANIFEST DESTINY—SOUTHERN INFLUENCE—INCREASING IMMIGRATION.

THE mercurial temperament of the pioneer San Franciscan lent itself to credulity. He was very easily induced to engage in enterprises of doubtful character and validity. On more than one occasion the growing City was almost depopulated by "rushes" to regions where gold was said to have been discovered in abundance. This trait was by no means peculiar to the townsman; it was a characteristic of all those engaged in the pursuit of mining, excepting the Chinese, who rarely deserted a field until they had cleaned it thoroughly. The whites, on the other hand, would abandon a region of moderate promise to try their fortunes in a new place which rumor asserted was richer. This propensity continued down to a late date. It was only one of the forms of the restlessness of pioneer days, and was productive of much discomfort to those who could not resist the call, but it did not even remotely possess the possibilities for mischief held out by filibustering. *A Restless People*

The Spanish power in Mexico was overthrown in 1822, and a republican constitution was adopted by the Mexican people, who were slow to develop a capacity for self government. Their inability did not pass unnoticed, and long before the vast region comprising New Mexico, Arizona and California was wrested from them by Americans, the European powers were eagerly considering the possibility of securing a share of the spoil in the event of a break-up of the republic which they regarded as inevitable. The third Napoleon was particularly intent upon profiting by the disintegration, and as later events disclosed was not averse to helping to promote that result. The evidence that the men who operated on behalf of France were inspired by him is not conclusive, but it is sufficiently strong to cause most Mexicans, and Americans who have given attention to the subject, to believe *Intrigues of Napoleon III.*

267

that he was cognizant of several movements during the Fifties which had a fatal outcome for their promoters.

Two Designing Frenchmen

In 1850 two titled Frenchmen, Count Gaston Raoul de Raoussett-Boulbon and another known as the Marquis de Pindray, were in San Francisco. The latter was said to have left France on account of a shady money transaction, and on his arrival in the City was ready to turn his hand to almost any sort of employment. Raoussett bought a lighter and hired a couple of men to assist him and did a fairly profitable business. Pindray soon took service as a vaquero, and Raoussett in a short time followed his example, investing his money in cattle purchased in the South, which he drove North, but the venture proved unprofitable. The adoption of the same pursuit by the two Frenchmen may have been a coincidence, but it is open to the suspicion that they were familiarizing themselves with an occupation, a knowledge of which might aid them in their future designs.

Plotting Against Mexico

The first demonstration against Mexico was made by Pindray, who formed a band of 150 men and started for Sonora with them. They professed to be colonists, but the purposes of their leader were under suspicion and he was assassinated before he reached Mexico. At this time Patrice Dillon was French consul in San Francisco. It is impossible to tell whether he acted without instructions, but he was undoubtedly engaged in an intrigue which had for its object the gaining of a foothold for France in Mexico. He found a ready instrument in Raoussett, who had conceived the idea of converting Sonora into a buffer state to prevent the United States from further encroaching on Mexico. Raoussett was sent by Dillon to the City of Mexico, where, in the course of a few months, he succeeded in convincing the authorities that his project was in the interest of Mexico, and they arranged to provide him with money to raise a band of men to assist him in carrying it out. Raoussett had no difficulty in securing 250 adventurers to assist him. They were chiefly Frenchmen and sailed with him for Guaymas, which place they reached in June, 1852.

Attempt to Capture Sonora

Meanwhile, however, a doubt had arisen in the minds of Mexicans regarding the integrity of Raoussett's purpose, and orders were conveyed to him to remain in Guaymas. Raoussett thereupon charged the Mexican government with duplicity and proceeded to defy Géneral Blanco, who had ordered him to refrain from proceeding to Sonora. Blanco then "denounced" Raoussett as an insurgent, and the latter attempted to secure the adhesion of the rancheros on the pretense that he was working for the independence of Sonora. Subsequently Raoussett captured Hermosillo, defeating Blanco in an engagement before that place. The Mexican general lost 200 men and fled, while the loss of the French adventurer was 17 killed and 23 wounded. The Frenchman lacked the ability to follow up his successes, and at Mazatlan was seized with a severe illness. Blanco, more successful in diplomacy than in war, succeeded in persuading the disheartened forces of Raoussett to return to San Francisco in a bark chartered for that purpose.

A Plotting French Consul

While in Mazatlan Dillon wrote to Raoussett urging him to renew his attempt. He returned to San Francisco and was made a hero of by the populace, who were disposed to regard the capture of Hermosillo as an extraordinary exploit. Another appeal was made to the French capitalists in San Francisco, who were about to furnish $300,000 when a false report that Sonora had been sold to the United States, which probably had its origin in the diplomacy which led to the treaty in

December, 1853, by which Mexico ceded territory embracing 45,535 square miles to the United States, caused the intriguers to withdraw their support.

Meanwhile Walker, who also aimed at the acquisition of Sonora, had sailed from San Francisco for Lower California October 15, 1853. On November 3 he seized La Paz and proclaimed the republic of Lower California. Walker's movements gave Santa Ana much more cause for alarm than those of the Frenchman, and he wrote to the Mexican consul at San Francisco, Luis del Valle, to recruit Frenchmen to a number not exceeding 3,000, who would be willing to take service with Mexico, and to ship them to Guaymas. Del Valle at once applied to Dillon, who entered into an arrangement with Raoussett, who eagerly embraced the opportunity to get a band of armed men into Mexican territory. But the French intriguers at this point encountered an obstacle in the shape of the determination of the pro-slavery element in San Francisco to prevent any colony being established by France on the American border. They were not disposed to sympathize with Mexico, and had even rejoiced over the victory of Hermosillo, obtained by Raoussett, but Walker's purposes, which were generally understood to be the conversion of the border states of Mexico into a slave holding republic with the view of permitting southern expansion, were more in harmony with their desires.

<small>Walker's Designs on Sonora</small>

In consequence they set in motion the machinery of the courts, and the British ship "Challenge," chartered to carry 800 men to Guaymas, was seized on March 29, 1854, for violation of the revenue laws. The Mexican consul was tried subsequently for violating the neutrality laws. Dillon, who was summoned as a witness, refused to testify, invoking his rights as a consul. Del Valle attempted to profit by the refusal, demanding that he be permitted to prove his innocence by a witness who would not testify. Dillon was forcibly brought into court, and the judge held that the French consul was here merely in his consular capacity, and that his domicile in the eyes of the law was in France. The French consul was then charged with violation of the neutrality laws, but pleaded that the men raised to be sent to Mexico were to colonize a part of that country with a view of preventing filibustering. The jury could not agree, standing ten for conviction and two for acquittal. In the following May a *nolle prosqui* was entered.

<small>Slavery Advocates Block French Plan</small>

There was great excitement in the City over the trial and the attitude of the French consul was severely deprecated, but the tenor of the criticisms indicates that they were not influenced by consideration for the neutrality laws. As a matter of fact the City was infected with the spirit of filibusterism, and the majority were indisposed to recognize any rights that their neighbors to the south might claim. In 1852, when William Walker proposed his scheme of establishing a republic in Lower California, it was hailed with applause, and scrip or promises to pay based on the revenues of the prospective new government was freely sold. The press voiced the same sentiment as that expressed in the "Annals:" "It is ever the fate of America to go ahead * * * So will America conquer and annex all lands. That is her manifest destiny."

<small>Mexico and Manifest Destiny</small>

When the news of the occupation of La Paz by Walker reached San Francisco the flag of the new republic was hoisted at the corner of Kearny and Sacramento streets and an office opened for recruits and more volunteers offered themselves than could be taken to the scene of action. The newspapers recorded all that was doing at great length, and there was great excitement, but no effort on the part of the authorities to prevent the departure of the filibusters. When the barque

<small>Helping Filibusters</small>

"Anita" sailed with its contingent no one offered to prevent its departure. The brig "Arrow" had been seized by General Hitchcock, commanding the United States forces on the Pacific, a couple of months earlier, September 30th, and released for want of sufficient legal evidence to show its destination. Other federal officers and the state and city authorities acted as though the matter did not concern them. Indeed a federal judge in the case of Colonel H. P. Watkins, who was convicted in the United States district court, openly sympathized with the prisoners and lamented that he was compelled to discharge his duty in fining the captain and another prisoner, who by the way escaped paying the fine by professing their inability to raise the amount imposed.

Career of Filibuster Walker

The subsequent adventures of Walker, Raoussett and the other filibusters are not a part of the history of San Francisco. They are not devoid of interest but their recital would consume more space than can be spared and besides they have been related in great detail by numerous writers. It is necessary to round out the story, however, by telling that the Lower California scheme came to naught, and that Walker and his cabinet returned to San Francisco in May, 1854, and were indicted by a grand jury, tried and promptly acquitted. Despite the fact that the whole affair was a wretched fizzle, in which Walker had exhibited some very despotic traits, he was made a hero of by the admiring San Franciscans, and they were quite ready to assist him when he embarked on his Nicaragua enterprise in May, 1855. This expedition, like those previously organized by him, also miscarried. After two years of varying success in that country he was compelled to leave. He went to New York, and after a stay in the North of a couple of years, he returned to New Orleans and from there made another attempt on Central America, fell into the hands of the Honduras military authorities and was tried and shot on September 25, 1860.

Fate of Raoussett

Raoussett met the same fate as Walker. While the trial of Patrice Dillon was pending he surreptitiously left the City in a small schooner carrying a few men, some arms and a quantity of ammunition. His purpose was to make himself master of Guaymas, with a view of heading off the United States, which he thought menaced Cuba, Canada and Mexico and threatened in a brief period to become master of the world. The little vessel was wrecked off the coast of Lower California and he and his comrades were nearly starved before they were able to reach the neighborhood of Guaymas towards the end of June, 1854. A number of the Frenchmen composing the band that had embarked on the "Challenge" had established themselves in Guaymas and he ordered them to seize the civil and military authorities of that place. They refused and endeavored to effect an arrangement with a general who was about to "pronounce," but the latter, while professing to acquiesce in the Frenchman's plans was secretly preparing to oppose him. When Raoussett attempted to capture Guaymas he was himself taken prisoner and promptly shot.

Crabb's Expedition

Another filibustering expedition, organized by Henry A. Crabb of Tennessee, who made his home in Stockton in 1850, where he took a prominent part in politics during several years, sailed from San Francisco to San Pedro in 1857. Crabb's objective was Sonora, and he proposed marching overland from San Pedro to that Mexican state with a band of one hundred men. His wife, a Mexican, had numerous relatives in Sonora, and he expected them to cooperate with him in his efforts. Before he started on his venture Crabb had thrown out intimations of his purpose to annex Sonora, and as he was a violent pro-slavery man, and in communication with some active advocates of the extension of the institution, it was not unreasonably assumed that he was receiving outside encouragement. Whatever he contemplated, his plans came to grief, for he was captured by Pesquiera, the governor, who refused to accept his explanation that the object of his visit to Sonora was merely to carry on mining, and ordered him shot. At first our minister to Mexico characterized the expedition of Crabb as that of filibusters, but a little later, at the end of May, 1857, he claimed that the party had no other object in entering Sonora than to secure homes. Nothing came of the claim, and no one believed the minister.

Occurrences of this sort were alternated with other excitements produced by the instability of the population, or that portion of it which manifested no disposition to adopt settled occupations and a not inconsiderable number who were ready on short notice to abandon what they were engaged upon on the chance of improving their condition. The earliest manifestation of this tendency was that furnished by the almost complete abandonment of the town when the news of the discovery of gold at Sutter's fort was received. It is not surprising that the announcement should have resulted in an exodus at that time, for the embryo City was not offering great inducements to the newcomers to help them make good their belief in its future. Things were proceeding in a humdrum fashion, and the rewards of the merchant, mechanic or laborer were not excessive. There was a wide margin for improvement, and when the possibility of picking up a competence in a few days began to be perceived, hardly any in the community felt that a greater profit might be derived from sticking to ordinary occupations than could be gained by resorting to the gold fields. *An Unstable Population*

But it is astonishing that after the vicissitudes of the mining occupation came to be generally understood, and when even the most credulous had begun to learn that persevering toil in commonplace industries in the long run held out more reliable rewards than searching for gold, the propensity to rush continued. The men who had resorted to the mines soon learned that untrustworthy reports easily gained circulation, and plenty of them were able to relate bitter experiences gained in pursuing myths. Stories of disappointments were oftener heard than tales of good luck, but the latter made an impression, while the former were easily forgotten. The miner who could exhibit a buckskin bag well filled with gold dust and nuggets was an infinitely greater object of interest than the small army of the unlucky who soon began to find their way to San Francisco which, when the mines began to pour out their treasures in earnest, began to prosper in a business way, holding out many inducements to the able and those willing to work. *The Restless Miners*

The steady stream of immigration, the ebb of the rush to the placers and other causes combined to make the City a very brisk place, and attractive to the man who had the money-making faculty, but as a whole the speculative tendency had possession of the community and it was easily deceived by accounts of rich finds, and occasionally with disastrous results. In the early part of 1851 there was a rush to the Klamath river country induced by a report that the sands of the beach near where the stream discharged itself into the ocean were composed of at least one-half pure metal. The most fabulous representations were made and eagerly believed. It was stated that a band of prospectors had found a patch of the metalliferous sand, which was estimated to contain gold to the value of $43,000,000, and these *Black Sand Swindle* figures were supposed to represent only one-tenth of the possible richness of this particular spot. Marvelous as it may seem these purely mythical statements were vouched for by men supposed to be reputable. The effect on the community was tremendous. The rush and excitement were as great as when the discovery of gold in California was announced. Shiploads of men went to the alleged wonderful country, only to learn that the black sands which were reputed to be immensely rich were really destitute of the precious metal, or contained so little of it that it could not be extracted by the most cunning devices known to the miners of those days.

A Rush to Australia
Despite this experience, which gave a rude shock to the business interests of San Francisco, greatly unsettling them, a year later, when the reports of the immense yields of the Australian mines began to be received, a large number of Californians left the state and made their way to Victoria, Ballarat and Bendigo. There was no exaggeration in this instance, Australia like California had enormously rich fields, and for many years they remained "a poor man's diggings," but there was no more assurance of their permanency when the fever first attacked San Francisco than there was when the Klamath river excitement lured from the City enough of its population to make their absence noticeable in the diminished crowds on the streets. There was one cause for rejoicing over the rush to Australia. A great many of the bad characters who had come to California from the island continent hastened to return when they learned that the chances of finding gold in the country they hailed from were as good as in the land which refused to welcome them.

The Fraser River Excitement
But the most serious of the rushes, so far as the fortunes of the rising City on the Bay of San Francisco was concerned, was that to Fraser river in British Columbia in 1858. The hegira commenced in the spring and continued until December. So many left the City that fears were entertained that it would be depopulated. After a while the new diggings began to have few attractions for the majority of those who expected to make their fortunes in them, and the most of them found their way back to San Francisco, and it is noted that on their return business renewed its activity, although it is not clearly apparent how that result could have been produced by the presence of a great number of "strapped" miners.

Uninterrupted Growth
Despite the speculative tendencies of the inhabitants of San Francisco, and the occurrence of startling events calculated to divert men from the pursuit of those ordinary occupations which demand the application of untiring industry to achieve success, the City continued to grow in wealth and population during the decade. Disastrous fires, reckless criminals, corrupt municipal management, intriguing filibusters, quarrelsome politicians and gold rushes were powerless to arrest its progress. In 1860 the census showed that the City had a population of 56,802, a more than fifty-fold growth since the occupation. But numbers by no means tell the whole story. There were other cities in the United States on the eve of the Civil war whose inhabitants exceeded those of San Francisco, but there was none of double its size which even remotely approached the metropolis of the Pacific in the possession of those features which go to the making of a great city.

Distinguishing Peculiarities
At no time after the gold rush began did San Francisco resemble the older communities. Five years after that event it contained more hotels, restaurants, theaters, saloons and other places created for the diversion of a restless pleasure-loving people than are found today in some cities of a quarter of a million inhabitants. They were not kept for occasional service, but were always in active requisition.

Although the greatest stars of the period found their way to the City by the Golden Gate at frequent entervals, such visits were inadequate to satisfy the demand for good dramatic performances, and stock companies were maintained, the excellence of which may be inferred from the fact that from their ranks sprang many whose subsequent successful careers stamped them as artists of merit. Grand opera also flourished and acquired something of a permanent character, the stay of visiting companies at times extending over months.

But it was in the possession of hotels and restaurants, far better than the average of the decade, that San Francisco found its chief claim for distinction. In 1853, it is stated, there were 160 hotels and public houses with a descriptive name, and 66 restaurants and coffee saloons. This formidable number included American dining rooms, English lunch houses, Spanish fondas, German wirthschafts, Italian osteria, and Chinese chow chows, and the cost of entertainment in them ranged from $5 to $12 for "a gentleman's dinner," to a couple of dollars for a satisfying meal. But the prices on the menus of popular restaurants are not always an index of the cost of living of the people generally; if they were we should conclude that the average man found it difficult to make ends meet on bigger wages than $15 a day. Some of the items read: "Roast duck, $5; broiled quail, $2; a dozen canned oysters, $1."

Numerous Hotels and Restaurants

With few exceptions all of the hotels and restaurants sold liquors. One of these exceptions was "The Fountain Head," whose proprietor employed 100 persons in catering for the patrons of his two establishments. Their salaries averaged $90 a month. According to a descriptive article published in the "Commercial Advertiser" of April 6, 1854, the monthly receipts of these two temperance houses aggregated $57,000; the expenditures were also on a liberal scale, the proprietor's potato bills being $3,000 monthly and his disbursements for ice and eggs amounting to $28,000 in five months. It is interesting to note that the St. Francis hotel, situated on the corner of Clay and Dupont street, was a fashionable hostelry in 1849. It was built of a dozen small houses originally intended for cottages. Its rooms were separated by the thinnest of board partitions without lath or plaster. On the next block stood the City hotel, built in 1846. It was the only public house in San Francisco up to the time of the discovery of gold. Both of these hotels were destroyed by fire. The Union hotel on Kearny street between Clay and Washington, was the first hotel built of brick. It was a four story structure and cost $250,000. It was burned in the fire of May 31, 1851, and subsequently rebuilt, but never regained its old time importance.

Temperance Restaurants Popular

Among the other hotels singled out for recognition were the Jones, on the corner of Sansome and California; the Oriental, corner of Bush and Battery; the Rossette, at Bush and Sansome; the International, on Jackson street between Montgomery and Kearny. The latter was conducted on the European plan, but the American method was more generally preferred by proprietors and customers, the rates ranging from $2 to $10 per day. These hotels were designed as much for the use of permanent guests as for transients, and down to the closing years of the decade 1850-60 their patronage was more largely that of home people than of strangers. Charles Warren Stoddard tells us that during the Fifties everybody in San Francisco boarded or kept a boarding house. Some of the latter sought to rival the hotels and as late as 1861 the name of Madame Parran's house on Clay

The Boarding Habit

street, near Powell, where a number of the leading lawyers of the City boarded, was as well known as that of the best hotel in the City.

The Tendency to Herd

Many memories cluster about the early hotels of San Francisco and reams have been written about their peculiarities. The story has been told of how dearly the privilege was bought of sleeping under cover in the most exciting period of the gold rush. Men sometimes paid as much as $30 a week for the use of a shelf or bunk in a shack or tent, and $8 a day for good board. The Parker house on Kearny street, facing the Plaza, paid a rental of $120,000 a year, and a canvas tent adjoining which housed the El Dorado saloon, netted its owner $40,000 a year. But the glories of the Oriental, and the wonders of the hotel which had for its foundation the submerged bulk of a ship, are not nearly so interesting as the fact that the gregarious or some other instinct of man in 1849 and the early Fifties impelled him to a course which produced the same condition in a new city with all out-doors in which to expand, as that witnessed in our own times and is erroneously attributed to enforced congestion.

Hotel Center in Early Days

The story of hotel and restaurant life in San Francisco is one of continuous improvement and mirrors the progress of the City. It also, when carefully followed, exhibits the development of a conservatism which later became as pronounced a characteristic of the people as their earlier instability. Before the breaking out of the Civil war most of the hotels of the earlier Fifties were destroyed or edged out by the encroachments of business, but the hotel and amusement center refused to move far from the district in which it had been established by the pioneers. The Occidental and Cosmopolitan hotels, although the City had spread to the south, and persisted in climbing hills which the prophets declared would be a barrier to expansion, were built within a half dozen blocks of the center of 1849; and a quarter of a century later the Palace was reared in the same neighborhood. Even the calamity of 1906 proved powerless to resist this conservatism. The new St. Francis is scarcely more than five minutes' brisk walk from the spot on which the St. Francis of 1849 stood, and a guest of the Fairmont could almost throw a stone into the district where restaurants and theaters flourished during the Fifties.

A Compact City

If the men who had much to do with shaping the destiny of San Francisco knew the lines about a "pent up Utica," and admired them, they never thought of applying them to themselves. Although the tendency to spread southward early manifested itself instead of allowing for expansion in that direction a course was deliberately adopted which later greatly hampered the City's growth. The influences and motives responsible for the attempt to contract the operations of the municipality are easily understood. The corruption of officials prior to the application of the drastic methods of the Vigilantes had caused the people to distrust themselves, and they easily fell in with the proposition of the framer of the Consolidation Act of 1856 to lop off a large part of the original county of San Francisco in order to form a compact political subdivision.

Cutting Loose from the Country

Horace Hawes was not gifted with much imagination, and if he had been the times and his environment would have militated against his taking a glance into the future, which would have permitted him to see that changed means of transportation would affect men's ideas concerning the desirability of packing people closely together. In cutting off all that part of the original county of San Francisco south of a line running through the southern extremity of Lake Merced, and its erection into San Mateo county, he doubtless thought that he was conferring a

MEIGGS WHARF, FOOT OF POWELL STREET, NORTH BEACH, AS IT APPEARED IN 1865

benefit on the remaining part which was consolidated with the City. Consolidation naturally suggested itself to an economical man, and Hawes was economical to the verge of parsimony; but no one criticized him adversely on that account at the time. The people who deemed it expedient to cut up the land into building lots of twenty-five feet and even less frontage were not expansive in their ideas. They leaned to the belief that the business of a city could be effected with more facility by contracting the area in which it was to be carried on than by spreading operations over a large surface.

Street cars were first used in San Francisco in 1863, several years after their introduction into American cities on the Atlantic seaboard. Up to that date "omnibuses" were employed. The first line of stages drawn by horses was used to carry passengers from North Beach to South Park and began operating in the early part of 1852. A road was opened along the bay shore, around the eastern and northern base of Telegraph hill, making communication easy, and the "busses" were regularly dispatched between the two points. The traffic was inconsiderable, and it was not until the advent of the tramway that the disposition to spread manifested itself, and then only feebly, for many years until a San Francisco invention solved the problem of climbing the hills that encircled the bay.

Early Transportation Facilities

The prestige given to South Park by this communication with North Beach endured well into the following decade. It was not much of a park as parks go in these days, but the people of the Fifties did not regard the term as a misnomer when applied to the oblong enclosure, surrounded by prim houses very much alike, but still having an air of gentility which caused the neighborhood to be regarded as fashionable. It soon had a rival in Rincon hill, which overlooked the bay, and maintained its supremacy until the Seventies when the cable cars began to climb Clay street; then it was deserted by people with pretensions, and surrendered to manufacture and commerce. It is now doomed to disappear entirely. Its integrity was early attacked by the commercial spirit which resented interference with southward march of business, and streets were cut through it which gave the houses an inaccessible appearance and made them undesirable for residence.

Fashionable Residence District

The same fate for a long while menaced Telegraph hill which survived threatened inroads only because the failure of Harry Meigg's project of rivalling Yerba Buena prevented North Beach from growing in population and importance as rapidly as that daring speculator imagined it would. Had his dream been realized there is no doubt that the assaults made upon the hill by those wishing to unite the region which had already won favor with the northern part of the City must have caused its complete demolition. A considerable portion along the edge of the bay was escarped for the purpose of making a roadway, and later there were further encroachments to increase the level area at its shore end, but the practical arrestment of business enterprise on the northern side of the City after the flight of Meiggs caused the retention of Telegraph hill until sentiment began to operate and now there is a strong probability that it will remain a permanent landmark, and a reminder of the days when it was an important signal station from which the welcome news of the arrivals of steamships bringing letters from "home" was announced.

Telegraph Hill

Even the success of Meiggs' scheme would have been ineffective to arrest the progress of the City southward and westward. The sand dunes were less formidable than they appeared to be to the forty-niners, and the successful use of the steam

Southward Movement of City

shovel soon pointed out the natural direction of extension for business purposes. Happy valley, as that part of the City lying between California street and Rincon Point was called, was assailed when the necessity for expansion exhibited itself and in the course of years not a suggestion of the early character of the soil was left. No pioneer has ever told how the area lying between California street and Rincon Point and the bay and the Mission Peaks came to be called Happy valley. Viewed from what is now known as Nob hill it appeared to be a mere waste of sand, although there were spots in it containing thick undergrowth as was notably the case in the place selected for a cemetery.

Early Street System

Through this waste of sand a broad street, to which the name of Market was given, was traced to run in a southwesterly direction from the bay. It did not follow the line of least resistance, but those who laid it out were apparently governed by the desire to avoid some of the embarrassments which would have been presented by a too strict adherence to the rectangular plan of the streets that were first surveyed. The pioneers of San Francisco were not wholly unmindful of the possibilities of conforming thoroughfares to topography; there was much criticism of the unloveliness of the formal squares or blocks, and it was pointed out that beauty and convenience might be made to go hand in hand, but the commercial spirit was the dominating factor in determining the matter and straight lines were decided upon. Hindsight is frequently more reliable than foresight, but it will be wise for those who take advantage of experience to criticize the failure of the pioneers to build for the future to keep in mind the fact that the builders of the City had many problems to deal with, and that the one which appealed to them most strongly for solution was that of making San Francisco a great commercial port and that object was constantly kept in the foreground.

No Desire to be the Capital

At no time was this idea subordinated to any other consideration. Few aspiring communities escaped more easily the desire to become a capital. On two or three occasions sporadic efforts were made to establish the seat of state government in San Francisco, but they never received the hearty support of the community. In 1850 the legislature which had been meeting at San Jose got tired of that place, and an agitation was started to transfer the capital to a spot that would be deemed more suitable. Numerous offers were made to tempt location, but San Francisco exhibited little or no concern, and was not even disposed to regard with alarm the proposal of Vallejo to start a city on the Straits of Carquinez which was to be provided with all the requisites of a great capital, including botanical gardens, universities and penitentiaries. Five or six years later, after the capital had been located at Sacramento, a flood compelled the legislators to find refuge in the City, and a movement was set on foot to offer inducements which would bring about its transfer to San Francisco, but it never gained force. Perhaps the inhabitants of the City were conscious of the jealousy of the interior which early asserted itself and concluded that any effort they might make would prove unavailing; but it is more than probable that the cause of the apathy concerning the matter was the same as that which made San Franciscans indifferent to the numerous attempts to divide the state, namely, the profound conviction that the destiny of the City was assured and could not be seriously affected by the machinations of politicians or by rivalry.

Confidence in Future

When Bret Harte wrote that San Francisco sat by the Golden Gate, "serene and indifferent to fate," he poetically expressed the unfaltering belief of the pioneer in the manifest destiny of the City. It was not, however, an unintelligent conviction, and was never responsible for the relaxation of energy which at times exhibited itself during the growth of the City. Other causes for the temporary arrestments of progress can easily be assigned, and they in no wise conflict with the assertion that on the whole the pioneers, and their immediate successors, made excellent use of their opportunities which in many respects were far inferior to those enjoyed by the regions on the other side of the Rockies which were helped by an unceasing stream of assimilable immigrants who assisted in the development of their resources.

The interdependence of city and country was clearly understood by the people of San Francisco who were perhaps keener to appreciate the possibilities of the soil than those who, by a variety of methods, some of them not altogether creditable, obtained possession of large quantities of land which they held for a rise in values. The people of the City at all times were averse to large holdings, and eager for the subdivision of the land, and they were settled in the determination that the big Spanish grants should never be made profitable by the introduction of cheap Oriental labor, fully realizing that the inevitable result of development by means of a servile and nonassimilable people would in the long run produce results not unlike those which for a period made the South a comparatively negligible industrial and commercial factor.

City and Country

Southern sentiment, which after its first defeat in the attempt to make a slave state of California nearly regained dominance, did not appear to have any other than political consequences. The offices and those occupations closely related to politics were swayed by Southerners, but their point of view was not largely shared by the mercantile element of San Francisco which preferred to mould itself on the methods of the more vigorous Northern states. The tremendous admiration entertained by San Franciscans for Henry Clay was largely due to their sympathy with his aspirations for American industrial emancipation. The people of San Francisco believed that the future of their City was linked with free labor. At times they appeared to vacillate, but the departure from the straight path never proceeded too far to be easily arrested. The vagaries of politics led them to side with a party whose leaders were not in accord with them, but when the crucial moment arrived they arrayed themselves without hesitation against the slaveholders; and in the same way, while they occasionally paltered with the proposition to hasten the state's development by means of cheap Chinese labor, when it became necessary to make a choice they were uncompromisingly against its introduction.

Advocates of Free Labor

It is necessary to make the connection perfectly clear so that the reader may comprehend that San Francisco encountered obstacles to her advancement which no other city of the Union was called upon to deal with. The first wave of emigration which swept into California nearly a quarter of a million people quickly receded. Afterward the tide ebbed and flowed placidly, and at the end of fourteen years of occupation its great area was occupied by less than four hundred thousand inhabitants, made up very largely of classes not disposed to enter upon the land.

Tide of Immigration

At the same time the older states of the Union were receiving continuous accessions of toilers to whom tilling of the soil was a congenial occupation, and incidentally their absorption was creating a labor condition which California must necessarily attain if her expectations of great industrial expansion were to be realized.

CHAPTER XXXII

RESOURCES THAT PROMOTED THE GROWTH OF SAN FRANCISCO

CHARACTER OF CALIFORNIA LANDS—A BIGGER HOME MARKET FOR THEIR PRODUCTS NEEDED—PAST DEPENDENCE ON THE OUTSIDER—UNORGANIZED MERCANTILISM—EARLY TRADE DEPRESSIONS—THE PANIC OF 1855—BANKING TROUBLES—PLENTY OF GOLD BUT NO CURRENCY—PRIVATE COINAGE—BUYING AND SELLING GOLD DUST—GOVERNMENTAL METHODS OF DEALING WITH THE PEOPLE—MERCHANT PRINCES OF PIONEER PERIOD—PIONEER STOCKS OF MERCHANDISE—LITTLE ATTEMPT TO DISPLAY GOODS—CREDIT SYSTEM AND COLLECTIONS—PIONEER IDEAS OF A TRANSCONTINENTAL RAILROAD—MUCH TALK OF CONNECTING EAST AND WEST—STATE PRIDE DEVELOPS SLOWLY—WAGON ROADS—HIGH FARE AND FREIGHT RATES—SEA AND RIVER NAVIGATION—CLIPPER SHIPS—PANAMA AND NICARAGUA ROUTES—THE PANAMA RAILROAD—SHIPPING OF THE PAST—BUSINESS DRAWBACKS.

ALTHOUGH mining was the only industry which largely contributed to the growth and prosperity of San Francisco during the early Fifties, those most interested in the development of the City did not deceive themselves concerning the probability of its becoming a diminishing resource. The exhaustion of the placers was freely discussed and the question asked what products could be made to take the place of gold when the fields should cease to yield large quantities of the precious metals. Later, when quartz mining began to make a showing there was a revival of the belief that the production of gold would always be California's most important industry, but it was not shared by observant men who recognized the possibilities of a thorough development of the vast area of fertile land which had been practically neglected up to the time of the occupation, and was not made much use of during the first few years after the discovery of gold.

Sources of Prosperity

There was a wide divergence of opinion respecting the agricultural capabilities of California in the early Fifties. They were relatively better appreciated before the gold rush began than while the excitement attending the great finds of the precious metal lasted. Among the immigrants who entered the state with the view of engaging in mining there were comparatively few who had previously worked on farms, and they were easily misled by appearances into the belief that most of the land was unfit for any other than grazing purposes. This view was to some extent shared by the immigrants who had been farmers and was only abandoned by them when actual experience demonstrated that there was no branch of agriculture which could not be profitably pursued within the borders of California.

Fertility of California Lands

Thus it happened that the pioneer merchants of San Francisco, while all their

280   SAN FRANCISCO

Agriculture Possibilities

energies were at first absorbed in the conduct of a trade unique in many particulars, inasmuch as it involved the exchange of a universally sought product for an infinite variety of commodities, rather than the complex operations attending the quest for markets in which to dispose of competing articles, were the first to recognize the need of industrial expansion, and did all in their power to bring about that result. That this was their attitude is made plain by the discussions in the legislature and the press in which the future of the port of San Francisco was always spoken of as dependent upon the development of the agricultural resources of the country, and the conversion of raw materials into finished products. It was the prevalence of this opinion as much as any other cause that kept California from meeting the fate which a section of the American people were desirous of imposing upon her from the date of acquisition. Had the course of events after 1846 not been interrupted by the discovery of gold it hardly admits of a doubt that the most of the immigrants attracted to the new territory would have been from the South and Southwest, and that they would have succeeded when the rupture between North and South finally came, in carrying California out of the Union. The influx of great numbers of men from those parts of the country where free labor prevailed, and where the conviction was very general that American prosperity depended on the creation of a condition which would relieve the country of the necessity of depending on foreigners, determined the future of California and set at naught the plans of politicians.

A Greater Market Needed

The early trade conditions, and the first feeble efforts at manufacturing in San Francisco very faintly indicated the aspirations of its inhabitants which were impossible of speedy realization because of economic obstacles that will only be overcome when the population of the state is great enough to permit it to manufacture on a scale which will make low cost of production possible. In tracing these efforts it will be seen that San Francisco was subject to drawbacks which at first seemed advantages, and that in reaching out to secure the benefits which close intercourse undoubtedly confers she subjected her growing industries to a competition which her sparse population and limited resources were not able to withstand.

Dependence on the Outside World

Turning back to the days of Forty-nine we find that the country was as dependent on the outside world for all those things which men desire as the native Californians were before their arrival. The commonest necessaries of life had to be brought from the "States" or Europe, and those artificial contributions to comfort demanded by man, whenever he can command the means to obtain them, were all derived from the same sources. As a consequence for several years the import trade of San Francisco was not merely the most important, it was practically the sole direct trade with other peoples, for the commodities imported were almost wholly paid for with the gold taken from the placers. In 1848 there were twelve mercantile establishments and a number of agencies for Eastern concerns and firms doing business in the Sandwich islands; and there were also several direct importers. Within the first eight weeks after the discovery at Sutter's fort fully $250,000 worth of gold dust had reached San Francisco, and in the ensuing eight weeks an additional $600,000 was received. The effect on trade was what might have been expected. The stocks on hand were rapidly cleaned out. So great was the demand for all sorts of commodities that the Russian American Company, whose managers in Alaska had early intelligence of the gold find, were enabled to clear shelves and warehouses of dead stock that had accumulated during the many years their establishment had been in operation.

In 1849 merchants were so eager to procure goods that they went out in boats to meet ships in the offing. It is related that a trader who adopted this plan of replenishing his stock hailed a ship just arrived, asking: "Have you woolen shirts?" "Yes," was the reply. "How many?" "About a hundred dozen." "What will you take for the lot?" "A hundred per cent over New York cost." "Done. Here's a hundred dollars to bind the bargain." The trade thus concluded, netted the purchaser more than the New York consignor or the ship, but all were satisfied. It is not surprising that the knowledge of this extraordinary demand should have resulted in a great movement of goods towards the new El Dorado. Soon ships were sailing toward the Golden Gate from all quarters of the globe bringing merchandise and men. Before the middle of the year 1849 the bay was filled with shipping. Over two hundred square rigged vessels lay at anchor in the harbor, and they had all brought goods, and as is usual in such cases, the importations were nearly all responsive to the same impulse, and not nicely adjusted to the requirements of the market. Nevertheless, although the merchants were obliged to pay the excessive rents and high prices for their goods, they made large profits.
_{Eager Traders}

An attempt was made in the fall of 1849 to organize a Merchants' Exchange, but while there were several subscribers to the project the hurly burly of the times prevented the consummation of the idea. Everybody was too busy to attend meetings, and those engaged in trade apparently were disposed to ignore methods prevalent in older communities. A reading room established by E. E. Dunbar, however, was much resorted to by men in business, and to some extent served the purpose for which exchanges are devised. The best of organization would not have materially improved the condition. The world knew that vast quantities of gold were being taken out, and just at that time the complaint of overproduction of manufactured articles was general, hence all sought to get their surplus commodities to the place where they could be exchanged for the gold. The desire of the local dealers to get rich quickly cooperated with the eagerness to unload, and the consequence was that San Francisco merchants were heavily overstocked. and in the spring of 1850 they were compelled to make great reductions in prices to realize, a course which saved some but resulted in many bankruptcies.

Unorganized Mercantilism

One of the effects of this overstocking was the creation of an auction business which survived many years in San Francisco, and was at one time so flourishing that the legislature, always on the lookout for opportunities to draw revenue from the City, sought to impose on it a special form of taxation. It first came into prominence through the necessity of speedily getting rid of the stocks of debtors, but later it was made use of by consignees to dispose of cargoes shipped by them without special knowledge of the needs of the market, a practice which tended to demoralize the regular conduct of business.

Auction Business

Despite these drawbacks merchandizing up to 1854 does not appear to have been an extra hazardous occupation. At least there was no perceptible diminution of the volume of trade. There were great fluctuations in prices and incautious operators occasionally went to the wall, but on the whole, owing to the high range of profits, there were relatively fewer fatalities than in many places in the Atlantic states where business was carried on in a conservative fashion. In 1853 there was a repetition of the earlier trouble of overstocking due to the practice of

Early Trade Depressions

282   SAN FRANCISCO

consignees flooding the market, and it became necessary to ship goods back to New York in order to relieve the glut. This depression passed away, and there were hopes of a complete recovery of business in 1854 which were disappointed, trading during that year being generally unprofitable.

The Panic of 1855

In 1855 as the result of bad banking methods several financial institutions failed, and the business community suffered severely. There were 197 failures with liabilities amounting to $8,000,000. The disaster had its origin in the indiscretion of a banking concern with its headquarters in St. Louis and a branch in San Francisco. The parent house had invested heavily in the Ohio and Mississippi Railroad and was drawing upon Page, Bacon & Co. of San Francisco for funds to meet demands upon it when it failed. At the time of the failure there was a million dollars worth of gold dust in transit to St. Louis, which successfully eluded the depositors of the San Francisco bank who tried to get it into their possession. The obligations of Page, Bacon & Co. in the City reached two millions, and the firm closed the doors of their establishment after paying out about $600,000. An attempt was made to sustain Page, Bacon & Co., but the manager of the bank, Henry Haight, was unable to make a satisfactory showing and the effort had to be abandoned. Adams & Co., another of the larger institutions, anticipated an expected run by putting up its shutters. A receiver was appointed, and there was a continuous legal battle which in the end dissipated all the funds of the depositors who received little of the money deposited by them.

Cause of Banking Troubles

The banking trouble of this period was largely attributed to the failure of the State to exercise a proper surveillance over the operations of financial concerns. Owing to the distrust of corporations which was excessive at the time of the adoption of the first constitution the state was prohibited granting charters for banking purposes, or of the issuance and circulation of bank notes; but there was no inhibition of the privilege of creating banks of deposit which exercised nearly all the functions of a chartered bank, such as receiving deposits, making loans, selling drafts and buying bullion, and between 1849 and 1852 five companies doing what was called an express banking business were in existence. They were S. F. Adams & Co., Page, Bacon & Co., Palmer, Cook & Co., Todd & Co., and Wells, Fargo & Co., and they all did a flourishing business, handling the bulk of the gold dust and bullion passing through San Francisco. There were also private banks and for some time mercantile houses possessing safes acted as depositaries.

First San Francisco Banks

Outside of the express companies the principal private banking firms in 1849 were those of Henry M. Naglee, Burgoyne & Co., B. Davidson, Thomas G. Wells and James King of William. Naglee in company with a man named Linton, established the first bank on the coast on Jan. 9, 1849. In April, 1854, this number had increased to a round dozen, the banks in operation being those of Burgoyne & Co., B. Davidson, James King of William, Tallant & Wilde, Page, Bacon & Co., Adams & Co., Palmer, Cook & Co., Drexel, Sailer & Church, Robinson & Co., Sanders & Brenham, Carothers, Anderson & Co., Lucas Turner & Co.

Gold in Plenty but no Money

Although California in the first year after the discovery of gold produced over ten million dollars worth of that metal, and in 1850 $41,273,106, the annual output increasing to $81,294,700 in 1852, it actually suffered from a dearth of money, and various expedients had to be resorted to in order to secure a medium for the transaction of business. Large quantities of foreign coin were in circulation and passed without much attention being paid to its real worth. Pieces which approximated in size to those of a familiar American coin were accepted without demur as an equivalent of the coin they resembled, and in a land of gold, over which the Stars and Stripes floated, for quite a period about the only gold coins obtainable were English sovereigns.

This neglect of the government at Washington was partly remedied by the establishment of private assay offices where coins were minted of various denominations. Ingots varying in size, stamped by an assayer appointed by the state under authority of an act passed by the legislature April 20, 1850, were the nearest approach to a legal money until the secretary of the treasury made a contract with the firm of Curtiss, Perry & Ward to commence the assaying of gold. Coins were emitted by this firm, and although they were not recognized by the government they circulated commercially, as did those put out by firms wholly unauthorized to coin money. *Private Coinage*

There was considerable profit in this private coinage, and although it might easily have lent itself to serious abuses there do not appear to have been any frauds of consequence perpetrated. Fifty dollar pieces called "slugs" were issued with the stamp of the United States assayer. They were octagonal in form and somewhat thicker than a double eagle. There were also twenty-five dollar and twenty, ten and five dollar pieces. Although not a legal tender they were freely received, and no objection was made to the fact that they were as a rule worth less than their face value. With his customary disregard of small things the argonaut was quite ready to permit those who furnished him with a convenient medium of exchange, for which there was urgent need, to make a liberal profit, and he never thought it worth his while to challenge what was unmistakably an invasion of a governmental function most jealously guarded by other nations than the United States. *Profits of the Private Coiner*

There was much looseness of thought concerning the rights of buyer and seller of gold dust and bullion which may be attributed to the carelessness of the miner as much as to the greed of those with whom he dealt. Until the branch mint began to supply legal tender coins it was the custom to make purchases with dust and scales were a part of the paraphernalia of every store. As a rule bargaining was not indulged in, and if the miner happened to be particularly flush he was more apt to give the storekeeper the benefit of overweight than to exact an advantage from him. Large sums of money were made by firms making a specialty of buying gold dust, and a scandal of considerable magnitude was raised by a charge against Page, Bacon & Co., that they had improperly "cleaned up" about $100,000, the implication being that they had cheated their customers by manipulating the scales and undervaluing the fineness of the metal. *Buying and Selling Gold Dust*

On this latter score there was ample ground for complaint against the negligence of the government which not only failed to act promptly in the matter of supplying a convenient medium of exchange, but took advantage of its own laches to compel importers to settle customs duties on a basis which involved a loss to the merchant in many instances. In July, 1848, the government consented to receive gold dust in payment of duties at a very low figure, permitting the payer the right of redemption which was kept open for one hundred and eighty days. In December of the same year gold dust was dull of sale at $10.50 an ounce, although the price had been fixed at a public meeting held in the previous September at $16 an ounce. In view of the fact that the importers of coin made profits ranging from fourteen *Governmental Incapacity* to thirty per cent, that coins worth 19 cents circulated at 25 cents, Spanish reals of 12½ cents were valued at 15 cents, that the owner of gold dust was compelled to sacrifice heavily in selling owing to the uncertainties attending its quality, and that interest on loans made in coin soared heavenward, the pioneer may justly claim that he was the victim of governmental incompetency at a time when it was universally acknowledged that the stream of gold he was pouring into the channels of trade was exerting a revivifying influence and starting the world anew on a career of progress.

Business Highly Speculative

The modern sensitiveness concerning the quality of money apparently did not trouble the argonauts whose chief concern was to gather gold and secure a circulating medium of some sort, but there is little room for doubt that the crudity of the banking and monetary systems of the early Fifties contributed largely to the business troubles of the period by converting what should have been ordinary transactions into speculative ventures. All speculation not forbidden by law may be regarded as legitimate, but there was little commerce of the sort we now term "legitimate" in California up to the crash of 1855. There was no certainty that the intelligent application of knowledge and the exertion of energy in any given enterprise would produce reasonable returns; everyday commercial affairs were invested with the same elements of uncertainty as the hunting of gold which might or might not be rewarded with success. It was largely a question of luck, because the practical isolation of the City and coast made the business men of San Francisco dependent on the caprice and judgment of outsiders who rushed in goods without any knowledge of the requirements of the people they were serving.

Early Merchant Princes

It is astonishing that so many men proved their ability by weathering commercial storms more numerous and violent than those encountered elsewhere. The fact that they did so can only be explained by the enormous output of gold which aggregated $345,950,117 up to the close of 1854, and reached the enormous sum of $639,191,997 at the close of the decade. This permitted the taking of profits which under any other condition would have been regarded as abnormal, and they provided a margin for contingencies which were frequently occurring, and many that were of a character which could not be foreseen by the most sagacious. Hence we are not surprised that even as early as 1853 there were instances of success in business which warranted the writer of the "Annals" in asserting that many who had resorted to mercantile pursuits had become "merchant princes." While the term was not pure hyperbole, for there were merchants who had amassed sufficient wealth to attain to influential positions in the community, it must not be taken too literally, or as connoting all that we now attach to the designation. Things are to be regarded relatively, and when the pioneer tells us that there were fine stores and as big and varied stocks in San Francisco in the early Fifties as there are now, we must weigh the assertion with the qualification "in proportion to population." There were big stores with big stocks of goods, and curiously enough they were conducted on lines very similar to those of a modern department store, but they bore no nearer resemblance to the great modern marts of trade than a large country store of today does to one of those institutions.

Display of Merchandise

In no particular has merchandizing changed more than in the mode of displaying goods. That is wholly a modern development and owes its growth as much to the improvement in the production of plate glass as to increased competition. When the hundreds of vessels which entered the harbor in 1849 and 1850 and 1851, and disgorged their cargoes into the mercantile establishments of the City, there were goods in abundance, and the enthusiastic annalist was warranted in speaking of the stocks as covering the range of human desire, but that range was limited, comparatively speaking. A merchant whose career in San Francisco began in the early Fifties, and who still actively pursues his calling declares, that a thoroughly equipped modern store probably carries fifty times as great a variety of articles as the biggest establishment did in 1854, and that the present method of conducting business would have seemed absurdly complex to the pioneer merchant; and that most of the devices now resorted to in order to tempt customers and promote trade would have been scorned by them in the early days when simplicity and directness of dealing were the rule.

The interior of a big store in San Francisco in the early Fifties presented a picture of profusion rather than variety, and in no case was there any serious effort made by employers or clerks to impress by display. Goods were piled where it was found convenient to bestow them rather than with reference to attracting the attention of customers to their existence. The staple articles, now usually hidden in warerooms to be brought forward when demanded, were most in evidence. Big piles of flannel shirts, and other garments which the customer could not help being aware were to be had, were as often as not in the foreground, while articles of luxury were concealed in parts of the store only penetrated by the inquisitive. Mountains of barrels were kept in sight, but the bijoutre and other luxuries had to be dragged forth when demanded. Window displays were so uncommon as to be almost unknown, and other means of advertising were equally neglected. The trained clerk was a rarity, the salesmen and accountants being principally recruited from the ranks of unsuccessful gold seekers, and very often the employer was as ignorant of the selling art as his employee.

<small>A Big Store in Early Days</small>

It is perhaps to this latter fact that the long persistence of a custom of colleeting bi-monthly, which grew out of the necessity of making remittances on the sailing days of steamers is owing. When the line established by the Pacific Mail Steamship Company succeeded in making its schedules of departures for Panama perfectly dependable, the 1st and 16th of each month were fixed as collection days, and every business house sent out men to dun customers. The practice was not abandoned when other facilities for remitting were provided, and still endures despite the fact that numerous mails are daily dispatched to the Atlantic states. It never met with adverse criticism until very recent years, and is still defended as a useful custom on the ground that it keeps debtors in mind of their obligations.

<small>Credit System and Collection Days</small>

The conservatism implied by the long endurance of a business device of this character contrasts forcibly with the intensely speculative character of pioneer trading days, and when investigated discloses the cause of some of the anomalies which have puzzled students of early Californian peculiarities. Accepting the warning which the evil results of wildcat banking at the East held out, the framers of the first constitution deliberately hedged about the business of banking with obstacles which made a safe system impossible. The people became obsessed by the idea that no representative of money was safe, and insisted that only the precious metals should be used as a medium of exchange. They deemed it impossible to devise a scheme by which a representative of the metals could be made absolutely safe, because they ignored the fact that the underlying cause of wildcat banking in the East was the scarcity of basic money. They did not see that the abundance of gold in Cali-

<small>Some Odd Contradictions</small>

fornia made the creation of reserves possible, and that proper laws under the conditions created by successful placer mining would have enabled them to obtain and maintain an absolutely safe circulation.

Getting in Touch with the East   The attitude of the commercial element of San Francisco, and the people generally, towards paper money after the outbreak of the Civil war was in seeming contradiction to the earnest efforts inaugurated at an early day to bring the coast in closer touch with the states on the other side of the Rocky Mountains. It is sometimes assumed that the need for a transcontinental railroad was first felt when the slaveholder rebellion threatened to sever California from the Union, but that is an error. Although California by her specific contract act appeared to advertise to the world that she had no confidence in the integrity of the government's greenbacks, her refusal to receive them had no such significance. Long before 1861 California was earnestly seeking closer financial relations with the Atlantic states, and the necessity of linking the country together, so as to lessen the drawbacks of an isolation which every observant person clearly perceived, was generally recognized.

Early Ideas Concerning Railroads   The spontaneity with which ocean transportation was provided after the discovery of gold no wise weakened the belief that California would be vastly benefited by land connection with all other parts of the Union. The Pacific Mail and other transportation companies speedily furnished facilities which undoubtedly for a considerable period made an overland project seem visionary rather than practical, but the multiplication of sea lines did not divert attention from the possibilities of a more direct and rapid transit. It is interesting to note that when this possibility was first discussed the scope of desire was very modest. There were some who had visions of more than one transcontinental railroad, but usually the talk revolved about "a railroad." In his retiring message in 1851 Governor McDougal spoke of the railroad that had already been started in western Missouri and expressed the hope that congress would aid in forwarding the gigantic project to completion. He pointed out that the government owned immense bodies of fertile lands which lay waste and untenanted and said that by granting those portions lying along the line of communication the value of the remainder of the public domain would be greatly enhanced.

Railroad Talk in 1854   In 1854 a writer in discussing the question of routes declared that whichever one was selected San Francisco would be "the chief terminus on the Pacific," but a little later he sounded a warning note and said that Puget Sound offered commercial advantages nearly as great as those of the Bay of San Francisco, and that it would be unfortunate if the northern section got the start as the result would be to divert immigration from California. "Later," he added, "let through lines terminate where they will; only let our City have the first one." In the same year on April 10, Governor Isaac J. Stevens of Washington territory, lectured in San Francisco on "The Great Interoceanic Highway," and pointed out what would be accomplished "when the long talked of Atlantic and Pacific Railroad was finished." Three routes were spoken of at that time. The first was the Southern. It seemed to be the favorite, probably because it appeared to be the one best calculated to advance the interests of the South; and the general impression was that it had the best show of receiving aid on that account. It would have traversed Texas, New Mexico and Arizona, and San Diego bay would have been its terminus. The second was the Middle route, which starting in Missouri was to have ended at

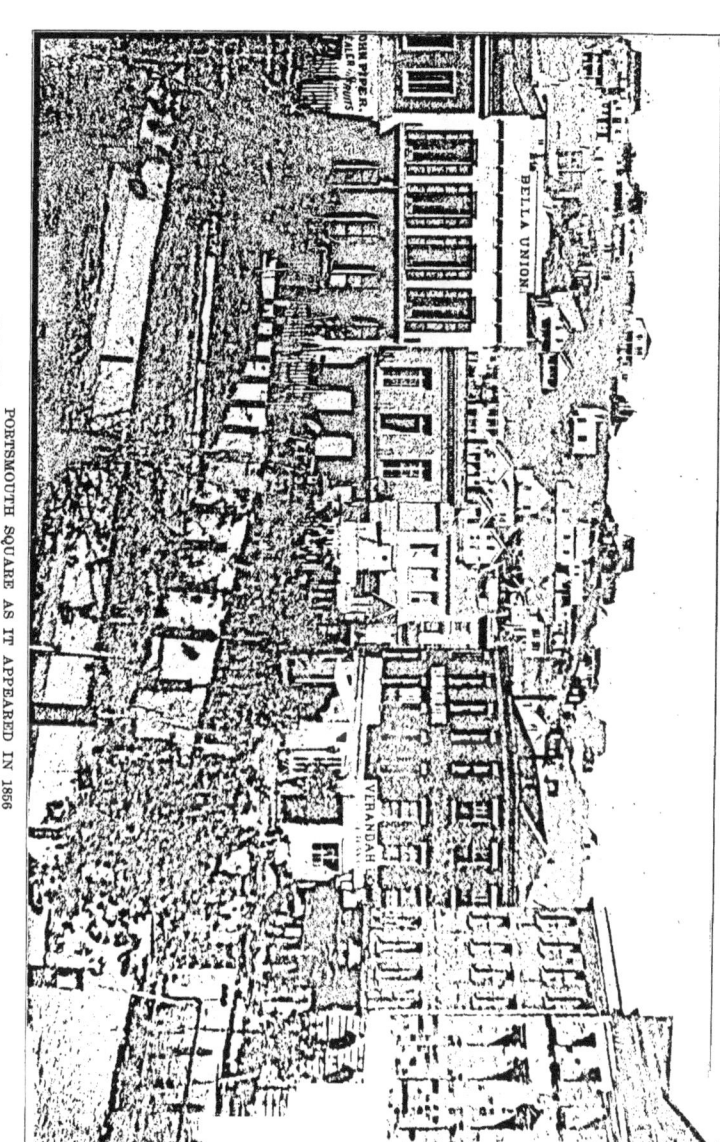

PORTSMOUTH SQUARE AS IT APPEARED IN 1866
Bella Union Theater at left; City Hall, formerly Jenny Lind Theater, on the right

some place on the Sacramento river, and the third was the Northern which would connect the basin of the St. Lawrence river with Puget Sound, passing along the lines of the Upper Missouri and Columbia rivers.

All of these projects were finally consummated, but not until many years after their enthusiastic advocates began talking of their possible accomplishment. The last spike of the first completed line which connected the Missouri river with Sacramento by rail was not driven until 1869, and not until after the scheme for its building had been made the battledore and shuttlecock of the politicians. The pro-slavery element was determined upon securing a line which would run south of the thirty-sixth parallel of latitude, and made it clear that unless that was conceded there should be no line at all. At no time was there any doubt expressed concerning the propriety of extending aid in the way of land grants. Northerners and Southerners were equally disposed to be liberal in that regard, the only hitch between them grew out of the choice of route. A Southern Transcontinental Line

That California had not as yet taken strong hold of the affections of the people of the state may be inferred from the fact that an important section of the community was quite ready to deprive the coast of the benefits of transcontinental communication rather than make any concessions which they thought would militate against the interests of the slaveholders. In the congress of 1858 lines were sharply drawn, and Broderick, who advocated the Central route was antagonized by Senator Gwin, who throughout the contest exhibited a far greater desire to advance the fortunes of the South than of the state he was chosen to represent. Perhaps the Southern contingent found some warrant for their action in the resolution passed at the first democratic meeting held in San Francisco on the 25th of October, 1849, which required candidates to vote for "an Atlantic and Pacific railroad through United States territory in preference to any other." Compliance with this demand would have necessitated adherence to the plan of Thomas H. Benton, but years afterward, when the situation had been completely changed by the purchase of the land comprising the present states of Arizona and New Mexico, the proviso lost its force, and the chief struggle was between the adherents of a route along the thirty-second parallel and those advocating a terminus at Sacramento. Undeveloped State Pride

Although discussion of transcontinental railway plans absorbed a great deal of public attention the people of San Francisco and the rest of the state did not concentrate all their hopes upon overland communication but were active supporters of schemes designed to put them in touch with the rest of the Pacific coast. They early appreciated the benefits to be derived from roads that would link the different sections of the coast together, and promoted enterprises which presented great difficulties owing to the vast distances intervening between the different nuclei of population. In 1848 when the news of the gold discovery reached Oregon, Burnett the first governor of California, organized a party which traveled overland from Oregon City to the Sacramento valley. The initial trip was attended with some difficulty, but the result was the mapping out of a road which was subsequently developed. In 1855 the legislature passed an act to build a wagon road over the Sierra, but it exceeded the debt limit provision in the organic law and was declared unconstitutional in 1857. Meanwhile, however, considerable work was done on the road, and obligations were incurred which the people by the decisive vote of Wagon Roads

288   SAN FRANCISCO

57,600 to 16,000 decided should be paid, sternly setting their faces against repudiation in any form.

Eager for Transportation Facilities

In 1855 the legislature was much occupied with the transportation question. The availability of the different passes was discussed and reports were made which showed the practicability of the state being entered by railroads at various points. A memorial was introduced at this session which had for its object anticipation of the service to be performed by a railroad or railroads. It proposed the establishment of an overland express by means of camels or dromedaries. The experiment was tried, but the "ships of the desert" did not prove a success, and horses were substituted for them, and later stage coaches were introduced. These facilities, however, were provided by individual effort, and were the only tangible results of the public discussions which continued during nearly twenty years. The political resolves adopted in 1849 were backed up by resolutions introduced and passed at almost every session of the legislature, the first being that suggested by John Bigler in 1850, urging on congress the importance of constructing a railroad from the Mississippi to the Pacific. The transportation literature of the period is voluminous, and only less entertaining than the story of the actual happenings after the railroad was finally built. Throughout it all there runs a vein of optimism which contrasts remarkably with the subsequent feeling engendered by the abuses which followed the advent of the first transcontinental line.

Benefits Expected

San Franciscans were more positive in the expression of the belief that a transcontinental line would work a great transformation in California than the other inhabitants of the state, but they failed to give their convictions practical effect. They were confident that it would make its fertile lands accessible to great numbers of immigrants who would produce on a scale which would speedily make San Francisco a trading port of consequence and a real metropolis. Its merchants had been long accustomed to viewing matters from the standpoint of the distributor, and they had visions of the development of a great Oriental traffic which would make the City the most prosperous one on the globe. No one apparently realized the possibility of the new method of communication destroying the advantages which came from comparative isolation. The railroad in the common belief would prove an unadulterated benefit; no one seemed to think of the possibility of its bringing trouble; even the laboring element of the community did not seriously regard the chance of its making a change in their condition.

High Freight and Fare Rates

We may discern the source of this optimism in the prevalent belief that in some fashion or other the transcontinental railway would bring relief from oppressive freight charges. How great a burden these were may be inferred from the message of Governor Bigler in 1854, in which he pointed out that the law allowed 20 cents per mile for passage, and 60 cents per ton for freight to steam navigation companies. He urged an amendment which would make a reduction of ten cents a mile for passage and 15 cents a ton for freight, and, evidently believing that the people were on the eve of securing the desired connection with the East, he warned the legislature that unless the reduction was made the railroad would be able to charge $500 for passage from the Missouri river to the coast; and $1,500 for hauling a ton of freight between the two points.

Ignorance Concerning Railroads

Theories respecting the management of railroads had not been highly developed at the time, but this recommendation, and the general attitude, indicates an almost total ignorance of the policy of "all the traffic will bear," which was subsequently elaborated by the organizers of what finally grew into the Southern Pacific system. That it could have been deemed possible for any sort of freight to bear a traffic charge of $1,500 a ton exhibits clearly that although the discussion was incessant, and took a range so wide as to even embrace the fear that unless the United States should hurry up Great Britain might get ahead of us by "building from Halifax to Lake St. Clair," it was not very illuminating. "Shall we yield the palm of building the longest railroad in the world to them?" asked a committee of the California senate, which reported a bill in May, 1852, granting the right of way to the United States for the construction of a road connecting the two oceans. "Never!" was the emphatic answer to its own query.

San Franciscans knew little about railroads in those days, and for that matter the fund of information concerning them was not large in the older communities. The first railroad in California was that built under the provisions of an act passed in 1853 and ran from Sacramento to Folsom. It was commenced in the early part of 1855 and was opened February 22, 1856. It did not prove profitable owing to the high cost of labor and the decline of the placer mines, and in 1865 fell into the hands of the Central Pacific after several vain efforts by different persons to make it pay. Until 1863, when the road between San Jose and San Francisco was opened, San Franciscans and California generally were utterly destitute of railroad experience, and it is not surprising that they raised false hopes for themselves, and made great blunders in dealing with the men who attained to knowledge more rapidly than they did, and made use of it to amass great wealth for themselves.

<small>Limited Railroading Experience</small>

The inaction of congress in promoting the railroad enterprise contrasts with the activity displayed by individuals in providing other means of transportation. The discovery of gold was promptly followed by a rush which called into requisition all sorts of sea craft, but this unorganized traffic was soon succeeded by regular lines. In a remarkably brief period there was as much certainty respecting the sailing days and arrivals of the steamships carrying passengers by way of the isthmus, or the Nicaragua routes as there is today. Not only was regularity secured in the traffic between San Francisco and the Atlantic states, great promptitude was also shown in the promotion of facilities for reaching the mining regions.

<small>Sea Transportation Regular</small>

After the sinking of "the steamboat" there was no steam navigation on the bay until speculators incited by the hope of profit, sent out an iron boat from the East, which was shipped in pieces and set up in San Francisco, making her first trip to Sacramento in September, 1849. This adventure was speedily followed by others. On the 9th of October a boat called "The Mint" started plying between San Francisco and the towns on the upper waters of the Sacramento. On the 26th a propeller called the "McKim" left the City for Sacramento. Prior to the appearance of these boats points on the Sacramento and San Joaquin rivers were reached by schooners and launches, their voyages often occupying as many as ten days. In 1854 the time had been reduced to about a half a day, and steamboats were making regular departures. The price of passage, which at first was $30 in the cabin and $20 on deck, was greatly reduced during the interval.

<small>An Early Traffic Combine</small>

In that year excessive competition brought about a combination which excited great indignation. The various steamboats plying on the bay, and on the inland waters, were brought under one management in a concern called the California Steam Navigation Company. It was organized with a capital of $2,500,000 in shares of $1,000 each. The merchants of the City denounced the amalgamation as

<small>The California Steam Navigation Company</small>

a dangerous monopoly, but took no practical steps to disrupt it by starting rival lines. The experience which led to the combination undoubtedly deterred fresh enterprises. At the height of the struggle between the companies, which later pooled their interests, passage became practically free, and on occasions the rivalry assumed the exaggerated form of offering meals to induce patronage. The rates of fare under the new arrangement were much lower than they were three or four years earlier, but they were still high enough to form a reasonable ground for protest. The cost of passage from San Francisco to Sacramento in the cabin was $10, on deck $7, and freight was carried at the rate of $8 a ton. To Marysville it was $12 in the cabin and $10 on deck, and freight was $15 a ton. The rate to Stockton for passengers was the same as that to Sacramento, but freight was taken at $2 a ton less.

Clipper Ships

The greatest development resulting from pioneer needs was that of the clipper ship. The story of the performances of these remarkable products of the skill of American shipbuilders is an ocean classic. Passages were made between New York and San Francisco by these vessels in as few as 89 days, the average being about 125 days. The "Flying Cloud" held the record up to 1854, making the trip from New York to San Francisco, around the Horn, in 89 days. In 1852, 72 vessels, averaging 1,000 tons burthen, all of them claiming to be clipper ships entered the port. But the glories of their performances were eclipsed by those of their rivals impelled by steam, and few but poets and "tars" lamented their disappearance. Indeed the sentimentally inclined pioneer was so impressed by the sight of a departing Pacific Mail steamer he was apt to indulge in superlatives and forget the clipper. It was the custom in the early days to see the steamer leave her wharf, and we have a vivid description of one of these events in the "Annals:" "Faster, proudly, triumphantly, with a continually accelerating speed. Oh it is a beautiful, a grand sight, such a majestic vessel exerting its enormous power and growing momently in strength and swiftness." The tribute was deserved, even though the majestic craft described would only make a good-sized launch for a modern liner such as now sails out of the port of San Francisco.

Travel by Way of Panama and Nicaragua

The distance from San Francisco to New York by way of Panama was about 5,700 miles and it required twenty-five days to make the trip. Up to the establishment of the Pony Express in 1860, all the Eastern mails, and for nearly twenty years up to the opening of the overland railroad most of the mails between the Atlantic and Pacific coast were carried by this route which was operated by the Pacific Mail Steamship Company. For a time it had a rival which made use of the waterways and territory of Nicaragua. A concern known as the Accessory Transit Company, the outgrowth of a contract originally made by Cornelius Vanderbilt and other New York capitalists with the Nicaraguan government, maintained an opposition line during four years which made semi-monthly passages between New York and San Francisco via Nicaragua. The Accessory Transit Company was later practically merged in the American Atlantic and Pacific Ship Canal Company in pursuance of a contract with the Nicaraguan government, which, among other things provided for the construction of a ship canal to connect the two oceans within a period of twelve years from April 11, 1850.

Nicaragua Ship Canal Project

This project had received governmental attention for many years, and it is not improbable that it might have been carried through had not the machinations of the filibuster Walker created complications which raised insuperable obstacles. In this work Walker was assisted by two California lawyers who sought to aid rivals of Vanderbilt in gaining possession of the steamship privilege which had become very profitable. The projectors of the ship canal disregarded their obligations, and juggled matters so that the Nicaraguan government received nothing for the concession. They made no effort to dig a canal, and thus furnished the excuse which Walker prompted Rivas, the president, to offer for canceling the contract and granting a new charter to Garrison, the rival of Vanderbilt, on the ground that the Accessory Transit Company had forfeited its rights. This new charter was granted by Rivas in February, 1856, but was kept a secret to permit Garrison to get in readiness new steamers to take the place of those which would be withdrawn. The proceeding was so complicated by chincanery that when Garrison sought to run the new line it at once became an object of distrust, and in a short time, although under the Vanderbilt regime it had done a profitable business, running semi-monthly steamers in and out of San Francisco, and carrying thousands of passengers, it was compelled to discontinue its operations.

Its rival the Pacific Mail continued to prosper. It had commenced the construction of a railroad across the Isthmus of Panama in 1850, but owing to excessive mortality among the working force, which hampered operations, the road was not opened until Jan. 23, 1855. The cost of the road, which was only 48 miles long, was originally estimated at only $2,000,000, but $7,000,000 were expended before it was finally completed. At one time it was feared by the projectors that the undertaking would swamp them, but the prospects of profit encouraged them to persevere, and profitable mail contracts ultimately repaired the losses incurred through the excessive cost of building. William H. Aspinwall, the moving spirit in the enterprise, was a New York millionaire who had interested himself in mail contracts before the discovery of gold. As early as 1845 a petition had been sent from Oregon asking for a mail service between that territory and New York. Aspinwall was a bidder at a subsequent call for proposals and received the contract through the default of parties who had bid lower than himself and associates. The service was to be monthly, by way of Panama, and subsequently, by act of congress in 1847, San Francisco was made a port of call. Aspinwall, together with Gardener Howland and Henry Chauncey incorporated the Pacific Mail Steamship Company April 12, 1848.

Building the Panama Railroad

Under the terms of the act of congress of 1847 the contractors carrying the mails to Oregon and California were to receive a subsidy of $200,000 per annum. They were to build the steamers to engage in the work under government supervision, and they were to be operated under the command of captains selected from the United States navy. The first steamers constructed were the "California," "Oregon" and "Panama," respectively 1,050, 1,120 and 1,058 tons burthen. They were propelled with side wheels and at that time there were few vessels on the Atlantic comparable with them in size, appointments or speed. The "California" was the first of the three to sail from New York, leaving that port for Panama via the Straits of Magellan on the 5th of October, 1848. While the "California" was making her way to the Pacific, preparations were made on the Atlantic side to establish a connection. A vessel named the "Falcon" was put in this service. She sailed from New York on the 1st of December, 1848, but the passengers she carried were obliged to wait twenty-five days in Panama for the arrival of the "California" whose passage occupied a much longer time than had been expected. The initial

The Pacific Mail Steamship Company

SAN FRANCISCO

Early Voyages of Pacific Mail Steamers

voyage of the "California" from Panama to San Francisco, owing to a coal shortage, took 28 days, but when she arrived in the port on the 28th day of February, 1849, she received a grand reception.

The time consumed in getting the passengers through from New York to San Francisco on this first trip was 89 days, including the detention of 25 days due to the failure to make connection with the "California." The 64 days of actual transit were subsequently largely reduced, but before it became possible to effect the reduction the company experienced great difficulty in maintaining its schedule. The crew of the "California" on her arrival in the harbor promptly deserted and made their way to the mines as did the most of the passengers. The next steamer of the line to arrive was the "Oregon." She left New York in December, 1848, and entered the harbor on the 1st of April, 1849, bringing 250 passengers who had made the long voyage through the Straits of Magellen. The "Panama" was to have been second, but did not enter until June 4, 1849, having 290 newcomers aboard.

First Arrivals by Steamer

Passenger lists are not, as a rule, very interesting, but those of the first two mail steamers entering the port of San Francisco contained so many names of men who afterward figured in the upbuilding of the City, they deserve reproduction if merely to emphasize the fact that fortune favors those who are prompt to seize an opportunity. Among the arrivals by the "California" whose names are part of the history of the city were General Persifer F. Smith, William Van Voorhees, Captain R. W. Heath, H. F. Williams, D. W. C. Thompson, Major Canby, Alexander Austin, Eugene Sullivan, E. T. Batters, Alfred Robinson, Mallachi Fallon, R. M. Price, Pacificus Ord, Levi Stowell and Cleveland Forbes. There were also four ministers, Sylvester Woodbridge, Presbyterian; O. C. Wheeler, Baptist; J. W. Douglas and S. H. Willey, Congregationalists. In the list of the "Oregon" are found the names of Dr. A. J. Bowie, R. P. Hammond, Dr. George F. Turner, Captain E. D. Keyes, Frederick Billings, F. D. Atherton, John Benson, A. K. P. Harmon, Rev. Albert Williams, Dr. Horace Bacon, D. N. Hawley, Captain M. R. Roberts, E. B. Vreeland, Dr. W. F. Peabody, John W. Geary, George H. Beach, William M. Lent, John T. Little, David Fay, J. Cowell, Samuel Blake, John T. Wright, A. J. Morell and Captain L. M. Goldsborough.

Rivals of Pacific Mail Company

In the last ten months of 1849 the passenger business of the Pacific Mail aggregated 3,959. It would have been extraordinary if such remunerative traffic had not tempted others to engage in the business. The Accessory Transit Company's efforts have already been mentioned, but there were numerous other rivals for patronage. In 1850 the number of steamers in the Panama trade had increased from 6 to 21 and the trips from 14 to 41, and the passengers carried from 3,959 to 7,118. In the succeeding year 30 steamers making 74 trips, and four lines in operation, were recorded. The number of steamers, however, does not begin to tell the story of increase, for the "Golden Gate" of 2,067 tons register, double the size of the first boats to ply in the Panama trade was put in service and she was able to accommodate 600 passengers.

Tonnage of Port in 1859

It would require a volume devoted to the special subject to tell the whole story of the maritime activities of the port in the first decade after the occupation. Here the attempt to describe them must be confined to the statement that in the closing year of the Fifties the tonnage of ocean arrivals aggregated 596,600 tons, of which 143,700 tons were steam. Of the total tonnage of 1859, 230,700 tons were registered as foreign and 365,900 as domestic. This expansion was nearly twelve fold during the decade, the registry showing a total of 50,000 tons in 1848; but the greatest increase occurred before the close of 1853, when 559,000 steam and sail tonnage was registered. After 1853 the greatest change noted was in the increase of steam tonnage, which rose from 98,400 to 143,700 tons in 1859.

The traffic indicated by these figures furnished ample justification for the decided strengthening of the belief, which at no time after the beginning of the gold rush had been at all weak, that San Francisco was destined to be a great commercial emporium. The point of view changed as new developments occurred. The disheartening effects of the disastrous fires of the first years of the City had passed away. No one in San Francisco at the beginning of the Sixties could be found to express himself as did a correspondent of the "Illustrated London News," who on July 5, 1851, describing the fire of May 3rd, said: "Whether San Francisco will ever *entirely* recover from the blow, is, I think, doubtful." There were no longer doubts about the future, but there was much uncertainty concerning how the future would work itself out. There was a great diversity of opinion, but it did not eventuate in the impairment of confidence, and to some extent the differences tended to promote the opposite feeling. The latter was based on the growing comprehension of the immense resources of the state, and in considering them all apprehension which might have been created by the diminishing returns from the mines disappeared.

After the drastic settlement of the municipal troubles in 1856 business men were freed from an incubus which affected initiative, and they were able to think intelligently and plan for the future. Their plans were not wholly dissociated from those of the rest of the mercantile world, but comparative isolation had its effect in shaping them, as it had in creating the opinion which frequently found expression later, that in some way California would be compelled to work out its own destiny. That this feeling should have existed is not at all surprising, and that it should have tended to obscure the possibilities of closer contact with the outside world is also not remarkable. There was steadfast faith in the future and it was not a faith wholly without works. The performances of the business men of San Francisco after 1856 were not spectacular, but they were effective, as was proved by the steady growth of the City after that date, not merely in population but in all those directions which contribute to the well being of a community anxious to take its place in the van of the army of civilization, and in the estimation of the outside world. Like the rest of the Union, the City of San Francisco, despite its remoteness from the political centers of the country, suffered from the depression produced by bad legislation on the eve of the Civil war. Its merchants received a severe blow, and the experiences of 1855 were repeated, but they passed through the crisis, and when the war did commence, fortuitous circumstances enabled them to recover from disaster more speedily than those of any other part of the Union.

CHAPTER XXXIII

JOURNALISM, LITERATURE, EDUCATION AND POLITICS OF PIONEER DAYS

NEWSPAPERS OF SAN FRANCISCO—PRESS AT TIME OF GOLD DISCOVERY—NEWS BEFORE THE AMERICAN CAME TO CALIFORNIA—THE FIRST NEWSPAPER MERGER—VIOLENCE OF EDITORIAL EXPRESSION—FREEDOM OF THE PRESS—EDITOR KILLED IN A DUEL—JOURNALISM AN UNPROFITABLE CALLING—DRIVING RIVALS FROM THE FIELD—NOT MUCH STRESS LAID ON NEWS—EDITORIAL WRITERS DURING THE FIFTIES—USE OF THE TELEGRAPH—NEWS RECEIVED BY STEAMER—MAILS RECEIVED BY STAGE AND PONY EXPRESS—JOURNALISM AND LITERATURE CLOSELY ALLIED—VARYING LITERARY STANDARDS—POLITICS AND LITERATURE—EARLY LIBRARIES—FIRST PUBLISHED BOOK—THE WEEKLY PAPERS—A WOMAN'S JOURNAL—GOLDEN ERA SCHOOL OF LITERATURE—EDUCATIONAL FACILITIES—THE PUBLIC SCHOOLS AND THE HIGHER EDUCATION—PAROCHIAL AND PRIVATE SCHOOLS—POLITICS AND THE SCHOOLS.

Newspapers of San Francisco

N TRACING the progress of events in San Francisco its public journals have been mentioned, not always in a manner calculated to impress one with the idea that journalism was an unmixed blessing. In the Fifties the newspapers were almost as turbulent as the times in which they were printed. Their editors and publishers were not always disposed to pour oil on the troubled waters. As a rule they pursued a course which might be fittingly described as adding fuel to the flames. In this respect, however, their conduct did not differ materially from that of those pursuing a like calling at the East, but the result oftener proved tragic in the new metropolis of the Pacific.

An Intensely Partisan Press

The early newspapers were intensely partisan and devoted a great deal of their space to the discussion of political questions. They were able to spare it because the art of news gathering had not been developed to any extent at the time, and the facilities for procuring intelligence were limited. Before the gold rush there was published under the auspices of Samuel Brannan a small sheet of four pages, fifteen by twelve inches in size. The editor, E. P. Jones, probably having in mind the former relations of Brannan with the Mormons, announced that sectarianism would be avoided in its columns. It was called "The Star," and it made its first appearance on January 7, 1847. On the 22d of May following, a weekly newspaper, printed in Monterey as early as August, 1846, from an old font of Spanish type, from which the w's were missing; was moved to Yerba Buena. It was published by Robert Semple, but appears to have been the selected organ of the military occupants of the country.

Effect of Gold Discovery on Journalism

These two papers filled the want of the period, and would probably have remained the sole exponents of public opinion for a long time had not the discovery of gold changed conditions, injecting energy into an occupation that hardly had an existence in San Francisco before 1849. The change did not come suddenly, for the editors and typesetters deserted their posts when the reports of the find at Sutter's fort reached them, and it was some months before they returned to their duties. Their desertion is one of the rare instances in American journalism of newspaper men abandoning their work, and was more due to the absence of that discipline which characterizes the modern news gathering organization than to the avarice of those employed in making these pioneer papers.

News Before the "Gringo" Came

Prior to 1849 news traveled very slowly in California. The journal of a navy chaplain, written in Monterey, states that, although gold was found in January, 1848, nothing was heard of the discovery until the ensuing May. When the news was received at the ancient capital it was through some such channel as had served for the dissemination of intelligence in California from the days when the chain of missions was first established. Who the bearer of the momentous bit of news was is not recorded, but it was probably someone who had occasion to visit Monterey on a business errand. At least it is certain that it was not specially transmitted to the little hamlet by the sea; that all came later.

Printers Desert Their Cases

The "Californian" temporarily suspended publication on the 29th of May, 1848, and in the following month the "Star" imitated its example. The subscribers of the "Californian" were treated to an apology, accompanied by an explanation that everyone had gone to the diggings. It is not impossible that the flight was for the purpose of getting information, for on the 15th of July, the "Californian" again made its appearance. The major part of the resumed issue was devoted to describing the rush to the diggings, but enough space was spared to announce that "the whole world was at war," and to give some faint idea of the extent of the revolutions in Europe which threatened to overturn all the monarchies of that continent.

A Journalistic Merger

Before the close of the year the "Star" and "Californian" were merged, and on the 4th of January, 1849, they dropped their hyphenated name and the "Alta California" was born. Other ventures soon followed. Some of them had an ephemeral existence, the support being less liberal than might have been expected, considering the free handed manner of the miners in getting rid of their "dust." On the 22d of January, 1850, the "Alta" was published as a daily, the first on the Pacific coast. The next day the "Journal of Commerce" imitated the example of the "Alta." A few weeks later the "Pacific News" entered the daily field and on the 1st of June a new candidate for favor, the "Herald," made its appearance and soon became very popular. On the first of August an evening paper, called the "Picayune," was issued. It was followed soon after by the "Balance" and the "Courier."

Intemperate and Violent Expression

From the beginning pioneer journalism was marked by violence of expression and a virulent personalism. In the columns of the "Herald" may be found the most scathing denunciations of the municipal officials who participated in the salary grab of that year. The men excoriated perhaps deserved all the epithets applied to them, but it is astonishing that at a time when those with grievances were so ready to resent them allowed the attacks to pass without other notice than that embodied in mild attempts at justification in the rivals of the "Herald," who were not so vigor-

SAN FRANCISCO   297

ous nor insistent in denouncing the salary grab as the paper which inaugurated the crusade.

What was called the freedom of the press received much more consideration in the Fifties than at present. In 1851 William Walker, the leader of the filibusters, was editor of the "Herald." He made a feature of attempting to reform the judiciary, and proceeded by direct methods in the accomplishment of his object. His assaults on a judge, Levi Parsons, who deserved what was said of him, caused him to be haled into court by Parsons, who fined him for contempt. Walker refused to pay and was committed to prison. Great excitement ensued, the community apparently siding with the editor, who was released on *habeas corpus*. It was urged that Parsons had abused his position, and that his remedy, if he had a grievance against Walker, was a libel suit. The legislature, as a result of the agitation growing out of the affair, began impeachment proceedings against Parsons, but after inquiry decided that the evidence did not afford sufficient grounds for such a course. *Freedom of the Press*

It is sometimes assumed that the journalism of the ante bellum period was of a solid character, and wholly free from the frivolities of the present day newspaper, but no candid investigator will reach such a conclusion. The editors of San Francisco in the Fifties did not differ essentially in their methods from the example set by their brethren in the Atlantic states, and the contemporary verdict was against their seriousness and veracity. In 1851 the writer of the "Annals," in summing up the newspaper situation, remarked, "A dozen daily papers by hint, innuendo, broad allusion and description, considerably assist in the promulgation and spreading of idle tales." This was not the verdict of a writer disposed to find fault with journalists, for he was one of the cult. He stated a simple fact which a modern critic, noting in the old files such attempts at facetiousness as the insertion of divorces in the lists of marriages and deaths, and the publication of family dissensions before they became public property by being carried into the courts, would say was amply supported by the evidence. These stories of domestic jars, which were often told in the tersest manner, however, provoked less trouble for the papers and their authors than the fiery comments of their editors on politicians, and their attacks on their rivals. These were productive of a number of duels, in which the editor usually got the worst of it, perhaps because he was more proficient with his pen than with a pistol. *Idle Gossip Disseminated*

In August, 1852, the senior editor of the "Alta," Edward Gilbert, was killed in a duel growing out of attacks made on the administration of Bigler, who found a champion in General J. W. Denver of Oak Grove, Sacramento county. Less than two years after the rival editors of the "Alta California" and "Times Transcript" exchanged shots, one of them receiving a bullet in his body. The affair of James King of William, which resulted in his death at the hands of a rival editor, has been described in another place. It is usually associated in the minds of pioneers with the Vigilante uprising of 1856, but the tragedy had a more direct connection with the most vicious feature of early journalism than it did with the punishment of criminals and the reformation of society. *Editor Killed in a Duel*

James King of William bore no resemblance to the twentieth century newspaper man. In his salutatory he announced that he had not adopted journalism from choice, but that necessity had driven him into the business. That he did not mean financial necessity may be inferred from the fact that he added that no one could be more fully sensible than himself of the folly of a newspaper enterprise as an *A Journalist from Necessity* investment of money. What he meant was contained in the menacing statement: "It has been whispered to us that some parties are about pitching into us. We hope they will think better of it. We make it a rule to keep out of a scrape as long as possible; but if forced into one we are 'thar,' *entiende?*"

Intemperate Language

It is not astonishing that this announcement and adherence to the policy outlined should have produced trouble, but it also brought circulation to the "Bulletin." In a month after the printing of the salutatory it printed nearly 2,500 copies, and in less than two months its circulation was the largest in the City, reaching nearly 3,500 copies, and its patronage went on increasing until its power and influence outstripped that of all of its rivals. It suited the temper of the times and the people who loved "scraps" more than news, and pleased a community which was hungry for diversion. The language used by James King of William was intemperate to a degree scarcely dreamed of in these days, and his comment took a wider range than is now permissible, as may be inferred from this quotation: "If the jury which tries Cora is packed, either hang the sheriff or drive him out of town and make him resign. If Billy Mulligan lets his friend Cora escape hang Billy Mulligan or drive him into banishment."

Invective Fails to Reform

The integrity of James King of William's motives was never assailed, and the Vigilante uprising indicates that his methods, no matter how extreme they may seem to us, were approved by a vast majority of the community. We may deprecate the fact that he covered with ridicule Broderick, who afterwards became, if not a popular idol, at least a greatly honored man, evidence of the inconsistency of a democracy. But changes in point of view do not blunt the point of truth. King charged Broderick with being connected with municipal steals, and declared that all of his efforts to secure power were for unholy purposes; and he covered with invective the boss' associates and others who were engaged in plundering the public. But curiously enough, virulent denunciation and unrelenting exposure did not move the people, who applauded James King of William's utterances, to resort to the peaceful remedy at their command. They did not act until the editor was killed, and their procedure then took on the appearance of meting out punishment to a rival newspaper rather than the satisfaction of justice.

Driven from the Newspaper Field

As a result of the killing of James King of William the "Herald" was driven out of business. Up to the time of the collision with the "Bulletin" the "Herald" had been a prosperous paper, and was well supported by the mercantile community. The "Herald" was unquestionably superior in many respects to the paper edited by James King of William and had enjoyed the favor of a fickle community for some years, but when the Vigilance Committee passed a resolution pledging all its members to withdraw their advertisements from the "Herald" it met with little opposition. The head of the Vigilante organization had the good sense to recognize that its action would be regarded, not as directed against the murderer of James King of William, but as an effort to curb the liberty of the press and to punish a paper for expressing its disapproval of the Vigilante movement, which he said it had a perfect right to do. His remonstrances, however, proved unavailing and the "Herald" was obliged to suspend publication.

Press Encourages Filibustering

While the press of pioneer days was never remiss in the duty of pointing out and denouncing municipal abuses, it was not so keen to expose or condemn attempted aggressions on neighboring countries. To the contrary it applauded and stimulated men like Walker in their efforts to steal from sister republics, and looked with tolerance on many things which are now made the objective of the assaults of the modern editor. The reformers of the Fifties pursued tactics which in many respects resembled those of the present-day advocates of the exemplary punishment of abusers of the public trust. They indulged in invective; made exposures, and called on the courts to put offenders in jail, but they rarely attempted to convince the good citizens, who were sufferers from maladministration of public affairs, that their inattention to civic duty was at the bottom of their trouble.

In the discussion of political questions the editors of the Fifties were particularly strong. Their columns contained many able presentations of the burning questions of the period, but they were not noted for their news gathering proclivities. This neglect was a feature of early journalism of which those responsible for it were wholly unconscious. It is related of a publisher, whose newspaper career began in pioneer days, that as late as 1877 he was under the impression that one man constituted an adequate reportorial force; but while his paper was never much burdened with news it always contained long and satisfying screeds on the principles of democracy.

Editorials a Leading Feature

Evidently there was no demand for what the modern calls news, or it would have been responded to in the Fifties, if competition were capable of producing such a result. At the close of 1853 there were twelve daily papers in San Francisco, two tri-weeklies, six weeklies, one Sunday Journal and a commercial sheet. Judging from the stirring accounts of the pernicious activity of the criminal class, the reporter would have found ample opportunity for the exercise of his talents in descriptive, had his inclination tended in that direction, but detail and artistic verisimilitude were not in his line. A striking characteristic of nearly all the reporting of the period was that sort of compactness which oftener results from inability to see things than the desire for conciseness. In short, reporting in the Fifties was a neglected art, or perhaps it would be nearer the truth to say that the newspapers had not discovered its possibilities. It can hardly be said that the pioneer editor's idea of journalism was derived from a study of French papers, but in many particulars the newspaper of the Fifties resembled those produced in Paris more nearly than the later products of this country. Great stress was laid on the necessity of providing theatrical criticism of the kind which deals in analysis of the motives of the playwright as well as the actor, and space was often found for abstruse discussions of mooted historical questions. Articles showing great erudition were favored, and there was relatively a much greater recognition of the value of classical models than at present.

Plenty of Rivalry

The editors of the Fifties were much addicted to literature, and as a rule esteemed the ability to produce a story or write verse, as of more consequence than the other qualities which later came to be in great demand in newspaper offices. An extended list of men who at one time or another wrote for the "Sacramento Union" in its palmy days, and afterward drifted to San Francisco, discloses the names of several who attained distinction in politics or at the bar, and the most of them were unusually facile producers, and not a few were masters of invective, a style in great demand, the possession of which established the reputation of the possessor as a great writer. Among the most noted of the writing editors of this period were Newton Booth, who became governor and later United States senator, Samuel Seabough, Lauren Upson, Joseph Winans, Henry Clay Watson, Noah Brooks, Mark Twain, Lauren E. Crane, Henry E. Highton, James L. Watkins, Charles Henry

Editorial Writers in the Fifties

Webb, A. P. Catlin, Theodore H. Hittell, Benjamin F. Washington and William Bausman. They were all forceful writers, but the most of them were more disposed to regard journalism as a stepping stone to something else rather than as a profession; and few of them had the all around training which would have qualified them to fill a reporter's position, although they were possessed of superior literary attainments.

Fixed Convictions of Editors

As vehicles for the expression of public opinion the early papers performed their part more thoroughly than the modern newspaper, which pays more attention to the gathering and dissemination of news than it does to the censorship of the acts of public officials. The sanctum in the Fifties was usually a political headquarters, and those who penetrated it did so to confer with the editor, who not infrequently assisted in the shaping of policies. Nonpartisan journalism of the modern kind was absolutely unknown. No San Francisco editor of the Fifties was without settled opinions when national questions were being discussed. Some of them were willing to put aside partisanism when municipal matters were concerned, but they were all ready to express themselves with vigor on the subject of the extension of slavery, which was the burning question of the day, and they would have regarded with surprise the assumption that abstention from a fixed conviction concerning it constituted an exhibition of independence.

Use of the Telegraph

In October, 1852, an ordinance was passed granting the right of way to the California Telegraph Company to construct a line between San Francisco, San Jose and other points in the interior, but it was late in the following year before it was completed. In September, 1853, a short line was constructed connecting San Francisco with Point Lobos, which was used for the purpose of giving information concerning shipping movements. Up to this time the earliest intelligence respecting arrivals was received from a station on Telegraph hill, which was supported by voluntary contributions. It does not appear that the telegraph was made much use of by the press at any time prior to the completion of the line between the Missouri and San Francisco, which occurred October 1, 1861.

News Received by Steamer

There was great rivalry during the period prior to the establishment of the Pony Express and the Overland Stage Line in the matter of presenting the news received by steamer from the Atlantic states. Condensations were made, and when there was intelligence of unusual importance great haste was made to get it on the streets. These condensations were followed by more careful digests in the regular issues of the paper. The most of these show excellent judgment in selection, and a better sense of proportion than is exhibited in the modern newspaper, which too frequently in the presentation of the news subordinates the interesting to the important.

Mails by Stage and Pony Express

In 1858 a stage line was established which connected San Francisco and St. Louis. It was known as the Butterfield route and ran through Arizona, New Mexico, Texas and Arkansas. Stages departed twice a week, but there was no gain in the matter of time over the steamship passage, but it gave the editor, and the people generally, improved mail facilities, there being eight arrivals monthly by stage as against two by steamer. Greater expedition in the transmission of special mail was secured by the establishment of what was known as the Pony Express. The best time made by the Butterfield route was 21 days, but by putting on relays of riders, who carried a mail pouch an average distance of 75 miles daily, the time between St. Joseph, Missouri, and Sacramento was reduced to nine days, and on

VIEW DOWN SACRAMENTO STREET TOWARD THE BAY IN 1856

extraordinary occasions to less than eight days. Lincoln's message of March, 1861, was brought through in 7 days and 17 hours.

The Pony Express was regarded as a great institution and deservedly so. It employed in its service nearly three hundred persons and over five hundred horses. There were eighty riders whose average performance was about 75 miles, but there is a record of one who rode 384 miles without stopping, except for meals and to change horses at stations. The rider's occupation was extra hazardous as well as arduous, for the country was infested with hostile Indians, but they were fearless men and did their work in a fashion that excited the admiration of the pioneer, who had a keen appreciation of the dangers and difficulties they encountered. When the first mail by this route reached Sacramento on April 13, 1858, both houses of the legislature adjourned, and when the bearer of the pouch arrived in San Francisco at one o'clock on the morning of April 14th, he was received with bands of music and a torchlight procession. The Pony Express carried two mails a week, limited to 200 letters. The postage was $5 for half an ounce, and all sorts of devices were resorted to by patrons to get the worth of their money. Tissue paper was generally used, and the newspapers with the aid of cipher codes were enabled to make a single letter go a great way in providing copy. A short time prior to the starting of the Pony Express a wire had been run from San Francisco to Stockton, and from thence through the San Joaquin valley and over the mountains to Los Angeles. The newspapers were active in promoting this enterprise, their object being to anticipate the arrival of the overland stage, but the successful operation of the Pony Express made the effort valueless so far as anticipating intelligence from the East was concerned and it was of very little value in developing a fresh source of news, for there was little of consequence happening in the southern counties of the state in the Fifties.

<small>The Pony Express</small>

Journalism and literature were so closely allied in the Fifties it is impossible to discuss them apart. Nearly all the editors of the decade were much more interested in *belle lettres* than news gathering, and in some fashion or other every man of letters who made his mark in California in the early days was usually identified with daily journalism. It may be said in general that they were responsive to the desire of the times, which sought entertainment in the columns of the press rather than news. A facetious account of an occurrence was apt to receive much more attention than one adhering strictly to facts, and if pointed with satire it was certain to obtain a wide recognition. Later writers have often expressed surprise that some of the brightest lights produced by California did not enjoy a greater degree of appreciation when they first wrote, and the failure is attributed to various causes, among them the inability of the pioneer element to recognize value in a local effort. The criticism is merely a variant on the saying that a prophet is without honor in his own land, and is not deserving of serious consideration because it implies something that was not true. It is no more possible to truthfully assert that Bret Harte, Mark Twain, J. Ross Browne and some others who made their impress were not appreciated, because the world subsequently recognized and made much of them, than it would be to say that Charles Dickens was neglected by the British because Americans bought more of his books and were more generally acquainted with his stories than his own countrymen.

<small>Journalism and Literature Allied</small>

The pioneers did not lack appreciation, nor were they disposed to neglect those who worked in the literary field. But the community was small, and its isolation

<small>Appreciative Pioneers</small>

deprived it of the stimulus which comes from general approbation. Without that it is impossible for a man to achieve literary or any other sort of reputation than the purely local. That the really creditable performances of early California writers were estimated at their real worth by San Franciscans, is proved by the fact that their first judgments were in many cases indorsed by the whole literary world, and the other fact that they not infrequently rated the productions of their authors above their real value only proves that like the rest of mankind they were not always able to distinguish between that which had enduring qualities, and the other kind, which like the average "best seller," obtains only temporary vogue.

Varying Literary Standards

But while the humor and other distinctive qualities of such men as Twain and John Derby were instantly appreciated by San Franciscans, it is apparent that they were very tolerant of productions which would now be deemed silly. One of the earliest "poets" of San Francisco, who attained the distinction of being regarded as a biting satirist, wrote some verses which won the applause of the City, and procured for him a place in the custom house. The collector of the port, whose name was King, had procured the dislike of the people after the fire of May 5, 1851, by removing the custom house treasure, under a heavy guard, to a new location. The ostentatiousness of the performance excited the mirth of the pioneers, and one of them, named Frank Ball, burst forth in song. This is a specimen verse:

"Come listen a minute, a song I'll sing,
Which I rather calculate will bring
Much glory and all that sort of thing,
On the head of our brave collector, King.
Ri tu di nu, Ri tu di nu,
Ri tu di nu di na."

Doggerel Appreciated

It is recorded that copies of this song sold freely at $1 a piece, but the most interesting fact connected with its publication is the disclosure of the extreme sensitiveness of a public official to ridicule. Apparently Collector King's vulnerable point was found by the poet. Indeed ridicule was a more potent weapon in 1851 than invective, and was resorted to by men with facile pens to accomplish their purposes. A Dr. D. G. Robinson, editor of the "Dramatic Mirror," attained such popularity by writing a lot of doggerel directed at the municipal officials and prominent men in the community that in the campaign of 1852 he was seriously proposed as the popular candidate for mayor.

Politics and Literature

It would be unwise to regard these manifestations of approval in any other light than as political ebullitions. They were not indicative of the literary status of the period, but they unmistakably point to the existence of a public opinion which could be easily aroused, and excite wonder that in a community so responsive it should have at any time been deemed necessary to resort to the drastic methods of the Vigilantes to effect reforms. We can better judge the trend of thought in literary matters by considering the efforts made for its advancement, and the support which was given to movements looking to the improvement of the public mind, than by considering it in its relation to politics. When we do this we discover that prompt attention was given by the pioneers to the importance of preserving data in order to secure historical accuracy. The California Society of Pioneers, organized in August, 1850, put forward as one of its principal objects "the collection and pres-

SAN FRANCISCO

ervation of information connected with the settlement and conquest of the country."

It has incidentally been noted that the volunteer fire organizations, some of which early housed themselves in substantial and attractive looking buildings, provided themselves with libraries for the use of members. On the 1st of March, 1853, the first public library, known as the Mercantile Library Association was formed. It was a movement in response to a general demand expressed in meetings and was followed by the collection of books. Its first officers were: David S. Turner, president; J. P. Haven, treasurer; C. E. Bowers, recording secretary; R. H. Stephens, corresponding secretary. Dr. H. Gibbons, E. E. Dunbar, J. B. Crockett, D. H. Haskell and E. P. Flint constituted the directory. The Mercantile Library Association had a checkered existence and contributed more than one item to the annals of the City before it passed out of existence, some of which will be dealt with later. In the ensuing year, December 11, 1854, a meeting was held in the office of the city tax collector to consider the propriety of starting a library which was to combine with the dissemination of books the promotion of the industrial arts. On March 6, 1855, a constitution and by-laws were adopted, and on March 29th the Mechanics institute was practically inaugurated by the election of officers. The first president was B. F. Heywood. The room of the library was on the fourth floor of a building on the corner of Montgomery and California streets from whence it moved to California near Sansome street. The beginnings of the library were exceedingly modest. For a time it was largely made up of public documents, but later it expanded and the field of its activities were so extended that it became an important factor in the growth and development of the City. Another library, which came into existence about the same time, was that of the Odd Fellows, which was organized in 1854. It was supported by voluntary contributions, and its fund for the purchase of books was limited. It was only designed to meet the literary needs of members of the association and never attained importance as a collection. There may have been private libraries worth mentioning as distinctive in the years preceding the Civil war, but they were unknown to fame. There were, however, book lovers who began to make collections at a very early date whose success will be referred to when the literary activities of a later period are described.

Early Libraries

If a directory may be dignified by the appellation "book," that published by Charles P. Kimball in 1850 deserves mention as the first emitted from a San Francisco press. It was a duodecimo of 136 pages and contained in the neighborhood of 2,500 names. Two years later James A. Parker issued a directory containing about 9,000 names, which may be consistently included in a discussion of the literature of the early Fifties because it contained a sketch of the rise and progress of the City, which a contemporary critic pronounced a creditable performance, and which he predicted "would become curious and interesting after the lapse of a few years," especially as San Francisco was "a rapidly increasing community."

The First Directory

San Francisco, however, was not dependent upon directories, libraries or daily newspapers for its literary pabulum. The weekly literary journal and magazines were early in the field, and they were well supplied with contributions which were oftener than otherwise voluntary, and under no circumstances were well paid for by the publisher, who was usually glad to make even financially, which he could not have done had he added payment for contributions to his "legitimate" expenditures. The first magazine published was "The Pioneer." It appeared in 1854.

The Literary Weeklies

Its founder was Ferdinand C. Ewer. Ewer contributed largely to his own publication, and wrote a story which had more than ordinary merit. His attainments were varied. Among other talents he possessed that of theatrical discernment, and greatly impressed Edwin Booth, whose future he predicted. Later Ewer took orders and built Grace church, from which he was called to the rectorship of Christ church in New York. He was infected by the High Church movement and preached a number of sermons on the failure of Protestantism which attracted much attention at the time.

Contributors to Literary Periodicals Among the contributors to Ewer's magazine were Colonel George Derby (the author of "Phoenixiana"), John Swett, Frank Soule (the author of the "Annals of San Francisco"), John S. Hittell and Stephen Massett. Edward Pollock, whose verses were considered of sufficient merit to be embraced in collections of poems, appeared occasionally in its pages. The "News Letter," established by Frederick Marriott in 1856, was in many respects a more virile publication than most of its contemporaries and predecessors. Its proprietor early developed the faculty of getting into trouble by using too much freedom in dilating upon the shortcomings of his fellow citizens who sometimes took a shortcut towards reparation by means of physical violence.

A Woman's Journal Quite a different publication was the "Hesperian," a journal issued by women. It made its appearance in 1859 and was to some extent the outcome of a feminist movement. The "Hesperian" furnishes an interesting example of the prevalence of sectional jealousy during the period. It differed from the purely literary ventures of the time in the matter of giving attention to local interests and took up the cudgels for San Francisco when a paper published in the City of Angels declared that it would be impossible for feminine literature to thrive in the atmosphere of the bay. The rejoinder of the "Hesperian" may not have completely refuted the assumption of the jealous southland, but it conclusively proved the loyalty of the editor of the magazine to San Francisco.

Local Color in Literature It has been remarked that the early productions of the writers for the magazines lacked local color, an assertion well borne out by an examination of the contents of the publications of the Fifties, which show a decided predilection on the part of authors for other places than California in which to set their scenes. All the writers, however, were not obnoxious to that charge. Some of them indeed, if the critics of the period may be depended upon applied it much too liberally. In a list of names provided by a diligent investigator of the literature of the Fifties we find those of many whose work was wholly devoted to depicting California peculiarities, which were not always tenderly treated.

Golden Era School of Writers In her "Story of the Files," Ella Sterling Cummins describes the period between 1852 and 1858 as "the Golden Era school of literature." A periodical known as the "Golden Era" flourished during those years, and at one time or another it contained contributions from all the early writers of note. It was edited by J. Macdonough Foard, Rollin M. Daggett, Joseph E. Lawrence, James Brooks, Gilbert A. Densmore, John J. Hutchinson, J. M. Bassett, Herr Wagner and E. T. Bunyan. They were all diligent contributors, but did not occupy its pages to the exclusion of outsiders, for Francis Bret Harte, Mark Twain, Joaquin Miller, Charles Warren Stoddard, Joseph T. Goodman, Orpheus C. Kerr, Thomas Starr King, Prentice Mulford and Richard Henry Savage were frequently represented by contributions. In addition to the numerous male contributors of the "Golden Era" there was a bright galaxy of feminine stars, among them Minnie Myrtle Miller, Ada Isaacs Menken, Ina Coolbrith, Alice Kingsbury and Anna M. Fitch, who hardly deserve to be included in the sweeping indictment of J. Macdonough Foard, who when asked to name the cause of the death of the "Golden Era" said: "I will tell you; we made our mistake when we let the women write for it. Yes, they killed it with their namby pamby school girl trash." There was a great deal of writing fairly deserving the designation "namby pamhy," but it was not all the product of feminine pens, nor was it altogether unappreciated. It was much the same sort of stuff emitted by Gleason's "Literary Companion" at the East, and that written by sentimental poets on the other side of the Atlantic. California's only offense was committed in not escaping the epidemic.

Early Educational Facilities

A community in which newspapers and magazines flourish, and whose citizens take an active interest in the creation of libraries, may naturally be trusted to vigilantly care for the education of the young. San Francisco was never deficient in this regard. From the establishment of the first public school on the 3d of April, 1848, to the present day, the record of the system has been one of continuous growth, which has scarcely been interrupted even by the calamitous fires that have at times visited the City. But while fire and earthquake were powerless to interfere with the orderly development of education, it is related that when the gold discovery was reported the schools had to be closed because parents deserted the City, taking their children with them and leaving no pupils for the teachers to expend their energies upon. The teacher of this first school was Thomas Douglas, who received a salary of $1,000 a year and taught both sexes. Prior to the opening of Douglas' school, under the auspices of the town council, a man named William Marston taught some 30 pupils, who paid for their tuition. Marston was not an educated man but was able to impart the rudiments of learning to his scholars, who were accustomed to assemble in a small shanty on the block between Broadway and Pacific streets west of Dupont. Late in 1847 a schoolhouse was built on the corner of Portsmouth square facing Clay street, and in it were held the first church meetings of the Protestants and of such organizations as the Odd Fellows. Still later it was made to do duty as a courthouse.

Birth of Public School System

The birth of the public educational system of the City practically dates from the foundation of a school by J. C. Pelton, who arrived from Massachusetts in the autumn of 1849, and furnished the Baptist church for the accommodation of pupils. Mr. Pelton was assisted by his wife. They at first depended on voluntary contributions which, however, were not generous enough to provide a proper support, and in the spring of 1851 they made application to the town council for relief, which was granted in the form of a salary allowance of $500 monthly, to be paid out of the city treasury, although the municipality did not interfere with the management. The Peltons had about 150 pupils, and their school was public in name if not actually a public institution.

Increased School Facilities

In 1851 the council passed an ordinance dated September 25th, providing for the creation of seven school districts and the erection of a schoolhouse in each district. A common school fund was arranged for, and a board of education, which was to consist of one alderman, one assistant alderman, two citizens and the mayor, who was to be ex-officio a member and president. The four members, other than the mayor, constituting the board were to be annually chosen by the common council. The ordinance creating the board gave it sole charge of the regulation of schools, purchase and erection of buildings, and further provided for a superintendent who was to be the executive officer and clerk of the board, and who, together with two members constituted a committee for the examination of teachers, whose qualifications had to be ascertained by them before appointment. The first board of education under this ordinance consisted of Charles J. Brenham; aldermen, Charles L. Ross and Joseph F. Atwell and citizens, John Wilson and Henry E. Lincoln.

School Attendance in the Fifties
In 1850 there was one school with two teachers and 150 pupils; in 1855 the number of schools had increased to nine and 1,638 pupils were taught by 29 teachers. The number of children of school age at this date was 4,694 and the average of daily attendance at the schools of those on the rolls was 83.38 per cent. In 1860 there were eleven schools and 68 teachers, and a daily attendance of 2,837 out of a total of 6,108 pupils of school age. The expenses of the department, which were $136,580 in 1855, had grown to $156,407 in 1860, a per capita cost of $55.13 of the average daily attendance.

Teachers and Their Methods
In the early days the number of pupils assigned to a teacher was 87. It was many years before a reformation was effected in this regard, although the number was conceded to be excessive. Pelton advocated a reduction to 40 in grammar classes, and 50 primary pupils, but successive boards of aldermen disregarded the arguments in favor of the change until the next decade. The first high school in San Francisco was opened August 16, 1856, with 35 boys and 45 girls. The "Bulletin," in its issue of December, 1859, in describing the exercises of graduation day spoke in high terms of the proficiency of the pupils and laid particular stress on the fact that the graduates showed a remarkable familiarity with the Constitution of the United States, and declared that on the whole they were a bright lot of scholars, well equipped for battling with the world and a credit to the American school system.

The Higher Education
San Francisco's interest in the higher education never took the form of attempting to induce the legislature to establish a university within its boundaries, but its citizens energetically assisted in the movement which ultimately secured for the state an institution which has taken high rank among the world's great establishments devoted to learning. In 1853 a Massachusetts clergyman named Henry Durrant arrived in the City with the purpose of founding a university. Under the auspices of the San Francisco and Congregational Association of California he opened the Contra Costa academy in Oakland, which was shortly afterward renamed, and in 1855 was incorporated as the College of California. A suitable site was secured in Oakland, on which a building was erected. In 1859 the college had three professors: Henry Durrant, Martin Kellogg and I. H. Brayton, and three instructors, and in 1860 the study of the classics was formally inaugurated.

Beginnings of a State University
It was this institution which finally developed into the University of California. The constitutional convention of 1849 placed at the disposal of the legislature for educational purposes, the 500,000 acres of land granted by congress for internal improvement, the proceeds of all escheated estates and the 16th and 36th sections of land, also granted by congress. In 1853 congress supplemented its grant for common schools with a gift of 46,080 acres for the support of a seminary of learning. This latter endowment was not taken advantage of until 1866, when the legislature, in order to secure the benefits of an act passed in 1862, which gave to several states a quantity of public land, California's share of which was 150,000

acres, established an agricultural, mining and mechanical arts college. Between the time when the subject of a university was first mooted in 1849 and the date when California's seat of the higher learning became a university in fact as well as name there was a great broadening of opinion respecting the utility of such institutions, but in that respect the people of California were not peculiar. The work of eradicating the idea that the state had no need of imparting more than a knowledge of the elementary branches of learning proceeded as slowly in the older communities as it did on the Pacific coast.

A short time after the Rev. Mr. Durrant's academy was projected the Order of Jesuits began the organization of the college which has since become a great institution under the name of St. Ignatius. Although Father Maraschi, the head of the order, commenced his work in this City on October 15, 1855, the College of St. Ignatius was not incorporated under the laws of the state until April 30, 1859. Its first degrees were conferred in 1863, and Augustus J. Bowie was the premier recipient of the honor. The college, during the Fifties, was situated on the site now occupied by the Emporium department store on Market street. When the ground was purchased it was not an uncommon thing for critics to comment on the boldness of the founders in going "so far out." St. Ignatius College

In addition to the public, and not a few private schools which were called into existence during the Fifties, the Catholics inaugurated a parochial system, which has since grown to large proportions. On the 13th of November, 1854, a number of Presentation nuns arrived in the City and opened a school in a frame shack near Meigg's wharf. There were about 200 pupils from the start, and they were given free tuition. In 1855 the Powell street convent was built and soon became an important addition to the educational facilities of the City. Parochial and Private Schools

The course of education, like that of true love, did not always run smoothly in the early days. Despite the liberality of the inhabitants the municipal authorities found so much use for the money raised by taxation that they were somewhat niggardly in making appropriations for the schools. The result of this was visible in the necessity imposed on the teachers of taking care of larger classes than could be easily instructed by one person. Salaries also were relatively low. In 1854 male teachers received $150 a month and female instructors $100. The board of directors during the decade were harassed by the squatters, who had no compunctions about planting themselves on a school or church lot, and were obliged to take precautions to prevent the City's property being stolen by them. A singular reflection on the shortsightedness of the guardians of the welfare of the City is contained in the fact that, although three or four years earlier great quantities of land were sold at ridiculously low prices to astute speculators, in 1853 a loan of $100,-000 had to be effected by the City to purchase school lots. Purchase of School Lots

The private schools of the early Fifties were numerous, and to some extent their operations were an embarrassment to the extension of the public school system. While devotion to the latter was an ingrained American idea, the bitterness imparted to the discussion of all questions by the Know Nothing element had created a quiet antagonism which manifested itself in various ways, chiefly in the spread of the doubt whether an educational system under public auspices would not lead to intolerance. This feeling, however, soon abated, and before the close of the decade had disappeared entirely. There was a Teacher's institute inaugurated in 1852 which held frequent meetings. It appears to have been attended by the male Know Nothingism and the Schools instructors only. Its members had the sagacity to avoid mixing in politics. It endured for a short time, when the meetings were abandoned.

A Little Prevision Exhibited

Although the City was compelled to buy back some property which it had sold for a song, in order to secure building lots in desirable locations, it did not wholly neglect the future. In 1852 sites for schools were set aside at the corner of Market and Fifth; at Harrison and Fourth; at Harrison and Folsom; at Bush and Stockton; at California and Mason; at Kearny and Filbert and at Taylor and Vallejo. If this prescience had been exhibited on a more extended scale the maintenance of the present school system would have been less onerous, for some of the properties mentioned have been diverted from their original use and are now producing revenue for the school department. But the failure to foresee the needs of the future was not peculiar to San Franciscans. It was common to the whole country. The American people of fifty or sixty years ago had expansive ideas, but very rarely planned in accordance with their beliefs. They had a vision, but in their waking moments they forgot their dreams and allowed them to materialize haphazard.

CHAPTER XXXIV

POLITICAL CONDITIONS AFTER PASSAGE OF CONSOLIDATION ACT

SAN FRANCISCO'S SEAL—RESPECTABLE ELEMENT REFORMED—PURITY OF BALLOT BOX—VIGILANTE'S DISCARD PRIMARY ELECTIONS—A SELF PERPETUATING NOMINATING COMMITTEE—SECRET SELECTIONS PRODUCE GOOD RESULTS—THE CONSOLIDATION ACT—MEASURES OF ECONOMY—MANY RESTRICTIONS—REFORMS EFFECTED—NATIONAL PARTIES—BRODERICK THE CHAMPION OF FREEDOM—BRODERICK REFUSES TO OBEY LEGISLATIVE INSTRUCTIONS—THE REPUBLICANS—TERRY KILLS BRODERICK IN A DUEL—CAREER OF TERRY—BAKER'S ORATION AT BRODERICK'S FUNERAL—TERRY BECOMES A CONFEDERATE GENERAL—OTHER POLITICAL DUELS—PACIFIC COAST REPUBLIC SUGGESTED—TALK ABOUT STATE DIVISION—POLITICAL REVOLUTION.

HE period between the discovery of gold at Sutter's fort and the outbreak of the Civil war was in many respects the most eventful in the history of San Francisco. It was filled with novel experiences and disasters which threatened the existence of the City. It was perhaps the one community in the country regarding which the prediction was frequently made, that it could not endure, and yet it surmounted all its troubles and continued to grow in population and wealth. Its great fires were invariably followed by pessimistic expressions, but the event always discredited the prophets. Under the circumstances it is not strange that a bumptious feeling should have arisen which inclined the people to believe that they were superior to fate, and to express their belief in the emblem on their municipal seal which depicts the Phoenix arising from its own ashes.

Seal of the Municipality

It is human nature to be proud of achievements, and the argonauts of the Fifties could boast the accomplishment of many. They committed mistakes which had to be remedied, but sooner or later they applied the remedy. The greatest blunder committed by the men of the Fifties, who were in a position to shape the destinies of the City, was that of neglecting civic affairs until the call for drastic measures became so imperative that they were obliged to resort to extra legal methods to cure an evil which might have been averted had they not neglected their political duties in their eager pursuit of personal business.

Pursuit of Wealth

The results which followed the Vigilante uprising in 1856 have been attributed to the exhibition of force which attended the movement, but the remarkable career of the people's party, which had its birth after the summary hanging of a few criminals, shows that the power of the ballot was existent, and that had it been as steadily invoked before Vigilante methods were resorted to, as it was afterward, it would have been as efficacious in preventing municipal corruption and repressing

Reformation of the Respectable Element

309

excessive crime as it has been in other communities in which the forms of law and order have seldom been departed from. The success of the people's party after 1856 was due to a reformation of the respectable element of the community, and not to the dread of the corrupt and criminal. When decent citizens refused to interest themselves in local affairs, and neglected to go to the polls, they abandoned the offices to an insignificant minority; when they resumed or inaugurated civic vigilance they had no difficulty in securing and maintaining control of municipal affairs. And it is worthy of note that this assumption of control was not accomplished by a change of machinery of government, but by the simple process of adopting precautions to prevent abuse of accepted methods.

There had been serious frauds committed at elections. Repeating, ballot-box stuffing and every device known to unscrupulous politicians had been practiced for years. Men who had scarcely received a vote were declared elected to office, and others who had been voted for by a majority of their fellow citizens were counted out, but as soon as the aroused respectability of the City did its duty these troubles promptly ceased and were unheard of until a period of security and decent government bred fresh neglect. The so-called better elements were able to get good results without resorting to Australian ballots or other devices to preserve the purity of elections. The latter was accomplished by the simple process of carefully watching and preventing manipulation. In other words the unceasing exercise of civic vigilance did the business.

Primary Methods Disregarded

The people's party set the example, which was followed in after years, of dispensing with the assistance of the rank and file of the electorate excepting on election days. Primaries were relegated to the political junk heap of the period, and a group of men originally selected from the executive committee of the Vigilance Committee undertook the important task of choosing candidates for municipal offices. In the beginning it was resolved that no one connected with the executive body of the Vigilance Committee should run for or accept an appointment to office, but this was later modified into an agreement that no member should antagonize the nominees of the people's party, which, of course, had the effect of keeping members of the committee from taking office only so long as the policy of disinterestedness was adhered to by those who had evolved the scheme of control.

Watching at the Polls

That the result for the time being was good there can be little doubt, and it is reasonably certain that the fact that a determined body of men had resolved to secure better municipal government had the desired effect of eliminating corruption, but there is no ground for the assumption that the terror of the Vigilante name deserves the credit of the reforms that were brought about. The platform of the people's party gives the true cause of the improvement. It is found in the demand that good citizens should devote at least a few weeks of their time to public affairs. The aroused sentiment of the community made compliance easy, and when men who were not office seekers, and who had no other object than to secure good government busied themselves about the polls the corrupt element found it impossible to carry out schemes which can only be successfully consummated when those whose business it is to prevent them refuse to go to the polls.

A Self Perpetuating Committee

The Vigilance Committee of 1856 had taken possession of the ballot boxes used in the preceding election, and had found that they contained false bottoms and sides, skillfully contrived to enable the manipulators to overwhelm the legitimate vote by mixing spurious with genuine ballots. The crudity of the frauds advertises the utter neglect of the better element to take any precautions against their perpetration. As a matter of fact none was taken and the ballot box stuffers did pretty much as they pleased. In the election following the lynching of Cora and Casey all this was changed. Honest ballot boxes were used, and care was taken to see that there should be no repeating, and the people's party ticket was elected to a man. The same result was witnessed in succeeding elections. The people acquiesced in the practice of what promised to be a self perpetuating committee selecting a ticket for them and then they voted for it by a large majority.

The testimony is unvarying that for six or eight years after 1856 good and capable men were elected to the municipal offices, and they succeeded in effecting a great reduction in expenditures. It may surprise those who elevate the means taken to accomplish an end above the end itself to learn that the theory of secret nomination inaugurated by the Vigilance Committee, and which was adhered to during the nearly eighteen years that the people's party retained power, was extolled by publicists as the best possible method of securing efficient and trustworthy officials. There appeared to be no uneasiness on the score of bossism; nor was there any fear that the republic would be undermined by invading the prerogative of the people of putting forward their own candidates. At the time we are speaking of results only counted.

<small>Secret Selections Produce Good Results</small>

It would be a mistake, however, to attribute all the real or fancied beneficial results which followed the success of the people's party to the selection of good men. The new charter, with which the City was provided through the energy of Horace Hawes, must be credited with a large share of the achievements which went by the name of reform. The Consolidation Act of 1856, which for many years remained the organic law of San Francisco, bristled with obstacles to extravagance. Its provisions reflected the temperament of its framer, who had the reputation of being close in all his dealings, and disinclined to enterprise. His cautious disposition was responsible for the reduction of the size of San Francisco by the cutting off of the territory known as San Mateo county, which the City later sought to annex. His theory, which met acceptance, was that rascality could be easier dealt with in a circumscribed than in a large area. In short the underlying principle of the Consolidation Act was the prevention of extravagance and corruption, and the introduction of the strictest economy.

<small>The Consolidation Act</small>

This latter object was attained not so much by the change in the structure of the government as by the introduction of a rigid system of checks, which made expenditures for any except the most ordinary purposes practically impossible. The double boards of aldermen and supervisors were superseded by a single body of twelve elected from twelve districts or wards, the theory of the abolitionists of the bi-cameral method, being that the necessity of providing sops for an increased number of municipal legislators offset any advantage which might be derived from their checking propensity. No confidence was reposed in the wisdom or integrity of the elective body which had its powers so carefully defined that they were almost non-existent.

<small>A Rigid System of Checks</small>

The act also cut salaries to the bone, and contained stringent provisions against the creation of any debt, or liability in any form whatsoever against the City and county, and they proved absolutely invulnerable to assault. The acceptance of an organic act of this character may be fairly attributed to the awakening of civic interest by the Vigilante uprising, but it would be a mistake to assume that it was

<small>Measures of Economy</small>

inspired by fear, and it would be a still greater blunder to attribute to that cause the metamorphosis of an extravagant method of administering public affairs into a system which practically banished even the thought of municipal improvement, for that was the outcome of the provisions of the Consolidation Act, which made it impossible to initiate an enterprise, no matter how desirable, without the intervention of the legislature.

Desirable Reforms Effected

Nevertheless, binding as were its provisions, the Consolidation Act effected desirable reforms, and did much to restore the credit of the City. It paved the way to the funding of its old indebtedness, and in a short time made San Francisco bonds equal to those of the state, whose credit stood high. Extravagance was curbed and taxation reduced, and the citizens were so well satisfied with the result that were quite ready to dispense with the accepted democratic form of selecting municipal officials, and allow a secret body to name candidates. They would perhaps have been able to justify their acquiescence in the new order of things if the only object of maintaining a municipal government were to secure effective administration, for that is all the reform regime accomplished. There was no consideration for the future, and hardly an adequate effort was made to keep in good shape those few improvements which had been acquired, chiefly through individual effort. In short the Consolidation Act inaugurated a policy the inevitable result of which, with the best of intentions on the part of the administrators, had to be dry rot.

National Politics

Side by side with the non-partisan movement for municipal government there was exhibited partisanship in national questions which frequently reached the point of violence. The lines between contending armies were never more clearly drawn than those which divided the advocates of the extension of slavery and the opponents of measures looking to that end. But the division at first only extended to opinion, and did not succeed in obliterating party lines. In the election of 1856 there were three parties, the republican, American and democratic. Although the latter was under the control of the pro-slavery element it triumphed in California. Despite the undoubted popular antagonism to the introduction of servile labor into the state, the same conditions of mind which prompted a large proportion of the people of the East to advocate compromise measures exhibited itself in California, and when the parting of the ways came there were many who urged that "the wayward sisters" should be allowed to go in peace. A great majority of the electorate of the state was vehemently opposed to having slavery foisted on California, but many of the majority were quite well satisfied to see it imposed on other sections of the Union. Without taking this attitude into consideration it is impossible to understand the ferment of the years preceding 1861, nor the complete about face which occurred when Sumter was fired upon.

The People and the Parties

The revulsion was not as sudden in California as might be inferred from the fact that the democratic party remained in the ascendant almost up to the moment of the beginning of hostilities, for the differences in its ranks were almost as acute as those between democrats and republicans at a later period. The national struggle is not a part of the history of San Francisco, but the attitude of San Franciscans towards the burning questions of the period explain many things which without a knowledge of the fluctuations and inconsistencies of the electorate would be obscure and cause misapprehension.

Extreme Partisanism

A careful study of the intimate connection of national politics with the domestic concerns of San Francisco will disclose the probability that most of the erratic

SAN FRANCISCO   313

doings, and much of the crime of the Fifties, was due to the evil influence of the partisanism begotten by the attempt to maintain and extend the institution of slavery. Sometimes the connection is difficult to trace, but there is sufficient evidence to support the presumption that if the slavery question had been out of the way the early records of the City would not have been blemished by the Hounds, nor by the uprisings of 1852 and 1856, which were as much directed against the machinations of politicians as against criminals. And in taking this ground, it is not necessary to assume that the pro-slavery element monopolized the political wickedness of the period, for the testimony points conclusively to a man who has been accounted a martyr to the cause of the Union as being a serious offender, adept in all the arts of the unscrupulous politician, and perhaps more responsible for the wretched condition of affairs which called the Vigilantes into existence than any other San Franciscan.

In making this assertion sight is not lost of the fact that during the Fifties the maxim of the end justifying the means was almost universally accepted in this country. The struggle was fierce and many of those who participated in it were fanatical in their devotion to the side espoused by them, and believed that in the game of politics, as in war, everything was fair; just as in the South to-day, where no compunctions are entertained by those who resort to fraud, and violence when necessary, to prevent the negro gaining power. Hence it is not astonishing to find that David C. Broderick, who undoubtedly indulged in the worst practices of the political boss, became the champion of freedom and finally laid down his life for the cause. It is not necessary to follow the career of Broderick in all its details. Reams have been written about a single episode in his life, and the writers have invariably sought to justify or condemn the actors; few have shown any disposition to recognize that idols often have feet of clay, and that the champions of a great cause may sometimes have the infirmities of very ordinary men. We know from the admissions of those who have extolled Broderick's virtues that during his period of bossism he sold offices to the highest bidder, professedly to raise funds for the party organization, and that he was the beneficiary in numerous unsavory water lot deals. They also tell us that he manipulated so well that he was in absolute control of the legislature, and that at times he was the dispenser of gubernatorial patronage. And after he had succeeded in his ambition and was seated in the United States senate we are informed that his first encounter with the president was over the dispensation of patronage.

Broderick the Champion of Freedom

But despite his blemished record and the objectionable methods by which he mounted the ladder of his ambition, no one will question the important part Broderick performed in keeping alive the sentiment in favor of free labor, which undoubtedly saved California from being carried out of the Union. No ordinary champion of the cause of freedom could have won in the fierce struggle waged in California during the years following the adoption of the constitution at Monterey. The pro-slavery element was unscrupulous and untiring in its efforts to keep California in line, but failed because it had to deal with a man who implicitly believed in fighting the devil with fire. As early as 1850 Broderick opposed a bill introduced in the legislature which was directed against the immigration of free negroes. In 1852 he opposed the Fugitive Slave Law; and in 1854 he fiercely antagonized a resolution which favored the same legislation. There were democrats enough of the uncertain kind in the state at the time to put it through, but Broderick by

The Champion of Free Labor

persistent efforts kept Californians apprised of the fact that the pro-slavery element was ceaselessly at work and defeated their machinations. When finally elected to the United States senate, although he seems to have made it his first business to dislodge the Southern contingent from the federal offices in San Francisco, and thereby incurred the undying enmity of all the inmates of what was popularly nicknamed "the Virginia Poor House," Broderick was soon found arrayed with the opponents of slavery. His speech on the Kansas troubles, his first discourse in the United States senate, of which he was the youngest member, being only 37 years of age, attracted national attention, and also made a marked man of him.

Broderick Arraigns President Buchanan

This speech was delivered in December, 1857, and was sensational in the extreme. In it Broderick expressed wonder at the forbearance of the people of Kansas, and declared that if they had taken the delegates to the Lecompton convention, which tried to force slavery on the Kansans, "and had flogged them, or cut their ears off," he would have applauded the act. Two or three months later in a speech he said: "How foolish for the South to hope to contend with success in such an encounter. Slavery is old, and decrepit and consumptive; freedom is young, strong and vigorous. The one is naturally stationary and loves ease; the other is migratory and enterprising." After an apostrophe to labor in which he derided the assumption that cotton was king, and declared that he represented a state in which toil was honorable, he concluded with a direct assault on the president: "I hope in mercy, sir, to the boasted intelligence of this age," he said, "the historian when writing a history of these times will ascribe this attempt of the executive to force this constitution upon an unwilling people to the fading intellect, the petulant passion and trembling dotage of an old man on the verge of the grave."

Legislative Instructions Disregarded

Although this bold arraignment of Buchanan procured for Broderick the hatred of the pro-slavery element at the East and in California, and was perhaps responsible for the legislative resolution instructing the two California senators, Gwin and Broderick, to vote for the Lecompton constitution, the latter was undoubtedly within the truth when he said, in refusing to abide by the instructions, "I am satisfied that four-fifths of the people of California repudiate the Lecompton fraud," but he might have added that they would have assumed a different attitude had he not, by the vigor of his advocacy of the cause of freedom, made them see a great white light. The legislature condemned Broderick for his position on the Lecompton measure and stigmatized his reflections on the president as a disgrace and humiliation to the nation, but in 1861 their successors expunged from the records an arraignment dictated by the federal officeholders, of whom nearly ninety-eight per cent were Southerners.

Republican Overtures to Broderick

Broderick left Washington for California in March, 1859, on the adjournment of congress. While passing through New York he was insulted by two men from New Orleans who sought a quarrel with him, but on this occasion he preferred the rule of the big stick to the uncertainties of the duel and baffled an undoubted effort to put him out of the way. By this time Broderick had almost ceased to be a democrat except in name. He had come to believe that the South was seeking war, but he found it difficult to shake off the party fetich. The democrats were hopelessly divided over the Lecompton measure and Horace Greeley, who visited California in 1859, sought to bring about a fusion of Broderick's adherents with the republicans, but the time was not ripe for such a movement. The relations of

SAN FRANCISCO   315

Broderick with Baker, the republican candidate for congress, however, became very intimate, and in stumping the state the senator naturally allied himself with the republicans by vigorously denouncing the Federal Brigade and charging that his colleague Gwin was "dripping with corruption."

Broderick's career was ended by a pistol shot he received in a duel with David S. Terry. The meeting took place on the 13th of September, 1859, and the victim died three days later. Volumes have been written about this affair of "honor," and opinions have varied with the bias of the writers. A part of the press vehemently expressed the view that Broderick was murdered, and intimated that he was the victim of a conspiracy. The assertion was made that many of his opponents were longing to shoot him, but there are features connected with the encounter which divest it of the appearance of deliberation, and will permit the unbiased to think that it was the outcome of a highly inflamed state of public opinion, and the propensity of the period to settle political quarrels by a resort to the code. *Broderick Killed by Terry*

Terry had served through the Mexican war as a mounted ranger and came to California from Texas in 1849. He was a lawyer, and like most Southerners took an active part in politics and early found himself in opposition to Broderick, whom he strongly opposed in the convention of 1854. After that event Terry, who had always theretofore acted with the democrats, left that party and joined the Native Americans and in 1855 was elected by them associate justice of the supreme court. On the death of Chief Justice Murray, Terry was appointed his successor, and three years later he was a candidate before the Lecompton convention to succeed himself, but was unable to secure the nomination. He held Broderick responsible for his defeat, and in his exasperation he made charges that the men who had defeated him while claiming to be Douglas democrats were in fact abolitionists. He concluded his charge with the remark: "Perhaps I am mistaken in denying their rights to claim Douglas as a leader; but it is the banner of the black Douglass whose name is Frederick and not Stephen they are under." *Terry's Early Career*

Broderick was ready to defend the right of the free negro to enter California, and he was consistently opposed to every effort to abridge the rights of those already in the state. He fought against the efforts to exclude negro testimony from the courts, and was ready to shed his blood to prevent the extension of slavery, but he was unable to brook the intimation that he could be led by a "nigger," and resented being called an abolitionist, consequently he became angry when he read the newspaper report of the speech in which the quoted words occurred. He was seated at the breakfast table in the International hotel in San Francisco, when he first saw the account, and remarked that when Terry was incarcerated by the Vigilance Committee he had paid $200 a week to a newspaper to defend him, and added, "I have said that I considered him the only honest man on the supreme bench, but now I take it all back." *Abolitionist a Term of Reproach*

There happened to be in the room a man named Perley whom Terry had seconded in a duel some years previously, and he at once demanded of Broderick whether he was referring to Terry. Broderick answered "Yes" and Perley challenged him, but his invitation was declined on the ground that he was not the equal in station of the challenged party. Two months later, September 8, 1859, Terry wrote to Broderick demanding a retraction. The message was carried to the senator by Calhoun Benham, and Broderick replied asking Terry to be specific as the remarks attributed to him might have been misrepresented. Terry wrote *Terry Demands a Retraction*

316   SAN FRANCISCO

again repeating the words used and Broderick acknowledged their correctness, and added, "you are the best judge as to whether the language affords good ground for offense." At this distance of time, when the passions of the antebellum period have burnt to ashes, we ought to be able to recognize that Broderick's answer was not one calculated to turn away wrath, and that it constituted a provocation which even in these days might cause a resort to violence, and must have inevitably called for a challenge when the duello was considered the proper tribunal for settling quarrels between gentlemen.

Meeting of Broderick and Terry
The meeting was arranged by Calhoun Benham and J. C. McKibben who represented Broderick. Broderick had the reputation of being one of the best shots in the state. The duel was fought with a pair of pistols of the most approved type of European weapons used for that purpose, and it was asserted that Terry was familiar with a defect in one of them which caused it to be quick on the trigger. When the combatants met it was disclosed that Broderick's seconds had brought no pistols. A city gunsmith however, had brought a new pair which had never before been fired. Terry won the choice of weapons, and the pistols brought by his seconds were used, but Broderick's second, McKibben, after snapping a cap on one of them declared himself satisfied and failed to exact a requirement of the code which called for tossing to decide who should have first choice of the pistols. Terry's second took one of the pistols and the one left was that which had the alleged defect to which allusion has been made. On his deathbed Broderick declared that he did not touch the trigger and that the movement of raising his arm caused it to explode and discharge the bullet into the ground. It is also asserted that Terry said to Benham immediately after Broderick fell that the wound was not mortal, "I have hit two inches too far out," he added, and this was reckoned against him as an indication of a deliberate intention to kill, and was taken as a complete refutation of the assumption that Terry did not know how to shoot, and had engaged in the affair under that disadvantage.

Colonel Baker's Oration
Broderick's funeral was attended by a majority of the citizens of San Francisco, and an oration was pronounced over his body by E. D. Baker, afterward United States senator, and a colonel in the Civil war, and one of the first officers to be killed in that conflict. It was an impassioned appeal, and was as much a political deliverance as a eulogy of the victim. Baker was a great orator and was as convincing as he was eloquent. His oration made a profound and lasting impression which was not speedily effaced, and it may be truly said of it that it proved as potent to destroy the secession sentiment which later manifested itself, as the eloquent addresses of Rev. Thomas Starr King.

Terry Becomes a Confederate General
Terry was indicted in San Francisco, but the case was transferred to another county and dismissed. He left the state during the Civil war and joined the Confederate army in which he reached the rank of brigadier general. He was wounded at Chickamauga and some years after the close of the rebellion he returned to California. His name will be again met with in the course of this narrative, for his career was turbulent and had a disastrous ending. But its vicissitudes need not blind us to the fact that he was the creature of circumstances in his earlier experiences in California, and that much that has been laid at his door may be more fairly charged against the institution of which he was a fanatical upholder, and to the exaggerated sentiment of state's rights than to his infirmities. But above all things fairness demands the statement that he was a brave man. His whole career,

no matter how erring, proves that, and disposes of the implication that he was a cowardly murderer.

The Broderick and Terry duel excited much comment because one of the actors had made himself obnoxious to the majority of San Franciscans by the part he took in the Vigilante uprising. There were other affairs growing out of the political differences of the times which have received no more than passing attention. In August, 1858, George Penn Johnson and William I. Ferguson, state senator from Sacramento, had an altercation over the Lecompton measure and a duel followed in which Ferguson received a wound from which he died on the 14th of September following. The state at the time seemed to be hopelessly divided and the struggle for supremacy between the opposing elements was fiercely maintained. {Political Duels}

The situation was complex. Governor Weller in 1860 in a message expressed apprehension for the preservation of the Union which he thought was being imperilled by assaults "on our cherished institutions," among which he included that of slavery. His idea respecting the solution of the problem, so far as California was concerned, was to side with neither North or South, but to erect "here upon the shores of the Pacific a mighty republic which may in the end prove the greatest of all." His suggestion was not received with enthusiasm by either side. In the election of 1859 Latham had received 62,000 votes, against his chief opponent John Currey, the anti Lecompton candidate, who had 31,000 while Stanford, the republican nominee had only 10,000. It was impossible to divine from these figures the impending revolution, which resulted in placing the republican party in power at the election in 1860. {Proposed Pacific Coast Republic}

The tragic death of Broderick played an important part in bringing about the change. It was made the most of by the orators of the republican party, particularly by Colonel Baker, whose glowing speeches in advocacy of the preservation of the Union were given point by recent events in San Francisco. One of his addresses in the City still holds its place in the estimation of critics as the greatest speech delivered in California. The results of his fervor were apparent in the complete transformation of California. In the election of November, 1860, the democratic candidate for the presidency received only 38,000 votes, and Lincoln 39,000; and when the new legislature met it professed devotion to the Union. In 1859 the legislature had censured Broderick by resolution for his action on the Lecompton measure; in 1861 its successor voted to expunge the resolution from the record. {A Political Revolution}

An event occurred in 1859, the significance of which has sometimes been misapprehended in later years. On the 19th of April in that year the legislature passed an act giving the consent of California to the segregation of the six southern counties, provided that the people of those counties should vote for separation at the next election, and the creation out of them of a new territory or state. The privilege was not availed of, nor is there any evidence that any desire for segregation existed outside of that felt by a small coterie of politicians, who thought their prospects of political preferment would be advanced in the event of their movement succeeding. There was no sectional rivalry involved, and San Francisco manifested no opposition to the scheme of division. Its attitude was one of indifference. That too, was the position maintained on the subject of the location of the state capital. At frequent times during the Fifties, schemes of removal were agitated, but the interest in them was mainly confined to the politicians. In 1860 {State Division Proposed} the legislature, owing to the flooding of Sacramento was compelled to seek refuge in San Francisco, and its presence revived the idea of locating the capital in the City. An ordinance was passed offering any square in the City other than the Plaza, and $150,000 for the construction of necessary buildings, but the proposition had little public sentiment back of it, and San Francisco remained a mere metropolis without the capital feature being added to its attractions or advantages.

CHAPTER XXXV

CONDITION OF THE CITY AT CLOSE OF THE PIONEER PERIOD

PUEBLO TITLES—VAN NESS ORDINANCE—VEXED QUESTIONS AFFECTING TITLES SETTLED
—CONTROL OF THE WATER FRONT—THE IMPENDING WAR—DOUBTS CONCERNING
CALIFORNIA'S AGRICULTURAL CAPABILITIES—MECHANIC'S INSTITUTE FAIRS—EXCES-
SIVE IMPORTS—SAN FRANCISCO AS A DISTRIBUTING POINT—MANUFACTURES IN 1860
—OBSTACLES TO GROWTH OF MANUFACTURING INDUSTRY—COMMERCE OF THE PORT
—EARLY DEPENDENCE ON WHEAT EXPORTS—FRUIT INDUSTRY IN ITS INFANCY—
MINERAL RESOURCES—EXHAUSTION OF PLACERS DISCUSSED—DISCOVERY OF THE
COMSTOCK LODE—OPTIMISM OF THE ARGONAUTS—APPEARANCE OF THE CITY IN
1861—GROWTH OF THRIFTY HABITS—DEPRESSION PRECEDING THE CIVIL WAR.

HE uncertainties attending land titles in the City, which were the cause of much friction during the Fifties were nearly all disposed of before the end of the decade. It however, required the intervention of the state legislature and the state's courts and action by the United States to bring about this result. The former was secured in 1858, that of the federal authorities later, but the matter was regarded as practically settled by the act of the legislature approved March 8, 1858. The trouble arose from the conflict of views respecting the original status of San Francisco lands within the limits of the charter of 1851, and particularly that part of them between the charter lines of 1850 and 1851. Two ordinances had been passed by the city council, one on June 20th and another on September 27, 1855. The object was to definitely decide the moot question whether the lands in dispute were public lands of the United States, or lands belonging to the City by virtue of the old Spanish or Mexican laws.

Pueblo Titles

The first of the two ordinances was passed during the term of Stephen P. Webb as mayor, and the other during the incumbency of James Van Ness, but only the latter's name was connected with the legislation in the popular mind, and the two measures were usually referred to as though they were one. Its main provisions have been described by a historian who made a legal examination of the question as follows: "That while the lands within the city limits should be entered by the mayor at the proper land office of the United States in trust for the occupants thereof; that the City should have such portions as were necessary for plazas, squares, streets and other public purposes, and that the remainder should belong to such persons as had been in actual *bona fide* possession thereof from the 1st of January, 1855, to June 20th of the same year, or could show by legal adjudication that they were entitled to such possession. It further provided for the laying out

The Van Ness Ordinance

320   SAN FRANCISCO

of streets, and for a liberal selection of grounds for public purposes, and likewise that application should be made to the legislature for its confirmation and ratification, and to congress for the relinquishment to the City of all the right, title and interest of the United States."

Confirmation of Pueblo Titles

As the state courts had decided that there had been some sort of a pueblo at San Francisco, and that the city lands were pueblo lands, and as the United States courts followed them in such decisions it was very important that the city ordinances should be confirmed by the state. This was done in March, 1858, and the acts of the commissioners appointed in accordance with the ordinances were duly ratified. As already stated congress supplemented the action of the legislature by a special relinquishment of any claim it might possess, and thus the vexed question of pueblo titles was finally settled.

Legislature and the Water Front

The action just recited furnishes an instance of the benevolent attitude of the legislature towards San Francisco. A year later a scheme was introduced in that body which aroused the indignation of the people and called forth bitter denunciations on the stump and in the columns of the press. It was regarded as an attempt to turn over the control of the water front to a corporation by authorizing it to construct a wall and collect tolls and wharfage for a period of fifty years. The opposition of Governor Latham, who intimated that it was urged from bad motives, at the same time calling attention to the fact that the City was up in arms against it, caused the project to be temporarily sidetracked, but in the ensuing year it was revived under the impression that the successor of Latham would be more favorable to the measure.

Control of the Harbor

In this expectation the legislature was disappointed. Despite the protests of the people of San Francisco the bulkhead bill was put through both houses, passing the senate by a vote of sixteen to thirteen and the assembly by forty-three to thirty. In the latter body the measure was advocated by several San Francisco members, who were charged with being under the influence of the projectors of the scheme who were the owners of the existing wharves and had organized under the name of the San Francisco Dock and Wharf Company. When the act came to Governor Downey he promptly vetoed it, accompanying his objections with a vigorous message in which he took the ground that it was unconstitutional and that if it were put into effect it would work an irreparable injury to the internal and external commerce of California, and to San Francisco, which was, and must forever remain, the metropolis of the state. The news of Downey's adverse action gave great satisfaction to San Francisco, and subsequently when he visited the City he was "the recipient of a great public demonstration." An attempt was made to pass the bill over the veto of the governor but it failed, and the schemers were forced to abandon plans which they had been urging on the legislature at several preceding sessions.

Effects Produced by Civil War

The antagonism to the bulkhead scheme was an early manifestation of the fear of monopoly which later took a strong hold upon the people of the entire state, and would have ripened into a crusade against real or imaginary vested rights much sooner than it did had not the outbreak of the Civil war produced conditions which for a time diverted attention from certain evils that later were attacked with great vigor. The mines were still producing great quantities of gold, the product in 1860 being $44,095,163, and the output to that date was nearly $640,000,000. The state, and especially San Francisco, was unable to escape the effects of the great depression which set in at the East after the crisis of 1857, and which affected

EMPEROR NORTON, A STREET CHARACTER OF EARLY DAYS
Photographed in 1875

THE COBWEB PALACE IN 1856
A place of resort a North Beach in the early days

England and Europe as severely as it did the United States. Business in San Francisco languished. Despite the fact that the people were rapidly learning that there were other great resources than placer mining, their dependence on the outside world showed little signs of abating. The major part of the immense quantity of gold extracted from the earth had gone to pay for supplies furnished by the people on the Eastern seaboard and by Europeans. Manufactures, even of the modest sorts were not pursued on a scale that could be regarded as important, although there was a vast improvement in that regard over the condition which existed when the gold rush began. There were foundries which supplied some of the immediate needs of the population, and artisans were plying their crafts on what may be called the custom plan. But the manufacturing outlook was by no means encouraging.

The first industrial fair held in California was conducted under the auspices of the Mechanics' institute. It was primarily intended to exhibit the progress of San Francisco in the mechanics arts, but when the opening day arrived, September 8, 1857, the visitors found that as much attention had been given to the display of agricultural and horticultural products as to the products of the workshops. Even at this late date the newspapers discussed the exhibits of the farms and orchards as if they thought it necessary to remove doubts considering the agricultural possibilities of the state. The impression that the unfamiliar appearing lands of the interior engendered and the doubts created by insufficient rainfall had to be argued away, and the critics of the fair were united in the expression of the belief that such displays as that made on this occasion would prove more potent than words to accomplish that object. First Industrial Fair

These fairs of the Mechanics' institute speedily took on another feature than the practical one of displaying progress in the fields of industry. They soon became the favorite resort of the people, who met each other socially in the pavilion erected for housing the displays. Good music was provided, and for many years these annual exhibitions were a popular institution reflecting credit on the management, and bringing profit to the institute. It cannot be affirmed of them that they accomplished the chief object for which they were held, for they did not greatly stimulate manufacturing, the exhibits not increasing greatly in number and variety during several years, but they kept alive the desire to make the City a great manufacturing center until a mistaken monetary policy destroyed the advantage which isolation gave to the City by overwhelming the struggling domestic producer with floods of imported goods. Social Side of Mechanics' Institute Fairs

Although there were numerous foundries and machine shops, they were operated on a small scale. In the vicinity of the City, brick yards were turning out fairly good building material, and the nearby forests were being cut down for that purpose. The lumber industry soon attained considerable importance in consequence, and despite the frequent conflagrations of the earlier years, redwood outside of the business district, which had not extended greatly during the decade, was generally employed in the construction of houses. There was some ship and boat building as early as 1852 and this branch of industry in some respects made better progress than many which seemed to give better promise. Slow Progress in Manufacturing

There is an economic fiction that all trade is beneficial, and it has been demonstrated to the satisfaction of an important school of economists that it is even desirable to have what is called an adverse trade balance than to sell more products Excessive Imports than are bought, but it derives no support from the early experience of California. It was to have been expected that the sudden influx of population which followed the discovery of gold would make impossible a concurrent growth of domestic production, and that dependence on the outside world for supplies would have to be for a longer period than in other countries where development proceeded in a more orderly fashion. This expectation in California was not disappointed by the result. Except in the production of the chief necessaries of life the state remained in a backward state for a long period, and had to struggle with an excess import business which had to be balanced by the product of her gold mines.

San Francisco a Distributing Point In 1858 the total exports of the port of San Francisco, and they virtually represented the surplus products of the state, were only $4,770,163, while the imports aggregated $7,120,506. These figures more nearly describe the condition of California's relations with the outside world at the time than those of later years do for the periods they stand for, because in the Fifties, and until the transcontinental railroad began to operate, the only mode of transportation to other countries was by sea. The port of San Francisco was practically the only shipping point in California, and its harbor received the ships with cargoes destined for distribution among the people of the state. Thus early San Francisco became a distributing center of great importance, and its merchants formed a habit of mind, from which they have not yet become completely emancipated, of elevating commerce rather than manufacturing to the first place in their consideration.

Obstacles to Manufacturing The manufacturing possibilities in the Fifties could not have seemed alluring to men accustomed to regarding a big market for products as a condition precedent to producing cheaply, and who kept in mind the great difference in the wages of labor in the Atlantic states and Europe. At the opening of the decade in 1860, the population of California was only 379,994, not a sufficiently large number of inhabitants to tempt operations on a great scale, even if they had been concentrated, but they were scattered over a wide area, and were practically as remote from San Francisco as the City now is from the Atlantic seaboard. As a result, production was confined to those things whose cost of carriage would have been great enough to offset the drawbacks incident to high wages and manufacturing on a small scale.

Manufactures in 1860 In the census of 1860 California was credited with a total investment of $22,043,096 in manufacturing enterprise, and a production of $68,253,228. As San Francisco was almost the only producing center at the time, the major part of the product must be credited to her account, but as under the term manufacturing, as employed in the census year 1860, all those small activities which represent an order business were embraced, it may be said that there was practically no manufacturing of the sort which was later developed. But that was also true of nearly all the older communities of the United States in the decade preceding the Civil war, the dependence upon foreigners for manufactured articles being almost as great in New York and Pennsylvania as it was in California at the time.

Rapid Agricultural Development It is not surprising, therefore, that the minds of men in San Francisco turned naturally to trade, and that a survey of the agricultural possibilities of California should have convinced them that the future of the port depended upon the development of the interior resources of the state, and that the likelihood of the creation of surpluses of grain, wool and other products of the soil would offer greater opportunities to profit by exchanging them for the wares of the established manufacturing communities of the old world, than could be secured by attempting to engage in rivalry with peoples where the conditions for profiting seemed more favorable. Thus it happened that the sentiment in favor of a domestic manufacturing industry which exhibited itself in an excessive display of admiration for Henry Clay and his policy gradually weakened, and for a time was almost dormant.

There was abundant reason for the increasing confidence in the future of California agriculture. Although the most sanguine could not have foreseen the development it has since attained, because men in the Fifties did not dream of the possibilities lying back of the expansion of human desire, the evidence of prolificness was so marked it could not help making an impression. The value of farm products which in 1850 was only $3,874,041 in 1860 had increased to $48,726,804. The increase in volume was not attended by the diversification of products which later marked the agricultural advancement of the state, but there was sufficient encouragement derived from every experiment in new fields to strengthen the belief that there was no crop which could not be successfully grown in California. The growth of this conviction had the effect of allaying the earlier apprehension that with the working out of the placer mines the state would become a slow-growing community, and that its progress would be greatly hampered by its remoteness from the great centers of population. The ownership of large tracts obtained through Spanish and Mexican grants, by single individuals, who manifested no disposition to improve or sell them contributed for a time to this fear; but as the years rolled on it was seen that although vast areas were thus controlled, there was still plenty of land which might be had for the taking and that the disposition to take it up and utilize it was increasing. In 1850 the census enumerators were able to find only 872 farms; in 1860 this number had increased to 18,726, and the area of improved land had been extended from 4,833,614 acres in the first to 6,385,724 acres in the last named year.

Dependence on Wheat Exports

The assumption that California would become a great agricultural state has been fully realized, but none of the things which the astute prognosticators of the Fifties predicted turned out as expected. In the early Fifties flour was imported from the East and the hungry miners were compelled to pay fabulous prices for it, but at the end of the decade there was shipped through the port of San Francisco flour and wheat equal to 558,546 centals. There was embraced in this quantity 58,926 barrels of flour, the manufacture of which attained to considerable importance later. The comments of the press at this period indicate that there was a general belief that wheat production would always be the great mainstay of California and that a large part of the importance of San Francisco would be dependent on that industry. The acute were able to see into the misty future only a short distance. San Francisco was a great exporter of wheat for several years after 1860. The trade attained its maximum development in 1881 when 24,862,095 centals were exported, but in 1908 the volume of shipments had fallen back to nearly the figures of 1860, the quantity of wheat and flour exported, reduced to terms of wheat being 719,535 centals.

Diversification of Agriculture

In 1860 there was no longer any object in restaurants announcing, as was done in the early Fifties, that potatoes would be served on certain days. They had ceased to be a luxury, the production having risen from 9,292 to 1,789,463 bushels. Indian corn, of which there was no record of production in 1850, had an output of 510,708 bushels in 1860, and of rye, which does not appear to have been raised at

Infancy of Fruit Industry

all before the occupation there was a product of 52,140 bushels. There was a revival of the nearly extinguished grazing industry after 1850, but the products which had formerly figured as the chief ones during the Spanish and Mission regime had lost their importance as exports. They were more than offset, however, by the development of the wool industry, which, after 1854, when a product of 175,000 pounds was reported, increased to 3,055,325 pounds in 1860, the most of which was exported.

Mineral Resources

At the close of the Fifties there was little thought of those branches of horticulture which have since become great sources of wealth to the state. That excellent fruit could be produced was well known, but that its production would become commercially important was not imagined even by the dreamers of great possibilities, of whom there were many in 1860. It was several years later before raisin culture was even suggested, and the orange in those days, although there were some few trees, was looked upon as a purely tropical product. The canning industry had its beginning in the Sixties, and it was not until the growing wealth of the United States created a demand for luxuries that its importance as a revenue producer was recognized. It is only by the light of later developments that the optimism of the Californians, and especially of the San Franciscan, can be fairly measured, and when that test is applied there is a disposition to credit the optimists of the later Fifties with intuition rather than prescience. Those things which they implicitly believed would happen did not always occur, but the failure to accurately divine the future of certain industries, when they built too sanguinely upon them, was usually compensated by the introduction and success of fresh ones which their own experience, and for that matter, that of all their countrymen, did not suffice to make them wise enough to foresee.

Exhaustion of the Placers

It could never have entered into the minds of the pioneers of the Fifties that their state would produce minerals in greater abundance after the exhaustion of the placers than when the diggings were making their greatest showing, but there was a certain degree of confidence in the future of the mining industry which was warranted by discoveries made long before the depletion of what were regarded as the chief because they were the easiest worked sources of supply. In 1852 a Frenchman named Chabot, who was operating near Nevada City, conceived the idea of washing down a gravel bank which he believed was rich in gold. With a good head of water he tried the experiment, and it was so entirely successful that in a comparatively brief period hydraulicking became quite common, and considerable quantities of gold were added to the supply obtained by the more primitive methods adopted immediately after the discovery. It was not long, however, before fears began to be entertained that the wholesale washing down of hills would prove injurious to agriculture, and ultimately the apprehension created by their denudation and the filling up of the rivers with detritus brought about a cessation of hydraulicking until means were devised which permitted the exploitation of gravel deposits without causing injury to the farmer.

Diminishing Output of Gold

As early as 1854 we find discussions of the probable exhaustion of the placers, and conjectures concerning the effect of a diminishing output on the future of San Francisco. There was a wide divergence of opinion, but through it all there was apparent distrust of mining as a perpetual and dependable resource. One writer who seemed to have given the subject anxious consideration, opined that "with the aid of proper scientific appliances" the placers might still be made to render a bounteous reward to the miner, and that "generations must pass before the California gold regions" give up all their treasures. "This may be more particularly said," he added, "of the gold-bearing quartz rocks and veins which in many places are exceedingly numerous and rich."

There was no disposition to underrate the future of the gold mining industry, but it was beginning to be perceived that its returns, even with rich quartz veins to draw upon, would be on a diminishing scale. In 1852 the gold output attained its maximum, the California production in that year reaching the enormous value of $81,294,700, but every succeeding twelvemonth's record showed smaller figures, and at the close of the decade the product was little more than half as great as it was eight years earlier. And thus while mining at the beginning of the Sixties was still the most important industry of the state, and as such was still the main dependence of the City, which was the provider of supplies, and had become a manufacturer of mining machinery, the demand for which had grown with the introduction of hydraulicking, and the exploitation of quartz veins, it was beginning to be understood that agriculture would gradually usurp preeminence and become the greatest source of the state's prosperity. Future of Mining Industry

This conviction was not strong enough to prevent the liveliest interest in mining operations. San Francisco, long after the realization of the expectation that agriculture would rival mining in importance, retained its early sympathies and point of view, and was disposed to give more attention to a reported strike than to the development of the resources of the soil. Its population was permeated with the mining man's desire for quick results, and the foot loose were always ready to rush to the region which held out hopes of making a speedy fortune. This propensity had at times affected the growth of the City, and it continually militated against its stability. There was a still more injurious characteristic to contend with. The men who had made money in the mines, or who had profited by the enormous production of gold in the earlier years were more disposed to expend their energies and capital in prosecuting doubtful mining schemes than in pushing slower but more certainly profitable enterprises. Men who were not afraid to put their money into a hole in the ground, looked with distrust upon projects that people in older communities would consider perfectly safe. Interest in Mining Persists

This condition of mind endured several years after the Fifties. During that decade it resulted in greatly stimulating prospecting which resulted in laying the foundation for the achievement of results in the future. Many excellent mines were opened which produced a steady if smaller output of the precious metal, and thus helped agriculture by providing a market for a growing population, which in turn was served by the trading and industrial activities of the people of San Francisco. The City long before the close of the decade had learned to take notice of the possibilities of the opening up of the region lying outside of the boundaries of the state and gave close attention to developments in Nevada, which later became a great customer for California products and an outlet for the surplus energy of its inhabitants with mining proclivities. Prospecting Stimulated

In 1853 the celebrated Comstock lode was found and the argentiferous quality of its ores ascertained. It was not, however, until 1859 that the richness of the discovery became known, and the usual rush resulted. Ores were extracted which indicated a yield of $1,595 a ton and $3,196 of silver. It was in this group of mines that the widely celebrated "Big Bonanza" was discovered some years later. The The Comstock Lode importance of these Nevada discoveries was at no time underrated by San Franciscans, but the most optimistic believer in mines as a source* of prosperity could not foresee to what the exploitation of the new mines would lead. The San Francisco manufacturer and merchant saw in their development the creation of new customers, and the enterprising a fresh field for investment, but no one dreamed that the abundance of their product would lead to a revolution in the monetary system of the world, and to political and sociological consequences which have still to be worked out.

Optimism of the Argonauts

Although San Franciscans were not sufficiently gifted with the prophetic faculty to indulge in detailed predictions of a sort that always harmonized with the event, they were possessed of an overweening optimism and faith in the future of their port, which enabled them to review their career and conclude the retrospect with words which breathed the spirit of "I told you so." In surveying the growth of their City from the time of the gold discovery at Sutter's fort down to the outbreak of the Civil war they had abundant cause for satisfaction. The population had increased fifty fold, and wealth had grown proportionately. The people had passed through many vicissitudes with courage unimpaired, and disaster, instead of discouraging, only spurred to new effort, and mistakes merely suggested methods of repairing them.

Comparison with Eastern Cities

The place which was only a hamlet twelve years earlier had reached a stage of development which entitled its inhabitants to claim that so far as those things go which contribute to the physical comfort of man, and to his enjoyment and elevation, it was far more advanced than many cities on the Atlantic seaboard which had been a far longer time in the upbuilding. It had provided itself with good hotels and restaurants in abundance; it had more than its share of theaters and other places of amusement, and it presented an attractive appearance to the stranger. The work of reducing its site to a condition which seemed adapted to growing requirements had advanced far enough to make a considerable section take on a real urban appearance, and there were ambitious projects for further extension.

San Francisco in 1861

Many miners who had made their "piles" in the early Fifties had gone back to their old homes. One of these returning to San Francisco in 1861 would have found many changes in the City he had left. Plenty of familiar landmarks remained to remind him of "the days of gold," but he would have missed much that was characteristic of the period when he thought that California could never be made a congenial place to dwell in; one in which a man would care to bring up a family. He would have been compelled to note that the City was furbishing up; that its streets were less like country roads, and that its stores had ceased to present the appearance of a water front emporium. If he ventured forth at night, he would not be compelled to carry a lantern as formerly, for the streets were fairly well lighted for the period. Gas had been introduced as early as 1854 through the energy and foresight of Peter Donohue, and its use had become more or less general. In 1855 the company had ten miles of mains and charged $15 per thousand cubic feet for the illuminant. There were not many consumers at that price, the number being only 563 in the year named. But the illuminant soon grew in favor and in 1856 there were 4,080 consumers who paid $12.50 a thousand for 32,623,790 cubic feet consumed by them. In 1860 the rate per thousand had fallen to $8.00, and 6,172 consumers paid for 60,000,000 cubic feet, and the boast was made that in San Francisco oil had been displaced by "the light of the future."

Eight dollars a thousand smacks of the extravagance of the earlier period but **Growth of Thrift**
San Franciscans paid it cheerfully and had something left to put in the bank, as
may be inferred from the establishment of a Savings and Loan Society in 1857
which, when its first report was made in 1858 showed deposits at the close of the
first half of the year amounting to $20,000. There were other evidences of thrift.
When the decade of 1860 opened Eastern life insurance companies began to take
notice of San Francisco, and reached the conclusion that the conditions were not
as bad as had once been imagined. Prior to 1860 all the companies made an extra
charge of $10 per $1,000 when according to policy holders the privilege of living
in San Francisco. Just how much the danger of living in the Pacific coast metropolis
had to do with this extra imposition is not clear; probably a good deal as the
inhabitants of Los Angeles had to pay the same penalty, on the ground that the
country below the 35th parallel was in the deadly tropics. The removal of the
discrimination paved the way to the development of a business which rapidly became important enough to call into existence a commission to weed out unreliable
companies.

Other changes the returning miner would have discovered in abundance, but **An Orderly City**
they were all of a sort which he, if he were conservative in his instincts, would
have regarded as for the better. He would have found a police force which had
taken the place of the constabulary of the days when only sporadic attempts were
made to keep the peace. It was not large in numbers, but its effectiveness was
shown in a greatly decreased criminal record, and in the preservation of order
under circumstances which were sometimes trying. In fact San Francisco before the
close of the Fifties had become a very orderly city and a model in many particulars
for other communities. There was a high tide of strenuous political feeling running,
but it was kept within bounds. Even in the matter of Chinese labor, which was
a very vexed subject in the interior, San Francisco remained tolerant while riotous
demonstrations were being made against the Oriental in the mining regions.

On the whole the people of San Francisco would have had good reason to be satis- **Depression on Eve of Civil War**
fied with themselves, and their accomplishments, if they could have escaped the
depression in which the whole nation was plunged on the eve of the Civil war; but
they were bound up with the rest of the Union and had to suffer with it. Curiously
enough, however, San Francisco was the earliest city to recover from the effects
of the depression, and her prompt recovery was due to the use of the metal which
had first attracted world wide attention to California. When the nation abandoned
gold California determined to stand by it. Gold was her fetich. It had made her
and she would have no other money. Her resolution had consequences about which
men differ, but it did not impair her devotion to the Union. Perhaps it strengthened
it for there came a time when the people of San Francisco, and the rest of the
state, were enabled to do a good turn for their country by adhering to what they
called "sound money."

A PERIOD OF EXPECTANCY AND GROWTH

1861-1871

CHAPTER XXXVI

SAN FRANCISCO'S ATTITUDE DURING THE CIVIL WAR

THE CITY LOYAL TO THE UNION—ATTEMPTS TO TURN OVER ITS DEFENSES TO THE CONFEDERATES—A MINISTER WHO UPHELD THE SOUTH—FIRE-EATING SOUTHERNERS—THE CALL FOR VOLUNTEERS—CONFEDERATE ATTEMPTS ON MEXICO CHECKED—DEPREDATIONS OF PRIVATEERS—HARBOR DEFENSES IN WRETCHED CONDITION—CONTRIBUTIONS TO THE SANITARY COMMISSION FUND—EAGERNESS FOR WAR NEWS—ATTEMPT TO CAPTURE A PACIFIC MAIL STEAMER—CONFEDERATE LAND PIRATES—A GREAT CHANGE OF SENTIMENT—MONUMENTS ERECTED TO HONOR BRODERICK AND BAKER—MONUMENT TO THOMAS STARR KING—THE NEGRO QUESTION—SENATORIAL ELECTION SCANDALS—MERCHANTS PROFIT THROUGH THE WAR.

Under Which Flag?

HOUGH far removed from the scene of hostilities during the Civil war San Francisco felt that it was more vitally interested in the outcome than any other city in the Union. The position of Baltimore may at times have seemed precarious to ardent Unionists, but the fact that it lay under the shadow of the capitol assured the thoughtful that all the forces at the command of the government would be exerted to hold it securely. But San Franciscans had no such assurance. The remoteness of California from the seat of government almost made it imperative that the question of its position in the great struggle should be settled by its own people independently of outside assistance, which indeed, neither North nor South was prepared to extend when the war actually began.

Although a majority of the people of California were undoubtedly devoted to the preservation of the Union, and inexorably opposed to the introduction of slavery into the state, there was a large and very active minority whose sympathies were with the South, and it included many able and influential men. The early California bar contained a number of Southerners whose political training was far superior to that of the men they were competing with, and the federal offices almost up to the last moment before the flag was fired upon in Charleston harbor were filled with persons who were devoted to the policy of the extension of slavery. But what their opponents lacked in political acumen they made up in earnestness and devotion to the cause of freedom, and those qualities proved equal to the task of circumventing the many cunning schemes devised to take the state out of the Union.

Southern Sympathizers

San Francisco was the key of the situation. At the election in 1860 it had given a plurality of its votes to the Lincoln electors, who received 6,825 of the 14,360 votes cast in the City, Breckenridge receiving 2,560, Bell 940 and Douglas 4,035. The complexion of the vote exhibited unmistakably that San Francisco was on the right

San Francisco Votes for Lincoln

side, but the position of the state was not so well assured. Governor Downey in his message to the legislature in 1861, had urged that California should by joint resolution express its disapprobation of any measures with which the Confederacy might be "justly dissatisfied, or their constitutional rights in the humblest degree affected," and he plainly intimated that he thought it would be an outrage to act in any manner subversive of the rights of those interested in slave property.

Mixed Opinions

There is no gainsaying that Downey's views reflected the sentiment of a large number of Californians who, while opposed to any action calculated to extend the institution of slavery were at the same time convinced that the South had constitutional rights which it would be an outrage to encroach upon, and a still greater number who were under the domination of the idea that it would be wisest to let the wayward sisters go in peace. The strong sentiment of unionism was a later development, and the danger, so far as California was concerned lay in the fact that while it was crystallizing it had to encounter a mind already made up, for the active Southerners were in no doubt as to the course which they meant to pursue, and were quite ready to act while their opponents were debating.

General Johnston's Attitude

The military commander of the department at the time of the outbreak of the war was Brigadier General Albert Sidney Johnston of Kentucky. His devotion to the secession cause was shown subsequently but he has been acquitted of complicity in an alleged plot to turn over the City defenses to the Confederates. Floyd, who was secretary of war under Buchanan, was charged with having arranged for the turning over of forts and arsenals in the South, and there was a rumor current in San Francisco that General Johnston had been sent to California to cooperate with the secession element of the City. There were detailed accounts of a plot in which Charles Doane, then sheriff of San Francisco, was to have taken part. Doane's inclinations were undoubtedly towards secession, but the story runs that he disappointed the expectations of the men who projected the movement, and that instead of lending aid to seize the forts Doane had arranged with David Scannell to secure the help of 1,000 firemen in the event of any attempt being made to seize United States property.

Plot to Seize the City

Johnston has denied knowledge of the alleged plot, but Scannell many years after the conclusion of the war intimated that the story was not entirely without foundation, and that there was a project of which cognizance was taken in an unofficial way, but which never came to a head. His expressions regarding the matter were too ambiguous to be accepted as confirmation of the current story which the historian Hittell, after investigation, dismissed as apocryphal. Johnson was superseded by General Edwin V. Sumner, who arrived in the City on the 24th of April, 1861, the same day that the news of the firing on Fort Sumter was received by Pony Express. As Johnson had been secretly apprised of the contemplated change he was not surprised and was entirely prepared to turn over the command.

Fort Sumter Fired Upon

The news of the firing on Sumter occasioned great excitement and called forth a demonstration a few days later which effectually put a quietus on all talk of turning over the City to the secessionists. A mass meeting was called for May 11th. The day was declared a public holiday and there was a great outpouring accompanied by evidences of loyalty in the shape of flying flags, and mottoes which proclaimed devotion to the Union. There were many impassioned speeches made, some of them by men who had been wavering before an overt act was committed by the South. They were brought into line, as they declared, by the assault on the

MASS MEETING, MAY 11, 1861, AT THE JUNCTION OF MARKET AND POST STREETS

The building on which he signs appear occupied the site on which the Crocker National Bank stands a present. At this meeting San Francisco declared in favor of adhesion to the Union

flag. The utterance attributed to General Dix, "If any man pull down the American flag, shoot him on the spot" was quoted, and there were intimations that any attempt of the kind in San Francisco would be summarily treated.

Although San Francisco thus furnished unequivocal evidences of loyalty, the strong union demonstrations did not wholly discourage the Southern element in the City. The Reverend Dr. Wm. A. Scott, the pastor of Calvary Presbyterian church, was in the habit of introducing into his sermons reflections on the Northern cause, and was accustomed to praying for all presidents. His attitude provoked a great deal of adverse comment, and it was feared in some quarters that he might be subjected to treatment which would cause him something more than humiliation; but the public indignation expended itself in a harmless effigy, which was hung up in front of the door of the church on Sunday morning, September 22, and labeled "Dr. Scott, the Reverend traitor." He had an unusually large congregation that morning, but he discreetly omitted the offensive prayer. A few days later he resigned his pastorate and on October 1st departed with his family for the South, where he remained until after the termination of the Civil war.

Loyal to the Union

The other clergymen, or at least those who gave expression to their sentiments publicly, were on the side of the Union. Among them was the gifted Unitarian clergyman, Thomas Starr King, whose earnest efforts were recognized at the time as an important factor in the creation of the sentiment which attached the state to the North. King, who came to San Francisco from Boston in 1860, was a lecturer of great power, and had the literary faculty highly developed. He was able to attract large audiences and generally made a powerful impression on his hearers when he threw himself into his subject. He labored indefatigably for the Union cause in the pulpit, on the rostrum and in the great work of gathering funds for the sanitary commission. He died in San Francisco in 1864, before the struggle for the preservation of the Union had ended. His fellow citizens many years later honored his efforts by erecting a bronze statue to his memory in Golden Gate Park.

Clergy on the Side of the Union

The preacher Scott had some encouragement in his defiant attitude from the fire eating portion of what was nicknamed the "chiv" element of the democratic party. The bar of San Francisco at the time had a considerable Southern representation in it, and in this contingent there were several very able men who embraced the cause of secession. With rare exceptions they refrained from displays of truculency, but occasionally one would break out in denunciation of the tyranny of the North. Edmund Randolph, who had identified himself with the filibuster Walker, was in this latter category. In a speech at a convention held in Sacramento in July, 1861, he defended the states that had seceded and passionately declared: "If this is rebellion, then I am a rebel." His words were applauded by the "chivs," but nothing came of his defiance.

Fire Eating Southerners

It is to the credit of the City that the mixed opinion prevalent resulted in no collisions of a serious character. Before the firing on Sumter great bitterness of feeling existed, and more than one quarrel over the Lecompton measure resulted in a resort to the arbitrament of the pistol. But the firing on the flag had a sobering effect and men acquired the habit of expressing themselves with prudence. Extremists like David S. Terry made haste to leave the state to cast in their fortunes with the South, and those who remained behind, recognizing the preponderance of Union sentiment, avoided trouble. It cannot be said, however, that there was much intolerance shown, for during the entire course of the war there were journals pub-

The People Come Together

lished in the City which betrayed an unmistakable sympathy with the cause of the South. There is an instance of legislative action in the case of a judge who was impeached and suspended from office for using seditious language, but the charge against him was in the nature of an echo of Vigilante days, for he was accused of having acted corruptly in the Terry case. If it were not for the survival of the acrimony growing out of the disturbances of 1856 he would probably not have been molested.

The Call for Volunteers

The first call for troops issued by the secretary of war in April, and a second one in the September following, were promptly responded to by the required quota, and the enlisted men were mustered in at once. San Francisco furnished her full share, and had the demand been for a larger number of men it could easily have been filled. The troops raised in California had little prospect of serving where the blows would fall thickest, but they had what was regarded as an extremely important duty mapped out for them, no more nor less than the holding for the Union the vast territorial area of Arizona, New Mexico and the State of California. It had been ascertained that the Confederate plans embraced the occupation of the territory mentioned and steps were actually taken to accomplish that result. A considerable force of Southerners marched from Texas and without much difficulty overran New Mexico and penetrated Arizona, but never succeeded in reaching the Colorado river, which was their objective.

Operations of Confederates

The operations of the Confederates in the southwest were more or less influenced by plans formed many years before the war of secession began. The slave owners of the South had long looked with covetous eyes upon the territory of Mexico and were desirous of extending their institution southward. The filibustering schemes of Walker and others were linked up with this desire, and there is abundant evidence that many who were hostile to the extension of slavery north or westward were disposed to regard the acquisition of Mexican territory as a welcome solution of a difficult problem. After the passage of the ordinance of secession by South Carolina and the other slave states the disposition to give effect to the desire crystallized rapidly, and what Walker had vainly essayed would have been accomplished had the Southern arms proved successful, and Mexico's free institutions would have been subverted.

Checking the South's Move on Mexico

The promptitude displayed by the federal government saved the situation. General Sumner was ordered to employ the troops at his command to checkmate the Confederate designs on the neighboring republic. It was with this object that a second call for troops was issued. It was at first contemplated sending them by sea to Mazatlan with the view of marching them across Mexican territory to Texas, and northward toward the American border to meet the Confederate force that had penetrated to Arizona, but this project was abandoned to avoid involving Mexico by converting neutral territory into a battleground. Thus it happened that the energies of the California troops were expended chiefly in Arizona, although at times it was found necessary to employ a portion of them in hunting down sympathizers in the southern part of the state who were bent on assisting the Confederates to enter California, or, as in the case of a band captured on Warner's ranch, who were on their way to join the Southern forces in Arizona.

Interest in the War

The remoteness of San Francisco from that part of the Union where military operations were carried on extensively in no wise abated the interest of the people in the doings of the combatants. Those who were not called upon to take part in

SAN FRANCISCO

the active work of saving the neighboring territory of Arizona, and the republic of Mexico from being overrun by Confederate troops went about their ordinary occupations, but a large part of the thought of the community was given up to the struggle, and there were active and successful efforts to help the cause by other means than fighting in the field. The war became the engrossing political issue, and until peace was concluded at Appomattox public sentiment was like tinder. Feeling ran high and suspicion was rife, but it never developed into intolerance. Occasionally an imprudent secession sympathizer would express himself too freely, and find himself immured in the military prison on Alcatraz island as the result of his indiscretion, but such cases were rare, and hardly warranted the vigorous denunciations of tyranny which they called forth, for the victim only needed to take the oath of allegiance to secure his liberty.

Perhaps the most disquieting feature connected with the long protracted hostilities was the knowledge possessed by San Franciscans that rebel privateers were scouring the Pacific and destroying American merchant vessels wherever they found them. In addition to the evil effect upon commerce of the depredations of the "Florida" and "Shenandoah," there was constant uneasiness growing out of the possibility that they might have the temerity to make a descent on the City. The information concerning these cruisers was comparatively limited, and their activities had created an exaggerated idea of their formidableness. The apprehension caused the legislature to take action, and in 1862 a bill was introduced appropriating $500,000 for the defense of the harbor. It did not become a law, but had the effect of inducing the authorities at Washington to send out the material for building a monitor. It was shipped to the coast in sections and put together in this city. Cruisers were also promised, but for a long time the City was wholly dependent upon its forts for protection and there was not much confidence in their strength.

Depredations of Privateers

As a matter of fact the defenses of San Francisco at the outbreak of the Civil war were more amusing than assuring. While not exactly following the traditions of the Spanish and Mexicans, the federal government had never greatly exerted itself to put the defenses of the port in first class condition. At the time of the occupation there were some vestiges of the ancient batteries, the guns of which had almost reached the stage of usefulness which many of them afterward attained when converted into hitching posts. No attempt was made to improve on this condition until July, 1854, when two lines of batteries inside the entrance to the harbor were begun, which were to be additions to the works at Fort Point and Alcatraz island. Point San Jose and Angel island were also to be fortified, and guns were to be mounted on Lime Rock Point opposite Fort Point. Not all of these projected defenses had been provided. Although military critics of the period were doubtful concerning the sufficiency of the scheme, some of those regarded as important were wholly neglected.

Wretched Harbor Defenses

The affair between the "Monitor" and "Merrimac" in Hampton Roads in March, 1862, had greatly unsettled opinion respecting the value of defenses. The accounts of the encounter received in San Francisco were calculated to create the impression that a new style of war vessel, invulnerable to such guns as were mounted on the forts in the harbor, had been invented and it was believed by some that British shipbuilders would not be slow to provide the Confederates with armored vessels which might steam past the batteries and shell and sack the City. The belief did not endure long even in the minds of the few who were first to entertain it, as

The Monitor and the Merrimac

336 SAN FRANCISCO

information deemed more accurate was soon received which dispelled the idea that heavily armored ships could be successfully sent into the Pacific.

Contributions to Sanitary Commission — An appeal made to the Californians by the Sanitary Commission was taken up with great enthusiasm by the people of San Francisco who, at a meeting held on the 6th of September, subscribed $6,000 to the fund for the care of sick and wounded soldiers. This was followed by the formation of committees for the purpose of receiving contributions, and in the course of ten days $160,000 in gold was remitted to the East to the head of the commission. This was followed by another remittance of $100,000 in October and a third one of $100,000 was made before the close of the year. Thomas Starr King was foremost in the movement and his eloquence greatly stimulated the enthusiasm of the donors. The generous response to the invitation to help made a profound impression at the East, and called forth from the Rev. Henry W. Bellows, the organizer of the commission, a compliment which was keenly appreciated by the people of San Francisco.

A Tribute to San Francisco's Generosity — In October, 1863, Dr. Bellows, in acknowledging the receipt of a remittance, declared that California had been the chief support of the commission and added that its organizers felt they could not get along without its assistance. He stated that the expense involved in carrying on the work was heavy, and that $50,000 monthly would be required, half of which amount he suggested might be contributed by the Pacific coast. The suggestion was promptly heeded by the San Francisco committee, which answered that it would provide $200,000 during 1864, and that the rest of the state could be depended upon to contribute an additional $100,000. When the message was received by Dr. Bellows he sent the following telegram: "Noble, tender, faithful San Francisco, City of the heart, commercial and moral capital of the most humane and generous state in the world." San Franciscans and Californians generally felt that their devotion was amply repaid by this tribute, and when the accounts of the commission were made up at the close of the war it was found that California had supplied nearly a million and a quarter of the $4,800,000 contributed by the people of the loyal North. Oregon and Nevada displayed equal liberality, their contribution aggregating a quarter of a million, which added to that of California formed nearly a third of the entire amount raised by the commission.

Eager for War News — The long protracted struggle did not touch the Pacific coast as closely as it did the people of the East, but the eagerness for news of the happenings of the war was as intense in San Francisco as in any other city of the Union. Telegraphic communication by this time had become well established, and the newspapers were promptly supplied with information concerning battles and other important occurrences. The dispatches were not as voluminous as a later generation has become accustomed to, but they were supplemented by detailed accounts scissored from the Eastern papers when they were received by mail. There was a great deal of vigorous discussion, and it is claimed that the modern method of emphasizing assertion by using the largest size type obtainable in the editorial columns had its birth at this period in a San Francisco office. Calvin B. McDonald, who wrote for the "American Flag," startled the readers of his paper and set the community agog by printing an editorial entirely in "caps." The vigor with which he expressed himself when denouncing the "copperheads" hardly needed such assistance and the innovation was only temporary.

The editors with secessionist proclivities, and the politicians afflicted with the same leanings were not slow in firing back, but their execution was slight. Occasionally they exceeded the limit of temperate discussion and provoked riots which never assumed serious proportions. It is surprising that the result was not otherwise, for the aggressive tactics of the "American Flag" and its personalities, made it almost impossible for the criticized editors to contain themselves in peace. The good sense of the community usually prevailed, and even as late as July, 1863, a convention of those opposed to the war against secession was permitted to meet at Sacramento, and its members were allowed to unburden their minds without molestation. Freedom of speech and of the press were recognized as desirable, and only under the great provocation of the assassination of Lincoln were there demonstrations resulting in mob violence. On the day of the death of the president the enraged people visited the offices of the "Democratic Press," the "Occidental" and the "News Letter" and destroyed their type and other property, but the editors escaped the summary punishment the mob designed inflicting upon them.

<small>Advocacy of Secession</small>

At this late day it seems difficult to realize that there should have been such fluctuations of opinion as those caused by the varying fortunes of the war. California, like the rest of the Union, had its moments of despondency and of exultation. These were reflected in a message of Governor Stanford to the legislature of 1863-4, in which he spoke of "the dissensions that had crept into loyal states, the doubts that prevailed as to our ultimate success, and the growing fear of intervention," all of which he declared were overcome by the glories of Gettysburg, Vicksburg and Port Hudson. While the victories to which he referred greatly elated the Unionists of California, they by no means suppressed the activities of the sympathizers with the Confederacy, who continued scheming and talking about Northern tyranny and denouncing the war as an unholy attempt on the part of the abolitionists to revolutionize the government with the view of centralizing power and subverting the rights of the states. In July, 1864, Charles L. Weller was thrown into Alcatraz prison by General Irwin McDowell for utterances which reflected those of a large section of the democratic party in the North and which had only a short time before been expressed in the platform formulated by San Francisco democrats at a public meeting.

<small>Sympathy for the South</small>

During the first years of the war there were secession sympathizers in San Francisco who had large hopes of converting the port into a base for rebel privateers, but these ideas were dissipated by observation of the undoubted loyalty of the majority of the citizens, and the realization that no project of importance could be carried out unless effective assistance could be had from the outside, but the Confederacy was at no time in a position to extend help of any sort. It was thought at one time that aid might be rendered by Great Britain or France, who did not disguise their wish that the Union should be dissolved, but this expectation was of short duration. In abandoning hopes of help, however, there were plotters who did not dismiss the belief that San Francisco's shipping facilities might be made to serve the Confederates and advance their fortunes.

<small>A Base for Rebel Privateers</small>

In the early part of 1863 a group of Confederate sympathizers, through the energy of a scamp named Harpending, had obtained letters of marque from Jefferson Davis, which authorized him to prey upon the commerce of the United States, to burn, bond or take any vessel flying the American flag or its citizens. Harpending, who was an ingenious rogue, as his later history in San Francisco proved, had

<small>Attempt to Steal a Mail Steamer</small>

suggested a plan of seizing a Pacific mail steamship, and after obtaining possession of it to capture other vessels and thus create a rebel navy in the Pacific. Harpending, who was a Kentuckian, was joined in the enterprise by Ridgley Greathouse, William C. Law, Alfred Rubery and Lorenzo C. Libbey. Rubery, an Englishman, next to Harpending, was the most active in the affair. Law was to be captain of the first steamer captured and Greathouse was to finance the seizure. Libbey was to act as mate.

Miscarriage of the Plot
The scheme was to purchase a schooner ostensibly for the Liberal party in Mexico, and to load it with a cargo for Manzanillo. The schooner "J. M. Chapman" was acquired for the purpose and her sailing was to be timed to intercept the Pacific mail steamship "San Francisco," bound to Panama with treasure. After capturing the "San Francisco" the would-be privateers intended to sail with her to the scene of the wreck of the "Golden Gate" off the Mexican coast, where another vessel of the company was engaged in an effort to recover treasure from the wrecked steamer. This ship was also to be seized and with the force thus augmented the work of sweeping American commerce from the Pacific was to be prosecuted.

The Privateers Captured
Harpending was an accomplished scoundrel and apparently entirely uninfluenced by any other consideration than a desire for personal gain, and that was the chief if not the only motive of his accomplices. The scheme was not well conceived and the vigilance of the revenue officials prevented it being carried out. On the 15th of March, 1863, when the "J. M. Chapman" was about to sail she was boarded and taken possession of by the United States authorities, the seizure being made by a boat's crew of the United States sloop of war "Cyane." When the papers of the "Chapman" were examined a proclamation to the people of California to throw off the authority of the United States was found, also a plan for the capture of Alcatraz. When the seizure was made all of the conspirators were on board excepting Law, who was prevented by intoxication from joining the gang. The prisoners were taken to Alcatraz, and were subsequently tried. Greathouse, Harpending and Rubery were found guilty and sentenced each to ten years imprisonment and a fine of $10,000 a piece. Rubery was pardoned by Lincoln through the intercession of John Bright of England, whose friendship for the Union cause earned for him the consideration of the president. The others were subsequently released on the ground that they were included in the amnesty proclamation issued by Lincoln December 3, 1863.

Rebel Land Pirates
The rebellion produced land robbers as well as sea pirates. On the night of June 30, 1864, the stage from Virginia City to Sacramento when near Placerville was attacked by a band of men who obtained a large quantity of bullion. The robbers gave a receipt to the driver in which the statement was made that the seizure was for the purpose of providing funds to be used in the work of obtaining recruits for the Confederate army. There is no evidence that they were authorized by anyone connected with the Confederacy to rob stage coaches, but they were part of a band trying to enlist men in Santa Clara county to join the rebel army. The contingent that made the descent on the coach was overtaken by a sheriff's posse on the following morning, and a fight ensued in which a deputy sheriff was killed. A few were captured, the remainder fled to Santa Clara county, where another fight took place, in which several of the robbers were killed and others taken as prisoners. The grand jury of El Dorado county returned indictments against Thomas B. Pool and nine others. Pool was convicted and hanged at Placerville September

29, 1865, and another of the gang was sentenced to twenty years imprisonment. The remainder of the band evaded punishment by the interposition of various technicalities.

Nothing more pertinently illustrates the great change in sentiment produced by the Civil war than the action taken by the legislature in 1863 in appropriating $5,000 to aid in the completion of a monument to David C. Broderick in Lone Mountain cemetery. A few years earlier the same body had denounced Broderick by resolution for ranging himself on the side of those opposed to the extension of slavery into the territories. The state government was then dominated by the Southern element, whose leaders were not backward in proclaiming the superiority of the "chivalry" of the South, to the "mud sills" of the North, a judgment which the democratic party of California, although the great majority composing it was made up of toilers, accepted without cavil. A resolution had previously been passed by the legislature, directing that the condemnation of his course in opposing the introduction of slavery into Kansas should be expunged from the record; the later action was taken because many of his fellow citizens had come to regard him as a martyr to the cause of the Union.

<small>A Great Change of Sentiment</small>

Although the memorial to Broderick was completed with the funds provided it is doubtful whether the sentiment of gratitude expressed in the resolutions accompanying it made a deep impression. The monument stands in an accessible part of the City, but despite the fact that volumes have been written about Broderick and his opponent Terry, it attracts little or no attention. Its existence and whereabouts are known to the old timers, but the younger generation never stray in its direction; nor are the footsteps of visitors ever guided to its precincts. Equal neglect of the memory of Colonel E. D. Baker, who fell at Ball's Bluff, is displayed by the careless San Franciscan. He too has been honored by a monument, but the stranger who has been thrilled by the glowing accounts of his devotion to the Union cause, as told in the histories of the Civil war, is never reminded that the ashes of the man who left the comfortable precincts of the United States senate chamber to defend his country on the battlefield, and who fell at the head of his command, are interred in a San Francisco cemetery.

<small>Monuments to Broderick and Baker</small>

Perhaps the neglect is not reprehensible. The stream of humanity flows in channels fixed by convention and usage. People do not visit cemeteries for recreation or study. The epitaphs on tombstones do not appeal to them. They are too apt to heed the injunction to let the dead past bury its own dead. Hence the failure to perpetuate memories that deserve to be kept fresh and green. Fortunately for posterity that of Thomas Starr King and his devotion to the cause of the Union is thus preserved. The legislature of 1864, which on the announcement of his death on March 4 of that year, adjourned for a period of three days out of respect to his memory, after resolving "that he had been a tower of strength to the cause of his country," honored themselves and the eloquent orator whose voice was always raised for freedom, but the bronze effigy of the dead patriot in Golden Gate Park will tell the story of his devotion to the Union to hundreds of thousands long after the early legislative records have been forgotten.

<small>Monument to Thomas Starr King</small>

There were other indications of the vastly changed sentiment of the people. Although the men who formed the constitution of California had gone on record as opposed to the introduction of slave labor into the new state, they had not wholly divested themselves of the spirit of illiberality begotten by race prejudice,

<small>The Negro Question</small>

and the legislature of 1850, finding no inhibition, passed laws prohibiting any black or mulatto person or Indian from giving testimony in any case in which a white person was a party. This discrimination stood on the statute books of California until 1863, when the law was repealed, but not until after a hard struggle, in which many compromises were suggested by men who were devoted Unionists, but could not suddenly abandon the beliefs of a lifetime. One of the half-way proposals which was rejected provided that negro testimony should only be accepted when corroborated by the evidence of whites. It was the same sort of prejudice which caused Broderick to resent the imputation that he was an abolitionist when he was making stalwart efforts for freedom. The opprobrious epithet of one day became a glorious appellation on the next.

Senatorial Election Scandals

The fires of war sometimes have a purifying effect, but they produced no such result on California politics. After the Vigilante uprising there was for several years something like an approach to good government in San Francisco, but its accomplishments were all of a repressive character. All efforts were concentrated upon the prevention of crime and the repression of corruption in the conduct of municipal affairs. The success achieved in this latter direction so far as the government of San Francisco was concerned was remarkable, but the regeneration did not extend to all sorts of politics and politicians. The earlier performances attending the election of United States senators were continued in a modified form after 1861. There were no longer demonstrations of the kind which marked the ante bellum selections of senators, but flagrantly corrupt methods were resorted to by candidates to secure votes. In the election to fill the place of Latham, who had succeeded Broderick, there was a tremendous scandal growing out of allegations of attempted bribery. It was reported that an interior member had been offered a bribe to desert Trenor W. Parks and give his vote to Timothy Guy Phelps, who lacked only five or six of having a majority on joint ballot. There was much recrimination, and charges were made that nominations for judicial positions were freely promised to secure votes. The whole affair was made the subject of an investigation by a republican caucus on January 27, 1863, which professed itself unable to get at the facts and dismissed the matter. A resolution was subsequently introduced in the assembly to investigate, but it was tabled by a decisive vote. The contest created great excitement in San Francisco and was made the subject of vigorous newspaper comment, some of which equalled in virulence the editorial utterances of the days preceding the Civil war.

Effects of Civil War on San Francisco Commerce

While the course of the rebellion engrossed much of the attention of the people of San Francisco and California, it by no means deprived domestic affairs of their interest. Those who lived through the exciting four years of the Civil war know that men went about their daily avocations in cities that were almost within hearing distance of the din of battle. General Sherman, whose early life was so closely identified with that of San Francisco, many years after the close of the struggle tersely described war as hell. He had in mind its horrible features: its cruelty, its disregard of life and of mine and thine, its brutalities and its destructiveness. He was a combatant, and those were the things which were forced on his attention; but there were other evils which the observer whose vision did not take in the battlefield had borne in upon him. The greatest of these was the callousness produced by the continued recital of killings and suffering. There are always some who escape this distressing influence, but the majority do not. A protracted war not infrequently, as was the case in the Netherlands, when it revolted against Spain, emphasizes the tendency of men to adapt themselves to circumstances and to profit from conditions. That was true of the East, where the necessity of procuring revenue to carry on the war caused the imposition of a tariff which called into existence new industries and turned the adversities of the nation into a source of material prosperity.

San Francisco by no means escaped this influence. The hearts of her people were in the right place and their sympathies were easily stirred. They responded promptly to the call of duty and were not unmindful of the sufferings and the sacrifices made by those who bore the brunt of the conflict. But there were adventitious circumstances which they were prompt to recognize and seek to turn to their advantage. The long delay in the construction of a transcontinental railroad promised to end by the government actively assisting in the promotion of an enterprise which up to that time seemed impossible of accomplishment through individual exertion. This in itself seemed to the isolated Californians a boon whose value to the whole country, and to themselves in particular, could not be overestimated, but there was something immediately at hand which for the time being turned their attention from the achievement of the future to a present benefit which they were able to seize because their principal product was gold; the metal which the whole world was eagerly struggling to obtain and which California determined to retain as a monetary medium no matter what happened to the rest of the universe or to the Union.

Profiting Through Adherence to Gold

CHAPTER XXXVII

EFFECTS OF ADHERENCE TO GOLD MONEY DURING THE WAR

CHANGING COMMERCIAL CONDITIONS—THE PANIC OF 1857—INCREASING EXPORTS—TAXATION OF CONSIGNED GOODS—THE WAR TAX—EQUAL TAXATION DEMANDED—WAR INCREASES EMIGRATION TO CALIFORNIA—ADHERENCE TO THE USE OF GOLD MONEY—THE SPECIFIC CONTRACT ACT—MERCHANTS PROFIT THROUGH RETENTION OF GOLD MONEY SYSTEM—GREENBACKS NOT DISTRUSTED—SPECULATION IN GREENBACKS—HIGH RATES OF INTEREST—ILLIBERAL BANKING LAWS—LARGE GOLD PRODUCTION—RESULT OF BAD BANKING METHODS—FIRST SAVING AND LOAN SOCIETY—FEDERAL EMPLOYES ARE PAID IN DEPRECIATED CURRENCY—PAYING DEBTS IN GREENBACKS—ATTEMPTS TO INDUCE ABANDONMENT OF GOLD MONEY—MANUFACTURING DISCOURAGED BY SPECULATION IN MONEY—GREAT EXPECTATIONS OF THE PEOPLE—LOOKING FORWARD TO RAILROAD CONNECTION WITH THE EAST.

HE great depression of 1857, which continued until the activities promoted by the Civil war caused the revival of business, had extended to California and was severely felt by the merchants of San Francisco. Its effects were somewhat different from those produced by previous panics whose origins could be traced to local causes. There was no severe crash, but a steady liquidation which forced many out of business and compelled those well intrenched to exercise caution. The industries of the state were expanding with the exception of gold mining which, however, still contributed large sums to the circulating medium of the world even if the continued adverse trade balance operated to prevent its retention in the United States. *The Panic of 1857*

So far as California was concerned there was a constant improvement in this latter particular. In the earlier years of the decade 1850-60 the manifests of vessels entering the port of San Francisco were largely made up of such articles as flour, butter, barley, lumber, hams, bacon, pork, beef, candles; in 1861 the state had reached the stage of providing itself with most of the commodities mentioned and was beginning to prove its resourcefulness by exporting, not on a great scale, but in sufficient quantity to indicate future possibilities. There was also a disposition shown to manufacture more extensively, and thus lessen the almost complete dependence on the East which had exhibited itself during the period when the dominating thought was that California was not of much account except as a mining and grazing country. *Changing Commercial Conditions*

The result of this changing commercial condition was visible in the growing list of exports, the variety of which was increasing as greatly relatively as the aggre- *Increasing Exports*

344   SAN FRANCISCO

gate value of the things exported. In 1858 the total exports were valued at only
$4,770,163; before the Civil war had fairly closed the shipments through the port
of San Francisco were nearly three times as great, the custom house returns showing their value to be $14,554,496. Concurrently, however, there was an increase
of imports by sea from $7,120,506 in 1858 to $15,271,104, but during the interval
there was a decided change in the character of the imports, many commodities formerly received in large quantities from the East and foreigners disappearing from
the list of things imported, their places being taken by articles whose variety and
quality advertised the growing opulence of the people of California.

Taxation of Consigned Goods   The large imports into San Francisco had at various times suggested to the
legislature that they might be made to prove a source of revenue to the state. In
1852 an attempt was made to levy a tax on consigned goods, but its imposition was
resisted. A grand jury found two hundred indictments against the violators of
the law but no attention was paid to its action. In the following year Governor
Bigler, in a message to the legislature, called attention to the resistance to the
payment of the tax, and urged the enforcement of the law. At the same time he
recommended that taxes should be collected from steamship companies trading to
California ports even though their ownership was in other states. In the legislature of 1861-62 an attempt was made to revive these schemes of taxation, but Governor Stanford interposed his veto and it was sustained.

State Short of Revenue   It does not appear that these fruitless attempts to impose a burden on the
commerce of the port of San Francisco were inspired by hostility to the City, or by
a desire to promote domestic industry by giving its products an advantage over
those shipped by outsiders. In the debates on the subject in the legislature allusions were made to the evils of the system of consigning goods, and there was also
some talk which indicated a feeling of antagonism against the City, but in the later
as in the earlier case the movement was due to the desire to find sources of revenue
to meet the growing demands made upon the state government. In a message in
1862 in which Stanford dealt with the subject of taxation he called attention to
the fact that while the excess of receipts over expenditures was a trifle over $91,000,
the general fund was much behind and he recommended a state tax larger than
the estimate required: 23 cents in addition to the 62 cents imposed by the revenue
act of May 19, 1861, on each $100 of valuation.

The War Tax   Part of this large demand was due to the necessity of meeting the call of the
federal government for a direct contribution of a quarter of a million dollars, but
the chief cause was the disposition early manifested by the legislature to indulge
in extravagant appropriations. In that particular the state authorities were as
reckless as those of San Francisco had been until the curb of the Consolidation Act
was applied. And if the vigorous denunciations of Governor Downey truthfully
represented the situation, the legislature was no more scrupulous than the worst
"boodling" boards of aldermen elected in San Francisco in the Fifties. The governor had no hesitation in asserting that funds obtained for the purpose of reclaiming swamp lands had been deliberately diverted, and were expended in the payment
of salaries and wages instead of being employed in the construction of levees, a
criticism which derived much force from the fact that the floods of 1861-2 compelled the legislature to desert Sacramento and repair to San Francisco.

Taxation Questions   It is during periods of depression that men's thoughts turn to questions of taxation. In the boom years when a valuable product like gold was secured by methods

which resembled those of the gambler rather than the well directed efforts of men forced to give their attention to the development of varied resources, little or no attention was paid to budgets or the means to be taken to meet them. But when the mines began steadily reducing their output soberer thoughts began to take possession of the public mind. There had been more or less discontent with the distribution of the taxation burden of the state prior to 1861, but it had usually betrayed sectional feeling. The miners sometimes protested that too much was demanded of them, and the grazing, or "cow counties," as they were called, found fault with the treatment accorded them; but both were always ready to join in any plan which would force the City to pay as big a tribute as its assumedly growing wealth would bear.

But in 1861 there was something like a fresh point of view introduced by an attempt to enforce the principle that all property should be taxed. A bill was introduced in the legislature in that year by James McM. Shafter which failed of passage, but the theory of which he sought to enforce later by promoting an action against the assessor of Marin county to have the claims to the possession of lands, the title to which was in the government, assessed and taxed like other property. His object was not to compel the government to pay taxes, but he sought to reach a class claiming lands which only required the patent of the government to complete the title to them. His purpose was achieved, as he secured a decision the chief value of which, however, did not consist in the amount of taxes derived, but in the arousing of attention to the drawbacks of large land holdings. The opposition to what later became known as land monopoly had its inception at this time, and it eventually took hold of the people to such an extent, that the demand for a change in the organic law, which had been urged at various times after 1852, had finally to be complied with.

Demand for Equal Taxation

But meanwhile events were shaping which deferred the accomplishment of this reform. The outbreak of the war had brought about conditions at the East which tended to start anew the flow of population toward the Pacific coast. The effect of the new accessions was as beneficial to San Francisco as the rushes to the Fraser river country had been injurious. In a comparatively brief period the City recovered a good deal of the briskness it had parted with during the depression which followed the panic of 1857. This result was undoubtedly greatly contributed to by the opening of mines on the Comstock lode, and to operations in California which tended to increase the waning confidence in mining as an important industry. The merchants of San Francisco were also beginning to reap the advantages derived from the depreciation of the legal tender notes issued by the government which enabled them to buy goods at greenback prices and sell them for gold.

War Promotes Emigration to California

There were many complications to grow out of the determination of California to adhere to the use of gold while the rest of the country was forced to resort to paper currency, but the majority of the people of the state, and more particularly the merchants of San Francisco, were profoundly convinced that it was the only safe course for them to adopt. Doubtless the possible advantage to be derived from an exchange which must always be in favor of the section with the most reliable currency had its influence in moulding public opinion, but the primary motive must be sought for in the extraordinary conservatism begotten by distrust of paper currency, which manifested itself in so pronounced a fashion when the state

The Use of Gold Money

constitution was framed, in which the issuance of paper money by banks was positively prohibited.

Greenback Currency Discountenanced

The wisdom of this early action was never disputed in San Francisco, and by some it was held that it afforded ample corroboration of the theory so much expatiated upon later, that the use of an inferior currency will drive out the superior. In the beginning, however, there was little evidence that this view was much considered in determining upon a policy which at one time threatened to create unfriendly feeling between the section of the Union using the greenbacks and California. Apparently the only object was to guard against the possibility of substituting for the money which had what was deemed fixity of value a variable currency worth so much to-day and less to-morrow. Thus it happened that the people of California, practically by unanimous consent, refused to use the legal tender money of the government, and by the sheer force of public opinion deterred the unscrupulous who might wish to profit by the depreciation of greenbacks to pay their obligations in paper currency, from resorting to such a course.

The Specific Contract Act

The so-called specific contract act was not passed by the legislature until 1863. That measure gave a certain sanction to a custom which had crystallized long before its passage and which all classes of citizens felt themselves in honor bound to observe. Occasionally there was a case of disregard of the obligation, but such departures from the standard set up by the merchants of San Francisco were extremely rare, as a resort to them procured for the offender business and social ostracism. But while there was little trouble on this score, there were other difficulties which arose to plague the law makers and to worry those who were apprehensive that California's monetary policy might be misconstrued into lack of devotion to the Union cause.

Governor Stanford Advocates Use of Paper Money

It was some such fear that impelled Governor Stanford in a message sent to the legislature in 1862 to criticize the action of the state treasurer, who had paid the state's proportion of the direct war tax in legal tender notes, which were then nearly 8 per cent below par in California. By this operation the state saved $4,400, the difference between the gold and currency price of an installment of $68,839 on the tax. The governor expressed chagrin and characterized the action of the treasurer as unauthorized, but the Washington authorities assured him that the legal tender notes had been advisedly received, and that payment in coin would have resulted in California contributing more than its share under the levy. The difference of opinion was referred to the legislature, but before it took any action in the premises Ashley had paid the remainder of the tax in government paper money and saved nearly $25,000. In order to take away the appearance of desiring to profit by the depreciation of the federal money the amount thus saved was appropriated as a recruiting fund to fill up the regiments of California volunteers in the field.

Merchants Profit

Meanwhile, however, the mercantile element was not so considerate of the effect of its action on the government credit. Merchants early began to take advantage of the difference in exchange, and before the close of 1862 the stock and exchange board organized in September, 1862, was actively dealing in currency, and continued to do so from that time forward until the resumption of specie payments by the government. The business transacted was by no means insignificant. It was not unusual for brokers to make sales of from $10,000 to $20,000 of currency on a single order, and while the operations of the board never reached the

SAN FRANCISCO

magnitude of those of the New York gold board, the fluctuations at times produced conditions as exciting as those which became common a few years later when mining stocks engrossed the attention of speculators.

One of the curious features of the trade in gold was the frequent exhibition of confidence in the ability of the government to redeem its obligations made by believers in the perpetuity of the Union. It was no uncommon occurrence for patriotic men to ostentatiously buy currency when it was greatly depreciated and put it away in their strong boxes. There was a period when greenbacks had fallen so low that $350 to $400 worth of gold would buy $1,000 worth of the government paper. At this time there were numerous transactions of the character mentioned, and the vaults of the banks were filled with small boxes containing currency and other valuable papers. In the Sixties there were no safe deposit companies, but all the banks were in the habit of accommodating customers by permitting them to use their fire and assumedly burglar proof vaults to store their tin boxes.

Greenbacks Not Distrusted

It is safe to say, however, that cold calculation was as influential as patriotism in producing these manifestations of confidence. The speculative propensities of Californians could not resist the temptation presented by the chance of a 35 cent paper dollar being converted into one worth a hundred cents in gold. Doubtless faith in the ultimate triumph of the Union cause was a powerful factor in every instance, even in the case of the gambler who was quite ready to take a three to one chance with his money. But whatever motive prompted the investment in the discredited paper the surrender to it resulted in great profits to a very considerable number of San Franciscans, who had the sagacity to buy greenbacks when they were very low priced, and hold them until the success of the Union arms caused the government's credit to rise, not as rapidly as it had fallen, but slowly and surely.

Speculation in Currency

Speculation in greenbacks was to some extent governed by interest rates. All those transactions of the sort involving the locking up of the purchased notes, and which were not prompted by purely patriotic motives, had to take this factor into consideration, for interest rates remained very high well in the Seventies. Despite the enormous gold product of the state the rates charged for the use of money were abnormally high. In 1849 men were as willing to pay ten per cent a month as they were to pay ten per cent per annum a quarter of a century later. As late as 1859 mortgage loans on real estate were made in many cases at 2 per cent a month, and occasionally 3 per cent. These can hardly be described as ruling rates, for in 1859 mortgages were recorded ranging from 1¾ per cent a month, for $40,000, and as high as 3 per cent a month for smaller amounts ranging from $1,000 to $4,000.

Greenbacks and Interest Rates

In 1860 the Hibernia bank began loaning at 2 per cent a month, which seems to have been the maximum rate during that and three subsequent years. There were some long term loans made by foreign capitalists at a much lower rate, but in 1864 the rates generally recorded ranged between 1¼ and 1½ per cent a month.. There is a record of a loan in 1867 of $35,000 at two per cent a month, but it was exceptional. In the following year there was evidence of brisk competition in money lending, and for the first time in the history of San Francisco financial dealings interest rates were quoted per annum instead of per month.

Interest Rates in 1860

How much of the blame for this anomalous condition of affairs is properly chargeable to the illiberal attitude of the framers of the state constitution in dealing with the matter of bank circulation it would be impossible to state. There had

Illiberal Banking Laws

been great abuses of the privilege of emitting paper money in the Eastern states, and there was a wholesome dread that something of the same sort would occur in California if precautions were not taken to make such a result impossible by absolutely prohibiting the issuance of bank notes. It was assumed that the great output of gold would provide a sufficient quantity of metallic money to satisfy all the requirements of a growing community, and that adherence to its use would ward off all the perils attendant upon wildcat banking. The possibility of adequate regulation received little recognition, nor does it appear that the difficulty of retaining gold in a country largely dependent on the outside world for consumable commodities of all sorts received due consideration.

Dependence on Metallic Money

The belief that California would always have an abundance of metallic money was justified by the event. When the test came it was seen that gold could be retained in sufficient quantities for purposes of circulation, but while the determination to adhere to gold accomplished that purpose there is a doubt whether the singular enjoyment was not dearly purchased. Although enough gold was preserved for circulation the surplus was steadily drawn from the state, being surrendered in exchange for commodities which would have been produced at home, if the opportunity presented to merchants to profit by buying goods for greenbacks and selling them for gold had not existed.

Gold Production

Up to the close of the Civil war the mines of California had produced about $785,000,000 worth of gold. How much of this vast quantity remained in the state it would be impossible to tell with precision, but it is estimated that the coin in circulation during the Civil war in the United States did not exceed $25,000,000, the most of which was probably used in this state. The $760,000,000 had been drawn away to other countries. It may be true, as the economists assert, that the Californians in parting with their gold had received in exchange things which they desired and needed more than the metal, but nevertheless it is obvious that the withdrawal of what the world persists in regarding as the great fructifying agency of production and commerce must have affected California injuriously. Had it been possible to retain any considerable portion of this vast sum the effect of its retention must have been to stimulate industry; but it was impossible to hold it while the population persisted in buying more of the products of the outside world than they were able to pay for with products of their own other than gold.

Results of Bad Banking Methods

So it happened that the extreme prudence of the argonauts failed to avert the consequences against which their precautions were taken. As related in the chapter dealing with the period between 1846 and 1861 San Francisco escaped from none of the disastrous consequences of bad banking except the issuance of the sort of curreney which required the constant use of a "bank note detector" to determine its value, or whether it possessed any at all. The other evils were all experienced at recurring intervals. There were failures which swept away the savings of depositors and caused the bankruptcy of merchants, and there were business depressions as acute as those produced by the scandalous wildcat banking of the Middle West. And while the people were experiencing these drawbacks they found their troubles accentuated by high rates of interest, which could have been avoided by the adoption of a rational banking system which might safely have included among its functions the providing of a safe circulating medium based on such reserves of gold as could easily have been commanded.

SCENE DOWN MARKET STREET IN 1865

Habits of thrift did not assert themselves very early in San Francisco. It was not until 1857 that the first savings and loan society was established in the City, and it required several years of consideration by the law makers before they ventured to pass an act providing for the formation of corporations for the accumulation and investment of funds and the savings of depositors. Such a law was passed in 1862, and under its provisions the institutions already in existence, the Savings and Loan Society and the Hibernia Savings and Loan Society, which had been established January 23, 1857, and April 12, 1859, respectively, commanded an increased degree of confidence, and greatly stimulated the saving habit. These banks and those which were later founded were of great assistance to the community, and in course of time, to some extent, overcame the early drawbacks due to a lack of system which did not invite the formation of surpluses that could be advantageously employed in the promotion of enterprises. *(First Savings and Loan Society)*

Very few Californians were disposed to consider the subject of the currency from any other standpoint than that of circulation. They were proud that their system, which forbade the issue of bank notes differed from that of every other state of the Union, and they gloried in the fact that they were unique in steadfastly adhering to "sound money." Writers of the period of the Civil war boasted that the currency question had given them no trouble until United States notes found their way to the coast, and they regarded as a supreme distinction their ability to avoid the suspension of specie payments. It would have been difficult to convince any considerable number that they were making a mistake in putting themselves out of touch with the rest of the Union, and that they were doing much to maintain the condition of isolation which they were eager to overcome by establishing rail connection with the region east of the Rocky Mountains. *(Results of Refusal to Use Greenbacks)*

There were some who, like Governor Stanford, urged the acceptance of the legal tender money of the government, but in most cases they were influenced by patriotic rather than financial or commercial motives. The majority, unshaken in the belief that the use of greenbacks would prove injurious, frowned upon their introduction and thus effectually prevented their circulation. That, however, did not interfere with their being made objects of speculation. Considerable amounts were regularly disbursed by the federal government and these were bought up by merchants who used them to meet their Eastern obligations, and later, when they had very greatly depreciated they were purchased in considerable quantities and hoarded in strong boxes against the day when the Union cause should triumph and the credit of the nation be fully restored. *(Currency Speculation)*

The depreciation seriously affected employes of the federal government stationed on the Pacific coast, who continued to receive their salaries in paper money. They had a real grievance, for their dollars were sometimes more than cut in half when converted into current coin. As the cost of many commodities at the time was not much less in California, and particularly in San Francisco, than in other sections of the country where the depreciated government money freely circulated, they found it difficult to make ends meet. Clothing and most articles brought from the East cost nearly as much in gold in California as they did in the places where they were manufactured, but products of the state were somewhat cheaper. Although frequent representations of the injustice worked by these conditions were made to the authorities at Washington no substantial relief could be afforded to the suffer- *(Payments in Depreciated Currency)*

ing government employes, but it was a common subject of comment at the time that none of the positions went begging.

Few Debts Paid with Greenbacks

It has been remarked that in the beginning the pressure of public opinion, unaided by legislation of any sort, sufficed to prevent any considerable number of debtors taking advantage of the situation to pay debts contracted in gold with the depreciated currency. But the temptation held out by the enormous difference in value beween metallic and paper money, which constantly increased until the culminating point was reached when a greenback dollar was only worth 35 cents in gold finally overcame the scruples of many, and the tendency to take advantage of the opportunity to profit began to assume proportions which threatened to destroy the policy of maintaining a metallic currency. This possibility, however, was averted by legislative action, which had the effect of firmly establishing a system of specie payments which enabled California to maintain gold payments throughout the entire period of greenback depreciation.

Action of the Legislature

In 1863 the legislature passed what was popularly known as the specific contract law. In reality it was a series of amendments to the civil practice act which provided that contracts might be made in writing in which the kind of money to be accepted in payment or fulfillment of a contract could be specifically prescribed. The legislation was not in direct response to a popular demand. John F. Swift, a member of the assembly from San Francisco, had introduced a resolution in the lower house on February 19th, the object of which was to make the government legal tender notes the circulating medium in the state. It was rejected by the decisive vote of 49 to 11, and instead the amendments providing for the specific contract system after considerable discussion were adopted and became a law April 27, 1863.

Opinion of Specific Contract Law

The course adopted by the legislature aroused a great deal of feeling and was strongly condemned by ardent Unionists, who feared that the state's action would be construed into opposition to the policy of the federal government. The determination of the people to retain metallic money, however, was steadfastly adhered to and the courts sustained their determination. The supreme court of the state decided that the amendments were constitutional, and the federal supreme court upheld the decision. The situation created by the variation in value of the gold and paper moneys had been profitably utilized by the merchants of San Francisco before the passage of the amendments, and the decisions determining their constitutionality, but the removal of uncertainty gave a great impetus to trade which for a while sufficed to remove all doubts respecting the prudence of the course.

Merchants Profit by Adherence to Gold

Buying the greenbacks and selling for gold enabled the merchants to make great profits, and their prosperity for a while obscured the fact which, by some, was clearly perceived later, that an obstacle had been placed in the way of the development of the resources of the state by making it an undesirable place for settlement by men of small means living in the East who might wish to emigrate to California, but who could not afford to make the sacrifice involved by the necessity of converting their depreciated into "sound" money, which they found on investigation would not go much further than greenbacks in the way of purchasing land and such articles as they would be forced to buy in order to make a start in a new home.

Coast States Imitate

The number who looked at the subject from this standpoint was comparatively limited. They were so few that they scarcely affected the general belief that the profits of the traders in exchanging their enhanced gold for the products bought in the East with greenbacks more than compensated for any drawbacks resulting from the cause mentioned. The law worked effectively. The disposition to shirk obligations was reduced to a minimum by the general resort to methods which virtually converted every credit sale into a specific contract to pay in gold. All bills were made out with the legend "terms payable in United States gold coin" conspicuously printed upon them, and greenbacks ceased to be offered in trade by anyone with the expectation that they would be received for any more than their quoted value. That the policy was generally regarded as wise may be inferred from the disposition shown by the peoples of the other Pacific coast states and territories to follow the example of California.

This general acceptance did not prevent renewed efforts to bring the currency of California in harmony with that of the rest of the country. The class who were solicitous that the relations of the state with the federal Union should remain harmonious were insistent that the specific contract legislation was unpatriotic, and they sought to bring about an abandonment of the gold policy. On the 6th of February, 1864, a telegram was sent to Salmon P. Chase, then secretary of the treasury, asking his opinion on the subject. His reply was that he would be gratified to see "the people of California declare in favor of one currency for the whole people," but his suggestion to repeal went unheeded. In 1865, on the 20th of December, a bill was introduced into the state senate providing for the repeal of the specific contract system, but it was defeated in the following February by a vote of 18 to 10. Attempts to Abandon Gold Money

Out of this refusal to repeal grew a scandal, the charge being made that the measure was beaten by the expenditures of money. It was charged that seven senators had received $12,000 each for their votes, but the editor of the paper making the accusation could or would not produce evidence to substantiate the charge. It was probably inspired by patriotic indignation that legal tender money of the United States should be made the football of speculators who, it was believed, were doing all in their power to profit by causing it to depreciate. The common supposition at the time in San Francisco was that large sums of money were made by those dealing in paper currency, and that the chief operators would not hesitate to expend money to defeat legislation which would put an end to their business. A Legislative Scandal

As late as 1870, when the question of fidelity to the Union could no longer be raised, the effort to make it absolutely impossible to introduce paper money into the state as a circulating medium was actively persisted in by the advocates of strict adherence to the gold system. In that year the speaker of the assembly declared that his constituents had sent him to Sacramento to secure the passage of a law which would make verbal as well as written contracts to pay in gold binding. The continued agitation of the subject was due to the growing conviction that the inflexible adherence of the people of California to metallic money was not redounding to the advantage of the state. It was urged that the opportunity which the merchant enjoyed of buying goods on a greenback basis, and selling them at gold prices, tended to discourage manufacturing; and that the effect necessarily must be to retard the growth of the state. It was also pointed out that the difference in the value of the two circulating mediums deterred men who desired to emigrate from the East to California from doing so, as it was well nigh impossible to con- Manufacturing Receives a Setback vince them that the shrinkage of their money when converted from greenbacks into gold was more nominal than real.

Dealings in Specie

There was not much discussion of the abstract propositions involved in the money problem despite the fact that San Francisco merchants and business men generally had a greater familiarity with exchange operations than the peoples of other American cities outside of New York. Their dealings with the Orient, which began early, had accustomed them to considering the precious metals as objects of purchase and sale. For many years San Francisco was the center of the large specie dealings with China. Mexican dollars were brought to the City by water, and reshipped from this port to the Orient. This trade was a source of profit to the transportation companies, and to the brokers who dealt in Mexican dollars. While it lasted the habit of thinking of metallic money as a mere commodity, subject only to the law of supply and demand became ingrained. In electing to stand by gold little consideration was given to the fear that the introduction of an inferior money would drive out the superior. The course adopted was dictated partly by the early distrust of paper money as a circulating medium, and the subsequent experience with hard money, which created the feeling that there is only one real kind of money; a feeling that still endures, as is evinced by the fact that metallic money still circulates in California to the exclusion of its paper representatives.

Experience on the Gresham Law

The successful effort of California to maintain a metallic currency during the long period while the paper money of the government was greatly depreciated has never received the attention it merits. Students of the money problem instinctively avoid the difficulties encountered in considering what is conceded to be a unique experience. Were the people of California able to maintain specie payments because they resolved to do so? If a mere resolution to that effect, and the enactment of laws giving effect to the resolution proved efficacious in the case of California, why would not a similar attitude on the part of the other states of the Union have produced the same result? Many years after the close of the Civil war questions of this sort were asked, and found a partial answer in the declaration attributed to Horace Greeley, that the only way to resume specie payments was to resume. The suggestion of the editor was acted upon, and the premium on gold, which had gradually approached the vanishing point, disappeared entirely.

Peculiar Conditions in California

Obviously, however, the conditions so far as the whole nation was concerned differed greatly from those existing in California. Although the enormous quantities of gold extracted from the soil of this state, prior to the beginning of hostilities, were nearly all exported, chiefly to the East, the dependence of the people of that section of the Union upon Europe for the greater part of the manufactured goods consumed by them resulted in a steady adverse trade balance, the payment of which drained from the country all the precious metals mined within its borders. California up to the end of 1860 had produced nearly $640,000,000, of which probably over $600,000,000 had been shipped to the Atlantic seaboard, but according to the best information available all of this vast sum, except a small quantity retained in hoards had been shipped out of the country.

Why Greenbacks Were Used

It is sometimes said that it was the inferior paper currency which caused the disappearance of the gold and silver at the outbreak of the Civil war, but this disregards the fact that the excuse for the issuance of legal tender currency by the government was the absolute necessity of providing a circulating medium of some sort. Metallic money had completely vanished before the government presses were set to work. The people of the East were compelled to resort to all sorts of expedients to provide themselves with currency. "Tokens" and "shin plasters" of all kinds, many of them emitted in defiance of law, and none of them by its authority, were gladly received and used until the federal government stepped into the breach and supplied the need. Business was nearly paralyzed, and would have been completely suspended, had not a money of some kind been provided. It was assumed by congress that the precious metals could not be secured in sufficient quantity to meet its obligations, hence its embarkation upon the doubtful experiment of a paper currency.

Rapid Decline of Gold Product

The conditions were wholly different in California. The beginning of the war found the people of the state abundantly provided, as far as mere monetary needs were concerned, with gold, and what was of more consequence the outlook for a continuance of the supply of the precious metal was favorable enough to warrant the belief that any inroad on the existing available amount would be repaired by the fresh production. The product of the mines in 1860 was $44,095,163, and there was every reason to believe that something like this rate of production would be maintained for some time to come. This expectation, however, was disappointed by the result, for after 1860 the output of the placers began to decline, dropping to $41,884,995 in 1861, to $38,854,668 in 1862, to $23,501,706 in 1863, to $24,071,423 in 1864 and in the closing year of the war to only $17,930,858.

Favorable Trade Balances

This diminishing production did not interfere with the successful maintenance of the metallic currency system. The output was still on a scale commensurate with the needs of the state, provided the people did not make the blunder of buying more than they were able to sell of other products than gold. That they succeeded in doing this is shown by the table of imports and exports, which exhibits a favorable balance of trade during the four years following 1865. In 1866 exports by sea amounted to $17,303,818 and imports $15,846,070; in 1867 exports increased to $22,465,903 and imports to $16,987,437. The year following there was a further increase of exports, but the imports showed a much larger gain, the figures being respectively $22,943,340 and $18,723,738. In 1869 exports fell off but they still exceeded the imports by over a million, the amounts being exports $20,888,092 and imports $19,714,001.

Great Expectations

It was in this latter year that the long hoped for transcontinental railroad was completed. Up to that time practically all of the trade of California with the East and foreign ports was conducted through the port of San Francisco. Over its wharves passed all the grain, wool and other products shipped out of the state. After 1869 another outlet was afforded which the sanguine expected would bring about an era of prosperity rivaling that which the discovery of gold had produced. Long before the close of the sixty decade, however, men had begun to ask themselves whether the years between the gold rush and the close of the Civil war had been as prosperous as they should have been. San Francisco had grown in population, but there was a feeling abroad that the resource which had been the mainstay of the City was decreasing, and that it could not be depended upon as a basis for future growth. The opinion was very general that the state needed immigrants to till its fertile soils, to provide workers to convert the raw materials which could be produced into finished fabrics, and to open the mines which were being developed but slowly, owing to the difficulty of procuring suitable labor.

A Hopeful People

In dwelling upon these expectations the newspaper commentators of the years immediately preceding the driving of "the last spike" which united the rails of the two companies, the Union and Central Pacific, that built the first overland railway, there was an occasional note of pessimism; but as a rule an abiding faith in the future was exhibited. Once in a while a warning was sounded, usually in the form of a speculative inquiry as to the possible effect of the diverging values of gold and greenbacks. It was asked whether a man with a few thousand dollars at his command would not hesitate to have their number vastly reduced by moving to a country with an appreciated money. Sometimes also the question would be asked whether the railroad, when completed, would be able to move passengers at a rate that would tempt emigrants to take advantage of the newly created facility. But these doubts were submerged in the general chorus of belief that the railroad was going to do great things for California, and that it would speedily transform what was becoming a dull place into an active, bustling and prosperous community.

CHAPTER XXXVIII

THE TRANSPORTATION PROBLEMS OF CALIFORNIA

EARLY FREIGHT AND FARE RATES—FIRST EXPERIENCES IN RAILROADING—PROPOSED TRANSCONTINENTAL RAILROADS—PROJECTORS OF THE FIRST OVERLAND RAILROAD ORGANIZATION OF THE CENTRAL PACIFIC—CONGRESSIONAL AID TO OVERLAND RAILROADS—GRANTS OF LAND AND FINANCIAL AID TO THE CENTRAL PACIFIC—GREAT HOPES BASED ON OPENING OF COMMUNICATION WITH EASTERN STATES—EVERYBODY FRIENDLY TO THE PROMOTERS OF THE RAILROAD—FRIENDLINESS CONVERTED INTO HOSTILITY—GREED OF THE CENTRAL PACIFIC MANAGERS—CAUSES OF HOSTILITY—EFFORTS TO ESTABLISH A MONOPOLY—ATTEMPT TO GRAB MINERAL LANDS—SHUTTING OUT COMPETITION—CONTRACT AND FINANCE COMPANY—OAKLAND WATER FRONT GRAB—COMPLETION OF THE FIRST OVERLAND LINE.

HEN the early experiences of Californians with railroads are reviewed it seems extraordinary that there should have been such great expectations based on the accomplishment of a single line. In 1854, as already related, Governor Bigler had called attention to the law which permitted steam navigation companies and railroads to charge passengers twenty cents per mile for passage, and shippers at the rate of 60 cents per ton for freight. He pointed out that with this latitude the hoped for transcontinental railroad could charge a passenger $500 for transportating him from California to the Missouri, and that a ton of freight hauled the same distance would cost the shipper $1,500. It apparently did not occur to him that such rates would be prohibitory, but with the zeal of a true reformer he recommended an amendment which was adopted, by which the passenger rate of fare was limited to a maximum of ten cents per mile, and freight to fifteen cents per ton.

Early Transportation Charges

His denunciation of monopolistic tendencies and his recommendation which was considered reasonable indicates the state of public opinion in California concerning the value and possibilities of railroad transportation. Perhaps it was not much behind that of the rest of the country, for in the Sixties the troubles which later made themselves felt had scarcely begun to be perceived even in those sections which had provided themselves with railway facilities on a limited scale. In California railroads were almost unknown. As early as February 22, 1856, a road from Sacramento to Folsom, the first one built in California, had been opened, but as it did not prove profitable it was not completed. The decline of the placer mines and the high cost of labor put an end to the project and there was nothing more done in the way of railroad building until the construction of the line from San Francisco to San Jose was taken in hand. That road was completed in 1863, and was built

Public Opinion Concerning Railroads

356   SAN FRANCISCO

originally without subsidy of any sort, but later when the Southern Pacific acquired possession the company induced the government to grant alternate sections of land for the extension of thirty miles beyond San Jose to Gilroy, which had been constructed with the aid of $300,000 worth of bonds issued by San Francisco which were afterward turned over to the Southern Pacific as a gift.

First Experiences in Railroading

These first experiences were not of the sort calculated to fire the imagination, but San Francisco persisted in believing that railroads, and especially an overland road, would make the port the greatest in the world. Just how far this belief was linked up with the manifest destiny idea it would be difficult to state, but there are traces of a connection in the prediction that the completion of a railway across the continent would lead to the conquest of China. This expectation was indulged in before the rapid influx of Chinese engendered the fear that the Orientals would occupy the state in such numbers that it would cease to be a habitable place for whites.

Beliefs of the First Comers

Whatever processes of reasoning brought about the result, it is a fact that the people of the Pacific coast, almost from the date of the first successful operation of a steam railroad, held unfalteringly to the belief that a transcontinental railway would prove of incalculable value as an assistant in the development of the then vast unknown region west of the Mississippi, and they were ready to make any sacrifice, and consent to any method to obtain their desire. It is sometimes assumed that the generosity of the government in dealing with the first transcontinental railroads was dictated by the necessities of war, but that does not correctly state the attitude of congress towards Pacific railroad projects. That body was ripe for the acceptance of any enterprise involving the granting of government aid, but the dissensions created by the schemes of the men bent on the extension of slavery and administrative incapacity prevented the carrying into execution any of the suggested projects.

The East and the Public Lands

When the scheme of building a transcontinental railroad was in a nebulous stage there was little or no opposition manifested at the East to the policy of dealing liberally with the West. It was usually regarded as highly desirable that the Pacific coast, and the region intervening between it and the Missouri, should be made accessible and habitable, and any aid within the power of the government to extend it was thought might with propriety be rendered. In 1835, when it was proposed to congress to build a road from Lake Michigan to the Columbia river, and thence south to San Francisco, the suggestion was not assailed, although the aid asked for demanded a pronounced exhibition of government generosity. Three years later another proposal was made to build to Puget Sound. It met no opposition, but failed because of inaction. In 1846 a proposal was made to build a road to the sound, the proponents demanding a strip of land sixty miles wide along its entire length. This would have required a grant of about 92,000,000 acres. The quantity of land asked for does not appear to have been regarded as excessive to secure the desired railroad, but the proposal was antagonized on the ground that a continuous strip of land sixty miles wide in the possession of a company would give it a dangerous monopoly.

Benton's Proposed Transcontinental Road

In 1849 Thomas Benton introduced a bill for what he called a Central National road from St. Louis to San Francisco, with a branch some point west of the Rocky Mountains to the Columbia river. His scheme called for a strip of land one mile wide on either side of the road, and a pledge of three-fourths of the proceeds of the public lands of California and Oregon, and one-half of the sales of other public lands in the United States as a pledge for construction, the same to be set aside until the road was paid for and in operation. There is no evidence that this proposal was regarded with disfavor by the people of the East. Those who gave it any attention and expressed themselves on the subject invariably assumed that a railroad of the importance which one connecting the East and West must attain, would be cheaply obtained if it could be secured by donating land which in the nature of things must remain valueless until railroad facilities were afforded.

The theory of the period, and that which prevailed for a long time afterward, was that the interests of the entire people would be best served by the lands of the government passing into private ownership. It cannot be said that the approval given to the schemes for the donation of land on a large scale was due to ignorance or to lack of consideration for posterity. There was at this early day a relatively small contingent of men apprehensive of the evils of land monopoly who expressed themselves freely against the policy of liberal grants, but by far the great majority of the people were firmly convinced that the prosperity of the country would be promoted by opening up the uninhabited sections of the Union to settlers, and that far more would be gained by making all the lands of the government accessible by providing railroad facilities than could possibly be secured by depending on the slow process of population pushing westward. Opening Public Lands

This was the general belief, but it was more firmly entertained in San Francisco than in any other part of the Union, although there were some who had quite early formed the impression that isolation had its advantages as well as its drawbacks. No such sentiment was expressed, however, at a convention held in the City on September 20, 1859, in pursuance of a resolution of the legislature. It was attended by delegates from Oregon and Washington as well as California, and was presided over by John Bidwell. Judah, afterward the engineer of the Central Pacific, was present as a delegate from Sacramento, and his knowledge of the subject largely influenced the convention which pronounced in favor of the Central as the best of the three proposed routes and urged upon congress the desirability of reaching a decision to promote construction at once. Advocacy of Railroad Project

Eighteen fifty-nine was not an opportune time to urge consideration of such a measure on congress. That body was more concerned about the extension of slavery than the opening of the country to settlement. Benjamin P. Judah, who had been selected by the convention for that purpose, visited Washington, but while his arguments in favor of an overland railroad were listened to with interest, the prevalent sectional jealousy raised insuperable obstacles. Judah and four of his fellow townsmen, Leland Stanford, Collis P. Huntington, Mark Hopkins and Charles Crocker, took a more active interest in the matter than most of those who had attended the convention, and were not disheartened by the inaction of congress. They believed in the project which Judah had advocated and kept it alive. They were not greatly encouraged by the people generally who were anxious enough to secure a transcontinental railroad, but were indisposed to embark or lend assistance to the enterprise which they believed was too great to be carried through by individuals. Originators of First Transcontinental Road

Doubtless the general belief was correct; but it did not persuade the group of Sacramentans to abandon their idea that the project was feasible and would sooner or later be carried out successfully. None of the four was rich, and perhaps that Small Capital for a Big Enterprise accounts for the tenacity with which they adhered to their plans. Huntington and Hopkins were dealers in hardware, Crocker had a dry goods store and Stanford sold groceries and provisions. The magnitude of the undertaking, and the smallness of the capital which the four could command, not infrequently subjected them to quiet ridicule, but they were not affected by it, probably because after studying the matter in all its aspects they concluded that their losses in the event of failure would be so small by comparison with the possible gains in the event of success they hardly deserved to be considered.

Organization of Central Pacific Company

On June 28, 1861, the Central Pacific railroad of California was organized under the general law which had been passed in 1860. Stanford was chosen president, Huntington, vice president, and Hopkins, treasurer. James Bailey, a jewelry dealer was made secretary and Judah, chief engineer. The capital stock of the corporation was fixed at $8,500,000, and 85,000 shares of $100 each were offered. Of this number Stanford, Huntington, Hopkins and Crocker took each 150 shares, and about 600 more were taken by others outside the group, but these latter holdings were all parted with later by their owners excepting the few shares held by Edwin Crocker.

Route Adopted

The engineer, Judah, had recommended as practicable three different routes: one through El Dorado county by way of Georgetown; one through Illinois town and Dutch Flat, and a third by way of Nevada City. The second of the three named was accepted as the best and adopted. It was the route subsequently followed by the Central Pacific. After the decision was reached Judah sailed from San Francisco for New York. On the steamer he met Aaron A. Sargent and enlisted his assistance in the undertaking; that of Senator McDougal was also secured, and the campaign for a land grant was inaugurated.

Congress Passes Pacific Railroad Bill

In the following January Sargent made a speech in the house of representatives in advocacy of the proposed transcontinental railroad, and asked for the appointment of a committee to prepare a Pacific railroad bill. There were already several measures before the house, all of which provided for the construction of a road through its entire length by a single company excepting one which proposed that the building of the road westward should be given to an Eastern company, while a Western organization should be authorized to build eastward. Sargent's effort to take advantage of this proposed arrangement was promptly antagonized by the advocates of all the rival projects, but the Rollins bill, by which name the two company proposal was known, after a struggle passed the house on May 6, 1862, by a vote of 79 ayes to 49 noes, and on June 20, with some amendments which were accepted, it passed that body and was approved by the president July 1, 1862.

Railroad Land Grants

The bill as passed authorized the Union Pacific to build from the Missouri river to the western boundary of Nevada. It fixed the capital stock of that company at 100,000 shares of $1,000 each, and provided that not more than 200 shares should be owned by any one person. In addition to a right of way of 200 feet on each side of the middle of the line of the road and necessary grounds for station buildings, etc., it granted five alternate sections of land per mile on either side of the road, or all the odd sections within the limits of ten miles which had not been sold or otherwise disposed of, and excepting all mineral lands, but giving the timber on the granted lands. The company as rapidly as it should complete forty consecutive miles was to receive sixteen $1,000 bonds bearing six per cent interest,

THE WHAT CHEER HOUSE, A FAMOUS HOSTELRY OF THE EARLY FIFTIES,
DESTROYED IN THE FIRE OF 1906
View Taken in 1865

MONTGOMERY STREET, LOOKING NORTH FROM MARKET STREET, IN 1865

and running thirty years. The bonds constituted a first mortgage which the company had to redeem at maturity or forfeit the road to the government.

The authorization to the Central Pacific provided for the construction of a road from the Pacific coast at or near San Francisco, or the navigable waters of the Sacramento to the eastern boundary of California upon the same terms as those granted to the Union Pacific. Provisions were inserted which would enable either company to continue building on the same terms in case one dropped out, and the difficulties of construction in the mountainous region were recognized by increasing the number of bonds to be issued for a distance of 150 miles westwardly from the base of the Rocky Mountains, and a similar distance eastwardly from the base of the Sierra from sixteen to forty-eight per mile. The gauge of the road was fixed at four feet, eight and a half inches, and two years were to be allowed for the completion of the first 100 miles and one year for each additional 100 miles on the eastern half, but this degree of expectation was reduced to one-half the time on the Central Pacific's portion of the line.

Central Pacific Construction Authorized

Ground was broken on the western end of the line in Sacramento January 8, 1863, and this exhibition of energy was followed by a campaign of solicitation in California which was pursued as zealously as that which succeeded so well in Washington. The four projectors of the enterprise allotted the arduous work before them among themselves. Huntington took the financial agency; Stanford assumed the duty of attending to legislative matters; Crocker was to superintend construction and Hopkins was to supervise the business of procuring supplies. They displayed remarkable ability in the new field they had entered and won speedy recognition from men who had shown some inclination a year or two earlier to deride the idea of so tremendous an enterprise being successfully carried out by a quartet of small tradesmen.

Ground Broken in 1863

The early success achieved by the projectors of the Central Pacific in securing support for their undertaking indicates the degree of enthusiasm produced by the prospect of a realization of the long deferred desire for a transcontinental connection by rail. Special legislation was required to secure authorization for communities to extend aid, but it was promptly granted in every instance, because the legislature had every reason to believe that the requests were spontaneous. Besides the legislators shared in the general feeling that the state would be vastly benefited by the building of the railroad. If there were any who had misgivings as to the policy of extending aid, or who thought that the projectors of the road were asking too much of the people, they failed to make themselves heard above the chorus of approval.

Enthusiasm for the Enterprise

In 1863 acts were passed authorizing Placer county to subscribe for stock to the amount of $250,000 to be paid for in gold bonds to run 20 years and bearing 8 per cent interest, and San Francisco was permitted to take $600,000 worth of stock in addition to $400,000 subscribed to the Western Pacific, the company to receive thirty year, seven per cent gold bonds. In the same year valuable privileges were given by Sacramento to the company. Extensive right of way, lands outside the City, a great portion of its water front, and the tract covered with water known as Sutter lake or the Slough, were embraced in the donation. Later the city of Sacramento was permitted to take 3,000 shares and to emit $300,000 worth of city and county bonds. The state was also persuaded without much difficulty to pay $200,000 on the completion of the first twenty miles, a similar sum for the second

State, County and City Aid Rendered

twenty and $100,000 on the completion of fifty miles. In return for this aid the railroad was to carry public messengers, transport convicts sent to the State's prison, materials for the building of the capitol and exhibits for state fairs, and was to convey munitions of war in time of insurrection or invasion. In April, 1864, an act was passed authorizing the Central Pacific to issue bonds to the amount of $12,-000,000, the interest on which was to be paid by the state, a tax of 8 cents on the hundred being provided to meet interest and create a fund for redemption, from which, however, the counties that had already subscribed were exempted.

Everybody Friendly
These liberal measures received the approbation of the people at a subsequent election. If it was suspected at the time that the four men who were pushing the enterprise were being too generously dealt with the suspicion was carefully concealed. There will always be found some to oppose a measure, no matter how popular, who, when subsequent developments indicate that a mistake has been made, are able to point to some expression of disapproval and say "I told you so." There were a few such in 1864, but the great majority were too eager for the success of the project to suggest any doubts, or to think that the men who had at last succeeded in putting the undertaking on a footing that promised success could be too greatly rewarded for their efforts. As a matter of fact the value of the land grants, and the importance of the financial aid rendered were hardly appreciated; and when they were the prevalent opinion was that the benefits likely to ensue would more than compensate the donors.

Friendliness Converted Into Hostility
This attitude of friendliness to the men back of the undertaking did not endure long. It was speedily converted into a hostility which was transmitted to their successors in the corporation, long after the original four had passed from the scene. That the antagonism the original four aroused was not undeserved is claimed by no one. Occasionally as it grew in intensity their actions were defended by some who attempted to present as an offset to the abuses and evils for which they were responsible the growing wealth of the state, which they declared was wholly due to the facilities created by the energy of the men who had built the transcontinental and other railroads of California. This development, not always commensurate with the expectations of the people, and certainly not as rapid as it would have been had the sole aim of the projectors been to advance the interests of California, it was urged, excused the monopolistic policy of the men who shrunk from the commission of no crime which would help secure their control of the destinies of the state.

Connecting Sacramento with San Francisco
The history of the growth of the corporation which at one time completely dominated the policies of the state, controlled executives, legislatures and courts, and for that matter the people who submitted to the domination with wide open eyes, is inseparably linked with that of San Francisco. In its inception it was apparently a Sacramento enterprise, but the projectors of the Central Pacific, although they were inland merchants, had a keen appreciation of the fact that all roads in California led to San Francisco, and that, no matter how advantageous it might seem to utilize the navigability of the Sacramento river, ultimately the terminus of the road must be in the metropolis. This was so clearly perceived that the Western Pacific, which was to run from San Jose by way of Alameda Creek, Livermore Pass and Stockton to Sacramento, was subsequently constructed under an assignment made in 1862 of its rights and franchises westward, the object being to provide a connecting link between Sacramento and San Francisco.

SAN FRANCISCO

The road to San Jose was begun in 1860 and was opened to traffic in January, 1864. Its construction was aided by the counties of San Francisco, San Mateo and Santa Clara to the amount of $600,000, half of which was contributed by San Francisco. The Western Pacific, which shared in the land grant and bond provision of the act of congress, passed July 1, 1862, also received a helping hand from San Francisco, $400,000 of the $1,000,000, the expenditure of which was authorized by the legislature of 1863 being devoted to that road. San Joaquin and Santa Clara counties also contributed $400,000. *[Railroad to San Jose]*

-The apparently liberal provisions of the act of 1862, by which congress authorized the construction of the Union and Central Pacific railroads, and the supplementary gifts received by those corporations failed to provide the funds necessary for the rapid prosecution of the work, and the energies of the promoters of the great enterprise were devoted to securing further concessions. Judah, who had in the earlier stages of the undertaking attended to the delicate duty of persuading the solons in Washington that great results would flow from the opening of the country, died in that city in November, 1863, and Huntington undertook the work and subsequently achieved the reputation of being the most successful manipulator of men ever known at the national capital. His earliest efforts were not attended with much difficulty, because he had no rivals to combat, but in later years he organized a lobby which moved to the accomplishment of its object without scruples and utterly regardless of public opinion and criticism. *[Huntington as a Lobbyist]*

Huntington and those associated with him in 1864 found congress easy game. They dwelt upon the necessity of saving California to the Union, and congressmen and senators affected to believe that the completion of the overland railroad was an absolute necessity to prevent the state falling into the hands of the Confederates. The time had passed for such apprehension, but the argument coupled with glowing accounts of the enormous benefits which would follow the opening of the country west of the Missouri, served its purpose, and on the 2d of July, 1864, the original act was amended so as to greatly increase the bonuses to the two companies, and at the same time it extended the period in which the Central Pacific was to have been completed. The new act increased the number of alternate sections from five to ten sections per mile on each side of the road within twenty miles of it, and reserved lands within twenty-five miles instead of fifteen on each side, and provided that mineral lands to be reserved should not include coal and iron. A modification of the provision respecting the carrying of the mails was also secured by which the government agreed to pay half in cash instead of applying the whole amount earned to the account of the loans. But the most extraordinary concession obtained was permission to issue mortgage bonds to an amount equal to those authorized by the earlier act. By this legislation the first bonds emitted were practically converted into a second mortgage, the holders of the later issue having first preference. *[Additional Favors and Land Grants]*

That the first provision made by congress for the building of the transcontinental railroad was not regarded as excessive, is shown by the credulous acceptance of an assault made on the Central Pacific by Lester L. Robinson, an engineer, who declared that the route of the road as mapped out by Judah was impracticable above Colfax. Robinson charged that the estimates made by Judah were not based on field notes, and that the purpose of the Central Pacific people was to build only far enough to connect with the Dutch Flat wagon road, and thus secure a monopoly of the freight and passenger business between the Nevada mines and California. *[Rivalry Between Carriers]*

Robinson was probably inspired to make this accusation by rival carriers, who realized that the route by rail to Folsom, and thence by stage through Placerville to Virginia City, would no longer be able to compete with the Central Pacific when that road determined upon following the north fork of the American river. Several transportation companies made common cause of their opposition, among them Wells, Fargo & Co., the California Steam Navigation Company, the California Stage Company and the Pacific Mail. Their apprehensions were better founded than Robinson's accusations, for as soon as the Central Pacific began to approach Dutch Flat, preparations were made by its managers to construct a wagon and stage road over the mountains from the end of its tracks into Carson valley, which when completed considerably decreased the cost and reduced the time occupied in traveling between California and Nevada.

The "Big Four"

Although Robinson's charges were promptly taken up by the press, a portion of which fell into the habit of calling the transcontinental railroad project "the Dutch Flat swindle," it is not probable that any considerable number of people in San Francisco in 1863 shared the distrust implied by the charge that the selected route was not feasible. It was nearly two years later before strong antagonism began to manifest itself and it was provoked chiefly by observation of the disposition shown by the four controlling spirits to secure for themselves all the profits of the enterprise. In the beginning the work of construction was performed by subcontractors, but very soon there were wheels within wheels in the corporation. A company was formed consisting of the "big four" and they let all the contracts to themselves. This action was denounced as swindling, and a great uproar was made over the unblushing disregard of the rights of stockholders.

Antagonism Benefits Railroad Projectors

If the press and the agitators had been hired to help the men they were denouncing they could not have served them more effectively than they did by exposing the facility with which the interests of the stockholders of the corporation could be undermined. It was not long after the outcry began that the communities which had subscribed to the stock exhibited a desire to get rid of it, a disposition which the Central Pacific managers assiduously cultivated. San Francisco, which had promised bonds to the amount of $600,000 for an equal amount of stock, made a proposition which the company accepted to surrender the stock on condition that the amount of the bonds should be reduced to $400,000. The transaction was denounced as sharp practice, but in the light of the subsequent fate of the stock it does not appear that the City suffered financially through the surrender of its shares. It is possible that the people might have profited in the end by clinging to their shares, but the fact that matters were so shaping themselves already at this early period that there seemed no hope of the stock ever being worth more than the paper on which the certificates were printed, justifies the assertion that it was the part of wisdom to save the $200,000 and the interest upon that amount.

Efforts to Establish a Monopoly

The policy of absorption which the transaction with the City of San Francisco indicated was extended, and it was soon perceived by the people that the object of the managers of the Central Pacific, who were rapidly becoming the sole owners of the road, was to absolutely monopolize the transportation facilities of the state. Their avaricious propensities were roundly denounced by the press, which as events subsequently proved, correctly voiced the opinion of the people. It was later urged that the newspaper and other criticism to which the Central Pacific was subjected was responsible for the policy adopted by the railroad of actively interfering in politics, but the weakness of the excuse is exposed by the fact that much of the early censure of the methods of Huntington, Stanford, Crocker and Hopkins was directed against the practice of manipulating elections in order to insure control of the legislature, of the courts and even of minor political subdivisions.

The activities of the Railroad, and by that term the people of California for many years knew not only the line operated by the Central Pacific corporation, but all subsidiary roads and connections controlled by its managers, were by no means confined to securing favors in the shape of gifts. They also devoted themselves to the work of debauching those who controlled the taxation system of the state. Every conceivable device was resorted to in order to escape bearing a fair share of the burden of taxation. In Placer county the value of the road was fixed by the assessor in 1864 at $6,000 a mile, and the district attorney demanded that it should be raised to $20,000. In the succeeding year, despite protests, the valuation was given by the assessor at $6,000. In 1866 the pressure was too great for the official, and the assessment was raised to $15,000. The corporation refused to pay, and after protracted litigation complaisant courts found defects in the revenue laws which were of such a character that it was deemed prudent by the state and protesting county to compromise on a basis of $6,000 a mile.

<small>Railroad Shirks Taxation</small>

In dealing with Placer and other counties the Railroad invariably pursued the Shylockian policy of exacting the full pound of flesh. It took care to value its property for taxation purposes at the lowest figure possible, but demanded the last cent promised by people who had contributed to the building of the road in the expectation that their generosity would be recompensed by an improvement of conditions. Like San Francisco, Placer ultimately was induced to part with its Central Pacific stock. It was obliged by an act of the legislature, passed in 1870, to sell it and apply the proceeds to the redemption of its bonds. San Joaquin was driven to the same course, but made a somewhat better bargain than Placer, which received a very small amount for its holdings.

<small>Railroad's Shylockian Policy</small>

There were other causes that produced friction. Foremost among these was the obvious intent of the Railroad to retain control of the minerals of the lands donated by act of congress. The provisions of the grant appeared clear enough, but the apprehension that they would be disregarded was so great that the legislature in 1865 passed a resolution asking the government to withhold patents until a determination should be reached which would clearly decide the rights of miners. In the meantime, however, patents for some 450,000 acres had been issued, which were later discovered to have been drawn in conformity with the provision of the act excluding mineral lands from the grants.

<small>Grabbing Mineral Lands</small>

Despite these differences, and the hostilities they engendered, there was no serious diminution of the confidence of the people that the completion of the transcontinental railroad would work a marvelous change in conditions. But there was a growing perception of the fact that if all the benefits obtainable from communication with the East were to be derived, it would be necessary to secure greater facilities than a single road could afford, and that competition would be required to prevent the Central Pacific holding a monopoly which would place the industries of the state absolutely under its control.

<small>Early Fears of Monopoly</small>

This feeling extended to all parts of the state with which the corporation had dealings, but was most acute in San Francisco where it was beginning to be perceived that the development of the state's resources was being lost sight of by the

<small>General Apprehension</small>

railroad managers in their eagerness to increase their wealth and power. Hence we find San Franciscans nearly three years before the opening of the first overland line which occurred in 1869 actively advocating, and to some extent assisting in the promotion of a rival transcontinental road. It cannot be said that San Francisco's assistance was very intelligently extended. It certainly was not of the sort calculated to secure active opposition, for it was permitted to develop into a scheme to exclude all rivals from California territory.

The Atlantic and Pacific Project

One of the remarkable contradictions of the Californian, and particularly the San Franciscan attitude toward the Railroad in the days preceding the driving of the last spike of the Central and Union Pacific, and during many years afterward, was furnished by the treatment accorded to what was known as the Atlantic and Pacific project. In July, 1866, a transcontinental road known by that name was authorized by congress. It was to start from Springfield, Missouri, and run through Albuquerque in New Mexico, to the headwaters of the Little Colorado, and thence as nearly as practicable along the 35th parallel of latitude to the Colorado and thence to the Pacific. The credit of the government was not extended to this enterprise, but liberal rights of way and land grants as extensive as those made to the Union and Central Pacific were promised.

A Rival Road Asked For

Although this project was advocated largely on the ground that it would provide a rival line, and thus destroy the possibility of monopoly, very little attention was paid by San Franciscans to the machinations of the Central Pacific managers designed to prevent any competing line entering the state. California's representatives and senators lent themselves to the scheme of the Central Pacific, and assisted in effectually excluding all rivalry for many years. At the instance of the corporation, in the same act which authorized the construction of the Atlantic and Pacific, a provision was inserted which gave the Southern Pacific railroad, a company incorporated in California in 1865 to build a road from San Francisco to San Diego, and thence to the state line, to connect with a road from the Mississippi river, the same right of way privileges and equal grants of land.

Helping to Shut Out Rivals

The purpose of this move was obvious and was the subject of comment, but called forth no opposition from the business interests of San Francisco. The prospects of obtaining communication with the South overshadowed the possibility or probability of excluding rivalry. A number of arguments were employed which appealed with more or less force to the somewhat limited business capacity of the people. It was urged that the interests of California would be best subserved by its own people retaining control of its transportation facilities, and the idea of an Eastern corporation exploiting the state was deprecated. But the arguments employed were of far less assistance to the schemes of the Central Pacific managers than the general apathy which was only disturbed by the evils of the immediate present and took little account of the future.

Bogus Rivalry of Southern Pacific

The Atlantic and Pacific Company after securing its congressional authorization made haste slowly to avail itself of its privileges. The land grant did not appear to greatly tempt investors, and the building of a road to the Colorado river held out no particular inducements to men who were far seeing enough to recognize that the objective of a transcontinental line should be the greatest city on the Pacific coast, and not an unknown place on the banks of a river whose only outlet to the ocean was through foreign territory. Further, the activities produced at the East by the disbursements of the tremendous sums borrowed from foreigners to

UNION COLLEGE, LOCATED AT THE SOUTHEAST CORNER OF SECOND AND
BRYANT STREETS, IN 1865
This was one of the earliest institutions of learning in the city

UNITED STATES CUSTOM HOUSE, 1868, ON CORNER OF BATTERY AND
WASHINGTON STREETS

carry on the war were subsiding, and the reaction caused by the heavy drain on the purse of the people to provide the necessary revenue was beginning to make men cautious. As a result of these various causes the Southern Pacific practically had the field to itself, and succeeded in preventing an outside corporation from entering California for many years, thus virtually placing all of the rail transportation facilities within the state, and those extending from it beyond its border, in the control of one set of men; for the bogus rival of the Central Pacific was the creation of the men who ran the latter.

Meanwhile the construction of the original road was proceeding rapidly, and its projectors were making enormous fortunes by resorting to methods which flagrantly disregarded the rights of stockholders. The Contract and Finance Company, by which the managers made the work of construction cost an immensely larger sum than it would have been necessary to expend, had the affairs of the corporation been honestly conducted, made tremendous earnings which were chiefly employed in the promotion of other enterprises, all of which were designed to strengthen the hold the little group of men engaged in the huge enterprise for which every dollar employed in the undertaking was provided by the people.

<small>The Contract and Finance Company</small>

In 1867 the western division of the transcontinental road had crossed the Sierra and reached the state boundary line 140 miles from Sacramento, the Union Pacific at the same time had built westward over the plains of Nebraska and had laid 550 miles of track. Although this still left a gap of more than a thousand miles between Omaha and San Francisco, the prospects of early completion were beginning to make themselves felt in attempts to interfere with the plans of the Central Pacific managers to absolutely control the situation. One of these obstacles came in the form of a company organized to build a road from Vallejo to Sacramento with a branch to Marysville from Davisville. It was named the California Pacific, and its purpose was to greatly shorten the route to San Francisco from Sacramento by the Western Pacific. The managers of the Central Pacific endeavored by every possible method to prevent the California Pacific entering Sacramento, but their efforts were unavailing. A bridge was built across the river in 1870, but in 1871 Milton S. Latham, the president of the road disposed of his interest and that of his friends to the Central Pacific, which by this time had so strengthened its resources that it was able to buy off and absorb every property which threatened rivalry or in any way menaced its absolute control of California's transportation facilities.

<small>Progress of the Central Pacific</small>

Whatever may be said in condemnation of the methods of Stanford, Huntington and Crocker, they planned boldly and with great forethought. Much credit has been bestowed on men who came on the scene later, for carrying out policies which their sagacity and absolutely unscrupulous mode of carrying out projected schemes alone made possible of accomplishment. Their achievements were extraordinary, but they do not indicate the vastness of their ambition. It is well nigh impossible in the light of the changed conditions produced by the growth of population, the enormous increase of capital and the weakening regard for vested rights, to believe that sane men should have entertained the idea of absolutely dominating a region of imperial proportions and resources, but there can be no doubt that these men were firmly convinced that their plans would culminate in giving them complete control over the economic destinies of California.

<small>Bold and Far Seeing Plans</small>

Audacious Schemes Carried Through

The audacity of many of their schemes is only matched by the success which attended their efforts to put them into execution. The phenomenal accomplishment of a group of four men, practically without capital, building 833 miles of railroad and making enough out of the operation to construct a rival line three times as long as the parent road has been referred to or rather foreshadowed, but it does not surpass, except as an exhibition of spectacular energy, the wonderful success attained in completely subjecting the people of the State of California to the will of the corporation. We have accounts of men in antiquity whose ambition led them to impose their rule on nations, but it is doubtful whether the worst of them were ever animated by motives as sordid as those which prompted the Central Pacific quartet to impose their rule on California. Even Alaric may be credited with a desire for glory; we know Theoderic did aim to be great; but the far reaching plans, the unscrupulous schemes and the wilful defiance of law, and the corruption practiced by the Central Pacific corporation were wholly influenced by the desire to place the people under a system which would make them perpetually yield tribute.

The Colton Trial

To this end their minds appear to have been wholly devoted, and when one of the number occasionally surrendered to the weakness of human vanity in a way that might interfere with the perfection of the plans for complete domination he was sternly rebuked by the man who ultimately came to the front as the guiding spirit of the corporation. The disclosures made during the trial of the case brought against the company by the widow of David Colton, who claimed to have been overreached in a bargain made by her after the death of her husband, a man high in the confidence of the magnates, show that Collis P. Huntington seriously disapproved of the ostentatious display of wealth by his partners, and that he regarded with contempt every deviation from the course they had mapped out for themselves to build up a vast railroad system which would give them absolute control of all the approaches to the State of California.

Needs of Future Underestimated

That some of the schemes of the magnates miscarried, or failed of realization, was not due to lack of capacity to plan and ability to execute the possible. They dreamed of commanding all the feasible methods of entering San Francisco, but they neglected to take into consideration the changes the future might bring in the way of overcoming obstacles which at the time they were working most actively must have seemed insuperable. In the Sixties it did not occur to anybody to assume that there would be an expansion of needs great enough to override difficulties which seemed to make impracticable methods and operations now performed with ease. Men were optimistic but their optimism was still dominated by practicability, and their plans for the future were usually based on observation of existing needs, and took no account of their increasing in geometrical ratio. When men spoke of the City as a metropolis destined one day to count its population by millions, they did not reduce their optimistic prediction to a thinkable form. They had no clearer conception of what such a city would require than the average man has of the word trillion or billion which simply means to him an enormous sum too great to be considered concretely. The men who under the inspiration of Huntington looked so far into the future rose above this restraint, but did not wholly escape its influence. They may have believed that San Francisco was destined to have its millions, but they laid many of their plans as if they were convinced that it could never increase its wants to such an extent that the provisions they made for meeting them could prove inadequate.

This is the impression produced by reading the comment on such operations as the effort to control the water front of Oakland and to secure possession of Goat island for terminal purposes. At this distance of time it may seem amusing to us that the people of San Francisco should have regarded with alarm the attempts of the Central Pacific to make their port difficult of access. But in the closing years of the Sixties there were no visions of Dumbarton Point bridges, and no one dreamed of the possibility of tunneling the bay. The only thought that suggested itself was that the machinations of the railroad managers might prove successful and that the City would be bottled up. And there is no doubt that the manipulators deemed the bottling scheme entirely practicable, and that they had little fear that the operation would prove disastrous to the port.

Bottling up a Port

That no apprehension of evil consequences entered the mind of the men who sought to gain complete control of Oakland's water front, after obtaining generous concessions from the legislature which enabled them to obtain for a trifle a large slice of that of San Francisco, is shown by the boldness they displayed in carrying out their plans. In 1868 they set in motion a scheme which made a long step toward the accomplishment of their object. A corporation was formed under the name of the Oakland Water Front Company, which designed acquiring all the existing wharves in that city and all the lands upon which wharves might be built. It named as trustees, Horace N. Carpentier, Leland Stanford, John B. Felton, Edward R. Carpentier, Lloyd Teris and Samuel Merritt. On the 31st of March, 1868, Horace Carpentier, who claimed to own by contract and deed from the city of Oakland, all the lands in front of it, between high tide and ship channel, executed a conveyance to the Water Front Company, and on the day following that concern deeded to the Western Pacific Railroad Company four hundred acres of the most valuable part of the city's frontage on the bay. The distrust created by the movement was in a measure allayed by the Western Pacific Company agreeing to convey to the city of Oakland certain wharf, dock and toll rights between Franklin and Webster streets, and within 18 months to extend and complete its road to and along the Oakland water front, and within three years to expend not less than $500,000 in making improvements.

Oakland Water Front

The people of Oakland, which was a very small city at the time, regarded the bargain as a good one. Their point of view was not the same as that of San Francisco. They were eager to have the railroad penetrate their town, and as the agreement resulted in the building of a road from Oakland to Niles on the main line of the Western Pacific, and in the construction of a line through Alameda to Haywards, and in some improvements on the water front the feeling was one of satisfaction not much tinged with apprehension. Even when all these various improvements were absorbed by the Central Pacific a year or two later no suspicion existed that the Carpentier blanket claim might be so stretched that the city would be prevented from giving to other companies the privilege of access to its water front.

Oakland Accepts a Mess of Pottage

At the same time that preparations were being made by the Central Pacific to control the approaches to San Francisco through Oakland, its emissaries were actively at work in the legislature securing from that body important privileges and donations. On the 28th of March, 1868, a bill was passed granting to the

Controlling Approaches to the City

Terminal Central Pacific Railway Company, submerged and tide lands which aggregated 150 acres, to be used for terminal purposes. It was over the lands thus granted that the first long wharf extending into the bay from Oakland was constructed. The act that donated the tide lands—they were appraised at the insignificant sum of $3 an acre—also accorded the privilege of reclaiming the intervening space and connecting it with the Oakland and Alameda shore. This has since been done, and much valuable land for the terminal purposes of the company has been created. The only condition exacted by the legislature was the expenditure of $100,000 upon improvements, and that a rail and ferry connection between San Francisco and the terminal lands should be provided within four years.

Mission Bay Lands Granted   Two days after the making of this grant the legislature, March 30, 1868, authorized the granting by a Board of Tide Land Commissioners of thirty acres of submerged land in Mission bay, south of Channel street, and outside of the old red water front line, together with a 200 feet wide right of way over state lands to enable the Western Pacific and Southern Pacific to reach the terminal which it was proposed to create by reclaiming the property. This improvement was not begun within the time provided and an extension was granted to the company in March, 1870, to which was attached a proviso that a first class road should be constructed from Oakland on the Bay of San Francisco to a point on the Straits of Carquinez, opposite the town of Vallejo. The construction of such a road would have given an all rail connection with the East by ferrying the trains over the waters of the strait. The road was subsequently constructed, but the people had to submit to many delays before their desires were realized, the railroad managers finding it more expedient to push their plans in other directions than to promote the interests of San Francisco by hastening all rail connection by a shortened route.

Greed of Railroad Managers   Any attempt to accurately describe the attitude of the public towards the railroad while these schemes were being projected and carried out would be misleading, because it was extremely contradictory. There was laudation of the corporation's enterprise, and on the other hand keen criticism of what some of the papers characterized as the "hoggishness" of the projectors of the transcontinental railroad. It was urged by some that the generosity of the government had provided more than sufficient funds to build the overland railroad, and that it was pure effrontery for the builders to endeavor to secure more favors by begging and manipulating legislatures, but the most vigorous condemnation was that directed against the creation of the Contract and Finance Company by which the men on the inside were enabled to enrich themselves at the expense of the stockholders. The language used in denouncing these machinations was of the plainest, and epithets were applied to the managers which were actionable, but they went on with their plans serenely indifferent to public opinion.

Indifference to Criticism   Perhaps their disregard of adverse opinion was not wholly without justification. There was unquestionably a strong sentiment in the community, and throughout the state generally, that the benefits which would result to California through the activities of the projectors of the first overland railroad, would more than repay the people for any toll that the manipulators might exact. There had already been developed at that time something like a perception of the fact that men who were at the back of quasi public enterprises were in a sense under obligation to deal fairly with the people, but it did not assert itself very strongly. The so-called best opinion was extremely conservative, and was uncompromisingly opposed to regulation. Very few were disposed to demand that men in dealing with the community or with stockholders should strictly observe the standard of honesty set up for individuals.

In short there was no public conscience in the Sixties of the kind we are now familiar with, but it developed with surprising rapidity in California in the next decade, so fast indeed, that it took a quarter of a century for the East to catch up with and absorb the ideas evolved while the state was under the domination of the men who later came to be comprehended in the term "the Railroad." No one in San Francisco on May 10, 1869, the day on which the last spike was driven at Promontory in Nevada, which connected the rails of the Central and Union Pacific railroads, suspected what the future held in store. He who would have predicted on that day that in less than a decade the men whose energies made the connection possible would in a few years become the most heartily despised and feared men in California, would have been deemed a lunatic.

Developing a Public Conscience

On that day at least, all San Francisco concurred in singing the praises of the men who had at last brought about a realization of the hopes entertained for twenty years. The railroad was at length completed, and the state was to enter upon an era of prosperity. Bands played their music, the militia and civic bodies marched to the inspiring strains of national and other airs, the Stars and Stripes floated to the breeze from innumerable business and other houses handsomely decorated to celebrate the event. No one on that May day in 1869 ventured to express a doubt that the people might be "paying dearly for their whistle." Good feeling ran so high it would have been deemed sacrilege to speak disparagingly of the man who, surrounded by an assemblage of about a thousand persons, drove the gold spike into the polished tie of California laurel, which had a plate of silver on which was engraved the names of the officers of the Union and Central Pacific companies. Every one on that day believed that the record on the silver plate conferred an undying fame on those whose names were inscribed upon its brilliant surface. No one dreamed that a few short years thereafter the men so honored on May 10, 1869, would be execrated by a majority of those who celebrated and rejoiced over the completion of the first transcontinental railroad.

The Driving of the Last Spike

CHAPTER XXXIX

LABOR CONDITIONS AND THE CHINESE QUESTION

ORGANIZATION OF A CENTRAL TRADES ASSEMBLY—STRIKE OF FOUNDRY EMPLOYES—
LABOR AND POLITICS—ATTEMPT TO PASS AN EIGHT HOUR LAW—FORMATION OF AN
EIGHT HOUR LEAGUE—TRADES UNIONS IN 1867—A WORKINGMEN'S CONVENTION—
LABOR LEADERS FAVOR POLITICAL ACTION—WORKINGMEN WIN IN PRIMARY ELEC-
TIONS—TRADE UNIONISM RECEIVES A BACKSET—WOMEN WORKERS—THE WORKING-
MEN AND THE CHINESE—RACE PREJUDICE IN EARLY DAYS—LEGISLATIVE INVESTI-
GATION IN 1852—SAN FRANCISCANS TOLERANT OF CHINESE—OPPOSITION TO CHI-
NESE IMMIGRATION—RAILROAD IMPORTS CHINESE LABORERS—FEW JAPANESE—AS-
SUMED NEED OF ORIENTAL LABOR—LAND MONOPOLY AND CHINESE LABOR.

IT IS sometimes assumed that the relations of employer and employed were not rudely disturbed in California until the late Seventies. Those who assert that such was the case have no warrant for doing so. The evidence is overwhelming that San Francisco was the center of difficulties created by the activities of trades unionism long before the opening of that decade. It is true that during the first few years following the gold discoveries the differences between the employer and the worker were adjusted without much friction, and it is even recorded that the losing party in successful strikes actually conceded that the success of their opponents did no serious harm and benefited the whole community by more thoroughly diffusing the gold gathered by the miners. But this condition did not endure very long. Indeed there were signs of its disturbance before the outbreak of the Civil war, but organization was lacking and the troubles were sporadic and were dealt with easily because employer and employed generally settled their differences without the intervention of outsiders. Shortly after the firing on Sumter, however, there were indications of unrest. The workingmen of San Francisco were undoubtedly in much better ease than most of their fellows at the East. Their nominal wages were considerably higher than those in the states on the other side of the Rockies, and the purchasing power of the money they earned was not impaired as was that of the workers on the Atlantic seaboard by the rapid advance in prices of all commodities. Although the merchants were getting rich by buying goods for greenbacks and selling them for gold, their profits were not made at the expense of the mechanic or artisan who had been able to maintain a satisfactory wage rate during the period of descending prices which followed the flush times of the Fifties and continued until San Francisco began to feel the effects of the disastrous panic and depression of the closing years of that decade.

Labor Conditions in the Sixties

371

Organization of Central Trades Assembly

The condition of the worker in San Francisco was generally satisfactory in 1863, but in that year the great demand for soldiers had lessened the available force of laborers and mechanics in the East to such an extent that they were able to effectively organize for the purpose of bettering themselves. Wages on the other side of the Rocky Mountains had been very low in the Fifties, and they were slow to move upward when prices under the influence of a depreciating currency began to soar. The situation was one suggesting the desirableness of organization, and a movement to that end became quite general and proved successful. The circumstances were wholly different in San Francisco, but the example of eastern success proved contagious and a movement was started in the City which resulted in the organization of a Central Trades Assembly in the fall of 1863. This assembly was conducted as a secret society and did not last very long. Its first president was John M. Day, a man who afterward figured in the Kearney movement. During the existence of the assembly there were numerous strikes, but it is probable that they would have taken place without its inspiration, for there had been reductions of wages in the earlier part of the year owing to a plethora of help, and as the oversupply was somewhat diminished later, the demand for a restoration to the former rates was not unreasonable.

Trades Assembly Collapses

The discussions of the labor situation in the press at that time revolved wholly about the law of supply and demand. One journal advised "labor to make no unreasonable demand" and it would have the sympathy and encouragement of the community; at the same time it warned the strikers that the opposite course would certainly result in injury to them by causing a general disturbance of the labor market if their persistence should bring competitors to the City to fill their places. It is not probable that considerations of this sort had much weight with the men bent upon effecting organization, but they influenced the working element sufficiently to make it lukewarm in its support of the assembly and it went to pieces in the following year.

Strike of Foundry Employes

In 1864 the foundrymen of San Francisco refused to accede to a demand for an increase of wages. At that time the boiler makers were receiving from $3.50 to $4 a day, and they asked for a raise to $4 and $5. The employers declared that the conditions would not justify the advance and declined to consent to a uniform increase. One concern offered to pay the increased wage demanded by seventeen of its employes, but positively refused to recognize the principle of compensating without reference to the qualifications or capacity of the worker. The employes would not recede from their position and "went out." Sympathetic resolutions were passed by other unions, but no financial aid was rendered to the strikers who were compelled to fight their battle without assistance. As the rate of wages paid to moulders was much lower at the East than in San Francisco the places of the strikers were filled by men brought from that section. No violence attended this strike, and the unsuccessful moulders union which was temporarily crippled by its want of success was speedily reorganized.

Labor and Politics

The failure of the moulders strike emphasized the argument that the difference in wage levels between East and West would not warrant aggression on the part of the employed, but the activity of a certain element in the unions was not wholly abated. Although the Central Trades Assembly had practically passed out of existence, some of its members who were dominated by the idea of creating a labor party, or at least of making the influence of labor felt in politics, continued their

FERRY LANDING AT FOOT OF PACIFIC STREET IN 1867

efforts. For two or three years there was an approach to harmony between employer and employed, and there was little or no agitation, but in 1867 there was a marked revival of effort to solidify the workers which developed into a political movement aimed at securing by legislation certain reforms which employers refused to concede to the demands of the workers.

In the legislature of 1865 an unsuccessful attempt had been made to pass an eight hour law. It failed because the petitions asking for the fixing of shorter hours of labor had been met by numerous remonstrances from mechanics who regarded the innovation as an encroachment on individual liberty, and insisted that the inevitable result of shortened hours of labor would be diminished wages and decreased production. In 1865 there was still a large proportion of workers who produced on their own account. The factory system had not developed to any extent, and the proportion of employers and employed was more nearly equal than later. The shoemaker who hired two or three men to assist him in producing, and the tailor who employed a few journeymen, were in close touch with their employes, and in many cases they were able to make the latter see that their interests were identical. These facts explain what later seemed an anomalous, but was really a perfectly natural condition of affairs.

Attempt to Pass an Eight Hour Law

The failure to pass an eight hour law did not discourage those who were seeking to bring about a reduction of hours of labor. An eight hour league was formed by the carpenters, which made itself felt to such an extent that Haight, the democratic governor had been met to the legislature of 1867-8, advocated the enactment of an eight hour law. Out of this league in 1867 was developed the Mechanics' State Council which devoted itself chiefly to the propagation of the eight hour idea, and in the same year the Industrial League of California, with branches in the northern and southern part of the state, was formed.

Eight-Hour League Formed

In January, 1867, the "Industrial Magazine" published a list of unions then in existence, all of which were holding regular meetings. They numbered twenty-six and embraced a great variety of trades. They were called: Industrial League No. 2; Eureka Typographical Union No. 21; Plumbers Protective Union; Bricklayers Protective Association; Stonecutter's Union; Operative Stone Mason's Society; Laborers Protective Association; Tinsmith's Protective Association; Moulders Association; Boiler Maker's Society; Plasterers Protective Association; Ship and Steamboat Joiners Association; Journeymen Shipwrights Association; Ship Caulkers Association; Journeymen Horseshoers Association; Shoemaker's Protective Association and Cartmen's Association. The magazine explained that this was not a complete list, as there were present at a convention which met on March 29, 1867, representatives from the Saddle and Harness Maker's Association, House Carpenters No. 1 and No. 2, also of the Coopers, Metal Roofers, Machinists, Riggers and Stevedore's unions.

Trades Unions in San Francisco in 1867

At this convention, which was attended by 140 delegates, thirty-two trades were represented. In the discussion of later political conditions it has been assumed that the disposition of workingmen to thoroughly organize did not manifest itself until the period immediately preceding the success of the workingmen's party when they elected Eugene Schmitz to the mayoralty of San Francisco. It will be seen from the list presented that this assumption is erroneous, and some account of the doings of the workingmen's deliberative body which met in 1867 will show that the political success of the workingmen's party organized by Abraham Ruef was

Working-men's Convention

anticipated thirty years earlier, and that the workers of that day inserted in their platforms demands which the country has since acceded to, and suggested changes which enthusiasts are now advocating as marvelous political reforms.

Eastern Advances Rejected

There was one feature of the deliberations which in a marked fashion indicated the aloofness of California at that period. A strong effort was made to induce the convention to send delegates to a national gathering, but a resolution to that effect was voted down after an extended debate which exhibited something like a consensus of opinion that the labor situation in California and the Pacific coast generally had peculiarities which made it desirable that those directly concerned should work out their problem without outside interference. Some of the arguments employed pointed to the fear that the possible result of a national federation of labor might be to reduce the California working man to the admittedly worse condition of the Eastern toiler, and intimations were freely thrown out that the aims and aspirations of the workers of the two sections might at times diverge if they did not actually conflict.

Political Action Favored

There was something like a divergence at the time, for the California organizers were strongly inclined to make a political machine of the affiliated unions, while the current of opinion ran strongly against such a movement in the East. The convention before it adjourned committed the unions to the policy of participation in political affairs. A resolution was unanimously adopted which provided for the creation of a committee consisting of one member from each delegation, whose duty it was made to draft a workingman's platform "embodying all justly needed reforms, calling the attention of the workmen to such measures of self protection as the exigencies of the time might require and urging the formation of workingmen's unions."

Faith Pinned to Primaries

This resolution was supplemented by another, in which the opinion was expressed "that the most advisable means of arriving at success in the object for which our convention has been convened is to act in our primary capacity as citizens, and to vote for proper representatives among ourselves at the primary elections, and they (sic) should therefore as citizens and favorable to the working classes elect only such delegates as this convention shall have recommended." In accordance with this resolution it was decided that the delegates from each of the San Francisco districts should nominate persons for the primary ticket. This was done and after some debate in which the qualifications of those put forward were freely discussed, a ticket was made up which was put forward as that of the workingmen. The primaries were held on June 5, 1867, and when the votes were counted it was found that the ticket framed by the convention had carried by a large majority.

Politicians Take the Hint

The success of the workingmen at the primaries produced a marked effect upon the politicians and resulted in the passage of the eight hour law and a mechanic's lien measure by the legislature of 1868. In the assembly the eight hour law was championed by the member from Mariposa county, who had conferred upon him the nickname of "the Mariposa blacksmith." His attitude, and the vigor with which he advocated their cause made a distinct impression on the workingmen, and they tendered him the nomination for congress. As he appeared inclined to accept, but subsequently withdrew his name, he was charged by the workingmen with having been bought off. The accusation was evidently inspired by observation of the fact that the workingmen's movement was distasteful to the railroad magnates, who had been subjected to severe criticism by members of the convention of 1867. The

SAN FRANCISCO

workingmen seemed to regard as ample corroboration of their suspicion the subsequent close relations of Wilcox, the Mariposa blacksmith, and the Central Pacific railroad.

When the Central Pacific railroad was completed in 1869 many who had found employment in the work of construction had to seek other occupations. The number of unemployed from this cause was augmented by a considerably increased immigration from various parts of the Union. At the same time Chinese were entering the state at the rate of about two thousand a month. This brought about a condition of affairs which worked disadvantageously to trades unionism. The disastrous results of the Black Friday of 1869 were being felt at the same time and a distinct check was given to progress. Under the circumstances the unions found it difficult to maintain their existence. The eight hour law was disregarded and wages were falling. When the decade 1870-80 opened the workingmen were no longer an active factor in politics, and many of the unions had almost ceased to preserve their organization.

A Backset to Trades Unions

A feature of the workingmen's movement of this period was the active interest taken in promoting the claims of women. The unions were not disposed to support demands for the suffrage, but they were quite ready to advocate the bestowal of clerical positions upon the sex. On January 10, 1870, a resolution was introduced in the state senate requesting the several state officers to give employment to women in their respective departments whenever practicable. It passed, but on a motion to reconsider was lost. Although this attempted legislation did not have its inception with the workingmen's organizations they made it quite clear in various ways that they were favorable to its adoption. Day, and a few other of the leading spirits of the workingmen's party of 1868 were thoroughly convinced that their cause would profit by being linked with that of the women and they acted on this theory, but without official indorsement of the unions.

Unions and Women Workers

No greater mistake was ever made in the discussion of a political question than that embodied in the very general assumption that the anti Chinese movement in California had its inspiration from organized labor. It is true that in the Sixties the trades unions and organizations of workingmen carried on an active propaganda against the introduction of Orientals, but their action had long been preceded by movements against the Chinese in no wise associated with hired labor. The earliest troubles grew out of the dissatisfaction of the miners, who were opposed to their working the placers, but the miners' unions were not labor organizations, their membership being made up in the early days of men who were working on their own account.

Unions and the Chinese

The hostility of this class was directed as much against certain other classes of foreigners as against the Chinese. Chileans, Peruvians and Mexicans were antagonized by the placer miners and frequently subjected to the same sort of mistreatment as the Orientals. The alignment was somewhat contradictory, for all Latins were not under the ban. The Frenchman, as often as otherwise, was *persona grata* in the mining camps, and curiously enough, Irish and Germans who had lived some time in the Eastern states before emigrating to the coast were regarded as Americans and made common cause with the latter against foreigners. The Know Nothing movement, which had a great vogue in California in the early Fifties, was directed not so much against all foreigners as against those who were regarded as undesirable, and was very much complicated by race prejudice, introduced into the

Anti-Foreign Movement of Miners

state by men from the slave holding section of the Union. General Persifer Smith of the United States army was an extreme exponent of the native American idea and proposed to prohibit all foreigners from mining for gold in the newly discovered diggings, but his views met with little sympathy. Other army officers influenced by what must be regarded as one of the earliest movements for the conservation of minerals, had proposed to regulate mining by compelling the miners to pay royalties, in the fixing of which citizens of the United States were to be favored, but this plan had a few advocates among civilians.

Chinese Testimony not Accepted

But while there was a wide divergence of opinion respecting who should be permitted to search for gold there was little or none concerning the status of certain races. The convention which framed the constitution, while effectively providing against the introduction of slavery, at the same time contributed to the existing prejudice against negroes, and the courts subsequently extended it to other races, among which the Chinese were included. Justice Hugh C. Murray, of the supreme court of California, in the case of George W. Hall, who had been convicted of murder on the testimony of a Chinese held that the word "Indian," as used in the statutes concerning witnesses, included not only the North American Indians but the whole Mongolian race. He admitted that the word as used in the statutes was specific, but argued that from the time of the discovery of America by Columbus all the countries washed by the Chinese waters were dominated by the Indies and that all who came from thence were Indians.

Early Race Prejudice

These refinements may seem very absurd to us, but at that time race distinctions were greatly exaggerated, and led to serious misconceptions. There is no doubt that very many miners were profoundly convinced that all Chinese were thieves, and this belief had its effect in stimulating hatred which often exhibited itself in unprovoked assaults on the Chinese. It is true that much of the ill feeling against the latter may have been provoked by their unremitting industry, and their exhibitions of an economy bordering on penuriousness, but these latter excited the animadversions of all other classes of citizens, and were in no sense the result of a trades union activity, nor in any wise due to feeling worked up by politicians. In short the Chinese were hated for their habits, which some call virtues, and the hatred was shared indiscriminately, even the ostracized and outlawed Mexicans making common cause against them.

Mexican Hatred of Chinese

One of the most atrocious crimes ever committed in California was perpetrated by a member of Joaquin Murietta's band of robbers named Garcia. It is related of him that he cut the throats of six Chinese after tying them together by their cues. He assigned no other reason for his brutality than the fact that they were such easy victims. On another occasion near the mission San Gabriel in Los Angeles county Garcia and Murietta surprised a couple of Chinese camping near the roadside. The wretched Orientals offered no resistance when they were robbed by the bandits, but the outlaws killed them for the pure lust of blood. Although Murietta and his gang rarely showed mercy to anyone who fell into their hands they were charged with being particularly vindictive in dealing with Chinese.

Early Predictions of Trouble

It should suffice to effectually dispose of the assumption that the antagonism to Chinese immigration was worked up by trades unions and politicians to relate that as early as 1854, when the question of excluding Chinese from the gold mines was discussed, the objections urged against their admission was based on the idea that "they were naturally an inferior race. both mentally and corporally, while

SAN FRANCISCO

their habits of living were particularly offensive to Americans." The man who thus summed them up was an American and not of the laboring class. He was not prejudiced and was apparently averse to considering the subject for he declared "it would be out of the question for him to discuss the general Chinese question," but he ventured the prediction that it would afford much opportunity for debate "by philosophers, statesmen, politicians and mere laborers in California for many years to come."

Still earlier than the date of this comment a committee had been appointed by Governor Bigler which made a report to the Legislature on the 28th of April, 1852, on the subject of Chinese immigration. The Chinese population of the State was then estimated to be about 22,000, the major part of them being at the mines, although there was a settlement of some consequence in San Francisco. The investigators entered into a detailed examination of the activities of the six companies, and showed that they each had a headquarters in the City, where the names of the new arrivals were recorded. These companies or tongs maintained a close supervision of the Chinese in the City and in the country, and they were not permitted to leave the United States without paying their debts, which were usually obligations to the tongs for moneys advanced in bringing the immigrants to America. It was estimated that the six companies had about $200,000 employed in the business of aiding immigrants who were all of the coolie class, and because of their ignorance were particularly amenable to the authority exercised over them by the leaders of their respective tongs. These facts and other details furnished by the report undoubtedly did much to increase the dislike felt for the Oriental, and there were numerous demonstrations against them in the mining towns, but in San Francisco, the place where the most trouble might have been expected if organized labor had been malignantly active, they were practically unmolested.

Legislative Report on Chinese in 1852

The records bear out the statement that, on the whole, San Francisco was much more tolerant of the Chinese in the Fifties than the people of the interior. There were at that time many in the City who believed with Governor McDougal that the Chinese could be made useful citizens by setting them at occupations for which they were peculiarly fitted. In 1851 he outlined an extensive project for the reclamation of swamp and overflowed lands, and actually recommended that further importations of Chinese should be made in order that such lands might be brought under cultivation. He spoke of the Chinese as "one of the most worthy classes of our newly adopted citizens, to whom the climate and character of these lands are particularly suited." The suggestion he threw out excited no adverse comment. It may have been passed over with silent contempt, for McDougal, who was an accidental governor, was not held in high esteem, but there was doubtless a considerable number of San Franciscans at the time who were inclined to look with favor on any scheme of providing cheap labor.

San Franciscans Tolerant of Chinese

But this acquiescent attitude did not extend to the mining regions. The Chinese were not merely harassed by the miners, who objected to their taking out gold, but they invoked legislative aid to make the industry as unprofitable for them as possible. Under interior pressure the Legislature imposed a license tax on foreign miners which was only collected from Chinese, and in 1855 an act was passed which levied a per capita tax of $50, collectible from the master, consignee or owner of the vessel, upon every Chinese imported. Much scandal grew out of this exaction, as those entrusted with the business of collecting the head tax were singularly re-

Miners' License Tax Imposed on Chinese

miss about turning the money into the treasury. The administration of the license tax law in the interior was not very creditable, and there was much recrimination and frequent exhibitions of violence. In 1859 Governor Weller was compelled to send an armed force to Shasta to quell anti Chinese riots. In a message which accompanied his call he declared that the "spirit of mobocracy must be crushed no matter at what cost." This sentiment met the hearty approval of the City press, even that portion of it which continually presented arguments against Chinese immigration applauding Weller's determination to suppress violence, and commending his action in sending riflemen to Shasta to quell the riotous miners.

Stanford and Chinese Immigration

It has been pointed out that the actions of Californians have not always squared with their professions of hostility to Chinese immigration. This accusation is fully borne out by the facts, but the inconsistency is easily explained. This is a practical, work-a-day world and the men in it are as apt to surrender to circumstances as to abide by their convictions. In January, 1862, Governor Leland Stanford, in a message to the Legislature took ground against Chinese immigration and declared that it should be discouraged by every legitimate means. He said "Asia with her numberless millions sends to our shores the dregs of her population. There could be no doubt," he added, "that the pretense of numbers of that degraded and distinct people would exercise a deleterious influence upon the superior race." Therefore, he declared, he would concur in any constitutional action having for its object the repression of immigration of the Asiatic races.

Railroad Imports Chinese Laborers

No one questioned the sincerity of his utterance, yet in a very short time thereafter the corporation of which Stanford was the president imported large numbers of Chinese for the purpose of constructing the Central Pacific railroad, and San Franciscans who were as thoroughly convinced as he was in 1862, did not hesitate to employ them in every occupation to which they could adapt themselves. And what may appear still more singular to those who have not investigated the subject, the attitude of the workingmen, no matter how denunciatory their resolutions in the Sixties, was that of acquiescence in the assumption that their assistance was needed in the development of the country.

Chinese Labor not Cheap

An investigator of the subject declares that the trades unionist of San Francisco was the first to discover "the possible menace of the overwhelming numbers of workers who, through many generations of discipline in the crowded Orient, have learned to live under conditions impossible to the workers of a younger civilization." This is an error. Long before organized labor asserted itself, thoughtful men in California sounded warnings and formulated arguments against Chinese immigration. And while they were pointing out its evils the workingmen in the City were the best patrons of Chinese labor, which was by no means as cheap as was sometimes implied.

Chinese Regarded as a Necessary Evil

But while workingmen and others were apparently contradicting themselves they were none the less earnest in their desire to remove the necessity which they imagined circumstances imposed upon them of depending upon the assumedly inferior people. The well-to-do did not hesitate to employ them as domestics; they were utilized as laborers; the vegetables they produced were consumed by all classes, and they did practically the laundering for the entire community. Nevertheless they were unwelcome and merely tolerated because they were thought to be indispensable for the time being, and must be put up with until a change in conditions would be effected by an influx of immigrants of another sort when the anxiously expected overland railroad should be completed.

But while all sections of the community when acting in an individual capacity did not hesitate to employ Chinese labor, this attitude was completely changed when it was incumbent on it to announce and act upon a definite policy. The "sand lot" has been charged with having forced on the constitutional convention of 1879 the insertion of an article on Chinese in the organic law which made it ridiculous in the eyes of the outside world, but there was nothing novel in it except its insertion in the organic law. The City Hall Commission of San Francisco on May 24, 1870, in asking for proposals to grade a portion of Yerba Buena park inserted in its advertisement this statement: "The statute provides that no Chinese or Mongolian shall be employed in doing any of the work bid or contracted for, and the failure to comply with the provision shall work a forfeiture of the contract." Thus it appears that the much ridiculed attempted discrimination against the Chinese in the constitution of 1879 was a settled policy years before the advent of Kearney; and furthermore it was adhered to tenaciously, despite the fact that it was in conflict with a treaty of the United States. These facts should have warned commentators against hastily assuming that the action of the convention was ludicrous.

Forbidden Employment on Public Works

Although the discussion of the period preceding the decade 1870, and the laws touching Chinese were always associated with the word Mongolian, it does not appear that there were others of that race here in sufficient numbers to give any concern. In 1863, when the legislature repealed the law of 1850, prohibiting the testimony of negroes, mulattoes and Indians in cases in which a white man was concerned, the new act contained an express inhibition against the testimony of "Chinese and Mongolians." In all the earlier descriptions of the cosmopolitan character of the population of San Francisco there is scarcely any mention of other Orientals than Chinese. In 1854 Captain Adams, of the United States navy, passed through the City on his way to Washington with the treaty which Commodore Perry had concluded with Japan, but up to that time no Japanese had appeared among the gold seekers, and if there were any here prior to 1872, when the embassy under the guidance of Charles E. de Long arrived in the City, the number was so small that little account was taken of them.

Few Japanese in Early Days

Shortly after the sand lot episode, James Bryce, in his "American Commonwealth," in discussing its attending features observed that they "belong more or less to all the newer and rougher commonwealths." To which he added: "There are several others peculiar to California—a state on which I dwell more willingly because it is in many respects the most striking in the whole Union, and has more than any other the character of a great country, capable of standing alone in the world. It has immense wealth in its fertile soil as well as in its minerals and forests. Nature is nowhere more imposing, nor her beauties more varied," and more to the same effect. In these expressions he was merely voicing the general conviction of Californians, who had an abiding faith in the great future of the state. In his last message to the legislature in 1856 Governor Bigler said: "California though the youngest of the Southern states, ranks at this among the first in the elements of true wealth, and the rapid progress made in the past warrants the hope that she will soon outstrip all competitors in the friendly struggle for commercial and agricultural supremacy in the markets of the world."

Boundless Resources of California

The Assumed Need of Chinese Labor

No Californian regarded this as an extravagant assumption; everyone believed in the boundless resources so much talked about, and all were convinced that the future progress of the state depended on the development of its resources, especially those of agriculture. This was particuarly true of the people of San Francisco, who looked forward to vast quantities of the products of the soil passing over the wharves of the port, and to an enormous expansion of trade with the outside world. But there was a keen perception of the fact that labor in abundance would be required to realize these dreams and that weakened the objection to the importation of Chinese. Consciousness of their undesirability still pervaded the community, but practical considerations of the present subordinated the belief that the presence of an alien race of an unassimilable character would prove a menace and an impediment to progress. Even the workingmen of the City, if their actions may be accepted as an index of their state of mind, acquiesced in the belief that all would prosper and do well if only the resources of the soil were developed as they should be and only could be by securing labor from some source or other.

Fear of Land Monopoly Settles Chinese Question

It needed further light on a subject which later became the burning one in city and country, to bring about a practical unanimity of, sentiment regarding Chinese immigration, and it can be truthfully said that in its elucidation the trades unions took but a subordinate part. The Chinese question might have endured indefinitely to plague the City, and impede the progress of the country, if the people had not awakened to the evils of monopoly, and had not borne in on them by observation the possibility of its perpetuation in California through the command of cheap Oriental labor. It was the dawning realization of what this latter contingency might impose upon the state, rather than the agitation of trades unionists, that must be credited with the final success of the anti Chinese crusade. Had not the people of California become convinced that cheap Chinese labor would indefinitely postpone the cutting up of the big land grants the unanimity of opinion which finally induced congress to adopt exclusion measures would never have been reached. It was the country and not the City that decided the matter, as will plainly be seen when the events which led to the sand lot uprising are carefully traced through the decade which followed the opening of the first overland railroad.

CHAPTER XL

THE MINING INDUSTRY AND MINING STOCK SPECULATION

SAN FRANCISCO AND THE MINING INDUSTRY—THE COMSTOCK LODE—DISCOVERY OF SILVER ORE—FOUNDATION OF SAN FRANCISCO'S FINANCIAL STRENGTH—CREATION OF A STOCK BOARD—PRIMITIVE DEALINGS IN STOCKS—MINING STOCK SPECULATION FROWNED UPON AT FIRST—THE SPECULATIVE FEVER TAKES HOLD—PROSPEROUS BROKERS—NEVADA STOCKS DEALT IN CHIEFLY—EXTENT OF THE MARKET—THE SUTRO TUNNEL SUGGESTED—THE ATTEMPT TO OVERREACH SUTRO PROVES UNSUCCESSFUL—MINERS STAND BY SUTRO AGAINST THE "BANK CROWD"—RELATIONS OF NEVADA AND SAN FRANCISCO—FAITH OF SAN FRANCISCANS IN MINING AS A SOURCE OF WEALTH—LEGITIMATE AND SPECULATIVE MINING.

ALTHOUGH the far seeing were predicting the future agricultural importance of California before the close of the Fifties, the mining industry was regarded by San Franciscans as the most important prop of the commerce of the port down to a much later date. The statistics of production amply supported this belief, which was only slightly disturbed by indications of a decreasing output. In 1859 the gold product was valued at $45,846,599. After that year it declined rapidly and in 1870 it had fallen to $17,458,133. But in the meantime a new factor began to operate which effectually deluded all classes by giving a fictitious importance to the waning industry.

San Francisco and the Mining Industry

In 1859 Henry Comstock, who had obtained some information respecting the operations several years earlier of two brothers named Grosh, in the neighborhood of Mount Davidson, rediscovered the lode which bears his name. The Grosh brothers had ascertained the argentiferous quality of the ores in 1853 but kept their discovery as secret as possible. They returned to the scene of their find in 1855 and again revisited it in 1857, when one of them met with an accident which resulted in his death. The survivor, in attempting to return to California after the accident had both of his legs frozen, and lost his life in the effort to remove them by amputation. The story runs that Comstock learned of the whereabouts of the lode from papers left by the Groshs, which enabled him to successfully relocate the ore body.

Discovery of Comstock Lode

The accounts concur in saying that Comstock and the other Washoe miners who followed him had no acquaintance with silver, and that their search was wholly for gold quartz. In June, 1859, Comstock and a companion, in following up the washouts of a ravine found outcroppings of an auriferous quartz which also contained a metal unknown to them. Specimens of this ore were carried to Nevada

Silver Ore Not Recognized

381

City and were there carefully assayed by J. J. Ott, who reported that the new discovery indicated a yield of $1,595 in gold and of $3,196 in silver. The news soon leaked out and caused great excitement and there was an immediate rush to the western part of Utah, now the state of Nevada; and Virginia City, Gold Hill, Silver City and Dayton were soon converted into lively mining towns.

Another Source of Wealth The rush did not affect San Francisco as some previous excitements of that character had. The new mines were not poor men's "diggings," as were the placers of California and the stories of the discoveries, although they gave accounts of ores of fabulous richness, appealed chiefly to the prospectors, a large and growing class in what had come to be known as the Golden State. The chief interest of the people of San Francisco at first centered about the idea that the new mining region would be another added source of wealth to the City as it was certain to be commercially tributary to the port of San Francisco. The territory was well known to San Franciscans, who realized that there was no probability of its developing along any other than mining lines, and it was reasonably assumed that the miners would be dependent upon California for agricultural products, and that their wants of other sorts would have to be satisfied by the merchants and manufacturers of San Francisco. This assumption was never disappointed by the event. Nevada for many years has been as much a part of California as if there was no political dividing line. Its development in the early days and subsequently was promoted by San Francisco capital, and the wealth of its mines was regularly poured into the City.

San Francisco the Miner's Mecca Men who struck it rich and made a fortune in the Comstock and other Nevada mines naturally gravitated towards San Francisco, and "the City" was the Mecca toward which the successful miners' footsteps naturally turned, as it was also the refuge of those who "went broke" in their quest of fortune; for as usual a large proportion of those who were in search of rich mines had their labor for their pains, the fickle goddess smiling only on the few.

Foundation of City's Financial Strength Undoubtedly a statistical presentation of the benefits derived from the opening of these mines would show that they played an important part in the laying of the foundation of the financial edifice of San Francisco, whose strength gave the City a commercial importance more than commensurate with its population rank. But concurrently with this contribution to the wealth and importance of San Francisco by the Nevada mines, whose treasures were largely poured into the coffers of the people near the Golden Gate, there was inflicted upon the City a plague whose effects were as disastrous in many respects as the ravages of a widespread disease.

Speculation in Comstock Mines It is probable that San Francisco might have become infected with the mania for speculation through some other medium, but it is doubtful whether any temptation more alluring than that offered by the Nevada mines could have presented itself to a people who had been blind votaries of chance for nearly twenty years. In the early days the successful placer miner felt that he had "struck it rich" if he washed out a few thousands in a few days; but the possibilities of the Nevada mines opened up visions of millions; dreams which sometimes resolved themselves into realities.

Stock Board Created At the time of the discovery of the Comstocks there were in San Francisco a number of brokers who dealt in California Navigation Company, wharf, gas, railroad, steamboat, telegraph and water stocks and in City scrip. Their business was on a modest scale and they were not organized. Their transactions were not strongly suggestive of speculation; they were more like plain buying and selling of merchandise than anything else, and there was little in them that hinted of dealings in futures. The extent of their operations can hardly be surmised for there is no record of them, but they were insignificant by comparison with those which were promptly developed when the business was systematized by the creation of a stock board.

In 1862 the directory gave the names of several brokers, some of which later became well known, among them W. Sharon, C. Sutro, George C. Hicox, Z. Holt, A. J. King, H. C. Logan, E. P. Peckham, John Perry, Jr., L. Ritter, T. C. Sanborn, C. H. West, L. Sloss, T. Vassault and F. H. Woods. Their offices were located on Montgomery street, principally between California and Washington, although some of them were found on the side streets adjacent. The most of them presented the same appearance as some of the survivals on Montgomery street, where domestic moneys are exchanged for foreign, and in the windows of which attractive displays of coins and bank notes are made, and saucers full of nuggets are exhibited. The old time broker's offices also announced that they bought and sold Mexican dollars, a trade of considerable importance in San Francisco for many years. *Early Stock Brokers*

These brokers had begun to buy and sell shares or feet in new mining locations before the discovery of the Comstocks, but their method of operating was very primitive. On receiving an order to purchase feet or shares a broker would hunt up his fellows to learn whether they knew of anyone who wished to sell, if so there was a transaction, or the inquiry paved the way for one in the future. It was a roundabout method, but served very well, despite its inconvenience, until what afterward became derisively known as the "mining stock industry" attained such proportions that the advantages of meeting together suggested themselves to the isolated brokers. This resulted in the formation on September 11, 1862, of the San Francisco Stock and Exchange Board, which was organized on that day by the election of J. B. E. Cavallier as president; John Perry, Jr., vice president; Franklin Lawton, secretary and H. Schmiedell, treasurer. *Primitive Methods of Selling*

The first board organized was not looked upon with favor. Curiously enough, considering San Francisco's earlier experience, there was a pronounced disposition to condemn speculation, and a merchant who showed any inclination to buy or sell the new mining securities was regarded with disfavor, and the chances were against his receiving accommodations at his bank if the banker knew of his weakness, and wholesale merchants were disinclined to extend credit to a retailer if he was suspected of speculative tendencies. The opinion of the conservative banker and merchant was evidently shared by the people generally, as may be inferred from the promptitude they showed in fastening the title of "The Forty Thieves" on the board which, unhappily for its reputation, consisted of exactly forty members. *Speculation Viewed with Distrust*

Despite the conservatism of merchants and bankers the Stock and Exchange Board waxed in strength and the business became so attractive that a rival organization, known as the San Francisco Board of Brokers was started, beginning its existence with 80 members on April 15, 1863, and three months later the Pacific Board of Brokers came into existence with a membership of forty. Thus in less than a year there were one hundred and sixty brokers at work in San Francisco catering for the speculatively inclined, with three separate organizations. This latter fact is accounted for by the feeling that the exclusiveness of the first board *Prejudice Speedily Overcome* had resulted in making the cost of seats too high. The formation of rival boards was avowedly for the purpose of bringing down the cost of doing a brokerage business, and it was contended with an air of sincerity that the rivalry was in the interest of the public.

Publication of Stock Transactions

Although the members of the first board formed soon became past masters in their chosen occupation, only two of the original forty had had any previous experience. It was not long, however, before they had their associates inducted into the mysterious art of parting the community from its earnings. On October 15, 1862, a little more than a month after the formation of the San Francisco Stock and Exchange Board the "Bulletin" published a record of its transactions. The innovation was a concession to a growing demand for information. The example of the evening paper was slowly and in some cases reluctantly followed by the other newspapers, but before the close of the year they were all printing the list of purchases and sales made on the board and no information they published was half so eagerly sought after as that which these tables furnished.

The Speculation Fever

The first record of the San Francisco Stock and Exchange Board is that of the purchase of five shares of Wide West and one of Real del Monte by P. C. Hyman from P. B. Cornwall. Before the close of the year 1862 the newspapers published daily long lists of sales, and announcements of the formation of new companies occupied an equal space in their columns. Perhaps the brokers were able to keep track of the new business with which they were flooded, but the community at large was hopelessly at sea concerning the character of the new companies daily offering themselves, but their ignorance in no wise interfered with the zest with which they entered into the game, which soon became a mere gamble in which the dice were nearly always loaded.

Prosperous Brokers

The community may have suffered but the brokers did not. The first board which had started with forty members had enlarged its membership to eighty. The original fee had been increased and seats were selling at $10,000 and $12,000, hence the rival institutions. As already related when greenbacks began to depreciate the San Francisco Stock and Exchange Board dealt in them largely. The orders ranged well up into the thousands and the scenes at times were as lively as those on the New York Gold Board. Much of the trading in currency was purely speculative, but there was a large volume of what was regarded as strictly legitimate business in the shape of purchases of the depreciated government money by merchants, which they used to meet their Eastern obligations. The quotations usually gave the selling price of the currency and not as in New York the premium on gold. During 1864, when the lowest point was touched United States currency sold at 35 cents on the San Francisco stock boards.

Dealings in Nevada Stocks

It is noteworthy that during most of the time when the speculation in Nevada stocks was rife comparatively little attention was paid to California mining stocks. There were numerous gold mines in the state which were being profitably worked by their owners, who showed no inclination to put them on the market, preferring to hold them as investments. The facts concerning the really paying properties were tolerably well known to the speculating public, and those mines listed which were not supported by an established reputation were distrusted and neglected. This suspicion did not extend to the Comstocks, the glamour of whose richness was such that every vein in the whole region was believed by the credulous to have been touched with a Midas wand; and those who did not believe were equally satisfied

SAN FRANCISCO IN 1865, LOOKING SOUTH FROM NOB HILL.

to buy because an actively manipulated "wildcat" was worth as much for speculative purposes as a real mine.

While the speculation of the Sixties was in no wise comparable with that which ensued when the big bonanza was uncovered in the early Seventies it was sufficiently active, especially during the later years of the first named decade to engross the attention of a large part of the community. In 1867 the business of the brokers had become so extensive that regular meetings were held by the San Francisco Stock and Exchange Board at 11 A. M. and 3 P. M., with informal sessions from 10:15 to 10:45 A. M. The business done, however, was not always on an ascending market. Hale & Norcross, which had sold as high as $3,600 was down to $650 on October 26, 1867. There were still transactions of considerable volume, the sales in October, 1867, aggregating $8,051,329, but they fell off heavily in the ensuing month, shrinking to $5,351,733.

Extent of the Speculative Market

An astonishing feature of the mining stock speculation of this period, and later during the Seventies, was the apparent utter disregard by the people who gambled of the transparent rigging of the market by unscrupulous manipulators. The most of those who entered the game displayed all the characteristics of the tyro who sits down to play with professional gamesters. They had abundant evidence that the cards were marked, but that did not discourage them. When there were struggles for control of mines, as was frequently the case, they did not hesitate to try their luck and clung, as it were, to the skirts of the manipulators, often with disastrous consequences.

Rigging the Market

In 1868 there was such a contest for control. A brief description of the varying fortunes of the contestants will illustrate the fierceness of the struggles which were constantly occurring at the time. In the early part of the year what in the parlance of the day was known as "the bank crowd," a group connected with the Bank of California attempted to wrest the control of Hale and Norcross from Charles L. Low. There was a continued buying of the stock which drove it up to $7,100 from $2,925, and a number were caught short. Those involved in the corner sought to secure terms by offering $8,000 to $10,000 a front foot, but protested that the extravagant demands made upon them were outrageous, but the bank crowd showed no mercy. Then the device of suspending Hale and Norcross from the list was resorted to on the ground that the stock was being withheld for election purposes, but this failed to interrupt the progress of the scheme for obtaining control. The last recorded transaction in Hale and Norcross on the board in this particular deal was $8,000, but $12,000 was being freely paid on the street, and in an open board, having its office in the Merchants Exchange, the announcement was made by a member that he was authorized to bid $100,000 for ten feet of the mine. The struggle began on the 8th of February and the election occurred on March 12, 1868. On the latter day Hale and Norcross could be bought for $2,900. The bank crowd had won its fight, and had elected as trustees Joseph Barron, Thomas Bell, Alvinza Hayward, George L. Mann, M. Morgenthou, Thomas Sunderland and Joseph Wallace.

Contests for Control of Mines

One of the boldest conceptions affecting the Nevada mining industry was formed in the early Sixties by a man whose name after 1864 frequently appears in the chronicles of the City. Adolph Sutro was born in Prussia in 1830 and in 1850 emigrated to America, arriving in San Francisco in that year, where he engaged in selling tobacco and cigars. In 1859 he joined the rush to the Washoe country, and

Sutro Suggests a Tunnel

in 1861 built a quartz mill at Carson river. While engaged in this business Sutro conceived the idea of piercing the mountain side with a tunnel so constructed that it would drain all the mines of the Comstock lode, and incidentally supply the ventilation necessary to enable the miners to successfully prosecute the work of extracting the valuable ores.

Sutro's Suggestion Welcomed

Despite the boldness of the suggestion its feasibility was not questioned, and the prospect of the enterprise being carried out was hailed with satisfaction. A company was formed in 1864 for the purpose of constructing the tunnel, and the legislature of Nevada granted the right of way, stipulating that it should be finished in eight years. This was followed by an arrangement with the various mines on the lode by which they agreed to pay a toll of $2 a ton on all the ores extracted by them when the tunnel should reach the stage of providing the promised benefits. The amount demanded for the service to be performed was insignificant by comparison with that which it would have cost the mining companies under the most favorable circumstances to unwater, remove waste, and ventilate their properties by machinery; and in some cases it was foreseen by the owners that the tunnel would make practicable the prosecution or continuance of operations which would be impossible without its aid.

Attempt to Overreach Sutro

In its inception Sutro's project was hailed by everybody connected with mining enterprises as a great benefaction. The men foremost in the undertakings of the coterie connected with the Bank of California in San Francisco gave him their support and helped him to get through congress an act which granted the tunnel project right of way through the public land crossed by it, and the right to purchase not exceeding two sections at the mouth of the tunnel, and at $5 per acre any public mineral land which it might cut, and within 2,000 feet of it except the Comstock mines as then known. There was also a provision in the act that fixed the rate which might be exacted at the amount agreed upon. With his interests thus well secured Sutro started in to raise the necessary funds to prosecute the undertaking when the men who at the outset had supported him suddenly began to oppose his efforts, their object being to obtain control. But they had mistaken their man. They had imagined Sutro to be somewhat visionary and pliable, and thought he would be content to accept a subordinate role with comparatively modest rewards. But he was not made of such stuff. The attempt to overreach and down him was so flagrant he had no difficulty in arraying public sentiment, more particularly that of the working miners, on his side. He also enlisted a portion of the press in his effort to maintain his rights, and altogether made it very lively for what he called "the bank crowd." On the lecture platform, in communications to the newspapers, and in every conceivable way he made the plea that, while he was attempting to benefit the mining industry and Nevada, the Bank of California was doing everything to obstruct the progress of the tunnel and destroy the enterprise.

Miner's Come to Sutro's Aid

The result of his campaign was remarkable. It had the effect of rallying to his aid the miners, who purchased some $50,000 of the tunnel stock, enough to provide him with sufficient funds to make a start. On the 19th of October, 1869, Sutro began operating and as the work on the tunnel progressed the difficulty of obtaining funds for the prosecution of the enterprise lessened, despite the continued hostility of the men whose efforts to obtain control he had so successfully balked. They continued their obstructive tactics until forced by circumstances to yield. In July, 1878. the tunnel had broken into the Savage shaft, but no agreement had yet been reached with the operators of the mines, who remained recalcitrant until 1879, when one of the pumps of the Savage property broke and in order to save the mine the owners turned the water into the tunnel.

Sutro's men were taken by surprise and had to flee from the tunnel, but they returned and under his direction a water tight bulkhead was constructed which effectually dammed the flow and the mines were threatened with destruction. This brought matters to a climax. The owners of the mines had to yield. Additional laborers were put on the work, the drain was reopened and widened, and soon millions of gallons were daily flowing through the tunnel and the Comstocks were kept comparatively free of water and great savings were effected. The cost of the tunnel with its laterals was about five million dollars. In order to secure this amount Sutro had to part with the controlling interest, but he retained enough of the stock to make him a rich man when he sold it and retired to San Francisco.

Mine Owners Surrender to Sutro

The story of the construction of the Sutro tunnel and the struggle for its control is as much a part of the history of San Francisco as though the mines it unwatered were within the boundaries of the City. The originator of the enterprise, and those who were interested in its success directly or indirectly, were all San Franciscans or hoped to enjoy the privilege of residing there at some future time. Those who were fortunate enough to obtain large rewards for their exertions as a rule found their way to the City and made it their home when they ceased active operations. The men engaged in merchandizing in Nevada made frequent visits to the metropolis, and they brought their wives with them to have a good time while they were engaged in purchasing goods. The relations of the people of Nevada generally were as intimate and as friendly as those of any part of California. Political boundaries even did not count, for it became the custom of San Francisco to provide the timber out of which United States senators and representatives in congress were constructed after October 31, 1864, when Nevada was admitted to the Union.

Relations of Nevada and San Francisco

The experience of Sutro has still another interest as it affords an illustration of the influence, not always beneficial, which mining success had in shaping the destinies of San Francisco. It was a fact not generally recognized at the time, that the acquisition of wealth gained in the pursuit of mining, or that derived from mining speculation, was not as freely used in the development of the varied resources of the state as if it had been amassed by the slower processes of the regions where the precious metals are not found. Men willing to plunge into enterprises with the attending uncertainties of mining, or who had gambled in stocks successfully were as a rule distrustful of undertakings with which they were unfamiliar. As a result their investments were confined to a narrow field, and they failed to give encouragement to industries which, even with the drawbacks attendant upon a restricted market, might have been sufficiently developed to accelerate the progress of the state and promote its prosperity. This conservatism affords an explanation of the endurance of the opinion throughout the Sixties and even later, that San Francisco's interests were peculiarly identified with those of the mines. They were in fact, but the neglected opportunities, had they been seized by the cautious, successful miner, and the reckless but fortunate speculator, would have produced conditions which might have effectually averted the protracted depression which followed the advent of the overland railroad. The feverish speculation of the earlier Seven-

San Francisco and the Mining Industry

ties, which those just described only faintly foreshadowed, postponed this trouble for a while, but it came later and with added intensity.

Steady Growth During the Sixties

San Francisco's growth during the sixty decade of the nineteenth century was tolerably constant; the population increased during the ten years from 56,802 in 1860 to 149,473 in 1870 and its assessable wealth in the last named year was $114,759,510, but expansion, as the events of the succeeding decade demonstrated, was not as healthy as it would have been had the development of industries been more symmetrical. But that was seemingly impossible while the mining regions continued to pour their treasure into the City. The placers of California were by no means exhausted, and the quartz mines of this and the neighboring territory were yielding in such a fashion as to suggest illimitable future possibilities. The Comstocks were turning out large quantities of bullion, and there was a prospect of new mines being found whose yield would more than offset the rapidly declining output of the placers. These expectations were not entirely visionary, for they had a seeming justification in such discoveries as that made at White Pine, Nevada, where argentiferous chlorides were found in 1868. There was the usual rush to the new camp; the merchants prospered selling outfits and merchandise to people in the new settlements, more bullion flowed into San Francisco and the speculative disposition was intensified.

Legitimate and Speculative Mining

There were of course some who regarded the situation with distrust, but the community generally did not foresee trouble, or look forward with hope to the day when the mining interest would be subordinated to industries less under the influence of chance. Queerly enough when the mines of Nevada and California finally ceased to be an object of overwhelming interest to San Franciscans, for a time they attached too little importance to mining as an adjunct of the scheme of general industrial development. The people of the City had become so accustomed to identifying the industry with speculation, that when stocks ceased to have any attractions they refused to think much about mines, but their development continued without interruption. The annual output of the precious metals in California had not greatly decreased since 1870, but the steady production of about sixteen or seventeen millions of gold annually did not appeal to the imagination of a highly impressionable people. Many of those who passed through the exciting events of the closing years of the Sixties, and the early Seventies, thought of the period as the culmination of an era of prosperity. But there were careful observers who discovered beneath the surface the signs of an impending trouble due to the indifference to general development; which they recognized as the necessary outcome of a too eager pursuit of an industry which has advanced more steadily, and upon much broader lines without the adventitious aid of speculation, than it did when nearly everyone believed that it was the mainstay of San Francisco prosperity.

BROADWAY WHARF IN 1865—ONE OF THE BUSIEST WHARVES IN THE CITY AT THAT TIME

CHAPTER XLI

COMMERCE, MANUFACTURES AND FINANCES OF SAN FRANCISCO

SAN FRANCISCANS VERY CONSERVATIVE—OPPOSITION TO CREATING A CLEARING HOUSE—OVERSHADOWING FINANCIAL IMPORTANCE OF THE CITY—EXPANSION OF SHIPPING INDUSTRY—CHANGE IN THE CHARACTER OF IMPORTS—SAN FRANCISCO A DISTRIBUTING CENTER—FISHERIES OF THE PACIFIC COAST—THE COD FISH INDUSTRY—THE ACQUISITION OF ALASKA—SEWARD'S GOOD BARGAIN—VALUE OF ALASKAN TRADE—TRADE WITH THE HAWAIIAN ISLANDS—COMMUNICATION WITH HAWAII—RECIPROCITY TREATY WITH THE ISLANDS—SAN FRANCISCO'S ATTITUDE TOWARD RECIPROCITY—PLANS FOR ANNEXATION—GROWING TRADE WITH THE ISLANDS—ORIENTAL TRADE—FIRST SHIP OF THE PACIFIC MAIL TO THE ORIENT—SAN FRANCISCO'S COASTWISE TRADE—RAPID GROWTH OF WHEAT EXPORTS—DIVERSIFICATION OF AGRICULTURE—WOOL INDUSTRY—WOOLEN AND OTHER MANUFACTURING INDUSTRIES—THE FUR SEAL CONTRACT—END OF CALIFORNIA'S ISOLATION.

Not Prone to Innovation

SAN FRANCISCO has at times incurred the censure of Eastern critics, and of the conservatively inclined of its own citizens for being too prone to resort to innovations. Occasionally it has earned this reputation but it is not open to the imputation that it is always disposed to act hastily and without due regard for established usages. It has been shown that owing to a prejudice against wildcat currency the convention which framed the first organic law of the state took precautions which made it impossible for banks to issue paper money, and that the people became so habituated to the use of the precious metals that they absolutely refused to abandon what they called "sound money" when patriotism, interest and convenience dictated its abandonment in favor of the depreciating money of the federal government.

Adherence to a Principle

The steadfast adherence to this determination, no matter whether it was mistaken or wise, may fairly be characterized as devotion to principle, for it is undoubtedly true that while many saw opportunities for profit through the difference in exchange, the majority of the people were profoundly convinced that their course was for the general good, and that their acceptance of the greenback currency would have had attached to it a taint of dishonesty, because, unlike the people of the East they were not forced to use what they regarded as an unsafe medium of exchange. But while this sentiment explains in part the failure of San Francisco to favor harmonizing its currency with that of the rest of the Union nothing but extreme conservatism can account for the indifference displayed by the financial and other business interests of the City in the matter of improving its banking methods, which were hopelessly destitute of system.

Clearing House Opposed

The institution known as the clearing house was established as early as October, 1853, in New York, but it was a quarter of a century later before San Francisco provided itself with such an establishment. The indisposition to adopt this great convenience was based on the narrow suspicion that banks might profit at each other's expense if their checks were cleared or settled at a common center. The fear that a rival would gain a knowledge of the volume of another bank's business, or who its customers were was paramount, and it operated for years to keep the people from that acquaintance with the transactions of its fiduciary institutions which it has been found is absolutely necessary to safeguard the interests of depositors and of the community generally.

Clearing House Established in 1876

It was not until 1876 that a clearing house was established in San Francisco, and it is therefore difficult to trace with any degree of exactness the fluctuations of business during the earlier years. The market reports in the newspapers, and the editorial comment on commercial subjects during the Sixties are largely inferential. The statistics employed are fragmentary, and it would be extremely difficult if not impossible to construct from them a statement of conditions except one framed in general terms.

Overshadowing Influence of San Francisco

In an effort to determine trade conditions in the City such data as the state at large furnishes are valuable and almost indispensable, for during the Sixties, and many years afterward, San Francisco was the center of all the commercial and financial activity of California, and it may be more truly said of it at that time that it was "the State" than it is now to say that Paris is France. Up to the year 1884 there was not a single incorporated savings bank in any part of California, outside of San Francisco, and the condition so far as other banks were concerned was not much better. The disposition of the machinery of finance marked the paramountcy of San Francisco so emphatically that no one ever thought of questioning it any more than they would have questioned the meaning of the person who spoke of "the City."

Stimulus of Rivalry Needed

There was only one city on the Pacific coast at the time, a fact not altogether fortunate for San Francisco as its people learned later when under the stimulus of rivalry they put forth exertions to promote the development of resources which they had neglected while they were under the hallucination that mining was California's most important industry, and that its prosecution would always suffice to set in motion the activities which would make the port the greatest on the Pacific and one of the most important in the world. That this narrow view was adopted, and that it gained strength during the period when mining stock speculation was rife is perceptible in the tone of the press; and it can be traced also in the gradual neglect of the manufacturing industries, which had attained some importance before the completion of the first overland railroad, despite the fact that an extraordinary impulse was given to importation by the advantage which the ability to buy goods at the East in depreciated government money afforded to merchants.

Expansion of Shipping Industry

We find the evidence of this expanding import trade in the statistics of ocean tonnage arrivals. In 1861 the total tonnage of foreign vessels entering the port of San Francisco was 205,600 tons, of which 83,300 were steam. In 1869 the steam tonnage had increased to 205,900 tons and the total entered aggregated 413,900 tons. The domestic tonnage showed a like increase, the steam rising from

SAN FRANCISCO

40,000 tons entered in 1861 to 119,200 tons, and steam and sail combined rose from 389,000 to 757,100 tons. These figures show a doubling of the shipping business of the port in the eight years prior to and including the year of the opening of the railroad, the entrances of all kinds being 1,171,000 tons in 1869 and 594,600 in 1861. This traffic was of a very miscellaneous character. It embraced an active intercourse with the Pacific coast ports of the United States to the north and south of San Francisco, a considerable over sea trade and a large business by way of the isthmus and vessels sailing around the Horn between San Francisco and Eastern ports. A fairly good idea of the importance of the trade may be gained from the statement that freight money to the amount of $8,109,600 was paid on inward cargoes by the merchants of San Francisco in 1864, of which $3,747,700 was on shipments from domestic and Atlantic ports; $2,380,000 on freights by the Panama steamers, and $1,981,000 on freight received by sailing vessels in the foreign trade. The amounts paid for like service during 1867, 1868 and 1869 were, respectively, $6,800,000, $8,064,000 and $8,949,000.

An inspection of the manifests of the vessels which brought the vast quantity of freight for which these large sums were expended discloses many remarkable changes in the character of the imports during the Sixties. In the 273,600 tons of goods imported in 1869 we find enumerated a great variety of articles, many of which, had the manufacturing spirit been as active as that which displayed itself in the development of the mineral industry, would not have appeared in the list. The press frequently called attention to the absurdity of a state like California, with an abundance of raw material at hand, drawing on the outside world for its supplies of such simple domestic articles as soap and candles, and deprecated the folly of dependence upon the East for furniture and other things which they assumed could be profitably produced in San Francisco if the necessary enterprise to engage in manufacturing had existed. *Change in Character of Imports*

While the records furnish ample evidence that the desirability of establishing manufacturing industries was not lost sight of during the Sixties, and that relatively more progress was made in that decade than during the Seventies, there are strong indications of the growth of the belief that the future of San Francisco would depend upon its importance as a distributing center. That this idea had a firm hold upon an important section of the community may be inferred from the great prominence given to arguments urging the importance of improving the harbor facilities, which were usually accompanied with gentle reminders that it is also desirable to produce as well as distribute, and occasionally by a rebuke directed against what was recognized as a growing disposition to let things shape themselves. How strongly predisposed to attach undue importance to the comparatively insignificant factor of making the port a sort of supply station, the people of the two first decades were, can be inferred from the general attitude toward the fisheries of the coast. The importance of the Pacific whaling industry had long been realized. Its promotion had much to do with shaping the policy which finally culminated in the occupation of California. Presidents dwelt upon it in messages and pointed out the desirability of obtaining San Francisco as a port in which the whalers might safely winter; and after the annexation of California and its erection into a state of the Union successive governors discussed ways and means of inducing the whalers who persisted in harboring in Honolulu, to give San Francisco the preference. *San Francisco as a Distributing Center*

Pacific Coast Fisheries

Through all their recommendations ran the idea that great advantages would be derived from selling "outfits" to the whalers, but very rarely was there a suggestion that the fisheries might prove a more direct source of wealth to the port. The endeavor to secure this class of patronage began to meet with some degree of success in the opening years of the Sixties, but the depredations of the "Shenandoah" and "Alabama" soon rendered Arctic whaling an extra hazardous occupation and the business of outfitting did not prosper greatly. In 1865 thirty-four whalers, whose combined tonnage was 11,000, visited the port, the largest number to call in any one year; but after that date there was a falling off, owing as much to the changes in the methods of pursuing the industry as to any other cause. In the ensuing decade San Francisco wrested from New Bedford the glory of being the principal seat of the whaling industry, but the victory was not due so much to the superior enterprise of San Franciscans as to the introduction of steam schooners, the use of which made San Francisco a desirable base of operations. During the Sixties something like an appreciation of the enormous value of the Pacific coast fisheries began to manifest itself in San Francisco. In 1865 the crew of a brig returning from a voyage to the Amoor while becalmed off Saghalien island amused themselves fishing and were greatly surprised to haul in some fine specimens of cod. Up to that time all the codfish consumed in California had been imported from the Atlantic coast. The manifests of arriving vessels show that it was a very popular article of diet, no miscellaneous cargo failing to contain large quantities of the salted and dried fish. The menus of restaurants and hotels of San Francisco and the interior of the state also furnish evidence of the esteem in which it was held and in the mining camps it always ranked as a "standby." Consequently when the "Towanda" entered the port bringing a portion of the catch of the crew great interest was excited and presently a number of small craft were dispatched to the fishing grounds.

The Alaskan Cod Fisheries

The first year of the exploitation of this industry resulted in a catch of 587 tons of Alaskan cod, and this success prompted the sending out of a larger fleet in the ensuing season, when the catch was 902 tons. Probably the people of San Francisco might have awakened to a full realization of the importance of the fisheries in the Sixties had not the excitement of the mining stock market so completely absorbed their attention. It was, however, by no means wholly neglected, for the catches continued to increase, but at no time did it make any strong appeal to the imagination of business men. Occasionally a hotel bill of fare ventured to proclaim the fact that Alaskan cod was being served, and the retail grocers were with difficulty persuaded that the Pacific product was as good as that taken from the New Foundland banks, but generally speaking, the average San Franciscan was as ignorant of the possibilities of the fisheries which have since attained such importance as he was of the doings of the Grand Llama.

Alaska Acquired in 1867

But the beginnings of the industry were a liberal education to a few and prepared them to receive with satisfaction the announcement of the consummation of the treaty with Russia, by which the United States acquired possession of Alaska. That treaty, negotiated by William H. Seward, was proclaimed on June 20, 1867. The dissemination of the news of the purchase called forth an extraordinary amount of uninformed comment, the newly purchased territory being regarded by most of the American people as a vast iceberg, or at least as a country with an impossible climate and destitute of resources. This ignorance was not wholly confined to the

East; the San Francisco press had its share of the fun; but there were some who sat up and took notice, and profited by their knowledge of the country, the most of which was derived from the reports of the venturesome fishermen and the earlier intercourse of the employes of the Russian American Company, whose relations with the people of California, particularly those living about its great bay, were quite intimate.

No one reading the comments in the message of Governor Low would have inferred the existence of information of value concerning Alaska. He spoke of the extension of the area of political freedom through the acquisition, but was apparently oblivious of future possibilities. He did not ridicule the payment of $7,200,000 for a vast snow and ice field as some did, nor on the other hand did he dwell upon the fact that within the vast territory, whose boundaries were all that part of the coast west of the 141st meridian of longitude west of Greenwich, including the Aleutian islands, and all of the coast and islands north of Queen Charlotte island, a region whose extreme length north and south is about 1,100 miles, and its greatest breadth east and west, about 800 miles, there might be found illimitable riches. He was simply reflecting public indifference to the acquisition of 580,000 square miles of territory, with a coast line, including that of the islands and inlets of nearly 8,000 miles. *Importance of Alaska Purchase*

It was this general ignorance which caused the erroneous assumption that William H. Seward merely made a lucky fluke in the purchase. Nothing is further from the truth. The secretary knew that he was consummating a profitable bargain. Political considerations may have had their influence in determining his course, but he knew that Alaska was possessed of valuable resources and unhesitatingly expressed confidence in their development. In 1869 Seward made a trip to Alaska, passing through this City while en route to the territory. He was accompanied by S. C. Hastings, an old time friend, whose guest he was while in San Francisco. The object of his visit to Alaska was to confirm his impressions regarding the value of the purchase. On his return to San Francisco he made a trip to San Diego, where he met William Sumner Dodge, who had been chosen mayor of Sitka, and obtained from him much valuable information concerning Alaskan resources, which prompted him to complain with some acerbity of the American disposition to speak without adequate information, and to predict that the territory would one day be regarded as one of the most valuable possessions of the United States. *Seward's Good Bargain*

His prediction has been amply justified by the result, and San Francisco for many years was the largest beneficiary of the sagacity of the far-seeing statesman. San Franciscans were the first to recognize the opportunities which the new territory held out, and some of them profited greatly by taking advantage of them at a time when most of their fellow citizens were absorbed in watching or helping to promote the mining speculation craze. Later, when the unappreciated territory suddenly acquired notoriety, owing to its proximity to the Klondike mines in British Columbia, whose rich placers suggested equally valuable deposits, the ports to the north of San Francisco began to reach out and prosper, and the rapid development of the states of Washington and Oregon may be said to date from that period. It was about that time also that the outside world realized that it had inventoried Uncle Sam's Alaskan possession improperly when it dismissed it with a line crediting it with being chiefly valuable because of the existence of its seal herds. *Value of Trade of Alaska*

SAN FRANCISCO

Non Contiguous Territory Trade

In the Sixties the term "non contiguous territory" was unfamiliar to San Franciscans, but they were not unacquainted with the value of the trade of what has since become a part of the national domain, to which that designation is applied. The relations of San Francisco with Hawaii date back to the period before American occupation of California was thought of by the most enthusiastic manifest destinarian. The Spanish in the pursuit of their purpose of monopolizing the whole region lying along the Pacific coast had considered the desirability of taking possession of the group, possibly with a view of utilizing its principal port as a calling place for its galleons, but chiefly with the idea of keeping anyone else from making use of the islands, but conditions prevented the materialization of the desire.

Trade with Hawaii

When the American missionaries established themselves in the group, they brought with them commercial habits as well as religious doctrine and the islands flourished. The fact that they had made Honolulu an attractive port for whalers has been mentioned. The business methods which brought about that result had put them in a position to profit considerably by the discovery of gold in California. Like the Russian American Company, which took advantage of the rush in 1849 to unload all its shopworn goods on the newcomers, the merchants of the Hawaiian islands were prompt to put in the newly created market all they had to spare, and they played quite a part in furnishing the much needed food supplies for the rapidly increasing mining population of California.

Washington Authorities Unconcerned

The trade thus established flourished and made closer the relations which it may be assumed would have in any event subsisted between the people of the group and San Francisco. The islands to all intents and purposes were even at this time as much American as though the Stars and Stripes floated over them. The policy of the United States in regard to them had not taken definite shape, possibly because the authorities at Washington were convinced that the political integrity of the group would not be assailed by foreigners, but more probably because up to the time of the attempted secession the statesmen and politicians were wholly absorbed in the conduct of domestic affairs, and gave little thought to what was happening beyond the borders and the coast of the United States.

Communication with the Islands

Meantime, however, the trade of San Francisco with the islands was becoming more active and the relations of San Franciscans and Hawaiians more intimate. As early as 1854 an attempt was made to establish a steamship line between Honolulu and San Francisco. It did not result in regular communication, but it kept alive the desire for it, and paved the way to its accomplishment later. Although regular trips of steamships did not begin until 1868, there were numerous sailing packets plying between the two ports, and the support they received was a constant incentive to further effort. In January, 1866, the California Steam Navigation Company dispatched the propeller "Ajax" to Honolulu but did not repeat the experiment. In 1867 the California, Oregon and Mexican Steamship Company made a third essay and dispatched a monthly steamer, continuing the service until 1870, when a new line was started with the aid of a subsidy from Australia which, however, was never successfully operated.

Reciprocity Treaty with Hawaii

This enterprise was the outcome of the efforts of the Hawaiian sugar planters to secure a reciprocity treaty with the United States. A measure of that character was then pending in the senate and it was thought that the decision of that body would be influenced by the menace of diverting the sugar trade to the British colonies. The first steamer of the subsidized line, the "Wonga Wonga," was adroitly

METROPOLITAN THEATER AS IT APPEARED IN 1865

CALIFORNIA THEATER, ON BUSH STREET ABOVE KEARNY, IN THE SIXTIES
The Free Public Library was maintained in this building until the McAllister Street wing of the City Hall, destroyed in the fire of 1906, was completed

used to give an object lesson to the slow moving senators. Instead of proceeding to San Francisco as originally designed, she was loaded with a cargo of pulp and sugar for Australia. The ruse had the intended effect. Although those familiar with the situation were perfectly aware that the Australian colonies offered no such market as the Hawaiian planters were seeking, there were plenty who feared that one might be developed and the islands be estranged.

In the Sixties and up to the time of the conclusion of the reciprocity treaty with the Hawaiian kingdom in 1875 there was very little concern felt in San Francisco regarding the political future of the islands. Their autonomy had been guaranteed by Great Britain and France, and the United States had practically assented. Trade had increased under the arrangement and there was no disposition to disturb it, but there were some who strongly advocated the adoption of the frequently mooted treaty proposition in the belief that it would result in directing to this port the sugars which were being grown in increasing quantities on the islands of the group. The chief advocates of the treaty, however, were more largely influenced by the prospect of making money by growing cane than by the hope of expanding the business of the port, although they did not fail to point out that there must be a great increase of trade in the event of the adoption of the treaty. {San Francisco's Attitude Toward Reciprocity}

Public sentiment on the subject was not strong enough to greatly influence the authorities at Washington, and it is probable that the reluctance to break through the tariff system would have indefinitely postponed the consummation of the desire of the Hawaiian planters for closer relations had not James G. Blaine reached the conclusion that the acquisition of the Hawaiian group was a military necessity, and that the quickest way to achieve that object was to so strengthen the commercial bond between the islands and the United States that the islands would be unable to resist manifest destiny and would come under the American flag when the time became ripe for annexation. {Plans for Annexation}

Ultimately everything came about as Blaine had planned, but his views were strenuously combatted by John Sherman and others, who were convinced that the convention as originally framed was a one sided affair which gave the island planters all the advantages without in the least benefiting the American consumers of sugar. The soundness of their arguments was fully demonstrated so far as the question of the price of sugar was concerned, but on the other hand the predicted expansion of trade occurred and that sufficed to effectually dispose of economic criticism until some years after the conclusion of the treaty. {Effects of the Treaty}

Meanwhile, however, the trade of Hawaii and the United States was steadily growing and before the close of 1870 several steamers were plying between San Francisco and Honolulu, where they connected with the subsidized Australian line, thus enabling the merchants of the former port to develop a trade with the antipodes, which later attained proportions that seemed to warrant the establishment of a direct line between San Francisco and Australasia. {A Growing Trade}

If the trade which seemed to most impress the imagination of early San Franciscans had been first mentioned it would have been a case of giving prominence to that which attained real importance only toward the close of the Sixties, when the overland railroad was approaching completion. The discovery of gold had been quickly followed by the arrival of ships from the Orient, most of which were in what might be called the roundabout trade. Many of them were foreign, but a fair proportion sailed under the American flag. They brought goods and many {San Francisco's Oriental Trade}

Chinese immigrants, but there was nothing like a regular trade developed until California began to produce on a scale which enabled her to export. This somewhat one sided trade continued throughout the Fifties and Sixties. In 1862 there were 42 arrivals from Hongkong, whose tonnage aggregated 36,800 and in the succeeding year there were 44, registering 34,300 tons. They were not large vessels, only sixteen of the arrivals in 1863 exceeding 1,000 tons burthen. The voyages varied from 35 to 85 days from Hongkong to San Francisco.

Pacific Mail Company Subsidized

As the transcontinental railroad approached completion congress began to interest itself in the subject of the extension of Oriental trade. An annual subsidy of $500,000 was voted to provide for a monthly service between San Francisco and Hongkong. The Pacific Mail Company, which was largely instrumental in securing the passage of the subsidy measure was awarded the contract and the side wheel steamer "Colorado," of 3,728 tons burthen, made the first trip, sailing from San Francisco on January 1, 1867. Her departure was made the occasion for a great celebration, in which speech making figured and glowing predictions of the future of the trade with the Orient were indulged in by the speakers, who also took occasion to dwell upon the enterprise of the mail company and the magnificence of the accommodations its vessels would afford to passengers.

First Trip Under the Subsidy

This first steamer carried as the chief part of her cargo 1,000 barrels of flour and $560,000 of specie for Hongkong. There was also a small amount for Japan. The "Colorado" carried a few passengers, including ex-Governor Low and the president of the New York chamber of commerce. She made a detour to Honolulu and completed the round trip in 78 days. On her return she made the passage from Yokohama to San Francisco in 21 days. This record has since been more than cut in half, but no succeeding exploit appealed more powerfully to the imagination than the first performance of the "Colorado," which foreshadowed the subsequent accomplishment of Jules de Verne's traveler, who made the circuit of the earth in eighty days. The rate of speed has been greatly accelerated since then, and if Phineas Fogg should again start on a voyage and forget to turn off his gas, his bill for the wasted illuminant would be less than half as much as it was in 1870.

Trade with the Orient

The first year under the subsidy the company made five trips and in 1869 the line was in working order, having increased its fleet of steamers to nine. The flour trade, which had shown shipments of 43,000 barrels in the first half of the decade Sixty, in the last half recorded exports for the period aggregating 150,000 barrels. The exports of specie had also expanded considerably. The term specie at this time included the Mexican dollar, large quantities of which were sold in San Francisco for shipment to China. The import trade with Oriental countries during the Sixties was given more thought apparently than that of exporting. The idea that San Francisco would become the world's great tea emporium had obtained a firm hold, and there were numerous articles in the press dwelling on its importance and predicting its future growth. But the prophets reckoned without taking bonded warehouses and transcontinental railroad methods into consideration. They were to learn much about these later. In 1870 they had every reason to pin their faith to the proposition that San Francisco was the natural distributing point, for during the few years preceding they had seen the tea imports from China and Japan increase threefold, rising from 1,144,830 lbs. in 1860, valued at $300,766, to 3,119,063 lbs. in 1870, appraised at $1,060,012. A fair proportion of this commodity was handled here but the exigencies of transcontinental rates and the facilities for bonding in a comparatively brief period made San Francisco a mere port òf call so far as tea and raw silk were concerned.

The trade by steamer and sailing vessels with the Orient in the Sixties although it filled so large a space in the public mind, not only in San Francisco, but in the commercial centers of the East, where such questions receive attention, was not comparable in importance with that of the port with other parts of the world, and particularly with the remainder of the coast. There were lines of steamers sailing to British Columbia before the opening of the Sixties, and during the Fraser river rush there was considerable rivalry for the traffic which that excitement promoted; but at the beginning of the decade conditions had become normal and steamers made regular sailings to Victoria. In May, 1861, Halladay & Flint established a regular service between San Francisco and Mexican ports, which was maintained until the rivalry of the Pacific Mail Company made the business unprofitable.

<small>Coastwise Trade</small>

Although the steam traffic was constantly gaining in importance there was no sign during the Sixties of the subsequent displacement of the ocean sailing vessel. The "windjammer" still held her own, and the pride in the swift performances of the clipper ships had only measurably abated. Large and constantly increasing quantities of merchandise were being brought to San Francisco via the isthmus, but the sails of ships in quest of grain cargoes continued to enliven the appearance of the bay, and to add to the importance of the port, for they usually brought cargoes which were distributed by San Francisco merchants. The arrivals increased with the development of California's wheat fields, which was proceeding with marvelous rapidity during the decade, and was beginning to earn for California the reputation of being one of the world's great granaries.

<small>Sailing Craft</small>

In 1858-9 the total receipts of wheat and flour in San Francisco reduced to terms of wheat was only 638,664 centals. In 1866-7 the quantity had increased 5,901,593 centals and before 1870 it had passed the ten million cental mark. The bulk of this product was shipped to Great Britain and other countries. It formed the chief cargo of most of the sailing vessels clearing from the port of San Francisco. In the season of 1869-70 5,922,776 centals (wheat and flour) were exported to foreign lands, and a not inconsiderable portion of the remainder was shipped to domestic ports, the regions which have since developed their cereal producing ability at that time being largely dependent on the flour sent to them from San Francisco. The growing importance of the cereal export trade by no means passed unnoticed in San Francisco. Although it was subordinated in the general esteem to the mining industry the cultivation of grain was duly commented upon in press and public speech, and glowing pictures of vast wheat fields were painted. Through all this comment one searches in vain for any signs of apprehension that the development along this line might result in fastening the large land holding system on the state. But that fear was soon to manifest itself and allay the pleasure with which San Franciscans were beginning to contemplate grain farms, whose size was reckoned by thousands of acres.

<small>Growth of Wheat Exports</small>

These fragmentary statistics permit the comment that despite occasional vicissitudes the business of the port of San Francisco and of its merchants was fairly good during the decade. In 1863 there was a dry year which interrupted mining and caused a crop shortage. The bad results were visible in a diminished trade for a period of short duration. During the decade there were frequent opportunities for felicitation on the growing importance of industries which, although in some

<small>Crop Diversification</small>

instances introduced in the time of the missions, had made but slow progress. It began to be noted that the production of wine and brandy would prove a source of wealth to the state and the output of 2,250,000 gallons in 1866 was cited as evidence of what might be expected when the capability of California to produce the best quality of wines was fully recognized. This product was nearly doubled before the close of the decade.

Fruit Canning

The fruit canning industry, which has since attained the distinction of being foremost among California's sources of revenue was also coming into prominence. The canner began his operations early in the Fifties, but they were on an inconsiderable scale until 1857, when Cutting & Co., who take rank as pioneer producers, introduced their process, and practically fixed the seat of the industry in San Francisco. In 1866 it was estimated that 19,000 cases were packed in the state, nearly all of which was put up in San Francisco. Excellent samples of raisins grown in the San Joaquin valley were exhibited about this time, and with their usual optimism the editors predicted that the day would come when they would contest with those of Malaga. As the output in 1870 was only reckoned at 1,200 boxes, valued at $1,350, they are entitled to be regarded as true prophets, for the product has grown to over 7,000,000 boxes annually and California now supplies the major part of the raisins consumed in the United States.

The Wool Industry

During the mission period, as already related, little attention was paid to the breed of sheep, but the neglected industry speedily attained importance after the occupation, and San Francisco began to be a wool market of considerable consequence. The wool produced in the Fifties was up to the standard of merino and this result was secured by crossing with the Mexican type. Later Southdowns and Shropshires were introduced which produced bigger animals, and following the experiments of Austrian growers Californians finally succeeded in producing a good grade of sheep by breeding from Leicester and Lincolns with fine merinos, the result being larger carcasses and an improved quality of mutton and a fairly good class of wool. The vast extent of the ranges caused sheep raising to extend rapidly, and before the close of the Sixties the wool crop, which was practically all marketed in San Francisco, had attained great importance. The clip of 1870 was estimated at 20,072,660 pounds, and growers and intermediaries were alike prosperous.

Manufacture of Woolen Textiles

The production of so large a quantity of raw material naturally had the effect of directing attention to the desirability of converting it into textile fabrics, and there were large plans laid to accomplish that end which had a measure of success for a time. There were many circumstances militating against profitable manufacturing in California, but it was believed that they were more than offset by the advantages which the state enjoyed. Among these latter were reckoned the remoteness from the producing centers of the East, which were compelled to obtain their supplies of raw material from a great distance while California mills would have theirs at hand. It was thought that the increased cost of fuel in California would be more than offset by the greater cost to the Eastern manufacturer of the raw material, and the cost to him of sending the finished fabric to California. It was also pointed out that owing to the equable climate the efficiency of the worker would be improved. On the whole it was assumed that California would become a great manufacturer of woolens, and that San Francisco would be the principal seat of the industry.

The Pioneer Woolen Mills had been established before the Sixties and was operated in a small way. Its business expanded and in 1868 it had 37 sets of carding machines, 150 looms, 13,000 spindles, 120 knitting and 18 sewing machines. It gave employment to about 700 men, women and children, and had a paid up capital of $1,000,000. Its chief products were blankets, cloths, tweeds, flannels, robes and shawls. The quality of the output was excellent, and for a time the blankets of this mill were regarded with favor beyond the borders of the state and were not entirely unknown at the East where they competed with the best that section could produce. There was running at the same time according to the census report from which this information is extracted, the Mission Woolen Factory, which employed 240 hands and consumed about 800,000 pounds of wool annually. The same authority puts the daily consumption of the Pioneer Mills at about 3,000 pounds. It also reports that there were mills in operation during the Sixties in Marysville, Los Angeles, Merced, Napa, Petaluma, San Jose, Santa Rosa, Stockton and Woodland, a total of twelve in the entire state. *Woolen Mills in San Francisco*

Writing of this period a special agent of the census remarked several years later: "When the youth of San Francisco in 1865 is considered, the progress which had been made in manufactures up to that time was little short of marvelous. There were in that year between 300 and 400 establishments in that City which were engaged in the various kinds of metal making, and employment was given to over 2,000 hands." This satisfactory condition was attained in spite of the great stimulus given to importation from the East by the temptation held out to merchants to profit by the advantages derived from the difference in the value of gold and paper money, and notwithstanding the prevalent high wages. While the isolation endured the standard of living and wages established in California apparently did not greatly interfere with its development. It was only when the necessity of meeting with the growing competition of the East arose that difficulty was experienced by manufacturers in maintaining their industries. *Condition of Manufacturing Industries*

That the difficulties they were to encounter were not clearly foreseen may be inferred from a statement contained in the announcement of the Seventh Industrial Exhibition of the Mechanics institute issued in July, 1869. In it the board of directors of the institute expressed the opinion that "in view of the completion of the Pacific railroad, the consequent influx of visitors (principally business men) from abroad, the extension and completion of various other lines within the state limits, the successful development of the China and Japan trade and commerce, and the great interest felt in the peculiarly fortunate geographical position of San Francisco by farseeing men from all parts of the world, the exhibition should be as comprehensive and general as possible, and that there should be greater number of exhibits, each exhibitor being satisfied with a smaller amount of space in order to advance the general good of the state at large." *High Hopes Entertained*

The circular expressed the optimism of the period and exhibits a total lack of apprehension concerning the effect of possible changes. Changes were expected, but they were all to contribute to the growth of the industries of the state and the prosperity of its inhabitants. It was thought that the greatly increased demand for space by manufacturers in the pavilion then located on Union square presaged the further expansion of all branches of manufacturing industry. The enterprising men who were to be brought by the new railroad were to come and establish themselves in the City and take advantage of its peculiarly fortunate *The Exploiter Not Feared* geographical position. It did not occur to the directors, and for that matter, any other San Franciscans, that they might also have in view the possibility of further exploiting a field to which the new Overland railroad would give them easier access.

Metal Industries Prosperous

San Franciscans at that time had ample reason to be proud of their progress in manufacturing. They saw in operation in their midst iron works whose out-turn of products made them worthy of notice. The Union Iron and Brass Works founded in 1849 was still in existence and prosperous, as were the Pacific Iron Works, the Fulton Foundry, the Vulcan Iron Works, the Miners Foundry, and the Golden State Iron Works, establishments without rivals nearer than 3,000 miles, enjoying the patronage of the mines constantly being opened, and whose demand for machinery was continuous and profitable. They regarded with great expectation the advent of a young marine engineer named George W. Dickie, because his coming was accompanied by the announcement that there was to be an expansion of the shipbuilding industry. Previously to 1870 there had been considerable shipping construction, but it consisted almost wholly of sailing vessels for coast and bay service and some steamboats for bay and river traffic, but the machinery for the latter was chiefly procured from the East. It was proposed to change this attitude of dependence and produce engines in San Francisco. There were several competent shipbuilders in the various yards of the port in 1870, among whom are mentioned in the local annals of the industry, Messrs. North, Gates, Collier, Tiernan, White, Turner, Middlemas and Boole. There was also some work done in the way of building engines for tugs, and small bay and coasting steamers, and providing boilers for the same, and there was sufficient repair work to keep several moderate sized establishments busy. The construction of larger vessels did not begin until later, but the outlook on the whole was fairly satisfactory at the close of the Sixties and the retrospect might be described by the same term.

Miscellaneous Manufactures

The reduction of ores had attained to some importance in the Sixties and there were several establishments where gold and silver were refined. The wire rope works of A. S. Halladie & Co. manufactured all the wire cable used on the coast, and turned out cables miles in length. There was a large demand for this product as wire cables were principally used for operating the hoisting machinery in the mines. A glass factory was in successful operation and employed over 50 hands, but the establishment which stood out most prominently was the big sugar refinery at Harrison and Eighth streets, the buildings of which were the largest in the state at the time and were an impressive feature of the landscape and seemed to emphasize the claim made that the City was a really important manufacturing center. These mills refined one thousand tons of raw sugar monthly. In addition to this company which was known as the San Francisco and Pacific Sugar Refinery there was a rival concern, the Bay Sugar Refinery, which had a plant capable of refining 50,000 pounds daily. It was situated at Union and Battery streets.

Encouraging Home Industry

The disposition to encourage manufacturing industries asserted itself very strongly during the Sixties. Whatever may have been the earlier belief regarding the impossibility of competing with the East because of the cost of fuel and the high rate of wages generally prevalent, it was modified to such an extent that the legislature was induced at times to offer premiums for its encouragement. This practice was strongly condemned by Governor Haight in a message to the legislature of 1869-70. He referred to several statutes which had been passed, giving

NUCLEUS HOTEL IN 1865

It stood on the site o the Hearst Building the presen home o the San Francisco Examiner corner of Third and Market Streets

premiums for the raising of silk cocoons, the planting of mulberry trees and the manufacture of woolen fabrics, and objected to the practice because "it was sustained by the same reasoning as that urged in favor of a protective tariff," and declared "that it merely resulted in forcing capital out of one channel into another." The encouragement he deprecated was not extended on a very great scale, but there is no evidence that any serious diversion of capital occurred in consequence. Perhaps it might have been well for the community if it had been diverted into the manufacturing channel instead of being directed into that of mining stock speculation which absorbed most of the floating capital during the seventy decade.

Almost at the beginning of the decade 1860-70, Governor Stanford in a message to the legislature declared that California from being "a state entirely at the mercy of others for the necessaries and comforts of life," had risen to an independent position, and in some productions took precedence of all other states in their annual aggregate yield. "As we now lead all other states in the production of wine and barley" we may some day "rival Louisiana in the production of sugar, Virginia in tobacco and Kentucky in hemp. . . . California may yet snatch from North Carolina the distinction of being the chief tar state." These predictions were based on what he said were promising experiments, but they were not all realized. But great store was set upon them, and many business castles in the air were built in San Francisco upon the expectations he voiced. The question of manufacturing tobacco of all kinds was investigated, and satisfactory experiments were made with the California product which was declared to be all that could be desired, but the industry has never thrived. Tobacco has never been grown in California in quantity, but the manufacture of cigars flourished for a while, the material used, however, being imported. The sugar industry has been an important one in San Francisco for many years, but the refineries have always operated with foreign or Hawaiian raw products. Tar and turpentine have never been produced on a scale to merit particular attention and North Carolina may still retain her old time distinction so far as California is concerned.

Message on Industries of California

But the mention of these failures only accentuate the fact that the resources of the country tributary to San Francisco were so great and varied that they sufficed to keep up the growth of the port and make its gains in wealth and population during the decade a source of wonderment to cities less fortunately situated. Opportunities were neglected during the period which would have been utilized by peoples trained along other lines, but there were some seized which were overlooked by the owners of capital in other sections of the Union who would gladly have taken advantage of them had they appreciated their importance. An instance of this sort was the good fortune of a group of San Franciscans in 1870 to obtain a lease from the government to take 100,000 male seals annually from the Pribilof islands. The privilege was first awarded to Hutchinson, Kohl & Co., but subsequently the Alaska Commercial Company was formed to forward the enterprise which was successfully conducted and laid the foundations for several large fortunes.

Alaskan Fur Seal Contract

In 1869 there was a panic in the New York gold market which gave a setback to business in the Eastern states, but its influence was not widely felt in San Francisco, which was still sufficiently insulated to resist shocks other than those of its own producing. The peculiar advantages already described served to ward off the evils of the depressions in other sections of the Union, or so modified them that recovery from their effects was not difficult. The completion of the Overland

End of Isolation Period

railroad, however, worked a change. It was scarcely noticeable at first, being obscured during the earlier Seventies by the discovery of the Bonanza mines and the tremendous speculation which ensued; but the decade did not complete half its course before San Franciscans were brought to a complete realization of the fact that they were firmly bound to the outside world by the rails which connected the Atlantic and Pacific sections of the Union, and that their City was no longer an isolated community.

CHAPTER XLII

NATIONAL, STATE AND MUNICIPAL POLITICS IN THE SIXTIES

THE LAST POLITICAL DUEL—CONTINUED SUCCESS OF THE PEOPLE'S PARTY—KEEPING DOWN TAXATION—PEOPLE'S PARTY SUFFERS DEFEAT—A LUKEWARM PERIOD—THE TAPE WORM TICKET AND BALLOT REFORM—LOCAL SELF GOVERNMENT DENIED—BUILDING A NEW CITY HALL ON THE INSTALLMENT PLAN—WATER SUPPLY—MOVEMENT TO SECURE MUNICIPAL CONTROL OF WATER SYSTEM—OPPOSITION TO CREATION OF DEBT—WIDENING OF KEARNY STREET—PROPOSAL TO CUT DOWN RINCON HILL—QUIETING OUTSIDE LAND TITLES—SECURING LAND FOR GOLDEN GATE PARK—THE LAND FOR PARK PURPOSES ORIGINALLY A DREARY WASTE OF SAND—WOODWARD'S GARDENS—ACTIVE BUILDING OPERATIONS—REAL ESTATE IN FAVOR—PRICES OF REAL ESTATE—MARKET STREET IN 1870—STREET CAR CONVENIENCES—CONGESTION OF POPULATION—BANKING AND BUSINESS CENTER—APPEARANCE OF CITY AT CLOSE OF SIXTIES.

THE Civil war produced many political changes in San Francisco. In the realignment over national issues the old differences between democrats were lost sight of for a time, and to all appearances a majority of the people were quite content to unite for one purpose, but the common desire for the preservation of the Union which found expression in the support given to the party of that name was by no means productive of harmony, nor did it cause men to lay aside their personal ambitions, or for that matter their old time prejudices. Changing fashions had somewhat modified the asperities of politics. There was less of the "plug ugly" spirit displayed on election days than during the Fifties, and the political duel became a thing of the past, the last one fought in the state being the affair between Charles W. Piercy, a Union democrat from San Bernardino and Daniel Showalter of Mariposa, in which Piercy was killed. The fatal quarrel was brought about by a charge made by Piercy that Showalter was a secessionist. It does not appear that the charge was unfounded, but Showalter resented it as much as if it were. *The Last Political Duel*

The legislature of 1863-4 availing itself of the opportunity to do mischief which the unrestrained powers granted to that body afforded, attempted to redistrict San Francisco in the interest of a candidate for United States senator in such a manner that success would have given the element which caused so much trouble during the previous decade control of local municipal politics. The picturesque designation of "short hairs" was conferred upon the supporters of this movement, and all sorts of evil intentions were attributed to them. That the name was not unaptly bestowed may be inferred from the fact that a fair proportion of those to *Political Corruption* whom it was applied were devotees of the prize ring or their admirers. The disturbance created by the effort in a measure refutes the commonly accepted assumption that the Vigilante expression of disapprobation in 1856 had made such a lasting impression that corruption did not dare to lift its ugly head during the sixty decade.

Continued Success of People's Party

The people's party first started in 1856 continued to prove successful at the polls until 1867. It has been eulogized because it introduced what its supporters were pleased to call an era of economy. If the failure to expend money for any other purpose than the mere maintenance of a form of government merits laudation the people's party and those who supported it deserve applause, but if the exacting requirements of present day reformers are accepted as a standard of measurement the performances, or rather nonperformances of the men who held municipal office in San Francisco will not demand a high meed of praise.

Keeping Down the Tax Rate

A writer whose comments reflect the spirit of the warmest admirers of the people's party declared that "it was in fact ahead of the times, and it had to give way to a system more in accord with the character of the people and their disposition to extravagance." This indictment was not fairly brought against the community for it was a long way from exhibiting any signs of a desire to plunge into extravagances; it was merely displaying restlessness over the fact that despite a not inconsiderable expenditure every year by the municipality there were absolutely no public improvements to show for what had been expended. About all the taxpayer gained in return for the demands made upon him was a not greatly improved administration of justice, and a sort of hand to mouth management of affairs which prevented the City from absolutely falling into decay. The spirit of what came later to be known as "Silurianism" had taken possession of San Francisco. Every proposed innovation was assailed as an effort to restore the control of the elements suppressed by the Vigilantes. The only thing that commended itself to the adherents of the people's party was a promise to keep down the tax rate.

Defeat of People's Party

Naturally such a sentiment could not endure permanently in a community with opportunities to expand and eager to make use of them. It is not surprising therefore that the people's party with its traditions of respectability and hostility to expenditure should have suffered defeat as it did in 1867, when the rival organization, which advocated improvements, succeeded in electing Frank McCoppin as mayor. Not that the democratic party, whose candidate he was, boldly came forth in support of a programme of improvement, for it did nothing of the sort, but McCoppin was known to favor the erection of a city hall, and he also had advanced ideas concerning the functions of a municipal government, all of which were regarded as a menace to the welfare of the City by those who had come to regard the Consolidation Act with all its restrictions as a most marvelous instrument, because it made it nearly impossible to enlarge the demands upon the taxpayer.

Union Party Defeated

National questions ceased to exert a dominating influence in city politics very soon after the close of the Civil war. There was no cessation of the effort, however, to make the Union party continue to do service for the local politicians, but their efforts were in vain. In the September election of 1866 the Union party suffered its first defeat. The democratic candidate for governor, Henry Haight, was elected. His success was chiefly due to dissensions within the ranks of the Union party. His rival was in the camp of Gorham and the element which dominated the republican party in the Seventies, and there was already more or less dissatisfaction with them because of their too close affiliations with the railroad. Haight was an original republican. He had voted for Fremont, and later for Lincoln, but when the latter was running for a second term the Californian labored and voted for McClellan. After his election Haight became a pronounced opponent to the reconstruction policies of the government. He was apprehensive that "a negro empire would be created on our Southern border," and was vigorously opposed to the creation of military districts which he declared would prove subversive of republican institutions.

The strenuous language employed by Haight was in no wise indicative of the strength of sentiment in California. Remoteness from the seat of government and the withdrawal of the influence exerted so dominantly in earlier years had permitted California, and particularly San Francisco, to fall into political habits which bordered on perfunctoriness. The politicians thundered, and the press argued, but the people were in no mood to subordinate their domestic concerns to national affairs. Haight in a message to the legislature of 1869-70, expressed the belief that the Pacific states would be a unit in favor of free trade, a specie currency and the exclusive right to manage their domestic concerns; and in January, 1870, the legislature refused to vote for the adoption of the Fifteenth Amendment by a decisive vote, but feeling did not run high in state or City.

Lukewarm Politics

An idea of the paramount desire of San Francisco is obtained from the statement made by George H. Rogers of San Francisco, who was speaker of the assembly in the legislature of 1869-70. He declared that his constituents had sent him to Sacramento to procure the simplification of the registry law. The legislature of 1865-6 had passed an act known as the Porter Primary Law of which great things had been expected by the reformers, but it in no wise satisfied their demands for the bosses had no difficulty in making ducks and drakes of its provisions. In a message to the legislature Haight called attention to an abuse perpetrated at Mare island by federal officials who compelled the employes to vote a ballot which was nicknamed the "tape worm ticket." These ballots were printed on paper nearly as thick as that used in ordinary playing cards, and like the latter had their backs decorated with scroll work which made them distinguishable at a distance. They were five or six inches long and about two-thirds of an inch wide, and the candidates' names were printed in the finest of type. The bosses compelled the job holders to plainly display these ballots before depositing them in the box. Any recalcitrancy would have been punished with discharge, consequently there was a solid vote for those whose names were dictated by the ring which controlled federal politics during the closing years of the decade Sixty.

The Tape Worm Ticket

Continuation of this abuse was made impossible by the passage of a uniform ballot law which provided for a ticket to be printed on paper the color of which was to be designated by the secretary of state. Size and style of type were also prescribed, and restrictions were placed on solicitors who were not permitted to importune a voter within one hundred feet of the polls. The law also forbade the opening of saloons on election days and threw about the ballot box numerous other precautions. On the whole, so far as mere secrecy of the ballot was concerned, this law seemed to fully meet every requirement, and undoubtedly it afforded abundant safeguards for holding a perfectly fair election, one which bosses could not control if the people chose to prevent their interference, a fact well attested by the success of various reform movements under the system, all of which were procured by the simple device

Ballot Reform Effected

of attention to duty, which proved so efficacious in the days following the Vigilante affairs. From which it may be concluded that the machinery of election is of less consequence in securing good results than the disposition or indisposition of the people to perform their civic duties.

Local Self Government Denied

That the desire for good government could be easily aroused in San Francisco was frequently shown during the Sixties, but the people were not entirely their own masters at the time, nor did they succeed in becoming so until the close of the ensuing decade when the constitution of 1879 was adopted, which for the first time gave something like local self government to the City. The struggle for this right was a long one. As early as 1862 the legislature had submitted an amendment against special and local legislation, but it was rejected by the legislature of 1863. Up to that time and for many years afterward the people of San Francisco were obliged to defer to the wishes of the rest of the state. There was hardly anything they could do without the sanction of the legislature, but despite the drawback of this restraint, and the restrictive features of the Consolidation Act, there was a strong sentiment prevalent that the system was the embodiment of political wisdom, as its effect was undoubtedly to prevent the community committing the indiscretion of running into debt, or overburdening the taxpayer.

Building on the Installment Plan

It was the prevalence of this latter sentiment which must be held responsible for the fatuous course which caused the community to embark on a scheme of building a city hall which would be a credit to San Francisco, on what might be called the installment plan. The hostility to debt creation was so great that a commission was formed with authority to build with the proceeds of a special annual tax levy. Operations on the new building were commenced in the early part of 1870. A portion of Yerba Buena park, which was used as a burial ground in the Fifties, was selected for a site, and the plans of an architect named Laver, who had attained a reputation as the builder of the New York state capitol at Albany were chosen. The cost as originally estimated was quite modest, but there were plenty of critics who declared that it would be largely exceeded. The most pessimistic, however, did not even remotely approach the truth in making their guesses.

The New City Hall

The result justified the apprehensions of the element which expressed the conviction that the new city hall would be an extravagantly costly affair, but the policy of building it piecemeal was as much responsible for the unsatisfactory result as any other cause. The edifice as originally designed was not altogether inharmonious, but succeeding commissions departed so much from the plans of the architect that when completed it was a rather incongruous affair. It was planned to have a tall tower and a mansard roof, but in place of the former there was substituted a lofty dome, and the French roof was never constructed. The most flagrant error committed by the commission was in selling the land fronting on Market street. This blunder was made in response to a demand for economy, and the result was to lessen the dignity of the structure, which would at least have been impressive because of its size, by placing it on a back street.

Fear of High Taxation

The experience of the taxpayer in the Fifties was not of the sort calculated to create enthusiasm for public improvements. It was largely responsible for the lack of interest taken in the proposal to make an attractive offer in order to secure the capital when stress of weather compelled the legislature to seek refuge in San Francisco during the winter of 1861-62, and it caused the men who were managing the destinies of the people's party to look with coldness upon all suggested improvements which would involve the expenditure of money out of the general purse. Their opposition sufficed to absolutely prevent progress, for the system pursued of putting forward candidates for office made a popular choice impossible. The selections were made by a practically self perpetuating body, and while the memory of the rascalities of the men suppressed by the Vigilantes endured the recommendations of this self-constituted custodian of the public welfare were accepted without much cavil.

While this strong predilection for economy existed throughout the greater part of the Sixties and operated to prevent improvements by the municipal authorities, it by no means put a stop to individual effort to make provision for the wants of the growing community. It was not until the opening years of the Seventies that the supervisors began to concern themselves about the matter of an ample water supply; but the prevision which the city authorities lacked was made good by the forethought of men who very early saw opportunities for profit in selling the indispensable fluid to the inhabitants of a growing community. The Spring Valley Water Company, as already related, in 1858 purchased a considerable tract of land in San Mateo county in a secluded and well forested region, and accumulated the waters of Pilarcitos creek and its tributaries, and also those of Upper San Mateo creek in a reservoir, the contents of which were conducted through tunnel, flume and pipe a distance of thirty-two miles to its Lake Honda reservoir and a reservoir on Market street which was subsequently destroyed by cutting through that thoroughfare. Lake Honda reservoir was located near the Almshouse tract, and had an elevation of 365 feet, and the Market street reservoir was near to where it was intersected by Buchanan street. The water was turned into these reservoirs during the winter 1862-63, and pipes distributed it in the North Mission and Hayes valley districts and part of the Western addition, and in the principal business parts of the City. In the fall of 1864 the foundation of the main dam of Pilarcitos was started and in the subsequent year a new Pilarcitos conduit line was conducted into San Francisco. In the latter part of the Sixties the San Andreas dam and its independent pipe line added to the supply of the City.

<small>The City's Water Supply</small>

In 1871 an investigation of the water supply of the City was made with a view to municipal control. The scant precipitation of the rainfall seasons of 1869-70 and 1870-71 had caused some apprehension respecting the sufficiency of the supply of water and on the 10th of April, 1871, the board of supervisors appointed a special committee consisting of General B. S. Alexander, U. S. A., and Professor George Davidson of the United States Coast Survey to investigate and make a report which they did in December of the same year. They reported that "the water supplies of the peninsula within reasonable distance are amply sufficient to furnish an abundant supply of pure, fresh water to provide for the wants of San Francisco for at least fifty years," and they also recommended that the City should own and have absolute control of its water supply.

<small>Municipal Water Supply Desired</small>

At this time the daily consumption of water in the City was only a little more than 6,000,000 gallons. The population was a trifle in excess of 150,000, and the computation on which the estimate of future needs was based was evidently made under the apprehension that the per capita consumption would not be greatly enlarged. In a very few years after 1871, it became necessary to go beyond the peninsula to augment the supply, and it was clearly seen that the increasing demands of the City would oblige it to develop additional sources in the remote Sierra.

<small>Consumption of Water</small>

There were few people in San Francisco in 1865 when the Mountain Lake Water Works were absorbed by the Spring Valley Company who anticipated such a necessity arising, nor in that year was it foreseen that the failure to acquire a municipal water system would lead to endless litigation. Two years later, however, the competitive advantage disappeared and evidence of dissatisfaction was abundant. In 1867 suits were brought against the water company, and there has been an intermittent attempt ever since to acquire the Spring valley system or to create a rival supply.

Opposition to Creation of Debt

The sentiment of the Sixties in San Francisco was decidedly individualistic. There was a profound distrust of collective management which militated against public improvement. "Don't run into debt," was a maxim and it was urged that the plan of sweeping before one's own front door was the ideal one to follow if financial difficulties were to be avoided. Extreme reluctance was manifested to carry out any project at the general expense which would directly or indirectly benefit private individuals. Considering the circumstances under which the realty of the City had been acquired by its owners it is not surprising that the system of opening streets at private charge should have been adopted, and that in consequence needed facilities were slowly provided and that the general result was a ragged and unsymmetrical development. But notwithstanding these drawbacks there was a constant improvement of the facilities for getting about and in the appearance of sidewalks and street pavements, although the latter result was hampered by considerations of economy, and the aversion for regulative measures which would interfere with the right of the individual to do as he pleased with his own property.

Widening of Kearny Street

Critics arose very early to protest against the utter disregard of the esthetic, and of the convenience of the future inhabitants of the City in laying out the City on a strictly rectangular plan, but they made little or no impression on the public mind. When the desire for improvement manifested itself it did not take the form of changing lines, but of widening streets, but comparatively few movements of that kind were inaugurated, and only one was carried out during the Sixties. The necessary permission to increase the width of Kearny street was obtained from the legislature of 1865-66, and the legal methods of assessing the beneficiaries and compensating the injured property holders were prescribed. The advantages to be derived from this improvement were so obvious that the project met with a minimum of opposition, and when it was effected it was regarded with great satisfaction and complacently quoted as an instance of the "go aheadativeness" of the people of San Francisco.

Proposal to Raze Rincon Hill

Another project authorized by the legislature at the session of 1867-68 which provided for the modification of the grade of Second and other streets was not so well accepted by the community. The object was to extend the business district southward by cutting through Rincon hill, which at this time, and until the invention of the cable system of propelling street cars was devised, was a favored residence district. The plan was prematurely put forward, a fact attested by the result which was to simply scarify the hill, and make it unfit for habitation without accomplishing the object aimed at of extending the business district in a southerly direction. Those who conceived the project peered a long way into the future, but did not reckon sufficiently with the disposition to move along the line of least resistance. Nearly half a century was permitted to elapse before steps were taken that

THOMAS STARR KING CHURCH ON GEARY STREET BETWEEN
GRANT AVENUE AND STOCKTON STREET
Dedicated in 1864

SAINT IGNATIUS COLLEGE, ON MARKET STREET BETWEEN FOURTH AND
FIFTH STREETS, AS IT APPEARED IN 1863
The site of the college is now occupied by a large department store building

promise to realize the idea of converting the Rincon hill region into a suitable quarter for business purposes.

The legislature which authorized the Rincon hill invasion passed an act which confirmed an ordinance of the board of supervisors, the object of which was to quiet outside land titles, and also to survey and dispose of the salt marsh and tide lands belonging to the state within the City and county of San Francisco. The effect of this last named act was to dispose of the state's reversionary interest, after the previous grants to the City for ninety-nine years, to the tide and marsh lands in the City of San Francisco. Two sales of these lands made before 1870 realized $813,000 of which $200,000 was appropriated to the State University. The remainder of the lands were sold for a sum which increased the total amount received by the educational institution to something over $1,500,000. Salt, Marsh and Tide Lands

The ordinance to quiet outside land titles has peculiar interest, because it represented a bit of bargaining by which the City managed to save out of the lands it had so easily parted with at an earlier period the tract which has since been converted into Golden Gate park. Up to the time of the passage of this ordinance, which was numbered 800, and was frequently referred to by those numerals, there was little or no attention given to the subject of public breathing places. There were some who protested that the City was behind the times and gave no consideration to the future, but the public generally exhibited indifference. The few gifted with forethought, when the question of determining the titles to the disputed outside lands came up, began to work up sentiment in favor of a park. Outside Land Titles

In 1864 Justice Field decided in favor of the City's claim to four square leagues, and on March 8, 1866, congress approved the decree. The City had disposed of all its title within the pueblo limits up to the charter line of 1851 by the Van Ness ordinance, and the act of congress therefore related practically only to the territory outside of the early boundary which was Divisadero street on the west, and Twenty-second and what is known as Napa street running to the bay on the south. The land outside the western boundary of 1851 was all claimed by squatters, or settlers as they called themselves, and their number included several persons very active in state and municipal politics whose influence was sufficient to prevent the municipality from profiting by the decision of the federal court and the act of congress which conferred ownership of the outside lands on the City. Securing Land for a Park

In this posture of affairs the desire to obtain a public park was made use of to effect a settlement. The claimants of the outside lands were convened, and they were asked how much of the land claimed by them they would be willing to surrender in exchange for a clear title from the City. The offers ranged from ten per cent to twenty-five per cent of their holdings. The committee appointed under the ordinance made an appraisement of the value of the claimed lands and fixed it at $12,087,306, and estimated that of the remainder for park and public purposes at $1,300,000. In the latter were embraced 1,013 acres for Golden Gate park valued at $801,593; Buena Vista park, 36 acres at $88,250; cemetery of 200 acres, $127,465; Mountain Lakes, 19 acres, $19,930; public square, 15 acres, $12,025; school lots, 68 acres, $115,077. An assessment of ten per cent was levied on the whole, which sufficed to pay 90 per cent of the appraised value of the part taken for public use, thus satisfactorily disposing of what had long been a vexed question, and clearing away the impediments to the growth of the City westward. The legis- A Dreary Waste of Sand

410   SAN FRANCISCO

lature on March 14, 1870, approved the settlement thus made by passing a suitable act which duly provided for the creation of Golden Gate park.

Boundaries of the New Park — The land for the new park was not selected with reference to its fitness for the purpose, but it was the best that could be obtained owing to the greediness of the claimants who were not by any means the sort of persons implied by the contemptuous term "squatter," but were rich and influential citizens. Had a decent liberality prevailed in the settlement in 1870, the park would have extended from Divisadero street to the ocean, not merely as a pan handle, but for the entire width from Fulton street on the north to Frederick street on the south. As it was the people were apparently gratified to get any recognition at all and proceeded to make the best of their bargain. The land between Stanyan street, the eastern boundary, and the Pacific was a dreary sand waste, of whose unpromising aspect the present generation can hardly form a conception, but persistent effort, and a tolerably liberal expenditure of public money, and some few gifts from individuals have made it one of the most attractive people's pleasure grounds in America.

Woodward's Gardens — The people did not begin to derive any benefit from the park thus acquired until the decade Seventy was well advanced. Throughout the greater portion of the Sixties, and well down toward the close of the decade 1880-90 the desire for open air recreation was ministered to by the enterprise of a man named Woodward, whose gardens, laid out on a more generous scale than those of Russ soon became the resort of the pleasure seeker on Sundays and holidays. The proprietor was under no illusions concerning the public taste. He recognized that the common folk, and they were all common in the Sixties, when they took an outing were in quest of amusement, and were not seeking fresh air. There was no lack of the latter in the denser parts of the City at any time in the Sixties, and except in the Chinese quarter there was not even a remote approach to congestion. Hence the term garden must be liberally interpreted. Not that there were no flowers, for there were a few, and there was some green grass which clothed terraces carefully guarded from encroachment. The real feature of the place was its attempt to provide as many and as varied forms of amusement as possible. There was a menagerie and an aquarium; an art gallery and a museum; there were swings and other provisions for the pleasure of the children, and regular performances were given in a pavilion and the visitor was afforded every opportunity to refresh the inner man with liquids and solids in a restaurant. An entrance fee of 25 cents for adults was charged, but the big crowds on Sundays to witness balloon ascensions and to enjoy the other attractions of the gardens show that the people did not begrudge the price.

Active Building Operations — The public improvements of a city are not difficult to recount for they are usually recorded, but it is a far different matter to attempt to deal with the accomplishments of private persons, who, despite the liberty of action enjoyed in a community in which little or no restraint is placed on the exercise of individual taste, manage to do things pretty much alike. The influx of people which followed the outbreak of the Civil war was followed by an era of active building, but there was nothing statistically startling or architecturally exceptional during the decade. The Russ, the Lick house and the Occidental hotel were added during this period and deserved the reputation which the people bestowed upon them, for they were fully abreast in most particulars of the best hostelries of the largest Eastern cities. The Lick house, which took its name from its builder and owner, was erected in 1862. It contained a banquet hall designed and executed chiefly by Lick himself, who was an expert worker in wood. It was spacious, and the decorations made it a notable room, surpassed in size and appearance by very few other dining places in the United States. Lick, who was one of the earliest pioneers of California, has the distinction of having been the most liberal citizen of San Francisco, his benefactions to science and the people generally earning for him a world wide reputation.

While it would be uninteresting to describe in detail the progress of the City as exemplified by its building operations, there are some facts which are worth noting because they mark changing conditions. In 1861 Judge H. C. Hastings put up a number of four room houses in the southern part of the City which he rented at $10 a month. They were not very pretentious affairs, but proved an excellent investment for the owner, who found no difficulty in renting them. This bit of enterprise was later regarded as important as it gave an impetus to the construction of small cottages by individual owners who profited by the example set by Hastings. In the year following an act was passed by the legislature under which all the savings and loan societies were organized. Their operations were already very considerable but from this time forward they greatly promoted thrift and the spirit of home building which they encouraged by a judicious loan system. *Home Building*

Investments in real estate were popular in San Francisco from the days of the military occupation. The sale of water front lots, which took place June 29, 1847, was preceded by an advertisement signed by General Kearny and Alcalde Edwin Bryant, in which it was announced that "the town itself is no doubt destined to become the commercial emporium of the western side of the North American continent." There was unwavering faith in the accuracy of this forecast, and a decided disposition to profit by securing land in a place so advantageously located. Many succeeded in procuring more than their share in the period when the chief object of the authorities seemed to be to get rid of all the land under their control, and much dissatisfaction was ocasioned by irregularities of procedure and the disappointment of those who were not as apt in grabbing as others. But these troubles finally ended and before the close of the Sixties the real estate business was established on a basis which indicated absolute confidence in the future of the City, although the variations in the volume of transactions at different times were considerable. In the movements of real estate toward the close of the decade can be traced the influence of excessive mining stock speculation. In 1867 the sales amounted to $17,000,000; two years later they were $30,000,000 and in 1873 they had dropped to $12,000,000. The propensity of fortunate speculators to invest some of their profits in real estate was very marked, and it was shared by men who had made money in legitimate mining operations. A large part of the buying between 1867 and the year when the maximum sales for this particular period was attained was by men of this class who looked upon San Francisco real estate as the very best sort of a nest egg. *Real Estate Investments*

The fluctuations in values during this period were not excessive. The dullness of the market scarcely had the effect of compelling sacrifices; its chief characteristic was lack of movement. Men bought as a rule to hold, and when times became dull they were content to wait. There was much buying by persons who contemplated a future rise in values which they did not intend to help bringing about by making improvements, but it was not sufficient to retard the advancement of the City in those directions to which the topography offered no serious obstacles. *Slight Fluctuations in Values*

412 SAN FRANCISCO

Mission Loses Its Distinctiveness

Before the close of the Sixties nearly all traces of the Spanish occupation had been effaced. There was still an isolated adobe but the low walled houses with their red curved tiles which a few years earlier had marked the Mission Dolores as a place to visit had practically disappeared. Instead of the Mission being a single street with amply spaced houses, in the rear of which cattle grazed in meadows, it had become an indeterminate sort of place practically connected with the more densely inhabited part of the City. There was still plenty of meadow land, but houses were being erected on many streets which were rapidly taking on the shape of thoroughfares, and the term "the Mission" no longer specifically described the place where the Indians once worshiped in the church which still survives, and the corral formerly visited by the amusement lovers of pioneer days to witness bear baiting and bull fights.

Real Estate Values in 1870-71

Some idea of the development of the City since the Sixties may be formed from a survey of real estate values in 1870-71. On streets like Mission, Howard and Folsom, which were 81½ feet wide, lots 80 to 90 feet deep between Fourth and Seventh streets sold at from $125 to $200 a front foot, and similar lots beyond Seventh and as far as Fourteenth at from $75 to $100. Further southerly to Twentieth street from $60 to $75, and on Valencia from $80 to $90. Van Ness avenue property at this time was rated at from $120 to $150 a front foot. In the Hayes and Berdman tracts where the streets were 69 feet wide and the lots 120 feet deep, the price per front foot ranged from $60 to $100. On Stevenson, Jessie, Minna, Natoma and like streets, which were only 38 feet wide, and the lots on which were only 70 to 80 feet deep, between Fourth and Seventh streets the value of a front foot was $50 to $60, and west of Seventh to Tenth, about $40. These figures are derived from a pamphlet the writer of which sought to establish that Oakland property was a far more desirable investment, as lots on the best streets could be bought as low as from $27.50 to $45 a front foot. They by no means understated the values of San Francisco real estate, and are corroborated by records of actual sales. There is a careful statement embodied in it which tells the reader that in discussing "San Francisco values certain favored localities where even residence property is held as high as $300 a front foot, are not included."

Market Street in 1870

In 1870 the future of Market street was clearly realized. At that time the single ferry slip located in the City at which the boats from Oakland landed and departed was at the foot of Pacific street, but it was urged that it should be placed "as near to the foot of Market as possible, because from that point alone the street car lines can be made to radiate to any part of the City." The location of the ferry at the foot of Pacific street was not the only cause of dissatisfaction. It was urged that while provision had been made for the safety of passengers there was an absolute disregard of comfort and it was roundly declared that the surroundings were unworthy of "the civilization of 1870." The inaction of the Harbor Commission was attributed to a desire to conform to the wishes of "the Railroad" whose managers interfered with proposed improvements because they did not regard the foot of Pacific street as the permanent location of the ferry slip, and had decided that it should be at the foot of Market street where it would better suit their convenience.

Early Street Car Conveniences

In 1870 there was no car line traversing lower Market street. The City Railroad Company which operated as far as the Mission district at that date still had its starting point at the corner of New Montgomery and Market streets. The San Francisco and Market street line had commenced operations as early as July 4,

1860. Its cars were dispatched from near the same downtown point and ran as far as the Mission Dolores. The Howard street line and one on Folsom street were started in the latter part of 1862. Before the decade had half run its course the omnibus had been practically discarded as a mode of conveyance in what may be called the down town part of the City. The Market street sand hills had been cut through from Kearny street with the assistance of the steam paddy as early as 1862, and street cars were running to Hayes Park at Laguna and Hayes street. The Omnibus Line in that year was operating cars between North Beach and South Park. The cars on this line were drawn by two horses and the fare charged was ten cents or four tickets for a quarter of a dollar. When the City Railroad Company introduced the one horse car, and dispensed with the services of a conductor, requiring passengers to deposit their fares in a box under the eyes of the driver, no one thought of protesting against the innovation. The desire to secure accommodations was so eager that no part of the community thought of dictating terms. The attitude of the people towards the railroad companies was one of thankfulness, and the suggestion that they should pay for the privilege of using the streets would have been scouted as ridiculous. Franchises had no present nor prospective value so far as appearances went; and if those who developed these early facilities for getting about ever thought that they had secured concessions which would prove a source of great future gain to them they carefully concealed the fact. Summing up the street car situation at the opening of the Seventies it may be said that at that time the citizen who cared to make use of such means of getting about could ride from the northern to the southern part of the City, and could reach points on Rincon hill and in the Mission district, and could get as far west as Lone Mountain, where the journey could be continued to the Cliff house by Concord "busses" if one desired to visit that resort. The transfer system was not thoroughly developed at the time, but there were arrangements by which a passenger for a single fare might ride from Lone Mountain to the Portrero or to Woodward's Gardens in the Mission.

The car facilities of the period while not in advance of the demand were always ahead of the population which slowly penetrated to the localities opened by them. As a rule it may be said that the conveniences for getting about were provided by the railroad companies in advance of active requirements, but the rapid growth of the sections traversed by their lines soon converted what at first was an accommodation to comparatively few patrons into a necessity which created demands which were not always responded to with promptness. While the complaints in the Sixties were not as acute as they have become during recent years protests against the long intervals between cars were not infrequent, but they usually came from those interested in building up the sections traversed, and the people who were led to pioneer the outlying districts tempted by the opportunity to acquire building lots cheaply, and by the desire to get away from the parts of the City which were already showing signs of congestion.

Facilities in Advance of Population

The great fire of 1906 effected so complete a redistribution of the population of San Francisco, it becomes difficult to realize that the City was well started on the road to a state of congestion in what is now one of the principal business and manufacturing sections. The streets south of Market in the Sixties were rapidly filling with houses which were beginning to assume the objectionable characteristics of the tenement system. There were no such large buildings as those in New York

Congestion South of Market Street

414 SAN FRANCISCO

in which enough human beings to fill a small town were crowded, but there was an unmistakable tendency in that direction, and it began to assert itself very strongly in the Seventies. During the Sixties, however, the crowding vice was confined to comparatively small structures. There were houses which sheltered three or four and sometimes more families, and boarding and lodging houses were multiplying rapidly, but there were still numerous homes of men of small means, mechanics and others, and it was not impossible to find within a stone's throw of Market street cottages the owners of which adorned their front yards with flowers.

Old Landmarks Disappearing

There was no longer any suggestion of the fact that the waters of the bay had once described a curve which extended from Telegraph to Rincon hills, washing the shores at what is now Montgomery street. The intervening space had all been filled in and was covered with buildings chiefly devoted to business purposes. There was little variation in the style of these structures which bore the impress of the caution begotten by the numerous fire experiences of the early Fifties. They were chiefly two storied structures built of brick without much attempt at ornamentation, and were all well guarded with iron doors and shutters which gave them a prison-like appearance. Those east of Sansome street were almost wholly occupied by wholesalers and commission merchants, while most of the retail trade was done on the streets west of Kearny, later encroached upon by "Chinatown."

Banking Center in the Sixties

The original banking center of the City was practically restricted to three blocks bounded by Washington and California on the north and south and by Battery and Kearny on the east and west. Some of the financial institutions were located in the narrower streets intersecting these blocks, but the most of the more pretentious concerns did business on Montgomery street between California and Washington. One of the earliest banks shared quarters with a livery stable on the corner of Kearny and Washington streets, and a savings bank received its deposits in a second story office. In 1866 the Bank of California erected a handsome stone building on the corner of California and Sansome streets. It was designed after classical models, and the San Franciscan of the period was prone to point to it as an illustration of the rapid development of the City, which in the brief period of fifteen or sixteen years had made such advances that its financial institutions were housed as "superbly" as any in the country.

An Architectural Innovation

Nearly about the same time the London and San Francisco bank erected its structure on the corner of California and Leidersdorf streets. Its iron front was the subject of much favorable comment of the same kind indulged in at the East, where the moulder's art was beginning to be looked upon as a wonderful substitute for the slower and more expensive products of a real architecture. These constructions determined the permanency of the early location of the financial district, the only changes made as the years advanced were those caused by the crowding out of the miscellaneous concerns doing business, their places being usurped by banks, insurance companies, brokers' offices and like activities, although in close proximity to them were some of the best hotels and places of amusement.

Appearance of City

In the closing years of the Sixties the City presented a compact appearance calculated to impress the stranger with its business importance. The tendency to spread out did not develop itself in real earnest until the difficulties presented by the hills, which bounded the originally built up section, were overcome by the introduction of the cable car. Up to that time a considerable part of the population lived in the upper stories of buildings whose ground floors were occupied by stores until the growth of trade warranted the devotion of the entire structure to the housing and display of goods. This practice was maintained in many of the business streets up to the eve of the great fire in 1906, and contributed greatly to the animation after nightfall of a quarter which in most other commercial cities is surrendered to quiet when the rush of the day has been suspsnded. Perhaps in the conditions this concentration created may be found the explanation of that "atmosphere" whose existence so many recognized, and which it was claimed persisted down to April 18, 1906, when it, together with many much more valuable assets were consumed by the flames which swept away more than three-fourths of the City.

CHAPTER XLIII

THE HARBOR, THE RAILROADS AND THE LAND MONOPOLISTS

FERRY SERVICE—HARBOR COMMISSION CREATED—SEA WALL PROVIDED FOR—BAD MANAGEMENT DRIVES AWAY SHIPPING—THE BULKHEAD LINE DEFINED—HUNTERS' POINT DRY DOCK—BLOSSOM ROCK REMOVED—COMPLAINT ABOUT PILOT LAWS—SEA ROUTES FROM SAN FRANCISCO—LINES TO COAST PORTS—STATE INTERDEPENDENCE NOT MUCH THOUGHT ABOUT—RAILROAD PLANS OF MONOPOLIZING—ALL TRAFFIC RIVALS FORCED OUT BY THE CENTRAL PACIFIC—MORE LAND GRABBING—ATTEMPT TO MAKE GOAT ISLAND A TERMINUS—FEAR OF GOAT ISLAND RIVALRY—CALIFORNIA RAILROADS IN 1870-71—INCREASING HOSTILITY TO RAILROAD MANAGEMENT—THE RAILROADS AND THE LABORING CLASS—LAND MONOPOLY AND TAXATION QUESTIONS—WOMAN SUFFRAGE ADVOCATED—AGITATION OF QUESTION OF REVISING THE CONSTITUTION.

Ferry Service in 1871

PAMPHLET published in Oakland in 1871 reproached the people of San Francisco with indifference to the charms of that suburb. It declared that thousands of people living in the City had never visited the side of the bay on which Oakland was situated, and that the most of them were "in blissful ignorance of the attractions" which it offered in the way of "recreation and invigorating trips to and from Oakland." That may have been true of the mere pleasure seeker, but the statistics of 1870 show that the travel between the two cities was already considerable at that time. During the year the El Capitan, which performed the ferry service, made twelve trips daily, carrying an average of 180 passengers or 4,320 a day. In addition to the service provided by the El Capitan boats were run on the Estuary or Creek line, as it was called, but they carried freight only.

Condition of Water Front

The condition of the water front at that time was not very attractive. The ferry slip was situated at the foot of Pacific street but it served no other purpose than embarking and debarking passengers. It was not only inconveniently situated, but it was unprovided with any of the conveniences demanded by travelers. It was in fact a makeshift, and to the observing it told the story of a mere marking of time, until the new power which was beginning to shape the politics and business affairs of the Pacific coast, could perfect its plans so as to absolutely control its destinies.

Harbor Commission Created

The improvement of the water front was one of the vast projects mapped out by the legislature for the people of San Francisco who had permitted its control to pass out of their hands. A sea wall was to be constructed and the harbor was in every way to be made worthy of the praise bestowed upon it by navigators from the day of the discovery of the bay. An elaborate program was laid out and a

418   SAN FRANCISCO

commission created which later developed into a political machine whose members
oftener paid more attention to pushing the fortunes of those who gave them their
appointments than they did to the shipping interests of the port. The act which
created the commission at first provided for the election of one member from San
Francisco but was subsequently amended by being increased to four members, all
appointed by the governor. To this board was assigned the duty of fixing rates
for dockage and wharfage. It was empowered to locate and to build wharves and
piers, quays and landings along the water front of the City, and to make regulations
concerning the property entrusted to it, designate anchorages, maintain a fair way,
and to do all other needful things required by the commerce of the port. The City
was practically divested of all authority the ex officio dignity conferred upon the
mayor, giving him no voice in the conduct of affairs or in the deliberations of the
commission whose meeting he attended only when some question touching the improvement or control over the street which ran along the front, 150 feet of the width
of which was placed under the jurisdiction of the state.

Sea Wall Provided For
Although the act was passed in 1863, not much progress was made during several years in building the sea wall for which specific provision was made. The first
contract for the construction of that improvement was let in 1867. The lowest bid
was $278 a lineal foot, making the cost of a mile of wall aggregate over a million
and a half. The work of construction and filling in proceeded very slowly during
the first years of the commissionership and finally ceased almost entirely, the politicians, as the years went on, becoming more and more expert in the practice of
dissipating the revenues without producing anything of consequence for the money
expended. More than forty-three years afterward only 11,700 feet of wall was
completed. The so called bulkhead scheme by which the legislature in 1860 sought
to confer upon the owners of the old wharves, who had organized under the name of
the San Francisco Dock and Wharf Company, the power to build a stone bulkhead
on the water front created a tremendous scandal, but it is doubtful whether its success could have done more injury to San Francisco, even if the worst fears of those
who opposed it had been realized, than has been inflicted on the City and state by
the bad management of successive harbor commissions, and the corruption which
attended the conduct of affairs by some of the boards.

Shipping Driven Away
The projectors of the bulkhead scheme may have designed monopolizing the
water front privileges of the port, but it is reasonably certain that they would
not have so managed affairs as to drive shipping to other points on the bay. That
was the net result of the mismanagement of the politically selected commission in
the closing years of the Sixties. In order to escape the high rates ship owners took
their vessels to Vallejo and Port Costa to load. In 1869 twenty-five vessels took
on nearly three-quarters of a million centals of wheat at Vallejo, and after that
date Port Costa was provided with facilities for loading wheat, causing the harbor
of San Francisco to be neglected and entailing an additional burden on shippers
which might have been avoided had the work of construction on the front been
pushed and the affairs of the port carefully administered.

Bulkhead Line Defined
Although there had been much quarreling over the arrangement of the water
front in the Fifties, and a great deal of interference on the part of the legislature
in that regard, it was not until the session of 1877-8 that an act was passed defining
the bulkhead line. Between this line and high water or shore line there was originally about 2,500 acres of submerged land. This was divided into city blocks and

EAST SIDE OF MONTGOMERY STREET, NORTH OF CALIFORNIA STREET, IN 1865

sold by the state. About two-fifths of it lying north of the Union Iron Works was reclaimed with tolerable promptness, but the remaining 1,500 acres lying south of the Sugar Refinery, and in the vicinity of Islais Creek, India Basin and Hunters' Point was left in the state in which it had been acquired by the purchasers who had no other purpose in mind when buying than to await the process of growth and the extension of the water front system to make their holdings valuable.

Before the passage of the act creating the Harbor Commission, and for many years afterward the water front of the port presented a ragged appearance. There were numerous wharves, but their alignment was by no means perfect, and very few of them were provided with sheds. The facilities for loading and unloading, however, were quite equal to the demands made upon them, and under private ownership they would probably have been extended as rapidly as required, and perhaps at a less cost to shipping than was subsequently entailed by the costly operations of the political custodians of the water front, who constantly lagged in the performance of their duty. In marked contrast to the flimsy construction adopted by the Harbor Commission which persisted in building wharves and warehouses of easily destructible materials down to a recent date, was the action of the San Francisco Dock Co., a private concern, which in 1867 excavated a graving dock out of the solid rock at Hunter's Point. It was 493 feet long, 164 feet wide and 24 feet deep over the sill. Ragged Appearance of Water Front

At the time of the construction of the Hunter's Point dock it was assumed that it would be able to accommodate shipping of the largest size. Up to 1873 the average length of the twenty largest vessels entering the harbor of San Francisco was about 390 feet, and the draft of the ships of greatest tonnage was many feet less than the water carried over the sill of this substantial dock. This modern view of the future of navigation was by no means confined to San Francisco, and it was apparently confirmed by the experience of the "Great Eastern," whose non success in the closing years of the Fifties gave rise to the impression that very large ships would not prove profitable. The "Great Eastern" measured 680 feet in length and her tonnage was nearly 19,000, but her failure caused her to be regarded as an abnormality, and this impression endured for several years. Hunter's Point Dry Dock

Considering the importance attached to the acquisition of San Francisco Bay by the politicians and statesmen who brought about that result, the federal authorities after it was achieved acted with great deliberation in the matter of making it perfectly safe for navigation. In 1826 the British ship "Blossom" had discovered a rock between Yerba Buena and Alcatraz islands which was covered with only five feet of water at low tide. For many years a buoy marked the dangerous obstruction, and it was not until 1870 that it was finally removed. The engineer who did the work was Alexis von Schmidt, who also has to his credit the construction of the stone dry dock at Hunter's Point. He excavated galleries 140 feet long and 40 feet transversely at a depth of about 30 feet below low tide, protecting the work by means of a cofferdam. On the 23d of May, 1870, with all of the people of San Francisco on the hill tops to view the spectacle, the mine was exploded. It was a great show, the rock and water being thrown in the air over 150 feet. The blast proved a complete success. The required depth of 24 feet was attained and the government accepted the work and paid the contract price, $75,000. Blossom Rock Removed

A constant cause of complaint in the management of the affairs of the harbor has been its pilotage system. As early as March 16, 1855, Governor Bigler, in a Pilot Laws message to the legislature, declared that one of the chief obstacles to San Francisco becoming a port of call for whalers was the excessive charge for pilotage. Eight dollars a foot was exacted, and as the average draught of the whalers was about 14 feet the amount demanded was $114; while to enter Honolulu it only cost $28. He urged a reduction in order that the desire to make San Francisco the headquarters of the whaling industry of the coast should not be balked. During this governor's administration he was called upon to deal with a question which arose out of the alleged negligence of a San Francisco pilot, who ran a Peruvian vessel under his charge on the Tonquin shoals. The bark was a total loss and her owners filed a libel in admiralty against all the pilots of San Francisco, six in number at that time. Impecuniosity was pleaded, and the affair was referred to Secretary of State Daniel Webster by the Peruvian *charge d'affaires*, who alleged that foreign vessels were by the law of California compelled to employ pilots, and that the latter in the Bay of San Francisco had made $271,000 during the preceding 15 months, and he urged that if they could not pay the state should. Bigler denied that foreign vessels were compelled to hire pilots. It was true, he said, that if they did not they had to pay one-half pilotage, but that was merely a port charge. So far as the contract with the pilot was concerned that was perfectly optional, and was no affair of the state.

Pilots Control Their Own Affairs

The matter was not pursued further by Webster, and after 1851 the pilots became a law unto themselves. They succeeded in persuading successive legislatures to exempt them from the jurisdiction of the Harbor Commission, and have always, with the assistance of powerful interests managed to control their own affairs. Various efforts were made during the Sixties to bring about a reformation, but they all failed. The pilot lobby at Sacramento was for many years a conspicuous feature and its success in persuading the legislature to refrain from making changes was not always attributed solely to the ability with which the hardships of a pilot's life were pictured before committees dealing with the subject of port affairs and the necessity of lightening the burdens of shippers.

The Sea Routes

During the Sixties interest in harbor affairs was more active than during several subsequent decades. Before the completion of the transcontinental railroad in 1869, and the construction of lines which permitted the traveler to visit most parts of the state without having recourse to water craft, the bay and the rivers emptying into it filled a larger space in the public mind than later. In 1870 San Francisco was not connected by rail with Los Angeles. If one wished to journey to that then remote place he was compelled to go by steamer, which made weekly and later semi weekly trips to San Pedro, or he took the stage, which occupied several days in making the trip. In that year petitions were being circulated in Los Angeles, asking that the right of way be granted the California Southern Coast Railroad Company through government lands, and for land grants and other aid in the construction of the road which was to run by the coast from San Francisco to San Diego with branches from Los Angeles and the lower counties to connect with the transcontinental road near the Colorado river.

Los Angeles and San Diego

At that time Los Angeles was less active in its attempts to secure railroad connection with the outside world than San Diego. The *dolce far nienti* feeling still held the inhabitants of the small town in its thraldom, and they amused themselves poking fun at their ambitious neighbor, who had persistently agitated for a transcontinental railroad from the time when Jefferson Davis was secretary of war, proclaiming the merits of San Diego harbor and extolling the charms of southern California climate. It is not surprising that San Francisco should have derived amusement from reading of the claims of San Diego to future greatness; but the fact that the people of Los Angeles were also amused and convinced that it was absurd to appeal to Eastern folks to make their homes in the southern part of the state by expatiating on the attractions of its climate may seem strange to those who have witnessed its rapid growth during recent years, chiefly because it offered inducements to the seeker after health.

As a matter of fact it was not given to the people of any part of California to peer far into the future. The round phrases of the optimistic, when not too closely analyzed, convey the impression that the people of the Sixties clearly perceived what railroads would do for them, but there is no evidence whatever that one man in a hundred in San Francisco had any conception of the marvelous changes which the multiplication of transportation facilities would bring about. Prophets who do not profess to be inspired must have experience on which to base their prophecies, and the opportunities for obtaining it in California were very limited before the opening of the Seventies. We need not wonder then that in 1870 San Francisco newspapers should have treated with something like amused contempt the dreams of the people of San Diego, and that they hardly gave more than a passing thought to the possibilities involved in the opening up of southern California, and that when they did think of the railroad in that connection it was to regard it in the light of a convenience which would enable the people of the South to more readily reach the metropolis on the Bay of San Francisco.

The South Disregarded

It may be said with equal truthfulness that no one in the Southland thought of railroads from the standpoint of the interdependence of California. The dream of the San Diegan and of the Angeleno was of communication with the East; and in that particular they resembled the San Franciscan, who built all his hopes of development on the section on the other side of the Rockies. He may have intuitively associated with the expected filling up of the state the idea of concurrent growth of its various parts but he rarely worked out the problem and would have been amazed if he had been told that the day was not far distant when remote Los Angeles would sustain relations so intimate with San Francisco that the weekly or semi weekly steamer sailings would be expanded into a daily train service, representing a great many more arrivals and departures than there are hours in the day.

Value of Interdependence

In a circular issued by the "Mechanics Institute" in July, 1869, the opening of the transcontinental railroad is dwelt upon at length, and predictions of the effects to be produced are freely made, but it contains no reference whatever to the results likely to follow the multiplication of railroad facilities within the borders of the state, many of which were already projected in 1869, and were in a fair way of realization at the beginning of the decade 1870-80. But in 1870 the desirability of more rapid connection with the Sacramento valley than the Central Pacific and Western Pacific would provide were beginning to be recognized, and a short route was surveyed. There was already in existence a line between San Francisco and Sacramento known as the California Pacific, which was operated partly by steamboat and partly by rail. It carried its passengers from the City to Vallejo on the steamer "New World," from which they were transferred to the train. There were two trips made daily excepting Sunday, when only one train

Route to Sacramento Shortened

was dispatched. The running time from San Francisco to Sacramento was four hours and to Marysville, which was its terminus, 5½ hours. By this route eighty miles in distance, and eight hours in time were saved between Marysville and San Francisco; and fifty-five miles and two hours in time between the City and the capital.

A Rival Line Projected

The new transcontinental line could permit no rival to retain such an advantage as these savings in time implied. Its managers recognized that they must gain possession in some manner of this advantageously situated railroad which appeared to command the natural western terminus of the overland road, the southern terminus of a line from Oregon and practically the whole outlet of Northern California and Nevada. Accordingly steps were taken to ascertain the possibility of locating a still shorter route between Sacramento and San Francisco. A survey was begun in September, 1870, with that object in view and before the end of November the engineers had run their lines as far as Benicia. The announcement of this result in the "Railroad Gazeteer" occasioned considerable surprise in San Francisco, as it had been supposed that the tule lands offered an insuperable obstacle to safe construction because of their softness, but it was found that there was a substratum of clay under the ooze which afforded a fine foundation for a roadbed.

Central Pacific Buys out a Rival

It was this discovery more than any other cause which induced the projectors of the California Pacific to sell out to the Central Pacific and abandon the railroad field in California. The California Pacific enterprise, which was organized in 1867, had been prosecuted with great vigor. It had made a strong fight to secure an entrance into Sacramento, and had succeeded in effecting its purpose notwithstanding the obstacles placed in its way by the men in control of overland road projects. It had successfully constructed a road from Vallejo to Marysville, with a branch to Sacramento, had bought a road built from Calistoga to Napa, and was making preparations to build feeders in various directions and contemplated extending its line northward into Oregon.

Latham Forced Out

In 1870 few San Franciscans imagined that this concern, headed by Milton S. Latham, would be compelled to succumb to its rival. Newspaper comment of the period indicates confidence in the strength of the California Pacific, and that there was a disposition to regard the survey of the line across the tules as a "bluff" made to bring Latham to terms. But he was under no illusions concerning the nature of the contest which would have to be waged to maintain the position of the California Pacific, and when the Terminal Company was formed by men connected with the Central Pacific, which had for its declared object the building of an air line from Sacramento to Oakland, he concluded to surrender and made a bargain for himself and friends by which, in exchange for a block of Central Pacific six per cent bonds, they turned over their majority holdings to the men in control of the western end of the transcontinental railroad.

Postponement of Air Line Project

This arrangement was made in the summer of 1871, and nothing more was heard of the projected air line for some time afterward. The menace had accomplished its purpose; a rival had been driven from the field and the improvement of communication with the Sacramento valley and the North could be deferred, while projects of extension in other directions were to be carried out. Just what these plans were the public was only permitted to guess, information of any kind being sparingly furnished. It was clear, however, that the energies of the railroad would be directed towards securing all the land which could be obtained through

ORPHAN ASYLUM AND ST. PATRICK'S CHURCH IN 1865
The Palace Hotel, Marke Street, is built on the site they occupied

the liberality of the government. The Southern Pacific Railroad Company was incorporated with that object in 1865 and at the beginning of the decade was pushing its line southward to head off the Atlantic and Pacific. On the formation of the company it was proposed to run the line through Santa Clara, Monterey and San Luis Obispo to Los Angeles and San Diego, but in 1871 several routes were spoken of in the papers and in circulars in which real estate operators were extolling the advantages of the property which they desired to sell.

The route through the San Benito pass to Gilroy was referred to as conforming to plans filed with the secretary of the interior as a basis for a land grant, but there was no show of vigor in that direction, and it was assumed that the tardiness with which the work was prosecuted indicated that the company had encountered great difficulties. Later it developed that the object was to utilize the San Francisco and San Jose railroad, incorporated in 1863, and which was acquired with its extension to Gilroy, for the purpose of securing from the government alternate sections of public land on the pretense that it was constructed with a view of forming part of the overland line designed to connect the Southwest with San Francisco. By this subterfuge the quartette obtained the public lands within the area of the eighty miles, and secured a large quantity of valuable redwood timber lands in Santa Clara and San Mateo counties from which they succeeded in ousting settlers. The action of the quartette was so flagrant in this case it came in for a great deal of criticism. But notwithstanding the fact that the road had originally been built to San Jose as a private enterprise, and that the extension to Gilroy was accomplished by the aid of a subsidy of $300,000 from the City of San Francisco, no serious effort was made in Washington to prevent the grabbing of the land.

A Successful Land Grab

One of the evil results of the grabbing policy of the railroad quartette was the creation of an intense suspicion which practically degenerated into hostility to all enterprise and improvement. The fear that "the Railroad" would ultimately gain possession of everything it planned to obtain interfered to prevent rational discussion of suggested projects. In 1869 it was proposed to unite Goat island with the eastern shore of the bay by constructing a solid causeway. The island contains about 300 acres of land which could be utilized for terminal purposes, and the Central Pacific sought to obtain possession of it with the view of creating facilities which would facilitate the speedy transfer of passengers to the City which was separated from the island by a comparatively narrow channel. In addition to the land which would be made available by grading the island, the railroad through its subsidiary corporation, the Terminal Company, which had received a grant of the shoal land extending northward from Goat island, could have added largely to this area by reclamation.

Trying to Secure Goat Island

At an earlier period the project of uniting the island with the mainland had been mooted and the desirability of carrying out such a plan was recognized. But when it took on the form of a concrete proposal that congress should grant the use of the island to the overland railroad for terminal purposes it was bitterly antagonized. The discussion was more notable for its extreme hostility to the managers of the railroad than sober consideration of the merits or demerits of the scheme. The fear of monopoly was very real at the time, and arguments against any movement which suggested a strengthening of the hold of the Central Pacific appealed very strongly to the people who could not have been persuaded that any way could be devised by which Goat island might be utilized for the benefit of the whole community. If the

Fears of Goat Island Rivalry

424   SAN FRANCISCO

railroad had any connection with it San Franciscans assumed that it would be used to their disadvantage, and incredible as it may seem at this stage of the development of the City, it was actually feared that if the island was ceded for terminal purposes it would result in the creation of a rival port which would prove injurious to San Francisco and perhaps eclipse its importance.

Engineers Block Goat Island Grab

A contracted view of this sort necessarily would have operated to prevent the consideration of any plan that had for its object the creation of terminal facilities which could be shared by all lines seeking to reach the City from the eastern side of the bay, even if the idea of union and regulation had been sufficiently developed at the time to suggest something of the sort. But there was no confidence in the regulative power of the people of the state at that time. That was a later development, and its growth was largely due to the antagonism which Stanford and his associates had created. When the Goat island project was uppermost every possible argument against its use was presented, but it is doubtful whether the scheme of the railroad to secure possession could have been blocked had not the United States engineers expressed the opinion that the closing or obstruction of the channel between the eastern shore of the bay would have the effect of diminishing its tidal area, and thus imperil the future of the harbor by shoaling the bar at its entrance. When this view became generally disseminated the project ceased to have any support and was abandoned.

Grabbing Everything in Sight

The cause of the apprehension of San Franciscans may be discovered in the tendency of the constructors of the Central Pacific to absolutely control all the railroads of California and everything directly or indirectly connected with them. There was no announcement of such a policy but the people were constantly being confronted with evidence of such an intention. The methods adopted to obtain control of the California Pacific were followed in many other cases. The owners of a desired property were menaced with opposition and they usually succumbed without making a serious effort to defend themselves. Latham undoubtedly was ambitious to build up a system, but he speedily realized that he would be unable to win in a contest with the men who were the recipients of the lavish bounty of the nation and state. On his retirement from the senate in 1863 he had promoted the construction of the North Pacific Coast road, but the venture had not proved successful. It was a narrow gauge affair, and it was thought at the time when it was first projected that the economies of that mode of building would make cheap roads very formidable rivals to those of the standard gauge, or rather of the gauge which was afterward standardized. The experience, however, proved disastrous, but Latham's later enterprise would have been a success had he not been driven out of it by the Central Pacific quartette.

California Railroads 1870-71

In 1870-71 the railroad facilities of the state may be described briefly as follows: (1) The Central Pacific, which commencing at Oakland, ran southerly to what was known as Vallejo's Mill, whence it ran eastwardly through Livermore pass, traversing the Sunol, Amador, Livermore, San Joaquin and Sacramento valleys to the Sierra, passing through Stockton and Sacramento on the route across the continent. Later when the California Pacific was organized through passengers were carried by way of Vallejo and the road by way of Livermore pass was devoted to local traffic and freight uses. (2) A branch running southerly from Vallejo's Mill to San Jose connecting with the line of the Southern Pacific which was built as far as Gilroy. (3) The California and Oregon, under construction by the Central

Pacific which had reached Tehema in 1871, and the company was preparing to make the connection between Sacramento and Oakland by the short route via Benecia already described, a plan which it later carried through. (4) The California Pacific from Vallejo to Sacramento with a branch to Marysville and steamer connection between Vallejo and San Francisco. (5) The Coast Route of the Southern Pacific with Los Angeles as its objective which, however, had reached no further south than Gilroy in 1871. (6) The San Joaquin branch of the Southern Pacific which intersected the main line at a point eight miles west of Stockton running southerly for a distance of twenty miles and penetrating a fertile region of the San Joaquin valley. (7) The North San Francisco and Humboldt operated from a point on the bay to Santa Rosa; an ambitious project designed to provide a system for all the coast counties north of the bay.

With one exception all these roads were in the possession of or under the control of the men who had built the Central Pacific, and they were making preparations which were recognized as having for their object the exclusion from the state of any rival railroad. As a consequence the men who a few years earlier were regarded with admiration, and whose enterprise was extolled on every hand, were generally execrated before the close of the Sixties. In 1870 Haight vetoed two senate bills empowering counties to aid in the construction of railways, but a few days afterward he succumbed to the argument that the people had the right to decide, and on April 4, 1870, he appended his signature to a measure which would have permitted San Francisco or any other county to subsidize railroads to the extent of five per cent. of the value of their taxable property. A year later the same governor fiercely assailed the policy of making land grants, and denounced Congress for making a gift of 50,000,000 acres to "a corporation composed of a few capitalists;" and before he went out of office he recommended the repeal of the five per cent. subsidy act, and denounced the excessively high rates which the railroads of California were permitted to charge for carrying passengers and hauling freight, and recommended a reduction even though it was true, as the railroads contended, that the maximum was never charged.

<small>Central Pacific Arouses Opposition</small>

This was a great change from the attitude of earlier years when Stanford, the governor, was applauded for throwing out suggestions which were subsequently acted upon by congress and the legislature. In his inaugural message in 1862 he asked "May we not therefore . . even at this time ask the national government to donate lands and loan its credit in aid of this portion of that communication which is of the very first importance, not alone to the states and territories west of the Rocky Mountains, but to the whole nation and is the great work of the age?" This utterance was hailed with satisfaction by every Californian, because they all believed that the overland railroad was to be constructed for the benefit of the people and to promote the development of the state; but when after a few years of experience they found that the interests of California were being disregarded, and that the men who had been so liberally dealt with by the government had become oppressors rather than benefactors there was a general revolt which culminated in an attempt to bind the corporation hard and fast, but which failed of success because the nation was not yet ripe for the regulative process, and California was not strong enough to accomplish the innovation while the rest of the country refused its moral support.

<small>A Decided Change of Opinion</small>

426 SAN FRANCISCO

Increasing Dissatisfaction

The ferment in labor circles contributed largely to the growing hostility to the railroad which was already being stigmatized as "the monopoly." Merchants and business men generally were disgruntled because they saw the disposition of the railroad to reach out after everything which promised profit. They viewed with disapprobation the practice of letting contracts to themselves inaugurated by the railroad managers, and freely denounced as "hoggishness" the care taken by the quartette to exclude everyone but the big four from the benefits so liberally showered upon them by the government and people. But by far the greatest provocation to dissatisfaction was the failure of the brisk times which were expected to follow the opening of the railroad to promptly materialize.

The Supply of Labor Excessive

This failure was emphasized by contrast with the flush times of the speculative period preceding the opening of the railroad. The briskness due to the activity in mining stocks had subsided before the driving of the last spike, and a reaction of the kind which usually follows excessive speculation had set in, a condition which was not helped by the panic of 1869 in the New York gold market, the evil effects of which communicated themselves to the entire country. Concurrent with this commercial relapse there was developed considerable labor discontent. The completion of the railroad in 1869 had released or thrown out of work a large number of men, and these unemployed had their ranks reinforced by immigrants from the East, who were impelled to seek their fortunes in what was coming to be known as the promised land. At the same time Chinese were pouring into the country at the rate of a couple of thousand a month.

Activity in Labor Circles

It is not surprising in view of these conditions that early in 1870 there were numerous meetings of the unemployed, and that they resulted in something like concert of action. In July of this year it was decided by some of those interested in forwarding the interests of the workingmen that political activity would forward their aims, but there was no approach to unanimity on this point. The Knights of St. Crispin favored nominating a ticket, but the Mechanics' States Council and Eight Hour League were opposed to such a course. The difference between the advocates of these opposing views was so acute that when it became apparent that political nominations would be made the Eight Hour League members withdrew. The proponents of political activity stood firm. They were largely influenced by outside pressure and perfected an organization which affiliated with the National Labor Union, and as the California branch of that body they maintaied their existence down to 1878.

Sand Lot Demands Anticipated

The formation of this body at this early date refutes the mistaken assumption that the so called Sand Lot troubles had their origin in 1877-78. An inquiry into the causes of dissatisfaction which culminated in the demand for a constitutional convention to form a new organic law discloses that every trouble later complained of by the workingmen and the people of the state generally was voiced in the protests formulated at a large meeting held in San Francisco in December, 1871, and in the platform of the State Labor Convention held in the succeeding January, which substantially resembled that adopted by the workingmen's party in 1877-78. These two political documents deserve a place in history, because they embodied demands which were voiced in San Francisco forty years before the rest of the Union recognized them as reforms, only, however, after having fiercely denounced them for a quarter of a century as vagaries of the San Francisco Sand Lot.

SAN FRANCISCO

It is good to look the facts squarely in the face and study their import. Proper consideration given to the lessons they convey may assist in determining whether the voice of the people is always worth listening to, and we may perhaps learn from such a study whether the ability to detect evils, and to force the adoption of legislative reforms, accomplishes the purpose of those who advocate them. But above all things it is worth while to get at the truth so that we may be under no illusions regarding the origins of the so called California workingmen's movement toward the close of the Seventies, which was in reality a struggle participated in by many who were not of the laboring class, and which had for its main object the removal of what was regarded as the chief impediment to the growth of the state.

<small>The Voice of the People</small>

All through the Sixties artisans and laborers, and many who were not in the ranks of the toilers, were uneasy over the influx of Chinese. The Eight Hour League was particularly strenuous in its opposition to this immigration, which oftener than otherwise was of the aided sort. There was much talk about the importation of coolies, and the impression might easily have been derived from this particular agitation that the principal grievance of those who complained against existing conditions was the rivalry of Chinese; but the newspaper comment of the period indicates clearly that the questions uppermost in the United States at the beginning of the second decade of the twentieth century bear a marked resemblance to those agitating California in 1870, and that chief among them was resentment against inequitable taxation. This state of mind was not engendered so much by the burden of taxation as by perception of the fact that its unequal distribution tended to the perpetuation of large land holdings. Venal assessors lent themselves with facility to the view that a piece of property which had been improved by the exertions of the owner was a fitter subject for taxation than large tracts of unimproved land, many of which were under the suspicion that they had been fraudulently obtained.

<small>Taxation Questions</small>

Thus it came about that the struggling settler was called upon to shoulder more than his share of the taxation load. It was recognized that while this condition persisted the owners of immense grants would not break up their estates. The consequences of their failure to do so were clearly foreseen by all classes; by the merchant as well as the mechanic. There was a firmly established belief that California could only become a great and prosperous state by cutting up the big ranches and settling on them small farmers. There were occasional lapses from this conviction which betrayed themselves in inconsistencies such as the glorification of big wheat fields; but, on the whole, even though the spectacular farming of the cereal period appealed to imaginative writers, there was a clear perception that the small farmer was essential to the development of the state, and that good policy demanded that the revenue machinery should not be so manipulated that California would be made impossible to that class.

<small>Large Landholders Favored</small>

And it was this perception and conviction which, more than any other cause, tended to the complete unification of Californians on the subject of Chinese immigration. It was impossible to escape the conclusion that the large land owners, if they were afforded the opportunity, would avail themselves of the cheap labor from the Orient to maintain their possessions intact. The interest in diversified farming was increasing rapidly, and before the close of the Sixties horticulture and viticulture were much in the minds of the people. The visions of future prosperity which contemplation of the expansion of these industries gave rise to were usually accompanied by suggestions that they could never be realized except by the utilization of

<small>Land Owners and Chinese</small>

cheap labor, and doubtless the most of those who held to this opinion were sincere in the belief that the conditions were so exceptional in California that its development would be postponed indefinitely unless some mode of profitably working the large grants and other tracts of land held by individuals could be found.

Henry George's Fear of Land Monopoly

We have some evidence of the force of this opinion in Henry George's "Progress and Poverty" which was the fruit of years of observation of the trend of affairs in California. George was profoundly convinced that the grants would not be broken up except by a system of taxation which would throw the entire burden of support of the state on the land. His single tax theory was developed under the influence of the belief that by that method alone could the tendency to monopolize the land be checked. He doubted the efficacy of any other plan to accomplish that object and was not at all in sympathy with the methods proposed by others to compel the cutting up of the ranches, although he was in substantial agreement with those who claimed that land monopoly was seriously injuring the state. His extreme free trade views prevented any point of contact between himself and the labor organizations, because they were all opposed to Chinese immigration, while the desire for consistency compelled him to assert that if his panacea were adopted all the world would be happy, and it would make no difference whether the state was filled with Orientals or occupied by whites.

Power to Equalize Taxes

Very few shared his views respecting the means of remedying the trouble, but there was complete accord on the point that something needed to be done, and the mode of doing it proposed by Governor Haight in a message to the legislature of 1869-70 seemed to meet with a modified acceptance, although it took several years of agitation before the state was ready to make the change. He recommended that the State Board of Equalization be given effective power to equalize assessments, and expressed himself as deciding in favor of a constitutional amendment making assessors hold by appointment instead of election. He declared that "the state land system was so framed as to promote the acquisition of the domain by capitalists and corporations, either as donations or at nominal prices." In 1870 there was not so much confidence in the ability of the electorate to select good officials as at present, and suggestions of the extension of the appointive power were not taken amiss.

Appointment of Assessors Urged

Perhaps the prevalent belief of the period that the assessors elected by the people were, as a rule, disposed to favor the big property owner at the expense of the small holder, had much to do with the temporary acquiescence in the not unwarranted assumption that assessors selected with especial reference to their possession of the necessary qualifications for the work, and with some regard for their personal integrity would perform their duties more faithfully. But the suggestion to appoint while not unfavorably received was never acted upon. As will be shown later the agitation which culminated in the adoption of the Constitution of 1879 proceeded on the assumption that a change in the organic law which would command a uniform system of assessing lands of like quality and similarly situated would accomplish its purpose, if the powers of the State Board of Equalization were so extended as to enable it to compel obedience to the provision.

Woman Suffrage Movement

Another indication of the spirit of unrest in California at the beginning of the Seventies was the attempt to persuade the legislature to submit an amendment to the constitution according to women the right to vote. A petition was presented in the assembly on March 2, 1870, and a committee of five was appointed to formulate such an amendment; but when it was submitted it was refused engrossment by a vote of 47 noes to 23 ayes. There was not much agitation of the subject in advance of the presentation of the petition, and the summary action of the legislature in refusing to submit the proposed amendment to the people was not regarded as an arbitrary act. The paramount political idea of the period was that stability of government could only be secured by avoiding precipitate action; and in the matter of changing the fundamental law every precaution was taken to prevent the evil effects of popular caprice, by compelling the electorate to carefully consider in advance the probable or possible effect of changes in the organic instrument.

CHAPTER XLIV

SOCIAL SIDE OF LIFE IN SAN FRANCISCO IN THE SIXTIES

THE VACATION HABIT STILL UNDEVELOPED—NEAR-BY ATTRACTIONS—GOLDEN GATE PARK BEFORE IT WAS RECLAIMED—THE CLIFF HOUSE AND WOODWARD'S GARDENS FAVORITE RESORTS—GRAND OPERA GREATLY APPRECIATED—FAVORITE OPERAS OF EARLY DAYS—CONCERTS POPULAR—THE REIGN OF MINSTRELSY—ACTORS OF PIONEER DAYS—THE DRAMA DURING THE SIXTIES—VOGUE OF BENEFIT PERFORMANCES—BIG PRICES PAID TO HEAR EDWIN FORREST—HARRIGAN AND OTHER CALIFORNIA FAVORITES—EARLY VAUDEVILLE—LOCATION OF OLD TIME THEATERS—SAN FRANCISCO'S FIRST DRAMATIC PERFORMANCE—SOCIETY IN THE FORMATIVE STAGE—FIRE AND MILITARY ORGANIZATIONS—PUBLIC CELEBRATIONS—SPORTS—POLITICAL TURNOUTS.

<small>A Stay at Home People</small>

HE resident of San Francisco in the Sixties was not much addicted to gadding about. In a preceding chapter the reproach brought by Oaklanders that there were many people living on the peninsula who had never taken advantage of the opportunity which a commodious ferry boat presented to visit the eastern shores of the bay was reproduced, and it appears from other sources that the San Franciscans were equally indifferent to the attractions of other parts of the outside world during the decade. In an article published in the editorial columns of the "Bulletin" in 1870 there is an enthusiastic description of the glories of a nearby Redwood forest, and an appreciation of the floral beauties of the fields which has for its peroration words of advice to get away from work and enjoy Nature. The declared purpose of the writer was to impress on readers the folly of making a daily grind of life when it is so easy to break away occasionally and get some real delight out of living.

<small>Vacation Habit Undeveloped</small>

As editors were still in the habit of writing eulogies on the delights, and the benefits resulting from the vacation habit many years after, which were accompanied with awful warnings against the dangers that menace men who refuse to rest, the investigator might easily commit the blunder of assuming that life in San Francisco was lived under the high pressure system at this particular period. But nothing would be further from the truth. It is true that the vacation habit was not general in the Sixties, but that was more due to the fact that getting about was not as easy as it is at present, and more particularly to the feeling that the comforts of the town far surpassed those offered by the country. Besides the equable climate marked out no special time for the business man to take a rest, or for the lounger to flee from the discomforts of the City. There was no season of the year in which a man could

432   SAN FRANCISCO

not work in perfect comfort, so it became the fashion to work on interruptedly until another fashion superseded it, and then men and women went to the country because it was the fashion to do so.

Country Resorts Still there were some who sought out the places where Nature might be enjoyed, and where the physical man might be built up. The various springs within a comfortable distance of the City had a fair share of patronage, and those who visited them were offered conveniences which were not so common at the time as they became later. Thus we find in an announcement of the attractions of the Calistoga Hot Springs that "an important advantage is the telegraph connecting the hotel with every part of the state." There was also an alluring intimation that the visitor to the hotel which was situated three and a half hours travel from San Francisco by boat and train would be met on the arrival of the latter at the terminus by the stages of "the renowned Foss and Connolly line." The stage had not yet become a thing of the past in city or country, and the people took as much interest in the statement that a new line of "busses" had been put on as they now do in the announcement that a new limited overland train, made up of palace sleeping, dining and observation cars will be dispatched daily.

Near By Attractions In a circular adorned by a rude wood cut which was disseminated in 1870 we find several interesting bits of information. It opens with the words "Roaring Ocean! Surging Breakers," and closes with the statement that the Cliff house can be reached by "new covered busses connecting with the Lone Mountain cars every half hour." It contained a neat touch which must have appealed strongly, namely, "Take you out in buggy time." That was a phrase full of significance to the San Franciscan of 1870, for it meant "going some, and then some," and to him who had no buggy it conveyed the joyful tidings that if he went to the Cliff he would not have to take everybody's dust. In the early Seventies the Cliff house had already achieved fame as a resort, and no traveler who visited the City failed to make a trip to see the seals. To have done so would have been, in the estimation of most San Franciscans at that time, a case of playing Hamlet and omitting the melancholy Dane.

The Park Before it Was Reclaimed In 1870 the expanse of land now covered by trees, shrubbery and lawns, and known as Golden Gate park, was a waste of sand. The dunes presented an unpromising appearance, and the landscape gardener who foresaw their redemption must have been gifted with a powerful imagination. Like the billows of the ocean the rolling hills stretched away in the direction of the City, and to the accustomed eye they gave evidence that they were not always in repose. But the outlook appeared to have no discouragement for those who were determined to create a park. Their faith in themselves was unbounded. They wrote letters to the papers describing what Holland had done in the way of converting water into land, and in resisting the encroachments of old ocean and said what the Dutch have done we can do and they and their successors energetically set to work to verify their predictions, and make the best of the bad bargain imposed on the City by the greedy squatters.

The Cliff House The attractions of the Cliff house were limited. The stranger enjoyed the novelty of seeing the huge seals disporting on the rocks in plain view from the porch, but the San Franciscan's visit to the resort was more intimately connected with the delight of speeding over the road behind a swift horse or a pair of them, and the refreshments served at the restaurant at the end of the sprint. Very often the drive was punctuated by stops at roadside houses, for the pleasure seeker in the

THE SAND DUNES OF GOLDEN GATE PARK BEFORE THEY WERE CONVERTED INTO A GARDEN
View from the old Seal Rock House, taken in 1865. The work of reclaiming the sand dunes was no begun until the seventies

Sixties was very apt to feel the same aversion for long periods between drinks as the governor of North Carolina whose name has come down to us in history as a stalwart objector to human drouth. During the period when speculation in mining stocks was brisk a good observer with an extended city acquaintance, by stationing himself at some vantage point on the Cliff house road could easily tell who had been lucky or unlucky in the contest between the bulls and the bears.

The popularity of Woodward's Gardens was of a different sort. Its attractions appealed to the family man, and papa and mama with their progeny thronged the resort on Sundays and holidays, and to some extent divided their Saturday afternoon between it and the theater matinees. The performances in the pavilion of the garden, a great barn-like structure, guiltless of decoration of any kind, with wooden stationary benches, were not neglected by the people, but from the stress laid upon the special attractions of the menagerie, such as the acquisition of a "Japanese rooster with a tail twenty-six feet long," and other astonishing natural history freaks, it is reasonable to suppose that the management regarded the histrionic features of their concern as subordinate to the main purpose of inducing the citizen of San Francisco to take some recreation in the open air which he had to do if he wished to take in all the sights, as the monkeys and other animals, those in cages and those in paddocks, were not crowded into a stuffy enclosure, but were placed where they could be seen without the accompanying infliction of bad odors. Then there was the aquarium and the aviary, both creditable in their arrangement and the variety of their exhibits, so on the whole Woodward's in the Sixties was pretty well abreast of the times, and served as an excellent substitute for a public park, even if an entrance fee was exacted.

<small>Popularity of Woodward's Gardens</small>

If the standard of the dramatic and musical performances at Woodward's Gardens was not high, that reproach cannot be brought against the professional caterers for the amusement of San Franciscans in the Sixties. Something has already been said about the extraordinary devotion of the pioneers to music and the drama. The development of this predilection was so rapid it almost denies the suggestion of evolution. It is true that for the first two or three years after gold was found at Sutter's fort the circus held triumphant sway in San Francisco, but its place was soon usurped by high class amusements. The sawdust ring gave way to grand opera, and no city in America was more eager to hear the latest production of the great composers than the new town by the Golden Gate. As early as 1851 there were regular performances of Italian and French opera, and in some years, as in 1858, there were as many as eleven seasons. A simple enumeration of the various companies visiting the City between 1851 and 1861 will indicate the strong hold music had on the populace during the decade. In 1851 and again in 1853 the Pellegrini Opera Company sang Italian opera; in 1853 the Planel French Opera Company was at the Adelphi; in 1854 Thillon's English Opera Company appeared at the Metropolitan and later in the same year a French company sang in the same house. In 1854 the San Franciscans seem to have surrendered to opera, for in addition to the companies mentioned Kate Hayes, a great local celebrity, gave Italian opera and Madame Anna Bishop made her first appearance singing in Norma, Sonnambula and Don Pasquale. The company to which she belonged gave two seasons as did also the Thillon English Opera Company, and in the same years Madame Barili-Thorn also sang. In 1855 Madame Bishop repeated her triumphs and formed an alliance with Madame Barili which was known as the Bishop-Thorn combination. Signora Gar-

<small>Grand Opera in San Francisco</small>

batas also appeared at the Metropolitan. In 1856-8 a French company sang at the Metropolitan and in 1859 Bianchi was at Maguire's opera house on Washington street and was followed in the same house later in the year by Lyster's English Opera Company which gave four seasons. The same company gave performances in Italian and English in 1860 at Maguire's.

Favorite Operas of the Fifties

From the same source that this information was derived we are able to resurrect the programmes and gain a knowledge of the class of music which appealed to the miners and the rather mixed population of San Francisco in the Fifties. In 1851 the San Franciscans heard Sonambula, Norma, La Fille du Regiment, Favorita, Dame Blanche, Gilles Ravasseur and The Barbieire de Seville. In 1854 The Crown Diamond, Daughter of the Regiment, Black Domino, Bohemian Girl, Lucia, Norma, Don Pasquale, El Maestro de Capella, The Enchantress, Cinderella, The Pride of the Harem, Linda de Chammonai, Der Freischutz, Judith, Martha, Jeanette's Wedding, Ernani, Lucrezia Borgia, Nabuco, Marie de Rohan and Fra Diavolo. In 1885 Robert La Diable was given five nights in succession and L Elisir d'Amore, Don Giovanni, I Duc Foscari, I Lombardi and La Gazza Ladra were sung. The list of 1860 repeats many familiar operas, Favorita, Lucia, Bohemian Girl, Traviata, Norma Maritana, Ernani, Lucrezia Borgia, Trovatore, Sonambula, Lurline, Der Freischutz, Fra Diavolo, Midas, Rigoletto and The Rose of Castile.

Heavy Operas Enjoy Favor

The habitual opera goer whose knowledge of the chronology of musical composition has not been cultivated will be surprised to find how nearly modern taste harmonizes with that of half a century ago. With few exceptions all the operas sung in the Fifties in San Francisco are still held in high esteem, and some of them ignored for a time have been resurrected very recently. But there is evidence of a vast difference in the taste of the two periods. Five nights of Meyerbeer's Robert La Diable would not be offered by the most venturesome twentieth century manager, nor would the bravest *prima donna* dare to sing Norma night after night as Madame Anna Bishop did with the enthusiastic approval of her audiences, but it may be fairly said that taken as a whole a repertoire could be reconstructed from the programmes of the Fifties, which with a few additions would satisfy the most exacting modern opera goer.

Opera in the Sixties

During the Sixties there was no abatement of this musical fervor. The very ample diary from which this information is extracted tersely states that "there was no opera in 1861." No explanation of the failure of the impressario to provide that form of amusement is given, but it was probably due to the disorganized condition of affairs at the East. In the following year, however, the purveyors of music resumed their activities. In 1868 Biscaccianti, who became a great favorite, made her appearance in Italian opera, and the Bianchi Company gave three seasons in May, July and August and in October to December. In the ensuing year the same company entertained the people week after week, and Madame d'Ormy's company sang Il Polutio. By the close of the year Signora Bianchi's name was a household word, and her latest programme made the interesting announcement that it was her twelfth season. It also contained the name of Roncovieri, a member of her company and the father of Alfred Roncovieri, superintendent of public instruction in 1912. In 1864 the Ghioni Italian Opera Company and the Richings' Opera Company sang in the City. Caroline Richings was then at the zenith of her popularity and the San Franciscans testified their liking for her by giving a good support to the company during four seasons between June 9th and October 31. In 1865 the Bianchi Com-

SAN FRANCISCO

pany gave its 13th season, and produced Faust which had its first representation in this City on May 17th. It had been performed several years earlier in Paris, but it was a novelty in San Francisco and was greatly appreciated, being sung three successive nights to crowded houses. Adelaide Phillips and Madame Anna Bishop also entertained the San Franciscans in 1865, the latter giving her twelfth season in that year. In 1866 there was a three months' season by the Brambilla Company, an English company known as Howsons, and Bianchi gave her 14th season. La Juive and Crispano e la Comare were produced. In 1867 there was a new candidate for favor—the Bonheur Italian Opera Company, and the Howsons and Bianchi companies also performed. In 1868 the principal musical event was the opening of a season of fifty nights by Parepa Rosa at the Metropolitan. In addition to this the Lyster Opera Company from Australia sang at the same opera house, the engagement extending into 1869. In 1870 Carandinis Opera Company from Australia won a measure of success from the general excellence of its performances, which, however, were not noteworthy because of the failure to present acceptable singers in the leading roles.

The popularity of concert singing was very decided in San Francisco, and some of the artists who achieved success in opera appear to have made their talent do double duty. The high rates of admission charged, and cheerfully paid, was doubtless the temptation. In 1852, 1853 and 1854 Kate Hayes was able to secure audiences at prices ranging from $5 to $2. Miska Hauser also sang to $5, $3 and $2 seats, and Madame Bishop's popularity was great enough to permit her to exact the same rates in 1854. But before the end of the decade Madame Elise Biscaccianti, who had obtained $5 for seats in 1852 was pleased to sing for a $1 admission. In the Sixties there was an evident inclination for classical and serious musical compositions. The Bianchis in 1866 sang Mozart's Grand Requiem Mass at the Metropolitan theater with a chorus of 15 tenors, 15 bassos, 8 sopranos and 4 contraltos. The orchestra was well balanced consisting of 34 pieces and was composed of 5 first violins, 4 second, 3 violos, 3 violoncellos, 2 contra bassi, 2 flutes, 2 clarionettes, 2 horns, 2 trumpets, 3 trombones, 2 bassoons, 2 oboes, 1 tympanum, 1 grande caisse and cymbals. A couple of years later the Parepa Rosa Company rendered The Creation on two succeeding Sunday nights, but the oratorio was by no means new to San Franciscans, Madame Anna Bishop having produced it by request in 1855, and also the Stabat Mater of Rossini.

Popularity of Concerts

It would grossly misrepresent the musical status and taste of the early San Franciscans to permit it to be supposed that they were wholly absorbed by the higher class of compositions. The people of the Fifties and the Sixties were many sided in their likes and dislikes and took with equal kindness to oratorio and negro minstrelsy. The veracious diarist has recorded for us a procession of minstrel companies between 1849 and 1870 which suggests an uninterrupted popularity enjoyed by the burnt cork artists during the period embraced between the two dates. Commencing with the Philadelphia Minstrels, who opened at the Bella Union on the night of October 22, 1849, we have the following formidable list: Philadelphia Minstrels, 1849-1851; Pacific Minstrels, Washington hall, 1849; Virginia Serenaders, Washington hall, 1850; Sable Harmonists, at the Jenny Lind in 1851; Buckley's New Orleans Serenaders at the Adelphi, 1852; Rainey and Donaldsons at the American, 1852; Buckley's Minstrels, 1852; Rainer's Operatic Serenaders at the American, 1852; Campbell's Minstrels, 1852; Buckley's Minstrels, Sable Harmonists,

Reign of the Minstrel

Tracy's Minstrels and Donnelly's Minstrels in 1853; Backus' Minstrels and Christy's Minstrels in 1854; Christy and Backus' Minstrels and the San Francisco Minstrels in 1855; the same companies in 1856; Max Zorers, Woods Minstrels, and San Francisco Minstrels in 1857; California Minstrels, San Francisco Minstrels, Christy's Minstrels and Lyceum Minstrels in 1858; San Francisco Minstrels, Wills and Hussey's Minstrels and Billy Burch's Minstrels in 1859; Hussey's Minstrels, Burch and Murphy's Minstrels and Billy Burch's Minstrels in 1860.

Minstrels of the Sixties

There is no mention of any company performing in 1861 but the popularity of minstrelsy remained unabated during the remainder of the decade with changing candidates for public favor. In 1862 there were four companies: Sam Pride's Colored Minstrels, W. H. Smith's Minstrels, San Francisco Minstrels and the Minstrel and Vaudeville Troupe. In 1863 the San Francisco Minstrels had the field all to themselves. In 1864 the San Francisco Minstrels shared popularity with Ben Cotton's and Murphy and Bray's Minstrels. In 1865 there were three troupes: the Wellington, the San Francisco and Hussey's New York Minstrels. In 1866 there was a company which described itself as a Minstrel Tournament, and Talbot's Minstrels. In 1867 the Wellington Minstrels, Leslie and Raynor's Minstrels and Dan Bryant and Joe Murphy's Minstrels in 1868. Smith & Co.'s Minstrels and the California Minstrels held forth and the latter company maintained its existence a couple of years longer and began to witness the waning of the popularity of a style of amusement which had attracted the American and had subtracted his dollars during many years. After the Seventies there were sporadic recurrences of the minstrel fever in San Francisco and towards the close of the decade there was a revival which lasted into the Eighties, but the palmy days of minstrelsy passed with the Seventies.

Actors of Pioneer Days

In reviewing the course of the drama in the Sixties the names of many actors who were favorites during the preceding decade are met with. James Stark, a tragedian who appeared with Mrs. Kirby at the Jenny Lind theater in 1850 made his appearance nearly every year during the Sixties. He was very versatile and gave the first representation of the roles of Brutus, Coriolanus, King Lear, Falstaff, Shylock, Sir Giles Overreach, Richelieu, Ingomar, Hamlet, and Virginius in San Francisco. Buchanan McKean, who had been a favorite in the City about the time of the second Vigilante episode, reappeared and performed in 1861, 2, 3 and 4 at the Metropolitan opera house. It is related of McKean that while acting Pizarro in February, 1856, he refused to finish the last act because Cora's child cried aloud in the audience. Cora was the man who committed the crime which brought the wrath of the San Franciscans to a head and set the Vigilance Committee in motion. McKean subsequently expressed himself very strongly on the subject of bringing children to playhouses. C. N. Thorne, Sr., a very popular actor during the Fifties, and familiarly known to the theatergoers of San Francisco, returned to the City in 1861 and was at the American and Metropolitan during the ensuing four years. Frank Mayo, a name not unknown to the present generation of theatergoers began his career in San Francisco during the turbulent year 1856 and returned to the City in 1858 and appeared frequently between that date and 1865. Edwin Adams, who made his appearance in 1867, became a great favorite. He was a tragedian of note and fully reciprocated the appreciation of the Californians. Mr. and Mrs. Charles Kean visited San Francisco in 1864 and in 1865 they played an extended engagement, the receipts of which averaged $1,100 a performance.

MARKET STREET IN 1866, LOOKING TOWARD TWIN PEAKS

SAN FRANCISCO

There were other favorites in the Sixties whose names are still more than a mere memory to the present generation. John Drew, the father of the present well known actor of that name appeared in 1859, and there is a significant mention of the fact that his burlesques at the Opera House were so popular that prices of admission were raised. He reappeared several times in 1860, 1861 and 1862. Matilda Heron appeared at the Opera House on Washington street in 1865 after several years absence from the City. Julia Dean Hayne, another celebrity who had first appeared in 1856 in "The Hunchback" returned to San Francisco in 1860, reappearing regularly every year until her death in New York in 1865. Charlotte Thompson and Mrs. D. P. Bowers and C. W. Couldock visited the City towards the end of the Sixties and played successful engagements. Drama During the Sixties

The sensationally and frivolously inclined were by no means neglected by managers in catering. There was for instance Ada Isaacs Menkin who made a thrilling descent from the highest part of the stage bound to the back of a galloping horse in the drama of Mazeppa. The actress had other talents than the ability to stay on a horse when tied to the animal; she also wrote poetry, which however, was not near so popular as her shapely form encased in tights. Dancing was by no means a neglected art, and the appreciation it commanded explains in part the strong hold maintained by the negro minstrel troops whose programmes always contained "terpsichorean" numbers. Ada Isaacs Menkin as Mazeppa

In the attitude of San Francisco audiences towards the dramatic profession there is discovered a note of fondness which one seeks for in vain in the reminiscences of the stage in other cities. There is a surprising number of artists who were literally appropriated by San Franciscans and virtually adopted. Edwin Adams, who had first appeared in San Francisco in 1867, when his health failed some years later, returned to the City and was given a rousing "welcome home" benefit which netted $3,000. It is said of him that the warmth of the appreciation of San Franciscans had so endeared the City to him that he constantly longed to make his home with its people. Mrs. Judah, who began her career as early as 1852, years after her practical retirement from the boards, when she could be induced to play a character part with some great actor or actors, would receive ovations calculated to disturb the equanimity of the star. Alice Kingsbury was another actress who obtained a strong hold on the affections of the people. The parts which she most preferred and which San Franciscans liked best to see her perform were "Fanchon" and "Topsy," but she was an excellent all around character impersonator and had marked literary inclinations. Actors and People

Lotta Crabtree who attained to extraordinary popularity during the Sixties, is another actress who had the endearing "our" applied to her by all San Franciscans. She was born in New York City in 1847 and was brought by her mother to California, and lived in La Porte, Plumas county, during her childhood. In 1856 she danced at the American theater and her career was fixed for her by the enthusiastic audience. In 1860 on the opening night of the Apollo New Melodeon on Market street, she began her professional career in real earnest, and in 1864 she had made such a reputation for herself that she received an invitation to appear at Niblo's in New York. While acting in the East, Lotta was always known as "the California Girl." Her success on the other side of the Rocky Mountains was as great as it had been in San Francisco, and when she returned to the City, San Franciscans appropriated her honors and made them part of its dramatic history. In 1869, at "Our Lotta" a farewell benefit Lotta was presented with a wreath of gold and a package of $20 gold pieces by her admirers. Later, in 1876, she reciprocated by presenting to the City the drinking fountain which marks the busiest spot in the City in which she won her first triumphs.

Benefit Performances

The early practice of throwing nuggets and coins on the stage did not persist many years in San Francisco, but the strong predilection for the drama found expression in many other ways, some of which, while not original, attained a relatively greater vogue than in many of the Eastern cities where appreciation of the actor and his art was not so highly developed as it was in this City in the Sixties. The number of benefit performances during this decade, and the one preceding it, was very great, and the reciprocal relations implied are in marked contrast to the matter of fact attitude of the public since catering amusement for the public has become a strictly business proposition. If an actor was popular they gave him a benefit to emphasize the fact; if he was out of luck and needed to have his purse replenished the public turned out to help fill it; if he died impecunious he was buried with the aid of a benefit. The manager had benefits when he did well because the theatergoers desired to show their appreciation of the ability with which he conducted his place of amusement; if he had a bad season a testimonial performance was given to make his balance sheet look better.

Appreciative Actors

But the benefit business was by no means a one sided affair. If the public was frequently invited to help the profession, it was by no means slow in calling upon actors and managers to help forward every movement of a public character. All the hospitals were constantly being helped in this fashion. Did a newly formed military company wish to provide itself with a stunning uniform a benefit was given, and the older organizations when they felt like furbishing up would apply to the actors, and never in vain. In the Fifties, and until the volunteer fire organizations gave place to a paid department in 1865, the various companies seemed to have benefits at regularly recurring intervals. On these occasions the organization to be benefited would turn out in full force, properly uniformed, and all their friends bought tickets and went to the show which would invariably be a bumper affair, evoking an enthusiasm which did much to promote that love of the drama which was so characteristic of San Francisco, and for many years gave it the reputation of being, in the parlance of the profession, "a great show town."

Edwin Forrest's Great Popularity

There were other modes in which the San Franciscan delighted to show his appreciation of the dramatic art and its exponents. In 1866 Edwin Forrest, esteemed as the greatest tragedian of his times, appeared in San Francisco. The opening night was May 11th, and as the demand for seats was great the expedient of auctioning them was resorted to by the management. R. I. Tiffany obtained first choice, paying $500 for the privilege, and $437 were paid as premiums for 58 other seats disposed of under the hammer. The remainder of the house was sold out in the regular way, and at good prices. The engagement was a great pecuniary success and when it was concluded the San Francisco critics were united in the opinion that Forrest was the greatest tragedian of the age. He played during the time he was at the Washington street opera house, Richelieu, in which part he made his first appearance; Virginius, Lear, Othello, Damon, Macbeth, Brutus, the Broker of Bogota and Jack Cade several times. In other plays of his repertory he appeared less frequently although he was urged to repeat them by his admirers.

SAN FRANCISCO

Among the actors who came from the East with Forrest was John McCullough. He played with the great actor on the opening night and took the part of De Mauprat in "Richelieu," making a distinctly favorable impression. He succeeded in winning many friends through his genial manners, among them the banker, William C. Ralston, who took a lively interest in the drama and conceived the idea that it would be a distinct advantage to the community to have a theater presided over by a man of real histrionic talent. Later when the opportunity presented itself Ralston, who for a period was the local Maecenas, was instrumental in promoting a movement which resulted in the building of the California theater, the management of which was tendered to McCullough. The new place of amusement was opened on January 18, 1869, by McCullough, who had associated with him Barrett, and for a period the theater had a remarkable success. Forrest had predicted that the mantle of his greatness would fall on the shoulders of McCullough, but the latter never realized this expectation. He had modeled himself closely upon his great patron, and his impersonations were characterized by so many of the peculiarities of Forrest, a strong disposition existed to accept him at the tragedian's valuation; but the critics, despite their partiality for McCullough as a fellow citizen, for he had virtually become a Californian, before a couple of years had passed were pleased to find fault with his imitativeness, and condemned as mannerisms tricks of rhetoric and action which only a short time previously they had extolled as the perfection of dramatic art.

John McCullough's San Francisco Career

Edward Harrigan, who at a later period developed the play illustrative of tenement house life in New York, and which had a great vogue for a while, commenced his theatrical career in the Bella Union theater in San Francisco in 1868. He was a great favorite and to some extent the precursor of the monologuist of the modern vaudeville stage. The minstrel troupes of the Sixties following the example, it is said, of a Philadelphia burnt cork "artist," usually included as a feature of their entertainments a stump speech which, as the name implies, parodied politics. Harrigan's "stunt" was more in the nature of singing, interspersed with remarks which he made with a naturalness suggesting spontaneity, and doubtless much of his talk had that element, for he was fond of chaffing the gallery and measuring his wits against those of "the gods." Annie Yeamans, who contributed so largely to the success of Harrigan's plays appeared at the Eureka theater in San Francisco in 1865. A local newspaper, when Harrigan's plays began to attract attention in New York in the late Seventies, stated that the versatility shown by Mrs. Yeamans in 1865 in Irish comedy parts helped to crystallize the idea which he already at that time entertained of writing a series of plays of the sort which met with such a warm welcome when they were produced in the Eastern metropolis.

Edward Harrigan

During the Fifties and Sixties Irish melodrama and comedy had a great vogue in San Francisco. In 1854 Mr. and Mrs. Barney Williams, "the Irish boy and the Yankee girl" took the town by storm. Charles Wheatleigh who had won considerable popularity in 1854 and 1856 returned to the City in 1860, and played engagements in every year of the decade in such pieces as "Arrah No Pogue" and the "Connie Soogah," the popularity of which showed no signs of waning until well into the Seventies. In 1869 John Brougham, an Irish American actor of considerable note, gratified the partiality for this school of acting and was very well received. In the same year John T. Raymond, who subsequently popularized the character of Colonel Sellars in Mark Twain's "Gilded Age," played an engagement in San

Irish Plays in the Sixties

Francisco, but he appears to have made no marked impression, although he found his way back to the City regularly every year between 1869 and 1876 when he was the star in Twain's play. Another American who afterward attained great prominence and won for himself an enduring fame appeared at the Opera House on July 8, 1861, in burlesque. They called him "Joe" Jefferson then; later when he attained his extraordinary success in "Rip Van Winkle" he became Joseph Jefferson.

<small>Compliments to Actors</small>

It would be an oversight to neglect mention of the fact that during the Sixties returning favorites frequently had their opening night ovations anticipated by demonstrations such as visiting delegations and serenades. These exhibitions of appreciation were usually reserved for the feminine professionals, and were not infrequently prompted by the desire to reciprocate courtesies as in the case of Madame Anna Bishop, who on her return to San Francisco in 1865, was serenaded at the Occidental hotel by the Philharmonic society as a testimonial of its appreciation of the part she had played in fostering the love of music in the City.

<small>Early Vaudeville</small>

Vaudeville had an early vogue in San Francisco, and there were numerous houses at different times devoted to that form of entertainment. They were usually known as music halls or "Melodeons," but while they enjoyed a large patronage they never were fashionable and nearly all of them during the Sixties were rather indiscriminately classed with, or put on the same plane as the dance hall, which was usually, when at all pretentious, conducted after the style of the Parisian "Cafe Chantant." There was not even a remote approach to exclusiveness, and as a result the audiences were rather mixed, a fact which tended to debar many from enjoying very good performances, as there was generally a fairly good supply of "talent" to draw upon for specialties. The demand for entertainment during this period was so marked that year after year an organization known as "The Old Folkes" gave successful concerts, filling houses night after night. As the Philharmonic and the Handel and Hayden society, the Amphion quartette and similar organizations devoted to the interpretation of classical compositions were in the habit of giving performances in public halls, at this time it may be said that the musical taste of San Franciscans was very catholic.

<small>Location of Theaters</small>

The theatrical business of San Francisco shared the vicissitudes of the City. So many houses of entertainment were burned during the early Fifties and reconstructed that chronologists found it necessary to distinguish them by prefixing the words "first" or "second" and sometimes "third." There was a great partiality exhibited for English names, but some departures in the direction of originality were made in the selection of designation. Jenny Lind, who became famous about the time of the gold discovery, was honored by having three separate theaters named after her. The first and second built in 1850 and 1851 were destroyed by fire, and the third was converted into a city hall. They were erected on the east side of the Plaza, now known as Portsmouth square, on the spot where the new Hall of Justice now stands. All the amusement places of the Fifties were in this vicinity. The Adelphi (first) was on the south side of Clay street, and the second of that name was on Dupont between Clay and Washington. The Italian theater was on the corner of Jackson and Kearny, the National on the north side of Washington near Kearny; Washington hall, opened December 24, 1849, was on Washington between Dupont and Kearny; the Phoenix Exchange opened March 24, 1850, was on Portsmouth square; on August 13, 1850, the Atheneum opened with model artists on Commercial street between Montgomery and Kearny; Armory hall, afterward the Olympic, was first on the corner of Washington and Sansome streets and was reopened on the corner of Sansome and Jackson in 1856; the American theater (first) erected in 1851 was on the northeast corner of Halleck and Sansome; it was rebuilt on the same spot December 4, 1854. On May 19, 1851, the Theater of Arts opened on Jackson near Dupont. The circuses were in the same neighborhood. Foley's Olympic, formerly Rowe's, which opened for bull fights in May, 1860, the Mission being considered too remote for such spectacles, was on Montgomery between Sacramento and California; his new amphitheater was on the west side of Portsmouth square, as was also Donati's museum opened in 1850.

There was no tendency to move from this location during the sixty decade, the most adventuresome manager penetrating no further south than Market between Second and Third streets. The Lyceum theater which was situated in the upper part of the building on the northwest corner of Montgomery and Washington streets was destroyed by fire in December, 1860. The Apollo Variety hall was opened on the south side of Market, near Third on November 14, 1860. In 1868 the second American theater, which had been used chiefly for French and German performances during the three or four years preceding was destroyed by fire. In 1857 the first Metropolitan theater on Montgomery between Washington and Jackson streets was destroyed by fire. It was rebuilt and reopened on the same site April 11, 1861. For many years it was the best theater building in San Francisco, and on its boards appeared many distinguished actors and noted singers. It was the fashionable opera house during several years, and its prestige survived until the construction of the California theater on Bush street between Kearny and Dupont, which opened on the night of January 18, 1869. The Academy of Music, on the north side of Pine, east of Montgomery, was opened by Maguire May 19, 1864, but only survived as a play house until August, 1866, when the building was sold and converted into stores. The Eureka theater was opened on December 18, 1862, on the east side of Montgomery between California and Pine; three years later it was converted into an anatomical museum. The Musical hall on the south side of Bush between Montgomery and Sansome which was much used for concerts was destroyed by fire January 23, 1860, and Platt's hall on Montgomery street on the site of the present Mills' building took its place.

<small>Amusement Center in the Sixties</small>

The first dramatic performance in San Francisco was given in Washington hall, on December 24, 1849, when "The Wife" was performed by a company driven out of Sacramento by the flood of that winter. The cast contains names which even old timers hesitate to say were those of actors deserving of having their names handed down to posterity, but the faithful diarist we have so freely drawn upon thought differently and has preserved them for us. They were J. B. Atwater as "St. Pierre," H. F. Daly as "Ferrado," J. H. McCabe as "Father Antonio," and Mrs. Frank Ray as "Mariana." The writer of the "annals" ignores this performance probably because he did not regard the actors as professionals. Between that eventful Christmas eve and the opening of the Seventies, San Francisco's hospitable boards welcomed all sorts of entertainments, but there was little variation in their character during the entire period. The records show that the City enjoyed all that was going, but the Fifties and the Sixties from beginning to end were given up to the same sort of operas, tragedies and melodramas. There was not much craving for novelty. The patrons of amusements found their greatest satisfaction in comparison. They did not care half so much to see a new play as they did to measure the perform-

<small>First Dramatic Performance</small>

ance of a new star against the achievement of some earlier favorite. They were exacting critics and singers and actors alike were apt to respect their judgment. And they were not slow to admit that their audiences generally were as sympathetic as their expressions were candid.

Society in a Formative Stage

It has been remarked of San Francisco that in the Sixties society was in the formative stage, and that the social diversions of the people were so few that they turned to the professional amusement caterer more readily than the people of other sections of the Union. The comment had some foundation in fact. "Society" is a slow growth; it does not admit of being imported in blocks. In new communities its progress beyond the church sociable function is not rapid. It retains the democratic impress until a new generation comes on the scene. Until the youngsters of the pioneers grew up, and compelled their parents to exercise circumspection in the matter of association people were not very particular as to whom they mingled with. The Sixties showed some diminution in the laxity of social view point, but San Franciscans were still far removed from that punctiliousness which exacts as a passport to familiar acquaintance some knowledge of antecedents, and there was as yet no approach to that form of exclusiveness which the owners of money create for themselves.

The Fire Fighting Organizations

The volunteer fire organizations, composed as they were in the Fifties, of the best as well as some of the worst men in the community, were nicely graduated in the popular mind. There were some companies which by common consent were classed as "high toned," while others were merely respectable. The same was true of the militia companies. Firemen and citizen soldiery were animated by the same motives. They were all zealous cooperators in fighting fire, and quite ready to work shoulder to shoulder for the common defense if called upon to do so, but there was a disposition to draw the line at other times, and in the language of a contemporary writer, care was taken in some of the more exclusive organizations "to not admit every Tom, Dick and Harry." But once admitted to a "high toned" company, Tom, Dick, or whatever his name may have been, belonged to the aristocracy and took part in its diversions.

Paid Fire Department Created

In 1865 the volunteer fire organizations of San Francisco were superseded by a paid fire department. The change was to some extent made necessary by the weakening of the volunteer spirit and the increasing demand for discipline and watchfulness imposed by the growth of the City. Buildings were being erected over a constantly extending area, and as they were largely constructed of frame the number of alarms became too numerous to permit an economic response under the old system. There was also a tendency on the part of the members of some companies to make their houses a lounging place, and a growing apprehension that skilful manipulation might convert them into parts of a political machine. These and other causes combined to make the most zealous volunteers of the early days welcome the abandonment of the old system and the substitution for it of the compensation plan.

Patriotic Firemen

When the volunteer fire organizations passed out of existence one of the most picturesque features of San Francisco life disappeared. For many years the handsome apparatus of the numerous companies had been the chief attraction of the parades organized to celebrate national holidays and signalize other occasions. The members took a great pride in making their displays effective and were always ready to turn out, and thus they contributed to keep the fires of patriotic feeling glowing brightly. The Fourth of July celebrations prior to 1865 were not perfunctory affairs. The community generally took an earnest interest in them, and the spirit engendered by the association of citizens in their engine houses had much to do with the existence of the strong disposition to give outward expression to patriotic feeling. After 1865 there was a distinct lessening of interest, and in the course of a few years Independence Day ceased to have anything more than a formal recognition.

The fires of patriotism were kept alive for a few years after the exit of the volunteer firemen by the militia companies which came into existence during the Civil war and retained popularity until the National Guard usurped their place. The soldiery produced by the old system was a very miscellaneous affair and was scarcely calculated to inspire confidence in it as an arm of the national defense. At first the militia was distinctively American. During the Fifties most of the militia organizations had the national impress, but during the Sixties a foreigner viewing a parade in San Francisco might easily mistake the participants for representatives of the various nations of the world. It is true that all the militia marched under the Stars and Stripes, but very often the company banners would so far surpass in gorgeousness of display the red, white and blue of the United States as to irresistibly suggest that the latter was a secondary consideration.

<small>Citizen Soldiery in the Sixties</small>

There was nothing that more conspicuously displayed the cosmopolitanism of San Francisco during the Sixties than these military organizations. Census figures conveyed but a faint idea of the truth; the marching foreign hosts, bearing arms, and insistently proclaiming their nationality hammered it home with a force which later exerted itself with such effect that the anomaly practically disappeared. A simple enumeration of the titles of the militia companies is all that is required to make clear the extent of a practice which bordered on the absurd, but which might easily have become vicious. The list of companies embraced the New York Volunteers, Michigan Volunteers, California Volunteers, First Infantry Battalion, Wallace Guards, Union Guard, Ellsworth Rifles, Irish Battalion, Independent National Guard, National Guard, San Francisco Schuetzen Verein, California Fusileers, California Rangers, Second Irish Regiment, McClellan Guard, Zouaves, Washington Light Infantry, Shield's Guard, Columbia Guard, Sixth German Regiment, San Francisco Cadets, State Guards, Ellsworth Zouave Cadets, Dragoons, Hibernia Greens, Liberty Guard, San Francisco Hussars, Governor's Guard, Sherman Guard, Veteran Corps, California Tigers, San Francisco Light Guard, Independent California Grenadiers, Mackenzie Zouaves, Excelsior Guards, Sumner Light Guard, Sarsfield Guard, I. R. A. Twenty-first Regiment, City Guard, Lafayette Guard, Laredo Guard, Guardia de Jaurez, Franklin Light Infantry, Germania Rifles and the Montgomery Guard.

<small>Foreigners and Their Military Companies</small>

These companies when they turned out made a brave display. Their uniforms were as varied as their names. Brilliant colors were highly favored, the wide, flowing red breeches of the French Zouaves being particularly affected. The disposition to copy the garb of foreign soldiers was general, even the American companies disdaining to wear the sober national blue. The company flags almost invariably were more costly and beautiful than the national colors, being adorned with bullion and fringe while in many instances the American ensign had to depend on the simple effectiveness of its design. As a spectacle the militia soldiery of the

<small>Showy Uniforms of Citizen Soldiery</small>

Sixties in San Francisco was decidedly more interesting than the plainly uniformed National Guard of the present day, but its appearance was far less inspiring.

Public Celebrations of School Children

In the Fifties a spectacle in which school children figured could be relied upon to excite as much interest and afford as much satisfaction as a display of soldiery. This partiality endured throughout the Sixties. The May day celebration at Woodward's Garden always drew a large concourse to that pleasure ground. On May 1, 1870, there was such a gathering to which all the school children were invited by the proprietor to attend free of charge, with their teachers, and asked to bring with them their singing book, "The Golden Wreath," and join in the grand concert at 11 A. M. The following selections were sung: "Spring Delights are Now Returning," "Full and Harmonious," "Ear, Far Upon the Sea," "Listen to the Mocking Bird," "Happy Land," "Come Let Us Ramble" and "Home, Sweet Home." It is interesting to note that "the young ladies, misses and teachers" were carried free by the City Railroad Company, and that they all had an opportunity to see "Mammoth Dick, the biggest ox in the world, height seven feet, weight 4,400 pounds," as he happened to be the leading attraction aside from the May day celebrants.

Amateur Theatricals Flourish

Amateur theatricals flourished during the Sixties, and there were several private organizations whose members considered themselves competent to produce ambitious plays. Not infrequently this unprofessional talent came to the fore. This usually happened when some quasi-public institution needed money. This was often the case with the Mercantile library, an institution whose precarious existence suggests that the reading habit was not very pronounced, or that its management was bad, for other libraries flourished while it languished. In 1865 an amateur benefit was given in which R. B. Swain and Wm. H. L. Barnes took part. The piece performed was "Rosedale," Barnes personating the leading character. The proceeds of the entertainment exceeded five thousand dollars, and for the time being relieved the embarrassment of the library, which, however, was soon again in trouble. Barnes was a prominent lawyer and a finished orator and reckoned among his other gifts that of literary composition. He was the author of a play "Solid Silver," which was staged by John McCullough. It was well received in San Francisco and in Eastern cities and earned for the writer several thousand dollars in royalties.

Outdoor Sports Suffer from Competition

Outdoor sports during the Sixties were deprived of some of their attractiveness by the reaction which followed the exciting conditions of the first decade, and to some extent by the increased facilities for betting which the stock exchange offered. There was still great interest taken in horse racing, but the business was not yet organized as in later days. Running races were the principal attraction, but trotting was growing in favor. The reference made to "buggy time" in a circular describing the delights of the Cliff house points to the predilection for that vehicle. The lovers of fast horses were numerous and there were many animals owned in the City whose performances excited general interest. Their owners were often their own drivers and they enjoyed no greater pleasure than a brush on the road with a rival. The road to the Cliff during the period was not infrequently the scene of spirited races which were usually impromptu, but none the less exciting on that account. Many of these races were between teams and the skill of the drivers was as much the admiration of those who witnessed them as the swiftness of the horses.

PORTSMOUTH SQUARE IN 1865
The building on the right is the old Jenny Lind Theater which was converted into a city hall

SAN FRANCISCO

Baseball became popular at an early date in San Francisco. In 1861 games were played on the sand lots which were afterward converted into Union square, at the Presidio Reservation at Twenty-fifth and Folsom and later at Seventh and Folsom streets. In 1868 the first league was formed with the Wide Awakes, the Pacifics and the Eagles making up the teams. The Wide Awakes were members of a club formed by the students of the college which afterward became the University of California. The first ball park in the City was started in 1867 by an Australian named Hatfield, a professional promoter, who furnished the capital to lay out a diamond at Twenty-fifth and Folsom streets. In the same year the Red Sox of Cincinnati visited the City, being the first Eastern team to invade San Francisco. In those days the pitcher stood forty-five feet from the plate and tossed the ball underhanded; the catcher was stationed twenty feet distant from the plate and the batsman was put out if the ball was caught on the first bound. The batter was also given three strikes and three balls, and then a warning which made four strikes for him before he was out. The game began to lose its interest for San Franciscans in 1870 and it was several years before it experienced a revival.

Baseball in the Sixties

Pugilism which excited an interest in California during the Fifties, suffered a decline during the ensuing decade. There were exhibitions of boxing with the gloves, but to a generation which had been accustomed to witnessing bare knuckle combats between heavyweights they proved tame. Toward the end of the Sixties there was a recrudescence of interest stimulated by the stock brokers, whose good fortune on the board usually exhibited itself in a desire for exciting diversions. The renewal of popularity enjoyed by "the manly sport" was only temporary, and interest subsided with the sagging of the stock market, but revived again when the bonanza excitement began in the early Seventies, and the contests became so serious an offense to the community that a law was passed absolutely prohibiting boxing.

Interest in Pugilism Declines

During the Sixties the exhibitions under the auspices of the Mechanics' institute were extremely popular and furnished a common meeting ground for people. The fairs were usually continued during several weeks, and as a band furnished good music every afternoon and evening the pavilion was well filled. The practice of buying season tickets was very general and the purchasers made good use of them. The socially inclined San Franciscan could attend in the certain assurance that he would meet his friends. Toward the close of the decade in 1869 the institute was reincorporated, and in the article stating the purpose of the society the idea of cultivating "a social feeling of friendship among the members" was given prominence. This object was diligently pursued for many years, but with the growth of the City was finally lost sight of, and the institute has devoted itself almost entirely to the creation of a great library of circulation and reference.

Popularity of Mechanic's Institute Fairs

In the Sixties politics were not wholly divorced from amusement. San Francisco in common with the rest of the country insisted on combining pleasure with instruction during a political campaign. Processions, chiefly after nightfall, were in great vogue, and the participants endeavored to make them interesting with the view of impressing the spectators. In the earlier years of the decade transparencies with mottoes were the principal features of these night parades. They were made by stretching muslin over frames of wood, and were illuminated by candles. Small ones borne by the individual members usually had the name of the favored candidate with pithy mottoes painted on the cloth on the four sides. Larger ones

Political Meetings and Torchlight Processions

carried by several men, and sometimes mounted on wheels, were more elaborate and often contained long extracts from platforms, or expressions of the candidate. The torch came into use later in the decade when coal oil had worked its way into favor. With its advent came a nearer approach to organization. During the transparency era the processions were in a measure spontaneous, but when the torch was adopted uniformed clubs were formed, and much attention was paid to securing applause by exhibitions of proficiency in marching, which was achieved by steady drilling to which more attention was paid by members, as a rule, than to the expounders of the principles of the organizations to which they adhered.

Old Time Parade Route
The route of these parades in the Sixties was not long enough to detract from their popularity, although they had an offset for their shortness in the inequalities of the street pavements traversed by the participants. The course traveled over was a little longer usually than that of the Pioneer parade of September 9, 1867, which headed by "Chris" Andrus' band marched down Montgomery street to Clay, along Clay to Sansome, thence to Maguire's opera house on Washington street, where the exercises of the day set aside for the celebration of the admission of the state to the Union consisted of a poem and an oration, the poet of this particular occasion being Charles Warren Stoddard, who enjoyed the distinction of himself being a pioneer. The appreciation of the privilege of forming part of the great federal Union was regularly exhibited by San Franciscans on each recurring anniversary, but there were great changes in the mode of celebration, and that of the eventful occasion in Delmonico's when the news was received and oceans of champagne flowed was never repeated.

Flourishing Fraternal Organizations
The flourishing condition of the Pioneer society mirrored that of other organizations. The Odd Fellows and Masons had gained largely in numbers during the Fifties, and the latter in 1860 began the construction of the temple on the corner of Post and Montgomery streets, a building which served the purposes of the order until it was destroyed in the great conflagration of 1906. During the decade the various charities of the City through their needs contributed greatly to the promotion of social intercourse, a fact readily inferred from the frequency of announcements in the newspapers of concerts, balls, amateur theatricals and other diversions provided for the purpose of raising funds for their maintenance. The responses to these calls were liberal, testifying alike to the generosity and amusement-loving propensities of the people who were never called upon in vain for aid.

Whole Souled Enjoyment of Spectacles
In the amusements of San Franciscans during the Sixties there was nothing particularly characteristic, but there was a whole souledness about their way of enjoying themselves which advertised the fact that the City, although it aspired to metropolitan greatness was not as yet disposed to affect sophistication. When Rosa Celeste in 1866 walked a tight rope from the Cliff house to Seal rock the whole town poured out to see her; and in 1864, on the occasion of a sham battle in which the militia displayed their valor on Washington's birthday of that year, the vantage places of Hayes valley were all occupied by eager spectators who were quite ready to extol the occasion as a great one, and to proclaim that the conduct of the citizen soldiery "reflected great credit on their military knowledge and hearing and inspired confidence in the defenders of our great country."

CHAPTER XLV

INCREASING INTEREST IN CIVICS AND A MORAL AWAKENING

PRECAUTIONS NEGLECTED IN PIONEER DAYS—RESTRAINT UPON EXTRAVAGANCE—THE INFLUENCE OF WOMEN—ABATEMENT OF THE DRINK HABIT—INCREASING RESPECT FOR LAW—BANDIT VASQUEZ—CRIME IN SAN FRANCISCO—KILLING OF CRITTENDEN BY LAURA D. FAIR—A MORAL AWAKENING FOLLOWS—THOMAS STARR KING'S CHURCH—ERECTION OF TEMPLE EL EMANUEL—GRACE CATHEDRAL—TEMPERANCE AND CHARITABLE ORGANIZATIONS—EDUCATIONAL WORK—GROWTH OF PUBLIC SCHOOL SYSTEM—MODE OF SELECTING TEACHERS—COURSE OF STUDIES—MODERN LANGUAGES TAUGHT—NIGHT SCHOOLS—PRIVATE AND PAROCHIAL SCHOOLS—THE HIGHER EDUCATION—THE STATE UNIVERSITY—LITERATURE—HIGHLY SEASONED WRITING—LITERATURE AS A CALLING—JOURNALISM IN THE SIXTIES—WOMEN REPORTERS NEWS GATHERING IN THE SIXTIES—ART AND ARTISTS IN THE SIXTIES—INTERIOR DECORATION—HOTELS AND RESTAURANTS—THE HOME FEELING BEGINNING TO DEVELOP.

HE drastic smoothing process adopted by the Vigilance Committee did something towards making the seamy side of life in San Francisco less obtrusively conspicuous than it was during the Fifties, but part of the bettered condition of the community must be apportioned to the Consolidation Act which provided for a larger police force and a better system of management. Swift and condign punishment has its value but the criminal element has a short memory and the force of awful example is soon weakened. The only really efficacious check is the constant watchfulness exercised by a well organized force especially created to guard the peace. The pioneers were singularly negligent in this regard, and the fact that they permitted the rapidly growing City to depend upon village methods for the prevention of crimes of violence and the security of property was largely responsible for the necessity imposed upon them of resorting to extra legal methods to accomplish what might have been more easily effected by living up to the motto that an ounce of prevention is worth a pound of cure.

Neglect of Preventive Measures

Horace Hawes sought to remedy the defect of inadequate guardianship of the peace by providing for an increase of the police force to 150 and the machinery for its management. His measure called the Consolidation Act, which went into effect in 1856 created a Police Commission consisting of the mayor and police judge and a chief of police, which latter position was made elective. This body was endowed with full power to appoint, promote, disrate or dismiss members of the force. At the first election under the new act James Curtiss, who had served as chief of

Increase of Police Force

447

the Vigilance Committee's force was elected, and held office until 1858, when he was succeeded by Martin Burke, who was followed by Patrick Crowley who held the position until 1874. The Consolidation Act, however, had a general defect which extended to that portion of it creating the Police Department. The latter was a vast improvement over the lack of system which it superseded, but the provisions of the act creating it were utterly destitute of flexibility, and had later to be remodeled to meet the growing needs of a city whose population was increasing with extraordinary rapidity.

Defects of Consolidation Act

The illiberality of the framer of the Consolidation Act caused more or less trouble in the Sixties, and until a charter framed more in accordance with the modern spirit was adopted in its stead; but its shortcomings, some of which a man of different temperament would have avoided, and others which no ordinary prescience could have detected, were outweighed by the benefits it conferred. As already noted it effectually put an end to extravagance and "graft," and its method of dealing with the police problem made impossible a repetition of the awful criminal record of 1855, during which year 489 men were killed in San Francisco.

Restraints upon Extravagance

When the Sixties opened "times were changed and men had changed with them." But the modifying influences were those of restraint rather than temperament. The determination to minimize the temptation to commit crime was pronounced, and for a while the tide ran strongly towards puritanism. "Wide open" gambling was no longer tolerated, and there was a great deal of talk about Sunday laws. The salutary effect of the restraining clauses in the Consolidation Act affecting expenditure were dwelt on with pride, and there was a strong disposition manifested by the city press to extend the benefits of the reformation to the rest of the state. Something of the kind was needed, for the state officials were complacently allowing such abuses as the payment of 75 cents per mile for the transportation of prisoners from the place where convicted to the state prison and similar extravagances.

Increased Attention to Civic Duty

But the most important change noted in the Sixties was the improved disposition of citizens to perform jury duty. Before the Vigilante uprising of 1856 there was a pronounced unwillingness on the part of business men to serve on juries. Every conceivable mode of evasion was resorted to by those engrossed in their private affairs to avoid sitting, and to this cause, as much as any other, is attributed the disrepute into which the courts fell in pioneer days. From editorials in the daily press the fact is gathered that until nearly the close of the Sixties there was not much shirking, but about that time there must have been something like a recrudescence of the bad habit as the papers contain frequent diatribes on the failure to secure the right sort of juries.

Influence of Women

Concerning the efficiency of restraint there can be no dispute, but there was a new factor operating to diminish crime far more potent than police or law. It is the fashion to cynically account for the troubles of man by assuming that there is usually a woman at the bottom of them, and it is undoubtedly true that there is much crime inspired by unbridled sexual passion and by feminine folly. But on the other hand the influence of family ties, and the presence of good women avert an immeasurably greater amount of criminality and folly than the bad provoke. No one who has attentively inquired into the causes of so many crimes of violence in the early Fifties in California will seriously contend that they were not largely due to the absence of self restraint which men impose on themselves

JUNCTION OF MARKET, POST AND MONTGOMERY STREETS AS IT APPEARED IN 1868, BEFORE THE GRAND AND PALACE HOTELS WERE ERECTED

in a society in which observance of the conventionalities is demanded by the presence of women. The free and easy manners of men easily degenerate into rudeness and quarrelsomeness. When the latter became tempered by the necessity of paying deference to woman there was a decided abatement of the tendency to fight at "the drop of the hat." When good women became numerous in San Francisco men began to lay aside the offensive weapons they had been ostentatiously carrying, and when it became possible for men to find society in other places than the bar room, drinking and gambling ceased to be the chief pleasures of life.

That San Francisco became a moral town and shook off all its earlier vices in the Sixties is not true, but there was a visible diminution of what may be termed the brazenness of evil. The free and easy spirit was not wholly obliterated; men still gambled and drank, but they no longer did so after the fashion of the cowboy who resents as an insult a declination to do as he does. Instead of attempting to force all to a common level, there was a growing disposition to respect the man who avoided drinking places and refused to gamble, and the number of the latter was soon great enough to deprive respectability of the singularity which attached to it in the days when to refuse to be "a hale fellow well met" stamped the objector as a person to be avoided. **Abatement of the Drinking Habit**

Nothing can more pertinently illustrate the great change that came over San Francisco after the last Vigilante affair than the patient attitude of the community towards the delays and technicalities of the law than the case of Horace Smith, who in January, 1861, killed a man named Samuel T. Newell. The circumstances of the murder were such that a few years earlier Smith would in all probability have received short shrift, but despite the fact that feeling ran high, his friends were permitted, after a change of venue had been denied by the court, to procure the passage of an act by the legislature which transferred the case to Placer county for trial. And when the San Francisco trial judge denied the right of the legislature to pass such an act and the supreme court affirmed its constitutionality, and the murderer secured an acquittal in the Placer county court, although there was a profound conviction that there was a miscarriage of justice and great disappointment, the public accepted the verdict. **Respect for Law**

There was much other evidence that a great change in sentiment had taken place in San Francisco and that a disposition to let bygones be bygones existed. The fact that the legislature in 1861 caused the resolutions of censure directed against Broderick in 1859 to be expunged from the records has already been mentioned, but the step was doubtless taken as a recognition of his services to the Union cause and there was a sharp division respecting the propriety of the action. But three years later when the proposition to appropriate $5,000 to aid in the completion of the monument to his memory in Lone Mountain cemetery in San Francisco was put forward it met with practically no opposition, and the little which exhibited itself was in no wise influenced by local considerations. There were still some echoes of Vigilante days; indeed they were heard in the legislature as late as 1877-78 when a bill was passed over the governor's veto authorizing the payment to Alfred A. Green a sum not exceeding $20,000 for services rendered in 1856 in establishing the Pueblo claim; but in San Francisco all the animosities engendered by the upheaval had practically disappeared. The proscribed, against whom no other offense had been urged than their sympathy with the Law **A Monument to Broderick**

450 SAN FRANCISCO

and Order party, who had returned to the City, mingled with their fellow citizens and freely participated in public affairs.

Most Orderly Place in the State

Satisfaction over the results achieved unquestionably had a part in producing this practical amnesty. San Francisco from the wickedest had suddenly been converted into the most orderly place in the state. The seat of criminal operations seems to have been transferred to the interior counties where the bandits became so bold that Governor Downey in 1860 recommended that highway robbery should be made a capital offense. The legislature, however, refused to act on his suggestion, and for a long period the state was infested with an organized band of robbers whose depredations extended over a wide area. The leader was one Tiburcio Vasquez, who was born in Monterey in 1835 of respectable parents. He commenced his criminal career in a quarrel in which a constable was killed. One of the men who was in the difficulty with him was summarily dealt with by the Monterey Vigilance Committee, the other escaped to Los Angeles where he was subsequently hanged for committing a murder.

Vasquez and his Band

In some manner Vasquez escaped prosecution on this occasion, but in 1857 he was convicted of horse stealing and sent to San Quentin prison from whence he escaped in June, 1859, by joining in an uprising of prisoners who succeeded in overpowering the guard. He was again arrested, and imprisoned for horse stealing, and remained in San Quentin until 1863. In 1867 he was again in San Quentin having been convicted of cattle stealing. After his release in 1871 he organized the band which during the early Seventies terrorized the state to such an extent that great rewards were offered for his capture. Meantime, however, he had committed crimes as daring and as cruel as those charged against the Murietta gang, and he and those with whom he associated succeeded in producing a feeling of insecurity which endured until tempted by the hope of gaining the offered reward for his capture experienced men engaged in the work of hunting him down which they successfully accomplished, killing him and dispersing the band in 1875.

Abuse of Pardoning Power

In a message to the legislature sent to that body in December, 1865, Governor Low called attention to an increase in the number of prisoners in San Quentin, which, however, he attributed to the greater security of the prison and not to more crime. Prior to that year the prisoners were not as carefully guarded as they were later, and escapes were frequent. The governor also intimated that the pardoning power had been too freely used, a criticism which the records show was fully deserved. His animadversions and the comments of the press indicate that the pardoning propensity was not as much due to the prevalence of the sentiment which moves the modern penologist to action as the exertion of what is known as the political "pull," and the pressure of influential persons in private life.

Crime Committed for a Bauble

Although the criminal records of the Sixties indicate that the entire decade was destitute of abnormal features viewed from the police standpoint there were at least two cases which fell in this period which were classed by them as "celebrated," and one of which was the outcome of a mode of life regarded with too much leniency by San Franciscans in pioneer days. The first of these is more remarkable because of the folly and cupidity of the criminal than for any other reason. A young man named Hill who had inherited a small fortune managed to get rid of it very quickly through gambling and dissipation. While he had money he dressed in a showy fashion, and wore a cluster pin in his shirt front which was reputed to be worth $1,500. On the 15th of February, 1865, he disappeared from his lodgings in the Mansion house on Dupont street near Sacramento, but as he frequently absented himself without explanation no comment was excited. Some weeks later a dog belonging to a gardener in the San Souci valley in the vicinity of Fulton and Baker streets was observed tugging at a rope which protruded from the sand. Investigation disclosed the body of a man who had apparently been killed with a blunt instrument of some sort, as there was a large jagged hole in his forehead. Inquiry developed that it was that of Hill. He had been despoiled of all his valuables, including the cluster pin. The police in working up the case discovered that Hill had gone out with a man named Thomas Byrnes, the son of a roadhouse keeper, on the night of his disappearance, and that the horses drawing the buggy had returned to the stable without any occupants in the vehicle. It was recalled that Byrnes had taken a monkey wrench saying that it might be needed. The explanation that the horses had run away was easily accepted by the stable keeper as no damage had been caused by the alleged runaway, and the occurrence passed unnoticed. Byrnes had originally planned to make it appear that Hill had been killed by being thrown out of the buggy, but he became afraid and buried the body after killing his victim. His crime was subsequently exposed when he attempted to pawn the cluster pin which he learned was a cheap imitation and worth about three dollars. Byrnes was tried and executed on September 3d of the following year.

On the 3d of November, 1870, a crime of a different sort was perpetrated. The perpetrator was Laura D. Fair, a woman whose character was pretty well known to the initiated, but who managed to maintain appearances sufficiently to be permitted to remain in respectable hotels, which was not a difficult matter at that time. With this woman a prominent lawyer named Alexander Crittenden had maintained improper relations for some time, causing an estrangement from his wife. Crittenden's infatuation finally succumbed to the pressure of friends, and he resolved to cut loose from the woman and return to his wife. Mrs. Fair was greatly exasperated and menaced him, but he disregarded her threats. Considering the fact that the woman had on two previous occasions attempted to kill men, once during the Civil war when she shot at a Union soldier and missed him, and at another time had discharged a pistol at a man in the Russ house, who had made a disparaging remark about her, Crittenden acted very incautiously, taking no steps to protect himself.

Lawyer Crittenden Killed by Laura D. Fair

On the date mentioned Laura D. Fair met Crittenden in a public place and shot him down. She was tried, found guilty and sentenced to be hanged on June 3, 1871. Extraordinary as it may seem, despite her notorious character, a by no means inconsiderable portion of the community took her part. No occurrence since the Vigilante outbreak in 1856 had created near so much excitement or caused a greater division of opinion. When the supreme court granted a new trial this difference was accentuated and finally when on her second trial she was acquitted on the ground of "emotional insanity," the singular verdict was accepted by many as just. It would be difficult to describe the motives which influenced those who sympathized with the Fair woman. There was nothing about her calculated to excite sympathy and mushiness had not yet become a San Francisco weakness. They knew that the husband whose name she bore had committed suicide on account of what were euphemistically called "family troubles," but in spite of this knowl-

Acquittal of the Murderess

edge and her subsequent career, which was made public during the course of the trial, there were plenty who openly expressed their satisfaction when she was acquitted.

A Moral Awakening

An effort to determine the cause of this attitude discloses that at bottom it was prompted by a feeling of resentment against the victim, whose treatment of his wife, while it had not apparently disturbed the community very greatly while he was committing his offense against society, was shocked into a sense of propriety by the culminating tragedy. In short the opinion not infrequently voiced, that "it served him right," was indicative of a revolt against the looseness of living which had long been condoned by a too tolerant community. Crittenden was a man of fine attainments, and enjoyed the friendship of a large circle, the members of which, if they gave his affair a thought, regarded it as an amiable weakness, or passed it over lightly as a shortcoming too common in San Francisco to be made much of by people who were not saints.

New Standards Recognized

There is no evidence that the moral awakening, if the dawning perception of the evil of loose living may be characterized as such, effected a complete reform, but it did unquestionably make those who committed offenses of the sort for which Crittenden paid so heavy a penalty less disposed to advertise their delinquencies. It is not surprising that this should have been the case, for during the decade much happened in San Francisco that tended to put its people on a plane resembling that of the communities of the older section of the Union. At one time the much talked of cosmopolitanism of the City was accepted as a blanket excuse which could be made to cover all sorts of departures from the straight path, but the influence of religion and education was constantly exerting itself and forcing the irreclaimable as well as the merely indifferent and careless to recognize the standards of respectability established in older and differently circumstanced cities of the United States.

A Changing View Point

It would be impossible to overlook the increasing importance of this factor in changing the view point of San Franciscans. There is nothing to show that during this period, when the "atmosphere" which in later years was supposed to envelop the City was being created, that its creators recognized that it was being "back fired" by those who elevated the orderly and the conventional above the unusual and the irregular. It is doubtful if those who seized upon the departures gave much thought to anything else than the production of literature which depicted a strange mode of life. They certainly, even in those sympathetic touches which seemed to condone that which in stricter communities would have been condemned, did not seek to set up as examples worthy of imitation the strange characters they described.

Hoping for Improvement

It is very clear from the matter of fact evidence which may be extracted from the newspapers of the Sixties that no one was particularly proud of any peculiar brand of wickedness which California or San Francisco may have developed, but that there was a very earnest desire generally entertained that the City should pursue her career soberly. There are even traces of a belief that the closer communication with the East, which the opening of the first overland railroad would bring about, would result beneficially by injecting new blood into the community. The hopes for the future were not all purely material. The religious and cultured were looking forward as joyfully to an era in which as a result of contact with the outside world much that was considered bad would have to disappear.

SAN FRANCISCO 453

Statistics and quotations cannot express the growth of this feeling, but the progress made in the strengthening of those supports which make the structure of society secure may be satisfactorily indicated by the recital of facts which show that long before the close of the sixty decade of the nineteenth century San Francisco had taken a long stride in the direction of stability, and that it had become a community more orderly in many respects than any other in the American Union. It is necessary to emphasize this claim, because the events of the Seventies were so grossly misrepresented, and misapprehended, by the outside world that the stigma of riotousness has been fastened upon San Francisco by historians who enjoy the reputation of being careful writers. {A Stable Community}

The evidence of the inaccuracy of their judgment will appear further on; here it is merely designed to show that in all those particulars which go to make up an orderly and law abiding people San Francisco had advanced greatly during the Sixties, and that when the seventy decade opened the City was well provided with churches and other religious institutions, and that its educational facilities were well abreast of those of the most progressive cities in the United States. Between 1860 and 1871 numerous fine and costly structures for religious purposes were erected. Some of these had been demolished before the fire of 1906, their abandonment being caused by the encroachments of business and the desire to relocate in neighborhoods which were more accessible to their congregations. One of the most noteworthy of these edifices was the First Unitarian, erected on the south side of Geary, between Grant avenue and Stockton street, on the spot now occupied by the Whitney building. It was built of stone at a cost of $65,000 and opened for services on the 10th of January, 1864. Thomas Starr King was its first pastor. He died on the 4th of March following, and his remains were interred in a marble sarcophagus which was in plain view of the passing throngs who were made familiar with the patriotic services of the distinguished preacher by its inscription, and the grateful remembrances of the people. This memorial was removed when the congregation took up its new quarters in the church on the corner of Geary and Franklin streets to a deservedly conspicuous position in front of that edifice. {Thomas Starr King's Church}

In the ensuing year the Jewish congregation El Emanuel began the construction of a temple on Sutter street between Stockton and Powell, which was dedicated on March 23, 1866, by the Rev. Elkan Cohn, who remained its rabbi until the time of his death. The two towers of El Emanuel, which were 165 feet high, were a conspicuous feature in all the early sky lines, and the architecture was concededly an excellent example of its type. While in course of erection much criticism was bestowed upon the architect, Patton, for resorting to imbrication, and predictions were freely made that the walls would not stand, but they went through the earthquakes of 1868 and 1906 without injury, although the interior of the building and the inflammable parts were destroyed in the fire of the latter year. After the great conflagration the temple, shorn of its towers, was restored, the walls being as sound as when they were put up forty years earlier. {Erection of Temple El Emanuel}

In 1860 the Episcopalians laid the corner stone of Grace cathedral on the southeast corner of California and Stockton streets. The ceremony was performed by Bishop Ingraham Kip and two years later, on September 28, 1862, the edifice was opened for public worship. The style was Gothic and it was a notable addition to the ecclesiastical architecture of the City. Its commanding position made it a conspicuous object in the landscape. It was destroyed in the conflagration of {Grace Cathedral Erected}

1906 and the site was subsequently sold, a gift of the entire block on California street between Jones and Taylor having been presented to the diocese by William H. Crocker, his brother George and his sister Mrs. Alexander, upon which a cathedral worthy of the metropolis of the Pacific coast was in course of construction in 1912. In 1867 a large frame edifice was put up on the northeast corner of Post and Powell streets for Trinity Episcopal congregation. Despite the destructible character of the material employed, the building presented a handsome appearance and was a costly construction, $75,000 being expended on its erection. It was opened for service September, 1867, and was used by the congregation until 1894, when a hotel called the Savoy was erected on its site.

Numerous Churches Built

In the Sixties the Methodists were particularly active. Three new congregations were formed and buildings provided. They were the Central, the Grace in the Mission and the Bush street. These additions were made in 1864, 1865 and 1869. In 1871 the Simpson Memorial church was erected. The other Protestant denominations were equally zealous and helped to swell the number of church edifices. New Catholic parishes were created, among them St. Josephs and St. Bridgets, and in 1869 the 50 vara on Golden Gate avenue (then Tyler street) between Jones and Leavenworth was purchased and the German population was provided with St. Boniface church. The first structure was a modest frame, but the congregation grew rapidly, a fact noted of all the Catholic parishes during the Sixties. In 1864 the archiepiscopal residence was built on the lot adjoining St. Mary's cathedral.

Activities of the Charitable

The religious activities of the City were not confined to the building of churches and the organization of new congregations. Thev were equally notable in the field of charity and general helpfulness. The metropolis of the state, which had once boasted a legislature of "a thousand drinks," and which was still far from accepting prohibition had a hall to house its Temperance Legion, in which meetings were held nightly to promote the cause. It was on Second street in a frame building close to Market. In 1862 the Ladies' Relief and Protective society began the construction of the home for the care of orphaned children on Franklin street between Geary and Post, which was occupied in April, 1864. This building was outside of the fire line and was still serving its original purpose in 1912. It would demand a good sized volume to do more than suggest the manifold accomplishments of the earnest workers of this period, but they may be condensed into the statement that they put their impress upon it and are entitled to a large part of the credit attaching to the undoubted change for the better which occurred in San Francisco during the Sixties.

Work of the Educators

Equally deserving of recognition is the work performed by the educators between 1860 and 1871. A brief sketch of the progress of the schools will show that the City was quick to accept new ideas, and that it did not shrink from innovations which promised results. When the sixty decade opened there were eleven public schools in San Francisco with 68 teachers; in 1870 the number of schools had been enlarged to fifty-five and there were 371 teachers. The greatest expansion was after the close of the Civil war, the number of schools having increased only by nine during the first half of the decade, while there were thirty-five additions between 1865 and 1870 and during the latter period the number of teachers was increased by 233, as against only 68 in the first five years of the Sixties. There were 22,151 enrolled pupils in 1870, as against 6,108 in 1860, and the average daily attendance rose from 2,837 in the earlier year to 15,394 in the first year of the Seventies. The expansion of the system was reflected in the greatly enlarged cost of maintenance, which increased from $156,407 in 1860 to $526,625 in 1870. But the community was growing more rapidly than the expenditures, for the cost per capita for all school purposes fell from $55.13 in 1860 to $33.56 in 1870.

The records of the earlier years do not deal with the value of school property, but in 1870 we find it estimated at $1,729,800. In that year the assessed value of all city property was only $114,759,510. This apparently indicates generous dealing with the school system and a disposition to provide facilities as rapidly as demanded, which was indeed the case during the Sixties. In 1870 the number of children of school age was given by the United States census marshals at 27,055. The age as fixed by law prior to 1865 was from four to eighteen. In 1865, when the first census was taken under the new law the number of children between five and seventeen—which years included the school age until 1873—was 21,013. As the average daily attendance was only 6,718 in 1865 and the number of school age children was 21,013, it is obvious that there was need for compulsory regulation. The daily attendance in 1870 averaged 15,394 out of a total of 27,055 of school age, a marked improvement over the first half of the decade.

Value of School Property

In 1860 the legislature passed an act creating a state board of education. One of its duties was to issue certificates of competency to teachers certified to by county boards of examination. The law was subsequently amended so that the state board not only granted state diplomas on credentials but framed questions in twenty branches of study to be submitted by county boards of examination, quarterly, to applicants for certificates which were of three grades, dependent upon the percentage secured by those taking the examination. A percentage of 85, or exceeding that rate, entitled an applicant to a first grade certificate. This continued to be the mode of selection during the Sixties without being subject to much adverse comment, but the method was abused in the next decade and a great scandal ensued which resulted in the adoption of a new system.

Mode of Selecting Teachers

The course of studies during the Sixties remained the same as that of the previous decade, but about the middle of the decade music and drawing were added, and the multifarious branches now dealt with were subsequently included. At any time before 1870 parents were satisfied to have their children instructed in arithmetic, grammar and spelling, a smattering of United States history and geography, and much stress was placed on cultivating the ability to write "a good hand." This accomplishment was rated very high by people of a practical turn, who did not foresee that chirography would later be almost superseded by the typewriting machine; and it was also esteemed as a mark of culture, the idea that illegibility and peculiarity in penmanship stamped the writer as original not yet having taken possession of the faddists.

Course of Studies in the Sixties

Although the ordinary course of studies was maintained during the Sixties a movement was inaugurated by J. C. Pelton in 1865 for the establishment of classes for instruction in the modern languages, German, French and Spanish. The innovation at first met with some opposition, but it was instituted and later an act of the legislature rendered the cosmopolitan schools, as they were called, secure against attack. Before the close of the decade there were three schools in which the languages enumerated were taught in addition to the regular branches. While the curriculum of the grammar schools was kept from being too greatly amplified dur-

Modern Languages in Public Schools

ing the Sixties, the necessity of an approach to the higher learning was recognized and high schools were provided. The first of these, opened August 16, 1856, was a mixed school made up of pupils of both sexes. In 1862 an agitation for segregation was begun which culminated in 1864 in the formation of separated boys' and girls' high schools. In 1866 a Latin high school was established with George W. Bunnell, afterward professor of Greek language and literature in the University of California, as its principal; it was, however, discontinued in 1868, the pupils being incorporated with those of the boys' high school.

Truancy Evil Dealt With

Pelton, who was superintendent of education in 1866, recommended in that year the establishment of a normal school in San Francisco, but his proposition was antagonized by legislators from other sections of the state, who urged that two universities and three state normal schools provided amply for instruction in pedagogy. Several years later a city normal school was created which had to undergo many vicissitudes before its incorporation in the state normal school system. Superintendent James Denman, who earned a high reputation as a zealous official and instructor, undertook in 1868 to deal with the evil of truancy displayed in the returns of the irregular attendance, but without success. He urged the appointment of truant officers and the desirability of a thorough investigation, but his recommendations went unheeded and nothing was done in the premises for several years.

Size of Classes

Among the troubles of workers in the educational field was that which arose out of the difficulty of making the public understand the limitations of the teacher. In the early days it was assumed that a teacher could take care of as many pupils as could be crowded into a classroom. The factor of attention to the individual pupil was almost wholly disregarded. As many as 87 scholars were assigned to one teacher. Pelton was vigorous in his opposition to this imposition and urged that forty grammar and fifty primary pupils were as many as could be properly taught by a single teacher, and these maximums were accepted after 1866. They were occasionally disturbed by capricious boards, but were never seriously departed from at any time.

Night Schools

Night schools were established at an early date in the City, and their facilities were taken advantage of by the not inconsiderable number whose appreciation of learning only began with the arrival of years of discretion, and of that equally large class desirous of overcoming the disadvantages of the illiterateness imposed upon them by the neglect of their natural guardians, or the shortcomings of their earlier environment. In these schools instructions were given in commercial branches to several classes. This addition to their sphere of usefulness was made after the establishment of the Commercial school in 1865, the scope of which was greatly broadened in subsequent years.

Private and Parochial Schools

The educational facilities of San Francisco during the Sixties were by no means confined to the public schools. There were many private institutions of varying degrees of excellence and a well developed Catholic parochial school system. Nothing approaching exact data respecting the operation of these schools is available, but they were numerous and their attendance was large. Their flourishing condition helps to explain the wide divergence between the number of children of school age which the census figures furnish, and the enrollment in the public schools. This chief cause of this disparity occasionally provoked comment, but it never approached the stage of serious controversy as in some cities of other parts of the Union, in which the parochial school became a burning question. Sometimes a zealous priest would comment on what he called the unfairness of taxing people to provide benefits for people who would not accept them, but the protest never took the concrete form, as it did in New York, of demanding that the parochial schools be accorded a share of the state's school moneys.

Instead of wasting time in profitless discussion the Catholic church authorities devoted themselves to strengthening the educational system provided by them. In 1862 a number of Dominican nuns were brought from Monterey and opened the first Catholic school for girls on Brannan street. The school was attached to the parish of St. Rose of Lima. In 1866 the Sisters of Notre Dame established a school for boys opposite the old Mission Dolores church. This institution prospered greatly and was ultimately converted into a college, and its preparatory classes were accredited to the University of California. In 1863 the Christian Brothers arrived in the City and took charge of St. Mary's college. St. Ignatius college, which had been incorporated under the laws of the state in 1859, continued to flourish, and in 1863 graduated a class at the head of which was Augustus J. Bowie, who enjoyed the distinction of receiving the first diploma from that institution. St. Mary's college was not chartered to grant degrees until 1872.

Catholic Schools and Colleges

Although the University of California is a state institution, and is housed in buildings in the trans-bay region, San Franciscans have always taken a lively interest in its fortunes and have done more to promote its growth than the people of any other section of the state. In fact its origins are distinctly San Franciscan, as a brief resume of its early struggles for recognition will show. In 1853 Rev. Henry Durant of Massachusetts, a Yale man, came to San Francisco for the purpose of founding a university. His visit was under the auspices of the San Francisco Congregational Association, which decided upon opening the Contra Costa academy in Oakland, which in 1855 was incorporated under the name of the College of California, a suitable site for which was obtained in California. No president was chosen but the Rev. Samuel H. Willey, who had been urging the establishment of an institution for the higher learning, was appointed vice president. In 1859 three professors, Henry Durant, Martin Kellogg and I. H. Brayton, and three instructors were chosen as the faculty, and in 1860 instructions were formally commenced, and classes were graduated from 1864 to 1869 inclusive. A tract of 160 acres had been secured in the meantime, about four miles north of Oakland, which at the instance of Frederick Billings was given the name of Berkeley, an appellation which attached to the town site.

University of California

The constitutional convention of 1849 had placed at the disposal of the legislature (1) five hundred thousand acres of land granted by congress for the purpose of promoting internal improvement after devoting it to the cause of education; (2) all escheated estates; (3) the 16th and 36th sections of land granted by congress and constituting 1/18 part of the soil of the state. By the terms of a constitutional provision these benefactions were inviolably appropriated to the support of the common schools. In addition to these provisions for the common school system, congress in 1853 gave to the state 56,080 acres for a seminary of learning, and in 1862, under the terms of what was known as the Morrill Act, California received 150,000 acres of public land for educational purposes, and the legislature in order to secure this endowment in 1866 passed an act to establish an agricultural, mining and mechanical arts college, and to select a board of directors, who personally

Resources of the University

selected a site of 160 acres a little to the north of the Berkeley grounds of the College of California.

Scope of University Broadened

Those most earnestly interested in the cause of the higher learning were anxious to broaden the scope of the institution created by the legislature, and in 1867 they made a proposition which resulted in the merging of the College of California in the state foundation. Rev. Dr. Horatio Stebbins, Professor Durant, Governor F. F. Low, John W. Dwinelle and John B. Felton on behalf of the college offered to turn over all its property to the state on condition that "it should forthwith organize and put into operation upon the site at Berkeley, a University of California, which shall include a college of mines, of civil engineering, of mechanics, a college of agriculture and an academical college of the same grade and with courses of instruction at least equal to those of Eastern colleges and universities." The offer was accepted and in 1869 the College of California discontinued its work and gave place to the new university, which opened its doors on September 23rd of that year.

Provision for Co-Education

Professor Durant was the first president of the new university. The honor was deservedly bestowed for his zeal in the furtherance of the cause of the higher education was unsurpassed. It should be remarked of the creation of the university that the public attitude towards it was extremely liberal and that the sentiment in favor of making it something more than a mere agricultural college and school of mechanics arts was very pronounced. It is also indicative of the spirit of the times that the legislature, when providing that no fees should be charged, also prescribed that the university should be opened to women on terms of equality with men. This provision respecting co-education was largely inspired by the discussion growing out of the separation of the sexes in the high schools of San Francisco which resulted in the success of the separatists who, however, conceded that the arguments which applied to younger students were not applicable to those of mature years. The advocates of women's suffrage, whose activities were quite pronounced during the Sixties, also exerted considerable influence in securing for the unenfranchised sex this valuable recognition which, perhaps, more than any other cause contributed to the final success of their movement in 1911. Many of the most vigorous champions of woman's suffrage in that year were graduates of the university and were in the van of the contest for "equal rights."

Literature and the Higher Education

In later years the University of California and the Leland Stanford, Jr., university established in the Eighties, made their impress on the City in various ways. The metropolis was too large to have imposed on it the peculiarities of a university town, but the proximity of two great institutions exerted an influence which could easily be recognized by the careful observer. But during the Sixties such advances as were made in literature and the arts were largely dissociated from the higher culture. It has been said that "the year 1868 witnessed the dawn of California literature—a dawn of radiant promise which paled and faded into a brief day that closed ominously." Concerning the concluding clause of the criticism there may be a difference of opinion, but regarding the first part, which assumes that nothing worthy the term literature was produced during the first twenty years after the American occupation, there is not much room for dispute. It is hardly possible to successfully attribute this to San Franciscan or Californian defects; the same indictment could be brought against the whole country with equal propriety. The twenty years preceding 1868 was the period in which namby-pambyism in writing was predominant. It was the era in which the choicest literary pabulum was

LADIES' PROTECTIVE AND RELIEF SOCIETY BUILDING, ERECTED IN 1864 ON FRANKLIN STREET BETWEEN GEARY AND POST STREETS

served out by writers who exerted their talents for the benefit of the readers of the New York "Ledger," Street & Smith's "Weekly," and Gleason's "Literary Companion." There were some rare exceptions in the East of escape from the influence of the "Bertha the Sewing Girl" style, but the general product was on that plane. Under the circumstances it would have been extraordinary if San Francisco had evolved a new school, for it must be borne in mind that the generation then inhabiting the City was imported and not a product of the soil. When J. Macdonough Foard, the editor of the "Golden Era," the first paper in California making literary pretensions, in after years declared that the admission of "schoolgirl trash" to its columns killed it, his indictment was against the literary taste of the period, and did not apply exclusively to the contributors of that pioneer journal.

Another of the early magazine editors furnished quite a different explanation of the drawbacks to which literature was subjected in the Sixties. J. H. Hutchings, who essayed an illustrated publication in 1858, which he called "Hutching's Illustrated California Magazine," declared that its demise in 1861 was due to the propensity of his contributors to go to the East for their subjects and to utterly disregard the value of local coloring. There seems to have been little foundation for this assumption as it is notorious that in after years there was a pronounced disposition to regard with disfavor the work of authors who colored their writings with California pigments which the outside world thought produced pictures true to Nature, but which most Californians insisted upon considering as burlesques until they were taught their error by people who had never been in the Golden State but knew literature when they met it face to face. *California Note in Literature*

The truth of the matter is that the Californians of the Fifties and Sixties, although somewhat prosaic and practical, demanded writing with a great deal of ginger in it. This requirement for literary seasoning was amply met by the writing editors of the daily newspapers who produced articles which fairly sizzled. The appreciation of this quality was very general, and a taste for virile expression existed, which can only be properly likened to that of the habitual drinker who pronounced all liquor, excepting that which burned as it was being swallowed, as stuff fit only for the consumption of infants. There was so much of that sort of writing in the daily papers it is not astonishing that the weeklies varied the feast, and introduced the "sweeter" stuff offered by women contributors. An intellectual feast composed wholly of curries and chutney needed something of the sort. *Highly Seasoned Writing*

Next in point of acceptability in the Sixties was the work of the cynic. The period produced one whose reputation was well established in California long before his merit was recognized by Eastern critics. Ambrose Bierce, who began his career in San Francisco in 1866 was for a long time a source of unfailing delight to the readers of a weekly paper, the "News Letter," the principal aim of which, for many years, was to make people uncomfortable and succeeded in doing so by telling the truth about them with a frankness almost brutal at times, or by delicately puncturing them with the rapier-like thrusts of Bierce, who was as satirical as he was cynical. In those days Bierce was responding to a demand. Had he been able to offer literature of the quality of that of his maturer years it is doubtful whether it would have been acceptable to the most of his readers, and yet, they unquestionably had as high an opinion of his merits as Mrs. Atherton, who has said that "he is the peer of Robert Louis Stevenson in weird, shadowy effects and the superior of that writer in expression." *Cynical and Satirical Literature*

Business Men Write for Magazines

There was no such ready perception in the case of some of the true lights of California literature. The public of San Francisco was not near so responsive to the work of Mark Twain, Charles Henry Webb, Bret Harte and Charles Warren Stoddard, all of them contributors to "The Californian" during its brief existence which lasted from 1864 to 1867. There were others whose productions were as well received by the editor, whose literary training had been received on the "New York Times," but their names never became distinguished through their writings, although some of them attained to prominence in other fields than those of literature. "The Californian" was among the first to seek for other qualifications in its contributors than the mere ability to write English, and in its brief career it introduced to its readers such men as William C. Ralston, William Sharon, Frank McCoppin and Hall McAllister. None of them apparently was seeking literary honors, but they regarded the "Californian" as a convenient vehicle for the dissemination of their peculiar views.

Literature as a Calling

It should be said of the literary development of the Sixties that it lacked the stimulus of an active demand. It has been noted by critics of the work of this and the preceding decade that the attempts at magazine publication were nearly all dismal failures, but the experience of San Francisco in that regard was not unique. The publication of purely literary journals at this particular time was a precarious business in other and more densely populated sections of the country. Nowhere in the United States was there anything like an approach to professional writing. Even Boston could hardly boast a purely professional class whose members subsisted wholly on the earnings of their pens. Outside of those performing the routine work of the newspaper office there were few men and less women who were able to support themselves by their literary labors.

Journalism in the Sixties

This was particularly true of San Francisco where the literary productions even of the best writers of the period were paid for at such figures that the authors came perilously near being in the class of voluntary contributors. It has been noted during recent years that the literary ranks have been largely recruited from the newspaper offices, but that source of supply had not reached a high stage of development in San Francisco at that time. The force needed to produce a daily paper in those days was absurdly small compared with the number employed by a modern journal which attempts to cover the news and print matter whose only excuse for its presentation is that it interests readers. Journalism in the Sixties was so intimately connected with what may for the sake of convenience be termed "literature," that a description of the condition of the former will furnish a fair idea of the advances made by the latter. It has been remarked by the author of "The Story of the Files," that the growing prosperity of the San Francisco newspapers proved a boon to the writers who contributed to the weekly and monthly periodicals, and she gives a list of women who, when the opportunity offered, engaged in the more prosaic work of reporting. But this movement was not perceptible until toward the close of the Seventies, when the superior qualifications of women for the performance of certain duties began to be recognized.

Employment of Women as Reporters

That they were not employed to any extent at an earlier period was by no means due to prejudice or failure to recognize their fitness. It is not impossible that some editors in the Sixties may have thought that newspaper work was not a proper occupation for the gentler sex, but it is improbable that the subject seriously occupied the mind of any one in charge of a daily journal of that period. The reason is simple. The scope of the newspaper was exceedingly limited, and the number of persons employed in producing a daily was small, and their rewards were small. A glance over the pages of the San Francisco dailies of any date between 1860 and 1870, and in fact down to the close of the latter decade, will show how little of the matter produced was of a sort to inspire the idea in the feminine mind that journalism opened a field for the employment of woman's talents.

When women entered journalism it was not as competitors with men, but to fill places in most instances deliberately created with the view of adding to the interest of the daily presentation of what may be characterized as news matter. In the Sixties the newspaper editor did not feel the impulse to add to the attractiveness of his sheet by making innovations. He more nearly conformed his methods to the ideas of those who assume that the proper function of a newspaper is to print only the news of serious import. Indeed some of the editors of the period went a step further and acted upon the assumption that instructive comment on political matters was of more importance, and far more interesting to the reader than mere news. That was true of the "Examiner," which during the years from its foundation in 1865 as an evening paper, down to the time of its purchase by George Hearst, paid far more attention to political discussion than the gathering and presentation of information.

News Gathering in the Sixties

The founder of the "Examiner," which was first published as an evening paper, was William S. Moss. It made its first appearance June 12, 1865. Moss had conducted a paper known as the "Democratic Press" which was wrecked by a mob during the Civil war for its too frequent expressions of sympathy with the cause of secession. Moss had associated with him William Penn Johnston and Philip A. Roach. Johnston was a prolific writer and deserved the reputation he attained of being a clear exponent of the principles of the party to which he belonged, but neither he nor Roach gave a rap for news unless it was political. It is related of Roach that on an occasion when some one found fault with the inadequacy of the paper viewed from the news point he referred the complainant to "our reporter." Perhaps the news gathering force of the "Examiner" was not as small as this story implies, but it did not greatly misrepresent the strength of the paper's reportorial force.

The "Examiner" Founded

About the same time that the "Examiner" made its appearance a candidate for public favor entered the journalistic field, but in a guise so modest at first that it was scarcely recognized as a newspaper, and indeed it did not proclaim itself as such until some months after it was launched. Its proprietors were Charles and M. H. de Young, two young men who had developed a fondness for amateur journalism in the pursuit of which they gained a practical knowledge of publishing. On the 27th of January, 1865, they began the publication of a sheet which so far as typography was concerned bore a close resemblance to the ordinary theatrical programme, but an examination of its contents disclosed the fact that it contained news of a general character. This new venture was called the "Dramatic Chronicle," and at first was distributed freely in places of amusement. It soon began to be looked for because it early fell into the habit of anticipating the contents of the next morning's dailies. It had no telegraphic facilities to speak of, but by the alertness of its proprietors it managed to pick up and present bits of information which attracted attention to its existence. War news was its particular forte and it managed to secure many interesting bits of intelligence in the

Founding of the "Chronicle"

few months intervening between the date of its birth and the treaty at Appomattox. Not only did the editors of the "Dramatic Chronicle" display alacrity in the presentation of news, they also made some bold innovations on which the paper subsequently based the claim that it was the first newspaper to appreciate the value of illustration as an adjunct of daily journalism. This claim rests on the fact that on the receipt of the intelligence of the assassination of Abraham Lincoln by Booth, it published a portrait of the murderer with a noose around his neck, and followed it up with a picture of the scene in the box of Ford's theater, Washington. The two pictures were engraved by an artist named Tojetti, who enjoyed a reputation as a mural decorator, and were electrotyped by a job concern which made a specialty of printing bill heads and pamphlets. The facilities for producing pictures were too restricted, and the operation too slow at the time to tempt a publisher to engage heavily in illustration, but from that time forward, whenever the occasion offered, the "Chronicle," which on August 18, 1868, dropped the prefix "Dramatic," and became the "San Francisco Chronicle," printed cartoons, maps and occasional scenes from life, the most ambitious venture in the latter direction being a three column cut of the destruction wrought by the Inyo earthquake in 1871.

The "Bulletin" During the Sixties

The "Evening Bulletin" which took a leading place in the journalism of San Francisco after the murder of its editor, James King of William, by Casey, maintained its position during the Sixties. Its directing spirit was George K. Fitch, upon whom the excesses of the men who maladministered municipal affairs before 1856 made so profound an impression that he could never escape its influence. The "Bulletin" was the leading champion of the Consolidation Act framed by Horace Hawes, and regarded it as the highest attainment in the way of city government. Its restrictive provisions particularly appealed to Fitch, and he resisted every movement which looked toward the creation of a public indebtedness. The influence of the "Bulletin" unquestionably was great during this period, and whatever credit attached to the comparative freedom from debt about which San Franciscans were prone to boast down to the time of the great conflagration in 1906, may be claimed by that journal.

A Vigorous Local Journal

The "Bulletin" during this period was well edited so far as the presentation of opinion was concerned. Matthew G. Upton and William Bartlett, who were the chief contributors to its editorial columns during the Sixties were incisive writers and Fitch shared that reputation with them, but he lacked the style which his two assistants possessed. The conduct of the paper in its news columns was marked by the same conservatism which its chief displayed in his attitude toward public improvement. It never made innovations in its news columns, but adhered steadily to the practice of presenting happenings in a matter of fact way. Its strength lay wholly in its editorial columns in which crusades against law breakers and the plans of politicians who were suspected of extravagant tendencies were carried on with relentless severity. There probably never was a paper more completely devoted to the affairs of the municipality, or which showed as intimate a knowledge of their intricacies as that possessed by the "Bulletin" when George K. Fitch was at its head.

The "Morning Call"

Associated with Fitch in the publication of the "Bulletin" were Loring Pickering and James A. Simonton, who, with him in 1856 founded the "Morning Call" whose destinies were directed by Pickering, Simonton chiefly concerning himself

SAN FRANCISCO

in managing the affairs of an associated press service which was in later years merged with the greater organization bearing that name. The "Morning Call" was conducted on lines wholly different from those of the "Bulletin." It made news gathering its principal aim, especially devoting itself to the local field, the obtrusive happenings of which it printed concisely. It rarely departed from the straight and narrow path dictated by the extreme cautiousness of its head, and made no effort to attract attention by the introduction of new features. During the entire decade it had the lead in the morning field and was generally regarded as a safe and conservative journal, although the weakness of its editorial policies were often made the subject of comment and ridicule.

The "Alta" whose foundation dated back to January, 1850, was still in existence during the Sixties, but it was no longer the virile sheet published under that name in the previous decade, although it was still a prosperous journal with a good circulation and ambitious enough to attempt to hold the field by absorbing competitors. Its publishers, however, were not enterprising in the news field and to some extent shared the views of the editors of the "Examiner," who were firmly convinced that their readers were more interested in comment and opinion than in what was going on in the world. Like the "Call" it received the associated press dispatches, and because it enjoyed that advantage it considered it unnecessary to supplement the news furnished by that organization with special matter, and even permitted itself to believe that its clientele was not interested in any other than the most important city happenings.

Peculiarities of the "Alta"

During the Sixties the weekly papers of San Francisco were inclined to take the lead in public censorship. The "News Letter" made exposures of abuses a leading feature in its columns. It was widely read, but greatly disliked by many who were not slow to impugn its motives, but scarcely ever attempted to controvert its statements. It dealt in innuendo, and was intensely personal. It was noted for its clever satire, and its literary qualities were more marked than those of most weekly journals published in the United States at that time. The "American Flag," founded in 1861 by D. O. McCarthy also made a specialty of exposures, but its chief feature was its virulent and persistent assaults on "copperheadism." Its career was short lived. Its editors were unable to realize that the war had terminated, and that the keen interest it had excited had abated and in 1867 it went out of existence.

Weekly Papers as Censors

About the time that mining stock speculation began to take hold of the San Francisco public a daily publication devoted to recording the fluctuations of the market appeared. It was conducted on these lines almost exclusively until 1875, when it was given a wider scope by Wm. M. Bunker, who purchased and renamed it the "Evening Report." During the recurring stock excitements the "Stock Report" was more sought after than its competitors in the evening news field who also featured mining stocks, but were not able to keep pace with the rapid emissions of the smaller and livelier publication.

Paper Devoted to Mining Stock Speculation

In 1870 there was founded in San Francisco a weekly newspaper known as the "Wasp," which claims the distinction of having been the first journal in the United States to print cartoons in colors. In addition to this feature the "Wasp" made essays in the field of light literature, but the columns to which its readers turned most readily were those devoted to showing up the foibles of prominent citizens. In addition to these daily and weekly journals, San Francisco during the

First Cartoons in Colors

464   SAN FRANCISCO

Sixties maintained religious journals, a daily wholly devoted to the presentation of commercial news, and a number of sheets printed in foreign languages, among the latter the "German Demokrat" and "Abend Post."

Newspaper Mortality

The publication mortality during the Sixties was not so great as it was during the first ten or twelve years after the occupation. Nothing more accurately measures the advances toward general stability between 1860 and 1871 than the secure hold which a few papers obtained and maintained after the year first named. In the fifty decade new candidates for public favor sprung up and disappeared with such rapidity that readers scarcely had time to get acquainted with their characteristics, but with the advent of the telegraph and the improvement of the news gathering service, the publication business was completely transformed. The introduction of these facilities made demands upon the publisher previously unknown, and it ceased to be possible to issue a "newspaper" with a scissors and paste pot and mere gray matter.

Newspapers Show Great Improvement

Before the taste for news and novelties was developed any man with a few dollars and the ability to write could produce what was called a newspaper, but which a very superficial examination discloses was usually very little better than a pamphlet containing for the information of its patrons some few easily obtained facts. It is sometimes assumed that the transformation in journalism which followed the necessity of keeping in mind the cash drawer has resulted in its deterioration, but it is very unlikely that the critics, if they had a reasonable familiarity with the "newspaper" of the period in which the expectation of reward was slight, would recommend that the counting room should be divorced from the rest of the establishment engaged in producing a daily journal. And the same comment may be applied to those publications which seek to make a feature of literature. When the rewards for producing what goes by that name were slight; when, as related by the writer of "The Story of the Files," a writer endeavored to eke out an existence on five dollars a week, it is not surprising that there should have been a flood of mushy stuff which went by the name of poetry, and stories which were even less meritorious than the verses collected and published under such titles as "The Golden Wreath."

Appreciation of Local Talent

It is astonishing that among all this chaff there should have been so many real grains of wheat. There was matter produced by a goodly list of writers whose fame scarcely spread beyond the borders of the state which, while not entitled to rank as great, vied in excellence with the best turned out by the better rewarded professionals of a later date. Fashions change in literature as they do in dress or manners, but the letters of Prentice Mulford and the humorous skits of Derby read as well today as when they were first written. The work of Samuel Seabough, Newton Booth, Charles Henry Webb, Noah Brooks, Lauren E. Crane, A. P. Catlin, James C. Watkins, E. G. Waite, George Frederick Parsons, all contemporaries of Mark Twain, and all of whom were contributors to San Francisco periodicals during this period, did not strike the same chord as that touched by the sage brush journalist, but it was not without reason at the time more esteemed than the best produced by Harte or Twain.

Art in the Sixties

Art during the Sixties did not attain to a high plane. The purchasers of good pictures were not numerous and the opportunities enjoyed by the public to see meritorious works were rare. A catalogue of an exhibition of paintings by Snow & Roos, No. 21 Kearny street, in 1869, notes that Thomas Hill displayed five

SAN FRANCISCO   465

canvases in the collection of 122 hung in the room dignified by the lofty title of art gallery. Among the names of exhibitors are those of A. Bierstadt, Bush, Moran, Narjot and Keith. Those of the remainder were scarcely a memory in the ensuing decade. There is mention of a Jupiter and Antiope, attributed to Guercino, 1630, but the collection was almost wholly made up of landscapes. If most of the writers of the Sixties were obnoxious to the charge that they avoided local coloring no such accusation can be brought against the painters of the period, for their subjects were almost wholly Californian. The brief description of this exhibition would be incomplete if it omitted reference to the fact that the catalogue accorded honorable mention to a dozen or so of "chromos," a form of art not so much looked down upon at that time as it is at present. In 1870 the only place in San Francisco where a permanent collection of pictures and statuary could be seen was in Woodward's Gardens. If the catalogue made a truthful statement European art was at a very low ebb at that time. It announced without reservation that "the art gallery is filled with statuary and paintings from the best artists of Italy, Germany, Holland and the United States." As a matter of fact, with the exception of a few canvases by Bierstadt and Virgil Williams, the 63 numbers were all Italian "pot boilers," and the statues were plaster casts. But the gallery nevertheless was a great attraction and the care with which the visitors inspected its contents indicated a growing appreciation of art even though the opportunities to gratify it were limited.

Charles Warren Stoddard in describing the interior of a house in the Fifties gave us a glimpse of the taste of the period which conveyed the impression that incongruities were not regarded with much disfavor. He tells of a drawing room on Rincon hill in a house with a shaky verandah and French windows, whose walls were innocent of plaster, muslin covered with paper being substituted. The lace draperies were almost overpowering, and satin lambrequins with "colossal cord and tassels of bullion" added to their magnificence. A plate glass mirror on the mantel reflected the Florentine carving on its elaborate gilt frame. There were bronzes on the mantel and tall vases of Sevres, and statutettes of bisque brilliantly tinted. At the two sides of the mantel stood pedestals of Italian marble surmounted by urns of the most graceful and elegant proportions, and profusely ornamented with sculptured fruits and flowers. There was an old fashioned square piano in its carven case, and cabinets from China and East India; also a lacquered Japanese screen, marble topped tables of filigreed teak and brackets of inlaid ebony. Curios there were galore. Some paintings there were, and these rocked softly upon the gently beaving walls. As for the carpet it was a bed of gigantic roses that might easily put to the blush the prime of summer in the queen's garden. *Interior Decoration and Adornment*

This description cannot be quoted as typical in every particular, for even in the Fifties there were houses inhabited by substantial citizens which did not lack laths and plaster, but it undoubtedly accurately pictures the propensity to select ornaments with reference to their beauty rather than to their surroundings. That this tendency was more prevalent in San Francisco than in other cities where fortunes were made with less rapidity is undoubtedly true, but it was not entirely unknown in other sections of the Union. Art culture is a slow process, and it is not strange that there should have been plenty of men whose ability to procure costly and beautiful articles exceeded their knowledge of how to dispose of them after they were obtained. But experience sufficient to make a showing is gained *Growth of Taste* with comparative ease, and before the Sixties had become a thing of the past, there were many tastefully arranged homes in San Francisco. The dominant note of life in the community, however, was not that of the home. The hotel and boarding house, and the restaurant, still flourished in the Sixties and gave San Francisco a distinctiveness which it has not wholly lost, and which, perhaps, constitutes a part of that much talked of atmosphere whose discoverers find it so difficult to describe. It was the perception of this tendency, allied with megalomania which inspired W. C. Ralston to engage in the construction of a hotel that was to be the largest in the world. The idea was conceived before the opening of the Seventies and was executed in all its comprehensiveness in the first half of that decade.

Hotels in the Sixties
It was a bold conception for there was no lack of hotels at the time. The Grand hotel on the corner of Market and New Montgomery street, whose foundations had been laid in 1869 had just been completed at a cost of. $400,000 and was justly regarded as a caravansary fully abreast in every particular, when it opened in the spring of 1870, of the best in the East. The Occidental, on the east side of Montgomery street, between Sutter and Bush, erected on the site of the Old Music Hall and a public school, and later occupying the whole block frontage on Montgomery street, was famous for its accommodations from the time of its opening in the early Sixties. The Russ house, also on Montgomery street, between Bush and Pine, which was opened in 1862, was still flourishing, and the Nucleus, which occupied the site now covered by the Hearst building, had just commenced to bid for favor in 1867. At this time it was just as possible to say of San Francisco as it was ten years earlier that no city outside of New York was as well provided with hotels and restaurants, and that the home instinct was less developed than in any other place in America.

CHAPTER XLVI

DISASTERS OCCURRING DURING THE EIGHTEEN SIXTY DECADE

OPTIMISTIC TRAITS OF SAN FRANCISCANS—DISASTROUS FIRES FAILED TO DISCOURAGE THEM IN THE EARLY DAYS—THE FAILURE TO TAKE PROPER PRECAUTIONS AGAINST FIRES—BRET HARTE'S JESTING PROPHECY—THE EARTHQUAKE OF 1868—EFFECTS OF THE SHOCK—BADLY CONSTRUCTED BUILDINGS SUFFER—THE DISTURBANCE CAUSES NO APPREHENSION—WHY SAN FRANCISCANS ARE NOT APPREHENSIVE—INCIDENTS OF THE DISTURBANCE OF 1868—NEWSPAPERS STATE REAL ESTATE ONLY TEMPORARILY AFFECTED—NO ATTEMPT TO CONCEAL THE FACTS—A NITRO GLYCERINE EXPLOSION—OCEAN DISASTERS IN THE FIFTIES AND SIXTIES—NO INTERRUPTION OF PROGRESS—SIGNS OF AN IMPENDING DEPRESSION AT THE CLOSE OF THE DECADE SIXTY.

THE most calamitous happenings of the Fifties were the great fires which threatened the existence of the City. Their seriousness can hardly be realized at this distance of time, but that they were staggering blows we can gather from published correspondence and other sources even if the indomitable spirit of the inhabitants induced them to make light of the disasters. There was no attempt at concealment, but what the "Annals" suppressed and the local papers avoided was disclosed by letters sent to papers and people in the outside world. The "Alta California" in speaking of the fire of May 3, 1851, said "the energies of the people have not been depressed by this great calamity," and told how "within a week the buildings began to rise upon the burnt district and every portion was alive with mechanics," but at the same moment a correspondent of the London "Times" was writing a letter to that paper which was printed on July 5, 1851, in which he said: "Whether San Francisco will ever *entirely* recover from the blow is, I think, doubtful," but his pessimism did not permit him to overlook the fact that "energy unlimited is here—such energy and elasticity as were never equalled in so large and so mixed a population."

The undiscouraged Pioneer

During the Sixties the City escaped destructive fires although there were frequent demands made upon the volunteer and later the paid fire departments. In a city constructed so largely of wood it would have been extraordinary if the records had told another story. The press in the days following the disasters of the Fifties had much to say about the folly of building with destructible materials, but its advice was only followed to a limited extent. As already related in the business portion of the City, the area of which was not very extensive, substantial structures of brick, and some of stone were erected, and they were provided with

Excessive Number of Fires

iron shutters and doors, but redwood continued to be the favorite building material. Insurance actuaries claim that owing to adherence to wooden construction the destruction by fires up to 1899 was excessive, showing an average loss between two and three times that expected in cities having ordinary fire protection.

A Redwood Fallacy

Despite this fact a mischievous belief grew up that redwood was not very inflammable; it hardly went so far as to invest that sort of timber with fire-defying qualities, but it was largely responsible for the successful resistance to municipal regulation in the direction of extension of the fire limits. This and the cupidity of property owners who constantly fought efforts to compel the use of more durable materials was responsible for numerous fires which, in the aggregate, made a formidable showing in the loss account of the City. It should be added that these two causes were reinforced by the prevalent opinion that houses constructed of wood were safer in a country subject to earthquakes than those of brick and stone, and to some extent by the conviction that frame buildings were better adapted to the climate than any other sort. These views combined did much to defer the discovery which was made in 1906 that any style of masonry construction may be securely followed in San Francisco provided the workmanship is good.

Lack of Precaution Against Fire

The effect of earthquakes upon walls was too much dwelt upon and the danger from fire too little considered in the Sixties, although candor compels the admission that the people of San Francisco at no time during the decade ever gave the subject much thought. There is nothing particularly remarkable about this attitude of apparent indifference. It does not indicate a spirit of levity as some assume. The absence of apprehension was no more singular than that displayed by people living in the cyclone regions of the East, which are annually visited by destructive storms. The inhabitants of earthquake countries would gladly dispense with the disturbing tremors, but they, unconsciously perhaps, become imbued with the belief that their disastrous effects are avoidable and hence they feel no alarm.

Bret Harte's Jocular Prophecy

Not only were San Franciscans destitute of real apprehension concerning them, but they could actually make earthquakes a subject for jesting. In Bret Harte's condensed novels published in 1867 there is a passage which can be read with amusement despite the fact that the humorous prediction had some point given to it forty years later by a great disaster. Milpitas was unknown to fame in those days, so the author selected Oakland as the butt for his wit, which was as much relished by contra costans of the late Sixties as by San Franciscans. "Towards the close of the nineteenth century," wrote Harte, "the City of San Francisco was totally engulfed by an earthquake. Although the whole coast line must have been much shaken, the accident seems to have been purely local and even Oakland escaped. Schwapelfure, the celebrated German geologist has endeavored to explain this singular fact by suggesting that there are some things the earth cannot swallow—a statement that should be received with some caution as exceeding the ordinary latitude of geological speculation."

The Earthquake of 1868

Perhaps no one in San Francisco recalled this jesting prediction when the City was subjected to a shaking far more serious in its results than its inhabitants had previously experienced, but the spirit it displayed was exhibited in a slightly different form. There was no levity, but there was an abundance of assurance and an utter absence of hysteria. The disturbance referred to happened on the morning of Wednesday, October 21, 1868. The first shock occurred at 7:54 and lasted thirty seconds. It was followed at 10:35 and 11:20 A. M., by less severe shakes, which were interspersed with minor tremors. The vibration of the first quake was from northeast to southwest. Two or three days after the disturbance the local press stated that the number of fatal casualties was six and that there were about three times as many who had suffered more or less serious injury.

The effects of the shock were not confined to San Francisco or the peninsula. The accounts show that the disturbance was felt more severely on the other side of the bay than in the City. In Oakland a part of the wharf at the foot of Broadway collapsed and a large quantity of coal was sunk in the waters of the bay. Several brick buildings suffered injury, the wall of one at Twelfth and Broadway falling with a great crash. At San Leandro the county jail tumbled down and the treasurer, whose office appears to have been in the building, was killed. At Redwood and San Jose the shock was severe but not much damage ensued. Reports from the Sacramento valley indicate that the tremors were hardly noticed in that region. In San Francisco the principal damage was confined to the old city front between Sansome street and the bay on the east and west, and between Folsom street and Pacific street on the north and south.

The Shock in Oakland

There is no estimate of the extent of the pecuniary damage but the press furnished ample details which permit the inference that in most cases the injuries suffered by property owners were directly due to their own carelessness in disregarding the necessity of building properly. On the day following the disturbance the "Chronicle" stated "after a careful analysis of the reports from every quarter we find there is not a single case where any well constructed building standing on solid ground was damaged. Our great hotels, our churches, our large and stately private residences have suffered no injury. None but old and dilapidated buildings resting upon insecure foundations have been seriously injured. The Occidental, the Lick house, the Russ house, Montgomery block all stood firm, and yet they belonged to a class of buildings popularly considered most liable to danger." To this comment may be added the statement that the Montgomery block, the only one of the four buildings mentioned which escaped the flames in 1906 passed through the ordeal of April 18th unscathed, and still stands to remind San Franciscans that proper construction may be depended upon to guard against earthquake injury.

Badly Constructed Buildings Suffer

It is not difficult to find support for the assertion that the disaster of October 21, 1868, did not dismay the people of San Francisco. The evidence is abundant that they did not for a moment lose their nerve. The first shock was experienced at 7:54 A. M., and at 1:30 P. M., the "Chronicle" issued an extra containing six columns of fine print, made up of short paragraphs narrating injuries and damages and filled with bits of human interest. One of the reporters very properly thought it worth while to note that "a club of juvenile baseball players were playing a game on the corner of Stockton and Filbert streets, and when the 10:30 shock came they waited for the earth to cease oscillating and went on with their game." Another note is worth reprinting because it brings out clearly the reason why San Francisco escaped a real disaster on October 21, 1868. It stated: "While the firemen were rescuing two men covered with debris at the corner of Clay and Sansome streets an alarm of fire was sounded, and a fire was discovered in the building on the northeast corner of Clay and Battery streets which was quickly suppressed." Evidently the firemen were not confronted with the bitter experience

An Undismayed People

of 1906 when all their energies went for naught because of the failure of the water supply.

An Exhibition of Newspaper Enterprise

It is sometimes said that the history made by the local reporter is undependable, but no such charge can be brought against the collection of facts presented in this extra which were gathered, written and printed while the ground was still shaking. It was an unvarnished tale, and by no means a rounded one, for it was absolutely destitute of embellishment. The writers adhered strictly to bald facts, and presented what they learned without considering its effect. One item narrated in half a dozen lines the discreditable action of a number of men in the Pacific Tannery and Boot and Shoe Company's works, who in their eagerness to escape from the building in which they were working pushed back the women, causing several of the latter to be injured. Another disposes of the scene in the county jail where pandemonium reigned because its custodian refused to release the prisoners by simply stating that the inmates filled the air with shrieks which could be heard a block distant. But the most of the items simply recorded injuries to persons and property, and such occurrences as the busy reporters were able to learn about in the brief interval between, perhaps nine and half past twelve o'clock. They noted that at Fifth and Folsom the street had subsided, that a house at Folsom and Fourteenth had sunk four feet and they told of numerous fallen chimneys and cracked walls. They even took pains to deny rumors, as for instance this in the brief statement: "The Denman school house is not as badly injured as reported." They also related that "the Chinese at the Pacific Woolen Mills refused to return to their work," implying that the managers did not deem the shock of sufficient consequence to interrupt operations; and they were observant enough to note and record that steps were promptly taken to prop up walls that appeared in need of support. Several of the injuries resulted from frightened people jumping from windows, and we are told that two horses dashed through the windows of a dry goods store on the corner of Fifth and Folsom streets.

Damage Not Serious

There were some incidents set down in black and white which might have been taken for granted, as for instance the statement that when the second shock at 10:30 was felt "women screamed violently." But there is real value in the information embodied in the brief note that "the school house on Post street is injured so that there can be no school for a day or two" as it permits the inference that the damage was not very serious. It is also interesting to learn that "one of the spires of the Sutter street synagogue was thrown to the ground and that the custom house walls were cracked, but the building, despite that fact, and notwithstanding the dubious character of its foundations, did service until it was torn down to make way for another edifice nearly forty years afterward.

Only a Temporary Check

Far more interesting perhaps than the relation of actual occurrences is the comment called forth by the event during the succeeding few days. The analysis of the results of the temblor has already been quoted, and it may be supplemented by the observation made a day later that "the severest shock San Francisco has ever experienced, or is ever likely to experience, has come and gone, resulting in less damage to life and property than attended the great earthquake in London in John Wesley's time." This sounds like making the best of a situation, and smacks of "whistling while passing through the woods," as does also the assertion made two days later that "the crowds that filled our streets on Tuesday did not wear an aspect of sadness or depression. In fact a stranger, ignorant of the cause of the excitement, would have supposed that the people were enjoying some great holiday." But the matter of fact record in the column devoted to real estate news printed on the ensuing Sunday to the effect that "the recent severe earthquake shock has caused a temporary dullness but no depression of values," indicates in the most unmistakable manner that San Franciscans had not lost confidence in their City; and a well displayed advertisement a week later, announcing that the "Chronicle" was about to issue an illustrated earthquake edition, which might be procured "in wrappers ready for mailing," shows that there was no disposition to conceal the facts of the disaster.

In this illustrated edition attention was called to a fact which, taken in connection with what happened about the time when the shock of 1906 occurred, may prove of special interest to seismologists. "The year 1868," said the writer, "will figure in history as the year of earthquakes. Tremendous phenomena in South America, the West Indies and the Sandwich islands were on a scale far transcending any of those hitherto famous events in history." This assumption would not, perhaps, be assented to by more recent students of the subject, but it was undeniably true that the year mentioned was attended by great disturbances in various parts of the earth, just as was that of the year 1906. There may be no connection between the two facts, but the editor was not entirely unwarranted in saying that the shake seemed to establish that San Francisco was in touch with the rest of the world.

<small>Facts not Concealed</small>

There was one other disaster during the Sixties which was attended with circumstances that make it noteworthy, because it recalls the time when California was still unfamiliar with a class of high explosives which afterward came into common use. On the 16th of April, 1866, a case of nitroglycerine which had been sent to San Francisco from New York with other express matter by way of Panama by Wells Fargo & Co., exploded in the company's office in this City in the building on the northwest corner of Montgomery and California streets. The dangerous package, which was in a leaking condition, was taken there for examination. The character of the contents was indicated on the box, but apparently no one about the office was familiar with the properties of nitroglycerine, which is not strange, as its invention or adaptation to explosive uses only dated back to 1863, and Nobel was still making experiments to develop its practicability. When the leak was noted an employe was directed to open the box and he proceeded to do so with a mallet and chisel. A terrific explosion followed which killed several persons and badly shattered the building. The force of the explosive was so great that a man who was on the sidewalk on the California street side of the building was instantly killed. The proximity of several establishments engaged in the manufacture of high explosives has made San Franciscans measurably familiar with the results of disasters of this character, but none of them since that date made so profound an impression as that which occurred in the heart of the City and made them acquainted with the dangerous substance which has since been so freely used in the prosecution of the mineral industries of the state.

<small>A Nitro Glycerine Explosion</small>

The fate of ships has always been a matter of universal rather than local interest, but the ports of arrival and departure, no matter where the tragedy of their disappearance or destruction occurs, are the places where the greatest impression is made by the disasters of the deep. San Francisco has had many tragic reminders of the hazards of the ocean. In the Fifties the steamer "Central America" was

<small>Ocean Disasters</small>

lost off the coast of Florida in 1857 while en route from Aspinwall to New York and 418 of her passengers were drowned, many of them from San Francisco. On the 22d of December, 1853, the steamer "San Francisco," when two days out from New York, encountered a fierce gale, in which her engines were disabled and it was found necessary to abandon her. The passengers and crew were all rescued before she went to the bottom. The Sixties were marked by several of these tragedies of the deep. In 1860 three wrecks occurred on the northern coast, and in 1865 the "Brother Jonathan," on her way to Victoria from San Francisco, was lost with 109 passengers and a crew of 54. In 1866 the "Columbus" was wrecked and a year later the "John T. Wright" was burned at sea. The "Forward" and the "Oregonian" were lost in 1868, and in 1869 the steamers "Gold Hunter," "Hermann," "Sierra Nevada" and "Tynemouth" (Br.), all sailing from the port of San Francisco, were wrecked and in the same year the "America" was burned. The most disastrous marine tragedy of the decade was the loss of the steamer "Golden Gate," on the 28th of February, 1862. She sailed from San Francisco for Panama on the 21st of the month and when seven days out a fire was discovered amidships which spread so rapidly that the cabin passengers could not get to the life boats in the forward part of the ship. The captain decided to beach the burning vessel, but only eighty of the 338 on board reached the shore. The "Golden Gate" had $1,400,000 of treasure on board. In 1870 another Pacific mail steamer, the "Golden City," was wrecked off the coast of Lower California, but the passengers and treasure to the amount of $790,000 were saved, but the vessel and cargo proved a total loss.

Progress Not Interrupted by Untoward Events

Crimes, disasters on sea and land, seismic disturbances, even scarcities which result in famines are but temporary afflictions and scarcely affect the progress of a country of great resources. California after the occupation never experienced the miseries of dearth, her fertile soil always responded freely to the efforts of the energetic. Even in dry years, before the diversification of the agricultural industry made the state less dependent upon the rainfall than when the cereals were the chief crop, the shortage of one section would be made good by the productivity of more favorably situated land. San Francisco experienced the benefit of this unvarying good fortune of the tillers of the soil, and profited by catering to the necessities of the miners. So it happened that in spite of what at the time appeared to be great calamities the City continued to prosper, increasing in wealth and population, making a showing at the end of the decade surpassed by that of no other community in the United States.

Signs of an Approaching Depression

But before the decade seventy was many months old there were signs of a halt in progress. There was discontent among the workingmen and meetings of the unemployed. The hopes built on the advent of the transcontinental railroad were found to be illusory. There was no rush from the East to fill up the vacant lands and to develop the general resources of the state, and the house of cards built upon this expectation tumbled to pieces. The trouble foreseen by thoughtful men and predicted was materializing, and the primary cause was accentuated by what may be called an industrial aberration which produced evil consequences far more serious in their immediate effect than would have ensued had the regular course of events not been interrupted.

A Gloomy Outlook

The story of the period which opened in 1871 is a checkered one. In the main it is one of trouble and depression. It had its years of fancied prosperity, during which some men grew fabulously rich, but the City and state as a whole suffered because the riches which were gained by industry and good fortune instead of being fairly distributed were absorbed by the few. By speculative methods, more unscrupulous than daring, a foolish people were beguiled of their earnings by men whose rewards would without a resort to roguery have been sufficient to satisfy the ordinary dreams of avarice. And thus there was added to the drawbacks from which the state was already beginning to suffer the evil of improvidence. The outlook in the early Seventies was indeed gloomy, but it cannot be said that San Franciscans generally perceived the impending trouble. At times they were under the delusion that the evils from which they suffered were benefits, but this optimism gradually disappeared and long before a remedy for the difficulties was sought there was no question about the existence of the disease. There was much difference of opinion respecting the best mode of curing it, but there was little as to the causes. These were freely admitted to be land monopoly, railroad extortion and speculation, and the eradication of these absorbed the attention of San Franciscans, and influenced the destiny of the City during several years following 1871.

CPSIA information can be obtained
at www.ICGtesting.com
Printed in the USA
BVHW06s0705131018
530023BV00001B/88/P